A Guide to
STATE-APPROVED SCHOOLS OF NURSING
RN

2006

Schools Offering Basic Registered Nursing Programs Meeting
Minimum Requirements Set by Law and Board Rules
In the United States

Fifty-Eighth Edition

NATIONAL LEAGUE *for* NURSING
61 Broadway
New York, NY 10006

National League for Nursing
61 Broadway, 33rd Floor
New York, New York 10006
212-363-5555 or 800-669-1656
www.nln.org

ISBN: 0-9779557-0-2

Printed in the United States of America.

PREFACE

The National League for Nursing proudly presents the new, updated, and fully revised edition of *State-Approved Schools of Nursing RN, 2006*. All schools that conducted programs in nursing education in the US from October 16, 2004 through October 15, 2005 are included in this edition. Since 1953, the NLN has maintained a comprehensive database of nursing education programs, allowing us to publish books and monographs on trends in the educational preparation of future RNs.

This volume contains listings of associate degree, diploma, and baccalaureate programs of nursing. Graduates of these three types of basic nursing education programs may have differences in preparation, but all are eligible to take the examination that leads to RN licensure. (Information on schools preparing licensed practical nursing personnel is issued in a separate publication, *State-Approved Schools of Nursing LPN/LVN, 2006*.)

The 2006 edition boasts a number of new features that enhance its utility for prospective nursing students, health planners, nurse administrators, nurse educators, and career and guidance counselors. In addition to providing key data on accreditation, enrollments, graduations, and faculty for each prelicensure nursing program, this volume offers a wealth of information to those interested in pursuing an RN degree about the variety of prelicensure programs in their region, state, or metropolitan area.

Prospective nursing students will find such added features as program acceptance rates, faculty-student ratios, tuition rates, and information on student demographics in a clear, easy-to-read format. This year's volume also contains more than 2,000 graphs that allow the reader to easily compare a program's tuition to that of comparable nursing programs in the same region.

The National League for Nursing is deeply indebted to many members of the nursing community for their assistance in compiling the information within this volume. Without the cooperation of the state boards of nursing, which generously provided information on the state-approved schools in their jurisdiction, this book would not be possible. Moreover, we are grateful to each school that contributed information through the NLN's *National Nursing Education Database* (NNED™) *Survey*.

Kathy A. Kaufman, PhD
Senior Research Analyst
National League for Nursing
March 2006

TABLE OF CONTENTS

DEFINITIONS

Acceptance rate Number of students accepted divided by the total number of applicants between October 16, 2004 and October 15, 2005.

Full-time faculty Total number of faculty or instructional staff employed by the nursing program as of October 15, 2005 on a full-time basis.

Part-time faculty Total number of faculty or instructional staff employed by the nursing program as of October 15, 2005 on a part-time basis.

Faculty-student ratio Total number of nursing school faculty (i.e. number of full-time faculty plus .5 times the number of part-time faculty) divided by the total number of students enrolled in all of the institution's prelicensure nursing programs as of October 15, 2005.

Enrollments Total enrollment in the nursing program as of October 15, 2005. (A student is considered enrolled after declaring nursing as a major.)

Graduations Total number of graduates between October 16, 2004 and October 15, 2005.

Tuition Annual tuition rates for full-time students for 2005-2006, unless otherwise footnoted.

Percent under age 25 Percentage of students enrolled as of October 15, 2005 who are under the age of 25.

Percent female Percentage of students enrolled as of October 15, 2005 who are female.

Percent minority Percentage of students enrolled as of October 15, 2005 who are minorities (i.e., not in the category "white non-Hispanic").

Region Four US geographic regions – Midwest, North Atlantic, South and West – as defined on the map that follows on page vi.

US Geographic Regions

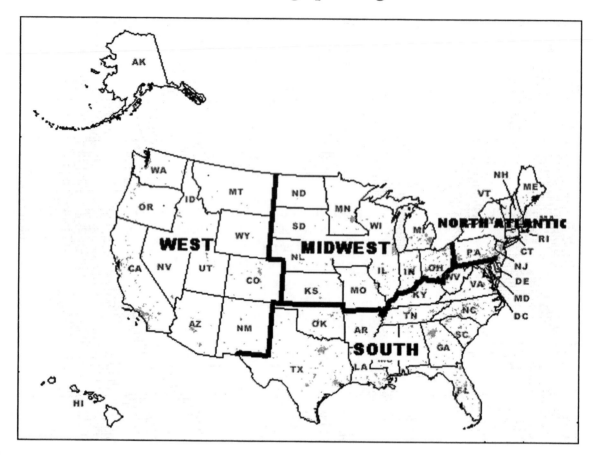

Alabama

AUBURN UNIVERSITY
Useful Facts*

107 Miller Hall
Auburn University, AL 36849
(334) 844-6757
Barbara Witt, EdD, RN

www.auburn.edu/academic/nursing/au_nursing.html

Acceptance rate	38.7%

Tuition		Student Demographics	
In state	$5,020	Female	88.6%
Out of state	$14,240	Under age 25	95.0%
Enrollments	580	Minority	10.1%
Graduations	73	Part-time	0.0%

Accreditation
Alabama Board of Nursing, National League for Nursing Accrediting Commission (NLNAC)

Degrees conferred
Baccalaureate

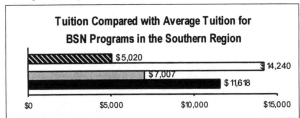

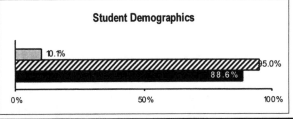

AUBURN UNIVERSITY - MONTGOMERY
Useful Facts*

PO Box 244023
Montgomery, AL 36124
(334) 244-3863
Barbara Witt, EdD, RN

www.aum.edu/home/academics/school/nursing

Acceptance rate	60.9%

Tuition		Student Demographics	
In state	$4,000	Female	90.8%
Out of state	$10,000		
Enrollments	422	Minority	46.2%
Graduations	52	Part-time	25.6%

Accreditation
Alabama Board of Nursing, Commission on Collegiate Nursing Education (CCNE)

Degrees conferred
Baccalaureate

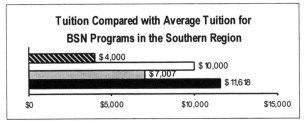

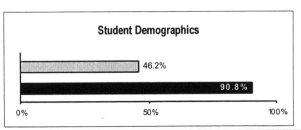

IDA V MOFFETT SCHOOL - SAMFORD UNIVERSITY

800 Lakeshore Drive
Brimingham, AL 35229
(205) 726-2861
Nena Sanders, DSN, RN

www.samford.edu

Accreditation
Alabama Board of Nursing, Commission on Collegiate Nursing Education (CCNE)

At the request of this nursing school, publication has been witheld. Please contact the school directly for more information.

Demographics Chart	■Female ☒Under age 25 ☐Minority	Distance Learning		¹The tuition reported for this program may be not be annualized. *Data reported between 2001 and 2004.

Alabama

JACKSONVILLE STATE UNIVERSITY
Useful Facts

700 Pelham Road North
Jacksonville, AL 36265
(256) 782-5428
Sarah Latham, DSN, MSN, RN

www.jsu.edu/depart/nursing

Acceptance rate		58.9%
Faculty-student ratio		1: 13
Faculty	Full time	20
	Part time	6

Tuition			**Student Demographics**	
In state	$4,040		Female	83.2%
Out of state	$8,080		Under age 25	66.0%
Enrollments	298		Minority	17.3%
Graduations	80		Part-time	0.0%

Accreditation
Alabama Board of Nursing, Commission on Collegiate Nursing Education (CCNE)

Degrees conferred
Baccalaureate degree

Minimum degree required
2 years college before applying to upper division

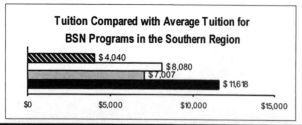

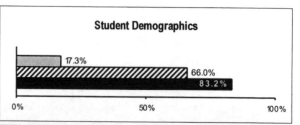

OAKWOOD COLLEGE

7000 Adventist Boulevard
Huntsville, AL 35896
(256) 726-7287
Carol Allen

www.oakwood.edu

Accreditation
Alabama Board of Nursing, National League for Nursing Accrediting Commission (NLNAC)

Degrees conferred
Baccalaureate

SPRING HILL COLLEGE
Useful Facts*

4000 Dauphin Street
Mobile, AL 36608
(251) 380-4492
Carol Harrison, BSN, MSN, EdD

camellia.shc.edu/nursing

Acceptance rate		100.0%

Tuition			**Student Demographics**	
In state	$8,490		Female	86.1%
Out of state	$8,490		Under age 25	95.0%
Enrollments	79		Minority	10.1%
Graduations	11		Part-time	0.0%

Accreditation
Alabama Board of Nursing, Commission on Collegiate Nursing Education (CCNE)

Degrees conferred
Baccalaureate

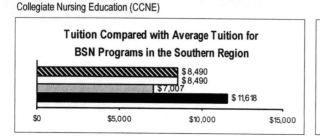

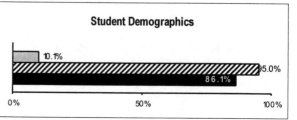

Key | Tuition Chart | ▨ Program - in state ☐ Program - out of state ▢ Average - in state ■ Average - out of state

Alabama

TROY STATE UNIVERSITY — *Useful Facts*

400 Pell Avenue
Troy, AL 36082
(334) 670-3428
Dr Bernita Hamilton, PhD, RN

www.spectrum.troy.edu/~nursing

Accreditation
Alabama Board of Nursing, National League for
Nursing Accrediting Commission (NLNAC)

Acceptance rate		90.0%
Faculty-student ratio		1: 10
Faculty	Full time	36
	Part time	19

Tuition	
In state	$4,004
Out of state	$8,008
Enrollments	153
Graduations	51

Student Demographics	
Female	86.2%
Under age 25	75.6%
Minority	22.7%
Part-time	0.8%

Degrees conferred
Baccalaureate degree

Minimum degree required
High school diploma or GED

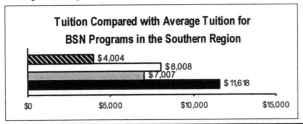

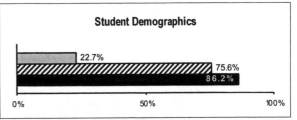

TUSKEGEE UNIVERSITY — *Useful Facts*

209 Basil O'Connor Hall
Tuskegee, AL 36088
(334) 727-8382
Doris Holeman, PhD, RN

www.tuskegee.edu

Accreditation
Alabama Board of Nursing, National League for
Nursing Accrediting Commission (NLNAC)

Acceptance rate		88.2%
Faculty-student ratio		1: 11
Faculty	Full time	8
	Part time	7

Tuition	
In state	$11,640
Out of state	$11,640
Enrollments	123
Graduations	17

Student Demographics	
Female	97.6%
Under age 25	99.2%
Minority	99.2%
Part-time	0.0%

Degrees conferred
Baccalaureate degree

Minimum degree required
High school diploma or GED

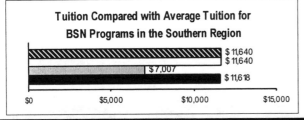

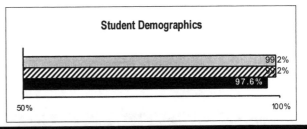

UNIVERSITY OF ALABAMA - BIRMINGHAM

1701 University Boulevard
Birmingham, AL 35401
(205) 934-5360
Rachel Booth, PhD, RN

www.uab.edu/son/sonintr2.htm

Accreditation
Alabama Board of Nursing

At the request of this nursing school, publication has been witheld.
Please contact the school directly for more information.

Demographics Chart	■ Female ▨ Under age 25 ☐ Minority	Distance Learning		¹The tuition reported for this program may be not be annualized.
				*Data reported between 2001 and 2004.

Alabama

UNIVERSITY OF ALABAMA - CAPSTONE COLLEGE OF NURSING

Box 870358
Tuscaloosa, AL 35487
(205) 348-1040
Sara Barger, PhD, RN, FAAN

www.nursing.ua.edu/

Acceptance rate   67.5%

Tuition		Student Demographics	
In state	$4,134	Female	90.3%
Out of state	$11,294		
Enrollments	748	Minority	20.4%
Graduations	66	Part-time	7.5%

Accreditation
Alabama Board of Nursing, Commission on
Collegiate Nursing Education (CCNE)

Degrees conferred
Baccalaureate

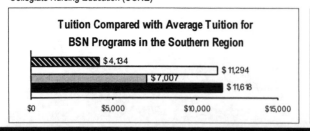

Tuition Compared with Average Tuition for BSN Programs in the Southern Region
$4,134 / $11,294 / $7,007 / $11,618

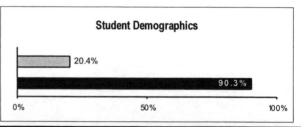

Student Demographics
20.4% / 90.3%

UNIVERSITY OF ALABAMA - HUNTSVILLE

301 Sparkman Drive
Huntsville, AL 35899
(256) 824-6345
Fay Raines, Phd

www.uah.edu

Acceptance rate   82.6%

Tuition		Student Demographics	
In state	$4,300	Female	93.6%
Out of state	$9,000	Under age 25	58.0%
Enrollments	396	Minority	30.6%
Graduations	114	Part-time	27.3%

Accreditation
Alabama Board of Nursing

Degrees conferred
Baccalaureate

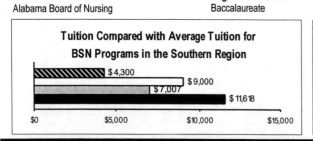

Tuition Compared with Average Tuition for BSN Programs in the Southern Region
$4,300 / $9,000 / $7,007 / $11,618

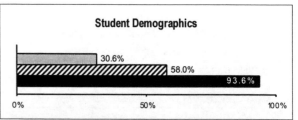

Student Demographics
30.6% / 58.0% / 93.6%

UNIVERSITY OF MOBILE

5735 College Parkway
Mobile, AL 36663-0220
(251) 442-2227
Elizabeth Flanagan, EdD, RN

umobile.edu

Acceptance rate	47.2%		
Faculty-student ratio	1: 9		
Faculty Full time	17		
Part time	5		

Tuition		Student Demographics	
In state	$10,230	Female	85.5%
Out of state	$10,230	Under age 25	65.8%
Enrollments	87	Minority	22.7%
Graduations	26	Part-time	0.0%

Accreditation
Alabama Board of Nursing, Commission on
Collegiate Nursing Education (CCNE)

Degrees conferred
Baccalaureate degree

Minimum degree required
High school diploma or GED

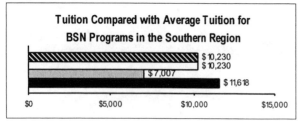

Tuition Compared with Average Tuition for BSN Programs in the Southern Region
$10,230 / $10,230 / $7,007 / $11,618

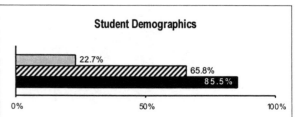

Student Demographics
22.7% / 65.8% / 85.5%

Key   Tuition Chart | ▨ Program - in state   ☐ Program - out of state   ▥ Average - in state   ■ Average - out of state

Alabama

UNIVERSITY OF NORTH ALABAMA — *Useful Facts**

Box 5054
Florence, AL 35632
(256) 765-4984
Birdie Bailey, PhD

www2.una.edu/nursing

Accreditation
Alabama Board of Nursing, National League for
Nursing Accrediting Commission (NLNAC)

Acceptance rate		42.0%
Faculty-student ratio		1: 11
Faculty	Full time	21
	Part time	13

Tuition	
In state	$3,528
Out of state	$7,056
Enrollments	308
Graduations	129

Student Demographics	
Female	89.2%
Under age 25	44.0%
Minority	14.9%
Part-time	12.1%

Degrees conferred
Baccalaureate

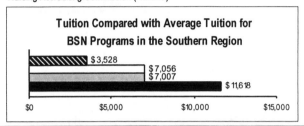
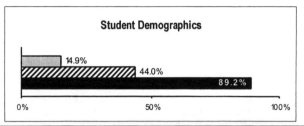

UNIVERSITY OF SOUTH ALABAMA — *Useful Facts**

USA Springhill Avenue
Mobile, AL 36688
(334) 434-3415
Debra Davis, DSN, RN

www.southalabama.edu/nursing

Accreditation
Alabama Board of Nursing

Acceptance rate	84.2%

Tuition	
In state	$3,560
Out of state	$7,120
Enrollments	291
Graduations	162

Student Demographics	
Female	84.2%
Minority	31.6%
Part-time	37.9%

Degrees conferred
Baccalaureate

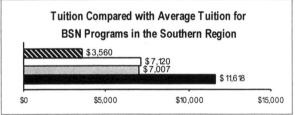
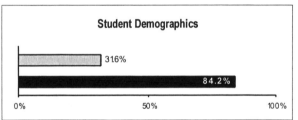

Alaska

UNIVERSITY OF ALASKA - ANCHORAGE — *Useful Facts*

3211 Providence Drive
Anchorage, AK 99508-8030
(907) 786-4571
Jean Ballantyne, PhD, RN

www.son.usaa.alaska.edu

Accreditation
Alaska Board of Nursing, National League for
Nursing Accrediting Commission (NLNAC)

Acceptance rate		92.4%
Faculty-student ratio		1: 7
Faculty	Full time	38
	Part time	16

Tuition	
In state	$3,360
Out of state	$10,290
Enrollments	224
Graduations	103

Student Demographics	
Female	88.6%
Under age 25	49.0%
Minority	22.7%
Part-time	19.8%

Degrees conferred
Bs in nursing science

Minimum degree required
High school diploma or GED

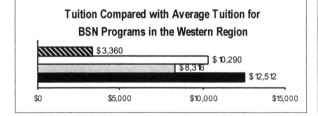
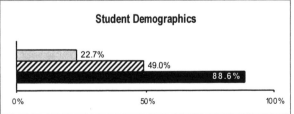

Demographics Chart	■ Female ▨ Under age 25 ☐ Minority	**Distance Learning** 💻	¹The tuition reported for this program may be not be annualized. *Data reported between 2001 and 2004.

Arizona

ARIZONA STATE UNIVERSITY

Box 872602
Tempe, AZ 85287
(480) 965-3244
Bernadette Melnyk, RN, PhD

www.asu.edu

Accreditation
Arizona State Board of Nursing

Degrees conferred
Baccalaureate

GRAND CANYON UNIVERSITY   *Useful Facts**

3300 West Camelback Road
Phoenix, AZ 85017
(602) 589-2431
Cynthia Russell, DNSc, RN, CS

www.grand-canyon.edu

Accreditation
Arizona State Board of Nursing

Degrees conferred
Baccalaureate

Acceptance rate	77.4%	
Enrollments	147	
Graduations	62	

Student Demographics
Female	93.4%
Under age 25	61.0%
Minority	8.9%

NORTHERN ARIZONA UNIVERSITY   *Useful Facts**

PO Box 15035
Flagstaff, AZ 86001
(928) 523-2671
Judith Sellers, DNSc, RN, FNP

www.nau.edu

Accreditation
Arizona State Board of Nursing

Degrees conferred
Baccalaureate

Enrollments	179

Student Demographics
Minority	60.4%
Part-time	0.0%

UNIVERSITY OF ARIZONA

1305 North Martin, PO Box 210203
Tucson, AZ 85721-0203
(520) 626-6152
Marjorie Isenberg, DNSc, RN, FAAN

www.arizona.edu

Accreditation
Arizona State Board of Nursing

Degrees conferred
Baccalaureate

UNIVERSITY OF PHOENIX   *Useful Facts*

4615 East Elwood
Phoenix, AZ 85040
(480) 557-1718
Beth Patton, RN, MA, MN

www.phoenix.edu

Accreditation
Arizona State Board of Nursing, Commission on
Collegiate Nursing Education (CCNE), National
League for Nursing Accrediting Commission
(NLNAC)

Acceptance rate	100.0%	
Faculty-student ratio	1: 262	
Faculty Full time	24	
Part time	0	
Enrollments	6285	
Graduations	45	

Degrees conferred
LPN or LVN

Minimum degree required
High school diploma or GED

Student Demographics
Female	89.7%
Under age 25	100.0%
Minority	59.3%
Part-time	0.0%

Key **Tuition Chart** | ▧ Program - in state ▢ Program - out of state ▨ Average - in state ■ Average - out of state

Arkansas

ARKANSAS STATE UNIVERSITY — Useful Facts

PO Box 910
State University, AR 72467
(870) 972-3074
Sue McLarry, PhD, RN

www.conhp.astate.edu/nursing/index.html

Acceptance rate	55.6%	
Faculty-student ratio	1: 9	
Faculty	Full time	35
	Part time	33

Tuition
In state $4,260
Out of state $10,950
Enrollments 270
Graduations 83

Student Demographics
Female 90.2%
Under age 25 64.1%
Minority 7.1%
Part-time 0.0%

Accreditation
Arkansas State Board of Nursing, National League for Nursing Accrediting Commission (NLNAC)

Degrees conferred
Baccalaureate degree

Minimum degree required
High school diploma or GED

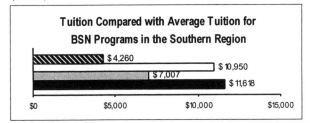

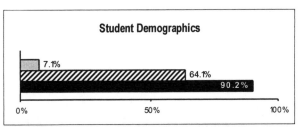

ARKANSAS TECH UNIVERSITY — Useful Facts

Dean Hall, Suite 224
Russellville, AR 72801
(479) 968-0383
Rebecca Burris, PhD, RN

www.nursing.atu.edu

Acceptance rate	47.5%	
Faculty-student ratio	1: 6	
Faculty	Full time	18
	Part time	3

Tuition
In state $4,290
Out of state $8,580
Enrollments 119
Graduations 51

Student Demographics
Female 89.0%
Under age 25 60.6%
Minority 3.7%
Part-time 0.0%

Accreditation
Arkansas State Board of Nursing, National League for Nursing Accrediting Commission (NLNAC)

Degrees conferred
Baccalaureate degree

Minimum degree required
High school diploma or GED

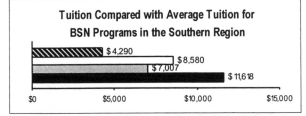

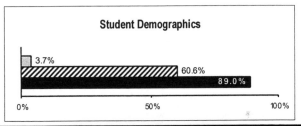

HARDING UNIVERSITY — Useful Facts*

900 East Center, Box 12265
Searcy, AR 72149
(501) 279-4476
Cathleen Schultz, PhD, RN, FAAN

www.harding.edu/nursing

Acceptance rate 73.9%

Tuition
In state $9,040
Out of state $9,040
Enrollments 317
Graduations 39

Student Demographics
Female 87.7%
Under age 25 89.3%
Minority 8.1%
Part-time 5.4%

Accreditation
Arkansas State Board of Nursing

Degrees conferred
Baccalaureate degree

Minimum degree required
Two years of prerequisites for BSN

Tuition Compared with Average Tuition for BSN Programs in the Southern Region

$9,040
$9,040
$7,007
$11,618

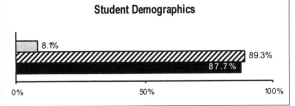

Demographics Chart	■ Female ▨ Under age 25 ☐ Minority	Distance Learning	¹The tuition reported for this program may be not be annualized. *Data reported between 2001 and 2004.

Arkansas

HENDERSON STATE UNIVERSITY

HSU Box 7803, 1100 Henderson Street
Arkadelphia, AR 71999-0001
(870) 230-5015
Rebecca Patterson, RN, DSN, APRN-BC

At the request of this nursing school, publication has been witheld.
Please contact the school directly for more information.

www.hsu.edu/dept/nsg/index.html

Accreditation
Arkansas State Board of Nursing, National
League for Nursing Accrediting Commission
(NLNAC)

UNIVERSITY OF ARKANSAS - FAYETTEVILLE

217 Ozark Hall
Fayetteville, AR 72701
(479) 575-3907
Thomas Kippenbrock, RN, EdD

At the request of this nursing school, publication has been witheld.
Please contact the school directly for more information.

www.uark.edu/coehp

Accreditation
Arkansas State Board of Nursing, Commission
on Collegiate Nursing Education (CCNE),
National League for Nursing Accrediting
Commission (NLNAC)

UNIVERSITY OF ARKANSAS - MONTICELLO   *Useful Facts*

358 University Drive, PO Box 3606
Monticello, AR 71656
(870) 460-1069
Larry Eustace, AASN, BSN, MSN, DSN, RN,
CNE

www.uamont.edu/nursing

Acceptance rate		45.2%	**Tuition**		**Student Demographics**	
Faculty-student ratio		1: 10	In state	$3,000	Female	81.7%
Faculty	Full time	9	Out of state	$6,750	Under age 25	66.2%
	Part time	1	**Enrollments**	78	Minority	10.0%
			Graduations	33	Part-time	2.8%

Accreditation
Arkansas State Board of Nursing, National
League for Nursing Accrediting Commission
(NLNAC)

Degrees conferred
Baccalaureate degree

Minimum degree required
64 college credit hours of prerequisite courses
with a 2.50 GPA or higher

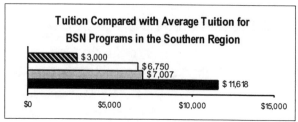

Tuition Compared with Average Tuition for BSN Programs in the Southern Region
- $3,000
- $6,750
- $7,007
- $11,618

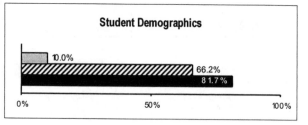

Student Demographics
- 10.0%
- 66.2%
- 81.7%

Arkansas

UNIVERSITY OF ARKANSAS - PINE BLUFF *Useful Facts**

1200 University Drive, Slot 4973
Pine Bluff, AR 71601
(870) 575-8220
Sheila Garland, PhD

www.uapb.edu

Acceptance rate	57.4%	**Tuition**		**Student Demographics**
		In state	$2,256	Female	91.7%
		Out of state	$5,256	Under age 25	40.0%
		Enrollments	62	Minority	95.0%
		Graduations	6	Part-time	11.7%

Accreditation
Arkansas State Board of Nursing, National
League for Nursing Accrediting Commission
(NLNAC)

Degrees conferred
Baccalaureate

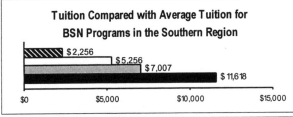

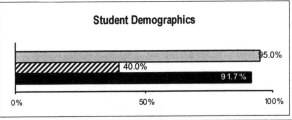

UNIVERSITY OF ARKANSAS FOR MEDICAL SCIENCES *Useful Facts**

4301 West Markham, Slot 529
Little Rock, AR 72205
(501) 686-5374
Linda Hodges, EdD, RN

www.nursing.uams.edu

Acceptance rate	53.1%	**Tuition**		**Student Demographics**
		In state	$3,816	Female	82.9%
		Out of state	$9,528	Under age 25	54.0%
		Enrollments	314	Minority	14.7%
		Graduations	136	Part-time	7.8%

Accreditation
Arkansas State Board of Nursing, Commission
on Collegiate Nursing Education (CCNE),
National League for Nursing Accrediting
Commission (NLNAC)

Degrees conferred
Baccalaureate

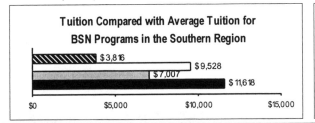

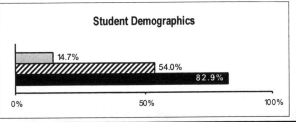

UNIVERSITY OF CENTRAL ARKANSAS

201 Donaghey Avenue
Conway, AR 72035
(501) 450-3119
Barbara Williams, PhD, RN

www.uca.eud/nursing

Accreditation
Arkansas State Board of Nursing, Commission
on Collegiate Nursing Education (CCNE)

At the request of this nursing school, publication has been witheld.
Please contact the school directly for more information.

Demographics Chart	■Female ▨Under age 25 ☐Minority	**Distance Learning**	†The tuition reported for this program may be not be annualized. *Data reported between 2001 and 2004.

California

AZUSA PACIFIC UNIVERSITY
Useful Facts

901 East Alosta Avenue
Azusa, CA 91702
(626) 815-5384
Aja Lesh, PhD, RN

www.apu.edu

Acceptance rate		23.0%
Faculty-student ratio		1:5
Faculty	Full time	31
	Part time	38

Tuition

In state	$21,550
Out of state	$21,550
Enrollments	253
Graduations	75

Student Demographics

Female	91.5%
Under age 25	93.2%
Minority	24.9%
Part-time	0.0%

Accreditation
California Board of Registered Nursing,
Commission on Collegiate Nursing Education
(CCNE)

Degrees conferred
Baccalaureate degree

Minimum degree required
High school diploma or GED

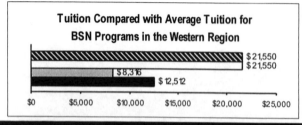

Tuition Compared with Average Tuition for BSN Programs in the Western Region
$21,550
$21,550
$8,316
$12,512

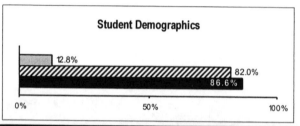

Student Demographics
12.8%
82.0%
86.6%

BIOLA UNIVERSITY
Useful Facts

13800 Biola Ave
La Mirada, CA 90639
(562) 903-4850
Rebekah Fleeger, PhD, RN

www.biola.edu/academics/undergrad/nursing

Acceptance rate		56.6%
Faculty-student ratio		1:8
Faculty	Full time	8
	Part time	5

Tuition

In state	$22,602
Out of state	$22,602
Enrollments	88
Graduations	27

Student Demographics

Female	94.3%
Under age 25	96.6%
Minority	11.5%
Part-time	0.0%

Accreditation
California Board of Registered Nursing, National
League for Nursing Accrediting Commission
(NLNAC)

Degrees conferred
Baccalaureate degree

Minimum degree required
High school diploma or GED

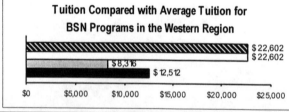

Tuition Compared with Average Tuition for BSN Programs in the Western Region
$22,602
$22,602
$8,316
$12,512

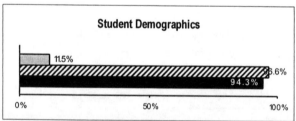

Student Demographics
11.5%
96.6%
94.3%

CALIFORNIA STATE UNIVERSITY - BAKERSFIELD
*Useful Facts**

9001 Stockdale Highway
Bakersfield, CA 93311
(661) 664-2029
Candace Meares, PhD, RN, CNAA

www.csub.edu

Acceptance rate	60.2%

Tuition[1]

In state	$276
Out of state	$440
Enrollments	128
Graduations	35

Student Demographics

Female	90.7%
Minority	34.2%
Part-time	0.0%

Accreditation
California Board of Registered Nursing

Degrees conferred
Baccalaureate

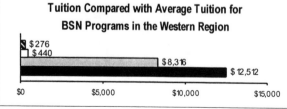

Tuition Compared with Average Tuition for BSN Programs in the Western Region
$276
$440
$8,316
$12,512

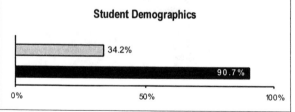

Student Demographics
34.2%
90.7%

Key Tuition Chart | ▨ Program - in state ☐ Program - out of state ☐ Average - in state ■ Average - out of state

California

CALIFORNIA STATE UNIVERSITY - CHICO
Useful Facts

1st and Orange Street, Holt Hall, Room 369
Chico, CA 95929-0200
(530) 898-5891
Sherry Fox, PhD, RN

csuchico.edu/nurs/nurs.html

Accreditation
California Board of Registered Nursing,
Commission on Collegiate Nursing Education
(CCNE), National League for Nursing Accrediting
Commission (NLNAC)

Acceptance rate		31.1%
Faculty-student ratio		1: 12
Faculty	Full time	11
	Part time	15

Tuition	
In state	$3,370
Out of state	$11,506
Enrollments	231
Graduations	81

Student Demographics	
Female	89.6%
Under age 25	64.6%
Minority	19.3%
Part-time	10.4%

Degrees conferred
Baccalaureate degree, MSN

Minimum degree required
High school diploma or GED

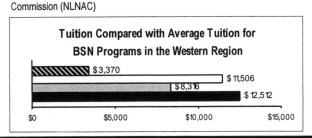

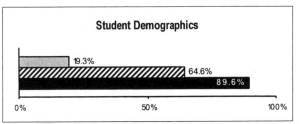

CALIFORNIA STATE UNIVERSITY - EAST BAY

25800 Carlos Bee Boulevard
Hayward, CA 94542
(510) 885-2925
Carolyn Fong, PhD, RN

www.csueastbay.edu

Accreditation
California Board of Registered Nursing, National
League for Nursing Accrediting Commission
(NLNAC)

At the request of this nursing school, publication has been witheld.
Please contact the school directly for more information.

CALIFORNIA STATE UNIVERSITY - FRESNO
Useful Facts

2345 East San Ramon Avenue, M/S MH25
Fresno, CA 93740
(559) 278-2429
Michael Russler, EdD, MSN, CFNP

www.csufresno.edu/nursing/nursing1.htm

Accreditation
California Board of Registered Nursing, National
League for Nursing Accrediting Commission
(NLNAC)

Acceptance rate		25.9%
Faculty-student ratio		1: 13
Faculty	Full time	16
	Part time	27

Tuition	
In state	$2,700
Out of state	$4,746
Enrollments	390
Graduations	119

Student Demographics	
Female	87.0%
Under age 25	50.7%
Minority	54.6%
Part-time	21.7%

Degrees conferred
Baccalaureate degree, MSN

Minimum degree required
High school diploma or GED

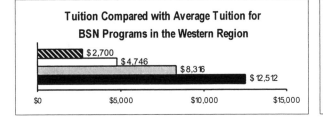

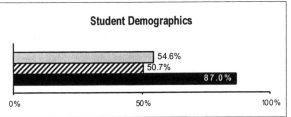

| Demographics Chart | ■ Female ▨ Under age 25 ☐ Minority | Distance Learning | ¹The tuition reported for this program may be not be annualized. *Data reported between 2001 and 2004. |

California

CALIFORNIA STATE UNIVERSITY - LONG BEACH

1250 North Bellflower Blvd
Long Beach, CA 90840-0301
(562) 985-8242
Christine Talmadge, PhD

www.csulb.edu

Accreditation
California Board of Registered Nursing

Degrees conferred
Baccalaureate

CALIFORNIA STATE UNIVERSITY - LOS ANGELES — *Useful Facts*

5151 State University Drive
Los Angeles, CA 90032
(323) 343-4700
Patricia Chin, DNSc, RN

calstatela.edu

Acceptance rate	17.7%	
Faculty-student ratio	1: 8	
Faculty Full time	12	
Part time	24	

Tuition		Student Demographics	
In state	$3,032	Female	87.6%
Out of state	$5,347	Under age 25	46.4%
Enrollments	194	Minority	82.4%
Graduations	125	Part-time	26.8%

Accreditation
California Board of Registered Nursing, National League for Nursing Accrediting Commission (NLNAC)

Degrees conferred
Baccalaureate degree

Minimum degree required
Prerequisite courses and admission tests

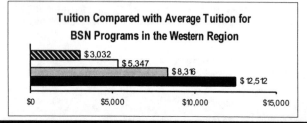
Tuition Compared with Average Tuition for BSN Programs in the Western Region: $3,032; $5,347; $8,316; $12,512

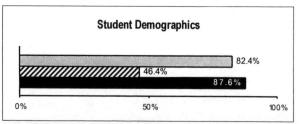
Student Demographics: 82.4%; 46.4%; 87.6%

CALIFORNIA STATE UNIVERSITY - SACRAMENTO — *Useful Facts**

6000 J Street
Sacramento, CA 95819
(916) 278-7543
Robyn Nelson, DNSc, RN

www.hhs.csus.edu/nrs

Acceptance rate	15.8%	Student Demographics	
		Female	89.8%
Enrollments	392	Minority	40.8%
Graduations	130	Part-time	5.7%

Accreditation
California Board of Registered Nursing, Commission on Collegiate Nursing Education (CCNE)

Degrees conferred
Baccalaureate

Minimum degree required
High school diploma or GED

CALIFORNIA STATE UNIVERSITY - SAN BERNARDINO — *Useful Facts**

HP-215, 5500 University Parkway
San Bernardino, CA 92407
(909) 880-5385
Marcia Raimes, PhD, MN, RN, CS

nursing.csusb.edu

Acceptance rate	26.0%	Tuition	Student Demographics
		In state $2,681	Female 85.6%
			Under age 25 67.0%
		Enrollments 264	Minority 57.1%
		Graduations 51	Part-time 0.0%

Accreditation
California Board of Registered Nursing, Commission on Collegiate Nursing Education (CCNE)

Degrees conferred
Baccalaureate

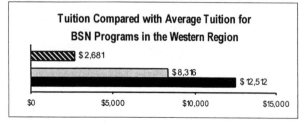
Tuition Compared with Average Tuition for BSN Programs in the Western Region: $2,681; $8,316; $12,512

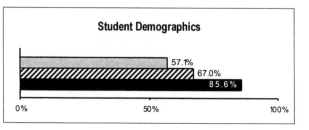
Student Demographics: 57.1%; 67.0%; 85.6%

Key Tuition Chart | ▧ Program - in state ☐ Program - out of state ▨ Average - in state ■ Average - out of state

California

CALIFORNIA STATE UNIVERSITY - STANISLAUS

801 West Monte Vista Avenue, DBH 260
Turlock, CA 95382
(209) 667-3141
Nancy Clark, EdD, RN, MSN, MPA

www.csustan.edu/nursing/index.htm

Accreditation
California Board of Registered Nursing

Degrees conferred
Baccalaureate

DOMINICAN UNIVERSITY OF CALIFORNIA   *Useful Facts**

50 Acacia Avenue
San Rafael, CA 94901
(415) 482-1830
Dottie Needham, DNS, APRN

www.dominican.edu

			Tuition		Student Demographics	
Acceptance rate	58.7%		In state	$24,254	Female	89.5%
			Out of state	$24,254	Under age 25	72.0%
			Enrollments	382	Minority	55.6%
			Graduations	36	Part-time	3.3%

Accreditation
California Board of Registered Nursing,
Commission on Collegiate Nursing Education
(CCNE)

Degrees conferred
Baccalaureate

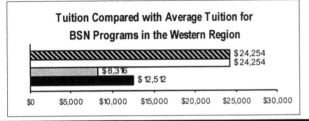

Tuition Compared with Average Tuition for BSN Programs in the Western Region: $24,254 / $24,254 / $8,316 / $12,512

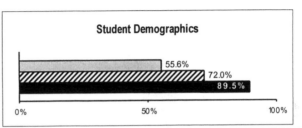

Student Demographics: 55.6% / 72.0% / 89.5%

HUMBOLDT STATE UNIVERSITY   *Useful Facts**

1 Harpst Street
Arcata, CA 95521
(707) 826-5731
Betty Jensen

www.humboldt.edu/~nurs

Enrollments 40

Accreditation
California Board of Registered Nursing

Degrees conferred
Baccalaureate

LOMA LINDA UNIVERSITY   *Useful Facts*

Loma Linda University
Loma Linda, CA 92350
(909) 558-4517
Helen King, PhD, RN

www.llu.edu/llu/nursing

				Tuition		Student Demographics	
Acceptance rate		59.5%		In state	$20,925	Female	86.4%
Faculty-student ratio		1:6		Out of state	$20,925	Under age 25	80.8%
Faculty	Full time	31		**Enrollments**	358	Minority	55.4%
	Part time	55		**Graduations**	90	Part-time	3.0%

Accreditation
California Board of Registered Nursing,
Commission on Collegiate Nursing Education
(CCNE)

Degrees conferred
Baccalaureate degree

Minimum degree required
None

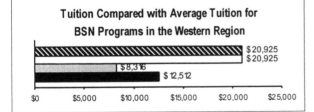

Tuition Compared with Average Tuition for BSN Programs in the Western Region: $20,925 / $20,925 / $8,316 / $12,512

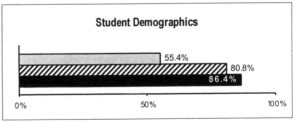

Student Demographics: 55.4% / 80.8% / 86.4%

Demographics Chart | ■Female ☒Under age 25 ☐Minority | **Distance Learning** | ¹The tuition reported for this program may be not be annualized.
*Data reported between 2001 and 2004.

California

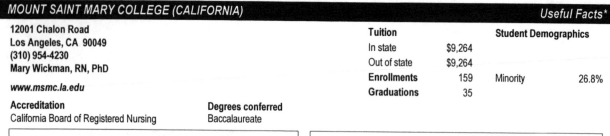

MOUNT SAINT MARY COLLEGE (CALIFORNIA)

12001 Chalon Road
Los Angeles, CA 90049
(310) 954-4230
Mary Wickman, RN, PhD

www.msmc.la.edu

Tuition		Student Demographics	
In state	$9,264		
Out of state	$9,264		
Enrollments	159	Minority	26.8%
Graduations	35		

Accreditation
California Board of Registered Nursing

Degrees conferred
Baccalaureate

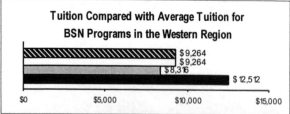

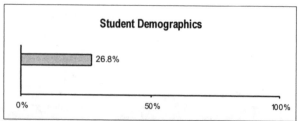

NATIONAL UNIVERSITY

11255 North Torrey Pines Road
La Jolla, CA 92037
(858) 642-8344
Nancy Saks, DNSc, RN

www.nu.edu/academics/schools/sohhs/nursing.html

				Tuition		Student Demographics	
Acceptance rate			64.4%	In state	$10,440	Female	79.2%
Faculty-student ratio			1: 4	Out of state	$10,440	Under age 25	41.7%
Faculty	Full time		6	Enrollments	72	Minority	29.6%
	Part time		52	Graduations	0	Part-time	0.0%

Accreditation
California Board of Registered Nursing,
Commission on Collegiate Nursing Education
(CCNE)

Degrees conferred
Baccalaureate degree

Minimum degree required
High school diploma or GED

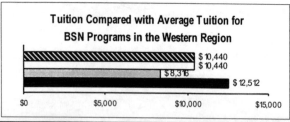

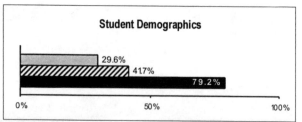

POINT LOMA NAZARENE UNIVERSITY

3900 Lomaland Drive
San Diego, CA 92106
(619) 849-2236
Dorothy Crummy, PhD, RN

www.ptloma.edu/nursing

Acceptance rate	75.0%		Student Demographics	
			Female	82.2%
			Under age 25	66.0%
		Enrollments	136	Minority	25.4%
		Graduations	38	Part-time	9.6%

Accreditation
California Board of Registered Nursing,
Commission on Collegiate Nursing Education
(CCNE)

Degrees conferred
Baccalaureate

SAMUEL MERRITT COLLEGE - SAINT MARY

3100 Summit Street, 3rd floor
Oakland, CA 94609
(510) 869-6611
Audrey Berman, PhD, RN, AOCN

www.samuelmerritt.edu

Faculty-student ratio		1: 5		Student Demographics	
				Female	90.1%
Faculty	Full time	45		Under age 25	54.4%
	Part time	60	Enrollments	353	Minority	55.0%
				Part-time	13.9%

Accreditation
California Board of Registered Nursing

Degrees conferred
Baccalaureate

Key | Tuition Chart | ⊠ Program - in state ☐ Program - out of state ▢ Average - in state ■ Average - out of state

California

SAN DIEGO STATE UNIVERSITY
Useful Facts*

5500 Campanile Drive
San Diego, CA 92182
(619) 594-6384
Patricia Wahl, PhD, RN, FAAN

www.rohan.sdsu.edu/dept/chhs/nursing

Acceptance rate	20.3%	

Student Demographics

Female	86.8%

Enrollments	288	
Graduations	73	

Minority	55.4%
Part-time	28.2%

Accreditation
California Board of Registered Nursing

Degrees conferred
Baccalaureate

SAN FRANCISCO STATE UNIVERSITY
Useful Facts*

1600 Holloway Avenue
San Francisco, CA 94132
(415) 405-3660
Beatrice Yorker, JD, MSN

www.nursing.sfsu.edu

Acceptance rate	21.8%

Tuition

In state	$786
Out of state	$4,387
Enrollments	227
Graduations	66

Student Demographics

Female	82.1%
Under age 25	5.0%
Minority	71.7%
Part-time	0.0%

Accreditation
California Board of Registered Nursing,
Commission on Collegiate Nursing Education
(CCNE)

Degrees conferred
Baccalaureate

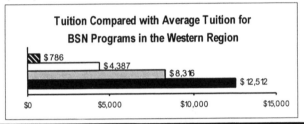

Tuition Compared with Average Tuition for BSN Programs in the Western Region

$786
$4,387
$8,316
$12,512

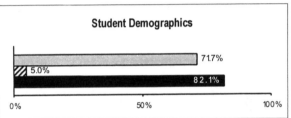

Student Demographics

71.7%
5.0%
82.1%

SAN JOSE STATE UNIVERSITY
Useful Facts*

One Washington Square
San Jose, CA 95192-0057
(408) 924-3132
Bobbye Gorenberg, DNSc, RN, C

www.sjsu.edu/depts/casa/depts/nurs.html

Acceptance rate	100.0%

Student Demographics

Enrollments	447	
Graduations	113	

Minority	71.2%
Part-time	20.5%

Accreditation
California Board of Registered Nursing

Degrees conferred
Baccalaureate

SONOMA STATE UNIVERSITY
Useful Facts

1801 East Cotati Avenue
Rohnert Park, CA 94928
(707) 664-2654
Liz Close, PhD, MSN, RN

www.sonoma.edu/nursing

Acceptance rate		22.1%
Faculty-student ratio		1:7
Faculty	Full time	9
	Part time	23

Tuition

Out of state	$10,170
Enrollments	135
Graduations	44

Student Demographics

Female	90.9%
Under age 25	52.5%
Minority	27.3%
Part-time	0.0%

Accreditation
California Board of Registered Nursing, National
League for Nursing Accrediting Commission
(NLNAC)

Degrees conferred
Baccalaureate degree

Minimum degree required
High school diploma or GED

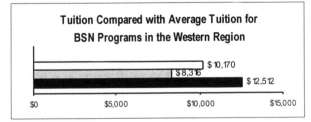

Tuition Compared with Average Tuition for BSN Programs in the Western Region

$10,170
$8,316
$12,512

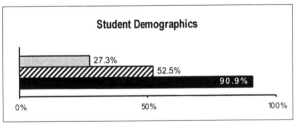

Student Demographics

27.3%
52.5%
90.9%

Demographics Chart | ■Female ☒Under age 25 ☐Minority | **Distance Learning** | †The tuition reported for this program may be not be annualized.
*Data reported between 2001 and 2004.

California

UNIVERSITY OF SAN FRANCISCO

Useful Facts*

2130 Fulton Street
San Francisco, CA 94115
(415) 422-2959
John Lantz, PhD, RN

www.usfca.edu/nursing

Acceptance rate   75.9%

Tuition	
In state	$18,860
Out of state	$18,860
Enrollments	4614
Graduations	67

Student Demographics	
Minority	77.6%

Accreditation
California Board of Registered Nursing

Degrees conferred
Baccalaureate

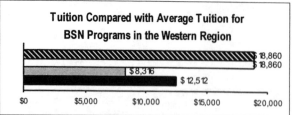

Tuition Compared with Average Tuition for BSN Programs in the Western Region

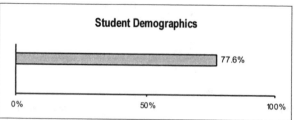

Student Demographics

Colorado

COLORADO STATE UNIVERSITY - PUEBLO

Useful Facts

2200 Bonforte Boulevard
Pueblo, CO 81001
(719) 549-2871
Rhonda Johnston, PhD, BC, APN, FNP, ANP, CNS

www.colostate-pueblo.edu

Faculty-student ratio		1: 19
Faculty	Full time	10
	Part time	2

Tuition	
In state	$2,524
Out of state	$13,542
Enrollments	212
Graduations	59

Student Demographics	
Female	86.1%
Under age 25	51.0%
Minority	24.7%
Part-time	3.4%

Accreditation
Colorado State Board of Nursing, National League for Nursing Accrediting Commission (NLNAC)

Degrees conferred
Baccalaureate degree

Minimum degree required
High school diploma or GED

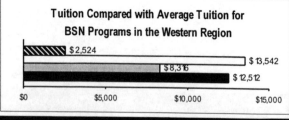

Tuition Compared with Average Tuition for BSN Programs in the Western Region

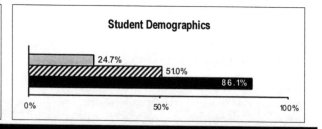

Student Demographics

DENVER SCHOOL OF NURSING

1401 19th Street
Denver, CO 80202
(303) 292-0015
Rebekah Lynch, PhD, RN, CNS

www.denverschoolofnursing.org

Accreditation
Colorado State Board of Nursing

Degrees conferred
Baccalaureate

Key   Tuition Chart | ▨ Program - in state   ☐ Program - out of state   ☐ Average - in state   ■ Average - out of state

Colorado

MESA STATE COLLEGE — *Useful Facts*

1100 North Avenue
Grand Junction, CO 81502
(970) 248-1398
Kristine Reuss, PhD, RN

mesastate.edu

Acceptance rate	40.0%	
Faculty-student ratio	1: 7	
Faculty Full time	14	
Part time	23	

Tuition	
In state	$2,359
Out of state	$9,546
Enrollments	178
Graduations	49

Student Demographics	
Female	87.7%
Under age 25	53.5%
Minority	11.0%
Part-time	0.0%

Accreditation
Colorado State Board of Nursing, Commission on Collegiate Nursing Education (CCNE)

Degrees conferred
Baccalaureate degree

Minimum degree required
High school diploma or GED

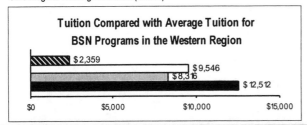
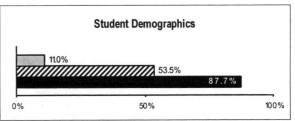

METROPOLITAN STATE COLLEGE OF DENVER — *Useful Facts*

PO Box 173362, Campus Box 72
Denver, CO 80217
(303) 556-2911
Nancy Case, RN, PhD

www.mscd.edu/~nursing

Acceptance rate	23.2%	
Faculty-student ratio	1: 9	
Faculty Full time	4	
Part time	22	

Tuition	
In state	$2,387
Out of state	$10,138
Enrollments	130
Graduations	31

Student Demographics	
Female	78.1%
Under age 25	6.3%
Minority	6.7%
Part-time	0.0%

Accreditation
Colorado State Board of Nursing, National League for Nursing Accrediting Commission (NLNAC)

Degrees conferred
Baccalaureate degree

Minimum degree required
BA or BS in a non-nursing field

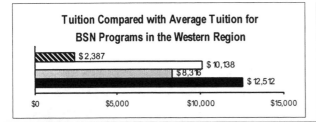
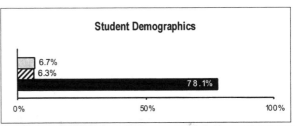

REGIS UNIVERSITY — *Useful Facts*

3333 Regis Boulevard
Denver, CO 80221
(303) 458-4181
Candace Berardinelli, PhD, RN, ANP

www.regis.edu

Acceptance rate	38.4%	
Faculty-student ratio	1: 10	
Faculty Full time	32	
Part time	84	

Tuition	
In state	$23,500
Out of state	$23,500
Enrollments	754
Graduations	307

Student Demographics	
Female	90.4%
Under age 25	38.5%
Minority	15.9%
Part-time	0.0%

Accreditation
Colorado State Board of Nursing, Commission on Collegiate Nursing Education (CCNE)

Degrees conferred
Baccalaureate degree

Minimum degree required
High school diploma or GED

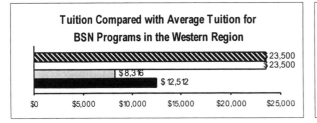
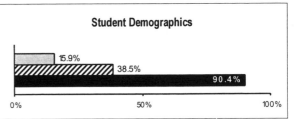

Demographics Chart: ■Female ▨Under age 25 ☐Minority | Distance Learning | ¹The tuition reported for this program may be not be annualized. *Data reported between 2001 and 2004.

Colorado

UNIVERSITY OF COLORADO - COLORADO SPRINGS - BETH-EL COLLEGE OF NURSING — *Useful Facts*

1420 Austin Bluffs Parkway, PO Box 7150
Colorado Springs, CO 80933
(719) 262-4418
Carole Schoffstall, PhD, RN

web.uccs.edu/bethel

Acceptance rate		22.7%
Faculty-student ratio		1: 9
Faculty	Full time	18
	Part time	35

Tuition	
In state	$7,053
Out of state	$19,075
Enrollments	320
Graduations	93

Student Demographics	
Female	91.6%
Under age 25	73.1%
Minority	21.5%
Part-time	14.1%

Accreditation
Colorado State Board of Nursing, Commission on Collegiate Nursing Education (CCNE)

Degrees conferred
Baccalaureate degree

Minimum degree required
BA or BS in a non-nursing field

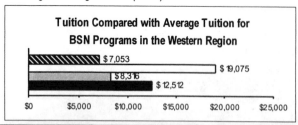

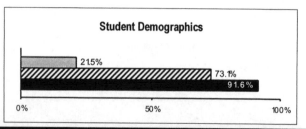

UNIVERSITY OF COLORADO AT DENVER AND HEALTH SCIENCES CENTER — *Useful Facts*

4200 E 9th Avenue
Denver, CO 80262
(303) 315-7754
Patricia Moritz, RN, PhD, FAAN

www.uchsc.edu/nursing

Acceptance rate		26.4%
Faculty-student ratio		1: 4
Faculty	Full time	47
	Part time	73

Tuition	
In state	$8,388
Out of state	$26,424
Enrollments	371
Graduations	136

Student Demographics	
Female	89.4%
Under age 25	36.4%
Minority	14.0%
Part-time	2.1%

Accreditation
Colorado State Board of Nursing, Commission on Collegiate Nursing Education (CCNE), National League for Nursing Accrediting Commission (NLNAC)

Degrees conferred
Nursing doctorate (ND), PhD, Baccalaureate degree, MSN, DNP

Minimum degree required
BA or BS in a non-nursing field

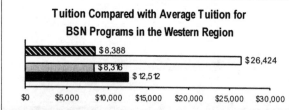

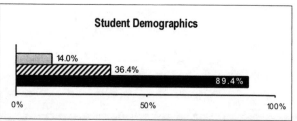

UNIVERSITY OF NORTHERN COLORADO — *Useful Facts**

Gunter Hall 3080
Greeley, CO 80639
(970) 351-1689
Margaret Andrews, PhD, RN, FAAN, CTN

www.unco.edu/hhs/son/son.htm

| Acceptance rate | 30.3% |

Tuition	
In state	$2,850
Out of state	$11,740
Enrollments	213
Graduations	94

Student Demographics	
Female	89.9%
Minority	14.1%
Part-time	0.0%

Accreditation
Colorado State Board of Nursing, Commission on Collegiate Nursing Education (CCNE)

Degrees conferred
Baccalaureate

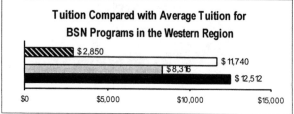

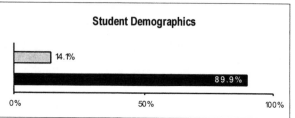

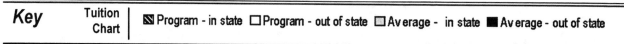

Key — Tuition Chart — ▨ Program - in state ☐ Program - out of state ☐ Average - in state ■ Average - out of state

Connecticut

FAIRFIELD UNIVERSITY

1073 North Benson Road
Fairfield, CT 06430
(203) 254-4150
Jeanne Novotny, PhD, RN, FAAN

www.fairfield.edu

Acceptance rate	65.4%

Tuition
In state	$26,585
Out of state	$26,585
Enrollments	257
Graduations	45

Student Demographics
Female	95.0%
Under age 25	84.0%
Minority	13.1%
Part-time	3.3%

Accreditation
Connecticut Board of Examiners for Nursing, Commission on Collegiate Nursing Education (CCNE), National League for Nursing Accrediting Commission (NLNAC)

Degrees conferred
Baccalaureate

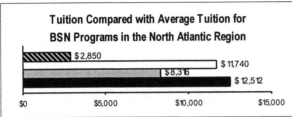

Tuition Compared with Average Tuition for BSN Programs in the North Atlantic Region

$2,850
$11,740
$8,316
$12,512

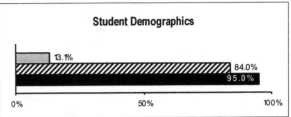

Student Demographics

13.1%
84.0%
95.0%

QUINNIPIAC UNIVERSITY

275 Mount Carmel Avenue
Hamden, CT 06518
(203) 582-8678
Janice Thompson, PhD, APRN, NP-C

www.quinnipiac.edu

Acceptance rate	46.5%
Faculty-student ratio	1: 10

Faculty	Full time	13
	Part time	46

Tuition
In state	$24,340
Out of state	$24,340
Enrollments	352
Graduations	54

Student Demographics
Female	94.6%
Under age 25	92.3%
Minority	9.4%
Part-time	0.6%

Accreditation
Connecticut Board of Examiners for Nursing, National League for Nursing Accrediting Commission (NLNAC)

Degrees conferred
Baccalaureate degree

Minimum degree required
High school diploma or GED

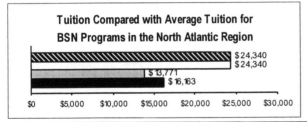

Tuition Compared with Average Tuition for BSN Programs in the North Atlantic Region

$24,340
$24,340
$13,771
$16,163

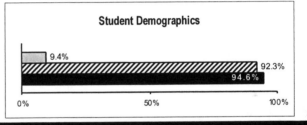

Student Demographics

9.4%
92.3%
94.6%

SACRED HEART UNIVERSITY

5151 Park Avenue
Fairfield, CT 06825
(203) 371-7715
Dori Sullivan, PhD, RN, CNA, CPHQ

nursing.sacredheart.edu

At the request of this nursing school, publication has been withheld. Please contact the school directly for more information.

Accreditation
Connecticut Board of Examiners for Nursing, Commission on Collegiate Nursing Education (CCNE)

Demographics Chart	■ Female ▨ Under age 25 ▢ Minority	Distance Learning		¹The tuition reported for this program may be not be annualized. *Data reported between 2001 and 2004.

Connecticut

SAINT JOSEPH COLLEGE - WEST HARTFORD

1678 Asylum Avenue
West Hartford, CT 06117
(860) 231-5258
Virginia Knowlden, EdD, RN

www.sjc.edu

Accreditation
Connecticut Board of Examiners for Nursing

Acceptance rate	94.9%

Tuition

In state	$17,430
Out of state	$17,430
Enrollments	90
Graduations	31

Student Demographics

Female	100.0%
Minority	14.8%
Part-time	37.5%

Degrees conferred
Baccalaureate

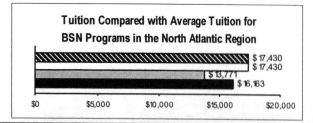

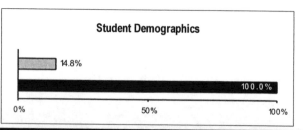

SOUTHERN CONNECTICUT STATE UNIVERSITY

501 Crescent Street
New Haven, CT 06515
(203) 392-6487
Cesarina Thompson, PhD

scsu.ctstateu.edu/departments/nursing

Accreditation
Connecticut Board of Examiners for Nursing

Acceptance rate	76.2%

Tuition

In state	$2,142
Out of state	$6,934
Enrollments	130
Graduations	40

Student Demographics

Female	93.6%
Minority	28.9%
Part-time	9.6%

Degrees conferred
Baccalaureate

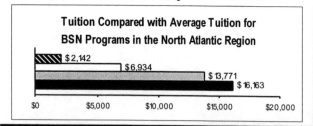

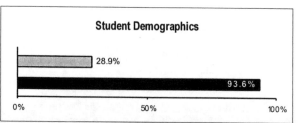

UNIVERSITY OF CONNECTICUT

231 Glenbrook Road
Storrs Mansfield, CT 06269
(860) 486-0537
Laura Dzurec, PhD

nursing.uconn.edu

Accreditation
Connecticut Board of Examiners for Nursing,
National League for Nursing Accrediting
Commission (NLNAC)

Acceptance rate	37.1%

Tuition

In state	$5,260
Out of state	$16,044
Enrollments	552
Graduations	77

Student Demographics

Female	90.6%
Under age 25	89.8%
Minority	21.3%
Part-time	1.7%

Degrees conferred
Baccalaureate

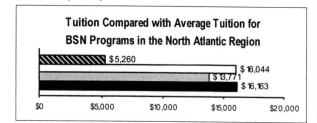

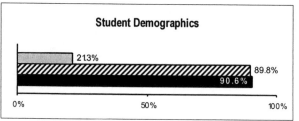

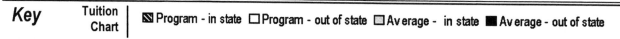

Key | **Tuition Chart** | ▨ Program - in state   ☐ Program - out of state   ☐ Average - in state   ■ Average - out of state

Connecticut

WESTERN CONNECTICUT STATE UNIVERSITY | Useful Facts

181 White Street, White Hall 107
Danbury, CT 06810
(203) 837-8557
Barbara Piscopo, EdD, RN

www.wcsu.edu/nursing

Accreditation
Connecticut Board of Examiners for Nursing,
Commission on Collegiate Nursing Education
(CCNE)

Acceptance rate		25.9%
Faculty-student ratio		1: 14
Faculty	Full time	18
	Part time	3

Degrees conferred
Baccalaureate degree, MSN

Tuition	
In state	$2,862
Out of state	$9,264
Enrollments	277
Graduations	32

Minimum degree required
None

Student Demographics	
Female	95.0%
Under age 25	20.8%
Part-time	29.2%

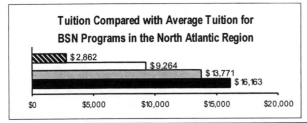

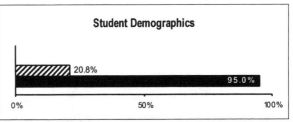

YALE UNIVERSITY | Useful Facts

100 Church Street South
New Haven, CT 06536
(203) 785-2393
Margaret Grey, DrPH, RN, FAAN

www.nursing.yale.edu

Accreditation
Connecticut Board of Examiners for Nursing,
Commission on Collegiate Nursing Education
(CCNE)

Acceptance rate		44.8%
Faculty-student ratio		1: 1
Faculty	Full time	57
	Part time	74

Degrees conferred
Certificate in Nursing

Tuition	
In state	$35,870
Out of state	$35,870
Enrollments	71
Graduations	76

Minimum degree required
BA or BS in a non-nursing field

Student Demographics	
Female	94.4%
Under age 25	56.3%
Minority	13.3%
Part-time	0.0%

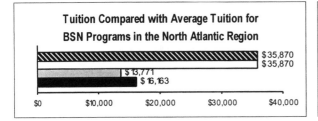

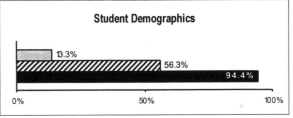

| Demographics Chart | ■ Female ▨ Under age 25 □ Minority | Distance Learning | | ¹The tuition reported for this program may be not be annualized. |
| | | | | *Data reported between 2001 and 2004. |

Delaware

DELAWARE STATE UNIVERSITY

*Useful Facts**

1200 North Dupont Highway
Dover, DE 19901
(302) 857-6750
Mary Warkins, PhD, RN

www.desu.edu

Accreditation
Delaware Board of Nursing, Commission on Collegiate Nursing Education (CCNE), National League for Nursing Accrediting Commission (NLNAC)

Acceptance rate	56.8%	

Degrees conferred
Baccalaureate

Tuition		Student Demographics	
In state	$4,646	Female	91.7%
Out of state	$10,303	Under age 25	80.0%
Enrollments	300	Minority	91.2%
Graduations	21	Part-time	13.3%

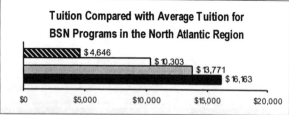

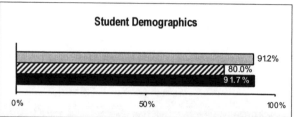

UNIVERSITY OF DELAWARE

Useful Facts

McDowell Hall, Rm 391
Newark, DE 19716
(302) 831-0655
Lisa Plowfield, PhD, RN

www.udel.edu/nursing

Accreditation
Delaware Board of Nursing, Commission on Collegiate Nursing Education (CCNE), National League for Nursing Accrediting Commission (NLNAC)

Acceptance rate		37.8%
Faculty-student ratio		1: 18
Faculty	Full time	31
	Part time	9

Degrees conferred
Baccalaureate degree

Tuition		Student Demographics	
In state	$6,614	Female	93.1%
Out of state	$16,770	Under age 25	92.6%
Enrollments	654	Minority	12.8%
Graduations	193	Part-time	4.7%

Minimum degree required
High school diploma or GED

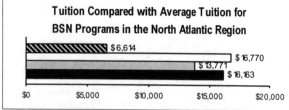

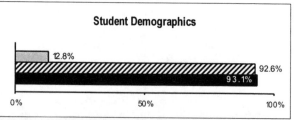

WESLEY COLLEGE

Useful Facts

120 North State Street
Dover, DE 19901
(302) 736-2512
Lucille Gambardella, PhD, RN, CS, APN-BC,CNE

www.wesley.edu

Accreditation
Delaware Board of Nursing

Acceptance rate		43.0%
Faculty-student ratio		1: 14
Faculty	Full time	8
	Part time	4

Degrees conferred
Baccalaureate degree

Tuition		Student Demographics	
In state	$13,585	Female	91.9%
Out of state	$13,585	Under age 25	68.9%
Enrollments	135	Minority	22.4%
Graduations	0	Part-time	2.2%

Minimum degree required
High school diploma or GED

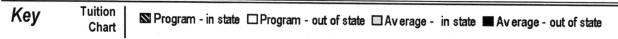

Key | Tuition Chart | ▨ Program - in state ☐ Program - out of state ☐ Average - in state ■ Average - out of state

District of Columbia

CATHOLIC UNIVERSITY OF AMERICA — *Useful Facts**

620 Michigan Avenue, NE
Washington, DC 20064
(202) 319-5403
Ann Marie Brooks, DNSc, RN, FAAN, FACHE

nursing.cua.edu

Accreditation
District of Columbia Board of Nursing, National
League for Nursing Accrediting Commission
(NLNAC)

Degrees conferred
Baccalaureate

Tuition		Student Demographics	
In state	$22,200	Female	94.7%
Out of state	$22,200	Under age 25	91.0%
Enrollments	134	Minority	19.5%
Graduations	33	Part-time	0.8%

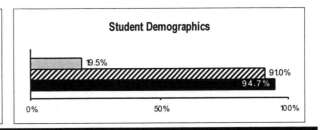

Tuition Compared with Average Tuition for BSN Programs in the North Atlantic Region
$22,200
$22,200
$13,771
$16,163

Student Demographics
19.5%
91.0%
94.7%

GEORGETOWN UNIVERSITY — *Useful Facts**

3700 Reservoir Road, North West
Washington, DC 20007
(202) 687-3118
Bette Keltner, PhD, RN, FAAN

www.georgetown.edu/schnurs

Accreditation
District of Columbia Board of Nursing

Degrees conferred
Baccalaureate

Acceptance rate 47.1%

Tuition		Student Demographics	
In state	$22,260	Female	93.5%
Out of state	$22,260	Under age 25	97.0%
Enrollments	316	Minority	20.9%
Graduations	64	Part-time	0.6%

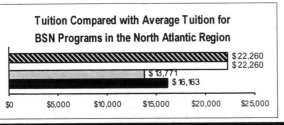

Tuition Compared with Average Tuition for BSN Programs in the North Atlantic Region
$22,260
$22,260
$13,771
$16,163

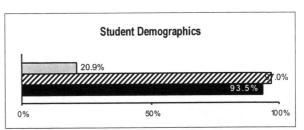

Student Demographics
20.9%
97.0%
93.5%

HOWARD UNIVERSITY — *Useful Facts**

501 Bryant Street, NW
Washington, DC 20059
(202) 806-7459
Dorothy Powell, EdD, RN, FAAN

www.nursing.howard.edu

Accreditation
District of Columbia Board of Nursing, National
League for Nursing Accrediting Commission
(NLNAC)

Degrees conferred
Baccalaureate

Acceptance rate 38.0%

Tuition		Student Demographics	
In state	$10,840	Female	89.5%
Out of state	$10,840	Under age 25	40.0%
Enrollments	341	Minority	98.5%
Graduations	66	Part-time	12.9%

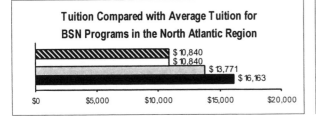

Tuition Compared with Average Tuition for BSN Programs in the North Atlantic Region
$10,840
$10,840
$13,771
$16,163

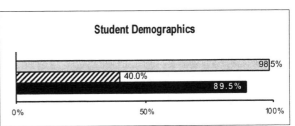

Student Demographics
98.5%
40.0%
89.5%

Demographics Chart | ■ Female ▨ Under age 25 ▢ Minority | **Distance Learning** | †The tuition reported for this program may be not be annualized.
*Data reported between 2001 and 2004.

District of Columbia

UNIVERSITY OF THE DISTRICT OF COLUMBIA
Useful Facts*

4200 Connecticut Avenue, NW, Building 44
Washington, DC 20008
(202) 274-5940
Susie Cato, MSN, MA, RN

www.udc.edu

Accreditation
District of Columbia Board of Nursing, National
League for Nursing Accrediting Commission
(NLNAC)

Degrees conferred
Baccalaureate

Tuition	
In state	$2,070
Out of state	$4,710
Enrollments	15
Graduations	6

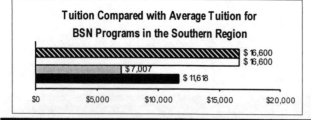

Tuition Compared with Average Tuition for BSN Programs in the North Atlantic Region
- $2,070
- $4,710
- $13,771
- $16,163

Florida

BARRY UNIVERSITY
Useful Facts*

11300 NE Second Avenue
Miami Shores, FL 33161
(305) 899-3800
Judith Balcerski, PhD, RN

www.barry.edu/nursing

Accreditation
Florida Board of Nursing

Degrees conferred
Baccalaureate

Acceptance rate 31.9%

Tuition		Student Demographics	
In state	$16,600	Female	84.3%
Out of state	$16,600	Under age 25	52.0%
Enrollments	273	Minority	73.5%
Graduations	86	Part-time	11.1%

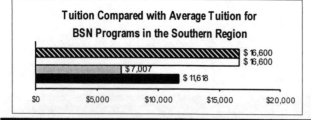

Tuition Compared with Average Tuition for BSN Programs in the Southern Region
- $16,600
- $16,600
- $7,007
- $11,618

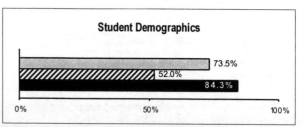

Student Demographics
- 73.5%
- 52.0%
- 84.3%

BETHUNE-COOKMAN COLLEGE
Useful Facts*

640 Dr Mary McLeod Bethune Boulevard
Daytona Beach, FL 32114
(386) 481-2100
Alma Yearwood Dixon, MSN, MPH, EdD, RN

www2.cookman.edu/academics/divisions/nursing/nursing.html

Accreditation
Florida Board of Nursing, National League for
Nursing Accrediting Commission (NLNAC)

Degrees conferred
Baccalaureate

Tuition		Student Demographics	
In state	$10,106	Female	89.3%
Out of state	$10,106	Under age 25	86.0%
Enrollments	244	Minority	95.7%
Graduations	12	Part-time	0.0%

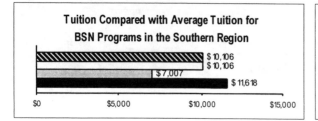

Tuition Compared with Average Tuition for BSN Programs in the Southern Region
- $10,106
- $10,106
- $7,007
- $11,618

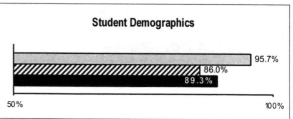

Student Demographics
- 95.7%
- 86.0%
- 89.3%

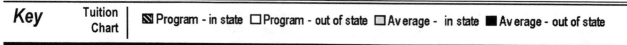

Key | Tuition Chart | ▨ Program - in state ☐ Program - out of state ▨ Average - in state ■ Average - out of state

Florida

FLORIDA A & M UNIVERSITY

103 Ware-Rhaney
Tallahassee, FL 32307
(850) 599-3017
Ruena Norman, PhD, RN

www.famu.edu/acad/colleges

Accreditation
Florida Board of Nursing, National League for
Nursing Accrediting Commission (NLNAC)

At the request of this nursing school, publication has been witheld.
Please contact the school directly for more information.

FLORIDA ATLANTIC UNIVERSITY

777 Glades Road
Boca Raton, FL 33431
(561) 297-3206
Anne Boykin, PhD, RN

www.fau.edu/nursing

Accreditation
Florida Board of Nursing, Commission on
Collegiate Nursing Education (CCNE)

At the request of this nursing school, publication has been witheld.
Please contact the school directly for more information.

FLORIDA GULF COAST UNIVERSITY — *Useful Facts**

10505 FGCU Boulevard South
Fort Myers, FL 33965
(239) 590-7505
Karen Miles, EdD, RN

www.fgcu.edu/chp/nursing

Accreditation
Florida Board of Nursing

Acceptance rate	83.2%	

Tuition
In state $2,813
Out of state $13,311
Enrollments 185
Graduations 74

Student Demographics
Female 88.2%
Minority 16.4%
Part-time 16.3%

Degrees conferred
Baccalaureate

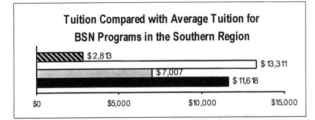
Tuition Compared with Average Tuition for BSN Programs in the Southern Region
$2,813 / $13,311 / $7,007 / $11,618

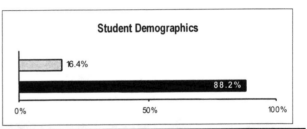
Student Demographics
16.4% / 88.2%

FLORIDA INTERNATIONAL UNIVERSITY — *Useful Facts*

11200 SW 8th St, HLS 2, RM 466
Miami, FL 33199
(305) 348-7726
Divina Grossman, PhD, RN, ARNP, FAAN

www.nursing.fiu.edu

Accreditation
Florida Board of Nursing, National League for
Nursing Accrediting Commission (NLNAC)

Acceptance rate	16.8%	
Faculty-student ratio	1:9	
Faculty	Full time	36
	Part time	41

Tuition
In state $3,560
Out of state $15,959
Enrollments 523
Graduations 200

Student Demographics
Female 71.4%
Under age 25 40.2%
Minority 87.7%
Part-time 6.0%

Degrees conferred
Baccalaureate degree

Minimum degree required
High school diploma or GED

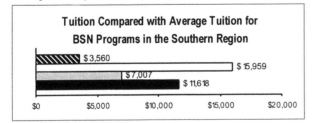
Tuition Compared with Average Tuition for BSN Programs in the Southern Region
$3,560 / $15,959 / $7,007 / $11,618

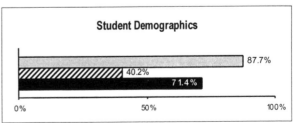
Student Demographics
87.7% / 40.2% / 71.4%

Demographics Chart ■ Female ▨ Under age 25 ☐ Minority | **Distance Learning** | ¹The tuition reported for this program may be not be annualized.
*Data reported between 2001 and 2004.

Florida

FLORIDA STATE UNIVERSITY
Useful Facts

102 Vivian M Duxbury Hall
Tallahassee, FL 32306
(850) 644-3299
Kathrine Mason, EdD

www.fsu.edu~nursing

Acceptance rate	25.0%
Faculty-student ratio	1: 11
Faculty Full time	27
Part time	16

Tuition		Student Demographics	
In state	$2,891	Female	91.5%
Out of state	$15,397	Under age 25	94.1%
Enrollments	389	Minority	24.5%
Graduations	183	Part-time	0.0%

Accreditation
Florida Board of Nursing, Commission on
Collegiate Nursing Education (CCNE)

Degrees conferred
Baccalaureate degree

Minimum degree required
Associate degree in a non-nursing field

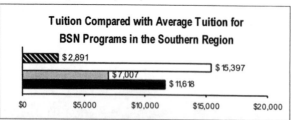

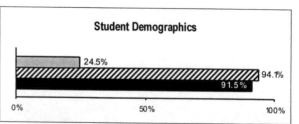

JACKSONVILLE UNIVERSITY
Useful Facts*

2800 University Boulevard North
Jacksonville, FL 32211
(904) 256-7280
Leigh Hart, PhD, RN, CCRN

www.ju.edu

Acceptance rate	77.1%

Tuition		Student Demographics	
In state	$9,295	Female	86.4%
Out of state	$9,295		
Enrollments	441	Minority	37.0%
Graduations	81	Part-time	12.3%

Accreditation
Florida Board of Nursing, Commission on
Collegiate Nursing Education (CCNE)

Degrees conferred
Baccalaureate

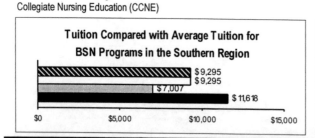

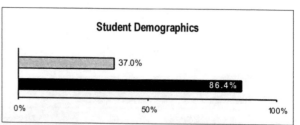

NOVA SOUTHEASTERN UNIVERSITY
Useful Facts

3200 South University Drive - 5th Floor
Fort Lauderdale, FL 33328
(954) 262-1962
Diane Whitehead, EdD, RN

www.nova.edu/nursing

Acceptance rate	19.9%
Faculty-student ratio	1: 16
Faculty Full time	11
Part time	2

Tuition		Student Demographics	
In state	$16,900	Female	11.5%
Out of state	$17,900	Under age 25	8.8%
Enrollments	196	Minority	57.7%
Graduations	48	Part-time	0.0%

Accreditation
Florida Board of Nursing, National League for
Nursing Accrediting Commission (NLNAC)

Degrees conferred
Baccalaureate degree

Minimum degree required
30 specific general education credits

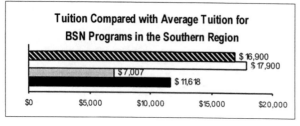

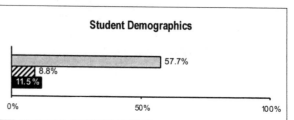

Key Tuition Chart   ▨ Program - in state   ☐ Program - out of state   ☐ Average - in state   ■ Average - out of state

Florida

PALM BEACH ATLANTIC UNIVERSITY SCHOOL OF NURSING

901 South Flagler Drive
West Palm Beach, FL 33416
(561) 803-2825
Linda Miller, BSN, MSN, EdD

www.pba.edu

Accreditation
Florida Board of Nursing

Degrees conferred
Baccalaureate

PENSACOLA CHRISTIAN COLLEGE
Useful Facts*

250 Brent Lane
Pensacola, FL 32503
(850) 478-8496
Teresa Haughton, MSN

www.pcci.edu

Accreditation
Florida Board of Nursing

Degrees conferred
Baccalaureate

Student Demographics

Enrollments	150		
Graduations	50	Part-time	0.0%

SOUTH UNIVERSITY
Useful Facts*

1760 North Congress Avenue
West Palm Beach, FL 33409
(561) 478-3378
Priscilla Bartolone, RN, MSN

www.southuniversity.edu

Accreditation
Florida Board of Nursing

Degrees conferred
Baccalaureate

Acceptance rate	71.1%	**Tuition**		**Student Demographics**	
		In state	$22,000	Female	98.2%
		Out of state	$22,000	Under age 25	5.0%
		Enrollments	56	Minority	62.3%
		Graduations	29	Part-time	0.0%

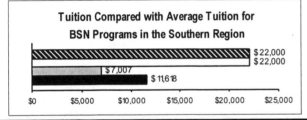

Tuition Compared with Average Tuition for BSN Programs in the Southern Region

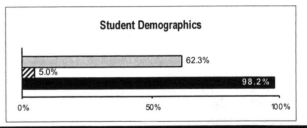

Student Demographics

UNIVERSITY OF CENTRAL FLORIDA
Useful Facts*

PO Box 162110
Orlando, FL 32816
(407) 823-2744
Jean Leuner, PhD, RN

www.cohpa.ucf.edu/nursing

Accreditation
Florida Board of Nursing, Commission on
Collegiate Nursing Education (CCNE), National
League for Nursing Accrediting Commission
(NLNAC)

Degrees conferred
Baccalaureate

Minimum degree required
Associate degree in a non-nursing field

Acceptance rate	21.4%	**Tuition**		**Student Demographics**	
Faculty-student ratio	1: 7	In state	$4,712	Female	90.7%
Faculty Full time	35	Out of state	$24,409	Under age 25	100.0%
Part time	20	Enrollments	322	Minority	30.8%
		Graduations	111	Part-time	0.0%

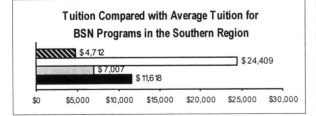

Tuition Compared with Average Tuition for BSN Programs in the Southern Region

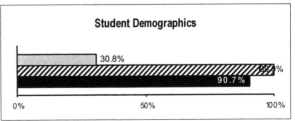

Student Demographics

Demographics Chart	■ Female ▨ Under age 25 ▢ Minority	Distance Learning 🖥️	⁺The tuition reported for this program may be not be annualized. *Data reported between 2001 and 2004.

Florida

UNIVERSITY OF FLORIDA
Useful Facts*

PO Box 100197, JHMHC
Gainesville, FL 32610-0197
(352) 392-3752
Kathleen Long, PhD, RNCS, FAAN

con.ufl.edu

Acceptance rate	46.8%

Enrollments	315	
Graduations	144	

Student Demographics

Female	92.3%
Minority	23.6%
Part-time	0.7%

Accreditation
Florida Board of Nursing

Degrees conferred
Baccalaureate

UNIVERSITY OF MIAMI
Useful Facts*

5801 Red Road
Coral Gables, FL 33146
(305) 284-2107
Nilda Peragallo, DrPH, RN, FAAN

www.miami.edu/nur

Acceptance rate	89.0%

Tuition

In state	$26,646
Out of state	$26,646
Enrollments	378
Graduations	118

Student Demographics

Female	88.4%
Minority	73.1%
Part-time	7.0%

Accreditation
Florida Board of Nursing, Commission on Collegiate Nursing Education (CCNE), National League for Nursing Accrediting Commission (NLNAC)

Degrees conferred
Baccalaureate

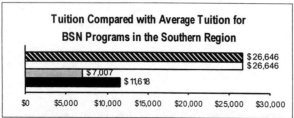

Tuition Compared with Average Tuition for BSN Programs in the Southern Region

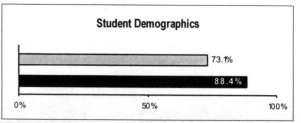

Student Demographics

UNIVERSITY OF NORTH FLORIDA
Useful Facts

4567 Saint Johns Bluff Road, South
Jacksonville, FL 32224
(904) 620-2684
Lillia Loriz, PhD, ARNP, GNP, BC

www.unf.edu/coh/cohnursi

Acceptance rate	11.6%	
Faculty-student ratio	1: 12	
Faculty	Full time	21
	Part time	3

Tuition

In state	$4,079
Out of state	$14,911
Enrollments	278
Graduations	139

Student Demographics

Female	88.7%
Under age 25	35.1%
Minority	16.0%
Part-time	0.0%

Accreditation
Florida Board of Nursing, Commission on Collegiate Nursing Education (CCNE), National League for Nursing Accrediting Commission (NLNAC)

Degrees conferred
Baccalaureate degree

Minimum degree required
Associate degree in a non-nursing field

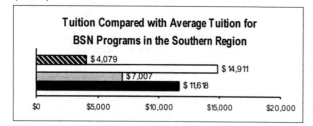

Tuition Compared with Average Tuition for BSN Programs in the Southern Region

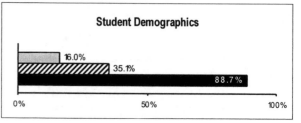

Student Demographics

Key — Tuition Chart — ⊠ Program - in state ☐ Program - out of state ☐ Average - in state ■ Average - out of state

Florida

UNIVERSITY OF SOUTH FLORIDA
Useful Facts*

12901 Bruce B Downs Blvd, MDC Box 22
Tampa, FL 33612
(813) 974-9091
Patricia Burns, PhD, RN, FAAN

www.hsc.usf.edu/nursing

Acceptance rate   19.3%

Tuition		Student Demographics	
In state	$3,402	Female	91.8%
Out of state	$17,563	Under age 25	49.0%
Enrollments	454	Minority	36.5%
Graduations	160	Part-time	6.4%

Accreditation
Florida Board of Nursing, Commission on
Collegiate Nursing Education (CCNE), National
League for Nursing Accrediting Commission
(NLNAC)

Degrees conferred
Baccalaureate

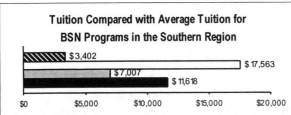

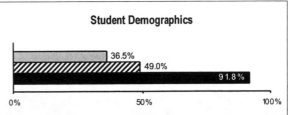

UNIVERSITY OF TAMPA

401 West Kennedy Boulevard
Tampa, FL 33606
(813) 253-3333
Nancy Ross, PhD, ARNP

www.ut.edu

Accreditation
Florida Board of Nursing, National League for
Nursing Accrediting Commission (NLNAC)

Degrees conferred
Baccalaureate

Georgia

ALBANY STATE UNIVERSITY
Useful Facts

504 College Drive
Albany, GA 31705
(229) 430-4724
Joyce Johnson, PhD, RN

www.asurams.edu

Acceptance rate		49.4%	Tuition		Student Demographics	
Faculty-student ratio		1:6	In state	$1,219	Female	88.6%
Faculty	Full time	9	Out of state	$4,877	Under age 25	45.5%
	Part time	2	**Enrollments**	62	Minority	97.7%
			Graduations	18	Part-time	22.7%

Accreditation
Georgia Board of Nursing, National League for
Nursing Accrediting Commission (NLNAC)

Degrees conferred
Baccalaureate degree

Minimum degree required
High school diploma or GED

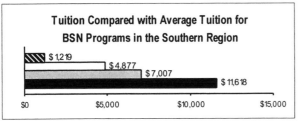

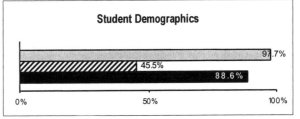

Demographics Chart	■ Female ▨ Under age 25 ☐ Minority	Distance Learning	💻	⁺The tuition reported for this program may be not be annualized. *Data reported between 2001 and 2004.

Georgia

ARMSTRONG ATLANTIC STATE UNIVERSITY — *Useful Facts**

11935 Abercorn Street
Savannah, GA 31419
(912) 927-5311
Camile Stern, PhD,RN

www.don.armstrong.edu

Accreditation
Georgia Board of Nursing, Commission on
Collegiate Nursing Education (CCNE)

Acceptance rate	35.1%

Degrees conferred
Baccalaureate

Tuition		Student Demographics	
In state	$2,322	Female	87.0%
Out of state	$9,290	Under age 25	54.0%
Enrollments	239	Minority	30.3%
Graduations	123	Part-time	3.0%

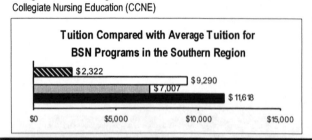

Tuition Compared with Average Tuition for BSN Programs in the Southern Region

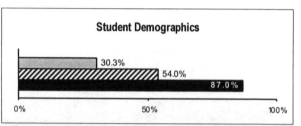

Student Demographics

BRENAU UNIVERSITY — *Useful Facts*

500 Washington Street
Gainesville, GA 30501
(770) 534-6206
Keeta Wilborn, PhD, RN

www.brenau.edu

Accreditation
Georgia Board of Nursing, National League for
Nursing Accrediting Commission (NLNAC)

Acceptance rate		33.1%
Faculty-student ratio		1: 8
Faculty	Full time	16
	Part time	6

Degrees conferred
Baccalaureate degree

Minimum degree required
High school diploma or GED

Tuition		Student Demographics	
In state	$23,800	Female	94.2%
Out of state	$23,800	Under age 25	29.5%
Enrollments	149	Minority	33.6%
Graduations	37	Part-time	41.0%

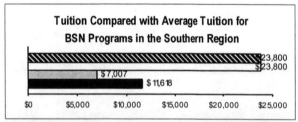

Tuition Compared with Average Tuition for BSN Programs in the Southern Region

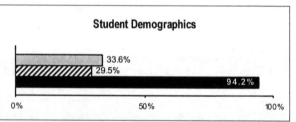

Student Demographics

CLAYTON COLLEGE AND STATE UNIVERSITY — *Useful Facts**

2000 Clayton State Blvd
Morrow, GA 30260
(770) 961-3481
Sue Odom, DSN, RN

www.healthsci.clayton.edu

Accreditation
Georgia Board of Nursing, Commission on
Collegiate Nursing Education (CCNE), National
League for Nursing Accrediting Commission
(NLNAC)

Acceptance rate		11.6%
Faculty-student ratio		1: 18
Faculty	Full time	6
	Part time	5

Degrees conferred
Baccalaureate degree

Tuition		Student Demographics	
In state	$2,802	Female	86.7%
Out of state	$9,770	Under age 25	40.0%
Enrollments	152	Minority	48.1%
Graduations	73	Part-time	5.2%

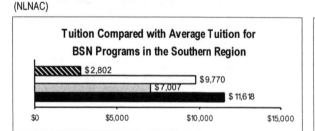

Tuition Compared with Average Tuition for BSN Programs in the Southern Region

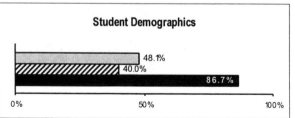

Student Demographics

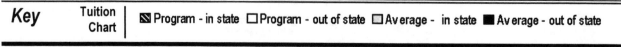

Key | Tuition Chart | ▧ Program - in state ▢ Program - out of state ▨ Average - in state ■ Average - out of state

Georgia

COLUMBUS STATE UNIVERSITY
Useful Facts

4225 University Avenue
Columbus, GA 31907
(706) 565-3649
June Goyne, RN, MSN, EdD, CEN

nursing.colstate.edu

Acceptance rate		34.7%
Faculty-student ratio		1:7
Faculty	Full time	14
	Part time	12

Tuition		
In state		$2,438
Out of state		$9,754
Enrollments		144
Graduations		48

Student Demographics	
Female	90.5%
Under age 25	73.7%
Minority	36.0%
Part-time	0.0%

Accreditation
Georgia Board of Nursing, National League for
Nursing Accrediting Commission (NLNAC)

Degrees conferred
Baccalaureate degree

Minimum degree required
High school diploma or GED

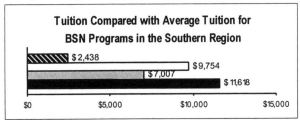

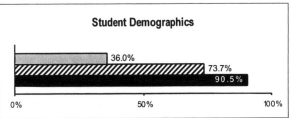

EMORY UNIVERSITY

1520 Clifton Rd NE
Atlanta, GA 30322
(404) 727-7976
Marla Salmon, RN, FAAN, ScD

www.nursing.emory.edu

At the request of this nursing school, publication has been witheld.
Please contact the school directly for more information.

Accreditation
Georgia Board of Nursing, Commission on
Collegiate Nursing Education (CCNE)

GEORGIA BAPTIST COLLEGE OF NURSING
Useful Facts

3001 Mercer University Drive
Atlanta, GA 30341
(678) 547-6798
Susan Gunby, RN, PhD

nursing.mercer.edu

Acceptance rate		32.7%
Faculty-student ratio		1:15
Faculty	Full time	29
	Part time	2

Tuition		
In state		$15,129
Out of state		$15,129
Enrollments		448
Graduations		79

Student Demographics	
Female	95.4%
Under age 25	70.6%
Minority	34.2%
Part-time	14.0%

Accreditation
Georgia Board of Nursing, Commission on
Collegiate Nursing Education (CCNE), National
League for Nursing Accrediting Commission
(NLNAC)

Degrees conferred
Baccalaureate degree

Minimum degree required
High school diploma or GED

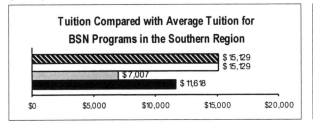

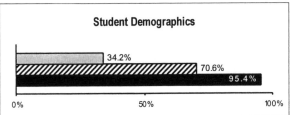

Demographics Chart	■ Female ▨ Under age 25 ☐ Minority	Distance Learning		[1]The tuition reported for this program may be not be annualized. [*]Data reported between 2001 and 2004.

Georgia

GEORGIA COLLEGE AND STATE UNIVERSITY

231 W Hancock Street
Milledgeville, GA 31061
(478) 445-4004
Cheryl Kish, EdD, RNC, WHNP

www.gcsu.edu/acad_affairs/school_healthsci

Accreditation
Georgia Board of Nursing, National League for
Nursing Accrediting Commission (NLNAC)

Acceptance rate		39.4%
Faculty-student ratio		1: 5
Faculty	Full time	22
	Part time	12

Degrees conferred
Baccalaureate degree

Tuition		**Student Demographics**	
In state	$1,576	Female	89.6%
Out of state	$6,304	Under age 25	53.3%
Enrollments	142	Minority	11.9%
Graduations	125	Part-time	31.1%

Minimum degree required
High school diploma or GED

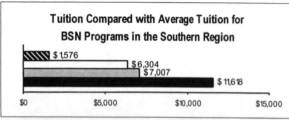

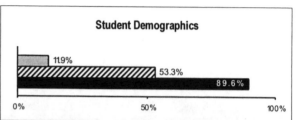

GEORGIA SOUTHERN UNIVERSITY

PO Box 8158
Statesboro, GA 30460
(912) 681-5455
Jean Bartels, PhD, RN

www.gasou.edu

Accreditation
Georgia Board of Nursing

Acceptance rate	62.7%

Degrees conferred
Baccalaureate

Tuition		**Student Demographics**	
In state	$1,876	Female	91.3%
Out of state	$9,380	Under age 25	83.0%
Enrollments	183	Minority	25.2%
Graduations	50	Part-time	0.0%

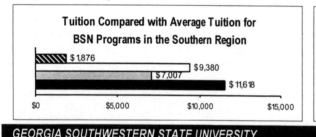

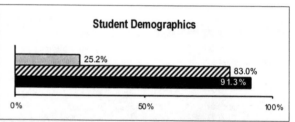

GEORGIA SOUTHWESTERN STATE UNIVERSITY

800 Wheatley St
Americus, GA 31709
(229) 931-2275
Maria Warda, PhD, MSN, BSN

www.gsw.edu

Accreditation
Georgia Board of Nursing, National League for
Nursing Accrediting Commission (NLNAC)

Acceptance rate		56.3%
Faculty-student ratio		1: 17
Faculty	Full time	1
	Part time	4

Degrees conferred
Baccalaureate degree

Tuition		**Student Demographics**	
In state	$2,438	Female	88.9%
Out of state	$9,754	Under age 25	73.3%
Enrollments	51	Minority	31.1%
Graduations	15	Part-time	0.0%

Minimum degree required
High school diploma or GED

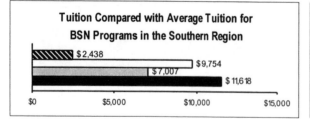

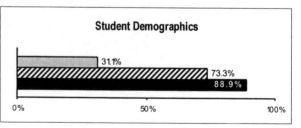

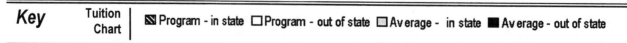

Key | Tuition Chart | ▧ Program - in state ▢ Program - out of state ▨ Average - in state ■ Average - out of state

Georgia

GEORGIA STATE UNIVERSITY　　　　　　　　　　　　　　*Useful Facts**

140 Decatur Street
Atlanta, GA 30303
(404) 651-2050
Alice Demi, RN, DSN, FAAN

chhs.gsu.edu/nursing

Acceptance rate	10.1%	

Tuition		
In state	$3,368
Out of state	$13,474
Enrollments	225
Graduations	88

Student Demographics	
Female	87.0%
Under age 25	46.0%
Minority	42.6%
Part-time	28.7%

Accreditation
Georgia Board of Nursing, Commission on
Collegiate Nursing Education (CCNE)

Degrees conferred
Baccalaureate

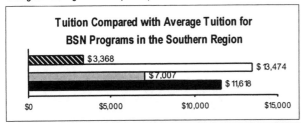
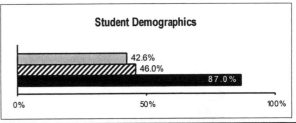

KENNESAW STATE UNIVERSITY

1000 Chastain Rd Building 16
Kennesaw, GA 30144
(770) 423-6173
David Bennett, PhD, RN

www.kennesaw.edu

Accreditation
Georgia Board of Nursing

At the request of this nursing school, publication has been witheld.
Please contact the school directly for more information.

LA GRANGE COLLEGE　　　　　　　　　　　　　　　　*Useful Facts*

601 Broad St
La Grange, GA 30240
(706) 880-8221
Celia Hay, PhD, RN

www.lagrange.edu

Acceptance rate	55.2%	
Faculty-student ratio	1: 13	
Faculty	Full time	3
	Part time	2

Tuition		
In state	$16,000
Out of state	$16,000
Enrollments	52
Graduations	14

Student Demographics	
Female	88.5%
Under age 25	50.0%
Minority	11.5%
Part-time	0.0%

Accreditation
Georgia Board of Nursing, National League for
Nursing Accrediting Commission (NLNAC)

Degrees conferred
Baccalaureate degree

Minimum degree required
High school diploma or GED

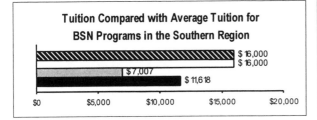
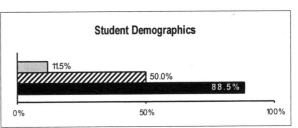

Demographics Chart	■Female ▨Under age 25 ☐Minority	**Distance Learning**	🖥	†The tuition reported for this program may be not be annualized. *Data reported between 2001 and 2004.

Georgia

MEDICAL COLLEGE OF GEORGIA
Useful Facts

997 St Sebastian Way (EG-1031)
Augusta, GA 30912
(706) 721-3771
Lucy Marion, PhD, RN, BC, FAAN

www.mcg.edu/son

Acceptance rate	39.2%	
Faculty-student ratio	1: 7	
Faculty	Full time	41
	Part time	16

Tuition		**Student Demographics**	
In state	$3,638	Female	91.5%
Out of state	$14,552	Under age 25	81.0%
Enrollments	349	Minority	9.2%
Graduations	185	Part-time	1.3%

Accreditation
Georgia Board of Nursing, National League for Nursing Accrediting Commission (NLNAC)

Degrees conferred
Baccalaureate degree

Minimum degree required
students must have all prerequisites and 2 years of undergraduate education; 150 enrolled in summer

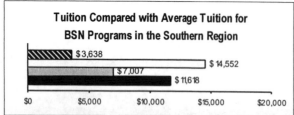

Tuition Compared with Average Tuition for BSN Programs in the Southern Region

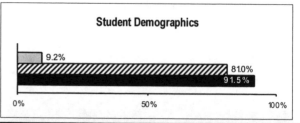

Student Demographics

PIEDMONT COLLEGE
Useful Facts*

PO Box 10
Demorest, GA 30535
(706) 776-0116
Barbara Crosson, EdD, RN

www.piedmont.edu

Acceptance rate	91.9%	
Faculty-student ratio	1: 7	
Faculty	Full time	6
	Part time	4

Tuition		**Student Demographics**	
In state	$13,500	Female	94.5%
Out of state	$13,500		
Enrollments	55	Minority	7.3%
Graduations	15	Part-time	0.0%

Accreditation
Georgia Board of Nursing, National League for Nursing Accrediting Commission (NLNAC)

Degrees conferred
Baccalaureate

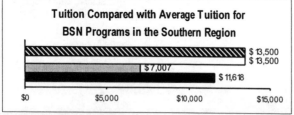

Tuition Compared with Average Tuition for BSN Programs in the Southern Region

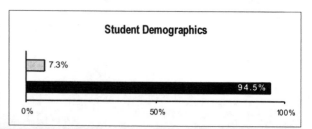

Student Demographics

STATE UNIVERSITY OF WEST GEORGIA
Useful Facts

1601 Maple Street
Carrollton, GA 30118
(678) 839-5624
Kathryn Grams, PhD, RN

www.westga.edu/~nurs

Acceptance rate	38.8%	
Faculty-student ratio	1: 9	
Faculty	Full time	18
	Part time	5

Tuition		**Student Demographics**	
In state	$2,438	Female	86.7%
Out of state	$9,754	Under age 25	73.3%
Enrollments	182	Minority	10.4%
Graduations	59	Part-time	29.2%

Accreditation
Georgia Board of Nursing, Commission on Collegiate Nursing Education (CCNE)

Degrees conferred
Baccalaureate degree

Minimum degree required
2 years of undergraduate prerequisites, minimum GPA of 2.75

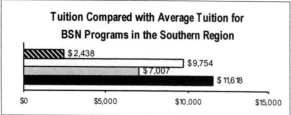

Tuition Compared with Average Tuition for BSN Programs in the Southern Region

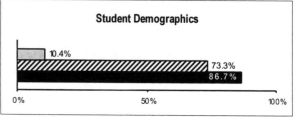

Student Demographics

Key | Tuition Chart | ▨ Program - in state ☐ Program - out of state ▤ Average - in state ■ Average - out of state

Georgia

VALDOSTA STATE UNIVERSITY
*Useful Facts**

1300 N Patterson St
Valdosta, GA 31698-0130
(229) 333-5959
Mary Ann Reichenbach, PhD, RN, MSN, MS, SB

www.valdosta.edu/nursing

			Tuition		Student Demographics	
Acceptance rate	69.8%		In state	$2,290	Female	88.9%
			Out of state	$7,714	Minority	13.8%
			Enrollments	335	Part-time	4.9%
			Graduations	46		

Accreditation
Georgia Board of Nursing

Degrees conferred
Baccalaureate

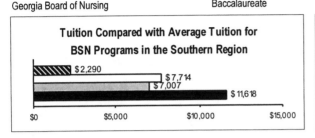

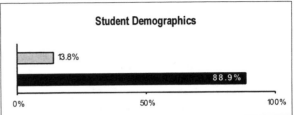

Hawaii

HAWAII PACIFIC UNIVERSITY

45-045 Kamehameha Highway
Kaneohe, HI 96734
(808) 236-5811
Carol Winters-Moorhead, PhD, RN

www. hpu.edu

Accreditation
Hawaii Board of Nursing, National League for
Nursing Accrediting Commission (NLNAC)

*At the request of this nursing school, publication has been witheld.
Please contact the school directly for more information.*

UNIVERSITY OF HAWAII - HILO
Useful Facts

200 W Kawili Street
Hilo, HI 96720
(808) 974-7761
Cecilia Mukai, PhD, RN-C, FNP

www.uhh.hawaii.edu/depts/nursing

				Tuition		Student Demographics	
Acceptance rate		45.5%		In state	$2,883	Female	91.7%
Faculty-student ratio		1: 6		Out of state	$7,944	Under age 25	61.1%
Faculty	Full time	6		Enrollments	47	Minority	58.8%
	Part time	4		Graduations	20	Part-time	0.0%

Accreditation
Hawaii Board of Nursing, National League for
Nursing Accrediting Commission (NLNAC)

Degrees conferred
Baccalaureate degree

Minimum degree required
High school diploma or GED

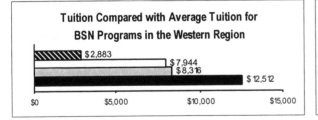

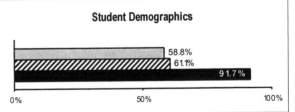

Demographics Chart	■Female ☒Under age 25 ☐Minority	Distance Learning	'The tuition reported for this program may be not be annualized. *Data reported between 2001 and 2004.

Hawaii

UNIVERSITY OF HAWAII AT MANOA
Useful Facts

2528 McCarthy Mall, Webster 425
Honolulu, HI 96822
(808) 956-8522
Mary Boland, DrPH, RN, FAAN

www.nursing.hawaii.edu

Acceptance rate	26.3%	
Faculty-student ratio	1: 6	
Faculty Full time	40	
Part time	15	

Tuition	
In state	$3,504
Out of state	$13,488
Enrollments	262
Graduations	97

Student Demographics	
Female	76.5%
Under age 25	57.9%
Minority	87.2%
Part-time	54.7%

Accreditation
Hawaii Board of Nursing, Commission on Collegiate Nursing Education (CCNE), National League for Nursing Accrediting Commission (NLNAC)

Degrees conferred
BS

Minimum degree required
None

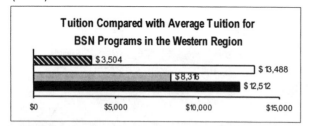

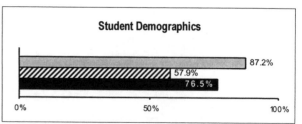

Idaho

BOISE STATE UNIVERSITY
Useful Facts

1910 University Drive
Boise, ID 83725
(208) 426-3600
Pam Springer, PhD, RN

nursing.boisestate.edu

Acceptance rate	21.3%	
Faculty-student ratio	1: 10	
Faculty Full time	37	
Part time	5	

Tuition	
Out of state	$7,056
Enrollments	275
Graduations	88

Student Demographics	
Female	82.4%
Under age 25	58.8%
Minority	8.3%
Part-time	0.0%

Accreditation
Idaho Board of Nursing, National League for Nursing Accrediting Commission (NLNAC)

Degrees conferred
Baccalaureate degree

Minimum degree required
High school diploma or GED

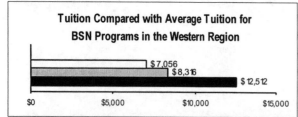

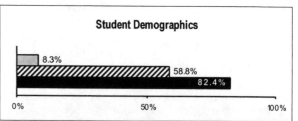

BRIGHAM YOUNG UNIVERSITY - IDAHO
Useful Facts*

175 Clarke Building
Rexburg, ID 83460
(208) 496-1325
Kathy Barnhill, MSN, RN, PhD

www.byui.edu

Tuition	
In state	$2,640
Out of state	$3,960
Enrollments	52
Graduations	11

Student Demographics	
Under age 25	80.0%

Accreditation
Idaho Board of Nursing

Degrees conferred
Baccalaureate

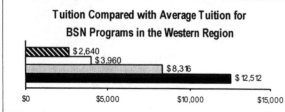

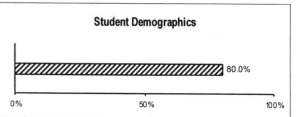

Key | Tuition Chart | ▨ Program - in state ☐ Program - out of state ▨ Average - in state ■ Average - out of state

Idaho

IDAHO STATE UNIVERSITY
Useful Facts*

650 Memorial Drive, Building 66
Pocatello, ID 83201
(208) 282-2185
Carla Dando, MSN, RN

nursing.isu.edu

Accreditation
Idaho Board of Nursing, Commission on
Collegiate Nursing Education (CCNE)

Acceptance rate	68.2%

Degrees conferred
Baccalaureate

Tuition
In state	$3,136
Out of state	$9,376
Enrollments	116
Graduations	49

Student Demographics
| Under age 25 | 71.0% |

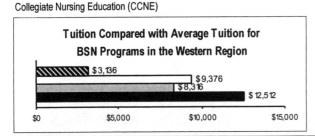

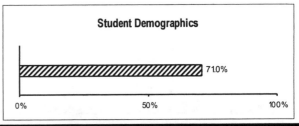

LEWIS-CLARK STATE COLLEGE
Useful Facts*

500 8th Avenue
Lewiston, ID 83501
(208) 792-2402
Donna Brandmeyer, EdD, RN

www.lcsc.edu/nurdiv/

Accreditation
Idaho Board of Nursing, Commission on
Collegiate Nursing Education (CCNE)

Acceptance rate	65.6%

Degrees conferred
Baccalaureate

Tuition
Out of state	$5,710
Enrollments	114
Graduations	41

Student Demographics
Female	86.2%
Under age 25	50.0%
Minority	1.2%
Part-time	3.4%

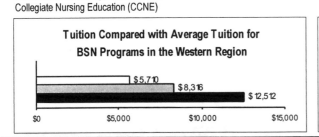

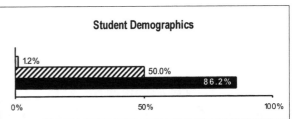

NORTHWEST NAZARENE UNIVERSITY

623 Holly Street
Nampa, ID 83686
(208) 467-8652
Patricia Kissell, PhD, RN

www.nnu.edu

Accreditation
Idaho Board of Nursing

Faculty
| Full time | 4 |
| Part time | 4 |

Degrees conferred
Baccalaureate

Demographics Chart	■Female ▨Under age 25 ▢Minority	**Distance Learning**	💻	†The tuition reported for this program may be not be annualized. *Data reported between 2001 and 2004.

Illinois

AURORA UNIVERSITY — *Useful Facts*

347 South Gladstone Ave
Aurora, IL 60506
(630) 844-5133
Maryanne Locklin, RN, APN, DNSc

www.aurora.edu

Accreditation
Illinois Department of Professional Regulation,
Commission on Collegiate Nursing Education
(CCNE), National League for Nursing Accrediting
Commission (NLNAC)

Acceptance rate	64.2%
Faculty-student ratio	1: 13
Faculty Full time	7
Part time	0

Degrees conferred
Baccalaureate degree

Tuition	
In state	$7,375
Out of state	$7,375
Enrollments	89
Graduations	53

Minimum degree required
High school diploma or GED

Student Demographics	
Female	91.2%
Under age 25	66.7%
Minority	21.1%
Part-time	3.5%

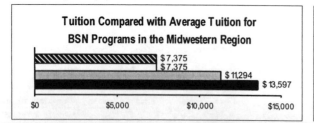

Tuition Compared with Average Tuition for BSN Programs in the Midwestern Region
$7,375 / $7,375 / $11,294 / $13,597

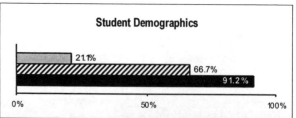

Student Demographics
21.1% / 66.7% / 91.2%

BLESSING-RIEMAN COLLEGE — *Useful Facts*

Broadway at 11th, PO Box 7005
Quincy, IL 62305
(217) 228-5520
Pamela Brown, RN, MS, PhD

www.brcn.edu

Accreditation
Illinois Department of Professional Regulation,
Commission on Collegiate Nursing Education
(CCNE), National League for Nursing Accrediting
Commission (NLNAC)

Acceptance rate	57.1%
Faculty-student ratio	1: 16
Faculty Full time	14
Part time	1

Degrees conferred
Baccalaureate degree

Tuition	
In state	$14,800
Out of state	$14,800
Enrollments	228
Graduations	29

Minimum degree required
High school diploma or GED

Student Demographics	
Female	94.8%
Under age 25	83.6%
Minority	4.6%
Part-time	7.5%

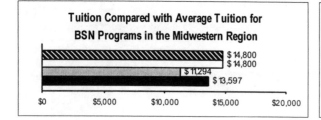

Tuition Compared with Average Tuition for BSN Programs in the Midwestern Region
$14,800 / $14,800 / $11,294 / $13,597

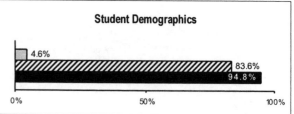

Student Demographics
4.6% / 83.6% / 94.8%

Key | Tuition Chart | ▨ Program - in state ☐ Program - out of state ▧ Average - in state ■ Average - out of state

Illinois

BRADLEY UNIVERSITY — *Useful Facts*

302 Burgess Hall
Peoria, IL 61625
(309) 677-2528
Francesca Armmer, PhD, RN

www.bradley.edu/academics/ehs/nur/nur_index.html

Acceptance rate	63.1%
Faculty-student ratio	1: 11
Faculty Full time	16
Part time	20

Tuition
In state — $18,700
Out of state — $18,700
Enrollments — 283
Graduations — 27

Student Demographics
Female — 94.3%
Under age 25 — 90.7%
Minority — 10.1%
Part-time — 6.0%

Accreditation
Illinois Department of Professional Regulation, National League for Nursing Accrediting Commission (NLNAC)

Degrees conferred
Baccalaureate degree

Minimum degree required
High school diploma or GED

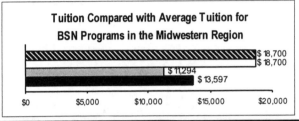

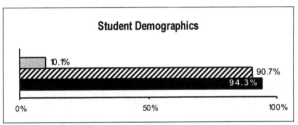

CHICAGO STATE UNIVERSITY — *Useful Facts**

9501 South King Drive
Chicago, IL 60628
(773) 995-3901
Linda Hureston, PhD, RN

www.csu.edu/collegeofhealthsciences

Acceptance rate	68.0%
Faculty-student ratio	1: 20
Faculty Full time	27
Part time	9

Tuition
In state — $4,248
Out of state — $7,944
Enrollments — 625
Graduations — 26

Student Demographics
Female — 95.1%
Under age 25 — 30.1%
Minority — 98.0%
Part-time — 9.9%

Accreditation
Illinois Department of Professional Regulation, National League for Nursing Accrediting Commission (NLNAC)

Degrees conferred
Baccalaureate degree

Minimum degree required
High school diploma or GED

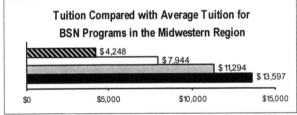

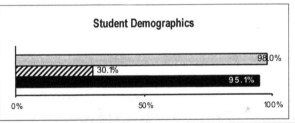

CONCORDIA UNIVERSITY AND WEST SUBURBAN — *Useful Facts**

3 Erie Court
Oak Park, IL 60302
(708) 763-6975
Rebecca Jones, DNSc, RN, CNAA

www.wscn.edu

Acceptance rate	27.7%

Tuition
In state — $18,100
Out of state — $18,100
Enrollments — 124
Graduations — 26

Student Demographics
Female — 91.1%
Under age 25 — 56.0%
Minority — 64.6%
Part-time — 21.1%

Accreditation
Illinois Department of Professional Regulation, Commission on Collegiate Nursing Education (CCNE)

Degrees conferred
Baccalaureate

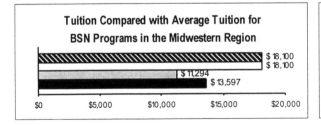

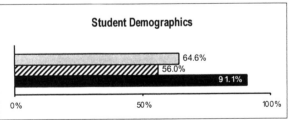

Demographics Chart | ■ Female ▨ Under age 25 □ Minority | **Distance Learning** | †The tuition reported for this program may be not be annualized.
*Data reported between 2001 and 2004.

IL — 39

Illinois

ELMHURST COLLEGE
*Useful Facts**

190 Prospect Ave
Elmhurst, IL 60126
(630) 617-3344
Linda Niedringhaus, PhD, RN

www.elmhurst.edu

Accreditation
Illinois Department of Professional Regulation

Acceptance rate 69.3%

Degrees conferred
Baccalaureate

Enrollments 122
Graduations 31

Student Demographics
Female 98.4%

Part-time 6.6%

ILLINOIS STATE UNIVERSITY
*Useful Facts**

Campus Box 5810
Normal, IL 61790
(309) 438-2174
Nancy Ridenour, RN, PhD, CS, FNC, FAAN

www.mcn.ilstu.edu

Accreditation
Illinois Department of Professional Regulation

Acceptance rate 72.4%

Tuition
In state $2,277
Out of state $5,710
Enrollments 164
Graduations 67

Degrees conferred
Baccalaureate

Student Demographics
Female 95.3%

Minority 4.8%
Part-time 9.4%

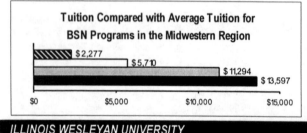

Tuition Compared with Average Tuition for BSN Programs in the Midwestern Region
$2,277
$5,710
$11,294
$13,597

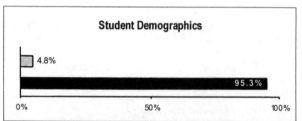

Student Demographics
4.8%
95.3%

ILLINOIS WESLEYAN UNIVERSITY
*Useful Facts**

PO Box 569
Rock Spring, GA 30739
(706) 764-3796
Larry Goins, MSN, RN, CS, BC

www.nwtcollege.org

Accreditation
Illinois Department of Professional Regulation

Acceptance rate 45.7%

Tuition
In state $20,284
Out of state $20,284
Enrollments 77
Graduations 30

Degrees conferred
Baccalaureate

Student Demographics
Female 98.7%
Under age 25 100.0%
Minority 7.8%
Part-time 0.0%

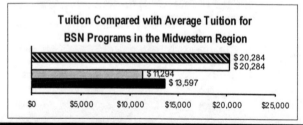

Tuition Compared with Average Tuition for BSN Programs in the Midwestern Region
$20,284
$20,284
$11,294
$13,597

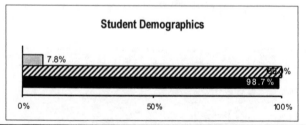

Student Demographics
7.8%
98.7%

LAKEVIEW COLLEGE
*Useful Facts**

903 North Logan Ave
Danville, IL 61832
(217) 477-2747
Jo-Ann Marrs, RN, FNP, EdD

lakeviewcol.edu

Accreditation
Illinois Department of Professional Regulation,
National League for Nursing Accrediting
Commission (NLNAC)

Acceptance rate 81.8%

Degrees conferred
Baccalaureate

Enrollments 56
Graduations 24

Student Demographics
Female 98.0%
Under age 25 30.0%
Minority 100.0%
Part-time 51.0%

Key | Tuition Chart | ▨ Program - in state □ Program - out of state ▢ Average - in state ■ Average - out of state

Illinois

LEWIS UNIVERSITY
*Useful Facts**

1 University Pkwy, Bow 404
Romeoville, IL 60446
(815) 836-5347
Jean Lytle, EdD, RN

www.lewisu.edu/nursing

Acceptance rate	100.0%		**Student Demographics**	
			Female	93.7%
			Under age 25	24.0%
Enrollments	769		Minority	29.1%
Graduations	159		Part-time	6.8%

Accreditation
Illinois Department of Professional Regulation

Degrees conferred
Baccalaureate

LOYOLA UNIVERSITY - CHICAGO
*Useful Facts**

6525 North Sheridan Rd
Chicago, IL 60626
(773) 508-3255
Sheila Haas, PhD, RN

www.luc.educ/schools/nursing

Acceptance rate	41.1%	**Tuition**		**Student Demographics**	
		In state	$18,266	Female	92.5%
		Out of state	$18,266	Under age 25	71.0%
		Enrollments	335	Minority	43.2%
		Graduations	118	Part-time	12.6%

Accreditation
Illinois Department of Professional Regulation

Degrees conferred
Baccalaureate

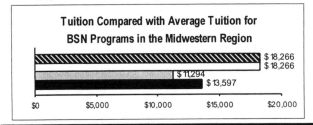

Tuition Compared with Average Tuition for BSN Programs in the Midwestern Region

- $18,266
- $18,266
- $11,294
- $13,597

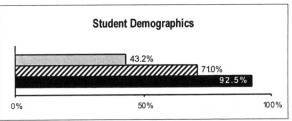

Student Demographics

- 43.2%
- 71.0%
- 92.5%

MACMURRAY COLLEGE
Useful Facts

446 East College Ave
Jacksonville, IL 62650
(217) 479-7083
Jo Brannan, PhD, RN

www.mac.edu/academ/nurs.htm

Acceptance rate	57.1%	**Tuition**		**Student Demographics**	
Faculty-student ratio	1: 17	In state	$15,000	Female	92.9%
Faculty Full time	5	Out of state	$15,000	Under age 25	69.4%
Part time	2	**Enrollments**	99	Minority	7.3%
		Graduations	11	Part-time	9.2%

Accreditation
Illinois Department of Professional Regulation,
Commission on Collegiate Nursing Education
(CCNE)

Degrees conferred
Baccalaureate degree

Minimum degree required
High school diploma or GED

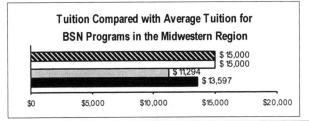

Tuition Compared with Average Tuition for BSN Programs in the Midwestern Region

- $15,000
- $15,000
- $11,294
- $13,597

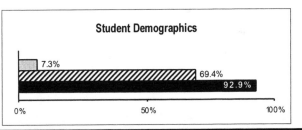

Student Demographics

- 7.3%
- 69.4%
- 92.9%

METHODIST COLLEGE OF NURSING

221 NE Glen Oak Ave
Peoria, IL 61636
(672) 309-5519
Sallie Tucker, RN, FAN, PhD

www.methodistcollegeofnursing.com

Accreditation
Illinois Department of Professional Regulation

*At the request of this nursing school, publication has been withheld.
Please contact the school directly for more information.*

| Demographics Chart | ■Female ▨Under age 25 ▢Minority | Distance Learning | | †The tuition reported for this program may be not be annualized.
*Data reported between 2001 and 2004. |

Illinois

MILLIKIN UNIVERSITY

Useful Facts*

1184 West Main St
Decatur, IL 62522
(217) 424-6348
Nancy Creason, PhD, RN

www.millikin.edu

Accreditation
Illinois Department of Professional Regulation

Degrees conferred
Baccalaureate

Acceptance rate	64.8%

Tuition		Student Demographics	
In state	$18,109	Female	95.9%
Out of state	$18,109	Under age 25	90.0%
Enrollments	122	Minority	12.4%
Graduations	28	Part-time	3.3%

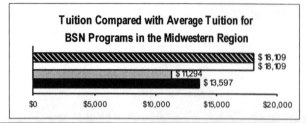

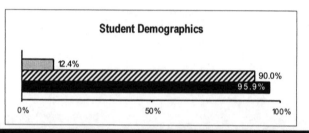

NORTH PARK UNIVERSITY

3225 W Foster Ave
Chicago, IL 60625
(773) 244-5693
Elizabeth Ritt, RN, EdD

www.northpark.edu

Accreditation
Illinois Department of Professional Regulation

Degrees conferred
Baccalaureate

NORTHERN ILLINOIS UNIVERSITY

Useful Facts*

1240 Normal Road
DeKalb, IL 60115
(815) 753-1375
Brigid Lusk, RN, PhD

www.niu.edu

Accreditation
Illinois Department of Professional Regulation

Degrees conferred
Baccalaureate

Acceptance rate	60.1%

Tuition		Student Demographics	
In state	$2,736	Female	96.1%
Out of state	$5,472		
Enrollments	390	Minority	17.5%
Graduations	133	Part-time	16.4%

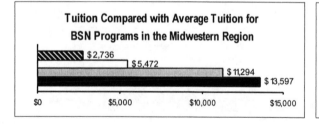

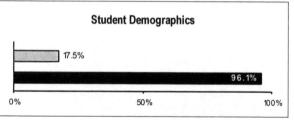

Illinois

OLIVET NAZARENE UNIVERSITY

1 University Ave
Bourbonnais, IL 60914
(815) 939-5345
Norma Wood, PhD, RN

www.olivet.edu/academics/divisions/nursing

Accreditation
Illinois Department of Professional Regulation,
Commission on Collegiate Nursing Education
(CCNE)

Acceptance rate	100.0%

Degrees conferred
Baccalaureate

Tuition
In state	$14,900
Out of state	$14,900
Enrollments	265
Graduations	36

Student Demographics
Female	97.8%
Under age 25	66.0%
Minority	13.1%
Part-time	0.5%

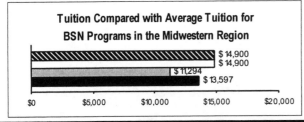

Tuition Compared with Average Tuition for BSN Programs in the Midwestern Region
$14,900
$14,900
$11,294
$13,597

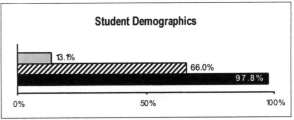

Student Demographics
13.1%
66.0%
97.8%

ROCKFORD COLLEGE

5050 E State St
Rockford, IL 61108
(815) 226-4196
Julie Luetschwager, DNSc, RN

rockford.edu

Accreditation
Illinois Department of Professional Regulation,
National League for Nursing Accrediting
Commission (NLNAC)

Acceptance rate		85.4%
Faculty-student ratio		1: 17
Faculty	Full time	6
	Part time	1

Degrees conferred
Baccalaureate degree

Tuition
In state	$22,450
Out of state	$22,450
Enrollments	109
Graduations	18

Minimum degree required
High school diploma or GED

Student Demographics
Female	92.6%
Under age 25	81.5%
Minority	21.4%
Part-time	18.5%

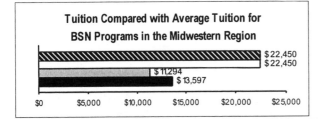

Tuition Compared with Average Tuition for BSN Programs in the Midwestern Region
$22,450
$22,450
$11,294
$13,597

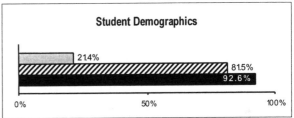

Student Demographics
21.4%
81.5%
92.6%

RUSH UNIVERSITY

600 S Paulina, Suite 1080
Chicago, IL 60612
(312) 942-7117
Lois Halstead, PhD, RN

www.rushu.rush.edu/nursing

Accreditation
Illinois Department of Professional Regulation,
Commission on Collegiate Nursing Education
(CCNE)

Acceptance rate		46.6%
Faculty-student ratio		1: 2
Faculty	Full time	80
	Part time	11

Degrees conferred
Baccalaureate degree

Tuition
In state	$24,260
Out of state	$24,260
Enrollments	173
Graduations	97

Minimum degree required
Bachelor's degree for Accelerated BSN Program

Student Demographics
Female	91.3%
Under age 25	54.3%
Minority	16.1%
Part-time	3.5%

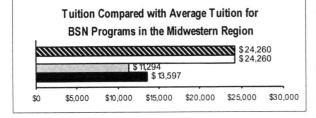

Tuition Compared with Average Tuition for BSN Programs in the Midwestern Region
$24,260
$24,260
$11,294
$13,597

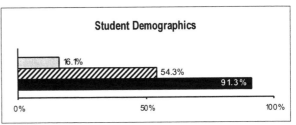

Student Demographics
16.1%
54.3%
91.3%

Demographics Chart	■ Female ▨ Under age 25 ☐ Minority	**Distance Learning**		⁺The tuition reported for this program may be not be annualized. *Data reported between 2001 and 2004.

Illinois

SAINT ANTHONY COLLEGE OF NURSING

5658 E State St
Rockford, IL 61108
(815) 395-5090
Terese Burch, PhD, RN

www.sacn.edu

Accreditation
Illinois Department of Professional Regulation,
Commission on Collegiate Nursing Education
(CCNE), National League for Nursing Accrediting
Commission (NLNAC)

Acceptance rate	28.2%
Faculty-student ratio	1: 9
Faculty Full time	13
Part time	2

Degrees conferred
Baccalaureate degree

Tuition	
In state	$15,400
Out of state	$15,400
Enrollments	125
Graduations	47

Minimum degree required
64 prerequisite college credits

Student Demographics	
Female	91.0%
Under age 25	56.6%
Minority	9.0%
Part-time	12.3%

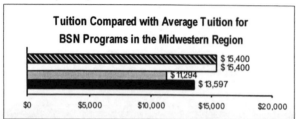

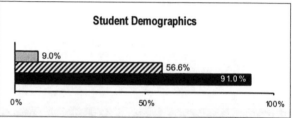

SAINT FRANCIS MEDICAL CENTER, COLLEGE OF NURSING

511 NE Greenleaf
Peoria, IL 61603
(309) 655-2206
Lois Hamilton, RN, PhD

www.sfmccon.edu

Accreditation
Illinois Department of Professional Regulation,
National League for Nursing Accrediting
Commission (NLNAC)

At the request of this nursing school, publication has been witheld.
Please contact the school directly for more information.

SAINT XAVIER UNIVERSITY

3700 W 103 St
Chicago, IL 60655
(773) 298-3706
Anne Bavier, PhD, RN, FAAN

www.sxu.edu/son

Accreditation
Illinois Department of Professional Regulation,
Commission on Collegiate Nursing Education
(CCNE)

At the request of this nursing school, publication has been witheld.
Please contact the school directly for more information.

Key | Tuition Chart | ▧ Program - in state ☐ Program - out of state ▨ Average - in state ■ Average - out of state

Illinois

SOUTHERN ILLINOIS UNIVERSITY - EDWARDSVILLE
Useful Facts*

Alumni Hall, Rm 2109, PO Box 1066
Edwardsville, IL 62026
(618) 650-3959
Marcia Maurer, PhD, RN

www.siue.edu/nursing

Acceptance rate	32.5%

Tuition		Student Demographics	
In state	$3,600	Female	90.4%
Out of state	$7,200	Under age 25	71.0%
Enrollments	318	Minority	18.8%
Graduations	111	Part-time	0.0%

Accreditation
Illinois Department of Professional Regulation,
Commission on Collegiate Nursing Education
(CCNE)

Degrees conferred
Baccalaureate

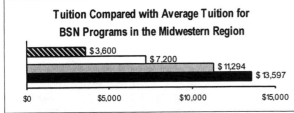

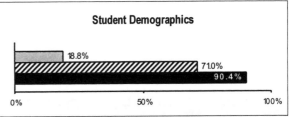

ST JOHN'S COLLEGE

421 N 9th St
Springfield, IL 62702
(217) 525-5628
Kathleen O'Neil, PhD, RN

www.st-johns.org/collegeofnursing

Accreditation
Illinois Department of Professional Regulation,
National League for Nursing Accrediting
Commission (NLNAC)

At the request of this nursing school, publication has been witheld.
Please contact the school directly for more information.

TRINITY CHRISTIAN COLLEGE
Useful Facts*

6601 W College Dr
Palos Heights, IL 60463
(708) 239-4723
Cynthia Sandler, PhD, RN

www.trnty.edu

Acceptance rate	85.7%

Tuition		Student Demographics	
In state	$16,250	Female	90.7%
Out of state	$16,250		
Enrollments	43	Minority	7.0%
Graduations	20	Part-time	4.7%

Accreditation
Illinois Department of Professional Regulation,
Commission on Collegiate Nursing Education
(CCNE)

Degrees conferred
Baccalaureate

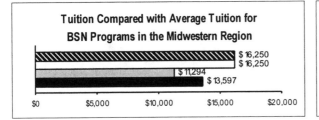

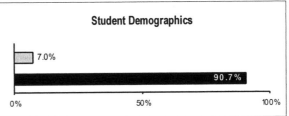

Demographics Chart	■ Female ☒ Under age 25 ☐ Minority	Distance Learning 🖥	⁺The tuition reported for this program may be not be annualized. *Data reported between 2001 and 2004.

Illinois

TRINITY COLLEGE OF NURSING

Useful Facts*

2122 25th Avenue
Rock Island, IL 61201
(309) 779-7710
Beth Cameron, ND, FNP

www.trinitycollege

Tuition		Student Demographics	
In state	$4,500		
Out of state	$4,500	Under age 25	25.0%
Enrollments	28		
Graduations	5		

Accreditation
Illinois Department of Professional Regulation

Degrees conferred
Baccalaureate

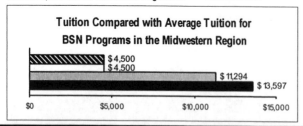

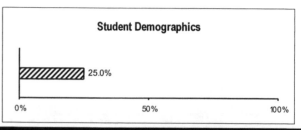

UNIVERSITY OF ILLINOIS - CHICAGO

Useful Facts*

845 S Damen
Chicago, IL 60612
(312) 996-7806
Joan Shaver, PhD, RN, FAAN

www.uic.edu/nursing

		Tuition		Student Demographics	
Acceptance rate	36.7%	In state	$2,842	Female	91.1%
		Out of state	$5,466	Under age 25	42.0%
		Enrollments	346	Minority	40.7%
		Graduations	139	Part-time	8.5%

Accreditation
Illinois Department of Professional Regulation,
Commission on Collegiate Nursing Education
(CCNE)

Degrees conferred
Baccalaureate

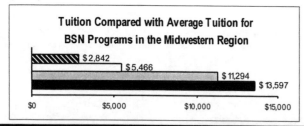

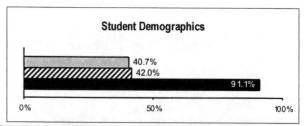

UNIVERSITY OF SAINT FRANCIS - JOLIET

Useful Facts

500 Wilcox Street
Joliet, IL 60435
(815) 740-3463
Maria Connolly, DNSc, APRN, FCCM

www.stfrancis.edu/conah

			Tuition		Student Demographics	
Acceptance rate		64.3%	In state	$18,170	Female	89.0%
Faculty-student ratio		1: 12	Out of state	$18,170	Under age 25	66.2%
Faculty	Full time	19	Enrollments	397	Minority	33.9%
	Part time	30	Graduations	67	Part-time	12.8%

Accreditation
Illinois Department of Professional Regulation,
Commission on Collegiate Nursing Education
(CCNE), National League for Nursing Accrediting
Commission (NLNAC)

Degrees conferred
Baccalaureate degree

Minimum degree required
High school diploma or GED

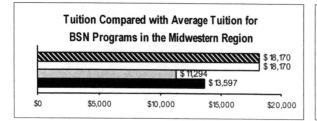

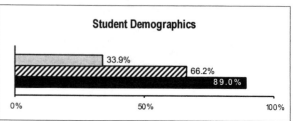

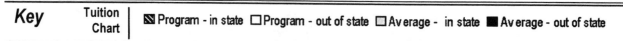

Key Tuition Chart | ▨ Program - in state ☐ Program - out of state ▤ Average - in state ■ Average - out of state

Indiana

ANDERSON UNIVERSITY — *Useful Facts*

1100 E 5th Street
Anderson, IN 46012
(765) 641-4383
Andrea Koepke, DNS

www.anderson.edu/academics/nurs/index.html

Acceptance rate	71.1%	
Faculty-student ratio	1: 17	
Faculty	Full time	10
	Part time	1

Tuition
In state $18,900
Out of state $18,900
Enrollments 178
Graduations 16

Student Demographics
Female 95.5%
Under age 25 81.5%
Minority 3.4%
Part-time 8.4%

Accreditation
Indiana State Board of Nursing, National League for Nursing Accrediting Commission (NLNAC)

Degrees conferred
Master's with joint degree, Baccalaureate degree

Minimum degree required
High school diploma or GED

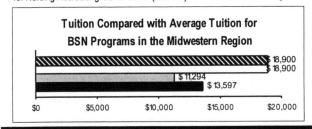

Tuition Compared with Average Tuition for BSN Programs in the Midwestern Region
$18,900 / $18,900 / $11,294 / $13,597

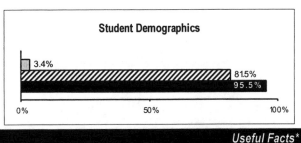

Student Demographics
3.4% / 81.5% / 95.5%

BALL STATE UNIVERSITY — *Useful Facts**

2000 University Ave
Muncie, IN 47306
(765) 285-5571
Linda Siktberg, PhD, RN

www.bsu.edu/nursing

Acceptance rate	71.9%	
Faculty-student ratio	1: 9	
Faculty	Full time	29
	Part time	8

Tuition
In state $5,752
Out of state $14,928
Enrollments 292
Graduations 70

Student Demographics
Female 92.3%
Under age 25 73.0%
Minority 5.0%
Part-time 0.0%

Accreditation
Indiana State Board of Nursing, National League for Nursing Accrediting Commission (NLNAC)

Degrees conferred
Baccalaureate

Tuition Compared with Average Tuition for BSN Programs in the Midwestern Region
$5,752 / $14,928 / $11,294 / $13,597

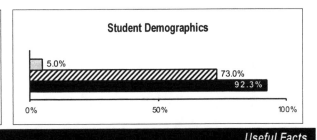

Student Demographics
5.0% / 73.0% / 92.3%

BETHEL COLLEGE — *Useful Facts*

1001 West McKinley
Mishawaka, IN 46545
(574) 257-2594
Ruth Davidhizar, RN, DNS, ARNP, BC, FAAN

www.bethelcollege.edu

Acceptance rate	83.3%	
Faculty-student ratio	1: 8	
Faculty	Full time	14
	Part time	20

Tuition
In state $15,800
Out of state $15,800
Enrollments 106
Graduations 30

Student Demographics
Female 92.7%
Under age 25 80.0%
Minority 9.1%
Part-time 0.0%

Accreditation
Indiana State Board of Nursing, National League for Nursing Accrediting Commission (NLNAC)

Degrees conferred
Baccalaureate degree

Minimum degree required
High school diploma or GED

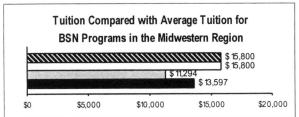

Tuition Compared with Average Tuition for BSN Programs in the Midwestern Region
$15,800 / $15,800 / $11,294 / $13,597

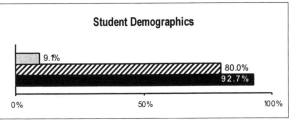

Student Demographics
9.1% / 80.0% / 92.7%

Demographics Chart	■ Female ▨ Under age 25 ☐ Minority	Distance Learning		†The tuition reported for this program may be not be annualized. *Data reported between 2001 and 2004.

Indiana

GOSHEN COLLEGE *Useful Facts*

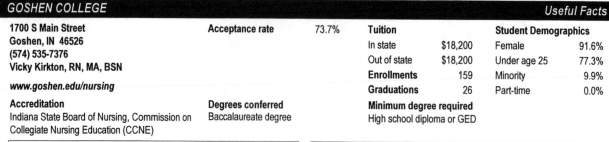

1700 S Main Street
Goshen, IN 46526
(574) 535-7376
Vicky Kirkton, RN, MA, BSN

www.goshen.edu/nursing

Acceptance rate	73.7%

Tuition

In state	$18,200
Out of state	$18,200
Enrollments	159
Graduations	26

Student Demographics

Female	91.6%
Under age 25	77.3%
Minority	9.9%
Part-time	0.0%

Accreditation
Indiana State Board of Nursing, Commission on Collegiate Nursing Education (CCNE)

Degrees conferred
Baccalaureate degree

Minimum degree required
High school diploma or GED

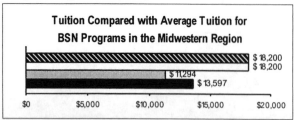

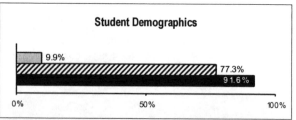

INDIANA STATE UNIVERSITY *Useful Facts*

749 Chestnut
Terre Haute, IN 47809
(812) 237-3683
Esther Acree, MSN, FNP

www.indstate.edu/site/nurs

Acceptance rate	100.0%
Faculty-student ratio	1: 22

Faculty	Full time	21
	Part time	0

Tuition

In state	$7,114
Out of state	$16,004
Enrollments	455
Graduations	52

Student Demographics

Female	89.7%
Under age 25	75.8%
Minority	10.5%
Part-time	14.7%

Accreditation
Indiana State Board of Nursing, National League for Nursing Accrediting Commission (NLNAC)

Degrees conferred
Baccalaureate degree

Minimum degree required
High school diploma or GED

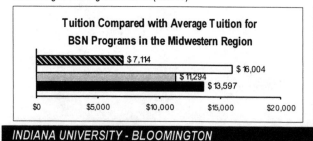

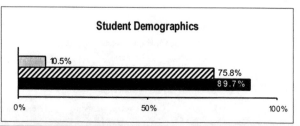

INDIANA UNIVERSITY - BLOOMINGTON *Useful Facts**

4201 Grant Line Road, LF-276
New Albany, IN 47150
(812) 941-2340
Lillian Yeager, RN

www.ius.indiana.edu/nursing

Tuition

In state	$4,475
Out of state	$11,153
Enrollments	98
Graduations	57

Student Demographics

Female	98.9%
Under age 25	67.0%
Part-time	2.2%

Accreditation
Indiana State Board of Nursing

Degrees conferred
Baccalaureate

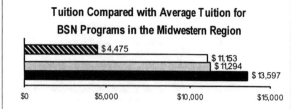

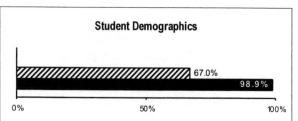

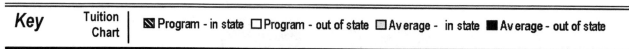

Key | Tuition Chart | ⬛ Program - in state ☐ Program - out of state ☐ Average - in state ⬛ Average - out of state

Indiana

INDIANA UNIVERSITY - EAST — *Useful Facts*

2325 Chester Boulevard
Richmond, IN 47374
(765) 973-8242
Karen Clark, EdD, RN

www.iue.edu/departments/nursing

Accreditation
Indiana State Board of Nursing, National League for Nursing Accrediting Commission (NLNAC)

Acceptance rate	50.6%
Faculty-student ratio	1: 11
Faculty Full time	15
Part time	0

Tuition
In state $4,475
Out of state $11,153
Enrollments 129
Graduations 28

Student Demographics
Female 93.0%
Under age 25 56.1%
Minority 2.6%
Part-time 0.0%

Degrees conferred
Baccalaureate degree

Minimum degree required
GPA criteria 28 credits minimum

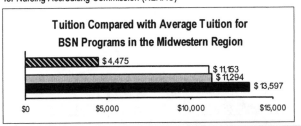
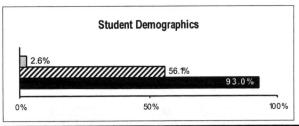

INDIANA UNIVERSITY - KOKOMO — *Useful Facts*

PO Box 9003
Kokomo, IN 46904
(765) 455-9288
Penny Cass, PhD, RN

www.iuk.edu/~konurse

Accreditation
Indiana State Board of Nursing, Commission on Collegiate Nursing Education (CCNE)

Acceptance rate	63.7%
Faculty-student ratio	1: 14
Faculty Full time	15
Part time	25

Tuition¹
In state $131
Out of state $353
Enrollments 182
Graduations 32

Student Demographics
Female 96.7%
Under age 25 56.9%
Minority 5.9%
Part-time 54.9%

Degrees conferred
Baccalaureate degree

Minimum degree required
31-32 credit hours as specified by the curriculum

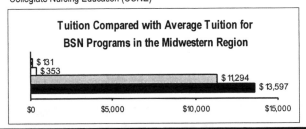
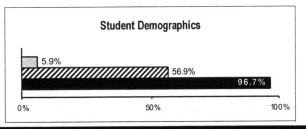

INDIANA UNIVERSITY - NORTHWEST — *Useful Facts*

3400 Broadway
Gary, IN 46408
(219) 980-6604
Linda Rooda, PhD, RN

www.iun.edu/~nurse

Accreditation
Indiana State Board of Nursing, Commission on Collegiate Nursing Education (CCNE), National League for Nursing Accrediting Commission (NLNAC)

Acceptance rate	35.0%
Faculty-student ratio	1: 12
Faculty Full time	15
Part time	9

Tuition
In state $3,932
Out of state $10,599
Enrollments 160
Graduations 35

Student Demographics
Female 92.8%
Under age 25 53.6%
Minority 31.2%
Part-time 0.0%

Degrees conferred
Baccalaureate degree

Minimum degree required
High school diploma or GED

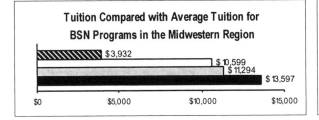
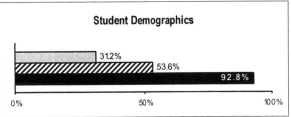

Demographics Chart ■Female ▨Under age 25 ☐Minority | Distance Learning | ¹The tuition reported for this program may be not be annualized. *Data reported between 2001 and 2004.

IN 49

Indiana

1111 Middle Drive
Indianapolis, IN 46202
(317) 274-1486
Marion Broome, PhD, RN, FAAN

nursing.iupui.edu

Accreditation
Indiana State Board of Nursing, Commission on Collegiate Nursing Education (CCNE), National League for Nursing Accrediting Commission (NLNAC)

Acceptance rate	34.4%
Faculty-student ratio	1: 6
Faculty Full time	99
Part time	95

Degrees conferred
Baccalaureate degree

Tuition[1]	
In state	$158
Out of state	$502
Enrollments	887
Graduations	303

Minimum degree required
High school diploma or GED

Student Demographics	
Female	92.5%
Under age 25	69.9%
Minority	7.5%
Part-time	16.5%

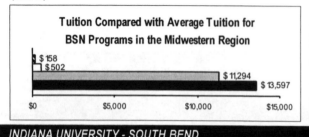

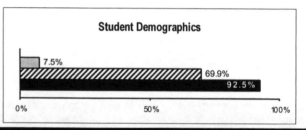

1700 Mishawaka Ave
South Bend, IN 46634
(574) 520-4207
Mary Jo Regan-Kubinski, PhD

www.iusb.edu/~nursing

Accreditation
Indiana State Board of Nursing, Commission on Collegiate Nursing Education (CCNE)

Acceptance rate	71.4%
Faculty-student ratio	1: 9
Faculty Full time	12
Part time	15

Degrees conferred
Baccalaureate

Tuition	
In state	$3,540
Out of state	$9,900
Enrollments	175
Graduations	28

Student Demographics	
Female	95.3%
Minority	8.7%
Part-time	30.2%

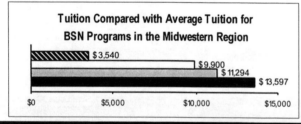

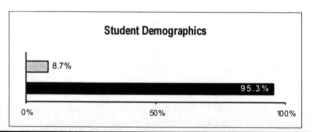

4201 S Washington Street
Marion, IN 46953
(765) 677-2267
Doris Scott, EdD

www.indwes.edu/academics/nursing

Accreditation
Indiana State Board of Nursing, Commission on Collegiate Nursing Education (CCNE)

Acceptance rate	96.9%

Degrees conferred
Baccalaureate

Tuition	
In state	$15,204
Out of state	$15,204
Enrollments	834
Graduations	213

Student Demographics	
Female	91.9%
Under age 25	93.3%
Minority	2.2%
Part-time	2.4%

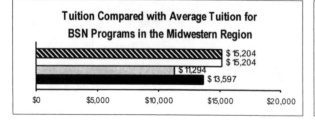

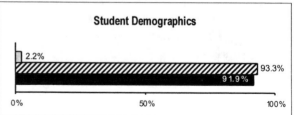

Key | Tuition Chart | ▨ Program - in state ☐ Program - out of state ☐ Average - in state ■ Average - out of state

Indiana

MARIAN COLLEGE

3200 Cold Spring Rd
Indianapolis, IN 46222
(317) 955-6155
Marian Pettengill, PhD, RN

www.marian.edu

Accreditation
Indiana State Board of Nursing, Commission on
Collegiate Nursing Education (CCNE)

*At the request of this nursing school, publication has been witheld.
Please contact the school directly for more information.*

PURDUE UNIVERSITY   *Useful Facts**

1337 Johnson Hall of Nursing	Acceptance rate	66.2%			Student Demographics	
West Lafayette, IN 47907					Female	95.9%
(765) 494-2849					Under age 25	93.0%
Pat Coyle-Rogers, PhD, RN			Enrollments	500	Minority	6.6%
www.nursing.purdue.edu			Graduations	96	Part-time	1.0%

Accreditation
Indiana State Board of Nursing

Degrees conferred
Baccalaureate

PURDUE UNIVERSITY - CALUMET CAMPUS   *Useful Facts*

2200 169th Street	Acceptance rate	58.0%	Tuition		Student Demographics	
Hammond, IN 46323	Faculty-student ratio	1: 10	In state	$5,409	Female	96.4%
(219) 989-2818	Faculty Full time	25	Out of state	$12,129	Under age 25	73.0%
Peggy Gerard, DNSc, RN	Part time	10	Enrollments	167	Minority	22.0%
nursing.calumet.purdue.edu			Graduations	22	Part-time	13.5%

Accreditation
Indiana State Board of Nursing, National League
for Nursing Accrediting Commission (NLNAC)

Degrees conferred
Baccalaureate degree

Minimum degree required
High school diploma or GED

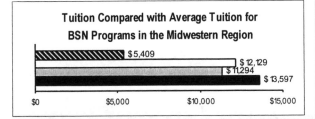

Tuition Compared with Average Tuition for BSN Programs in the Midwestern Region
$5,409
$12,129
$11,294
$13,597

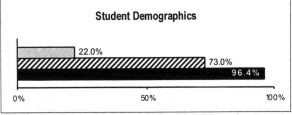

Student Demographics
22.0%
73.0%
96.4%

PURDUE UNIVERSITY - NORTH CENTRAL

1401 S US 421
Westville, IN 46391
(219) 785-5324
Elizabeth Hayes, MS, RN

www.pnc.edu

Accreditation
Indiana State Board of Nursing

Degrees conferred
Baccalaureate

Demographics Chart	■ Female ▨ Under age 25 ▢ Minority	Distance Learning		†The tuition reported for this program may be not be annualized. *Data reported between 2001 and 2004.

Indiana

SAINT MARY'S COLLEGE

Havican Hall, Room 6
Notre Dame, IN 46556
(574) 284-4680
Ella Harmeyer, MS, RN

www.saintmarys.edu/~nursing

Accreditation
Indiana State Board of Nursing, National League
for Nursing Accrediting Commission (NLNAC)

Degrees conferred
Baccalaureate

Acceptance rate	97.4%

Tuition	
In state	$16,994
Out of state	$16,994
Enrollments	101
Graduations	20

Student Demographics	
Female	100.0%
Under age 25	99.9%
Minority	2.0%
Part-time	0.0%

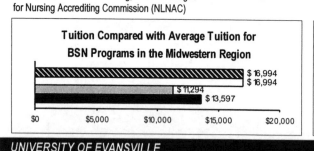

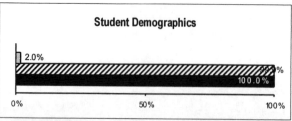

UNIVERSITY OF EVANSVILLE

1800 Lincoln Avenue
Evansville, IN 47722
(812) 488-2592
Charlotte Niksch, RN, MSN

www.evansville.edu

Accreditation
Indiana State Board of Nursing, National League
for Nursing Accrediting Commission (NLNAC)

Degrees conferred
Baccalaureate degree

Minimum degree required
High school diploma or GED

Acceptance rate		74.8%
Faculty-student ratio		1: 10
Faculty	Full time	7
	Part time	5

Tuition	
In state	$21,120
Out of state	$21,120
Enrollments	98
Graduations	12

Student Demographics	
Female	95.9%
Under age 25	96.9%
Minority	5.2%
Part-time	1.0%

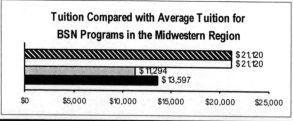

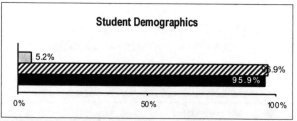

UNIVERSITY OF INDIANAPOLIS

1400 E Hanna Avenue
Indianapolis, IN 46220
(317) 788-3206
Sharon Isaac, EdD, RN, MSN, BSN

www.uindy.edu

Accreditation
Indiana State Board of Nursing, Commission on
Collegiate Nursing Education (CCNE)

Degrees conferred
Baccalaureate degree

Minimum degree required
High school diploma or GED

Acceptance rate		73.0%
Faculty-student ratio		1: 9
Faculty	Full time	22
	Part time	28

Tuition	
In state	$17,980
Out of state	$17,980
Enrollments	227
Graduations	23

Student Demographics	
Female	92.8%
Under age 25	97.1%
Minority	10.1%
Part-time	13.7%

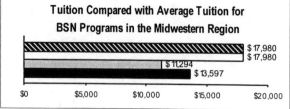

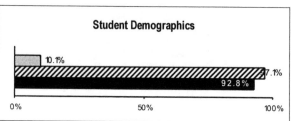

Key | Tuition Chart | ▨ Program - in state ☐ Program - out of state ▨ Average - in state ■ Average - out of state

Indiana

UNIVERSITY OF SAINT FRANCIS (INDIANA) — *Useful Facts*

2701 Spring Street
Fort Wayne, IN 46808
(260) 434-7644
Lorene Arnold, WHNP, MSN, RNC

www.sf.edu

Accreditation
Indiana State Board of Nursing, Commission on Collegiate Nursing Education (CCNE)

Acceptance rate		96.4%
Faculty-student ratio		1: 14
Faculty	Full time	28
	Part time	32

Tuition

In state	$16,750
Out of state	$16,750
Enrollments	288
Graduations	29

Student Demographics

Female	93.4%
Under age 25	87.9%
Minority	4.3%
Part-time	8.5%

Degrees conferred
Baccalaureate degree

Minimum degree required
High school diploma or GED

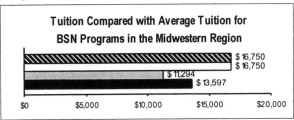

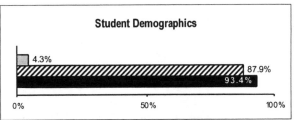

UNIVERSITY OF SOUTHERN INDIANA — *Useful Facts*

8600 University Blvd
Evansville, IN 47712
(812) 465-1151
Nadine Coudret, EdD, MSN

health.usi.edu

Accreditation
Indiana State Board of Nursing, Commission on Collegiate Nursing Education (CCNE)

Acceptance rate		50.0%
Faculty-student ratio		1: 9
Faculty	Full time	27
	Part time	6

Tuition

In state	$4,243
Out of state	$10,117
Enrollments	283
Graduations	51

Student Demographics

Female	94.5%
Under age 25	72.8%
Minority	0.4%
Part-time	19.1%

Degrees conferred
Baccalaureate degree

Minimum degree required
BA or BS in a non-nursing field

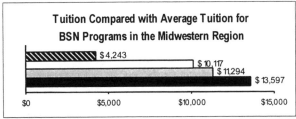

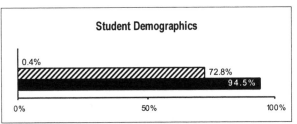

VALPARAISO UNIVERSITY — *Useful Facts**

836 LaPorte Avenue
Valparaiso, IN 46383
(219) 464-5289
Janet Brown, PhD, RN

www.valpo.edu/nursing

Accreditation
Indiana State Board of Nursing, Commission on Collegiate Nursing Education (CCNE)

Acceptance rate	77.2%

Tuition

In state	$21,000
Out of state	$21,000
Enrollments	225
Graduations	38

Student Demographics

Female	94.1%
Under age 25	84.0%
Minority	6.6%
Part-time	5.0%

Degrees conferred
Baccalaureate

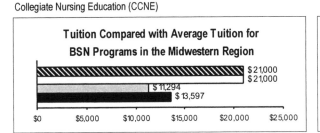

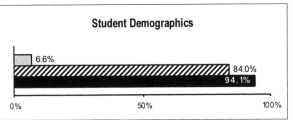

Demographics Chart ■Female ▨Under age 25 ☐Minority | **Distance Learning** | †The tuition reported for this program may be not be annualized.
*Data reported between 2001 and 2004.

Iowa

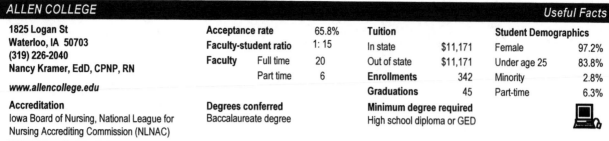

ALLEN COLLEGE — Useful Facts

1825 Logan St
Waterloo, IA 50703
(319) 226-2040
Nancy Kramer, EdD, CPNP, RN

www.allencollege.edu

Acceptance rate		65.8%
Faculty-student ratio		1: 15
Faculty	Full time	20
	Part time	6

Tuition	
In state	$11,171
Out of state	$11,171
Enrollments	342
Graduations	45

Student Demographics	
Female	97.2%
Under age 25	83.8%
Minority	2.8%
Part-time	6.3%

Accreditation
Iowa Board of Nursing, National League for Nursing Accrediting Commission (NLNAC)

Degrees conferred
Baccalaureate degree

Minimum degree required
High school diploma or GED

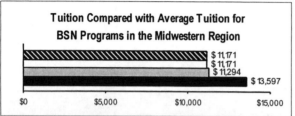

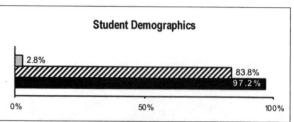

BRIAR CLIFF COLLEGE — Useful Facts

3303 Rebecca St
Sioux City, IA 51104
(712) 279-1758
Barbara Condon, MSN, RN, CNS

www.briarcliff.edu/nursing

Acceptance rate		93.8%
Faculty-student ratio		1: 18
Faculty	Full time	8
	Part time	1

Tuition	
In state	$16,560
Out of state	$16,560
Enrollments	153
Graduations	21

Student Demographics	
Female	93.1%
Under age 25	79.3%
Minority	9.5%
Part-time	6.9%

Accreditation
Iowa Board of Nursing, National League for Nursing Accrediting Commission (NLNAC)

Degrees conferred
Baccalaureate degree

Minimum degree required
2.5 cumulative GPA

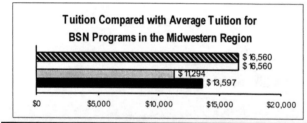

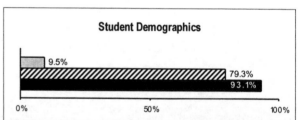

CLARKE COLLEGE — Useful Facts*

1550 Clarke St
Dubuque, IA 52001
(319) 588-6361
Mary Mooney, DNSc, ARNP

www.clarke.edu

Acceptance rate	80.0%

Tuition	
In state	$14,000
Out of state	$14,000
Enrollments	79
Graduations	25

Student Demographics	
Female	96.2%
Under age 25	55.0%
Part-time	40.5%

Accreditation
Iowa Board of Nursing

Degrees conferred
Baccalaureate

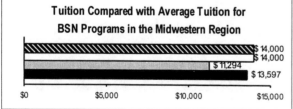

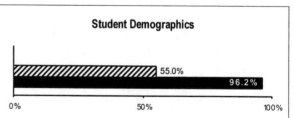

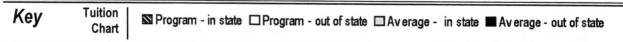

Key — Tuition Chart

▨ Program - in state   ☐ Program - out of state   ☐ Average - in state   ■ Average - out of state

Iowa

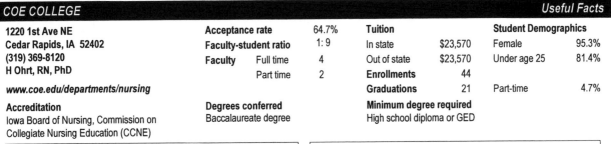

COE COLLEGE

1220 1st Ave NE
Cedar Rapids, IA 52402
(319) 369-8120
H Ohrt, RN, PhD

www.coe.edu/departments/nursing

Accreditation
Iowa Board of Nursing, Commission on
Collegiate Nursing Education (CCNE)

Acceptance rate		64.7%
Faculty-student ratio		1 : 9
Faculty	Full time	4
	Part time	2

Degrees conferred
Baccalaureate degree

Tuition	
In state	$23,570
Out of state	$23,570
Enrollments	44
Graduations	21

Minimum degree required
High school diploma or GED

Student Demographics	
Female	95.3%
Under age 25	81.4%
Part-time	4.7%

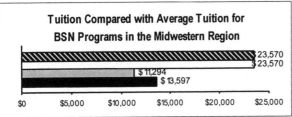

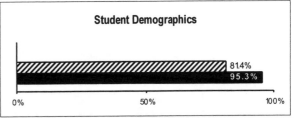

GRAND VIEW COLLEGE

1204 Grandview Ave
Des Moines, IA 50316
(515) 263-2866
Jean Logan, PhD

www.gvc.edu

Accreditation
Iowa Board of Nursing

Acceptance rate	82.1%

Degrees conferred
Baccalaureate

Tuition	
In state	$12,790
Out of state	$12,790
Enrollments	134
Graduations	73

Student Demographics	
Female	89.5%
Under age 25	63.0%
Minority	8.6%
Part-time	6.7%

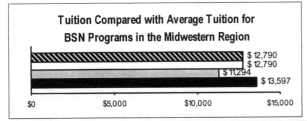

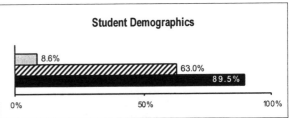

IOWA WESLEYAN COLLEGE

601 N Main
Mount Pleasant, IA 52641
(319) 385-6343
Judith Hausner, RN, PhD

www.iwc.edu

Accreditation
Iowa Board of Nursing, National League for
Nursing Accrediting Commission (NLNAC)

Acceptance rate		100.0%
Faculty-student ratio		1 : 7
Faculty	Full time	4
	Part time	11

Degrees conferred
Baccalaureate degree

Tuition	
In state	$16,950
Out of state	$16,950
Enrollments	70
Graduations	7

Minimum degree required
High school diploma or GED

Student Demographics	
Female	89.2%
Under age 25	58.5%
Minority	10.8%
Part-time	9.2%

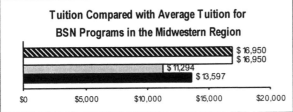

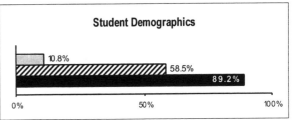

Demographics Chart	■Female ☒Under age 25 ☐Minority	Distance Learning		†The tuition reported for this program may be not be annualized.
				*Data reported between 2001 and 2004.

Iowa

LUTHER COLLEGE

700 College Dr
Decorah, IA 52101
(563) 387-1057
Donna Kubesh, PhD, RN

www.luther.edu

Accreditation
Iowa Board of Nursing, Commission on
Collegiate Nursing Education (CCNE)

Acceptance rate	45.8%

Tuition
In state	$20,310
Out of state	$20,310
Enrollments	109
Graduations	27

Student Demographics
Female	97.2%
Under age 25	97.0%
Minority	2.8%
Part-time	0.9%

Degrees conferred
Baccalaureate

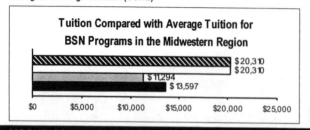

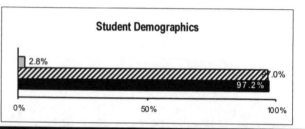

MORNINGSIDE COLLEGE

1501 Morningside Ave
Sioux City, IA 51106
(712) 274-5154
Mary Kovarna, RN, MSN

www.morningside.edu

Accreditation
Iowa Board of Nursing, National League for
Nursing Accrediting Commission (NLNAC)

Acceptance rate	93.9%
Faculty-student ratio	1: 14

Faculty	Full time	5
	Part time	4

Tuition
In state	$17,170
Out of state	$17,170
Enrollments	95
Graduations	15

Student Demographics
Female	94.6%
Under age 25	91.4%
Minority	6.5%
Part-time	1.1%

Degrees conferred
Baccalaureate degree

Minimum degree required
None

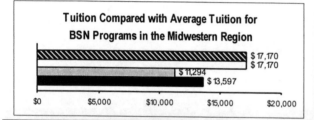

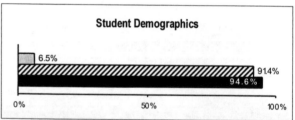

MOUNT MERCY COLLEGE

1330 Elmhurst Dr, NE
Cedar Rapids, IA 52402
(319) 368-6471
Mary Tarbox, EdD, RN

mtmercy.edu

Accreditation
Iowa Board of Nursing

Tuition
In state	$13,190
Out of state	$13,190
Enrollments	87
Graduations	34

Student Demographics
Female	95.2%
Under age 25 •	80.0%
Minority	3.6%
Part-time	45.2%

Degrees conferred
Baccalaureate

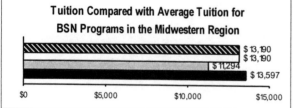

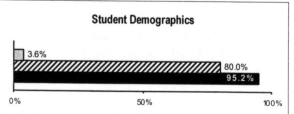

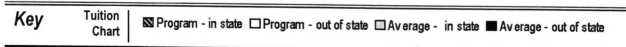

Key Tuition Chart ▨ Program - in state ☐ Program - out of state ☐ Average - in state ■ Average - out of state

Iowa

ST AMBROSE UNIVERSITY

518 West Locust Street
Davenport, IA 52803
(563) 333-6000
Dolores Hilden, RN, PhD

www.sau.edu

Accreditation
Iowa Board of Nursing

Degrees conferred
Baccalaureate

UNIVERSITY OF IOWA   *Useful Facts**

101F Nursing Building
Iowa City, IA 52242
(319) 335-7009
Melanie Dreher, PhD, RN, FAAN

www.nursing.uiowa.edu

Accreditation
Iowa Board of Nursing

Degrees conferred
Baccalaureate

Student Demographics

Enrollments	470		
Graduations	184	Part-time	24.1%

Kansas

BAKER UNIVERSITY   *Useful Facts**

1500 South West Tenth Street
Topeka, KS 66604
(785) 354-5853
Kathleen Harr, DNSc, RN

www.bakeru.edu

Accreditation
Kansas State Board of Nursing, Commission on
Collegiate Nursing Education (CCNE)

Degrees conferred
Baccalaureate

Acceptance rate	32.7%	**Tuition**		**Student Demographics**	
		In state	$10,250	Female	95.4%
		Out of state	$10,250	Under age 25	76.0%
		Enrollments	131	Minority	3.9%
		Graduations	54	Part-time	2.3%

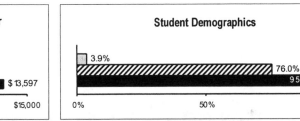

Tuition Compared with Average Tuition for BSN Programs in the Midwestern Region

- $10,250
- $10,250
- $11,294
- $13,597

(axis: $0, $5,000, $10,000, $15,000)

Student Demographics

- 3.9%
- 76.0%
- 95.4%

(axis: 0%, 50%, 100%)

BETHEL COLLEGE (KANSAS)

300 East 27th Street
North Newton, KS 67117
(316) 284-5377
Gregg Schroeder, MSN, ARNP

www.bethelks.edu

Accreditation
Kansas State Board of Nursing

Degrees conferred
Baccalaureate

Demographics Chart	■ Female ▨ Under age 25 ☐ Minority	**Distance Learning** 	†The tuition reported for this program may be not be annualized. *Data reported between 2001 and 2004.

Kansas

EMPORIA STATE UNIVERSITY

1127 Chestnut Street
Emporia, KS 66801
(620) 343-6800
Judith Calhoun, PhD, ARNP

www.emporia.edu/ndn

Accreditation
Kansas State Board of Nursing, National League for Nursing Accrediting Commission (NLNAC)

Acceptance rate	39.0%
Faculty-student ratio	1: 10
Faculty Full time	10
Part time	0

Degrees conferred
Baccalaureate degree

Tuition	
In state	$2,638
Out of state	$9,990
Enrollments	101
Graduations	28

Minimum degree required
High school diploma or GED

Student Demographics	
Female	92.1%
Under age 25	81.2%
Minority	100.0%
Part-time	0.0%

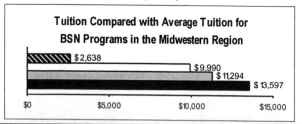

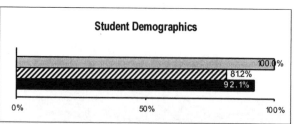

FORT HAYS STATE UNIVERSITY

600 Park Street
Hays, KS 67601
(785) 628-4511
Liane Connelly, PhD, MSN, BSN, RN, CNAA, BC, COI

www.fhsu.edu/nursing

Accreditation
Kansas State Board of Nursing, Commission on Collegiate Nursing Education (CCNE)

Acceptance rate	66.7%
Faculty-student ratio	1: 23
Faculty Full time	15
Part time	4

Degrees conferred
Baccalaureate degree

Tuition	
In state	$3,052
Out of state	$9,575
Enrollments	383
Graduations	43

Minimum degree required
High school diploma or GED

Student Demographics	
Female	89.2%
Under age 25	88.8%
Minority	4.8%
Part-time	3.3%

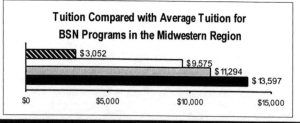

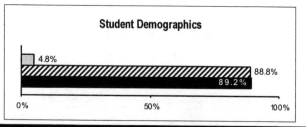

KANSAS WESLEYAN UNIVERSITY

100 East Claflin Avenue
Salina, KS 67401
(785) 827-5541
Patricia Brown, RN, PhD

www.kwu.edu

Accreditation
Kansas State Board of Nursing, National League for Nursing Accrediting Commission (NLNAC)

Acceptance rate	66.7%
Faculty-student ratio	1: 9
Faculty Full time	5
Part time	4

Degrees conferred
Baccalaureate degree

Tuition	
In state	$15,800
Out of state	$15,800
Enrollments	22
Graduations	0

Minimum degree required
High school diploma or GED

Student Demographics	
Female	81.8%
Under age 25	72.7%
Minority	23.8%
Part-time	4.5%

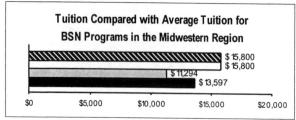

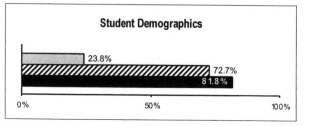

Key Tuition Chart | ◳ Program - in state ☐ Program - out of state ▢ Average - in state ■ Average - out of state

Kansas

MID AMERICA NAZARENE UNIVERSITY | *Useful Facts**

2030 E College Way
Olathe, KS 66062
(913) 791-3383
Palma Smith, PhD, RN

www.mnu.edu

Accreditation
Kansas State Board of Nursing

Degrees conferred
Baccalaureate

Acceptance rate	88.9%	

Tuition
In state	$10,150
Out of state	$10,150
Enrollments	92
Graduations	31

Student Demographics
Female	97.8%
Under age 25	79.0%
Minority	10.1%
Part-time	11.2%

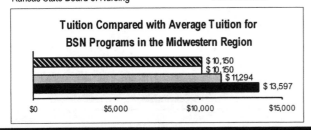
Tuition Compared with Average Tuition for BSN Programs in the Midwestern Region
$10,150
$10,150
$11,294
$13,597

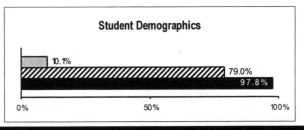
Student Demographics
10.1%
79.0%
97.8%

NEWMAN UNIVERSITY

3100 McCormick Ave
Wichita, KS 67213
(316) 942-4291
Anthony Chipas, PhD

www.newmanu.edu

Accreditation
Kansas State Board of Nursing

Degrees conferred
Baccalaureate

PITTSBURG STATE UNIVERSITY | *Useful Facts**

1701 S Broadway
Pittsburg, KS 67213
(620) 235-4432
Mary Carol Pomatto, ARNP, EdD

www.pittstate.edu/nurs

Accreditation
Kansas State Board of Nursing, Commission on
Collegiate Nursing Education (CCNE)

Degrees conferred
Baccalaureate

Acceptance rate		88.2%
Faculty-student ratio		1: 7
Faculty	Full time	14
	Part time	6

Tuition
In state	$2,100
Out of state	$6,464
Enrollments	125
Graduations	82

Student Demographics
Female	94.6%
Under age 25	90.2%
Minority	6.3%
Part-time	0.0%

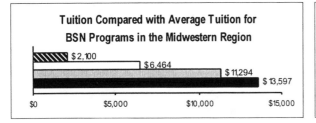
Tuition Compared with Average Tuition for BSN Programs in the Midwestern Region
$2,100
$6,464
$11,294
$13,597

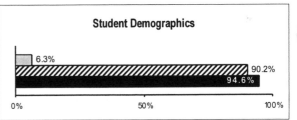
Student Demographics
6.3%
90.2%
94.6%

Demographics Chart | ■ Female ▨ Under age 25 ☐ Minority | **Distance Learning** | †The tuition reported for this program may be not be annualized.
*Data reported between 2001 and 2004.

Kansas

SOUTHWESTERN COLLEGE - WINFIELD
Useful Facts*

100 College Street
Winfield, KS 67156
(316) 229-6306
Martha Butler, PhD, RN

www.sckans.edu/nursing

Accreditation
Kansas State Board of Nursing, Commission on
Collegiate Nursing Education (CCNE)

Acceptance rate	80.0%

Degrees conferred
Baccalaureate

Tuition
In state	$14,618
Out of state	$14,618
Enrollments	74
Graduations	38

Student Demographics
Female	91.2%
Under age 25	25.0%
Minority	8.8%
Part-time	5.9%

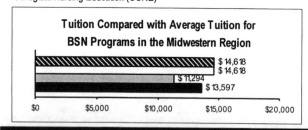

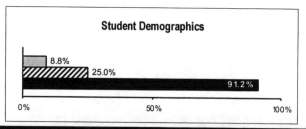

UNIVERSITY OF KANSAS
Useful Facts*

3901 Rainbow Blvd
Kansas City, KS 66160
(913) 588-1619
Karen Miller, PhD, RN, FAAN

www2.kumc.edu/son

Accreditation
Kansas State Board of Nursing, Commission on
Collegiate Nursing Education (CCNE)

Acceptance rate	40.3%

Degrees conferred
Baccalaureate

Tuition
In state	$3,527
Out of state	$11,003
Enrollments	301
Graduations	129

Student Demographics
Female	91.8%
Under age 25	65.0%
Minority	13.6%
Part-time	6.2%

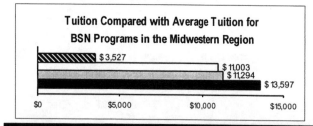

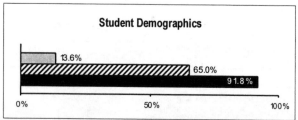

WASHBURN UNIVERSITY
Useful Facts

1700 SW College
Topeka, KS 66621
(785) 670-1213
Cynthia Hornberger, PhD, RN, MBA

www.washburn.edu/sonu

Accreditation
Kansas State Board of Nursing, Commission on
Collegiate Nursing Education (CCNE)

Acceptance rate		32.3%
Faculty-student ratio		1: 9
Faculty	Full time	18
	Part time	15

Degrees conferred
Baccalaureate degree

Tuition
In state	$4,920
Out of state	$11,130
Enrollments	232
Graduations	87

Minimum degree required
None

Student Demographics
Female	87.9%
Under age 25	100.0%
Minority	6.1%
Part-time	0.9%

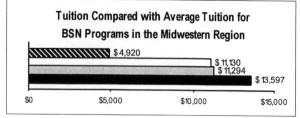

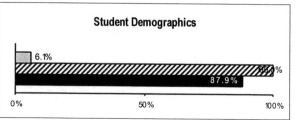

Key | Tuition Chart | ▨ Program - in state ☐ Program - out of state ☐ Average - in state ■ Average - out of state

Kansas

WICHITA STATE UNIVERSITY
Useful Facts*

1845 Fairmount
Wichita, KS 67260-0041
(316) 978-3610
Juanita Tate, PhD, MSN, RN

www.wichita.edu/nursing

Accreditation
Kansas State Board of Nursing, Commission on
Collegiate Nursing Education (CCNE)

Acceptance rate	34.5%

Degrees conferred
Baccalaureate

Tuition		**Student Demographics**	
In state	$3,909	Female	88.7%
Out of state	$11,363	Under age 25	58.0%
Enrollments	204	Minority	14.1%
Graduations	100	Part-time	1.1%

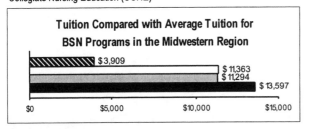

Tuition Compared with Average Tuition for BSN Programs in the Midwestern Region

$3,909
$11,363
$11,294
$13,597

$0 $5,000 $10,000 $15,000

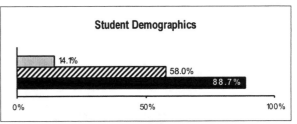

Student Demographics

14.1%
58.0%
88.7%

0%   50%   100%

Kentucky

BELLARMINE COLLEGE
Useful Facts*

2001 Newburg Rd, Miles Hall
Louisville, KY 40205
(502) 452-8414
Margaret Miller, PhD, MA, MSN, BSN, RN

www.bellarmine.edu

Accreditation
Kentucky Board of Nursing

Acceptance rate	76.0%

Degrees conferred
Baccalaureate

Tuition		**Student Demographics**	
In state	$12,480	Female	94.7%
Out of state	$12,480	Under age 25	40.0%
Enrollments	170		
Graduations	56	Part-time	33.5%

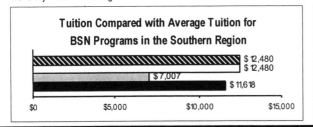

Tuition Compared with Average Tuition for BSN Programs in the Southern Region

$12,480
$12,480
$7,007
$11,618

$0 $5,000 $10,000 $15,000

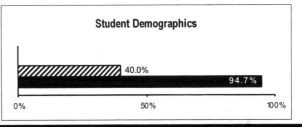

Student Demographics

40.0%
94.7%

0%   50%   100%

BEREA COLLEGE
Useful Facts*

2190 College Sta
Berea, KY 40404
(606) 985-3384
Pamela Farley, RN, PhD

www.berea.edu

Accreditation
Kentucky Board of Nursing

Degrees conferred
Baccalaureate

		Student Demographics	
		Female	92.5%
		Under age 25	99.0%
Enrollments	40		
Graduations	17	Part-time	0.0%

Demographics Chart	■Female ☑Under age 25 ☐Minority	Distance Learning		¹The tuition reported for this program may be not be annualized. *Data reported between 2001 and 2004.

Kentucky

EASTERN KENTUCKY UNIVERSITY

521 Lancaster, 220 Rowlett
Richmond, KY 40475
(859) 626-1942
Peggy Tudor, RN, MSN

www.adn.eku.edu

Accreditation
Kentucky Board of Nursing

Faculty-student ratio		1: 27
Faculty	Full time	18
	Part time	15

Degrees conferred
Baccalaureate

Tuition	
In state	$2,190
Out of state	$6,030
Enrollments	350
Graduations	115

Student Demographics

Part-time   18.7%

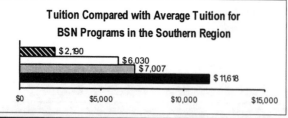

Tuition Compared with Average Tuition for BSN Programs in the Southern Region

- $2,190
- $6,030
- $7,007
- $11,618

KENTUCKY CHRISTIAN UNIVERSITY

100 Academic Parkway
Grayson, KY 41143
(606) 474-3271
Gail Wise, EdD, RN, C

www.kcu.edu

Accreditation
Kentucky Board of Nursing

Degrees conferred
Baccalaureate

MOREHEAD STATE UNIVERSITY

Reed Hall 234
Morehead, KY 40351
(606) 783-2296
Erla Mowbray, PhD, RN

www.moreheadstate.edu/nursing/index.aspx?id=5178

Accreditation
Kentucky Board of Nursing, Commission on Collegiate Nursing Education (CCNE), National League for Nursing Accrediting Commission (NLNAC)

Acceptance rate		41.7%
Faculty-student ratio		1: 9
Faculty	Full time	18
	Part time	6

Degrees conferred
Baccalaureate degree

Minimum degree required
High school diploma or GED

Tuition	
In state	$4,320
Out of state	$11,480
Enrollments	122
Graduations	26

Student Demographics

Female	87.0%
Under age 25	80.6%
Minority	3.7%
Part-time	12.0%

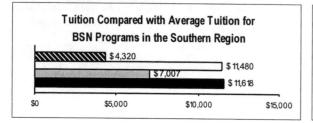

Tuition Compared with Average Tuition for BSN Programs in the Southern Region

- $4,320
- $11,480
- $7,007
- $11,618

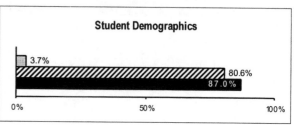

Student Demographics

- 3.7%
- 80.6%
- 87.0%

Kentucky

MURRAY STATE UNIVERSITY
Useful Facts*

120 Mason Hall
Murray, KY 42071
(270) 762-2193
Marcia Hobbs, RN, DSN

murraystate.edu/nursing

Accreditation
Kentucky Board of Nursing, Commission on
Collegiate Nursing Education (CCNE)

Degrees conferred
Baccalaureate

		Student Demographics	
Acceptance rate	62.9%		
Tuition			
In state	$3,984	Female	86.9%
Out of state	$10,836	Under age 25	80.0%
Enrollments	248	Minority	5.2%
Graduations	58	Part-time	16.2%

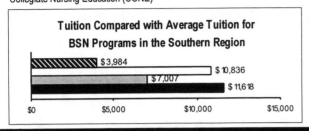

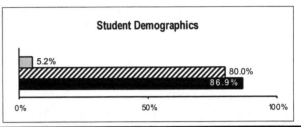

NORTHERN KENTUCKY UNIVERSITY
Useful Facts*

Nunn Drive, HC 303
Highland Heights, KY 41099
(859) 572-5248
Margaret Anderson, EdD, RN, CNAA

www.nku.edu/nursing

Accreditation
Kentucky Board of Nursing, National League for
Nursing Accrediting Commission (NLNAC)

Degrees conferred
Baccalaureate

		Student Demographics	
Acceptance rate	30.7%		
Tuition			
In state	$4,680	Female	96.1%
Out of state	$5,970	Under age 25	33.0%
Enrollments	664	Minority	4.7%
Graduations	0	Part-time	0.2%

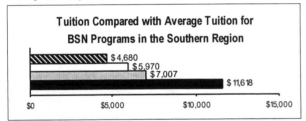

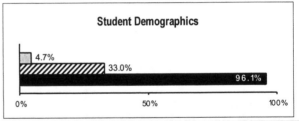

SPALDING UNIVERSITY
Useful Facts*

851 South Fourth Street
Louisville, KY 40203
(502) 585-7125
Br. Ignatius Perkins, OP, RN, MSN, EdD,
FAAN

www.spalding.edu/nursing

Accreditation
Kentucky Board of Nursing, Commission on
Collegiate Nursing Education (CCNE)

Degrees conferred
Baccalaureate

		Student Demographics	
Acceptance rate	100.0%		
Tuition			
In state	$13,500	Female	92.5%
Out of state	$13,500		
Enrollments	120	Minority	20.8%
Graduations	69	Part-time	0.0%

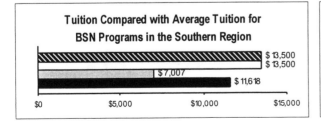

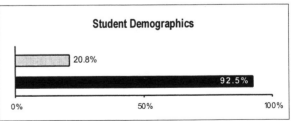

Demographics Chart	■Female ☑Under age 25 ☐Minority	Distance Learning	†The tuition reported for this program may be not be annualized. *Data reported between 2001 and 2004.

Kentucky

THOMAS MORE COLLEGE

333 Thomas More Parkway
Crestview Hills, KY 41017
(859) 344-3413
Lisa Torok, RN, MSN, PhD

www.thomasmore.edu

Accreditation
Kentucky Board of Nursing, National League for
Nursing Accrediting Commission (NLNAC)

*At the request of this nursing school, publication has been witheld.
Please contact the school directly for more information.*

UNIVERSITY OF KENTUCKY

Useful Facts*

760 Rose Street, Rm 315
Lexington, KY 40536
(606) 323-6533
Carolyn Williams, RN, FAAN, PhD

www.mc.uky.edu/nursing

Accreditation
Kentucky Board of Nursing

Degrees conferred
Baccalaureate

		Student Demographics	
		Female	93.6%
Enrollments	287		
Graduations	108	Part-time	9.8%

UNIVERSITY OF LOUISVILLE

Useful Facts*

555 S Floyd Street
Louisville, KY 40292
(502) 852-8387
Cynthia McCurren, PhD, RN

www.louisville.edu

Accreditation
Kentucky Board of Nursing

Degrees conferred
Baccalaureate

Acceptance rate	86.3%	**Tuition**		**Student Demographics**	
		In state	$3,447	Female	85.9%
		Out of state	$9,746		
		Enrollments	178	Minority	16.3%
		Graduations	116	Part-time	5.6%

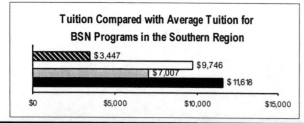

Tuition Compared with Average Tuition for BSN Programs in the Southern Region

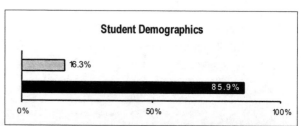

Student Demographics

WESTERN KENTUCKY UNIVERSITY

Useful Facts

1906 College Heights Blvd, #11036
Bowling Green, KY 42101
(270) 745-3579
Donna Blackburn, PhD, RN

www.wku.edu/dept/academic/chhs/nursing

Accreditation
Kentucky Board of Nursing, Commission on
Collegiate Nursing Education (CCNE)

Degrees conferred
Baccalaureate degree

Minimum degree required
High school diploma or GED

Acceptance rate	27.2%	**Tuition**		**Student Demographics**	
Faculty-student ratio	1: 10	In state	$5,316	Female	85.7%
Faculty Full time	40	Out of state	$12,732	Under age 25	72.4%
Part time	16	Enrollments	220	Minority	5.1%
		Graduations	94	Part-time	0.0%

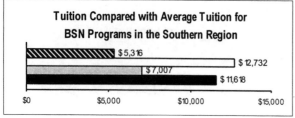

Tuition Compared with Average Tuition for BSN Programs in the Southern Region

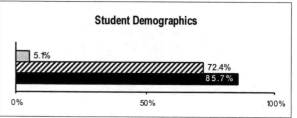

Student Demographics

Key | Tuition Chart

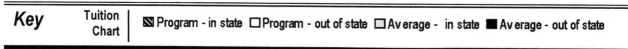

◩ Program - in state ☐ Program - out of state ☐ Average - in state ■ Average - out of state

Louisiana

DILLARD UNIVERSITY

2601 Gentilly Boulevard
New Orleans, LA 70122
(504) 816-4717
Sharon Hutchinson, PhD, MN, RN,C

www.dillard.edu

Accreditation
Louisiana State Board of Nursing, National
League for Nursing Accrediting Commission
(NLNAC)

At the request of this nursing school, publication has been withheld.
Please contact the school directly for more information.

GRAMBLING STATE UNIVERSITY   *Useful Facts**

PO Box 1192, 1 Cole Street
Grambling, LA 71245
(318) 274-2672
Betty Smith, PhD, RN

www.gram.edu

Accreditation
Louisiana State Board of Nursing, National
League for Nursing Accrediting Commission
(NLNAC)

Acceptance rate	61.2%	

Degrees conferred
Baccalaureate

Tuition		Student Demographics	
In state	$3,554	Female	89.1%
Out of state	$8,904	Under age 25	74.0%
Enrollments	367	Minority	94.2%
Graduations	29	Part-time	5.4%

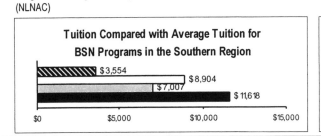

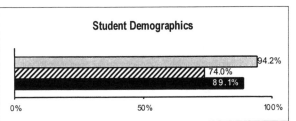

LOUISIANA COLLEGE   *Useful Facts**

1140 College Drive, Box 556
Pineville, LA 71359
(318) 487-7127
Phyllis Chelette, PhD, RN, MPH, CNAA

www.lacollege.edu

Accreditation
Louisiana State Board of Nursing, Commission
on Collegiate Nursing Education (CCNE)

Acceptance rate	100.0%	

Degrees conferred
Baccalaureate

Tuition		Student Demographics	
In state	$4,425	Female	84.3%
Out of state	$4,425	Under age 25	90.0%
Enrollments	89	Minority	11.2%
Graduations	13	Part-time	1.1%

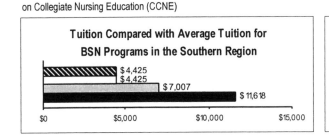

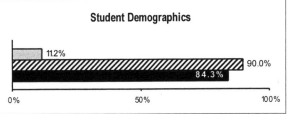

| Demographics Chart | ■ Female ▨ Under age 25 ▢ Minority | Distance Learning | | ¹The tuition reported for this program may be not be annualized.
*Data reported between 2001 and 2004. |
|---|---|---|---|---|

Louisiana

LOUISIANA STATE UNIVERSITY HEALTH SCIENCES CENTER
Useful Facts*

1900 Gravier Street
New Orleans, LA 70072
(504) 568-4106
Elizabeth Humphrey, EdD, RN

lsuhsc.edu/school/nursing

Accreditation
Louisiana State Board of Nursing, Commission on Collegiate Nursing Education (CCNE)

Acceptance rate	39.1%

Degrees conferred
Baccalaureate

Tuition		Student Demographics	
In state	$2,384	Female	87.8%
Out of state	$4,084	Under age 25	78.0%
Enrollments	459	Minority	15.4%
Graduations	120	Part-time	3.9%

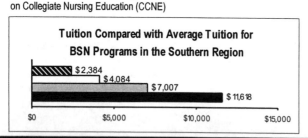

Tuition Compared with Average Tuition for BSN Programs in the Southern Region
- $2,384
- $4,084
- $7,007
- $11,618

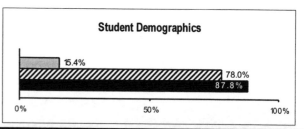

Student Demographics
- 15.4%
- 78.0%
- 87.8%

MCNEESE STATE UNIVERSITY
Useful Facts

PO Box 90415
Lake Charles, LA 70609
(337) 475-5822
Peggy Wolfe, PhD

www.mcneese.edu/colleges/nursing

Accreditation
Louisiana State Board of Nursing, National League for Nursing Accrediting Commission (NLNAC)

Acceptance rate	64.3%		
Faculty-student ratio	1: 35		
Faculty	Full time	29	
	Part time	9	

Degrees conferred
Baccalaureate degree

Minimum degree required
High school diploma or GED

Tuition		Student Demographics	
In state	$1,113	Female	79.8%
Out of state	$3,033	Under age 25	83.4%
Enrollments	991	Minority	21.0%
Graduations	62	Part-time	14.2%

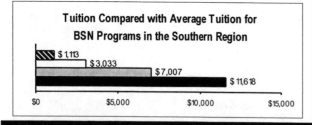

Tuition Compared with Average Tuition for BSN Programs in the Southern Region
- $1,113
- $3,033
- $7,007
- $11,618

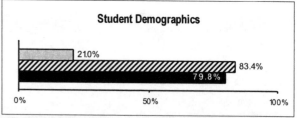

Student Demographics
- 21.0%
- 83.4%
- 79.8%

NICHOLLS STATE UNIVERSITY
Useful Facts

College Station, PO Box 2057
Thibodaux, LA 70310
(985) 448-4687
Velma Westbrook, DNS, RN

www.nicholls.edu/nursing

Accreditation
Louisiana State Board of Nursing, Commission on Collegiate Nursing Education (CCNE), National League for Nursing Accrediting Commission (NLNAC)

Acceptance rate	76.7%		
Faculty-student ratio	1: 12		
Faculty	Full time	25	
	Part time	0	

Degrees conferred
Baccalaureate degree

Minimum degree required
DK/NA

Tuition		Student Demographics	
In state	$3,390	Female	85.8%
Out of state	$8,838	Under age 25	72.7%
Enrollments	261	Minority	15.1%
Graduations	112	Part-time	49.2%

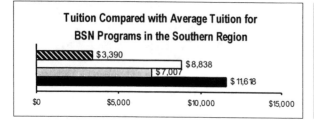

Tuition Compared with Average Tuition for BSN Programs in the Southern Region
- $3,390
- $8,838
- $7,007
- $11,618

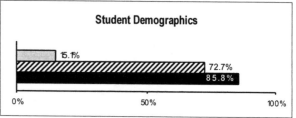

Student Demographics
- 15.1%
- 72.7%
- 85.8%

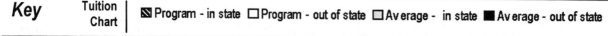

Key — Tuition Chart

▧ Program - in state ▢ Program - out of state ▨ Average - in state ■ Average - out of state

Louisiana

NORTHWESTERN STATE UNIVERSITY

1800 Line Avenue
Shreveport, LA 71101
(318) 677-3100
Norann Planchock, PhD, APRN, BC, FNP

www.nsula.edu/nursing

Accreditation
Louisiana State Board of Nursing, Commission
on Collegiate Nursing Education (CCNE)

At the request of this nursing school, publication has been witheld.
Please contact the school directly for more information.

OUR LADY OF HOLY CROSS COLLEGE

4123 Woodland Drive
New Orleans, LA 70131
(504) 398-2213
Patricia Prechter, RN, EdD

www.olhcc.edu

Accreditation
Louisiana State Board of Nursing, National
League for Nursing Accrediting Commission
(NLNAC)

At the request of this nursing school, publication has been witheld.
Please contact the school directly for more information.

SOUTHEASTERN LOUISIANA UNIVERSITY · Useful Facts

SLU 10781
Hammond, LA 70402
(985) 549-3772
Donnie Booth, PhD, MPH, BS, RN

www.selu.edu/academics/nursing

Accreditation
Louisiana State Board of Nursing, National
League for Nursing Accrediting Commission
(NLNAC)

Acceptance rate	33.6%	
Faculty-student ratio	1: 37	
Faculty Full time	46	
Part time	13	

Degrees conferred
Baccalaureate degree

Tuition	
In state	$4,319
Out of state	$7,992
Enrollments	1941
Graduations	154

Minimum degree required
High school diploma or GED

Student Demographics	
Female	86.1%
Under age 25	83.1%
Minority	24.6%
Part-time	22.0%

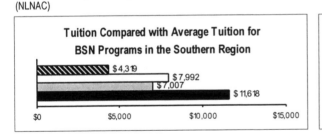

Tuition Compared with Average Tuition for BSN Programs in the Southern Region

$4,319
$7,992
$7,007
$11,618

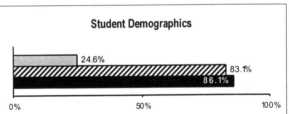

Student Demographics

24.6%
83.1%
86.1%

Demographics Chart	■Female ☒Under age 25 ☐Minority	Distance Learning	¹The tuition reported for this program may be not be annualized. *Data reported between 2001 and 2004.

LA · 67

Louisiana

SOUTHERN UNIVERSITY AND A&M COLLEGE, BATON ROUGE   *Useful Facts*

PO Box 11784
Baton Rouge, LA 70813
(225) 771-3266
Janet Rami, PhD, RN

www.subr.edu

Accreditation
Louisiana State Board of Nursing, Commission
on Collegiate Nursing Education (CCNE),
National League for Nursing Accrediting
Commission (NLNAC)

Acceptance rate	72.6%
Faculty-student ratio	1: 85
Faculty Full time	5
Part time	6

Degrees conferred
Baccalaureate degree

Tuition	
In state	$1,796
Out of state	$4,692
Enrollments	678
Graduations	69

Minimum degree required
None

Student Demographics	
Female	90.1%
Under age 25	76.8%
Minority	92.5%
Part-time	17.4%

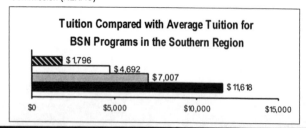

Tuition Compared with Average Tuition for BSN Programs in the Southern Region

$1,796
$4,692
$7,007
$11,618

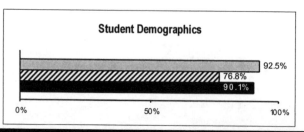

Student Demographics

92.5%
76.8%
90.1%

UNIVERSITY OF LOUISIANA - LAFAYETTE

PO Box 42490
Lafayette, LA 70504
(337) 482-6808
Gail Poirrier, DNS, RN

www.nursing.louisiana.edu

Accreditation
Louisiana State Board of Nursing, National
League for Nursing Accrediting Commission
(NLNAC)

*At the request of this nursing school, publication has been withheld.
Please contact the school directly for more information.*

UNIVERSITY OF LOUISIANA - MONROE

700 University Avenue
Monroe, LA 71209
(318) 342-1640
Linda Reid, MSN, RN

www.ulm.edu/nursing

Accreditation
Louisiana State Board of Nursing, Commission
on Collegiate Nursing Education (CCNE)

*At the request of this nursing school, publication has been withheld.
Please contact the school directly for more information.*

Key   Tuition Chart   ▨ Program - in state   ☐ Program - out of state   ☐ Average - in state   ■ Average - out of state

Maine

HUSSON COLLEGE — Useful Facts*

One College Circle
Bangor, ME 04401
(207) 941-7079
Mildred Padgett, MSN

www.husson.edu/academics/health/programs.html

Accreditation
Maine State Board of Nursing

Degrees conferred
Baccalaureate

Acceptance rate	83.3%	

Tuition[1]		Student Demographics	
In state	$316	Female	92.2%
Out of state	$316	Under age 25	90.0%
Enrollments	171	Minority	9.1%
Graduations	43	Part-time	18.2%

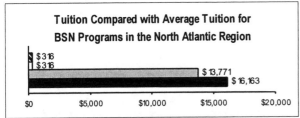

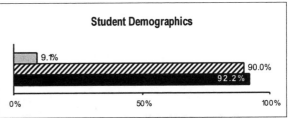

SAINT JOSEPH'S COLLEGE

278 Whites Bridge Road
Standish, ME 04084
(207) 893-7970
Margaret Hourigan, RN, EdD, CNAA, BC

www.sjcme.edu

Accreditation
Maine State Board of Nursing, Commission on
Collegiate Nursing Education (CCNE)

At the request of this nursing school, publication has been witheld.
Please contact the school directly for more information.

UNIVERSITY OF MAINE — Useful Facts*

5724 Dunn Hall
Orono, ME 04469
(207) 581-2599
Therese Shipps, RN, DNSc

www.umain.edu/nursing

Accreditation
Maine State Board of Nursing, Commission on
Collegiate Nursing Education (CCNE)

Degrees conferred
Baccalaureate

Acceptance rate	70.0%	

Tuition		Student Demographics	
In state	$4,380	Female	92.6%
Out of state	$12,450	Under age 25	61.0%
Enrollments	446	Minority	0.8%
Graduations	64	Part-time	11.5%

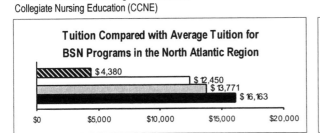

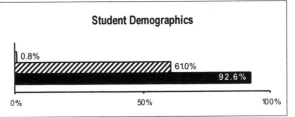

Demographics Chart	■ Female ▨ Under age 25 ☐ Minority	Distance Learning	[1]The tuition reported for this program may be not be annualized. *Data reported between 2001 and 2004.

Maine

UNIVERSITY OF MAINE - FORT KENT

25 Pleasant Street
Fort Kent, ME 04743
(207) 834-7584
Rachel Albert, PhD, RN

www.umfk.maine.edu/programs/nursing/main.htm

Accreditation
Maine State Board of Nursing

Acceptance rate		81.5%

Tuition

In state	$3,120
Out of state	$7,590
Enrollments	169
Graduations	8

Student Demographics

Female	88.9%
Under age 25	66.0%
Part-time	5.6%

Degrees conferred
Baccalaureate

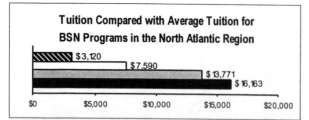

Tuition Compared with Average Tuition for BSN Programs in the North Atlantic Region

$3,120
$7,590
$13,771
$16,163

Student Demographics

66.0%
88.9%

UNIVERSITY OF SOUTHERN MAINE

PO Box 9300
Portland, ME 04104
(207) 780-4404
Jane Kirschling, RN, DNS

www.usm.maine.edu/conhp

Accreditation
Maine State Board of Nursing, National League
for Nursing Accrediting Commission (NLNAC)

Acceptance rate		61.3%

Tuition

In state	$4,620
Out of state	$12,780
Enrollments	612
Graduations	126

Student Demographics

Female	90.8%
Under age 25	51.0%
Minority	6.8%
Part-time	26.8%

Degrees conferred
Baccalaureate

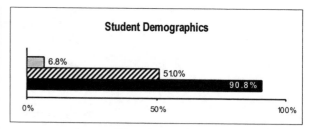

Tuition Compared with Average Tuition for BSN Programs in the North Atlantic Region

$4,620
$12,780
$13,771
$16,163

Student Demographics

6.8%
51.0%
90.8%

Maryland

BOWIE STATE UNIVERSITY

14000 Jericho Park Road
Bowie, MD 20715
(301) 860-3219
JoAnne Joyner, DNSc, RN, CS

www.bowiestate.edu

Accreditation
Maryland Board of Nursing, National League for
Nursing Accrediting Commission (NLNAC)

Degrees conferred
Baccalaureate

Key | Tuition Chart | ▨ Program - in state ☐ Program - out of state ▥ Average - in state ■ Average - out of state

Maryland

COLUMBIA UNION COLLEGE
Useful Facts*

7600 Flower Plaza
Takoma Park, MD 20912
(301) 891-4144
Gina Brown, PhD, RN

www.cuc.edu

Accreditation
Maryland Board of Nursing, National League for Nursing Accrediting Commission (NLNAC)

Degrees conferred
Baccalaureate

Acceptance rate	35.4%	

Tuition		**Student Demographics**	
In state	$15,433	Female	91.3%
Out of state	$15,433	Under age 25	60.0%
Enrollments	269		
Graduations	34	Part-time	0.0%

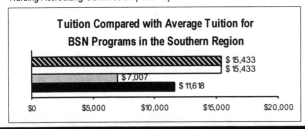

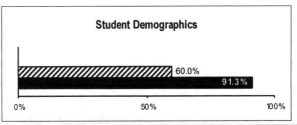

COPPIN STATE COLLEGE
Useful Facts*

2500 West North Avenue
Baltimore, MD 21216
(410) 951-3990
Marcella Copes, PhD

www.coppin.edu/nursing/

Accreditation
Maryland Board of Nursing, National League for Nursing Accrediting Commission (NLNAC)

Degrees conferred
Baccalaureate

Acceptance rate	16.6%	

Tuition		**Student Demographics**	
In state	$3,370	Female	95.8%
Out of state	$8,347	Under age 25	47.0%
Enrollments	195	Minority	98.4%
Graduations	45	Part-time	45.3%

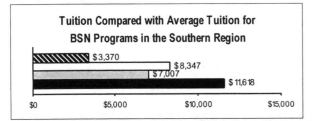

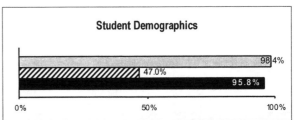

JOHNS HOPKINS UNIVERSITY
Useful Facts

525 N Wolfe St
Baltimore, MD 21205
(410) 955-7544
Martha Hill, PhD, RN, FAAN

www.son.jhmi.edu

Accreditation
Maryland Board of Nursing, Commission on Collegiate Nursing Education (CCNE), National League for Nursing Accrediting Commission (NLNAC)

Degrees conferred
BS

Minimum degree required
60 prerequisite credits

Acceptance rate	60.2%	
Faculty-student ratio	1: 4	
Faculty	Full time	70
	Part time	99

Tuition		**Student Demographics**	
In state	$23,784	Female	91.3%
Out of state	$23,784	Under age 25	19.9%
Enrollments	468	Minority	20.8%
Graduations	232	Part-time	2.8%

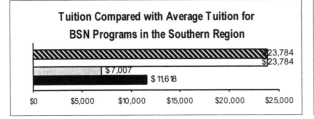

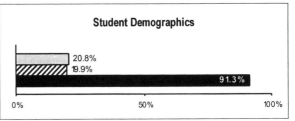

Demographics Chart	■ Female ▨ Under age 25 ▢ Minority	Distance Learning	†The tuition reported for this program may be not be annualized. *Data reported between 2001 and 2004.

Maryland

SALISBURY STATE UNIVERSITY
*Useful Facts**

1101 Camden Ave
Salisbury, MD 21801
(410) 543-6366
Susan Battistoni, PhD

www.salisbury.edu/schools/henson/nursingdept

Accreditation
Maryland Board of Nursing

Acceptance rate	79.7%

Tuition		Student Demographics	
In state	$3,216	Female	97.2%
Out of state	$8,272	Under age 25	80.0%
Enrollments	148	Minority	100.0%
Graduations	53	Part-time	3.4%

Degrees conferred
Baccalaureate

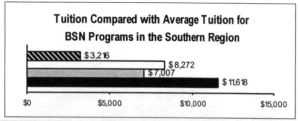

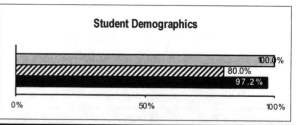

TOWSON UNIVERSITY
*Useful Facts**

8000 York Rd
Towson, MD 21252
(410) 704-4212
Jacquelyn Jordan, PhD, RN

www.towson.edu

Accreditation
Maryland Board of Nursing, Commission on
Collegiate Nursing Education (CCNE)

Acceptance rate	47.2%

Tuition		Student Demographics	
In state	$4,720	Female	92.0%
Out of state	$11,150		
Enrollments	199	Minority	26.1%
Graduations	68	Part-time	18.8%

Degrees conferred
Baccalaureate

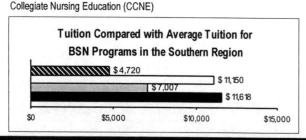

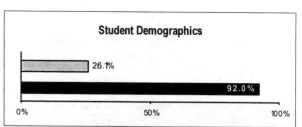

UNIVERSITY OF MARYLAND - BALTIMORE
Useful Facts

655 W Lombard St
Baltimore, MD 21201
(410) 706-6741
Janet Allan, PhD, RN, CS, FAAN

www.nursing.umaryland.edu

Accreditation
Maryland Board of Nursing, National League for
Nursing Accrediting Commission (NLNAC)

Acceptance rate		31.1%
Faculty-student ratio		1: 5
Faculty	Full time	99
	Part time	71

Tuition		Student Demographics	
In state	$6,890	Female	86.6%
Out of state	$17,960	Under age 25	50.0%
Enrollments	727	Minority	40.5%
Graduations	390	Part-time	9.5%

Degrees conferred
Baccalaureate degree

Minimum degree required
Completion of Prerequisite course work

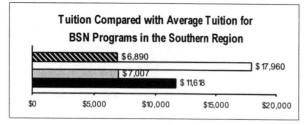

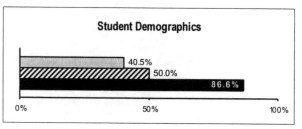

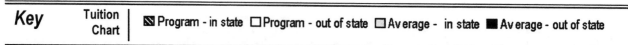

Key   Tuition Chart | ▨ Program - in state   ☐ Program - out of state   ☐ Average - in state   ■ Average - out of state

Maryland

VILLA JULIE COLLEGE | *Useful Facts*

1525 Greenspring Valley Rd
Stevenson, MD 21153
(443) 334-2312
Judith Feustle, ScD, RN

www.vjc.edu

Acceptance rate	15.9%	
Faculty-student ratio	1: 14	
Faculty	Full time	12
	Part time	34

Tuition	
In state	$14,674
Out of state	$14,674
Enrollments	392
Graduations	113

Student Demographics	
Female	93.5%
Under age 25	70.3%
Minority	21.2%
Part-time	16.1%

Accreditation
Maryland Board of Nursing, National League for Nursing Accrediting Commission (NLNAC)

Degrees conferred
Baccalaureate degree

Minimum degree required
High school diploma or GED

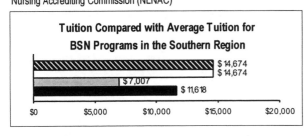

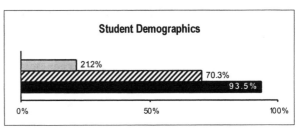

Massachusetts

AMERICAN INTERNATIONAL COLLEGE | *Useful Facts**

1000 State Street
Springfield, MA 01109
(413) 205-3519
Anne Glanovsky, PhD, RN

www.aic.edu.academics

Acceptance rate	69.6%

Tuition	
In state	$13,600
Out of state	$13,600
Enrollments	237
Graduations	22

Student Demographics	
Female	96.5%
Under age 25	17.0%
Minority	25.1%
Part-time	0.0%

Accreditation
Massachusetts Board of Registration in Nursing, National League for Nursing Accrediting Commission (NLNAC)

Degrees conferred
Baccalaureate

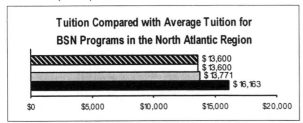

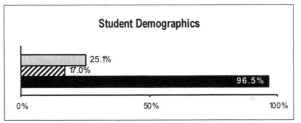

BOSTON COLLEGE | *Useful Facts**

140 Commonwealth Ave
Chestnut Hill, MA 02467
(617) 522-1710
Barbara Munro, PhD, RN, FAAN

www.bc.edu/nursing

Acceptance rate	30.7%

Tuition	
In state	$27,080
Out of state	$27,080
Enrollments	277
Graduations	43

Student Demographics	
Female	96.8%
Under age 25	99.0%
Minority	11.9%
Part-time	0.0%

Accreditation
Massachusetts Board of Registration in Nursing, Commission on Collegiate Nursing Education (CCNE)

Degrees conferred
Baccalaureate

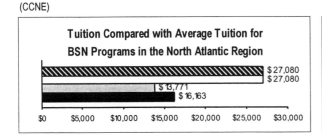

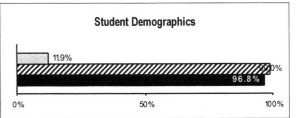

Demographics Chart	■ Female ▨ Under age 25 ☐ Minority	Distance Learning	†The tuition reported for this program may be not be annualized. *Data reported between 2001 and 2004.

Massachusetts

COLLEGE OF OUR LADY OF THE ELMS · *Useful Facts**

291 Springfield St
Chicopee, MA 01013
(413) 594-2761
Marjorie Childers, PhD, RN, CS

www.elms.edu

Accreditation
Massachusetts Board of Registration in Nursing

Acceptance rate 73.8%

Enrollments 117
Graduations 24

Degrees conferred
Baccalaureate

Student Demographics
Female	90.6%
Under age 25	73.0%
Part-time	26.5%

CURRY COLLEGE · *Useful Facts*

1071 Blue Hill Ave
Milton, MA 02186
(617) 333-2281
Linda Caldwell, DNSc, APRN-BC

www.curry.edu

Accreditation
Massachusetts Board of Registration in Nursing,
Commission on Collegiate Nursing Education
(CCNE)

Acceptance rate 68.4%
Faculty-student ratio 1: 22
Faculty Full time 13
Part time 27

Tuition
In state	$21,900
Out of state	$21,900
Enrollments	587
Graduations	88

Minimum degree required
None

Degrees conferred
Baccalaureate degree

Student Demographics
Female	7.4%
Under age 25	57.2%
Minority	11.4%
Part-time	19.9%

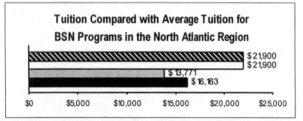

Tuition Compared with Average Tuition for BSN Programs in the North Atlantic Region

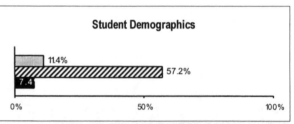

Student Demographics

ENDICOTT COLLEGE · *Useful Facts**

376 Hale St
Beverly, MA 01915
(978) 232-2327
Sherry Merrow, EdD, RN

www.endicott.edu

Accreditation
Massachusetts Board of Registration in Nursing,
National League for Nursing Accrediting
Commission (NLNAC)

Acceptance rate 52.2%

Tuition
In state	$14,550
Out of state	$14,550
Enrollments	99
Graduations	6

Degrees conferred
Baccalaureate

Student Demographics
Female	96.5%
Under age 25	87.0%
Part-time	2.3%

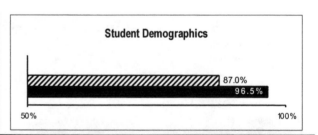

Tuition Compared with Average Tuition for BSN Programs in the North Atlantic Region

Student Demographics

FITCHBURG STATE COLLEGE · *Useful Facts**

160 Pearl St
Fitchburg, MA 01420
(978) 665-3221
Sophia Harrell, PhD

www.fsc.edu

Accreditation
Massachusetts Board of Registration in Nursing

Enrollments 292
Graduations 70

Degrees conferred
Baccalaureate

Student Demographics
Female	93.0%
Part-time	3.0%

Key | **Tuition Chart** | ▨ Program - in state ☐ Program - out of state ▥ Average - in state ■ Average - out of state

Massachusetts

MASSACHUSETTS COLLEGE OF PHARMACY AND HEALTH SCIENCES — *Useful Facts*

179 Longwood Ave
Boston, MA 02115
(617) 735-1461
Jeannine Muldoon, PhD, RN

www.mcphs.edu

Acceptance rate	63.6%	
Faculty-student ratio	1: 7	
Faculty Full time	7	
Part time	1	

Tuition
In state $20,400
Out of state $20,400
Enrollments 53
Graduations 0

Student Demographics
Female 92.5%
Under age 25 86.8%
Minority 44.0%
Part-time 15.1%

Accreditation
Massachusetts Board of Registration in Nursing

Degrees conferred
Baccalaureate degree

Minimum degree required
High school diploma or GED

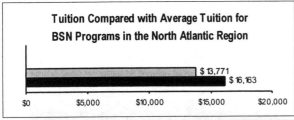

Tuition Compared with Average Tuition for BSN Programs in the North Atlantic Region

$13,771
$16,163

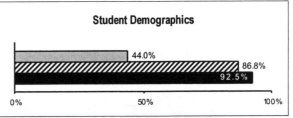

Student Demographics

44.0%
86.8%
92.5%

NORTHEASTERN UNIVERSITY — *Useful Facts**

102 Robinson Hall, 360 Huntington Ave
Boston, MA 02115
(617) 373-3649
Nancy Hoffart, PhD, RN

www.bouve.neu.edu/nursing

Acceptance rate	33.9%

Tuition
In state $26,750
Out of state $26,750
Enrollments 586
Graduations 97

Student Demographics
Female 92.5%
Under age 25 93.0%
Minority 21.6%
Part-time 0.0%

Accreditation
Massachusetts Board of Registration in Nursing,
Commission on Collegiate Nursing Education
(CCNE)

Degrees conferred
Baccalaureate

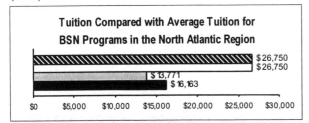

Tuition Compared with Average Tuition for BSN Programs in the North Atlantic Region

$26,750
$26,750
$13,771
$16,163

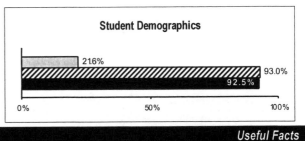

Student Demographics

21.6%
93.0%
92.5%

REGIS COLLEGE — *Useful Facts*

235 Wellesley Street
Weston, MA 02493
(781) 306-6601
Marie McCarthy, MS, RN

www.regiscollege.edu

Acceptance rate	100.0%	
Faculty-student ratio	1: 2	
Faculty Full time	15	
Part time	35	

Tuition
In state $21,525
Out of state $21,525
Enrollments 74
Graduations 0

Student Demographics
Female 100.0%
Under age 25 97.3%
Minority 31.3%
Part-time 0.0%

Accreditation
Massachusetts Board of Registration in Nursing,
National League for Nursing Accrediting
Commission (NLNAC)

Degrees conferred
Bachelor of Science Degre

Minimum degree required
High school diploma or GED

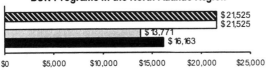

Tuition Compared with Average Tuition for BSN Programs in the North Atlantic Region

$21,525
$21,525
$13,771
$16,163

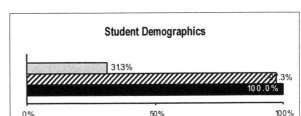

Student Demographics

31.3%
97.3%
100.0%

Demographics Chart ■Female ▨Under age 25 ▢Minority | **Distance Learning** | ¹The tuition reported for this program may be not be annualized.
*Data reported between 2001 and 2004.

Massachusetts

SALEM STATE COLLEGE

352 Lafayette Street
Salem, MA 01970
(978) 542-6805
Mary Farrell, PhD, RN, CCRN

www.salemstate.edu/nursing

Accreditation
Massachusetts Board of Registration in Nursing,
Commission on Collegiate Nursing Education
(CCNE), National League for Nursing Accrediting
Commission (NLNAC)

Acceptance rate		32.1%
Faculty-student ratio		1: 18
Faculty	Full time	27
	Part time	30

Degrees conferred
Baccalaureate degree

Tuition	
In state	$910
Out of state	$7,050
Enrollments	771
Graduations	62

Minimum degree required
High school diploma or GED

Student Demographics	
Female	94.6%
Under age 25	72.4%
Minority	20.7%
Part-time	24.0%

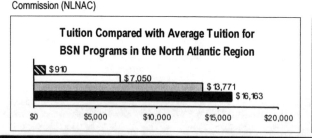

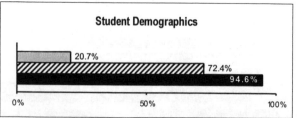

SIMMONS COLLEGE

300 The Fenway
Boston, MA 02115
(617) 521-2139
Judy Beal, DNSc, RN

www.simmons.edu

Accreditation
Massachusetts Board of Registration in Nursing,
Commission on Collegiate Nursing Education
(CCNE)

Acceptance rate	40.5%

Degrees conferred
Baccalaureate

Tuition	
In state	$23,760
Out of state	$23,760
Enrollments	345
Graduations	31

Student Demographics	
Female	100.0%
Under age 25	40.0%
Minority	25.1%
Part-time	58.9%

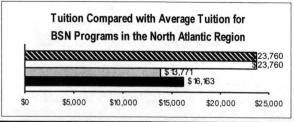

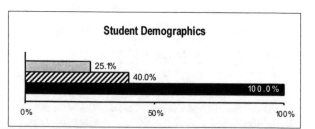

UNIVERSITY OF MASSACHUSETTS - BOSTON

100 Morrissey Blvd
Boston, MA 02125
(617) 287-7511
Brenda Cherry, PhD, RN

www.nursing.umb.edu

Accreditation
Massachusetts Board of Registration in Nursing

Acceptance rate	47.5%

Degrees conferred
Baccalaureate

Tuition	
In state	$1,714
Out of state	$9,758
Enrollments	546
Graduations	141

Student Demographics	
Female	89.4%
Under age 25	44.0%
Minority	30.5%
Part-time	44.2%

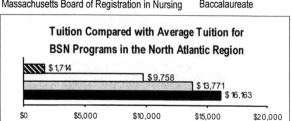

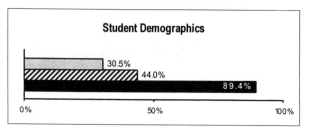

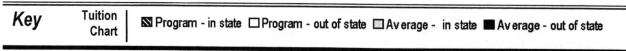

Key | Tuition Chart | ▨ Program - in state ☐ Program - out of state ☐ Average - in state ■ Average - out of state

Massachusetts

UNIVERSITY OF MASSACHUSETTS - DARTMOUTH
*Useful Facts**

285 Old Westport Road
North Dartmouth, MA 02747
(508) 999-8586
Nancy Dluhy, PhD, RN

www.umassd.edu

Acceptance rate	46.4%

Tuition
In state	$1,417
Out of state	$8,099
Enrollments	426
Graduations	80

Student Demographics
Female	93.0%
Minority	10.3%
Part-time	5.5%

Accreditation
Massachusetts Board of Registration in Nursing, National League for Nursing Accrediting Commission (NLNAC)

Degrees conferred
Baccalaureate

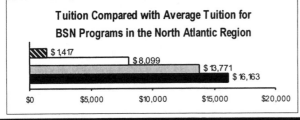
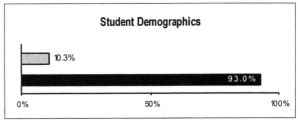

UNIVERSITY OF MASSACHUSETTS - LOWELL
*Useful Facts**

3 Solomont Way, Suite 2
Lowell, MA 01854
(978) 934-4467
May Futrell, PhD, FAAN

www.uml.edu/dept/nursing

Acceptance rate	33.2%

Tuition
In state	$1,454
Out of state	$8,567
Enrollments	276
Graduations	65

Student Demographics
Female	97.2%
Part-time	0.0%

Accreditation
Massachusetts Board of Registration in Nursing, Commission on Collegiate Nursing Education (CCNE)

Degrees conferred
Baccalaureate

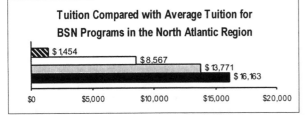
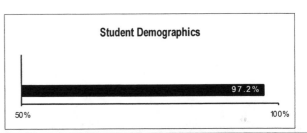

WORCESTER STATE COLLEGE
Useful Facts

486 Chandler St
Worcester, MA 01602
(508) 929-8129
Helen Rogers, DNSc, RN

www.worcester.edu

Acceptance rate		36.8%
Faculty-student ratio		1: 17
Faculty	Full time	8
	Part time	12

Tuition
In state	$970
Out of state	$7,050
Enrollments	239
Graduations	38

Student Demographics
Female	92.3%
Under age 25	64.5%
Minority	8.3%
Part-time	0.0%

Accreditation
Massachusetts Board of Registration in Nursing, National League for Nursing Accrediting Commission (NLNAC)

Degrees conferred
Baccalaureate degree

Minimum degree required
High school diploma or GED

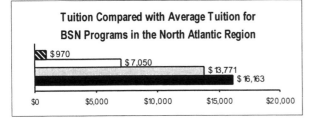
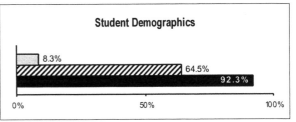

Demographics Chart	■Female ☑Under age 25 ☐Minority	Distance Learning	†The tuition reported for this program may be not be annualized. *Data reported between 2001 and 2004.

Michigan

ANDREWS UNIVERSITY

Andrews University, Marsh Hall
Berrien Springs, MI 49104-0200
(616) 471-3364
Karen Allen, PhD, RN, FAAN

www.andrews.edu/nrsg

			Student Demographics	
			Female	88.6%
Enrollments	116		Minority	60.7%
			Part-time	0.0%

Accreditation
Michigan/DCH/Bureau of Health Professions,
National League for Nursing Accrediting
Commission (NLNAC)

Degrees conferred
Baccalaureate

CALVIN COLLEGE

3201 Burton St SE
Grand Rapids, MI 49546
(616) 526-7076
Mary Doornbos, RN, PhD

www.calvin.edu/academic/nursing

Accreditation
Michigan/DCH/Bureau of Health Professions

Degrees conferred
Baccalaureate

EASTERN MICHIGAN UNIVERSITY

311 Marshall
Ypsilanti, MI 48197
(734) 487-2310
Barbara Scheffer, EdD, RN

www.emich.edu/nursing

Acceptance rate		30.0%	Tuition[1]		Student Demographics	
Faculty-student ratio		1: 11	In state	$182	Female	90.6%
Faculty	Full time	21	Out of state	$561	Under age 25	65.4%
	Part time	0	Enrollments	234	Minority	17.4%
			Graduations	86	Part-time	1.3%

Accreditation
Michigan/DCH/Bureau of Health Professions,
Commission on Collegiate Nursing Education
(CCNE)

Degrees conferred
Baccalaureate degree

Minimum degree required
High school diploma or GED

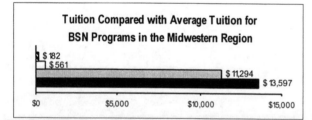

Tuition Compared with Average Tuition for BSN Programs in the Midwestern Region

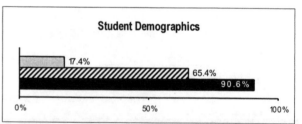

Student Demographics

FINLANDIA UNIVERSITY

601 Quincy Street
Hancock, MI 49930
(906) 487-7305
Frederika De Yampert, MSN, RN

www.finlandia.edu

Accreditation
Michigan/DCH/Bureau of Health Professions

Degrees conferred
Baccalaureate

Key | Tuition Chart | ⬚ Program - in state ⬜ Program - out of state ▨ Average - in state ■ Average - out of state

Michigan

GRAND VALLEY STATE UNIVERSITY — *Useful Facts**

301 Michigan St NE
Grand Rapids, MI 49503
(616) 331-7161
Phyllis Gendler, PhD, RN, NP

www.gvsu.edu/kcon

Acceptance rate		74.4%
Faculty-student ratio		1: 11
Faculty	Full time	36
	Part time	31

Tuition	
In state	$4,830
Out of state	$10,420
Enrollments	578
Graduations	182

Student Demographics	
Female	90.7%
Under age 25	91.1%
Minority	7.9%
Part-time	32.4%

Accreditation
Michigan/DCH/Bureau of Health Professions,
Commission on Collegiate Nursing Education
(CCNE)

Degrees conferred
Baccalaureate

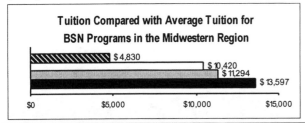

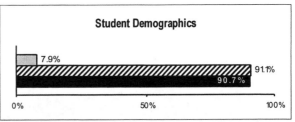

HOPE COLLEGE

105 E 14th Street
Holland, MI 49423
(616) 395-7420
Susan Dunn, PhD, RN

www.hope.edu/academic/nursing

Accreditation
Michigan/DCH/Bureau of Health Professions

Degrees conferred
Baccalaureate

LAKE SUPERIOR STATE UNIVERSITY — *Useful Facts*

650 West Easterday Avenue
Sault Sainte Marie, MI 49783
(906) 635-2288
Steven Merrill, RN, PhD

www.lssu.edu

Acceptance rate		67.6%
Faculty-student ratio		1: 7
Faculty	Full time	10
	Part time	6

Tuition	
In state	$6,488
Out of state	$12,476
Enrollments	95
Graduations	30

Student Demographics	
Female	88.5%
Under age 25	71.8%
Minority	14.1%
Part-time	0.0%

Accreditation
Michigan/DCH/Bureau of Health Professions,
National League for Nursing Accrediting
Commission (NLNAC)

Degrees conferred
Baccalaureate degree

Minimum degree required
High school diploma or GED

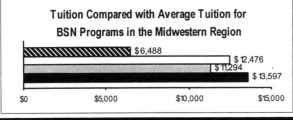

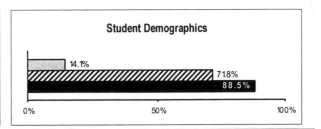

MADONNA UNIVERSITY

Diponio Building, 36200 Schoolcraft Road
Livonia, MI 48150
(734) 432-5465
Teresa Thompson, PhD, RN

www.madonna.edu

*At the request of this nursing school, publication has been witheld.
Please contact the school directly for more information.*

Accreditation
Michigan/DCH/Bureau of Health Professions,
National League for Nursing Accrediting
Commission (NLNAC)

| Demographics Chart | ■Female ☒Under age 25 ☐Minority | Distance Learning | †The tuition reported for this program may be not be annualized. *Data reported between 2001 and 2004. |

Michigan

MICHIGAN STATE UNIVERSITY · *Useful Facts**

A230 Life Sciences
East Lansing, MI 48824
(517) 355-6527
Marilyn Rothert, PhD, RN, FAAN

www.msu.edu/unit/nurse

Accreditation
Michigan/DCH/Bureau of Health Professions

Degrees conferred
Baccalaureate

Acceptance rate		50.6%

Tuition			Student Demographics	
In state	$7,256		Female	89.2%
Out of state	$18,954		Under age 25	90.0%
Enrollments	295		Minority	14.3%
Graduations	85		Part-time	0.0%

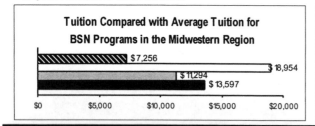

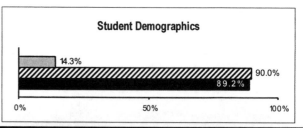

NORTHERN MICHIGAN UNIVERSITY · *Useful Facts**

New Science Building, Room 2301
Marquette, MI 49855
(906) 227-2834
Kerri Schuiling, PhD(c), MSN, CNH, WHNP, RN

www.nmu.edu

Accreditation
Michigan/DCH/Bureau of Health Professions,
Commission on Collegiate Nursing Education
(CCNE)

Degrees conferred
Baccalaureate

Acceptance rate		48.5%

Tuition			Student Demographics	
In state	$4,468		Female	90.0%
Out of state	$7,460			
Enrollments	215		Minority	6.9%
Graduations	49		Part-time	12.1%

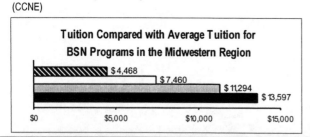

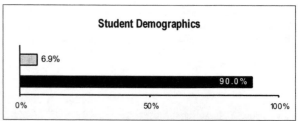

OAKLAND UNIVERSITY · *Useful Facts**

428 O'Dowd Hall
Rochester, MI 48309
(248) 370-4081
Linda Thompson, DrPH, RN, FAAN

www.2.oakland.edu/nursing

Accreditation
Michigan/DCH/Bureau of Health Professions,
Commission on Collegiate Nursing Education
(CCNE)

Degrees conferred
Baccalaureate

Acceptance rate		57.5%

Tuition			Student Demographics	
In state	$4,224		Female	90.3%
Out of state	$9,876			
Enrollments	462		Minority	9.1%
Graduations	102		Part-time	6.8%

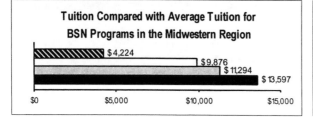

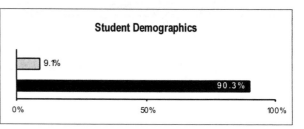

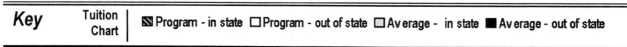

Key — Tuition Chart | ◩ Program - in state ☐ Program - out of state ☐ Average - in state ■ Average - out of state

Michigan

SAGINAW VALLEY STATE UNIVERSITY | Useful Facts

7400 Bay Road
University Center, MI 48710
(989) 964-4145
Janalou Blecke, RN, PhD

www.svsu.edu

Acceptance rate		71.1%
Faculty-student ratio		1: 16
Faculty	Full time	14
	Part time	6

Tuition	
In state	$6,474
Out of state	$12,645
Enrollments	279
Graduations	77

Student Demographics	
Female	89.4%
Under age 25	51.0%
Minority	7.2%
Part-time	24.5%

Accreditation
Michigan/DCH/Bureau of Health Professions,
Commission on Collegiate Nursing Education
(CCNE), National League for Nursing Accrediting
Commission (NLNAC)

Degrees conferred
Baccalaureate degree

Minimum degree required
High school diploma or GED

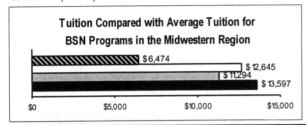

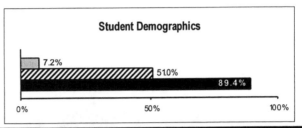

UNIVERSITY OF DETROIT MERCY | Useful Facts

4001 W McNichols
Detroit, MI 48221
(313) 993-1208
Suzanne Mellon, PhD, RN

www.udmercy.edu

Acceptance rate		35.1%
Faculty-student ratio		1: 16
Faculty	Full time	31
	Part time	24

Tuition	
In state	$21,900
Out of state	$21,900
Enrollments	702
Graduations	163

Student Demographics	
Female	87.5%
Under age 25	69.7%
Minority	24.5%
Part-time	14.8%

Accreditation
Michigan/DCH/Bureau of Health Professions,
Commission on Collegiate Nursing Education
(CCNE), National League for Nursing Accrediting
Commission (NLNAC)

Degrees conferred
Baccalaureate degree

Minimum degree required
High school diploma or GED

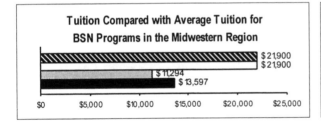

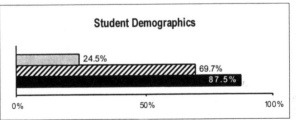

| Demographics Chart | ■Female ☑Under age 25 ☐Minority | Distance Learning | ¹The tuition reported for this program may be not be annualized. |
| | | | *Data reported between 2001 and 2004. |

Michigan

UNIVERSITY OF MICHIGAN
Useful Facts

400 North Ingalls
Ann Arbor, MI 48109
(734) 764-7185
Ada Hunshaw, PhD, RN, FAAN

www.nursing.umich.edu

Accreditation
Michigan/DCH/Bureau of Health Professions, Commission on Collegiate Nursing Education (CCNE)

Acceptance rate	52.7%
Faculty-student ratio	1: 8

Faculty		
	Full time	34
	Part time	92

Degrees conferred
Baccalaureate degree

Tuition	
In state	$8,932
Out of state	$27,320
Enrollments	617
Graduations	206

Minimum degree required
Please note admission to second career program requires BA or higher.

Student Demographics	
Female	92.2%
Under age 25	89.3%
Minority	16.5%
Part-time	5.7%

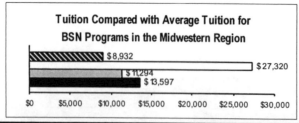

Tuition Compared with Average Tuition for BSN Programs in the Midwestern Region
$8,932
$27,320
$11,294
$13,597

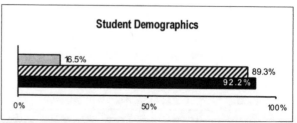

Student Demographics
16.5%
89.3%
92.2%

UNIVERSITY OF MICHIGAN - FLINT
Useful Facts

2180 WSW, 303 East Kearsley Street
Flint, MI 48502
(810) 762-3420
Linda Knecht, MSN, RN

www.umflint.edu/nursing

Accreditation
Michigan/DCH/Bureau of Health Professions, Commission on Collegiate Nursing Education (CCNE), National League for Nursing Accrediting Commission (NLNAC)

Acceptance rate	42.1%
Faculty-student ratio	1: 9

Faculty		
	Full time	12
	Part time	39

Degrees conferred
Baccalaureate degree, MSN

Tuition	
In state	$6,574
Out of state	$13,148
Enrollments	276
Graduations	83

Minimum degree required
High school diploma or GED

Student Demographics	
Female	89.7%
Under age 25	60.3%
Minority	12.8%
Part-time	30.9%

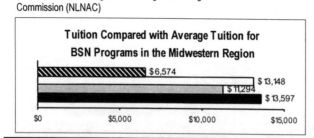

Tuition Compared with Average Tuition for BSN Programs in the Midwestern Region
$6,574
$13,148
$11,294
$13,597

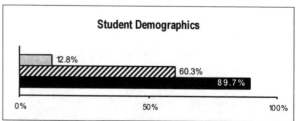

Student Demographics
12.8%
60.3%
89.7%

WAYNE STATE UNIVERSITY
Useful Facts*

5557 Cass Avenue
Detroit, MI 48202
(313) 577-4070
Barbara Redman, PhD, RN, FAAN

www.wayne.edu

Accreditation
Michigan/DCH/Bureau of Health Professions

Degrees conferred
Baccalaureate

Student Demographics

Enrollments	412
Part-time	17.2%

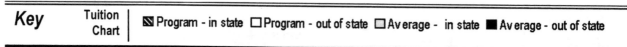

Key Tuition Chart ▨ Program - in state ☐ Program - out of state ☐ Average - in state ■ Average - out of state

Michigan

WESTERN MICHIGAN UNIVERSITY — *Useful Facts**

1903 West Michigan Avenue
Kalamazoo, MI 49008
(269) 387-8162
Marie Gates, PhD, RN

www.wmich.edu/hhs/nurs/index.html

Accreditation
Michigan/DCH/Bureau of Health Professions,
Commission on Collegiate Nursing Education
(CCNE)

Degrees conferred
Baccalaureate

Acceptance rate	63.9%

Tuition		Student Demographics	
In state	$5,066	Female	94.3%
Out of state	$13,221		
Enrollments	264	Minority	9.6%
Graduations	58	Part-time	25.0%

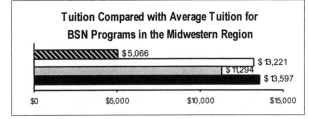

Tuition Compared with Average Tuition for BSN Programs in the Midwestern Region

$5,066
$13,221
$11,294
$13,597

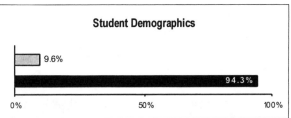

Student Demographics

9.6%
94.3%

Minnesota

BETHEL COLLEGE (MINNESOTA) — *Useful Facts*

3900 Bethel Dr #97
St Paul, MN 55112
(651) 638-6368
Sandra Peterson, PhD, RN

www.bethel.edu/college/dept/nursing/index.html

Accreditation
Minnesota Board of Nursing, Commission on
Collegiate Nursing Education (CCNE)

Degrees conferred
Baccalaureate degree

Minimum degree required
High school diploma or GED

Acceptance rate	70.5%

Tuition		Student Demographics	
In state	$21,190	Female	92.0%
Out of state	$21,190	Under age 25	96.4%
Enrollments	112	Minority	6.3%
Graduations	53	Part-time	0.0%

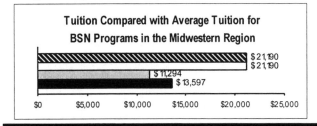

Tuition Compared with Average Tuition for BSN Programs in the Midwestern Region

$21,190
$21,190
$11,294
$13,597

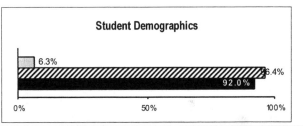

Student Demographics

6.3%
96.4%
92.0%

COLLEGE OF SAINT CATHERINE — *Useful Facts*

2004 Randolph Ave
St Paul, MN 55105
(651) 690-6583
Alice Swan, DNSc, RN

minerva.stkate.edu/offices/academic/nursing.nsf

Accreditation
Minnesota Board of Nursing, National League for
Nursing Accrediting Commission (NLNAC)

Degrees conferred
Baccalaureate degree

Minimum degree required
High school diploma or GED

Acceptance rate		40.7%
Faculty-student ratio		1: 9
Faculty	Full time	50
	Part time	18

Tuition		Student Demographics	
In state	$22,464	Female	99.1%
Out of state	$22,464	Under age 25	70.3%
Enrollments	251	Minority	15.6%
Graduations	104	Part-time	0.0%

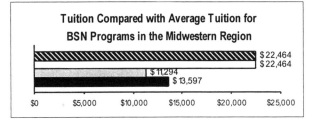

Tuition Compared with Average Tuition for BSN Programs in the Midwestern Region

$22,464
$22,464
$11,294
$13,597

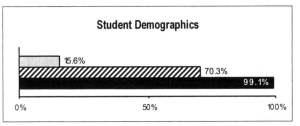

Student Demographics

15.6%
70.3%
99.1%

Demographics Chart ■ Female ▨ Under age 25 ☐ Minority | **Distance Learning** | †The tuition reported for this program may be not be annualized.
*Data reported between 2001 and 2004.

Minnesota

COLLEGE OF SAINT SCHOLASTICA　　　　*Useful Facts**

1200 Kenwood Ave
Duluth, MN 55811
(218) 723-6025
Martha Witrak, PhD, RN, CS

www.css.edu

Accreditation
Minnesota Board of Nursing

Acceptance rate	93.2%

Tuition

In state	$17,080
Out of state	$17,080
Enrollments	142
Graduations	59

Student Demographics

Female	90.8%
Under age 25	71.0%
Part-time	0.7%

Degrees conferred
Baccalaureate

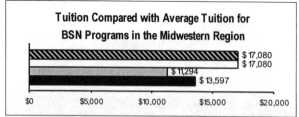

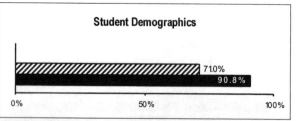

COLLEGE OF ST BENEDICT　　　　*Useful Facts**

37 College Ave South
St Joseph, MN 55105
(320) 363-5249
Kathleen Twohy, PhD

www.csbsju.edu/nursing

Accreditation
Minnesota Board of Nursing

Acceptance rate	80.0%

Tuition

In state	$18,015
Out of state	$18,015
Enrollments	120
Graduations	63

Student Demographics

Female	92.0%
Minority	0.9%
Part-time	6.3%

Degrees conferred
Baccalaureate

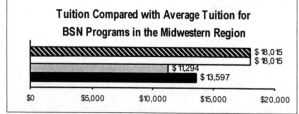

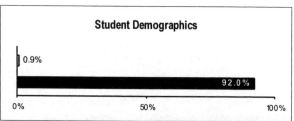

CONCORDIA COLLEGE

901 8th Street South
Moorhead, MN 56562
(218) 299-4060
Polly Kloster, PhD, RN

www.cord.edu

Accreditation
Minnesota Board of Nursing

Degrees conferred
Baccalaureate

Key Tuition Chart ▨ Program - in state ☐ Program - out of state ☐ Average - in state ■ Average - out of state

Minnesota

GUSTAVUS ADOLPHUS COLLEGE AND ST OLAF COLLEGE

1520 St Olaf Avenue
Northfield, MN 55057
(507) 646-3265
Rita Glazebrook, PhD, RN, CNP

www.stolaf.edu/depts/nursing

Acceptance rate 76.9%

Tuition		Student Demographics	
In state	$22,590	Female	93.8%
Out of state	$22,590	Under age 25	100.0%
Enrollments	81	Minority	1.2%
Graduations	38	Part-time	0.0%

Accreditation
Minnesota Board of Nursing, Commission on
Collegiate Nursing Education (CCNE), National
League for Nursing Accrediting Commission
(NLNAC)

Degrees conferred
Baccalaureate

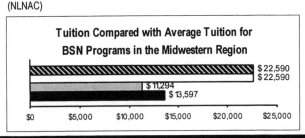

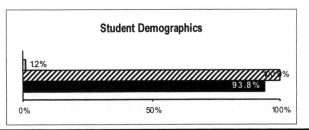

METROPOLITAN STATE UNIVERSITY

700 East 7th St
St Paul, MN 55106
(651) 793-1376
Marilyn Loen, PhD, RN, GNP

www.metrostate.edu

Faculty	Full time	7
	Part time	10

Accreditation
Minnesota Board of Nursing

Degrees conferred
Baccalaureate

MINNESOTA STATE UNIVERSITY - MANKATO

360 Wissink Hall
Mankato, MN 56001
(507) 389-6827
Mary Bliesmer, DNSc, APRN, BC

www.mnsu.edu/dept/nursing/welcome.html

Acceptance rate		42.1%
Faculty-student ratio		1: 11
Faculty	Full time	16
	Part time	20

Tuition		Student Demographics	
In state	$4,682	Female	89.0%
Out of state	$10,030	Under age 25	83.8%
Enrollments	296	Minority	10.1%
Graduations	117	Part-time	0.7%

Accreditation
Minnesota Board of Nursing, Commission on
Collegiate Nursing Education (CCNE)

Degrees conferred
BS with nursing major

Minimum degree required
None

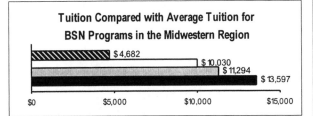

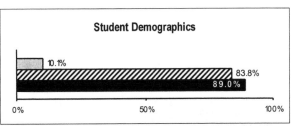

MINNESOTA STATE UNIVERSITY - MOORHEAD

1104 south 7 Avenue
Moorhead, MN 56563
(218) 477-2695
Barbara Matthees, PhD, RN

www.mnstate.edu/home

Faculty	Full time	6
	Part time	3

Accreditation
Minnesota Board of Nursing, Commission on
Collegiate Nursing Education (CCNE)

Degrees conferred
Baccalaureate

Demographics Chart	■Female ☑Under age 25 ☐Minority	Distance Learning	⁺The tuition reported for this program may be not be annualized. *Data reported between 2001 and 2004.

Minnesota

UNIVERSITY OF MINNESOTA - MINNEAPOLIS
Useful Facts*

6-101 WDH, 308 Harvard St
Minneapolis, MN 55455
(612) 624-5959
Sandra Edwardson, PhD

www.nursing.umn.edu

Accreditation
Minnesota Board of Nursing

Degrees conferred
Baccalaureate

Tuition		Student Demographics	
In state	$4,951	Female	86.2%
Out of state	$11,882	Under age 25	69.0%
Enrollments	205	Minority	8.7%
Graduations	99	Part-time	5.1%

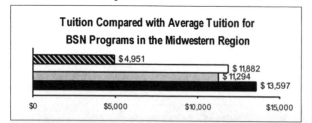

Tuition Compared with Average Tuition for BSN Programs in the Midwestern Region
$4,951 / $11,882 / $11,294 / $13,597

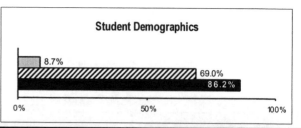

Student Demographics
8.7% / 69.0% / 86.2%

WINONA STATE UNIVERSITY
Useful Facts*

303 Stark Hall, 175 W Mark St
Winona, MN 55987
(507) 457-5122
Timothy Gaspar, PhD, RN

www.winona.edu/nursing

Accreditation
Minnesota Board of Nursing, Commission on
Collegiate Nursing Education (CCNE)

Degrees conferred
Baccalaureate

		Tuition		Student Demographics	
Acceptance rate	59.4%	In state	$4,014	Female	95.8%
		Out of state	$7,960	Under age 25	79.5%
		Enrollments	288	Minority	2.1%
		Graduations	139	Part-time	3.4%

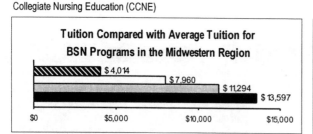

Tuition Compared with Average Tuition for BSN Programs in the Midwestern Region
$4,014 / $7,960 / $11,294 / $13,597

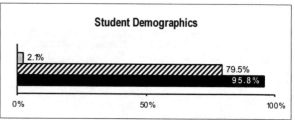

Student Demographics
2.1% / 79.5% / 95.8%

Mississippi

ALCORN STATE UNIVERSITY
Useful Facts

15 Campus Drive
Natchez, MS 39120
(601) 304-4302
Mary Hill, DSN, RN

www.alcorn.edu

Accreditation
Mississippi Board of Nursing, National League
for Nursing Accrediting Commission (NLNAC)

Degrees conferred
Baccalaureate degree

Minimum degree required
56 credit hours of prerequisites

				Tuition		Student Demographics	
Acceptance rate			24.8%	In state	$4,899	Female	86.3%
Faculty-student ratio			1: 12	Out of state	$11,109	Under age 25	69.9%
Faculty	Full time		15	Enrollments	87	Minority	46.6%
	Part time		5	Graduations	30	Part-time	2.7%

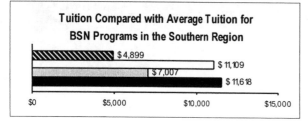

Tuition Compared with Average Tuition for BSN Programs in the Southern Region
$4,899 / $11,109 / $7,007 / $11,618

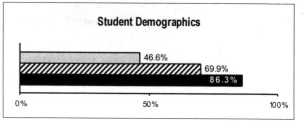

Student Demographics
46.6% / 69.9% / 86.3%

Key — Tuition Chart

▨ Program - in state ▢ Program - out of state ▤ Average - in state ▮ Average - out of state

Mississippi

DELTA STATE UNIVERSITY — *Useful Facts**

PO Box 3343
Cleveland, MS 38733
(662) 846-4268
Maureen Gruich, PhD, RN

www.deltastate.edu

Acceptance rate	62.5%	

Tuition		Student Demographics	
In state	$3,348	Female	82.6%
Out of state	$7,965	Under age 25	44.0%
Enrollments	39	Minority	30.4%
Graduations	27	Part-time	13.0%

Accreditation
Mississippi Board of Nursing, Commission on
Collegiate Nursing Education (CCNE)

Degrees conferred
Baccalaureate

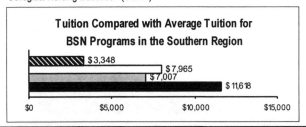

Tuition Compared with Average Tuition for
BSN Programs in the Southern Region

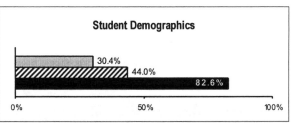

Student Demographics

INSTITUTION OF HIGHER LEARNING

3825 Ridgewood Road
Jackson, MS 39211

www.ihl.state.ms.us

Accreditation
Mississippi Board of Nursing

Degrees conferred
Baccalaureate

MISSISSIPPI COLLEGE — *Useful Facts*

PO Box 4037
Clinton, MS 39058
(601) 925-3278
Mary Padgett, PhD, RN

www.mc.edu/academics/nursing

Acceptance rate	41.0%	
Faculty-student ratio	1: 19	

Faculty		
	Full time	16
	Part time	3

Tuition		Student Demographics	
In state	$11,400	Female	85.4%
Out of state	$11,400	Under age 25	87.5%
Enrollments	339	Minority	33.3%
Graduations	50	Part-time	9.8%

Accreditation
Mississippi Board of Nursing, National League
for Nursing Accrediting Commission (NLNAC)

Degrees conferred
Baccalaureate degree

Minimum degree required
High school diploma or GED

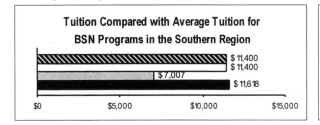

Tuition Compared with Average Tuition for
BSN Programs in the Southern Region

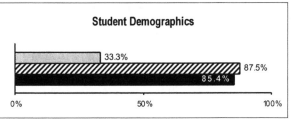

Student Demographics

Demographics Chart	■Female ☑Under age 25 ☐Minority	Distance Learning	[1]The tuition reported for this program may be not be annualized. *Data reported between 2001 and 2004.

Mississippi

MISSISSIPPI UNIVERSITY FOR WOMEN — *Useful Facts*

1100 College Street MUW-910
Columbus, MS 39701
(662) 329-7299
Sheila Adams, EdD

www.muw.edu/nursing

Acceptance rate		23.6%
Faculty-student ratio		1: 6
Faculty	Full time	32
	Part time	3

Tuition	
In state	$3,690
Out of state	$8,914
Enrollments	103
Graduations	36

Student Demographics	
Female	90.3%
Under age 25	94.2%
Minority	6.8%
Part-time	0.0%

Accreditation
Mississippi Board of Nursing, Commission on Collegiate Nursing Education (CCNE), National League for Nursing Accrediting Commission (NLNAC)

Degrees conferred
Baccalaureate degree

Minimum degree required
High school diploma or GED

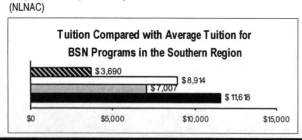

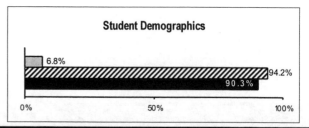

UNIVERSITY OF MISSISSIPPI MEDICAL CENTER — *Useful Facts**

2500 North State Street
Jackson, MS 39216
(601) 984-6220
Anne Peirce, PhD, RN

www.umc.edu

Acceptance rate	45.7%

Tuition	
In state	$2,378
Out of state	$5,197
Enrollments	210
Graduations	131

Student Demographics	
Female	90.4%
Under age 25	82.0%
Minority	15.3%
Part-time	2.8%

Accreditation
Mississippi Board of Nursing

Degrees conferred
Baccalaureate

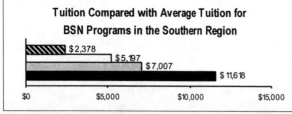

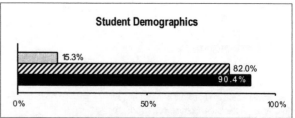

UNIVERSITY OF SOUTHERN MISSISSIPPI — *Useful Facts**

PO Box 5095
Hattiesburg, MS 39406
(601) 266-5445
Gerry Cadenhead, PhD, RN

www.nursing.usm.edu

Acceptance rate	76.1%

Tuition	
In state	$2,870
Out of state	$5,972
Enrollments	336
Graduations	178

Student Demographics	
Female	81.7%
Under age 25	62.0%
Minority	9.6%
Part-time	2.0%

Accreditation
Mississippi Board of Nursing

Degrees conferred
Baccalaureate

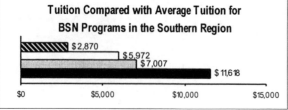

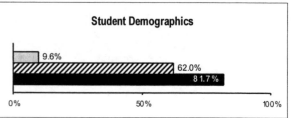

Key | Tuition Chart | ▨ Program - in state ☐ Program - out of state ☐ Average - in state ■ Average - out of state

Mississippi

WILLIAM CAREY COLLEGE | Useful Facts

498 Tuscan Avenue
Hattiesburg, MS 39401
(601) 318-6478
Mary Stewart, PhD, RN

www.wmcarey.edu

Acceptance rate		60.0%
Faculty-student ratio		1: 13
Faculty	Full time	20
	Part time	3

Tuition[1]	
In state	$270
Out of state	$270
Enrollments	275
Graduations	110

Student Demographics	
Female	79.6%
Under age 25	60.0%
Minority	43.3%
Part-time	24.8%

Accreditation
Mississippi Board of Nursing, National League for Nursing Accrediting Commission (NLNAC)

Degrees conferred
Baccalaureate degree

Minimum degree required
High school diploma or GED

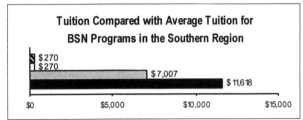

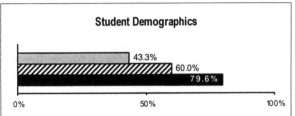

Missouri

AVILA COLLEGE | Useful Facts*

11901 Wornall Road
Kansas City, MO 64145
(816) 501-3672
Susan Fetsch, PhD, RN

www.avila.edu/catalog/degrees/nursing

Acceptance rate		97.3%
Faculty-student ratio		1: 10
Faculty	Full time	7
	Part time	4

Tuition	
In state	$14,700
Out of state	$14,700
Enrollments	92
Graduations	25

Student Demographics	
Female	87.5%
Under age 25	74.0%
Minority	32.5%
Part-time	0.0%

Accreditation
Missouri State Board of Nursing, Commission on Collegiate Nursing Education (CCNE)

Degrees conferred
Baccalaureate

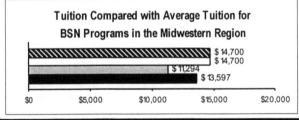

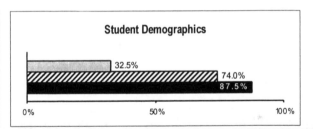

BARNES - JEWISH COLLEGE OF NURSING & ALLIED HEALTH

8001 Natural Bridge Road
Saint Louis, MO 63110
(314) 454-8416
Elizabeth Buck

www.barnesjewish.org

Accreditation
Missouri State Board of Nursing

Degrees conferred
Baccalaureate

| Demographics Chart | ■ Female ⊠ Under age 25 ☐ Minority | Distance Learning | [1]The tuition reported for this program may be not be annualized. *Data reported between 2001 and 2004. |

Missouri

CENTRAL METHODIST UNIVERSITY

411 Central Methodist Square
Fayette, MO 65248
(660) 248-6363
Shirley Peterson, PhD, MSN, BSN, RN

www.centralmethodist.edu

Acceptance rate	79.6%	
Faculty-student ratio	1: 16	
Faculty	Full time	5
	Part time	13

Tuition		
In state	$14,490	
Out of state	$14,490	
Enrollments	187	
Graduations	41	

Student Demographics	
Female	91.2%
Under age 25	77.9%
Minority	13.2%
Part-time	0.0%

Accreditation
Missouri State Board of Nursing

Degrees conferred
Baccalaureate degree

Minimum degree required
High school diploma or GED

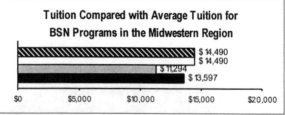

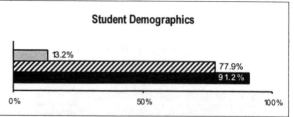

CENTRAL MISSOURI STATE UNIVERSITY

HC-106
Warrensburg, MO 64093
(660) 543-4775
Elaine Frank-Ragan, RN

www.cmsu.edu

Tuition		
In state	$2,208	
Out of state	$4,224	
Enrollments	98	
Graduations	51	

Student Demographics	
Part-time	7.0%

Accreditation
Missouri State Board of Nursing

Degrees conferred
Baccalaureate

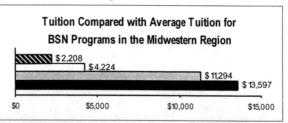

DEACONESS COLLEGE OF NURSING

6150 Oakland Avenue
Saint Louis, MO 63139
(314) 768-3861
Julia Raithel, PhD, RN

www.deaconess.edu

Acceptance rate	49.0%	
Faculty-student ratio	1: 28	
Faculty	Full time	12
	Part time	14

Tuition		
In state	$5,915	
Out of state	$5,915	
Enrollments	297	
Graduations	42	

Student Demographics	
Female	93.3%
Under age 25	79.8%
Minority	20.0%
Part-time	14.0%

Accreditation
Missouri State Board of Nursing, Commission on
Collegiate Nursing Education (CCNE), National
League for Nursing Accrediting Commission
(NLNAC)

Degrees conferred
Baccalaureate degree

Minimum degree required
High school diploma or GED

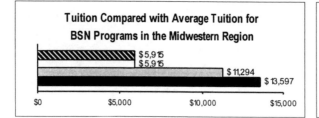

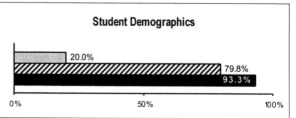

Key	Tuition Chart	▨ Program - in state ☐ Program - out of state ☐ Average - in state ■ Average - out of state

Missouri

GRACELAND UNIVERSITY
Useful Facts

1401 West Truman Rd
Independence, MO 64050
(816) 833-0524
Patricia Trachsel, PhD, RN

www.graceland.edu

Acceptance rate	47.3%
Faculty-student ratio	1: 15
Faculty Full time	13
Part time	0

Tuition
In state	$16,000
Out of state	$16,000
Enrollments	200
Graduations	72

Student Demographics
Female	88.7%
Under age 25	42.3%
Minority	8.7%
Part-time	4.2%

Accreditation
Missouri State Board of Nursing, Commission on Collegiate Nursing Education (CCNE), National League for Nursing Accrediting Commission (NLNAC)

Degrees conferred
Baccalaureate degree

Minimum degree required
High school diploma or GED

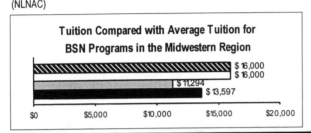
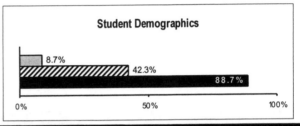

LESTER L COX COLLEGE
Useful Facts*

1423 North Jefferson
Springfield, MO 65802
(417) 269-3401
Julie Luetschwager, DNSc, RN

www.coxcollege.edu

Acceptance rate	17.6%

Tuition
In state	$8,910
Out of state	$8,910
Enrollments	89
Graduations	14

Student Demographics
Female	81.5%
Minority	3.1%
Part-time	12.3%

Accreditation
Missouri State Board of Nursing, Commission on Collegiate Nursing Education (CCNE)

Degrees conferred
Baccalaureate

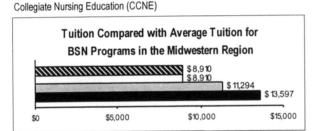
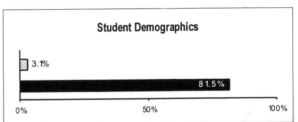

MARYVILLE UNIVERSITY - SAINT LOUIS
Useful Facts

13550 Conway Road
Saint Louis, MO 63141
(314) 529-9478
Mary Curtis, PhD, RN

www.maryville.edu

Acceptance rate	28.2%
Faculty-student ratio	1: 12
Faculty Full time	13
Part time	35

Tuition
In state	$17,000
Out of state	$17,000
Enrollments	381
Graduations	73

Student Demographics
Female	93.4%
Under age 25	66.4%
Minority	10.7%
Part-time	38.5%

Accreditation
Missouri State Board of Nursing, Commission on Collegiate Nursing Education (CCNE), National League for Nursing Accrediting Commission (NLNAC)

Degrees conferred
Baccalaureate degree, MSN

Minimum degree required
High school diploma or GED

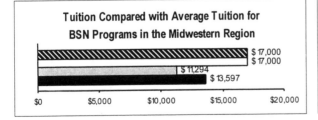
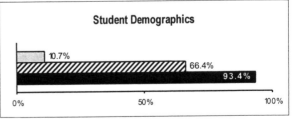

Demographics Chart	■Female ☒Under age 25 ☐Minority	Distance Learning	¹The tuition reported for this program may be not be annualized. *Data reported between 2001 and 2004.

Missouri

MISSOURI SOUTHERN STATE COLLEGE
Useful Facts

3950 East Newman Road
Joplin, MO 64801
(417) 625-3148
Grace Ayton, MN, RN, BC

www.mssu.edu

Acceptance rate		47.7%
Faculty-student ratio		1: 10
Faculty	Full time	9
	Part time	2

Tuition	
In state	$3,750
Out of state	$7,500
Enrollments	100
Graduations	47

Student Demographics	
Female	84.0%
Under age 25	44.7%
Minority	14.9%
Part-time	0.0%

Accreditation
Missouri State Board of Nursing, National
League for Nursing Accrediting Commission
(NLNAC)

Degrees conferred
Baccalaureate degree

Minimum degree required
High school diploma or GED

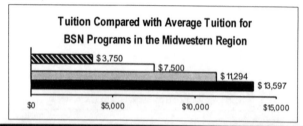
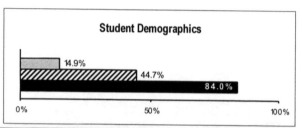

MISSOURI WESTERN STATE COLLEGE
Useful Facts*

4525 Downs Drive
Saint Joseph, MO 64507
(816) 271-4415
Kathleen Andrews, RN, PhD, CCRN

www.missouriwestern.edu/nursing

Acceptance rate		59.3%
Faculty-student ratio		1: 10
Faculty	Full time	14
	Part time	13

Tuition	
In state	$4,778
Out of state	$8,408
Enrollments	213
Graduations	73

Student Demographics	
Female	90.7%
Minority	5.4%
Part-time	1.0%

Accreditation
Missouri State Board of Nursing, Commission on
Collegiate Nursing Education (CCNE)

Degrees conferred
Baccalaureate

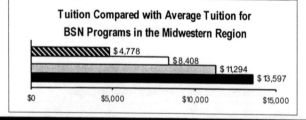
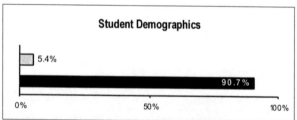

RESEARCH COLLEGE OF NURSING
Useful Facts*

2300 East Meyer Blvd
Kansas City, MO 64132
(816) 276-4721
Nancy DeBasio, PhD, RN

www.researchcollege.edu

Acceptance rate	72.3%

Tuition	
In state	$17,950
Out of state	$17,950
Enrollments	177
Graduations	90

Student Demographics	
Female	87.0%
Under age 25	80.0%
Minority	14.2%
Part-time	1.1%

Accreditation
Missouri State Board of Nursing, Commission on
Collegiate Nursing Education (CCNE)

Degrees conferred
Baccalaureate

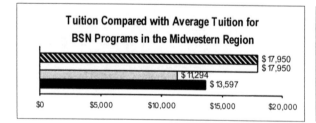
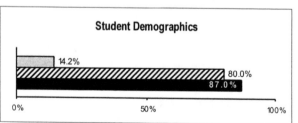

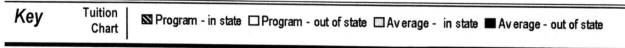

Key — Tuition Chart — ▨ Program - in state ☐ Program - out of state ☐ Average - in state ■ Average - out of state

Missouri

SAINT LOUIS UNIVERSITY
Useful Facts*

3525 Caroline Street
St Louis, MO 63104
(314) 977-8910
Joan Hrubetz, PhD, RN

www.slu.edu/colleges/nr

Accreditation
Missouri State Board of Nursing

Degrees conferred
Baccalaureate

Acceptance rate	51.3%

Tuition		Student Demographics	
In state	$23,360	Female	93.6%
Out of state	$23,360	Under age 25	84.0%
Enrollments	356	Minority	12.1%
Graduations	124	Part-time	2.6%

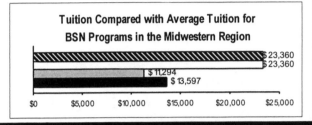

Tuition Compared with Average Tuition for BSN Programs in the Midwestern Region
$23,360
$23,360
$11,294
$13,597
$0 $5,000 $10,000 $15,000 $20,000 $25,000

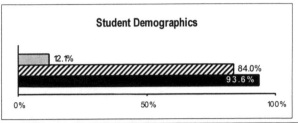

Student Demographics
12.1%
84.0%
93.6%
0% 50% 100%

SAINT LUKE'S COLLEGE
Useful Facts*

4426 Wornall Road
Kansas City, MO 64111
(816) 932-2233
Helen Jepson, EdD, RN

https://www.saintlukeshealthsystem.org/app/hpsaintlukescollege.asp

Accreditation
Missouri State Board of Nursing

Degrees conferred
Baccalaureate

Enrollments	111
Graduations	47

SOUTHEAST MISSOURI STATE UNIVERSITY
Useful Facts*

One University Plaza, Mail Stop 8300
Cape Girardeau, MO 63701
(573) 651-5154
A Hart, RN

www.semo.edu

Accreditation
Missouri State Board of Nursing

Degrees conferred
Baccalaureate

Acceptance rate	44.8%

		Student Demographics	
		Female	87.2%
Enrollments	210	Minority	5.4%
Graduations	55	Part-time	0.0%

SOUTHWEST MISSOURI STATE UNIVERSITY - SPRINGFIELD

300 Professional Building
Springfield, MO 65804
(417) 836-5310
Kathryn Hope, RN, PhD

www.smsu.edu/nursing

Accreditation
Missouri State Board of Nursing

Degrees conferred
Baccalaureate

Demographics Chart	■Female ☒Under age 25 ☐Minority	Distance Learning	†The tuition reported for this program may be not be annualized. *Data reported between 2001 and 2004.

Missouri

TRUMAN STATE UNIVERSITY

100 East Normal Street
Kirkville, MO 63501
(660) 785-4569
Stephanie Powelson, PhD

nursing.truman.edu

Accreditation	Degrees conferred
Missouri State Board of Nursing	Baccalaureate

Acceptance rate — 38.0%

Tuition		Student Demographics	
In state	$1,772	Female	97.1%
Out of state	$3,172	Under age 25	90.0%
Enrollments	170	Minority	7.6%
Graduations	39	Part-time	0.0%

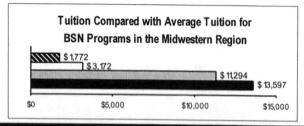

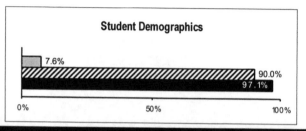

UNIVERSITY OF MISSOURI - COLUMBIA

S218 Nursing School Bldg
Columbia, MO 65211
(573) 882-0758
Rosemary Porter, RN

nursing.missouri.edu

Accreditation	Degrees conferred
Missouri State Board of Nursing, Commission on Collegiate Nursing Education (CCNE)	Baccalaureate

Acceptance rate — 53.4%

Tuition		Student Demographics	
In state	$6,276	Female	88.0%
Out of state	$9,447	Under age 25	70.0%
Enrollments	316	Minority	6.7%
Graduations	154	Part-time	5.3%

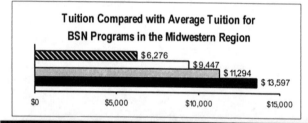

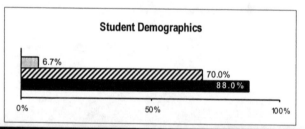

UNIVERSITY OF MISSOURI - KANSAS CITY

2220 Holmes Street
Kansas City, MO 65211
(816) 235-1752
Nancy Mills, RN

www.umkc.edu

Accreditation	Degrees conferred
Missouri State Board of Nursing	Baccalaureate

UNIVERSITY OF MISSOURI - ST LOUIS

8001 Natural Bridge Road
Saint Louis, MO 63121
(314) 516-5373
Jerry Durham, RN

www.umsl.edu

Accreditation	Degrees conferred
Missouri State Board of Nursing	Baccalaureate

Acceptance rate — 39.0%

		Student Demographics	
		Female	92.6%
		Under age 25	36.0%
Enrollments	258	Minority	23.9%
Graduations	72	Part-time	22.9%

Key | Tuition Chart | ▨ Program - in state ☐ Program - out of state ☐ Average - in state ■ Average - out of state

Missouri

WILLIAM JEWELL COLLEGE
*Useful Facts**

500 College Hill
Liberty, MO 64068
(816) 415-7605
Nelda Godfrey, PhD, APRN, BC

www.jewell.edu

Accreditation
Missouri State Board of Nursing, Commission on Collegiate Nursing Education (CCNE)

Acceptance rate		73.2%
Faculty-student ratio		1: 8
Faculty	Full time	12
	Part time	22

Tuition	
In state	$16,500
Out of state	$16,500
Enrollments	191
Graduations	26

Student Demographics	
Female	94.2%
Under age 25	63.0%
Minority	5.3%
Part-time	0.0%

Degrees conferred
Baccalaureate

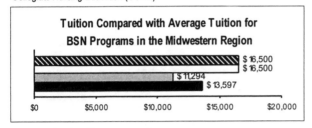

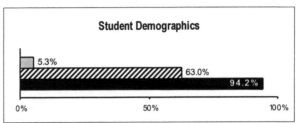

Montana

CARROLL COLLEGE

1601 N Benton Avenue
Helena, MT 59625
(406) 447-5494
Cynthia Gustafson, PhD, RN

www.carroll.edu

Accreditation
Montana State Board of Nursing, Commission on Collegiate Nursing Education (CCNE)

At the request of this nursing school, publication has been witheld.
Please contact the school directly for more information.

MONTANA STATE UNIVERSITY - BOZEMAN
*Useful Facts**

Sherrick Hall, PO Box 173560
Bozeman, MT 59717
(406) 994-3784
Elizabeth Nichols, DNS, RN

www.montana.edu/wwwnu

Accreditation
Montana State Board of Nursing, Commission on Collegiate Nursing Education (CCNE)

Faculty-student ratio		1: 9
Faculty	Full time	39
	Part time	35

Enrollments	500
Graduations	109

Degrees conferred
Baccalaureate

Demographics Chart	■Female ☑Under age 25 ☐Minority	Distance Learning	¹The tuition reported for this program may be not be annualized.
			*Data reported between 2001 and 2004.

Nebraska

BRYAN LGH MEDICAL CENTER

5035 Everett
Lincoln, NE 68506
(402) 481-8602
Kay Maize, RN, MS, MSN, EdD

www.bryanlghcollege.org

Accreditation
Nebraska Dept of Health & Human Services
Regulation

Acceptance rate	27.2%	
Faculty-student ratio	1: 11	
Faculty Full time	29	
Part time	4	

Degrees conferred
Baccalaureate degree

Tuition¹	
In state	$221
Out of state	$221
Enrollments	143
Graduations	0

Student Demographics	
Female	94.4%
Under age 25	86.7%
Minority	2.9%
Part-time	95.8%

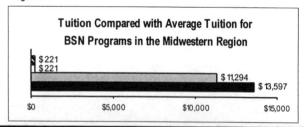

Tuition Compared with Average Tuition for BSN Programs in the Midwestern Region

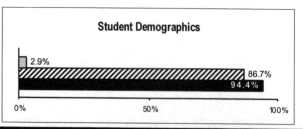

Student Demographics

CLARKSON COLLEGE

101 South 42nd Street
Omaha, NE 68131
(402) 552-3373
Linda Christensen, JD, MSN, RN

www.clarksoncollege.edu

Accreditation
Nebraska Dept of Health & Human Services
Regulation, National League for Nursing
Accrediting Commission (NLNAC)

Acceptance rate	55.0%	
Faculty-student ratio	1: 10	
Faculty Full time	34	
Part time	4	

Degrees conferred
Baccalaureate degree

Tuition	
In state	$10,350
Out of state	$10,350
Enrollments	366
Graduations	69
Minimum degree required	
CNA	

Student Demographics	
Female	93.7%
Under age 25	76.0%
Minority	10.9%
Part-time	21.0%

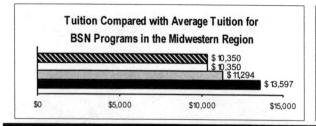

Tuition Compared with Average Tuition for BSN Programs in the Midwestern Region

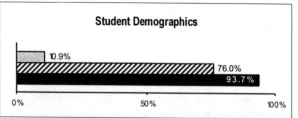

Student Demographics

CREIGHTON UNIVERSITY

2500 California Plaza
Omaha, NE 68178
(402) 280-2004
Eleanor Howell, PhD, RN

nursing.creighton.edu

Accreditation
Nebraska Dept of Health & Human Services
Regulation, Commission on Collegiate Nursing
Education (CCNE)

Acceptance rate	39.5%	
Faculty-student ratio	1: 10	
Faculty Full time	42	
Part time	10	

Degrees conferred
Baccalaureate

Tuition	
In state	$20,354
Out of state	$20,354
Enrollments	461
Graduations	203

Student Demographics	
Female	90.8%
Under age 25	79.0%
Minority	11.5%
Part-time	1.9%

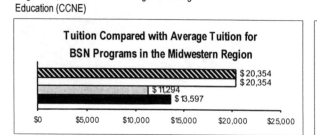

Tuition Compared with Average Tuition for BSN Programs in the Midwestern Region

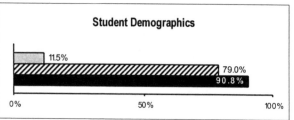

Student Demographics

Key | Tuition Chart

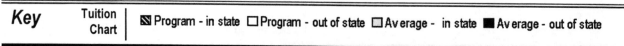
Program - in state ☐ Program - out of state ☐ Average - in state ■ Average - out of state

Nebraska

MIDLAND LUTHERAN COLLEGE
Useful Facts

900 N Clarkson
Fremont, NE 68025
(402) 941-6280
Nancy Harms, RN, PhD, MSN, BSN, BS

www.mlc.edu

Acceptance rate		80.6%
Faculty-student ratio		1: 7
Faculty	Full time	8
	Part time	3

Tuition	
In state	$18,140
Out of state	$18,140
Enrollments	63
Graduations	21

Student Demographics	
Female	93.7%
Under age 25	90.5%
Minority	3.2%
Part-time	1.6%

Accreditation
Nebraska Dept of Health & Human Services
Regulation, National League for Nursing
Accrediting Commission (NLNAC)

Degrees conferred
Baccalaureate degree

Minimum degree required
High school diploma or GED

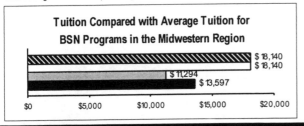

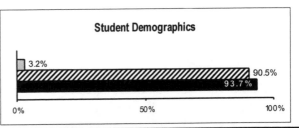

NEBRASKA METHODIST COLLEGE OF NURSING AND ALLIED HEALTH

8501 West Dodge Road
Omaha, NE 68114
(402) 354-7027
Marilyn Valerio

www.methodistcollege.edu

Accreditation
Nebraska Dept of Health & Human Services
Regulation

Degrees conferred
Baccalaureate

UNION COLLEGE
Useful Facts*

3800 S 48th Street
Lincoln, NE 68506
(402) 486-2600
Jeff Joiner, RN

www.ucollege.edu

Acceptance rate		100.0%
Faculty-student ratio		1: 12
Faculty	Full time	6
	Part time	3

Tuition	
In state	$10,940
Out of state	$10,940
Enrollments	91
Graduations	12

Student Demographics	
Female	85.2%
Under age 25	90.0%
Minority	11.8%
Part-time	2.3%

Accreditation
Nebraska Dept of Health & Human Services
Regulation, Commission on Collegiate Nursing
Education (CCNE)

Degrees conferred
Baccalaureate

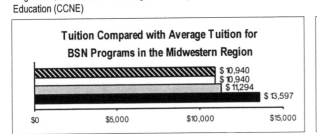

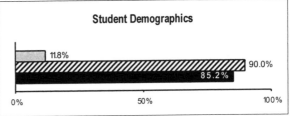

Demographics Chart	■Female ☑Under age 25 ☐Minority	Distance Learning	¹The tuition reported for this program may be not be annualized.
			*Data reported between 2001 and 2004.

Nebraska

UNIVERSITY OF NEBRASKA MEDICAL CENTER

985330 Nebraska Medical Center
Omaha, NE 68198
(402) 559-4109
Virginia Tilden, DNSc, RN, FAAN

www.unmc.edu/nursing

Accreditation
Nebraska Dept of Health & Human Services
Regulation, Commission on Collegiate Nursing
Education (CCNE)

Acceptance rate   36.8%

Degrees conferred
Baccalaureate

Tuition		Student Demographics	
In state	$4,063	Female	93.5%
Out of state	$11,900	Under age 25	68.0%
Enrollments	598	Minority	5.4%
Graduations	194	Part-time	3.2%

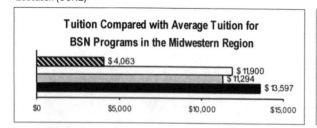

Tuition Compared with Average Tuition for BSN Programs in the Midwestern Region
- $4,063
- $11,900
- $11,294
- $13,597

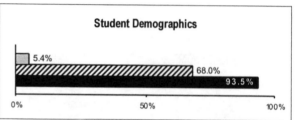

Student Demographics
- 5.4%
- 68.0%
- 93.5%

Nevada

UNIVERSITY OF NEVADA - LAS VEGAS

Box 453018, 4505 Maryland Pkwy
Las Vegas, NV 89154
(702) 895-5307
Carolyn Yucha, PhD, RN

www.unlv.edu

Accreditation
Nevada State Board of Nursing, National League
for Nursing Accrediting Commission (NLNAC)

Acceptance rate	40.7%	
Faculty-student ratio	1: 6	
Faculty	Full time	27
	Part time	6

Degrees conferred
Baccalaureate degree

Minimum degree required
High school diploma or GED

Tuition		Student Demographics	
In state	$3,038	Female	86.6%
Out of state	$12,505	Under age 25	64.8%
Enrollments	191	Minority	47.5%
Graduations	122	Part-time	10.6%

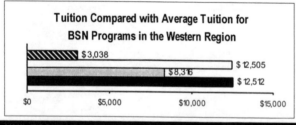

Tuition Compared with Average Tuition for BSN Programs in the Western Region
- $3,038
- $12,505
- $8,316
- $12,512

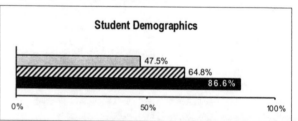

Student Demographics
- 47.5%
- 64.8%
- 86.6%

UNIVERSITY OF NEVADA - RENO

Mail Stop 134
Reno, NV 89557
(775) 784-4684
Julie Johnson, PhD, RN

www.unr.edu

Accreditation
Nevada State Board of Nursing

Acceptance rate   75.0%

Degrees conferred
Baccalaureate

Tuition		Student Demographics	
In state	$3,278	Female	88.6%
Out of state	$4,956	Under age 25	10.0%
Enrollments	92	Minority	11.7%
Graduations	44	Part-time	0.0%

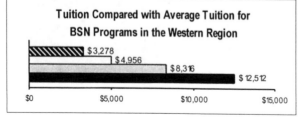

Tuition Compared with Average Tuition for BSN Programs in the Western Region
- $3,278
- $4,956
- $8,316
- $12,512

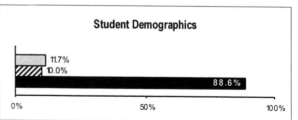

Student Demographics
- 11.7%
- 10.0%
- 88.6%

Key   Tuition Chart   ⊠ Program - in state   ☐ Program - out of state   ☐ Average - in state   ■ Average - out of state

New Hampshire

COLBY-SAWYER COLLEGE   *Useful Facts**

100 Main St
New London, NH 03257
(603) 526-3626
Kathleen Thies, PhD, RN

www.colby-sawyer.edu

Accetance rate	93.8%	

Tuition		Student Demographics	
In state	$18,960	Female	92.9%
Out of state	$18,960	Under age 25	80.0%
Enrollments	30		
Graduations	12	Part-time	3.6%

Accreditation
New Hampshire Board of Nursing

Degrees conferred
Baccalaureate

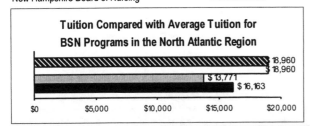
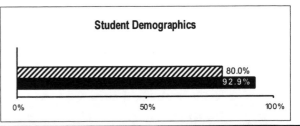

SAINT ANSELM COLLEGE   *Useful Facts**

100 Saint Anselm Dr
Manchester, NH 03102
(603) 641-7084
Kathleen Perrin, PhD

www.anselm.edu

Acceptance rate	62.5%	

Tuition		Student Demographics	
In state	$21,410	Female	96.9%
Out of state	$21,410	Under age 25	99.0%
Enrollments	225	Minority	1.3%
Graduations	50	Part-time	1.8%

Accreditation
New Hampshire Board of Nursing, Commission
on Collegiate Nursing Education (CCNE)

Degrees conferred
Baccalaureate

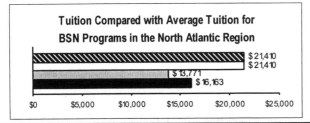
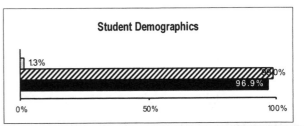

UNIVERSITY OF NEW HAMPSHIRE

217 Hewitt Hall
Durham, NH 03824
(603) 862-4715
Raelene Shippee-Rice, PhD, RN

www.unh.edu

Accreditation
New Hampshire Board of Nursing

Degrees conferred
Baccalaureate

| Demographics Chart | ■Female ▨Under age 25 ☐Minority | Distance Learning | | †The tuition reported for this program may be not be annualized.
*Data reported between 2001 and 2004. |
|---|---|---|---|---|

New Jersey

BLOOMFIELD COLLEGE

467 Franklin St
Bloomfield, NJ 07003
(973) 748-9000
Neddie Serra, EdD, RN

www.bloomfield.edu

Accreditation
New Jersey Board of Nursing, Commission on
Collegiate Nursing Education (CCNE)

Acceptance rate		36.3%
Faculty-student ratio		1: 11
Faculty	Full time	7
	Part time	9

Tuition			**Student Demographics**	
In state	$10,800		Female	90.6%
Out of state	$10,800			
Enrollments	127			
Graduations	28		Part-time	55.1%

Degrees conferred
Baccalaureate

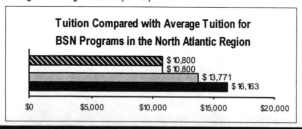

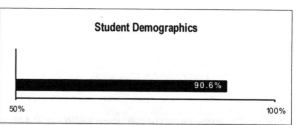

FAIRLEIGH DICKINSON UNVERSITY

1000 River Road, Dickison Hall Rm 444
Teaneck, NJ 07666
(201) 692-2890
Minerva Guttman, EdD, RN, NP

www.fdu.edu

Accreditation
New Jersey Board of Nursing

Acceptance rate		55.3%

Tuition			**Student Demographics**	
In state	$16,346		Female	90.6%
Out of state	$16,346			
Enrollments	158		Minority	61.3%
Graduations	35		Part-time	31.7%

Degrees conferred
Baccalaureate

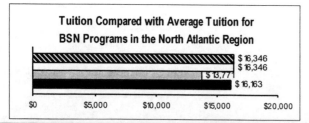

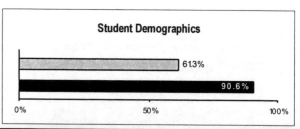

FELICIAN COLLEGE

262 South Main Street
Lodi, NJ 07644
(201) 559-6030
Muriel Shore, EdD, RN, CNAA, BC

www.felician.edu.

Accreditation
New Jersey Board of Nursing, Commission on
Collegiate Nursing Education (CCNE)

At the request of this nursing school, publication has been witheld.
Please contact the school directly for more information.

Key | Tuition Chart | ▨ Program - in state ☐ Program - out of state ▨ Average - in state ■ Average - out of state

New Jersey

RUTGERS THE STATE UNIVERSITY OF NEW JERSEY - CAMDEN   *Useful Facts**

Ackerson Hall 180 University Avenue
Newark, NJ 07102
(973) 353-5293
Joanne Stevenson, PhD, RN

www.camden.rutgers.edu

Accreditation
New Jersey Board of Nursing, Commission on
Collegiate Nursing Education (CCNE)

Acceptance rate	50.0%

Tuition	
In state	$500
Out of state	$10,178
Enrollments	95
Graduations	45

Student Demographics	
Female	91.0%
Minority	26.9%
Part-time	7.5%

Degrees conferred
Baccalaureate

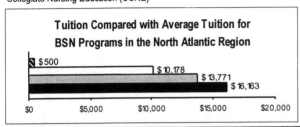
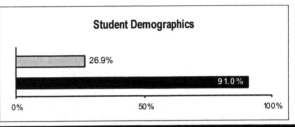

RUTGERS, THE STATE UNIVERSITY

180 University Avenue
Newark, NJ 07102
(973) 353-5293
Felissa Lashley, PhD, RN, FACMG, FAAN

nursing.rutgers.edu

Accreditation
New Jersey Board of Nursing, Commission on
Collegiate Nursing Education (CCNE)

At the request of this nursing school, publication has been witheld.
Please contact the school directly for more information.

SETON HALL UNIVERSITY

400 South Orange Ave
South Orange, NJ 07079
(973) 761-9015
Phyllis Hansell, EdD, RN, FAAN

www.shu.edu

Accreditation
New Jersey Board of Nursing, Commission on
Collegiate Nursing Education (CCNE), National
League for Nursing Accrediting Commission
(NLNAC)

At the request of this nursing school, publication has been witheld.
Please contact the school directly for more information.

THE COLLEGE OF NEW JERSEY   *Useful Facts**

PO Box 7718
Ewing, NJ 08628
(609) 771-2451
Susan Bakewell-Sachs, PhD, RN, APRN, BC

www.tcnj.edu/~nursing

Accreditation
New Jersey Board of Nursing, Commission on
Collegiate Nursing Education (CCNE)

Acceptance rate	30.6%

Tuition	
In state	$6,621
Out of state	$11,562
Enrollments	261
Graduations	34

Student Demographics	
Female	92.3%
Under age 25	95.0%
Minority	30.4%
Part-time	1.2%

Degrees conferred
Baccalaureate

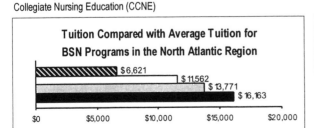
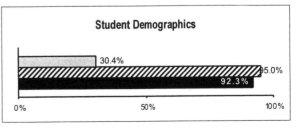

Demographics Chart	■Female ▨Under age 25 ▢Minority	Distance Learning	†The tuition reported for this program may be not be annualized. *Data reported between 2001 and 2004.

New Jersey

UNIVERSITY OF MEDICINE AND DENTISTRY OF NEW JERSEY - NEWARK · *Useful Facts*

65 Bergen Street, Suite 1143
Newark, NJ 07101
(973) 972-4322
Sara Torres, PhD, RN, FAAN

sn.umdnj.edu

Acceptance rate		35.0%
Faculty-student ratio		1:9
Faculty	Full time	54
	Part time	25

Tuition	
In state	$9,960
Out of state	$14,130
Enrollments	418
Graduations	115

Student Demographics	
Female	84.1%
Under age 25	52.1%
Minority	54.5%
Part-time	0.0%

Accreditation
New Jersey Board of Nursing, National League
for Nursing Accrediting Commission (NLNAC)

Degrees conferred
Baccalaureate degree

Minimum degree required
The generic BSN program: no minimum degree
required. Accelerated BSN: BS in non-nursing field

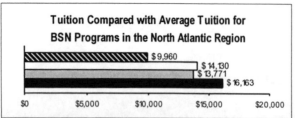
Tuition Compared with Average Tuition for BSN Programs in the North Atlantic Region

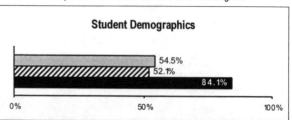
Student Demographics

UNIVERSITY OF MEDICINE AND DENTISTRY OF NEW JERSEY - RAMAPO

505 Ramapo Valley Road G-445
Mahwah, NJ 07430
(201) 684-7737
Kathleen Burke, PhD, RN

sn.umdnj.edu/

Accreditation
New Jersey Board of Nursing

Degrees conferred
Baccalaureate

WILLIAM PATERSON UNIVERSITY · *Useful Facts*

300 Pompton Rd
Wayne, NJ 07470
(973) 720-2673
Julie Bliss, EdD, RN

ww2.wpunj.edu/cos/nursing

Acceptance rate		25.6%
Faculty-student ratio		1:16
Faculty	Full time	17
	Part time	20

Tuition	
In state	$8,740
Out of state	$13,856
Enrollments	429
Graduations	71

Student Demographics	
Female	85.3%
Under age 25	47.2%
Minority	54.9%
Part-time	14.9%

Accreditation
New Jersey Board of Nursing, Commission on
Collegiate Nursing Education (CCNE)

Degrees conferred
Baccalaureate degree, MSN

Minimum degree required
High school diploma or GED

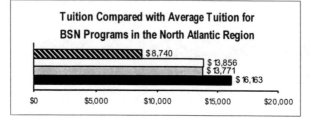
Tuition Compared with Average Tuition for BSN Programs in the North Atlantic Region

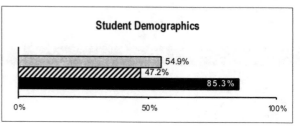
Student Demographics

Key	Tuition Chart	▨ Program - in state ☐ Program - out of state ☐ Average - in state ■ Average - out of state

New Mexico

NEW MEXICO STATE UNIVERSITY — Useful Facts

MSC 3185, PO Box 30001
Las Cruces, NM 88003
(505) 646-3812
Mary Hoke, PhD, MSN, RN-BC, APRN-BC

www.nmsu.edu/~nursing

Acceptance rate	44.9%
Faculty-student ratio	1: 9
Faculty Full time	22
Part time	18

Tuition
In state $4,206
Out of state $13,530
Enrollments 292
Graduations 84

Student Demographics
Female 82.7%
Under age 25 63.3%
Minority 61.4%
Part-time 5.8%

Accreditation
New Mexico Board of Nursing, Commission on Collegiate Nursing Education (CCNE)

Degrees conferred
Baccalaureate degree

Minimum degree required
High school diploma or GED

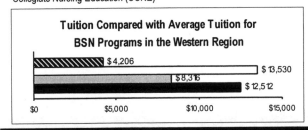
Tuition Compared with Average Tuition for BSN Programs in the Western Region

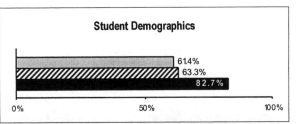
Student Demographics

UNIVERSITY OF NEW MEXICO - ALBUQUERQUE — Useful Facts

MSC09 5350, 1 University of New Mexico
Albuquerque, NM 87131
(505) 272-6284
Sandra Ferketich, PhD, RN, FAAN

hsc.unm.edu/consg

Acceptance rate	34.6%
Faculty-student ratio	1: 4
Faculty Full time	46
Part time	8

Tuition
In state $4,108
Out of state $13,437
Enrollments 223
Graduations 115

Student Demographics
Female 88.8%
Under age 25 59.6%
Minority 40.3%
Part-time 0.4%

Accreditation
New Mexico Board of Nursing, Commission on Collegiate Nursing Education (CCNE)

Degrees conferred
Baccalaureate degree

Minimum degree required
BA/BS in a non-nursing field for the Accelerated Students

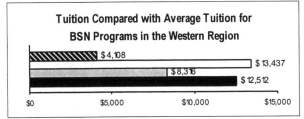
Tuition Compared with Average Tuition for BSN Programs in the Western Region

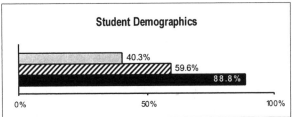
Student Demographics

New York

ADELPHI UNIVERSITY — Useful Facts*

1 South Ave, Alumnae Hall
Garden City, NY 11530
(516) 877-4511
Patrick Coonan, EdD, RN, CNAA

www.adelphi.edu/nurs

Acceptance rate	44.9%
Faculty-student ratio	1: 15
Faculty Full time	25
Part time	82

Tuition
In state $19,720
Out of state $19,720
Enrollments 1000
Graduations 138

Student Demographics
Female 88.5%
Under age 25 52.3%
Minority 62.2%
Part-time 18.2%

Accreditation
New York State Board of Nursing, Commission on Collegiate Nursing Education (CCNE)

Degrees conferred
BS in Nursing

Minimum degree required
High school diploma or GED

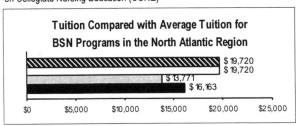
Tuition Compared with Average Tuition for BSN Programs in the North Atlantic Region

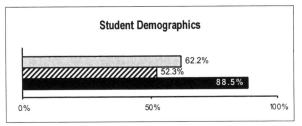
Student Demographics

Demographics Chart	■ Female ▨ Under age 25 ☐ Minority	Distance Learning	†The tuition reported for this program may be not be annualized. *Data reported between 2001 and 2004.

New York

COLLEGE OF MOUNT ST VINCENT

6301 Riverdale Ave
Riverdale, NY 10471
(718) 405-3353
Barbara Cohen, EdD, RN

www.cmsv.edu

Tuition	
In state	$14,510
Out of state	$14,510
Enrollments	388
Graduations	96

Accreditation
New York State Board of Nursing

Degrees conferred
Baccalaureate

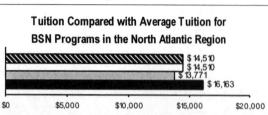

Tuition Compared with Average Tuition for BSN Programs in the North Atlantic Region
- $14,510
- $14,510
- $13,771
- $16,163

COLLEGE OF NEW ROCHELLE

29 Castle Pl
New Rochelle, NY 10805
(914) 654-5454
Donna Demarcat, RN, EdD

www.cnr.edu

Acceptance rate   72.0%

Tuition		Student Demographics	
In state	$9,600	Female	97.9%
Out of state	$9,600	Under age 25	20.0%
Enrollments	404	Minority	80.2%
Graduations	91	Part-time	27.4%

Accreditation
New York State Board of Nursing, Commission on Collegiate Nursing Education (CCNE)

Degrees conferred
Baccalaureate

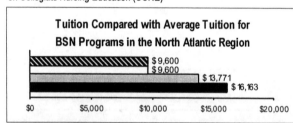

Tuition Compared with Average Tuition for BSN Programs in the North Atlantic Region
- $9,600
- $9,600
- $13,771
- $16,163

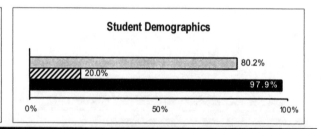

Student Demographics
- 80.2%
- 20.0%
- 97.9%

COLUMBIA UNIVERSITY

617 W 168th St Box 6
New York, NY 10032
(212) 305-3582
Mary O'Neil, PhD

www.columbia.edu

Student Demographics

Enrollments	409		
Graduations	228	Part-time	57.9%

Accreditation
New York State Board of Nursing

Degrees conferred
Baccalaureate

DAEMEN COLLEGE

4380 Main St
Amherst, NY 14226
(716) 839-8387
Mary Lou Rusin, EdD, RN

www.daemen.edu

Accreditation
New York State Board of Nursing, National League for Nursing Accrediting Commission (NLNAC)

At the request of this nursing school, publication has been witheld. Please contact the school directly for more information.

Key | Tuition Chart | ▨ Program - in state ☐ Program - out of state ☐ Average - in state ■ Average - out of state

New York

DOMINICAN COLLEGE — Useful Facts*

470 Western Hwy
Orangeburg, NY 10962
(914) 398-4998
Maureen Creegan, EdD, RN

www.dc.edu

Accreditation
New York State Board of Nursing

Degrees conferred
Baccalaureate

Tuition
In state $11,250

Enrollments   186
Graduations   91

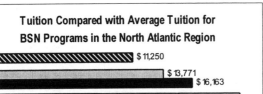

Tuition Compared with Average Tuition for BSN Programs in the North Atlantic Region

$ 11,250
$ 13,771
$ 16,163

D'YOUVILLE COLLEGE — Useful Facts*

320 Porter Ave
Buffalo, NY 14201
(716) 881-3200
Verna Kieffer, DNS, RN

www.dyc.edu

Accreditation
New York State Board of Nursing

Degrees conferred
Baccalaureate

Acceptance rate   48.8%

Tuition		Student Demographics	
In state	$12,350	Female	92.8%
Out of state	$12,350	Under age 25	33.0%
Enrollments	162	Minority	29.0%
Graduations	40	Part-time	20.3%

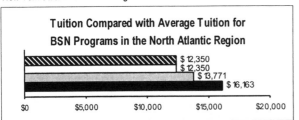

Tuition Compared with Average Tuition for BSN Programs in the North Atlantic Region

$ 12,350
$ 12,350
$ 13,771
$ 16,163

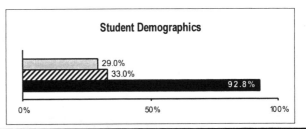

Student Demographics

29.0%
33.0%
92.8%

ELMIRA COLLEGE — Useful Facts*

One Park Place
Elmira, NY 14901
(607) 735-1800
Lois Schoener

www.elmira.edu

Accreditation
New York State Board of Nursing, National
League for Nursing Accrediting Commission
(NLNAC)

Degrees conferred
Baccalaureate

Enrollments   160

Demographics Chart | ■ Female ▨ Under age 25 ☐ Minority | **Distance Learning** | ¹The tuition reported for this program may be not be annualized.
*Data reported between 2001 and 2004.

New York

HARTWICK COLLEGE — *Useful Facts**

One Hartwick Drive
Oneonta, NY 13820
(607) 431-4785
Sharon Dettenrieder, MSN, RN

www.hartwick.edu/academic.nurs.html

Accreditation
New York State Board of Nursing, Commission on Collegiate Nursing Education (CCNE)

Degrees conferred
Baccalaureate

Acceptance rate	93.1%

Tuition		Student Demographics	
In state	$27,400	Female	87.5%
Out of state	$27,400	Under age 25	79.0%
Enrollments	81	Minority	14.1%
Graduations	23	Part-time	0.0%

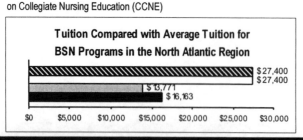

Tuition Compared with Average Tuition for BSN Programs in the North Atlantic Region
$27,400 / $27,400 / $13,771 / $16,163

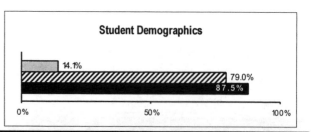

Student Demographics
14.1% / 79.0% / 87.5%

HERBERT H LEHMAN COLLEGE

250 Bedford Park Blvd
Bronx, NY 10468
(718) 960-8794
C Georges, EdD, RN, FAAN

www.lehman.cuny.edu

Accreditation
New York State Board of Nursing

At the request of this nursing school, publication has been withheld. Please contact the school directly for more information.

HUNTER COLLEGE - CUNY

425 East 25 Street
New York, NY 10010
(212) 481-7596
Diane Rendon, EdD, RN

www.hunter.cuny.edu

Accreditation
New York State Board of Nursing

Degrees conferred
Baccalaureate

KEUKA COLLEGE — *Useful Facts*

141 Central Avenue
Keuka Park, NY 14478
(315) 279-5273
Linda Rossi, EdD, APRN-BC

www.keuka.edu/academic/nurse/dvnurse.html

Accreditation
New York State Board of Nursing, National League for Nursing Accrediting Commission (NLNAC)

Degrees conferred
BS

Faculty-student ratio		1: 10
Faculty	Full time	4
	Part time	20

Tuition		Student Demographics	
In state	$17,800	Female	100.0%
Out of state	$17,800	Under age 25	0.0%
Enrollments	138		
Graduations	41	Part-time	0.0%

Minimum degree required
Must have their Associates (be RNs) to Enter Program

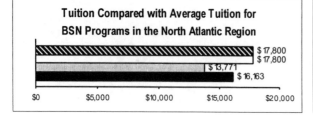

Tuition Compared with Average Tuition for BSN Programs in the North Atlantic Region
$17,800 / $17,800 / $13,771 / $16,163

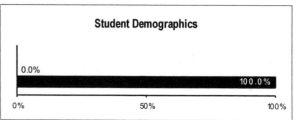

Student Demographics
0.0% / 100.0%

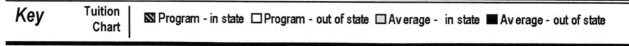

Key Tuition Chart — ⬚ Program - in state ☐ Program - out of state ☐ Average - in state ■ Average - out of state

New York

LONG ISLAND UNIVERSITY - CW POST CAMPUS OF LIU

CW Post Campus of LIU
Brookville, NY 11548
(516) 299-3065
Minna Kapp, EdD, MBA, RN

www.liu.edu/nursing

Accreditation	Degrees conferred
New York State Board of Nursing	Baccalaureate

MEDGAR EVERS COLLEGE - CUNY

1150 Carroll Street
Brooklyn, NY 11225
(718) 270-6222
Georgia McDuffie, PhD

www.mec.cuny.edu/academic_affairs/science_tech_school/nursing/nurse_home.htm

Accreditation	Degrees conferred
New York State Board of Nursing, National League for Nursing Accrediting Commission (NLNAC)	Baccalaureate

MERCY COLLEGE

555 Broadway
Dobbs Ferry, NY 10522
9146747865
Mary McGuinness, RN, PhD

www.mercy.edu

Accreditation	Degrees conferred
New York State Board of Nursing	Baccalaureate

MOLLOY COLLEGE - William J Casey Center

1000 Hempstead Avenue
Rockville Centre, NY 11571
(516) 678-5000
Bernadette Curry, PhD, RN

www.molloy.edu/academic/nursing

Accreditation	Degrees conferred
New York State Board of Nursing	Baccalaureate

MOUNT SAINT MARY COLLEGE (NEW YORK)

330 Powell Avenue
Newburgh, NY 12550
(845) 569-3138
Elizabeth Scannell-Desch, PhD, RN, OCNS

www.msmc.edu

Accreditation	Degrees conferred
New York State Board of Nursing	Baccalaureate

NAZARETH COLLEGE

4245 East Avenue
Rochester, NY 14618
(716) 389-2710
Margaret Andrews, PhD, RN

www.naz.edu/dept/nursing

Accreditation	Degrees conferred
New York State Board of Nursing	Baccalaureate

Demographics Chart	■ Female ▨ Under age 25 ▢ Minority	Distance Learning		†The tuition reported for this program may be not be annualized. *Data reported between 2001 and 2004.

New York

NEW YORK INSTITUTE OF TECHNOLOGY

1855 Broadway @ 61st Street
New York, NY 10023
(212) 261-1700
Susan Neville, PhD

www.nyit.edu

Accreditation
New York State Board of Nursing

Degrees conferred
Baccalaureate

NEW YORK UNIVERSITY

Useful Facts

246 Greene St
New York, NY 10003
(212) 998-5303
Terry Fulmer, PhD, RN, FAAN

www.nyu.edu/nursing

Accreditation
New York State Board of Nursing, National League for Nursing Accrediting Commission (NLNAC)

Acceptance rate		48.4%
Faculty-student ratio		1 : 7
Faculty	Full time	25
	Part time	93

Tuition	
In state	$29,890
Out of state	$29,890
Enrollments	515
Graduations	111

Minimum degree required
High school diploma or GED

Degrees conferred
BS with major in Nursing

Student Demographics	
Female	92.8%
Under age 25	61.6%
Minority	43.3%
Part-time	16.1%

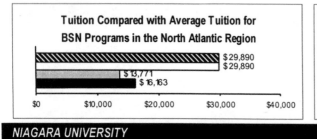

Tuition Compared with Average Tuition for BSN Programs in the North Atlantic Region
- $29,890
- $29,890
- $13,771
- $16,163

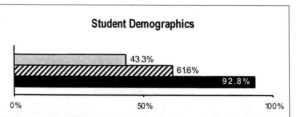

Student Demographics
- 43.3%
- 61.6%
- 92.8%

NIAGARA UNIVERSITY

Useful Facts*

Po Box 2203
Niagara University, NY 14109
(716) 286-8312
Dolores Bower, PhD, RN

www.niagara.edu/nursing

Accreditation
New York State Board of Nursing

Degrees conferred
Baccalaureate

Tuition	
In state	$14,000
Out of state	$14,000
Enrollments	126
Graduations	46

Student Demographics	
Female	94.4%
Under age 25	85.0%
Minority	6.9%
Part-time	0.0%

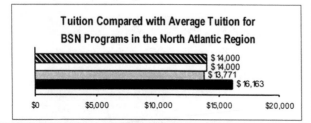

Tuition Compared with Average Tuition for BSN Programs in the North Atlantic Region
- $14,000
- $14,000
- $13,771
- $16,163

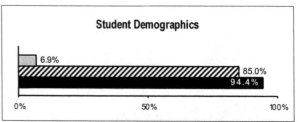

Student Demographics
- 6.9%
- 85.0%
- 94.4%

PACE UNIVERSITY

Useful Facts*

861 Bedford Rd -L28
Pleasantville, NY 10570
(914) 773-3341
Harriet Feldman, PhD, RN, FAAN

www.pace.edu

Accreditation
New York State Board of Nursing

Degrees conferred
Baccalaureate

Acceptance rate	68.1%
Enrollments	321
Graduations	135

Student Demographics	
Female	94.3%
Minority	52.7%
Part-time	19.6%

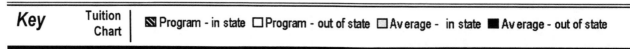

Key Tuition Chart — ▨ Program - in state ☐ Program - out of state ☐ Average - in state ■ Average - out of state

New York

ROBERTS WESLEYAN COLLEGE — *Useful Facts*

2301 Westside Dr
Rochester, NY 14624
(585) 594-6686
Susanne Mohnkern, PhD, RN

www.roberts.edu

Accreditation
New York State Board of Nursing, National League for Nursing Accrediting Commission (NLNAC)

Acceptance rate	72.8%
Faculty-student ratio	1: 20
Faculty Full time	9
Part time	3

Tuition
In state	$18,350
Out of state	$18,350
Enrollments	208
Graduations	43

Minimum degree required
High school diploma or GED

Degrees conferred
Baccalaureate degree

Student Demographics
Female	86.3%
Under age 25	54.7%
Minority	21.6%
Part-time	2.9%

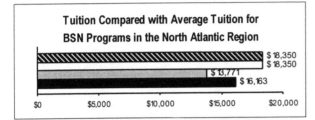

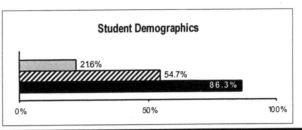

SAINT FRANCIS COLLEGE

180 Remsen Street
Brooklyn, NY 11201
(718) 489-5280
Susan Saladino, PhD, RN

www.stfranciscollege.edu

Accreditation
New York State Board of Nursing

Degrees conferred
Baccalaureate

SAINT JOHN FISHER COLLEGE — *Useful Facts**

3690 East Ave
Rochester, NY 14618
(585) 385-8472
Mary Beth Culross, PhD, RN

www.sjfc.edu

Accreditation
New York State Board of Nursing

Acceptance rate	92.3%

Tuition
In state	$16,200
Out of state	$16,200
Enrollments	115
Graduations	24

Degrees conferred
Baccalaureate

Student Demographics
Female	96.0%
Under age 25	72.0%
Minority	16.5%
Part-time	9.9%

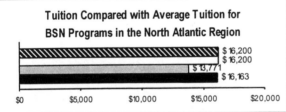

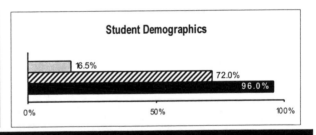

SAINT JOSEPH COLLEGE - NEW YORK

245 Clinton Ave
Brooklyn, NY 11205
(718) 399-0185
Barbara Sands, PhD, RN

www.sjcny.edu

Accreditation
New York State Board of Nursing, National League for Nursing Accrediting Commission (NLNAC)

At the request of this nursing school, publication has been witheld. Please contact the school directly for more information.

Demographics Chart | ■ Female ☒ Under age 25 ☐ Minority | **Distance Learning** | ¹The tuition reported for this program may be not be annualized.
*Data reported between 2001 and 2004.

New York

STATE UNIVERSITY OF NEW YORK - BINGHAMTON

PO Box 6000
Binghamton, NY 13902
(607) 777-4964
Joyce Ferrario, PhD, RN

www.binghamton.edu

Accreditation
New York State Board of Nursing

Degrees conferred
Baccalaureate

STATE UNIVERSITY OF NEW YORK - BROCKPORT   *Useful Facts**

350 New Campus Dr
Brockport, NY 14420
(585) 395-5323
Linda Snell, MSN, RN

brockport.edu/nursing

Accreditation
New York State Board of Nursing, Commission
on Collegiate Nursing Education (CCNE)

Degrees conferred
Baccalaureate

Acceptance rate	100.0%	

Tuition		**Student Demographics**	
In state	$3,400	Female	94.6%
Out of state	$8,300	Under age 25	50.0%
Enrollments	121	Minority	17.0%
Graduations	45	Part-time	1.8%

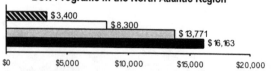

Tuition Compared with Average Tuition for BSN Programs in the North Atlantic Region
$3,400 / $8,300 / $13,771 / $16,163

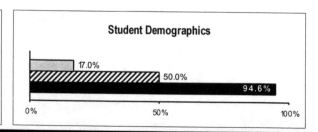

Student Demographics
17.0% / 50.0% / 94.6%

STATE UNIVERSITY OF NEW YORK - PLATTSBURGH   *Useful Facts*

101 Broad St
Plattsburgh, NY 12901
(518) 564-3124
Zoanne Schnell, PhD, RN

www.plattsburgh.edu

Accreditation
New York State Board of Nursing, Commission
on Collegiate Nursing Education (CCNE)

Degrees conferred
Baccalaureate degree

Acceptance rate	31.2%		
Faculty-student ratio	1: 33		
Faculty	Full time	10	
	Part time	2	

Tuition		**Student Demographics**	
In state	$4,350	Female	93.0%
Out of state	$10,610	Under age 25	100.0%
Enrollments	363		
Graduations	29	Part-time	0.0%

Minimum degree required
High school diploma or GED

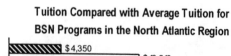
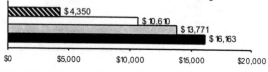

Tuition Compared with Average Tuition for BSN Programs in the North Atlantic Region
$4,350 / $10,610 / $13,771 / $16,163

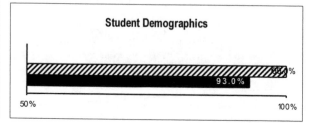

Student Demographics
93.0%

Key | Tuition Chart | ▨ Program - in state ☐ Program - out of state ☐ Average - in state ■ Average - out of state

New York

STATE UNIVERSITY OF NEW YORK - STONY BROOK
*Useful Facts**

Health Care Center, Level 2, Rm 235
Stony Brook, NY 11794
(631) 444-3260
Lenora McClean, EdD, RN

www.uhmc.sunysb.edu/nursing

Accreditation
New York State Board of Nursing

Degrees conferred
Baccalaureate

Acceptance rate	26.1%

Tuition		Student Demographics	
In state	$3,400	Female	86.2%
Out of state	$8,300		
Enrollments	210	Minority	31.4%
Graduations	108	Part-time	0.0%

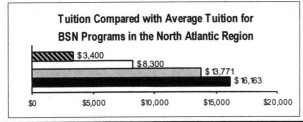

Tuition Compared with Average Tuition for BSN Programs in the North Atlantic Region

- $3,400
- $8,300
- $13,771
- $16,163

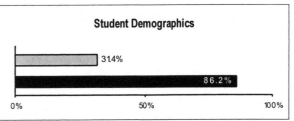

Student Demographics

- 31.4%
- 86.2%

STATE UNIVERSITY OF NEW YORK - SYRACUSE

750 East Adams Street
Syracuse, NY 12540
(315) 464-4277
Elvira Szigeti, RN

www.upstate.edu/con

Accreditation
New York State Board of Nursing

Degrees conferred
Baccalaureate

STATE UNIVERSITY OF NEW YORK - UTICA/ROME

PO Box 3050
Utica, NY 13504
(315) 792-7295
Jeannine Muldoon, PhD, RN

www.sunyit.edu

Accreditation
New York State Board of Nursing

Degrees conferred
Baccalaureate

STATE UNIVERSITY OF NEW YORK AT BUFFALO
*Useful Facts**

3435 Main St, 1030 Kimball Tower
Buffalo, NY 14214
(716) 829-2533
Mecca Cranley, PhD, RN

nursing.buffalo.edu

Accreditation
New York State Board of Nursing

Degrees conferred
Baccalaureate

Acceptance rate	81.6%

Tuition		Student Demographics	
In state	$3,400	Female	90.0%
Out of state	$8,300		
Enrollments	315	Minority	34.0%
Graduations	94	Part-time	8.1%

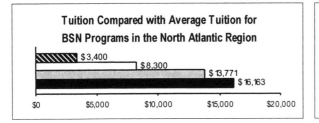

Tuition Compared with Average Tuition for BSN Programs in the North Atlantic Region

- $3,400
- $8,300
- $13,771
- $16,163

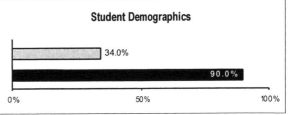

Student Demographics

- 34.0%
- 90.0%

Demographics Chart	■ Female ▨ Under age 25 ☐ Minority	Distance Learning	†The tuition reported for this program may be not be annualized. *Data reported between 2001 and 2004.

New York

SUNY COLLEGE OF NEW PALTZ

75 South Manheim Boulevard
New Paltz, NY 12561
(845) 257-2121
Ellen Abate

www.newpaltz.edu

Accreditation
New York State Board of Nursing

Degrees conferred
Baccalaureate

SUNY HEALTH SCIENCE CENTER - BROOKLYN

450 Clarkson Ave, Box 22
Brooklyn, NY 11203
(718) 270-7632
Mary Graham, EdD, MED, BS

www.downstate.edu

Accreditation
New York State Board of Nursing, National
League for Nursing Accrediting Commission
(NLNAC)

Degrees conferred
Baccalaureate

THE COLLEGE OF STATEN ISLAND

2800 Victory Blvd, Marcus Hall
Staten Island, NY 10314
(718) 982-3810
Mary O'Donnell, RN, PhD

www.csi.cuny.edu/nursing

Faculty-student ratio		1: 11
Faculty	Full time	17
	Part time	33

Accreditation
New York State Board of Nursing, National
League for Nursing Accrediting Commission
(NLNAC)

Degrees conferred
Baccalaureate

THE SAGE COLLEGES

Useful Facts

45 Ferry Street
Troy, NY 12180
(518) 244-2384
Glenda Kelman, PhD, RN, APRN, BC

www.sage.edu

Acceptance rate		68.2%
Faculty-student ratio		1: 6
Faculty	Full time	14
	Part time	38

Tuition

In state	$19,200
Out of state	$19,200
Enrollments	201
Graduations	37

Student Demographics

Female	100.0%
Under age 25	48.0%
Minority	18.7%
Part-time	8.7%

Accreditation
New York State Board of Nursing, Commission
on Collegiate Nursing Education (CCNE),
National League for Nursing Accrediting
Commission (NLNAC)

Degrees conferred
BS (w/major in nursing)

Minimum degree required
High school diploma or GED

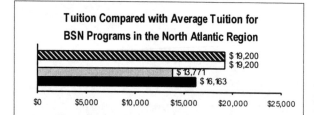

Tuition Compared with Average Tuition for
BSN Programs in the North Atlantic Region

$19,200
$19,200
$13,771
$16,163

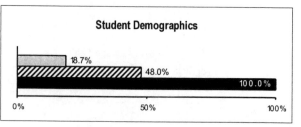

Student Demographics

18.7%
48.0%
100.0%

Key | Tuition Chart | ⧅ Program - in state   ☐ Program - out of state   ▨ Average - in state   ▪ Average - out of state

New York

UNIVERSITY OF ROCHESTER | *Useful Facts**

601 Elmwood Ave, Box SON
Rochester, NY 14627
(585) 275-8902
Patricia Chiverton, EdD, RN

www.urmc.rochester.edu/son

Acceptance rate	34.3%	**Tuition**		**Student Demographics**	
		In state	$26,900	Female	82.5%
		Out of state	$26,900	Under age 25	17.0%
		Enrollments	130	Minority	17.0%
		Graduations	53	Part-time	15.8%

Accreditation
New York State Board of Nursing, National
League for Nursing Accrediting Commission
(NLNAC)

Degrees conferred
Baccalaureate

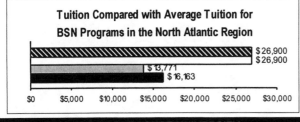

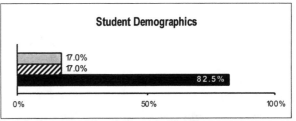

UTICA COLLEGE OF SYRACUSE UNIVERSITY | *Useful Facts*

1600 Burrstone Rd
Utica, NY 13502
(315) 792-3180
Mary Maroney, PhD, RN

www.utica.edu/academic/hhs/nursing/homepage/nursing.htm

Acceptance rate	87.9%	**Tuition**		**Student Demographics**	
Faculty-student ratio	1: 13	In state	$22,030	Female	87.8%
Faculty Full time	7	Out of state	$22,030	Under age 25	82.6%
Part time	8	**Enrollments**	141	Minority	35.6%
		Graduations	15	Part-time	0.0%

Accreditation
New York State Board of Nursing, National
League for Nursing Accrediting Commission
(NLNAC)

Degrees conferred
Baccalaureate degree

Minimum degree required
High school diploma or GED

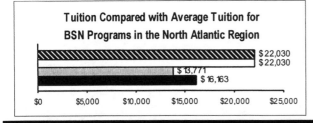

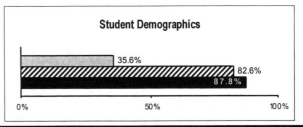

WAGNER COLLEGE | *Useful Facts*

631 Howard Ave
Staten Island, NY 10301
(718) 390-3445
Lauren O'Hare, EdD, RN

www.wagner.edu

Acceptance rate	85.7%	**Tuition**		**Student Demographics**	
Faculty-student ratio	1: 10	In state	$25,350	Female	91.7%
Faculty Full time	7	Out of state	$25,350	Under age 25	90.2%
Part time	17	**Enrollments**	152	Minority	14.4%
		Graduations	24	Part-time	1.5%

Accreditation
New York State Board of Nursing, National
League for Nursing Accrediting Commission
(NLNAC)

Degrees conferred
Baccalaureate degree, Second Degree
Accelerated

Minimum degree required
High school diploma or GED

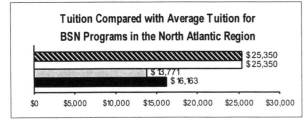

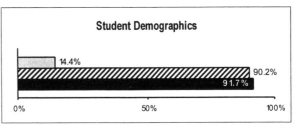

Demographics Chart	■ Female ▨ Under age 25 ☐ Minority	Distance Learning	¹The tuition reported for this program may be not be annualized. *Data reported between 2001 and 2004.

New York

YORK COLLEGE

Sci Bldg RM 110, 94-20 Guy R Brewer Blvd
Jamaica, NY 11451
(718) 262-2054
Reuphenia James, RN, EdD

www.york.cuny.edu

Accreditation
New York State Board of Nursing, National
League for Nursing Accrediting Commission
(NLNAC)

Degrees conferred
Baccalaureate

North Carolina

BARTON COLLEGE

PO Box 5000
Wilson, NC 27893
(252) 399-6401
Kim Larson, MPH, RN

www.barton.edu/nursing

Accreditation
North Carolina Board of Nursing, National
League for Nursing Accrediting Commission
(NLNAC)

*At the request of this nursing school, publication has been witheld.
Please contact the school directly for more information.*

DUKE UNIVERSITY

Box 3322 Medical Center
Durham, NC 27710
(919) 684-3786
Mary Champagne, PhD, RN

www.nursing.duke.edu

Accreditation
North Carolina Board of Nursing

Degrees conferred
Baccalaureate

EAST CAROLINA UNIVERSITY   *Useful Facts*

133 Rivers Building
Greenville, NC 27858
(252) 328-6099
Phyllis Horns, DSN, RN, FAAN

www.ecu.edu/nursing

Accreditation
North Carolina Board of Nursing, National
League for Nursing Accrediting Commission
(NLNAC)

Acceptance rate	41.7%	
Faculty-student ratio	1 : 7	
Faculty	Full time	64
	Part time	17

Degrees conferred
Baccalaureate degree

Tuition			Student Demographics	
In state	$2,135		Female	90.3%
Out of state	$12,649		Under age 25	82.7%
Enrollments	500		Minority	15.4%
Graduations	225		Part-time	3.8%

Minimum degree required
High school diploma or GED

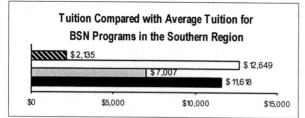

Tuition Compared with Average Tuition for BSN Programs in the Southern Region

$2,135
$12,649
$7,007
$11,618

$0 $5,000 $10,000 $15,000

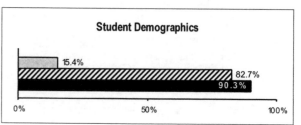

Student Demographics

15.4%
82.7%
90.3%

0%   50%   100%

Key | Tuition Chart | ⬛Program - in state ☐Program - out of state ☐Average - in state ■Average - out of state

North Carolina

FAYETTEVILLE TECHNICAL COMMUNITY COLLEGE

2201 Hull Road
Fayetteville, NC 28303
(910) 678-8482
Kathy Weeks, MSN, RN

www.faytechcc.edu

Faculty-student ratio		1: 8
Faculty	Full time	17
	Part time	14

Accreditation
North Carolina Board of Nursing

Degrees conferred
Baccalaureate

LENOIR-RHYNE COLLEGE   *Useful Facts*

PO Box 7292
Hickory, NC 28603
(828) 328-7282
Linda Reece, PhD, RN

www.lrc.edu/nur

Acceptance rate		89.9%
Faculty-student ratio		1: 14
Faculty	Full time	12
	Part time	12

Tuition	
In state	$18,130
Out of state	$18,130
Enrollments	248
Graduations	26

Student Demographics	
Female	92.3%
Under age 25	81.5%
Minority	8.5%
Part-time	6.0%

Accreditation
North Carolina Board of Nursing, Commission on Collegiate Nursing Education (CCNE), National League for Nursing Accrediting Commission (NLNAC)

Degrees conferred
Baccalaureate degree

Minimum degree required
Diploma

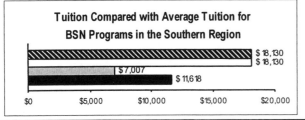

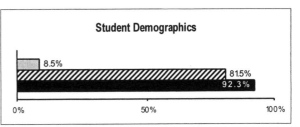

NORTH CAROLINA AGRICULTURAL & TECHNICAL UNIVERSITY   *Useful Facts*

1601 East Market Street - Noble Hall
Greensboro, NC 27411
(336) 334-7750
Patricia Price-Lea, PhD

www.ncat.edu/nursing/index.html

Acceptance rate		51.9%
Faculty-student ratio		1: 13
Faculty	Full time	24
	Part time	4

Tuition	
In state	$920
Out of state	$5,713
Enrollments	343
Graduations	46

Student Demographics	
Female	89.1%
Under age 25	80.9%
Minority	93.5%
Part-time	10.9%

Accreditation
North Carolina Board of Nursing, National League for Nursing Accrediting Commission (NLNAC)

Degrees conferred
Baccalaureate degree

Minimum degree required
850 SAT, 3.0 high school grade point average

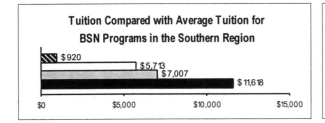

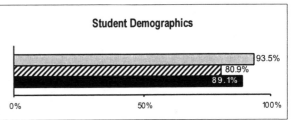

Demographics Chart	■ Female ▨ Under age 25 ☐ Minority	**Distance Learning**	[computer icon]	[1]The tuition reported for this program may be not be annualized. *Data reported between 2001 and 2004.

North Carolina

NORTH CAROLINA CENTRAL UNIVERSITY
Useful Facts*

PO Box 19798
Durham, NC 27707
(919) 530-5336
Betty Dennis, DrPH, MSN, RN

www.nccu.edu

Accreditation
North Carolina Board of Nursing, National
League for Nursing Accrediting Commission
(NLNAC)

Acceptance rate 31.3%

Degrees conferred
Baccalaureate

Tuition		Student Demographics	
In state	$3,032	Female	80.0%
Out of state	$11,954	Under age 25	15.0%
Enrollments	100	Minority	90.0%
Graduations	50	Part-time	0.0%

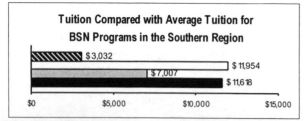

Tuition Compared with Average Tuition for BSN Programs in the Southern Region
$3,032
$11,954
$7,007
$11,618

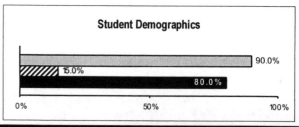

Student Demographics
90.0%
15.0%
80.0%

QUEENS UNIVERSITY OF CHARLOTTE
Useful Facts*

1900 Selwyn Avenue
Charlotte, NC 28274
(704) 337-2542
William Cody, PhD, RN

www.queens.edu

Accreditation
North Carolina Board of Nursing, Commission on
Collegiate Nursing Education (CCNE)

Faculty-student ratio 1: 7
Faculty Full time 6
Part time 7

Degrees conferred
Baccalaureate

Tuition		Student Demographics	
In state	$18,028	Female	96.6%
Out of state	$18,028	Under age 25	49.0%
Enrollments	67	Minority	36.8%
Graduations	22	Part-time	19.0%

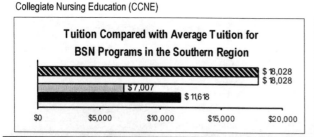

Tuition Compared with Average Tuition for BSN Programs in the Southern Region
$18,028
$18,028
$7,007
$11,618

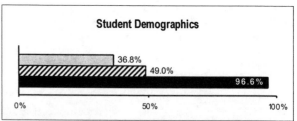

Student Demographics
36.8%
49.0%
96.6%

UNIVERSITY OF NORTH CAROLINA - CHAPEL HILL
Useful Facts*

Carrington Hall, Campus Box 7460
Chapel Hill, NC 27599
(919) 966-3731
Linda Cronenwett, PhD, RN, FAAN

www.unc.edu/dept/nursing

Accreditation
North Carolina Board of Nursing, Commission on
Collegiate Nursing Education (CCNE)

Acceptance rate 56.0%

Degrees conferred
Baccalaureate

Tuition		Student Demographics	
In state	$2,814	Female	93.1%
Out of state	$14,098		
Enrollments	307	Minority	13.2%
Graduations	181	Part-time	4.1%

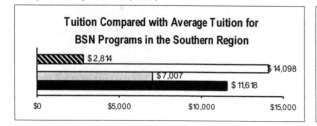

Tuition Compared with Average Tuition for BSN Programs in the Southern Region
$2,814
$14,098
$7,007
$11,618

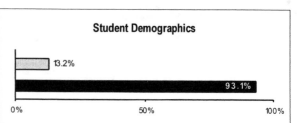

Student Demographics
13.2%
93.1%

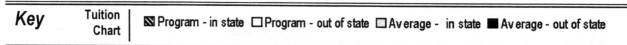

Key Tuition Chart ⬛ Program - in state ☐ Program - out of state ☐ Average - in state ■ Average - out of state

North Carolina

UNIVERSITY OF NORTH CAROLINA - CHARLOTTE | Useful Facts

9201 University City Blvd
Charlotte, NC 28233
(704) 687-6130
Pamala Larsen, PhD, RN, CRRN

www.health.uncc.edu

Acceptance rate		41.5%
Faculty-student ratio		1: 5
Faculty	Full time	29
	Part time	23

Tuition	
In state	$3,480
Out of state	$13,900
Enrollments	220
Graduations	112

Student Demographics	
Female	95.5%
Under age 25	80.6%
Minority	15.3%
Part-time	3.2%

Accreditation
North Carolina Board of Nursing, Commission on Collegiate Nursing Education (CCNE)

Degrees conferred
Baccalaureate degree

Minimum degree required
High school diploma or GED

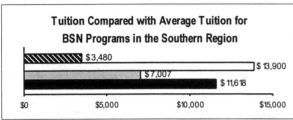
Tuition Compared with Average Tuition for BSN Programs in the Southern Region

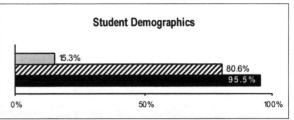
Student Demographics

UNIVERSITY OF NORTH CAROLINA - GREENSBORO | Useful Facts

PO Box 26170
Greensboro, NC 27402
(336) 334-5177
Lynne Pearcey, PhD, RN, CNAA

www.uncg.edu/nur

Acceptance rate		39.3%
Faculty-student ratio		1: 22
Faculty	Full time	48
	Part time	9

Tuition	
In state	$2,028
Out of state	$13,296
Enrollments	1132
Graduations	151

Student Demographics	
Female	91.9%
Under age 25	87.0%
Minority	29.4%
Part-time	8.5%

Accreditation
North Carolina Board of Nursing, Commission on Collegiate Nursing Education (CCNE), National League for Nursing Accrediting Commission (NLNAC)

Degrees conferred
Master's with joint degree, PhD, Baccalaureate degree, MSN

Minimum degree required
High school diploma or GED

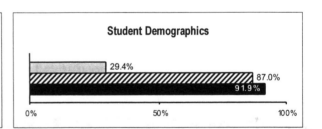
Tuition Compared with Average Tuition for BSN Programs in the Southern Region

Student Demographics

UNIVERSITY OF NORTH CAROLINA - WILMINGTON | Useful Facts

601 S College Road
Wilmington, NC 28403
(910) 962-7410
Virginia Adams, PhD, RN

www.uncw.edu/son

Acceptance rate		40.2%
Faculty-student ratio		1: 6
Faculty	Full time	22
	Part time	7

Tuition	
In state	$1,928
Out of state	$11,863
Enrollments	163
Graduations	60

Student Demographics	
Female	94.2%
Under age 25	87.1%
Minority	5.8%
Part-time	0.0%

Accreditation
North Carolina Board of Nursing, Commission on Collegiate Nursing Education (CCNE), National League for Nursing Accrediting Commission (NLNAC)

Degrees conferred
Baccalaureate degree

Minimum degree required
High school diploma or GED

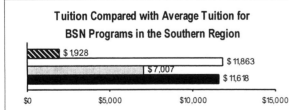
Tuition Compared with Average Tuition for BSN Programs in the Southern Region

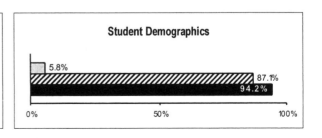
Student Demographics

Demographics Chart	■ Female ▨ Under age 25 ▢ Minority	Distance Learning	†The tuition reported for this program may be not be annualized. *Data reported between 2001 and 2004.

North Carolina

WESTERN CAROLINA UNIVERSITY — *Useful Facts**

209 Moore Hall
Cullowhee, NC 28723
(828) 227-7467
Vincient Hall, PhD, RN

www.wcu.edu

Accreditation
North Carolina Board of Nursing

Degrees conferred
Baccalaureate

Tuition		Student Demographics	
In state	$918	Female	90.8%
Out of state	$8,188		
Enrollments	157	Minority	6.7%
		Part-time	2.3%

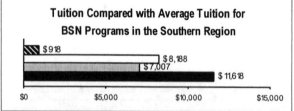

Tuition Compared with Average Tuition for BSN Programs in the Southern Region
$918 / $8,188 / $7,007 / $11,618

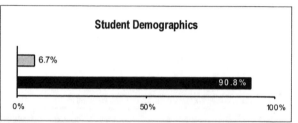

Student Demographics
6.7% / 90.8%

WINSTON-SALEM STATE UNIVERSITY — *Useful Facts**

Campus Box 19523
Winston-Salem, NC 27110
(336) 750-2307
Joanette McClain, PhD, RN

www.wssu.edu

Accreditation
North Carolina Board of Nursing, Commission on Collegiate Nursing Education (CCNE)

Degrees conferred
Baccalaureate

			Tuition		Student Demographics	
Faculty-student ratio		1: 13	In state	$1,774	Female	88.2%
Faculty	Full time	23	Out of state	$8,192	Under age 25	26.8%
	Part time	24	Enrollments	460	Minority	63.8%
			Graduations	191	Part-time	0.0%

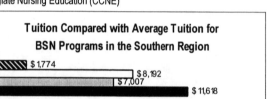

Tuition Compared with Average Tuition for BSN Programs in the Southern Region
$1,774 / $8,192 / $7,007 / $11,618

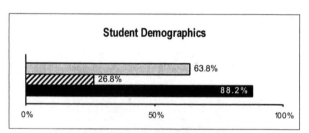

Student Demographics
63.8% / 26.8% / 88.2%

North Dakota

DICKINSON STATE UNIVERSITY — *Useful Facts*

291 Campus Dr
Dickinson, ND 58601
(701) 483-2133
Mary Anne Marsh, PhD, RN

www.dsu.nodak.edu/catalog/nursing

Accreditation
North Dakota Board of Nursing, National League for Nursing Accrediting Commission (NLNAC)

Degrees conferred
Baccalaureate degree

Minimum degree required
A/ASPN or ADRN

			Tuition		Student Demographics	
Acceptance rate		86.8%	In state	$3,329	Female	93.5%
Faculty-student ratio		1: 4	Out of state	$8,888	Under age 25	71.7%
Faculty	Full time	8	Enrollments	46	Minority	6.5%
	Part time	6	Graduations	21	Part-time	13.0%

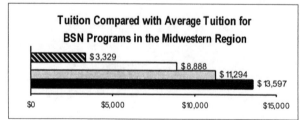

Tuition Compared with Average Tuition for BSN Programs in the Midwestern Region
$3,329 / $8,888 / $11,294 / $13,597

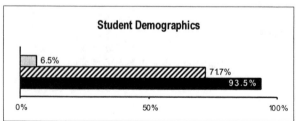

Student Demographics
6.5% / 71.7% / 93.5%

Key — Tuition Chart

▪ Program - in state □ Program - out of state □ Average - in state ■ Average - out of state

North Dakota

JAMESTOWN COLLEGE
Useful Facts

6010 College Lane
Jamestown, ND 58405
(701) 252-3467
Jacqueline Mangnall, PhD(c), RN

www.jc.edu

Acceptance rate		69.2%
Faculty-student ratio		1: 8
Faculty	Full time	5
	Part time	7

Tuition
In state $10,000
Out of state $10,000
Enrollments 71
Graduations 26

Student Demographics
Female 94.4%
Under age 25 76.1%
Part-time 0.0%

Accreditation
North Dakota Board of Nursing, National League
for Nursing Accrediting Commission (NLNAC)

Degrees conferred
Baccalaureate degree

Minimum degree required
High school diploma or GED

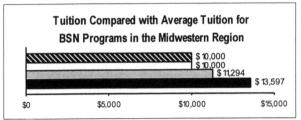

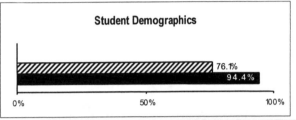

MEDCENTER ONE COLLEGE OF NURSING
Useful Facts

512 N 7th Street
Bismarck, ND 58501
(701) 323-6734
Karen Latham, PhD, RN

www.medcenterone.com/college/nursing.htm

Acceptance rate		50.4%
Faculty-student ratio		1: 8
Faculty	Full time	11
	Part time	2

Tuition
In state $8,400
Out of state $8,400
Enrollments 93
Graduations 39

Student Demographics
Female 84.8%
Under age 25 60.9%
Minority 5.4%
Part-time 4.3%

Accreditation
North Dakota Board of Nursing, Commission on
Collegiate Nursing Education (CCNE)

Degrees conferred
Baccalaureate degree

Minimum degree required
High school diploma or GED

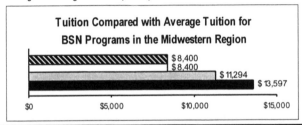

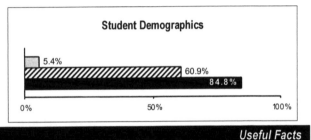

MINOT STATE UNIVERSITY
Useful Facts

500 University Ave West
Minot, ND 58707
(701) 858-3101
Elizabeth Pross, RN, PhD

www.minotstateu.edu/nursing

Acceptance rate		85.7%
Faculty-student ratio		1: 3
Faculty	Full time	30
	Part time	16

Tuition
In state $3,160
Out of state $8,437
Enrollments 109
Graduations 34

Student Demographics
Female 91.4%
Under age 25 59.0%
Minority 12.1%
Part-time 13.3%

Accreditation
North Dakota Board of Nursing, National League
for Nursing Accrediting Commission (NLNAC)

Degrees conferred
Baccalaureate degree

Minimum degree required
High school diploma or GED

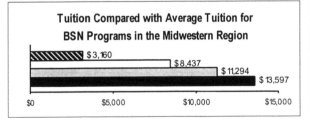

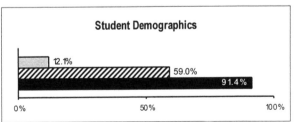

Demographics Chart	■Female ▨Under age 25 ☐Minority	Distance Learning	¹The tuition reported for this program may be not be annualized. *Data reported between 2001 and 2004.

North Dakota

UNIVERSITY OF MARY

7500 University Dr
Bismarck, ND 58504
(701) 255-7500
Betty Rambur, DNSc, RN

www.umary.edu/nursing

Accreditation
North Dakota Board of Nursing, Commission on
Collegiate Nursing Education (CCNE)

At the request of this nursing school, publication has been witheld.
Please contact the school directly for more information.

UNIVERSITY OF NORTH DAKOTA

Useful Facts*

PO Box 9025
Grand Forks, ND 58202
(701) 777-4555
Elizabeth Nichols, RN, DNS, FAAN

www.und.nodak.edu/dept/nursing

Accreditation
North Dakota Board of Nursing

Degrees conferred
Baccalaureate

Acceptance rate	33.8%

Tuition		Student Demographics	
In state	$2,754	Female	84.9%
Out of state	$7,354	Under age 25	75.0%
Enrollments	266	Minority	9.0%
Graduations	82	Part-time	13.2%

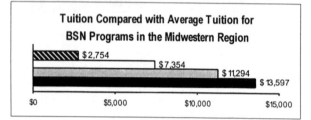

Tuition Compared with Average Tuition for BSN Programs in the Midwestern Region

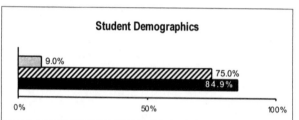

Student Demographics

Ohio

CAPITAL UNIVERSITY

Useful Facts*

2199 East Main Street
Columbus, OH 43209
(614) 236-6703
Doris Edwards, EdD, RN

www.capital.edu

Accreditation
Ohio Board of Nursing

Degrees conferred
Baccalaureate

Acceptance rate	80.5%

Tuition	
In state	$16,000
Out of state	$16,000
Enrollments	237
Graduations	83

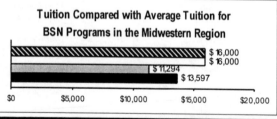

Tuition Compared with Average Tuition for BSN Programs in the Midwestern Region

CASE WESTERN RESERVE UNIVERSITY

10900 Euclid Avenue
Cleveland, OH 44106
(216) 368-2545
May Wykle, PhD, RN, FAAN, FGSA

fpb.case.edu

Accreditation
Ohio Board of Nursing, National League for
Nursing Accrediting Commission (NLNAC)

At the request of this nursing school, publication has been witheld.
Please contact the school directly for more information.

Key | Tuition Chart | ▨ Program - in state ☐ Program - out of state ☐ Average - in state ■ Average - out of state

Ohio

CEDARVILLE UNIVERSITY *Useful Facts**

251 North Main Street
Cedarville, OH 45314
(937) 766-7716
Irene Alyn, PhD, RN

www.cedarville.edu

Acceptance rate	81.8%

Tuition

In state	$11,424
Out of state	$11,424
Enrollments	235
Graduations	55

Student Demographics

Female	94.0%
Under age 25	98.0%
Minority	6.4%
Part-time	0.0%

Accreditation
Ohio Board of Nursing

Degrees conferred
Baccalaureate

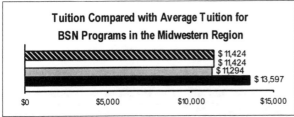

Tuition Compared with Average Tuition for BSN Programs in the Midwestern Region: $11,424 / $11,424 / $11,294 / $13,597

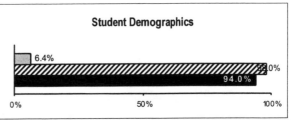

Student Demographics: 6.4% / 98.0% / 94.0%

CLEVELAND STATE UNIVERSITY *Useful Facts**

2121 Euclid Avenue Rt 915
Cleveland, OH 44115
(216) 523-7237
Noreen Frisch, RN, PhD, FAAN

www.csuohio.edu/nursing

Acceptance rate	36.7%
Faculty-student ratio	1: 9

Faculty	Full time	22
	Part time	6

Tuition

In state	$6,792
Out of state	$9,216
Enrollments	218
Graduations	100

Student Demographics

Female	89.4%
Under age 25	35.0%
Minority	20.4%
Part-time	1.1%

Accreditation
Ohio Board of Nursing, National League for
Nursing Accrediting Commission (NLNAC)

Degrees conferred
Baccalaureate

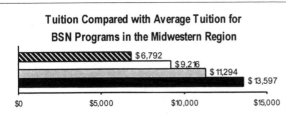

Tuition Compared with Average Tuition for BSN Programs in the Midwestern Region: $6,792 / $9,216 / $11,294 / $13,597

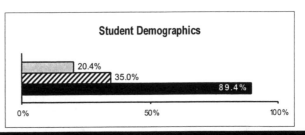

Student Demographics: 20.4% / 35.0% / 89.4%

COLLEGE OF MOUNT ST JOSEPH *Useful Facts*

5701 Delhi Road
Cincinnati, OH 45233
(513) 244-4511
Darla Vale, DNSc, RN, CCRN

www.mju.edu

Acceptance rate	95.3%
Faculty-student ratio	1: 19

Faculty	Full time	11
	Part time	20

Tuition

In state	$18,400
Out of state	$18,400
Enrollments	394
Graduations	59

Student Demographics

Female	89.7%
Under age 25	56.1%
Minority	14.5%
Part-time	0.0%

Minimum degree required
High school diploma or GED

Accreditation
Ohio Board of Nursing, National League for
Nursing Accrediting Commission (NLNAC)

Degrees conferred
Baccalaureate degree

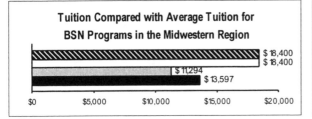

Tuition Compared with Average Tuition for BSN Programs in the Midwestern Region: $18,400 / $18,400 / $11,294 / $13,597

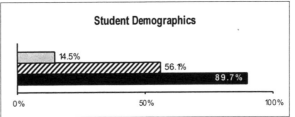

Student Demographics: 14.5% / 56.1% / 89.7%

Demographics Chart	■ Female ▨ Under age 25 ☐ Minority	Distance Learning	¹The tuition reported for this program may be not be annualized. *Data reported between 2001 and 2004.

Ohio

FRANCISCAN UNIVERSITY - STEUBENVILLE

1235 University Boulevard
Steubenville, OH 43952
(740) 283-6324
Carolyn Miller, DrPH, MPH, BSN, RN

www.franciscan.edu

Accreditation
Ohio Board of Nursing, National League for Nursing Accrediting Commission (NLNAC)

Acceptance rate		80.0%
Faculty-student ratio		1: 13
Faculty	Full time	8
	Part time	10

Degrees conferred
Baccalaureate degree

Tuition	
In state	$16,070
Out of state	$16,070
Enrollments	166
Graduations	33

Minimum degree required
High school diploma or GED

Student Demographics	
Female	93.2%
Under age 25	95.7%
Minority	5.6%
Part-time	0.0%

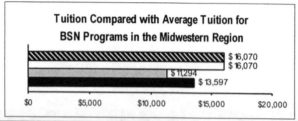

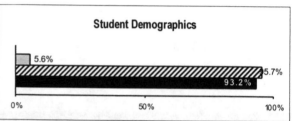

KENT STATE UNIVERSITY

113 Henderson Hall
Kent, OH 44242
(330) 672-3777
Julie Johnson, PhD, RN, FAAN

www.kent.edu/nursing

Accreditation
Ohio Board of Nursing, Commission on Collegiate Nursing Education (CCNE)

At the request of this nursing school, publication has been withheld. Please contact the school directly for more information.

LOURDES COLLEGE

6832 Convent Boulevard
Sylvania, OH 43560
(419) 824-3794
Elizabeth Schriner, PhD, RN, BC

lourdes.edu

Accreditation
Ohio Board of Nursing, Commission on Collegiate Nursing Education (CCNE)

Acceptance rate		67.3%
Faculty-student ratio		1: 38
Faculty	Full time	13
	Part time	3

Degrees conferred
Baccalaureate degree

Tuition	
In state	$8,856
Out of state	$8,856
Enrollments	554
Graduations	43

Minimum degree required
High school diploma or GED

Student Demographics	
Female	92.5%
Under age 25	73.7%
Minority	13.4%
Part-time	30.0%

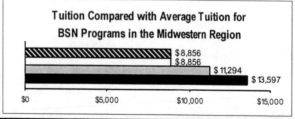

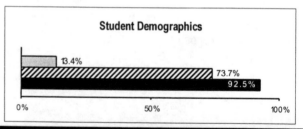

MALONE COLLEGE

515 25th St, NW
Canton, OH 44709
(330) 471-8366
Loretta Reinhart, PhD, MSN, RN

www.malone.edu

Accreditation
Ohio Board of Nursing

At the request of this nursing school, publication has been witheld. Please contact the school directly for more information.

Key | Tuition Chart | ▨ Program - in state ☐ Program - out of state ☐ Average - in state ■ Average - out of state

Ohio

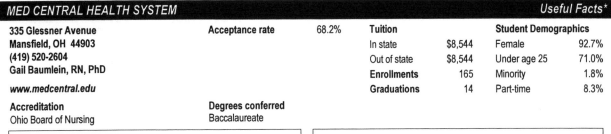

MED CENTRAL HEALTH SYSTEM — *Useful Facts**

335 Glessner Avenue
Mansfield, OH 44903
(419) 520-2604
Gail Baumlein, RN, PhD

www.medcentral.edu

Accreditation
Ohio Board of Nursing

Degrees conferred
Baccalaureate

Acceptance rate	68.2%

Tuition	
In state	$8,544
Out of state	$8,544
Enrollments	165
Graduations	14

Student Demographics	
Female	92.7%
Under age 25	71.0%
Minority	1.8%
Part-time	8.3%

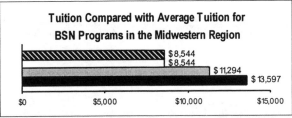
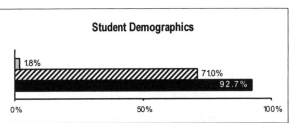

MEDICAL UNIVERSITY OF OHIO AT TOLEDO — *Useful Facts**

3015 Arlington Avenue
Toledo, OH 43614
(419) 383-5858
Jeri Milstead, PhD, RN, FAAN, CNAA, CNS

www.meduohio.edu

Accreditation
Ohio Board of Nursing, Commission on
Collegiate Nursing Education (CCNE)

Degrees conferred
Baccalaureate degree, Consortium w/2
other coll

Acceptance rate	82.5%
Faculty-student ratio	1: 8
Faculty Full time	50
Part time	5

Tuition	
In state	$6,430
Out of state	$15,242
Enrollments	415
Graduations	162

Student Demographics	
Female	88.6%
Under age 25	71.6%
Minority	6.4%
Part-time	0.9%

Minimum degree required
High school diploma or GED

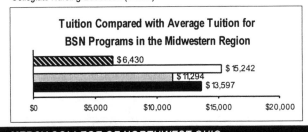
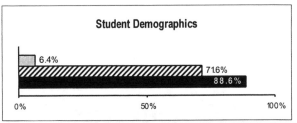

MERCY COLLEGE OF NORTHWEST OHIO — *Useful Facts*

2221 Madison Ave
Toledo, OH 43624
(419) 251-1583
Maria Nowicki, PhD, RN

www.mercycollege.edu

Accreditation
Ohio Board of Nursing, Commission on
Collegiate Nursing Education (CCNE)

Degrees conferred
Baccalaureate degree

Acceptance rate	81.9%
Faculty-student ratio	1: 37
Faculty Full time	13
Part time	0

Tuition	
In state	$7,650
Out of state	$7,650
Enrollments	176
Graduations	26

Student Demographics	
Female	93.2%
Under age 25	83.8%
Minority	8.3%
Part-time	14.2%

Minimum degree required
High school diploma or GED

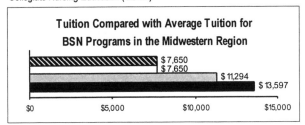
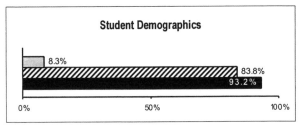

Demographics Chart	■ Female ▨ Under age 25 ☐ Minority	Distance Learning	†The tuition reported for this program may be not be annualized. *Data reported between 2001 and 2004.

Ohio

MOUNT CARMEL COLLEGE OF NURSING

127 S Davis Ave
Columbus, OH 43222
(614) 234-5032
Ann Schiele, PhD, RN

www.mccn.edu

Accreditation
Ohio Board of Nursing, National League for
Nursing Accrediting Commission (NLNAC)

Degrees conferred
Baccalaureate

OTTERBEIN COLLEGE

One Otterbein College
Westerville, OH 43081
(614) 823-1614
Judy Strayer, PhD, RN, CNS

www.otterbein.edu

Accreditation
Ohio Board of Nursing, Commission on
Collegiate Nursing Education (CCNE), National
League for Nursing Accrediting Commission
(NLNAC)

At the request of this nursing school, publication has been witheld.
Please contact the school directly for more information.

THE OHIO STATE UNIVERSITY
*Useful Facts**

1585 Neil Avenue
Columbus, OH 43210
(614) 292-8900
Carole Anderson, PhD, RN, FAAN

www.con.ohio-state.edu

Accreditation
Ohio Board of Nursing

Degrees conferred
Baccalaureate

Acceptance rate	51.6%

Tuition	
In state	$4,137
Out of state	$12,087
Enrollments	407
Graduations	137

Student Demographics	
Under age 25	82.0%

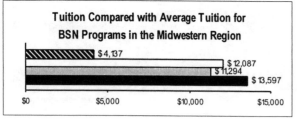

Tuition Compared with Average Tuition for
BSN Programs in the Midwestern Region

$4,137
$12,087
$11,294
$13,597

$0 $5,000 $10,000 $15,000

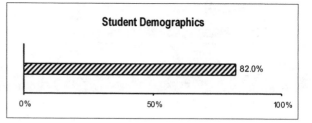

Student Demographics

82.0%

0% 50% 100%

Key | Tuition Chart | ▨ Program - in state ☐ Program - out of state ☐ Average - in state ■ Average - out of state

Ohio

THE UNIVERSITY OF AKRON — *Useful Facts*

209 Carroll Street
Akron, OH 44325
(330) 972-7552
Cynthia Capers, PhD, RN

www3.uakron.edu/nursing/index.html

Accreditation
Ohio Board of Nursing, Commission on
Collegiate Nursing Education (CCNE), National
League for Nursing Accrediting Commission
(NLNAC)

Acceptance rate		49.0%
Faculty-student ratio		1 : 8
Faculty	Full time	55
	Part time	23

Degrees conferred
MSN, PhD, Baccalaureate degree

Tuition	
In state	$7,549
Out of state	$16,274
Enrollments	545
Graduations	160

Minimum degree required
High school diploma or GED

Student Demographics	
Female	89.0%
Under age 25	60.9%
Minority	9.4%
Part-time	6.2%

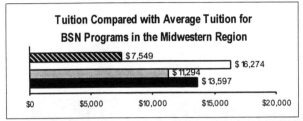

Tuition Compared with Average Tuition for BSN Programs in the Midwestern Region
$7,549
$16,274
$11,294
$13,597

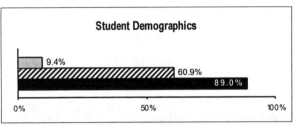

Student Demographics
9.4%
60.9%
89.0%

UNIVERSITY OF CINCINNATI — *Useful Facts**

PO Box 210038
Cincinnati, OH 45221-0038
(513) 558-5330
Andrea Lindell, RN, DNSc

www.nursing.uc.edu

Accreditation
Ohio Board of Nursing, Commission on
Collegiate Nursing Education (CCNE)

Acceptance rate 76.8%

Degrees conferred
Baccalaureate

Tuition	
In state	$6,336
Out of state	$17,943
Enrollments	388
Graduations	150

Student Demographics	
Female	92.7%
Minority	18.6%
Part-time	10.6%

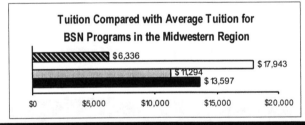

Tuition Compared with Average Tuition for BSN Programs in the Midwestern Region
$6,336
$17,943
$11,294
$13,597

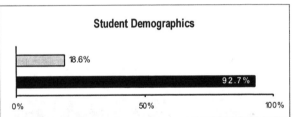

Student Demographics
18.6%
92.7%

URSULINE COLLEGE

2550 Lander Road
Cleveland, OH 44124
(440) 646-8166
Carol Waggoner, PhD

www.ursuline.edu

Accreditation
Ohio Board of Nursing

Degrees conferred
Baccalaureate

Demographics Chart	■ Female ▨ Under age 25 ▢ Minority	**Distance Learning**	¹The tuition reported for this program may be not be annualized. *Data reported between 2001 and 2004.

Ohio

WALSH UNIVERSITY

Useful Facts

Aultman Sci Ctr, 2020 E Maple St
North Canton, OH 44720
(330) 490-7250
Janis Campbell, PhD, RN

www.walsh.edu

Acceptance rate		100.0%
Faculty-student ratio		1: 28
Faculty	Full time	7
	Part time	5

Tuition	
In state	$16,000
Out of state	$16,000
Enrollments	263
Graduations	33

Student Demographics	
Female	91.3%
Under age 25	83.3%
Minority	4.9%
Part-time	16.3%

Accreditation
Ohio Board of Nursing, National League for
Nursing Accrediting Commission (NLNAC)

Degrees conferred
Baccalaureate degree

Minimum degree required
High school diploma or GED

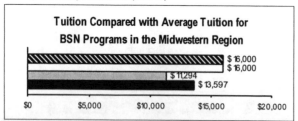

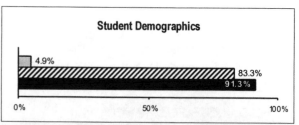

WRIGHT STATE UNIVERSITY

Useful Facts

3640 Colonel Glenn Highway
Dayton, OH 45435
(937) 775-3133
Patricia Martin, PhD, RN

www.nursing.wright.edu

Acceptance rate		72.8%
Faculty-student ratio		1: 10
Faculty	Full time	42
	Part time	27

Tuition	
In state	$9,152
Out of state	$17,652
Enrollments	563
Graduations	172

Student Demographics	
Female	88.0%
Under age 25	82.1%
Minority	12.4%
Part-time	8.1%

Accreditation
Ohio Board of Nursing, Commission on
Collegiate Nursing Education (CCNE)

Degrees conferred
Baccalaureate degree

Minimum degree required
High school diploma or GED

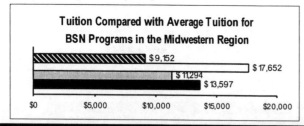

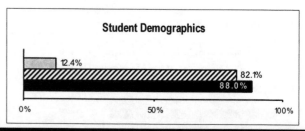

XAVIER UNIVERSITY

3800 Victory Parkway
Cincinnati, OH 45207
(513) 745-3815
Susan Schmidt, PhD, RN, COHN-S, CNS

www.xu.edu

Accreditation
Ohio Board of Nursing

Degrees conferred
Baccalaureate

Key | Tuition Chart | ▨ Program - in state ☐ Program - out of state ▨ Average - in state ■ Average - out of state

Ohio

YOUNGSTOWN STATE UNIVERSITY — *Useful Facts*

One University Plaza
Youngstown, OH 44555
(330) 941-3292
Patricia Hoyson, PhD, RNCNS

www.ysu.edu

Acceptance rate		82.8%
Faculty-student ratio		1: 10
Faculty	Full time	21
	Part time	15

Tuition
In state $4,999
Out of state $10,207
Enrollments 298
Graduations 58

Student Demographics
Female 80.7%
Under age 25 60.2%
Minority 11.5%
Part-time 0.0%

Accreditation
Ohio Board of Nursing, National League for Nursing Accrediting Commission (NLNAC)

Degrees conferred
Baccalaureate degree

Minimum degree required
High school diploma or GED

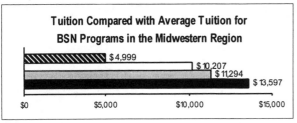

Tuition Compared with Average Tuition for BSN Programs in the Midwestern Region

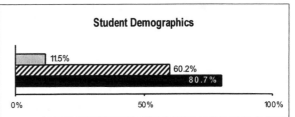

Student Demographics

Oklahoma

EAST CENTRAL UNIVERSITY — *Useful Facts*

1100 E 14th St
Ada, OK 74820
(580) 310-5429
Joseph Catalano, PhD, RN

www.ecok.edu/dept/nursing

Acceptance rate		50.0%
Faculty-student ratio		1: 7
Faculty	Full time	11
	Part time	17

Tuition
In state $3,208
Out of state $7,841
Enrollments 133
Graduations 49

Student Demographics
Female 87.2%
Under age 25 48.1%
Minority 25.8%
Part-time 0.0%

Accreditation
Oklahoma Board of Nursing, National League for Nursing Accrediting Commission (NLNAC)

Degrees conferred
Baccalaureate degree

Minimum degree required
None

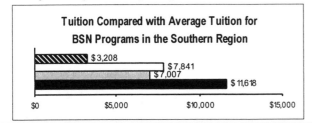

Tuition Compared with Average Tuition for BSN Programs in the Southern Region

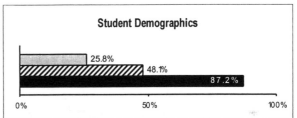

Student Demographics

LANGSTON UNIVERSITY — *Useful Facts*

PO Box 1500
Langston, OK 73050
(405) 466-3411
Carolyn Kornegay, RN, PhD

www.lunet.edu

Acceptance rate		41.7%
Faculty-student ratio		1: 8
Faculty	Full time	15
	Part time	9

Tuition
In state $2,085
Out of state $6,510
Enrollments 154
Graduations 44

Student Demographics
Female 90.3%
Under age 25 51.3%
Minority 35.8%
Part-time 27.9%

Accreditation
Oklahoma Board of Nursing, National League for Nursing Accrediting Commission (NLNAC)

Degrees conferred
Baccalaureate degree

Minimum degree required
High school diploma or GED

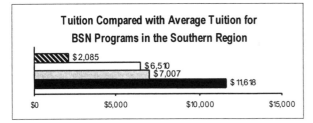

Tuition Compared with Average Tuition for BSN Programs in the Southern Region

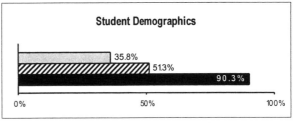

Student Demographics

Demographics Chart	■ Female ▨ Under age 25 ▢ Minority	Distance Learning 🖥	¹The tuition reported for this program may be not be annualized. *Data reported between 2001 and 2004.

Oklahoma

NORTHWESTERN OKLAHOMA STATE UNIVERSITY

709 Oklahoma Blvd, Carter Hall
Alva, OK 73717
(580) 327-8489
Frankie Buechner, RN, MN, EdD

www.nwosu.edu

Accreditation
Oklahoma Board of Nursing, National League for
Nursing Accrediting Commission (NLNAC)

At the request of this nursing school, publication has been witheld.
Please contact the school directly for more information.

OKLAHOMA BAPTIST UNIVERSITY

Useful Facts*

500 W University
Shawnee, OK 74804
(405) 878-2081
Lana Bolhouse, PhD, RN

www.okbu.edu

Accreditation
Oklahoma Board of Nursing, National League for
Nursing Accrediting Commission (NLNAC)

Acceptance rate	95.1%

Degrees conferred
Baccalaureate

Tuition		Student Demographics	
In state	$12,286	Female	92.1%
Out of state	$12,286	Under age 25	92.0%
Enrollments	139	Minority	17.4%
Graduations	23	Part-time	1.4%

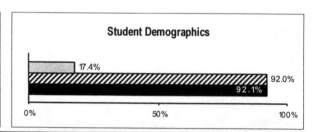

OKLAHOMA CITY UNIVERSITY

Useful Facts

2501 N Blackwelder
Oklahoma City, OK 73106
(405) 208-5900
Marvel Williamson, PhD, RN

www.okcu.edu\nursing

Accreditation
Oklahoma Board of Nursing, National League for
Nursing Accrediting Commission (NLNAC)

Acceptance rate		100.0%
Faculty-student ratio		1: 10
Faculty	Full time	10
	Part time	8

Degrees conferred
Master's with joint degree,
Baccalaureate degree, MSN

Minimum degree required
High school diploma or GED

Tuition		Student Demographics	
In state	$16,700	Female	91.3%
Out of state	$16,700	Under age 25	47.8%
Enrollments	140	Minority	33.0%
Graduations	44	Part-time	14.8%

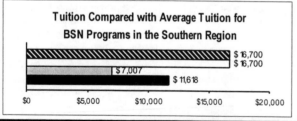
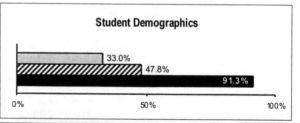

OKLAHOMA WESLEYAN COLLEGE

2201 Silver Lake Rd
Bartlesville, OK 74006
(918) 335-6218
Elizabeth von Buchwald, RN, MS, BSN

bwc.edu

Accreditation
Oklahoma Board of Nursing

At the request of this nursing school, publication has been witheld.
Please contact the school directly for more information.

Key   Tuition Chart | ▨ Program - in state   ☐ Program - out of state   ☐ Average - in state   ■ Average - out of state

Oklahoma

ORAL ROBERTS UNIVERSITY — *Useful Facts*

7777 South Lewis
Tulsa, OK 74171
(918) 495-6198
Kenda Jezek, PhD, RN

www.oru.edu

Accreditation
Oklahoma Board of Nursing, National League for Nursing Accrediting Commission (NLNAC)

Acceptance rate		100.0%
Faculty-student ratio		1:6
Faculty	Full time	7
	Part time	9

Degrees conferred
Baccalaureate degree

Tuition	
In state	$14,600
Out of state	$14,900
Enrollments	70
Graduations	24

Minimum degree required
High school diploma or GED

Student Demographics	
Female	95.7%
Under age 25	95.7%
Minority	15.7%
Part-time	0.0%

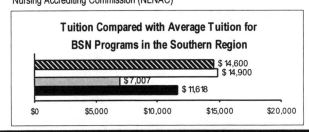

Tuition Compared with Average Tuition for BSN Programs in the Southern Region
$14,600
$14,900
$7,007
$11,618

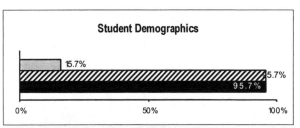

Student Demographics
15.7%
95.7%
95.7%

SOUTHERN NAZARENE UNIVERISTY — *Useful Facts**

6729 NW 39th Expressway
Bethany, OK 73008
(405) 491-6610
Carol Dorough, EdD (ABD), MSN, RN

www.snu.edu

Accreditation
Oklahoma Board of Nursing

Degrees conferred
Baccalaureate

Tuition	
In state	$8,850
Out of state	$8,850
Enrollments	81
Graduations	18

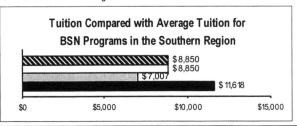

Tuition Compared with Average Tuition for BSN Programs in the Southern Region
$8,850
$8,850
$7,007
$11,618

SOUTHWESTERN OKLAHOMA STATE UNIVERSITY — *Useful Facts**

100 Campus Dr
Weatherford, OK 73096
(580) 774-3261
Patricia Meyer, PhD, RN

www.swosu.edu/depts/nursing/index.htm

Accreditation
Oklahoma Board of Nursing, National League for Nursing Accrediting Commission (NLNAC)

Acceptance rate	43.6%

Degrees conferred
Baccalaureate

Tuition[1]	
In state	$117
Out of state	$268
Enrollments	88
Graduations	29

Student Demographics	
Female	85.9%
Under age 25	62.0%
Minority	8.5%
Part-time	0.0%

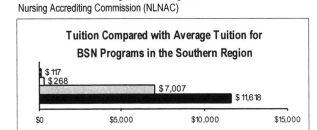

Tuition Compared with Average Tuition for BSN Programs in the Southern Region
$117
$268
$7,007
$11,618

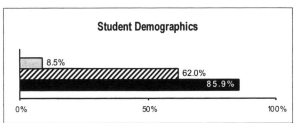

Student Demographics
8.5%
62.0%
85.9%

Demographics Chart	■ Female ▨ Under age 25 ☐ Minority	Distance Learning	[1]The tuition reported for this program may be not be annualized. *Data reported between 2001 and 2004.

Oklahoma

THE UNIVERSITY OF TULSA

600 S College Ave
Tulsa, OK 74104
(918) 631-3116
Susan Gaston, PhD, RN

At the request of this nursing school, publication has been witheld.
Please contact the school directly for more information.

www.cba.utulsa.edu/depts/nursing

Accreditation
Oklahoma Board of Nursing, National League for
Nursing Accrediting Commission (NLNAC)

UNIVERSITY OF CENTRAL OKLAHOMA   *Useful Facts*

100 N University Drive
Edmond, OK 73034
(405) 974-5176
Linda Steele, RN, PhD

nursing.ucok.edu

Accreditation
Oklahoma Board of Nursing, National League for
Nursing Accrediting Commission (NLNAC)

Acceptance rate	47.4%
Faculty-student ratio	1:9
Faculty Full time	13
Part time	10

Tuition¹	
In state	$142
Out of state	$319
Enrollments	162
Graduations	76

Student Demographics	
Female	94.3%
Under age 25	65.0%
Minority	12.9%
Part-time	10.2%

Degrees conferred
Baccalaureate degree

Minimum degree required
High school diploma or GED

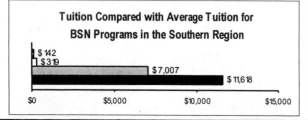

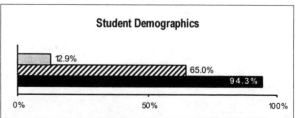

UNIVERSITY OF OKLAHOMA   *Useful Facts*

PO Box 26901
Oklahoma City, OK 73190
(405) 271-2420
Patricia Kenner, DNS, RNC, FAAN

www.ouhsc.nursing.edu

Accreditation
Oklahoma Board of Nursing, National League for
Nursing Accrediting Commission (NLNAC)

Acceptance rate	36.0%
Faculty-student ratio	1:7
Faculty Full time	73
Part time	19

Tuition	
In state	$2,862
Out of state	$10,755
Enrollments	542
Graduations	261

Student Demographics	
Female	86.6%
Under age 25	71.5%
Minority	28.2%
Part-time	2.0%

Degrees conferred
Baccalaureate degree

Minimum degree required
High school diploma or GED

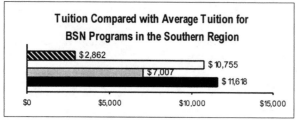

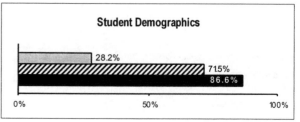

Key | Tuition Chart | ▨ Program - in state ☐ Program - out of state ▥ Average - in state ■ Average - out of state

Oregon

LINFIELD COLLEGE

2255 North West Northrup Avenue
Portland, OR 97210
(503) 413-7694
Brenda Smith, PhD, RN

www.linfield.edu

Acceptance rate	48.5%

Tuition

In state	$20,330
Out of state	$20,330
Enrollments	375
Graduations	111

Student Demographics

Female	93.3%
Under age 25	38.0%
Minority	11.6%
Part-time	2.3%

Accreditation
Oregon State Board of Nursing

Degrees conferred
Baccalaureate

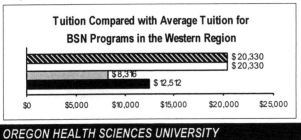

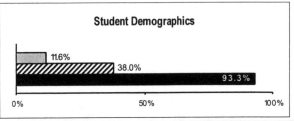

OREGON HEALTH SCIENCES UNIVERSITY

3455 South West US Veterans Hospital Rd
Portland, OR 97239
(503) 494-7444
Kathleen Potempa, RN, DNSc, FAAN

www.ohsu.edu/son

Acceptance rate	50.5%

Tuition

In state	$2,616
Out of state	$4,644
Enrollments	497
Graduations	198

Student Demographics

Female	92.1%
Minority	13.3%
Part-time	3.0%

Accreditation
Oregon State Board of Nursing

Degrees conferred
Baccalaureate

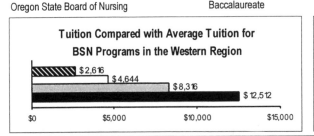

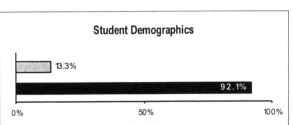

UNIVERSITY OF PORTLAND

5000 North Willamette Boulevard
Portland, OR 97203
(503) 943-7211
Terry Misener, RN, PhD, FAAN

www.up.edu

Acceptance rate	17.6%

Tuition

In state	$23,200
Out of state	$23,200
Enrollments	469
Graduations	99

Student Demographics

Female	91.9%
Under age 25	83.8%
Minority	16.7%
Part-time	2.8%

Accreditation
Oregon State Board of Nursing

Degrees conferred
Baccalaureate

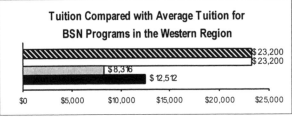

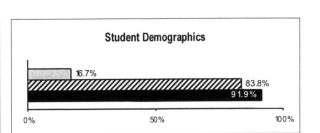

| Demographics Chart | ■ Female ▨ Under age 25 ▢ Minority | Distance Learning | †The tuition reported for this program may be not be annualized.
*Data reported between 2001 and 2004. |
|---|---|---|---|

Oregon

WALLA WALLA COLLEGE — *Useful Facts*

10345 South East Market Street
Portland, OR 97216
(503) 251-6115
Lucille Krull, RN, PhD, FNP

nursing.wwc.edu

Accreditation
Oregon State Board of Nursing, National League for Nursing Accrediting Commission (NLNAC)

Acceptance rate	69.4%
Faculty-student ratio	1:9
Faculty Full time	10
Part time	9

Degrees conferred
BS in Nursing (not BSN)

Tuition	
In state	$18,696
Out of state	$18,696
Enrollments	132
Graduations	45

Minimum degree required
High school diploma or GED

Student Demographics	
Female	82.6%
Under age 25	62.9%
Minority	13.6%
Part-time	0.8%

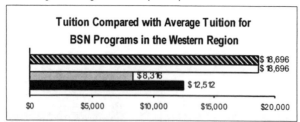

Tuition Compared with Average Tuition for BSN Programs in the Western Region

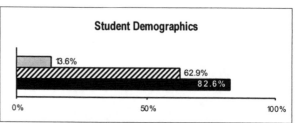

Student Demographics

Pennsylvania

ALVERNIA COLLEGE — *Useful Facts*

400 St Bernadine Street
Reading, PA 19607
(610) 796-8306
Karen Thacker, RN, MSN, CS

www.alvernia.edu

Accreditation
Pennsylvania State Board of Nursing, Commission on Collegiate Nursing Education (CCNE)

Acceptance rate	58.9%
Faculty-student ratio	1:23
Faculty Full time	9
Part time	7

Degrees conferred
Baccalaureate degree

Tuition	
In state	$18,900
Out of state	$18,900
Enrollments	285
Graduations	32

Minimum degree required
High school diploma or GED

Student Demographics	
Female	91.9%
Under age 25	61.3%
Minority	17.4%
Part-time	0.6%

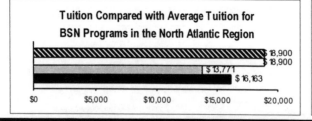

Tuition Compared with Average Tuition for BSN Programs in the North Atlantic Region

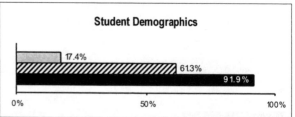

Student Demographics

BLOOMSBURG UNIVERSITY — *Useful Facts*

400 E Second Street, Room 3109, MCHS
Bloomsburg, PA 17815
(570) 389-4426
Mary Alichnie, PhD, RN

departments.bloomu.edu/nursing

Accreditation
Pennsylvania State Board of Nursing, Commission on Collegiate Nursing Education (CCNE)

Acceptance rate	28.7%
Faculty-student ratio	1:14
Faculty Full time	21
Part time	3

Degrees conferred
Baccalaureate degree

Tuition	
In state	$4,906
Out of state	$12,266
Enrollments	312
Graduations	44

Minimum degree required
High school diploma or GED

Student Demographics	
Female	92.5%
Under age 25	95.8%
Minority	3.7%
Part-time	5.6%

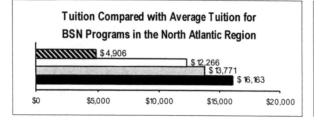

Tuition Compared with Average Tuition for BSN Programs in the North Atlantic Region

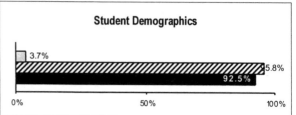

Student Demographics

Key Tuition Chart | ▨ Program - in state ☐ Program - out of state ☐ Average - in state ■ Average - out of state

Pennsylvania

CARLOW COLLEGE

3333 5th Ave
Pittsburgh, PA 15213
(412) 578-6115
Michele Upvall, RN, PhD, FNP

www.carlow.edu

Acceptance rate		100.0%
Faculty-student ratio		1: 14
Faculty	Full time	12
	Part time	17

Tuition	
In state	$15,806
Out of state	$15,806
Enrollments	280
Graduations	70

Student Demographics	
Female	99.0%
Under age 25	82.1%
Minority	15.7%
Part-time	0.0%

Accreditation
Pennsylvania State Board of Nursing,
Commission on Collegiate Nursing Education
(CCNE)

Degrees conferred
Baccalaureate degree

Minimum degree required
High school diploma or GED

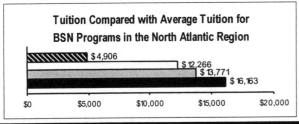

Tuition Compared with Average Tuition for BSN Programs in the North Atlantic Region — $4,906; $12,266; $13,771; $16,163

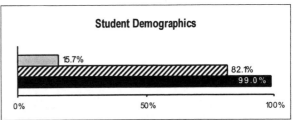

Student Demographics — 15.7%; 82.1%; 99.0%

CEDAR CREST COLLEGE

100 College Drive
Allentown, PA 18104
(610) 606-4606
Laurie Murray, RN, DSN

www.cedarcrest.edu.academic.nur

Acceptance rate		100.0%
Faculty-student ratio		1: 16
Faculty	Full time	14
	Part time	10

Tuition	
In state	$20,596
Out of state	$20,596
Enrollments	296
Graduations	51

Student Demographics	
Female	95.3%
Under age 25	21.5%
Minority	18.5%
Part-time	58.4%

Accreditation
Pennsylvania State Board of Nursing, National
League for Nursing Accrediting Commission
(NLNAC)

Degrees conferred
Baccalaureate degree

Minimum degree required
High school diploma or GED

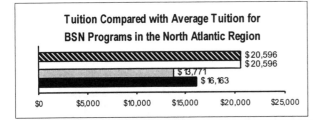

Tuition Compared with Average Tuition for BSN Programs in the North Atlantic Region — $20,596; $20,596; $13,771; $16,163

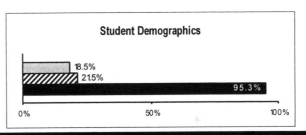

Student Demographics — 18.5%; 21.5%; 95.3%

COLLEGE MISERICORDIA

301 Lake Street
Dallas, PA 18612
(570) 674-6357
Donna Snelson, RN, MSN, CS

miseri.edu/academics/undergrad/healthweb/nurseweb/depthome.html

Acceptance rate	76.4%

Tuition	
In state	$17,850
Out of state	$17,850
Enrollments	340
Graduations	60

Student Demographics	
Female	89.6%
Under age 25	35.0%
Minority	2.7%
Part-time	34.6%

Accreditation
Pennsylvania State Board of Nursing,
Commission on Collegiate Nursing Education
(CCNE)

Degrees conferred
Baccalaureate

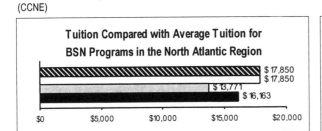

Tuition Compared with Average Tuition for BSN Programs in the North Atlantic Region — $17,850; $17,850; $13,771; $16,163

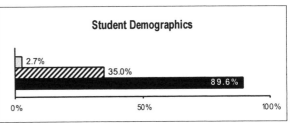

Student Demographics — 2.7%; 35.0%; 89.6%

Demographics Chart	■ Female ▨ Under age 25 ☐ Minority	Distance Learning	¹The tuition reported for this program may be not be annualized. *Data reported between 2001 and 2004.

Pennsylvania

DESALES UNIVERSITY

2755 Station Avenue
Center Valley, PA 18034
(610) 282-1100
Kerry Cheever, PhD, RN

www.desales.edu

Accreditation
Pennsylvania State Board of Nursing, National
League for Nursing Accrediting Commission
(NLNAC)

Acceptance rate	65.5%	
Faculty-student ratio	1: 12	
Faculty	Full time	9
	Part time	13

Tuition
In state	$20,000
Out of state	$20,000
Enrollments	185
Graduations	9

Degrees conferred
Baccalaureate degree

Minimum degree required
High school diploma or GED

Student Demographics
Female	85.6%
Under age 25	78.1%
Minority	7.5%
Part-time	8.8%

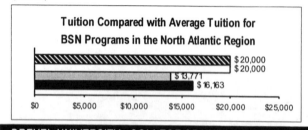

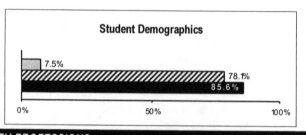

DREXEL UNIVERSITY - COLLEGE OF NURSING AND HEALTH PROFESSIONS

245 North 15th Street, Mail Stop 501
Philadelphia, PA 19104
(215) 762-4943
Gloria Donnelly, PhD, RN, FAAN

www.drexel.edu

Accreditation
Pennsylvania State Board of Nursing,
Commission on Collegiate Nursing Education
(CCNE), National League for Nursing Accrediting
Commission (NLNAC)

Acceptance rate	45.8%	
Faculty-student ratio	1: 26	
Faculty	Full time	32
	Part time	1

Tuition
In state	$22,700
Out of state	$22,700
Enrollments	846
Graduations	194

Degrees conferred
Baccalaureate degree

Minimum degree required
BA or BS in a non-nursing field

Student Demographics
Female	86.9%
Under age 25	64.7%
Minority	38.8%
Part-time	4.4%

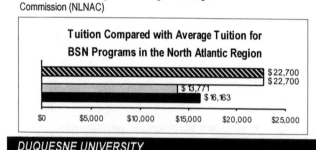

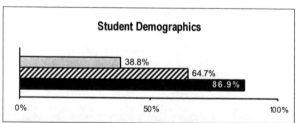

DUQUESNE UNIVERSITY

600 Forbes Ave
Pittsburgh, PA 15282
(412) 396-6554
Eileen Zungolo, EdD, RN, FAAN

www.nursing.duq.edu

Accreditation
Pennsylvania State Board of Nursing,
Commission on Collegiate Nursing Education
(CCNE)

Acceptance rate	66.2%	
Faculty-student ratio	1: 8	
Faculty	Full time	24
	Part time	37

Tuition
In state	$20,231
Out of state	$20,231
Enrollments	358
Graduations	95

Degrees conferred
Baccalaureate degree

Minimum degree required
High school diploma or GED

Student Demographics
Female	90.4%
Under age 25	93.6%
Minority	11.7%
Part-time	0.3%

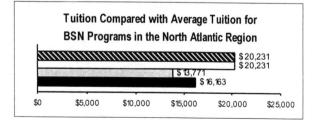

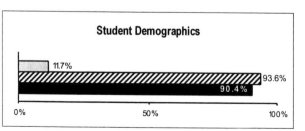

Key Tuition Chart | ▨ Program - in state ☐ Program - out of state ☐ Average - in state ■ Average - out of state

Pennsylvania

EAST STROUDSBURG UNIVERSITY — *Useful Facts*

200 Prospect St
East Stroudsburg, PA 18301
(570) 422-3563
Cecile Champagne, DNSc, RN

www3.esu.edu/academics/hshp/nurs/home.asp

Accreditation
Pennsylvania State Board of Nursing, National League for Nursing Accrediting Commission (NLNAC)

Acceptance rate	40.8%
Faculty-student ratio	1: 15
Faculty Full time	6
Part time	6

Degrees conferred
Baccalaureate degree

Tuition
In state	$4,810
Out of state	$12,026
Enrollments	138
Graduations	39

Minimum degree required
High school diploma or GED

Student Demographics
Female	89.8%
Under age 25	89.1%
Minority	4.7%
Part-time	0.8%

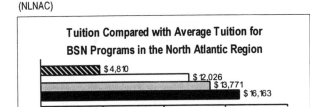

Tuition Compared with Average Tuition for BSN Programs in the North Atlantic Region: $4,810; $12,026; $13,771; $16,163

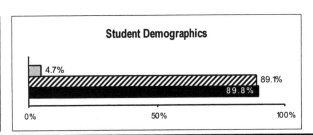

Student Demographics: 4.7%; 89.1%; 89.8%

EDINBORO UNIVERSITY OF PENNSYLVANIA — *Useful Facts*

295 Meadville St
Edinboro, PA 16444
(814) 732-2900
Patricia Nosel, MN, RN

www.edinboro.edu

Accreditation
Pennsylvania State Board of Nursing, Commission on Collegiate Nursing Education (CCNE)

Acceptance rate	58.0%
Faculty-student ratio	1: 13
Faculty Full time	21
Part time	0

Degrees conferred
Baccalaureate degree

Tuition
In state	$4,810
Out of state	$9,620
Enrollments	277
Graduations	62

Minimum degree required
High school diploma or GED

Student Demographics
Female	86.9%
Under age 25	71.2%
Minority	9.2%
Part-time	5.4%

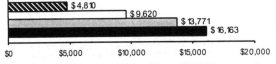

Tuition Compared with Average Tuition for BSN Programs in the North Atlantic Region: $4,810; $9,620; $13,771; $16,163

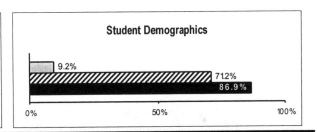

Student Demographics: 9.2%; 71.2%; 86.9%

GANNON UNIVERSITY — *Useful Facts**

109 University Square
Erie, PA 16541
(814) 871-5463
Carolynn Masters, PhD, RN, CARN

www.gannon.edu

Accreditation
Pennsylvania State Board of Nursing, Commission on Collegiate Nursing Education (CCNE)

Faculty Full time	13
Part time	8

Degrees conferred
Baccalaureate

Tuition
In state	$19,320
Out of state	$19,320

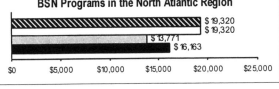

Tuition Compared with Average Tuition for BSN Programs in the North Atlantic Region: $19,320; $19,320; $13,771; $16,163

Demographics Chart	■ Female ▨ Under age 25 ☐ Minority	Distance Learning	¹The tuition reported for this program may be not be annualized. *Data reported between 2001 and 2004.

Pennsylvania

HOLY FAMILY COLLEGE

9801 Frankford Avenue
Philadelphia, PA 19114
(215) 637-7700
Christine Rosner, PhD, RN

www.holyfamily.edu

Accreditation
Pennsylvania State Board of Nursing,
Commission on Collegiate Nursing Education
(CCNE), National League for Nursing Accrediting
Commission (NLNAC)

At the request of this nursing school, publication has been witheld.
Please contact the school directly for more information.

INDIANA UNIVERSITY OF PENNSYLVANIA   *Useful Facts**

1010 Oakland Avenue
Indiana, PA 45623
(724) 357-2557
Jodell Kuzneski, RN

www.iup.edu

Enrollments	273
Graduations	59

Accreditation
Pennsylvania State Board of Nursing

Degrees conferred
Baccalaureate

LA SALLE UNIVERSITY   *Useful Facts**

1900 West Olney Ave
Philadelphia, PA 19141
(215) 951-1431
Zane Wolf, PhD, RN, FAAN

www.lasalle.edu/academ/nursing/index.htm

Accreditation
Pennsylvania State Board of Nursing,
Commission on Collegiate Nursing Education
(CCNE)

Degrees conferred
Baccalaureate

Acceptance rate	32.6%	**Tuition**		**Student Demographics**
Faculty-student ratio	1: 11	In state	$22,760	Female	88.4%
Faculty Full time	20	Out of state	$22,760	Under age 25	52.0%
Part time	84	**Enrollments**	702	Minority	46.0%
		Graduations	95	Part-time	41.1%

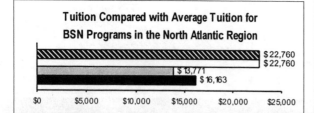

Tuition Compared with Average Tuition for BSN Programs in the North Atlantic Region

$22,760
$22,760
$13,771
$16,163

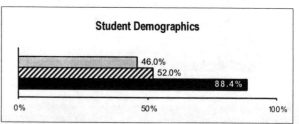

Student Demographics

46.0%
52.0%
88.4%

LYCOMING COLLEGE   *Useful Facts**

700 College Pl, Box 21
Williamsport, PA 17701
(570) 321-4224
Doris Parrish, PhD, RN

www.lycoming.edu

Accreditation
Pennsylvania State Board of Nursing

Degrees conferred
Baccalaureate

Tuition		**Student Demographics**	
In state	$20,032	Female	100.0%
Out of state	$20,032		
Enrollments	21		
Graduations	14	Part-time	16.7%

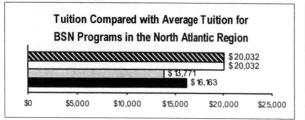

Tuition Compared with Average Tuition for BSN Programs in the North Atlantic Region

$20,032
$20,032
$13,771
$16,163

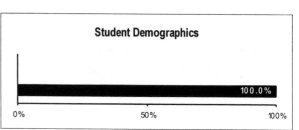

Student Demographics

100.0%

Key | Tuition Chart | ⊠ Program - in state ☐ Program - out of state ☐ Average - in state ■ Average - out of state

Pennsylvania

MANSFIELD UNIVERSITY *Useful Facts*

212 C Elliot Hall
Mansfield, PA 16933
(570) 662-4522
Janeen Bartlett Sheehe, DNSc, RN

www.mnsfld.edu

Accreditation
Pennsylvania State Board of Nursing, National
League for Nursing Accrediting Commission
(NLNAC)

Acceptance rate	64.3%	
Faculty-student ratio	1: 17	
Faculty Full time	8	
Part time	7	

Tuition
In state $4,810
Out of state $12,206
Enrollments 193
Graduations 32

Student Demographics
Female 90.2%
Under age 25 75.1%
Minority 7.6%
Part-time 1.7%

Degrees conferred
Baccalaureate degree

Minimum degree required
High school diploma or GED

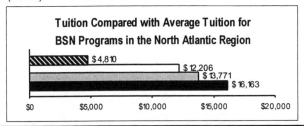
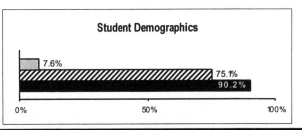

MARYWOOD UNIVERSITY *Useful Facts**

2300 Adams Avenue
Scranton, PA 18509
(570) 348-6211
Robin Gallagher, DNSc, CRNP

www.marywood.edu/departments/nursing

Accreditation
Pennsylvania State Board of Nursing, National
League for Nursing Accrediting Commission
(NLNAC)

Acceptance rate	94.2%	
Faculty-student ratio	1: 11	
Faculty Full time	4	
Part time	8	

Tuition
In state $20,700
Out of state $20,700
Enrollments 89
Graduations 8

Student Demographics
Female 94.4%
Under age 25 65.0%
Minority 6.7%
Part-time 7.9%

Degrees conferred
Baccalaureate

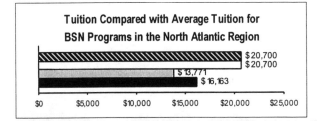
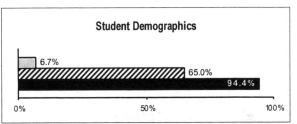

MESSIAH COLLEGE *Useful Facts**

One College Avenue
Grantham, PA 17027
(717) 691-6029
Sandra Jamison, DNS, RN

www.messiah.edu

Accreditation
Pennsylvania State Board of Nursing

Degrees conferred
Baccalaureate

Tuition
In state $15,000
Out of state $15,000
Enrollments 168
Graduations 54

Student Demographics
Female 95.8%
Minority 2.4%
Part-time 12.6%

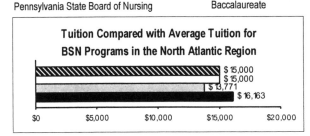
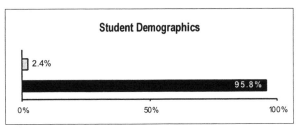

**Demographics
Chart** | ■Female ▨ Under age 25 ☐ Minority | **Distance
Learning** | †The tuition reported for this program may be not be annualized.
*Data reported between 2001 and 2004.

Pennsylvania

MORAVIAN COLLEGE
*Useful Facts**

801 Ostrum Street
Bethlehem, PA 18018
(610) 861-1607
Janet Sipple, RN, EdD

www.moravian.edu

Student Demographics
Female	91.9%
Minority	13.5%
Part-time	0.0%

Enrollments   128

Accreditation
Pennsylvania State Board of Nursing

Degrees conferred
Baccalaureate

NEUMANN COLLEGE
Useful Facts

One Neumann Drive
Aston, PA 19014
(610) 558-5560
Kathleen Hoover, PhD, RN

www.neumann.edu

Acceptance rate	71.3%
Faculty-student ratio	1: 14
Faculty Full time	14
Part time	7

Tuition	
In state	$16,590
Out of state	$16,590
Enrollments	245
Graduations	58

Student Demographics
Female	92.9%
Under age 25	83.0%
Minority	14.9%
Part-time	14.1%

Accreditation
Pennsylvania State Board of Nursing, National
League for Nursing Accrediting Commission
(NLNAC)

Degrees conferred
BS with Major in Nursing

Minimum degree required
High school diploma or GED

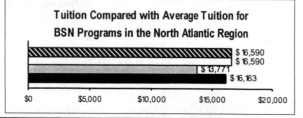

Tuition Compared with Average Tuition for BSN Programs in the North Atlantic Region

$16,590
$16,590
$13,771
$16,163

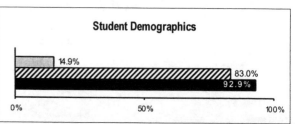

Student Demographics

14.9%
83.0%
92.9%

PENNSYLVANIA COLLEGE OF TECHNOLOGY
Useful Facts

One College Avenue
Williamsport, PA 17701
(570) 327-4525
Pamela Starcher, RN, MN, PhD(c)

www.pct.edu

Acceptance rate	14.3%
Faculty-student ratio	1: 5
Faculty Full time	17
Part time	32

Tuition	
In state	$10,080
Out of state	$12,660
Enrollments	7
Graduations	0

Student Demographics
Female	100.0%
Under age 25	57.1%
Minority	14.3%
Part-time	28.6%

Accreditation
Pennsylvania State Board of Nursing, National
League for Nursing Accrediting Commission
(NLNAC)

Degrees conferred
Baccalaureate degree

Minimum degree required
High school diploma or GED

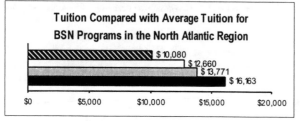

Tuition Compared with Average Tuition for BSN Programs in the North Atlantic Region

$10,080
$12,660
$13,771
$16,163

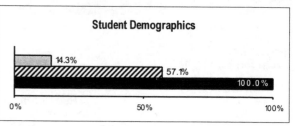

Student Demographics

14.3%
57.1%
100.0%

Key   Tuition Chart   ▨ Program - in state   ☐ Program - out of state   ▧ Average - in state   ■ Average - out of state

Pennsylvania

PENNSYLVANIA STATE UNIVERSITY | Useful Facts

201 Health and Human Dev East
University Park, PA 16804
(814) 863-0247
Paula Milone-Nuzzo, RN, PhD, FAAN, FHHC

www.hhdev.psu.edu/nurs/nurs.htm

Accreditation
Pennsylvania State Board of Nursing,
Commission on Collegiate Nursing Education
(CCNE), National League for Nursing Accrediting
Commission (NLNAC)

Acceptance rate	46.0%	
Faculty-student ratio	1: 10	
Faculty	Full time	64
	Part time	42

Degrees conferred
BS Nursing

Tuition	
In state	$11,508
Out of state	$21,744
Enrollments	461
Graduations	121

Minimum degree required
High school diploma or GED

Student Demographics	
Female	90.0%
Under age 25	98.0%
Minority	7.2%
Part-time	0.0%

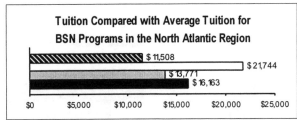

Tuition Compared with Average Tuition for BSN Programs in the North Atlantic Region

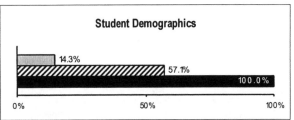

Student Demographics

ROBERT MORRIS UNIVERSITY

6001 University Boulevard
Coraopolis, PA 15108
(412) 299-2426
Lynda Davidson, PhD, RN

www.rmu.edu

Accreditation
Pennsylvania State Board of Nursing

Degrees conferred
Baccalaureate

SAINT FRANCIS UNIVERSITY

117 Evergreen Drive, Schwab Hall
Loretto, PA 15940
(814) 472-3027
Jean Samii, PhD, RN

www.francis.edu

Accreditation
Pennsylvania State Board of Nursing

Degrees conferred
Baccalaureate

TEMPLE UNIVERSITY | Useful Facts*

3307 North Broad Street
Philadelphia, PA 19140
(215) 707-8327
Jill Derstine, EdD, RN,FAAN

www.temple.edu/nursing

Accreditation
Pennsylvania State Board of Nursing,
Commission on Collegiate Nursing Education
(CCNE)

Acceptance rate	36.7%

Degrees conferred
Baccalaureate

Tuition	
In state	$9,828
Out of state	$17,526
Enrollments	323
Graduations	133

Student Demographics	
Female	87.7%
Under age 25	50.0%
Minority	49.7%
Part-time	12.3%

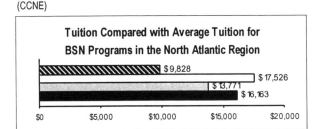

Tuition Compared with Average Tuition for BSN Programs in the North Atlantic Region

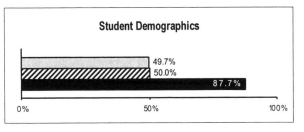

Student Demographics

Demographics Chart	■Female ☒Under age 25 ☐Minority	**Distance Learning**	†The tuition reported for this program may be not be annualized. *Data reported between 2001 and 2004.

Pennsylvania

THOMAS JEFFERSON UNIVERSITY
Useful Facts*

130 S 9th Street, 12th Floor
Philadelphia, PA 19107
(215) 503-8390
Mary Schaal, RN

www.jefferson.edu

Accreditation
Pennsylvania State Board of Nursing

Acceptance rate   76.7%

Degrees conferred
Baccalaureate

Tuition		Student Demographics	
In state	$17,500	Female	79.2%
Out of state	$17,500	Under age 25	50.0%
Enrollments	247	Minority	21.7%
Graduations	146	Part-time	12.3%

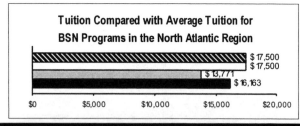

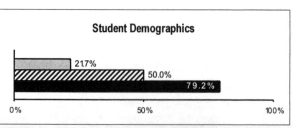

UNIVERSITY OF PENNSYLVANIA - PRESBYTERIAN
Useful Facts*

420 Guardian Drive
Philadelphia, PA 19104
(215) 898-8283
Afaf Meleis, PhD, FAAN

www.nursing.upenn.edu

Accreditation
Pennsylvania State Board of Nursing,
Commission on Collegiate Nursing Education
(CCNE)

Acceptance rate   46.4%

Degrees conferred
Baccalaureate

Tuition		Student Demographics	
In state	$26,282	Female	92.3%
Out of state	$25,078	Under age 25	76.0%
Enrollments	455	Minority	27.5%
Graduations	85	Part-time	1.5%

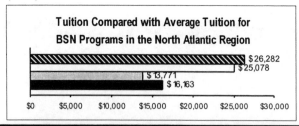

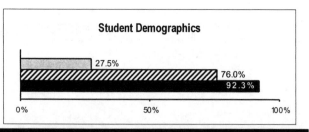

UNIVERSITY OF PITTSBURGH
Useful Facts*

3500 Victoria Street
Pittsburgh, PA 15261
(412) 624-1291
Ellen Beam Rudy, PhD, RN, FAAN

www.nursing.pitt.edu

Accreditation
Pennsylvania State Board of Nursing

Degrees conferred
Baccalaureate

Tuition	
In state	$7,872
Out of state	$17,168
Enrollments	572

Tuition Compared with Average Tuition for
BSN Programs in the North Atlantic Region

- $7,872
- $17,168
- $13,771
- $16,163

$0 $5,000 $10,000 $15,000 $20,000

Key   Tuition Chart | ▨ Program - in state   ☐ Program - out of state   ▤ Average - in state   ■ Average - out of state

Pennsylvania

UNIVERSITY OF SCRANTON
*Useful Facts**

800 Linden Street
Scranton, PA 18510
(570) 941-7903
Patricia Harrington, RN, EdD

academic.scranton.edu/department/nursing/

Accreditation
Pennsylvania State Board of Nursing,
Commission on Collegiate Nursing Education
(CCNE)

Acceptance rate	74.1%	

Degrees conferred
Baccalaureate

Tuition	
In state	$19,200
Out of state	$19,200
Enrollments	240
Graduations	35

Student Demographics	
Female	96.4%
Under age 25	68.0%
Minority	8.2%
Part-time	5.5%

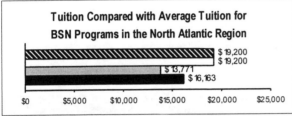
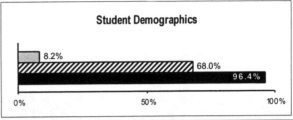

VILLANOVA UNIVERSITY
Useful Facts

800 Lancaster Avenue
Villanova, PA 19085
(610) 519-4909
M Fitzpatrick, EdD

www.nursing.villanova.edu

Accreditation
Pennsylvania State Board of Nursing,
Commission on Collegiate Nursing Education
(CCNE), National League for Nursing Accrediting
Commission (NLNAC)

Acceptance rate		51.1%
Faculty-student ratio		1: 9
Faculty	Full time	45
	Part time	33

Degrees conferred
Baccalaureate degree

Minimum degree required
BA or BS in a non-nursing field

Tuition	
In state	$28,450
Out of state	$28,450
Enrollments	564
Graduations	149

Student Demographics	
Female	96.0%
Under age 25	88.1%
Minority	12.6%
Part-time	2.5%

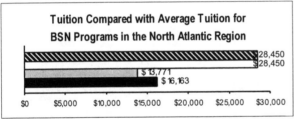
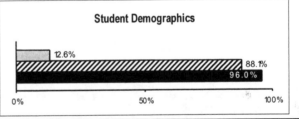

WAYNESBURG COLLEGE
*Useful Facts**

51 W College Street
Waynesburg, PA 15370
(724) 852-3356
Nancy Mosser, EdD, RN, BC

www.waynesburg.edu

Accreditation
Pennsylvania State Board of Nursing,
Commission on Collegiate Nursing Education
(CCNE)

Acceptance rate	61.5%	

Degrees conferred
Baccalaureate

Tuition	
In state	$14,200
Out of state	$14,200
Enrollments	218
Graduations	93

Student Demographics	
Female	84.2%
Under age 25	29.0%
Minority	2.0%
Part-time	0.0%

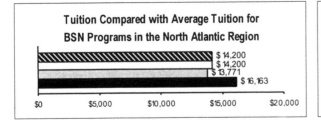
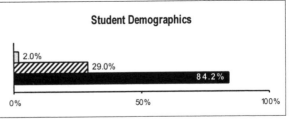

Demographics Chart	■Female ▨Under age 25 □Minority	Distance Learning		†The tuition reported for this program may be not be annualized. *Data reported between 2001 and 2004.

Pennsylvania

WEST CHESTER UNIVERSITY

Sturzebecker Health Sci Ctr, S New St
West Chester, PA 19383
(610) 436-2331
Ann Stowe, DNSc, RN

www.wcupa.edu

Accreditation
Pennsylvania State Board of Nursing

Degrees conferred
Baccalaureate

Tuition		Student Demographics	
In state	$3,618	Female	94.7%
Out of state	$9,046		
Enrollments	245		
Graduations	38		

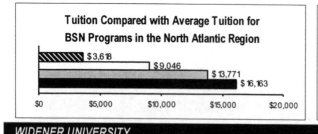

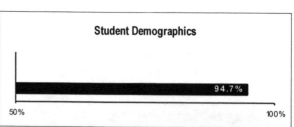

WIDENER UNIVERSITY

One University Place
Chester, PA 19013
(610) 499-4214
Marguerite Barbiere, RN, EdD

www.widener.edu

Accreditation
Pennsylvania State Board of Nursing, National
League for Nursing Accrediting Commission
(NLNAC)

Degrees conferred
Baccalaureate degree

Minimum degree required
High school diploma or GED

		Tuition		Student Demographics	
Acceptance rate	65.8%	In state	$24,600	Female	90.9%
Faculty-student ratio	1: 13	Out of state	$24,600	Under age 25	75.1%
Faculty Full time	29	Enrollments	515	Minority	30.4%
Part time	23	Graduations	70	Part-time	18.3%

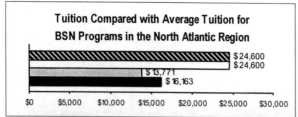

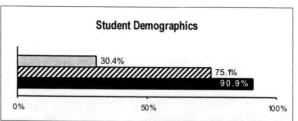

WILKES UNIVERSITY

109 South Franklin Street
Wilkes-Barre, PA 18766
(570) 408-4071
Joyce Chmil, RNC, CCRN

www.wilkes.edu

Accreditation
Pennsylvania State Board of Nursing

Degrees conferred
Baccalaureate

Tuition		Student Demographics	
In state	$15,050		
Out of state	$15,050		
Enrollments	83		
		Part-time	34.6%

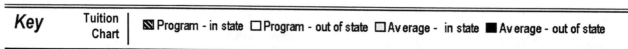

Key — Tuition Chart — ▧ Program - in state ☐ Program - out of state ☐ Average - in state ■ Average - out of state

Pennsylvania

YORK COLLEGE OF PENNSYLVANIA — *Useful Facts*

Country Club Road
York, PA 17405
(717) 815-1420
Jacquelin Harrington, DEd, RN

www.ycp.edu

Accreditation
Pennsylvania State Board of Nursing, National League for Nursing Accrediting Commission (NLNAC)

Acceptance rate		27.8%
Faculty-student ratio		1: 16
Faculty	Full time	18
	Part time	36

Degrees conferred
BS MS major in nuring

Tuition	
In state	$10,050
Out of state	$10,050
Enrollments	579
Graduations	97

Minimum degree required
ADN or Diploma

Student Demographics	
Female	93.8%
Under age 25	80.0%
Minority	3.8%
Part-time	21.7%

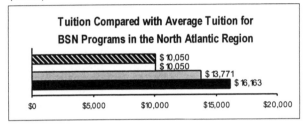

Tuition Compared with Average Tuition for BSN Programs in the North Atlantic Region

$10,050
$10,050
$13,771
$16,163

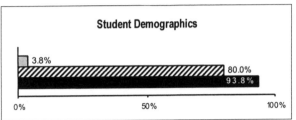

Student Demographics

3.8%
80.0%
93.8%

Rhode Island

RHODE ISLAND COLLEGE — *Useful Facts**

600 Mount Pleasant Avenue
Providence, RI 02908
(401) 456-8482
Patricia Thomas, PhD, RNC

www.ric.edu

Accreditation
Rhode Island Board of Nurse Registration & Nursing Education

Acceptance rate	67.9%

Degrees conferred
Baccalaureate

Tuition	
In state	$2,676
Out of state	$7,600
Enrollments	339
Graduations	129

Student Demographics	
Female	84.0%
Under age 25	43.0%
Minority	17.3%
Part-time	37.7%

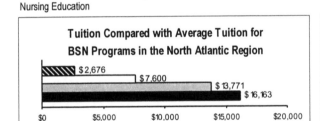

Tuition Compared with Average Tuition for BSN Programs in the North Atlantic Region

$2,676
$7,600
$13,771
$16,163

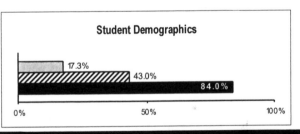

Student Demographics

17.3%
43.0%
84.0%

SALVE REGINA UNIVERSITY

100 Ochre Point Avenue
Newport, RI 02840
(401) 341-3198
Sandra Solem, PhD, RN

www.salve.edu

Accreditation
Rhode Island Board of Nurse Registration & Nursing Education, National League for Nursing Accrediting Commission (NLNAC)

At the request of this nursing school, publication has been witheld. Please contact the school directly for more information.

Demographics Chart	■ Female ▨ Under age 25 ☐ Minority	Distance Learning	¹The tuition reported for this program may be not be annualized. *Data reported between 2001 and 2004.

Rhode Island

UNIVERSITY OF RHODE ISLAND

Useful Facts*

White Hall, 2 Heathman Road
Kingston, RI
(401) 874-5300
Dayle Joseph, RN, EdD

www.uri.edu/nursing

Accreditation
Rhode Island Board of Nurse Registration &
Nursing Education, Commission on Collegiate
Nursing Education (CCNE)

Acceptance rate	68.6%

Degrees conferred
Baccalaureate

Tuition
In state	$3,464
Out of state	$11,906
Enrollments	428
Graduations	84

Student Demographics
Female	88.6%
Minority	20.7%
Part-time	9.5%

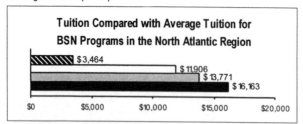

Tuition Compared with Average Tuition for BSN Programs in the North Atlantic Region
- $3,464
- $11,906
- $13,771
- $16,163

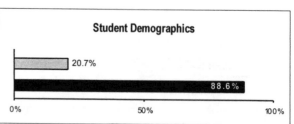

Student Demographics
- 20.7%
- 88.6%

South Carolina

BOB JONES UNIVERSITY

1700 Wade Hampton Blvd
Greenville, SC 29614
(864) 242-5100
Kathleen Crispin, EdD, RN

www.bju.edu

Accreditation
South Carolina State Board of Nursing

*At the request of this nursing school, publication has been witheld.
Please contact the school directly for more information.*

CHARLESTON SOUTHERN UNIVERSITY

Useful Facts

PO Box 118087
Charleston, SC 29406
(843) 863-7075
Marian Larisey, PhD, RN

www.csuniv.edu

Accreditation
South Carolina State Board of Nursing, National
League for Nursing Accrediting Commission
(NLNAC)

Acceptance rate		26.7%
Faculty-student ratio		1:8
Faculty	Full time	8
	Part time	2

Degrees conferred
Baccalaureate degree

Tuition
In state	$15,998
Out of state	$15,998
Enrollments	76
Graduations	16

Minimum degree required
High school diploma or GED

Student Demographics
Female	97.4%
Under age 25	77.6%
Minority	11.8%
Part-time	0.0%

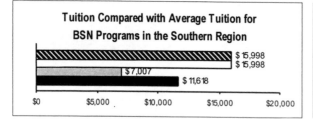

Tuition Compared with Average Tuition for BSN Programs in the Southern Region
- $15,998
- $15,998
- $7,007
- $11,618

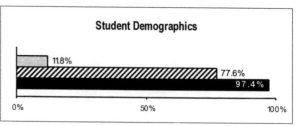

Student Demographics
- 11.8%
- 77.6%
- 97.4%

Key — Tuition Chart

▧ Program - in state ☐ Program - out of state ☐ Average - in state ■ Average - out of state

South Carolina

CLEMSON UNIVERSITY

508 Edwards Hall
Clemson, SC 29634
(864) 656-7622
Rosanne Pruitt, PhD, RN, FNP

www.hehd.clemson.edu/nursing

Accreditation
South Carolina State Board of Nursing,
Commission on Collegiate Nursing Education
(CCNE), National League for Nursing Accrediting
Commission (NLNAC)

*At the request of this nursing school, publication has been witheld.
Please contact the school directly for more information.*

FRANCIS MARION UNIVERSITY

PO Box 100547
Florence, SC 29501
(803) 661-1690
Sylvia Lufkin

www.fmarion.edu

Accreditation
South Carolina State Board of Nursing

Degrees conferred
Baccalaureate

LANDER UNIVERSITY

Useful Facts*

320 Stanley Ave
Greenwood, SC 29649
(864) 388-8278
Betsy McDowell, PhD, RN, CCRN

www.lander.edu/nursing

Accreditation
South Carolina State Board of Nursing, National
League for Nursing Accrediting Commission
(NLNAC)

Degrees conferred
Baccalaureate

			Tuition		Student Demographics	
Acceptance rate	95.7%		In state	$5,856	Female	92.6%
			Out of state	$12,024	Under age 25	66.0%
			Enrollments	139	Minority	8.4%
			Graduations	29	Part-time	3.7%

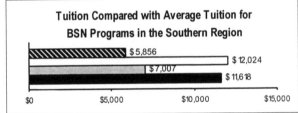

Tuition Compared with Average Tuition for BSN Programs in the Southern Region

$5,856
$12,024
$7,007
$11,618

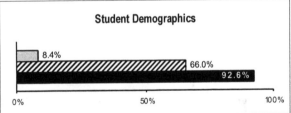

Student Demographics

8.4%
66.0%
92.6%

Demographics Chart	■ Female ▨ Under age 25 ☐ Minority	Distance Learning	¹The tuition reported for this program may be not be annualized. *Data reported between 2001 and 2004.

South Carolina

MEDICAL UNIVERSITY OF SOUTH CAROLINA

99 Johnathan Lucas St
Charleston, SC 29425
(843) 792-3941
Gail Stuart, PhD, APRN, FAAN

www.musc.edu/nursing

Accreditation
South Carolina State Board of Nursing,
Commission on Collegiate Nursing Education
(CCNE), National League for Nursing Accrediting
Commission (NLNAC)

Acceptance rate		27.9%
Faculty-student ratio		1: 5
Faculty	Full time	36
	Part time	1

Degrees conferred
Baccalaureate degree

Tuition		**Student Demographics**	
In state	$13,750	Female	88.4%
Out of state	$37,215	Under age 25	62.6%
Enrollments	199	Minority	15.7%
Graduations	159	Part-time	6.1%

Minimum degree required
60 credit hours of prerequisites

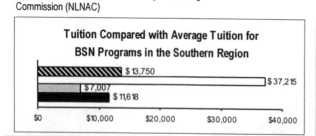

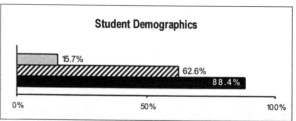

SOUTH CAROLINA STATE UNIVERSITY

300 College St, PO Box 7158
Orangeburg, SC 29117
(803) 536-8605
Sylvia Whiting, RN, BSN, MS, PhD

www.sc.edu

Accreditation
South Carolina State Board of Nursing

Acceptance rate		67.9%

Degrees conferred
Baccalaureate

Tuition		**Student Demographics**	
In state	$4,556	Female	94.4%
Out of state	$8,820	Under age 25	60.0%
Enrollments	74	Minority	95.8%
Graduations	29	Part-time	0.0%

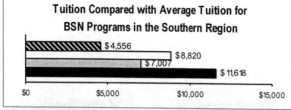

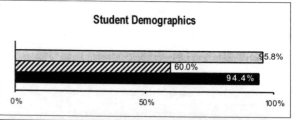

UNIVERSITY OF SOUTH CAROLINA - AIKEN

471 University Parkway
Aiken, SC 29801
(803) 641-3263
Julia Ball, RN, PhD

www.usca.edu

Accreditation
South Carolina State Board of Nursing, National
League for Nursing Accrediting Commission
(NLNAC)

Acceptance rate		87.0%
Faculty-student ratio		1: 9
Faculty	Full time	15
	Part time	23

Degrees conferred
Baccalaureate degree

Tuition		**Student Demographics**	
In state	$6,186	Female	92.9%
Out of state	$12,346	Under age 25	66.7%
Enrollments	181	Minority	22.0%
Graduations	38	Part-time	2.8%

Minimum degree required
High school diploma or GED

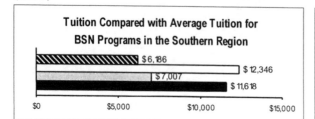

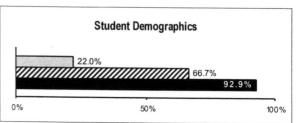

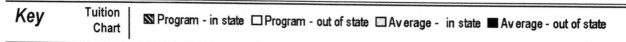

Key — Tuition Chart — ▨ Program - in state ☐ Program - out of state ☐ Average - in state ■ Average - out of state

South Carolina

UNIVERSITY OF SOUTH CAROLINA - COLUMBIA   *Useful Facts*

1601 Greene St
Columbia, SC 29208
(803) 777-3119
Peggy Hewlett, PhD

www.sc.edu/nursing

Accreditation
South Carolina State Board of Nursing,
Commission on Collegiate Nursing Education
(CCNE)

Acceptance rate		36.2%
Faculty-student ratio		1: 20
Faculty	Full time	33
	Part time	15

Degrees conferred
Baccalaureate degree

Tuition	
In state	$6,914
Out of state	$18,556
Enrollments	807
Graduations	88

Minimum degree required
Data is for Upper Division students; must have
completed first 2 years towards BSN degree

Student Demographics	
Female	92.9%
Under age 25	91.1%
Minority	23.7%
Part-time	9.9%

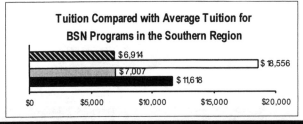

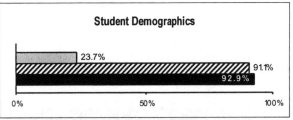

UNIVERSITY OF SOUTH CAROLINA - UPSTATE   *Useful Facts*

800 University Way
Spartanburg, SC 29303
(864) 503-5444
Marsha Dowell, PhD, RN

www.uscupstate.edu/academic/mbsn/index.shtml

Accreditation
South Carolina State Board of Nursing, National
League for Nursing Accrediting Commission
(NLNAC)

Acceptance rate		39.2%
Faculty-student ratio		1: 10
Faculty	Full time	35
	Part time	15

Degrees conferred
Baccalaureate degree

Tuition	
In state	$6,416
Out of state	$13,254
Enrollments	373
Graduations	150

Minimum degree required
High school diploma or GED

Student Demographics	
Female	88.6%
Under age 25	66.9%
Minority	29.6%
Part-time	5.7%

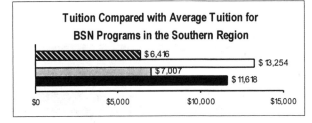

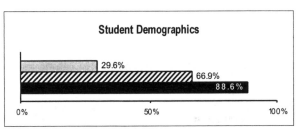

South Dakota

AUGUSTANA COLLEGE

2001 South Summit Avenue
Sioux Falls, SD 57197
(605) 274-4729
Margot Nelson, RN, PhD

www.augie.edu

Accreditation
South Dakota Board of Nursing, Commission on
Collegiate Nursing Education (CCNE)

At the request of this nursing school, publication has been witheld.
Please contact the school directly for more information.

Demographics Chart	■Female ▨ Under age 25 ☐Minority	Distance Learning	¹The tuition reported for this program may be not be annualized. *Data reported between 2001 and 2004.

South Dakota

MOUNT MARTY COLLEGE — *Useful Facts*

1105 West 8th Street
Yankton, SD 57078
(605) 668-1594
Ruth Stephens, PhD, RN

www.mtmc.edu/academic/division/nsg

Accreditation
South Dakota Board of Nursing, National League
for Nursing Accrediting Commission (NLNAC)

Acceptance rate	87.2%
Faculty-student ratio	1: 9
Faculty Full time	8
Part time	9

Degrees conferred
Baccalaureate degree

Tuition	
In state	$14,050
Out of state	$14,050
Enrollments	118
Graduations	26

Minimum degree required
High school diploma or GED

Student Demographics	
Female	89.7%
Under age 25	83.8%
Minority	3.4%
Part-time	4.3%

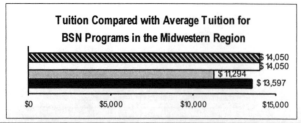

Tuition Compared with Average Tuition for BSN Programs in the Midwestern Region

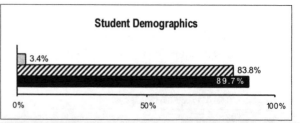

Student Demographics

PRESENTATION COLLEGE — *Useful Facts*

1500 North Main Street
Aberdeen, SD 57401
(605) 229-8472
Linda Burdette, MS, RN, CNP

www.presentation.edu/nursing

Accreditation
South Dakota Board of Nursing, National League
for Nursing Accrediting Commission (NLNAC)

Acceptance rate	92.9%
Faculty-student ratio	1: 10
Faculty Full time	12
Part time	20

Degrees conferred
Baccalaureate degree

Tuition	
In state	$11,400
Out of state	$11,400
Enrollments	199
Graduations	31

Minimum degree required
High school diploma or GED

Student Demographics	
Female	94.1%
Under age 25	41.4%
Minority	2.8%
Part-time	12.9%

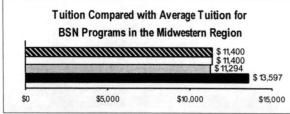

Tuition Compared with Average Tuition for BSN Programs in the Midwestern Region

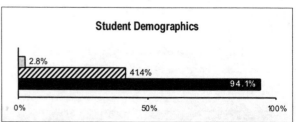

Student Demographics

SOUTH DAKOTA STATE UNIVERSITY — *Useful Facts**

Box 2275 Rotunda Lane, NFA 255
Brookings, SD 57007-0098
(605) 688-5178
Roberta Olson, PhD, RN

www.sdstate.edu/nursing

Accreditation
South Dakota Board of Nursing

Acceptance rate	66.7%

Degrees conferred
Baccalaureate

Tuition	
In state	$1,348
Out of state	$4,288
Enrollments	381
Graduations	157

Tuition Compared with Average Tuition for BSN Programs in the Midwestern Region

$ 1,348
$ 4,288
$ 11,294
$ 13,597

$0 $5,000 $10,000 $15,000

Key Tuition Chart | ▨ Program - in state ☐ Program - out of state ☐ Average - in state ■ Average - out of state

Tennessee

AUSTIN PEAY STATE UNIVERSITY — Useful Facts*

PO Box 4658
Clarksville, TN 37044
(931) 221-7737
Kathy Martin, PhD, RN

www.apsu.edu

Acceptance rate		67.2%

Tuition
In state	$4,224
Out of state	$12,712
Enrollments	167
Graduations	68

Student Demographics
Female	86.0%
Under age 25	44.0%
Minority	18.6%
Part-time	0.0%

Accreditation
Tennessee State Board of Nursing, National League for Nursing Accrediting Commission (NLNAC)

Degrees conferred
Baccalaureate

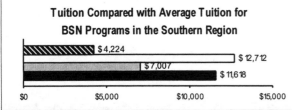

Tuition Compared with Average Tuition for BSN Programs in the Southern Region

$4,224
$12,712
$7,007
$11,618

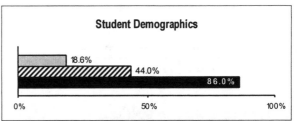

Student Demographics

18.6%
44.0%
86.0%

BAPTIST COLLEGE OF HEALTH SCIENCES — Useful Facts*

1003 Monroe Avenue
Memphis, TN 38104
(901) 572-2842
Veta Plumb, DNSc

www.bchs.edu

Acceptance rate		100.0%
Faculty-student ratio		1:7
Faculty	Full time	28
	Part time	9

Tuition
In state	$4,800
Out of state	$4,800
Enrollments	239
Graduations	93

Student Demographics
Female	95.5%
Under age 25	55.0%
Minority	27.8%
Part-time	14.2%

Accreditation
Tennessee State Board of Nursing, Commission on Collegiate Nursing Education (CCNE)

Degrees conferred
Baccalaureate

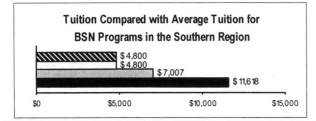

Tuition Compared with Average Tuition for BSN Programs in the Southern Region

$4,800
$4,800
$7,007
$11,618

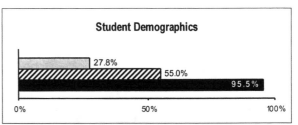

Student Demographics

27.8%
55.0%
95.5%

BELMONT UNIVERSITY — Useful Facts*

1900 Belmont Boulevard
Nashville, TN 37212
(615) 460-6117
Debra Wollaber, PhD, RNC

www.belmont.edu

Enrollments	143
Graduations	27

Student Demographics
Female	95.1%
Part-time	16.8%

Accreditation
Tennessee State Board of Nursing

Degrees conferred
Baccalaureate

Demographics Chart	■Female ☒Under age 25 ☐Minority	Distance Learning	¹The tuition reported for this program may be not be annualized. *Data reported between 2001 and 2004.

Tennessee

CARSON NEWMAN COLLEGE

1646 Russell Avenue
Jefferson City, TN 37760
(865) 471-3425
Patty Kraft, EdD, RN, BC-FNP

www.cn.edu

Tuition		Student Demographics	
In state	$12,900	Female	88.3%
Out of state	$12,900	Under age 25	93.0%
Enrollments	131	Minority	3.1%
Graduations	11	Part-time	7.8%

Accreditation
Tennessee State Board of Nursing, Commission on Collegiate Nursing Education (CCNE)

Degrees conferred
Baccalaureate

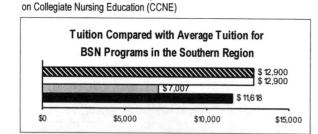

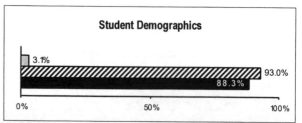

CUMBERLAND UNIVERSITY

One Cumberland Square
Lebanon, TN 37087
(615) 444-2562
Leanne Busby, DSN, RNC, FAANP

www.cumberland.edu

Acceptance rate 100.0%

Tuition		Student Demographics	
In state	$11,000	Female	93.1%
Out of state	$11,000	Under age 25	85.0%
Enrollments	74	Minority	6.9%
Graduations	21	Part-time	4.2%

Accreditation
Tennessee State Board of Nursing, National League for Nursing Accrediting Commission (NLNAC)

Degrees conferred
Baccalaureate

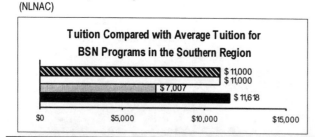

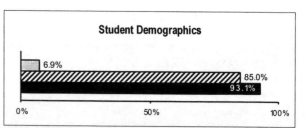

EAST TENNESSEE STATE UNIVERSITY

Box 70617 East Tennessee State University
Johnson City, TN 37614
(423) 439-7051
Patricia Smith, EdD, RN

www.etsu.edu/nursing

Accreditation
Tennessee State Board of Nursing, National League for Nursing Accrediting Commission (NLNAC)

At the request of this nursing school, publication has been witheld. Please contact the school directly for more information.

FISK UNIVERSITY

1000 Seventeenth Avenue N
Nashville, TN 37208
(615) 329-8665
Jana Lauderdale, PhD, RN

www.fisk.edu

Accreditation
Tennessee State Board of Nursing

Degrees conferred
Baccalaureate

Key — Tuition Chart: ▨ Program - in state ☐ Program - out of state ☐ Average - in state ■ Average - out of state

Tennessee

KING COLLEGE   *Useful Facts*

1350 King College Road
Bristol, TN 37620
(423) 652-4748
Johanne Quinn, PhD, RN

www.king.edu

Acceptance rate		100.0%
Faculty-student ratio		1: 18
Faculty	Full time	10
	Part time	5

Tuition	
In state	$16,626
Out of state	$16,626
Enrollments	220
Graduations	41

Student Demographics	
Female	91.0%
Under age 25	51.9%
Minority	1.5%
Part-time	0.0%

Accreditation
Tennessee State Board of Nursing, Commission on Collegiate Nursing Education (CCNE)

Degrees conferred
Baccalaureate degree

Minimum degree required
None

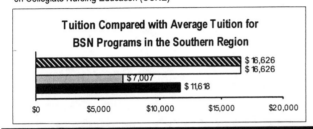
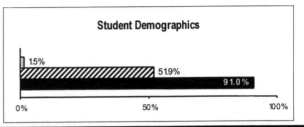

LIPSCOMB UNIVERSITY

3901 Granny White Pike
Nashville, TN 37204
(615) 343-3241
Linda Norman, DSN, RN

www.lipscomb.edu

Accreditation
Tennessee State Board of Nursing

Degrees conferred
Baccalaureate

MIDDLE TENNESSEE STATE UNIVERSITY   *Useful Facts*

Box 81 1301 East Main Street
Murfreesboro, TN 37132
(615) 898-2437
Lynn Parsons, DSN, RN, CNA

www.mtsu.edu/nursing

Acceptance rate		29.1%
Faculty-student ratio		1: 12
Faculty	Full time	23
	Part time	9

Tuition	
In state	$3,352
Out of state	$11,840
Enrollments	330
Graduations	116

Student Demographics	
Female	92.8%
Under age 25	93.8%
Minority	7.7%
Part-time	0.0%

Accreditation
Tennessee State Board of Nursing, Commission on Collegiate Nursing Education (CCNE), National League for Nursing Accrediting Commission (NLNAC)

Degrees conferred
Baccalaureate degree

Minimum degree required
High school diploma or GED

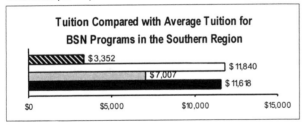
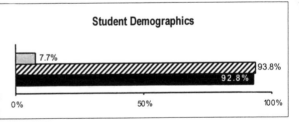

Demographics Chart	■Female ☒Under age 25 ☐Minority	Distance Learning	[computer icon]	¹The tuition reported for this program may be not be annualized. *Data reported between 2001 and 2004.

Tennessee

MILLIGAN COLLEGE *Useful Facts**

PO Box 500
Milligan College, TN 37682
(423) 461-8655
Melinda Collins, MSN, RN

www.milligan.edu

Accreditation
Tennessee State Board of Nursing, Commission on Collegiate Nursing Education (CCNE)

Acceptance rate	100.0%	
Faculty-student ratio	1: 13	
Faculty Full time	5	
Part time	4	

Tuition
In state	$12,750
Out of state	$12,750
Enrollments	92
Graduations	5

Student Demographics
Female	93.5%
Under age 25	85.9%
Minority	3.3%
Part-time	0.0%

Degrees conferred
Baccalaureate

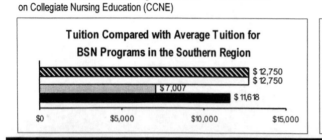
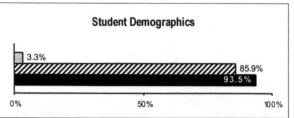

TENNESSEE STATE UNIVERSITY *Useful Facts*

3500 John A Merritt Boulevard, Box 9596
Nashville, TN 37209
(615) 963-5254
Mary Graham, EdD

www.tnstate.edu

Accreditation
Tennessee State Board of Nursing, National League for Nursing Accrediting Commission (NLNAC)

Acceptance rate	38.0%	
Faculty-student ratio	1: 7	
Faculty Full time	26	
Part time	14	

Tuition
In state	$4,414
Out of state	$13,726
Enrollments	124
Graduations	29

Student Demographics
Female	90.4%
Under age 25	67.3%
Minority	67.3%
Part-time	0.0%

Degrees conferred
Baccalaureate degree

Minimum degree required
None

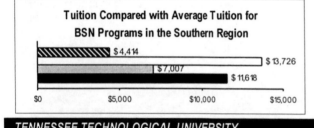
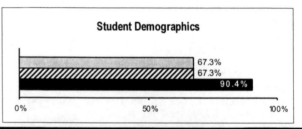

TENNESSEE TECHNOLOGICAL UNIVERSITY *Useful Facts*

805 Quadrangle
Cookeville, TN 38505
(931) 372-3203
Sheila Green, APRN, BC, PhD

www.tntech.edu/nursing

Accreditation
Tennessee State Board of Nursing, Commission on Collegiate Nursing Education (CCNE)

Acceptance rate	33.6%	
Faculty-student ratio	1: 8	
Faculty Full time	9	
Part time	7	

Tuition
In state	$3,678
Out of state	$13,018
Enrollments	99
Graduations	43

Student Demographics
Female	90.9%
Under age 25	91.9%
Minority	3.1%
Part-time	0.0%

Degrees conferred
Baccalaureate degree

Minimum degree required
None

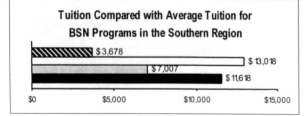
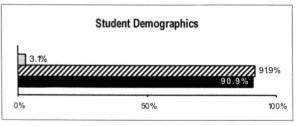

Key   Tuition Chart   ▨ Program - in state   ☐ Program - out of state   ☐ Average - in state   ■ Average - out of state

Tennessee

TENNESSEE WESLEYAN COLLEGE — *Useful Facts*

9821 Cogdill Road, Ste 2
Knoxville, TN 37932
(865) 777-5100
Ruth Heins, RN, MS, EdD

twcnet.edu

Acceptance rate	44.2%
Faculty-student ratio	1: 8
Faculty Full time	8
Part time	6

Tuition	
In state	$12,000
Out of state	$12,000
Enrollments	92
Graduations	29

Student Demographics	
Female	87.8%
Under age 25	44.4%
Minority	3.3%
Part-time	0.0%

Accreditation
Tennessee State Board of Nursing, Commission on Collegiate Nursing Education (CCNE)

Degrees conferred
Baccalaureate degree

Minimum degree required
Prenursing courses

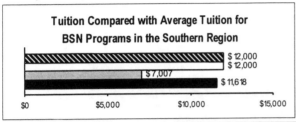

Tuition Compared with Average Tuition for BSN Programs in the Southern Region
$12,000 / $12,000 / $7,007 / $11,618

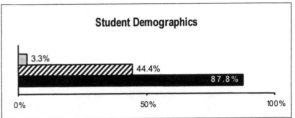

Student Demographics
3.3% / 44.4% / 87.8%

THE UNIVERSITY OF MEMPHIS — *Useful Facts*

102 Newport Hall
Memphis, TN 38152
(901) 678-2020
Marjorie Luttrell, PhD, RN

nursing.memphis.edu

Acceptance rate	39.9%
Faculty-student ratio	1: 10
Faculty Full time	28
Part time	25

Tuition	
In state	$5,000
Out of state	$10,064
Enrollments	398
Graduations	90

Student Demographics	
Female	89.8%
Under age 25	69.7%
Minority	28.3%
Part-time	15.7%

Accreditation
Tennessee State Board of Nursing, Commission on Collegiate Nursing Education (CCNE), National League for Nursing Accrediting Commission (NLNAC)

Degrees conferred
Baccalaureate degree

Minimum degree required
High school diploma or GED

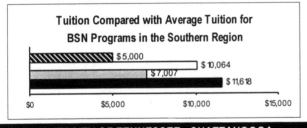

Tuition Compared with Average Tuition for BSN Programs in the Southern Region
$5,000 / $10,064 / $7,007 / $11,618

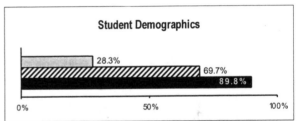

Student Demographics
28.3% / 69.7% / 89.8%

THE UNIVERSITY OF TENNESSEE - CHATTANOOGA — *Useful Facts**

615 McCallie Ave, Dept 1051
Chattanooga, TN 37403
(423) 425-4646
Katherine Lindgren, PhD, CCRN, CNA-Assist

www.utc.edu/academic/nursing

Acceptance rate	37.3%

Tuition	
In state	$4,094
Out of state	$12,350
Enrollments	140
Graduations	58

Student Demographics	
Female	91.0%
Under age 25	60.0%
Minority	13.4%
Part-time	0.0%

Accreditation
Tennessee State Board of Nursing, Commission on Collegiate Nursing Education (CCNE)

Degrees conferred
Baccalaureate

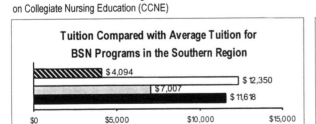

Tuition Compared with Average Tuition for BSN Programs in the Southern Region
$4,094 / $12,350 / $7,007 / $11,618

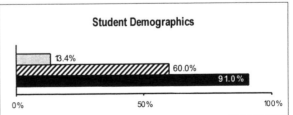

Student Demographics
13.4% / 60.0% / 91.0%

Demographics Chart	■ Female ▨ Under age 25 ☐ Minority	Distance Learning	¹The tuition reported for this program may be not be annualized.
			*Data reported between 2001 and 2004.

Tennessee

THE UNIVERSITY OF TENNESSEE - KNOXVILLE

1200 Volunteer Boulevard
Knoxville, TN 37996
(865) 974-7583
Joan Creasia, PhD

www.nightingale.con.utk.edu

Acceptance rate	51.1%	

Tuition		**Student Demographics**	
In state	$4,016	Female	86.9%
Out of state	$8,832	Under age 25	78.0%
Enrollments	249	Minority	7.6%
Graduations	122	Part-time	0.9%

Accreditation
Tennessee State Board of Nursing, National
League for Nursing Accrediting Commission
(NLNAC)

Degrees conferred
Baccalaureate

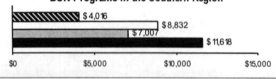

Tuition Compared with Average Tuition for BSN Programs in the Southern Region

$4,016 · $8,832 · $7,007 · $11,618

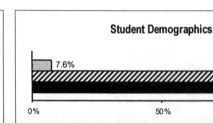

Student Demographics

7.6% · 78.0% · 86.9%

THE UNIVERSITY OF TENNESSEE - MARTIN

Gooch Hall 136
Martin, TN 38238
(731) 881-7131
Nancy Warren, PhD, RN

www.utm.edu

Acceptance rate		42.8%
Faculty-student ratio		1: 9
Faculty	Full time	14
	Part time	3

Tuition		**Student Demographics**	
In state	$3,744	Female	89.7%
Out of state	$12,798	Under age 25	89.7%
Enrollments	132	Minority	8.5%
Graduations	53	Part-time	0.0%

Accreditation
Tennessee State Board of Nursing, National
League for Nursing Accrediting Commission
(NLNAC)

Degrees conferred
Baccalaureate degree

Minimum degree required
Math 140 , Psych I, Psych II, Zoo, Micro, Chem

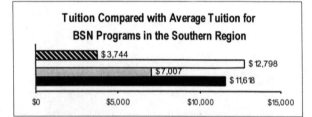

Tuition Compared with Average Tuition for BSN Programs in the Southern Region

$3,744 · $12,798 · $7,007 · $11,618

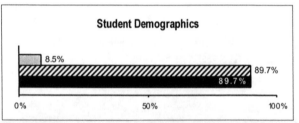

Student Demographics

8.5% · 89.7% · 89.7%

THE UNIVERSITY OF TENNESSEE - MEMPHIS

877 Madison Avenue
Memphis, TN 38163
(901) 448-6135
Donna Hathaway, RN

www.utmem.edu

Accreditation
Tennessee State Board of Nursing

Degrees conferred
Baccalaureate

Key | Tuition Chart | ▨ Program - in state ▢ Program - out of state ▢ Average - in state ▪ Average - out of state

Tennessee

UNION UNIVERSITY

1050 Union University Drive
Jackson, TN 38305
(731) 661-5200
Tharon Kirk, MSN, APRN, BC

www.uu.edu/union/academ/sonursed.htm

Accreditation
Tennessee State Board of Nursing, Commission on Collegiate Nursing Education (CCNE)

Degrees conferred
Baccalaureate

Acceptance rate	83.3%

Tuition		Student Demographics	
In state	$13,950	Female	91.2%
Out of state	$13,950	Under age 25	83.0%
Enrollments	177	Minority	13.2%
Graduations	61	Part-time	4.4%

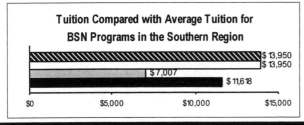

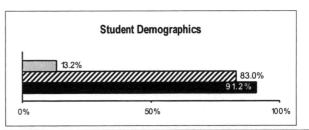

UNIVERSITY OF PHOENIX - NASHVILLE

616 Marriott Drive, Suite 150
Nashville, TN 37214
(615) 872-0188
Kim Hickok, MS, ARNP, BC

phoenix.19gi.com

Accreditation
Tennessee State Board of Nursing

Degrees conferred
Baccalaureate

Texas

ABILENE INTERCOLLEGIATE SCHOOL OF NURSING

2149 Hickory St
Abilene, TX 79601
(915) 672-2441
Cecilia Tiller, RN

www.acu.edu

Accreditation
Texas Board of Nurse Examiners

Degrees conferred
Baccalaureate

Acceptance rate	92.3%

		Student Demographics	
Enrollments	101		
Graduations	34	Part-time	0.0%

BAYLOR UNIVERSITY

3700 Worth St
Dallas, TX 75246
(214) 820-3361
Phyllis Karns, PhD, RN, MSN, BSN

baylor.edu

Accreditation
Texas Board of Nurse Examiners

Degrees conferred
Baccalaureate

Acceptance rate	0.7%

Tuition		Student Demographics	
In state	$12,128	Female	95.3%
Out of state	$12,128		
Enrollments	191		
Graduations	82	Part-time	2.1%

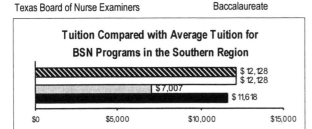

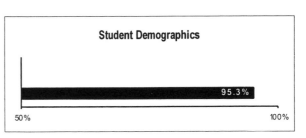

Demographics Chart	■ Female ▨ Under age 25 ☐ Minority	Distance Learning	†The tuition reported for this program may be not be annualized. *Data reported between 2001 and 2004.

Texas

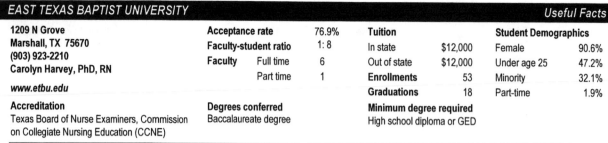

EAST TEXAS BAPTIST UNIVERSITY · *Useful Facts*

1209 N Grove
Marshall, TX 75670
(903) 923-2210
Carolyn Harvey, PhD, RN
www.etbu.edu

Acceptance rate		76.9%
Faculty-student ratio		1: 8
Faculty	Full time	6
	Part time	1

Tuition
In state $12,000
Out of state $12,000
Enrollments 53
Graduations 18

Student Demographics
Female 90.6%
Under age 25 47.2%
Minority 32.1%
Part-time 1.9%

Accreditation
Texas Board of Nurse Examiners, Commission on Collegiate Nursing Education (CCNE)

Degrees conferred
Baccalaureate degree

Minimum degree required
High school diploma or GED

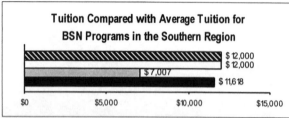

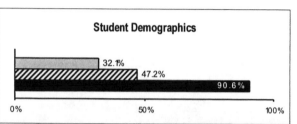

HOUSTON BAPTIST UNIVERSITY · *Useful Facts*

7502 Fondren Road
Houston, TX 77074
(281) 649-3300
Nancy Yuill, PhD, RN
www.hbu.edu

Acceptance rate		10.0%
Faculty-student ratio		1: 9
Faculty	Full time	10
	Part time	5

Tuition
In state $15,000
Out of state $15,000
Enrollments 99
Graduations 31

Student Demographics
Female 91.8%
Under age 25 81.4%
Minority 57.7%
Part-time 0.0%

Accreditation
Texas Board of Nurse Examiners, National League for Nursing Accrediting Commission (NLNAC)

Degrees conferred
Baccalaureate degree

Minimum degree required
High school diploma or GED

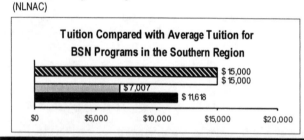

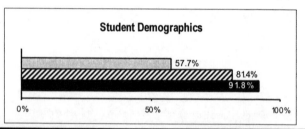

LAMAR UNIVERSITY · *Useful Facts*

PO Box 10081
Beaumont, TX 77710
(409) 880-8817
Eileen Curl, PhD, RN
dept.lamar.edu/nursing

Acceptance rate		25.0%
Faculty-student ratio		1: 9
Faculty	Full time	33
	Part time	2

Tuition
In state $3,834
Out of state $10,458
Enrollments 225
Graduations 59

Student Demographics
Female 82.0%
Under age 25 69.6%
Minority 27.2%
Part-time 1.4%

Accreditation
Texas Board of Nurse Examiners, National League for Nursing Accrediting Commission (NLNAC)

Degrees conferred
Baccalaureate degree

Minimum degree required
High school diploma or GED

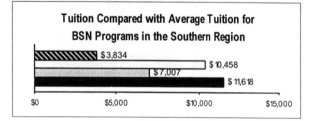

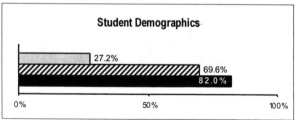

Key | Tuition Chart | 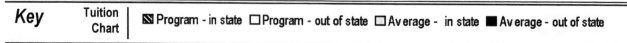 ▨ Program - in state ☐ Program - out of state ☐ Average - in state ■ Average - out of state

Texas

MIDWESTERN STATE UNIVERSITY — Useful Facts*

3410 Taft Blvd
Wichita Falls, TX 76308
(940) 397-4594
Susan Sportsman, PhD, RN, CAN

www.mwsu.edu

Accreditation
Texas Board of Nurse Examiners

Degrees conferred
Baccalaureate

Acceptance rate	100.0%

Tuition
In state	$2,096
Out of state	$8,456
Enrollments	167
Graduations	60

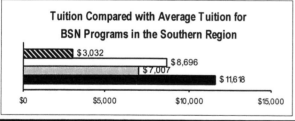

Tuition Compared with Average Tuition for BSN Programs in the Southern Region
- $2,096
- $8,456
- $7,007
- $11,618

PRAIRIE VIEW A&M UNIVERSITY

1801 Main Street Suite 801
Houston, TX 77002
(713) 797-7009
Betty Adams, PhD, RN

pvamu.edu/nursing

Accreditation
Texas Board of Nurse Examiners, National League for Nursing Accrediting Commission (NLNAC)

At the request of this nursing school, publication has been withheld. Please contact the school directly for more information.

STEPHEN F AUSTIN STATE UNIVERSITY — Useful Facts

1496 North Street
Nacogdoches, TX 75962
(936) 468-1492
Glenda Walker, DSN, RN

www.sfasu.edu

Accreditation
Texas Board of Nurse Examiners, National League for Nursing Accrediting Commission (NLNAC)

Degrees conferred
Baccalaureate degree

Acceptance rate		48.0%
Faculty-student ratio		1: 8
Faculty	Full time	22
	Part time	1

Tuition
In state	$3,032
Out of state	$8,696
Enrollments	180
Graduations	99

Minimum degree required
None

Student Demographics
Female	82.8%
Under age 25	97.1%
Minority	19.7%
Part-time	0.0%

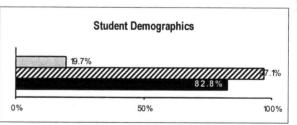

Tuition Compared with Average Tuition for BSN Programs in the Southern Region
- $3,032
- $8,696
- $7,007
- $11,618

Student Demographics
- 19.7%
- 97.1%
- 82.8%

TARLETON STATE UNIVERSITY

Box T-0500, 201 St Felix
Stephenville, TX 76402
(254) 968-9139
Elaine Evans, PhD, RN

www.tarleton.edu

Accreditation
Texas Board of Nurse Examiners

Degrees conferred
Baccalaureate

Demographics Chart | ■ Female ▨ Under age 25 ☐ Minority | **Distance Learning** | †The tuition reported for this program may be not be annualized.
*Data reported between 2001 and 2004.

Texas

TEXAS A&M INTERNATIONAL UNIVERSITY

5201 University Boulevard
Laredo, TX 78041
(956) 326-2450
Susan Walker, PhD, RN, CS

www.tamiu.edu/cson

Faculty-student ratio		1: 5
Faculty	Full time	14
	Part time	8

Tuition	
In state	$2,520
Out of state	$9,144
Enrollments	96
Graduations	32

Student Demographics	
Female	81.6%
Under age 25	25.3%
Minority	95.4%
Part-time	0.0%

Accreditation
Texas Board of Nurse Examiners, National League for Nursing Accrediting Commission (NLNAC)

Degrees conferred
Baccalaureate degree, MSN

Minimum degree required
High school diploma or GED

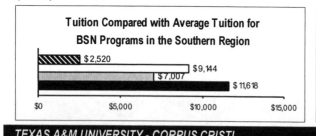

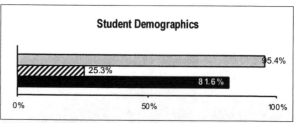

TEXAS A&M UNIVERSITY - CORPUS CRISTI

6300 Ocean Drive FC151
Corpus Christi, TX 78412
(361) 825-2649
Mary Hamilton, RN, PhD

www.conhs.tamucc.edu/nursing

Acceptance rate		46.7%
Faculty-student ratio		1: 17
Faculty	Full time	30
	Part time	15

Tuition	
In state	$4,180
Out of state	$15,596
Enrollments	630
Graduations	72

Student Demographics	
Female	87.5%
Under age 25	82.5%
Minority	50.0%
Part-time	13.3%

Accreditation
Texas Board of Nurse Examiners, Commission on Collegiate Nursing Education (CCNE)

Degrees conferred
Baccalaureate degree

Minimum degree required
None

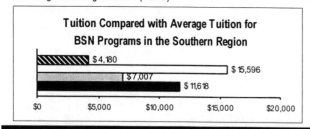

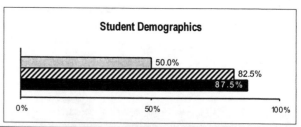

TEXAS CHRISTIAN UNIVERSITY

2900 West Bowie
Fort Worth, TX 76129
(817) 257-6756
Paulette Burns, PhD

www.hsn.tcu.edu

Acceptance rate		55.0%
Faculty-student ratio		1: 13
Faculty	Full time	29
	Part time	13

Tuition	
In state	$20,000
Out of state	$20,000
Enrollments	472
Graduations	97

Student Demographics	
Female	94.1%
Under age 25	100.0%
Minority	18.3%
Part-time	0.8%

Accreditation
Texas Board of Nurse Examiners, Commission on Collegiate Nursing Education (CCNE)

Degrees conferred
Baccalaureate degree

Minimum degree required
High school diploma or GED

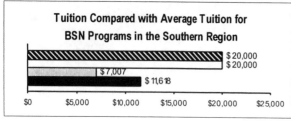

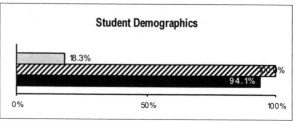

Key Tuition Chart | ▧ Program - in state ▢ Program - out of state ▨ Average - in state ■ Average - out of state

Texas

TEXAS TECH UNIVERSITY HEALTH SCIENCES CENTER — *Useful Facts*

3601-4th Street
Lubbock, TX 79430
(806) 743-2738
Alexia Green, PhD, RN, FAAN

www.ttuhsc.edu/son

Accreditation
Texas Board of Nurse Examiners, Commission on Collegiate Nursing Education (CCNE), National League for Nursing Accrediting Commission (NLNAC)

Acceptance rate		40.6%
Faculty-student ratio		1: 10
Faculty	Full time	44
	Part time	3

Tuition	
In state	$1,500
Out of state	$9,780
Enrollments	448
Graduations	233

Student Demographics	
Female	88.1%
Under age 25	87.2%
Minority	22.3%
Part-time	11.9%

Degrees conferred
Baccalaureate degree

Minimum degree required
Pre-licensure BSN-no prior degree required/Second Degree-baccalaureate non-nursing degree minimum

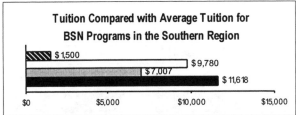

Tuition Compared with Average Tuition for BSN Programs in the Southern Region
$1,500 / $9,780 / $7,007 / $11,618

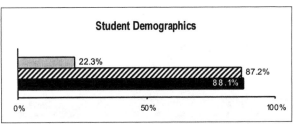

Student Demographics
22.3% / 87.2% / 88.1%

TEXAS WOMAN'S UNIVERSITY — *Useful Facts**

PO Box 425498
Denton, TX 76204
(940) 898-2401
Carolyn Gunning, PhD, RN

www.twu.edu/nursing

Accreditation
Texas Board of Nurse Examiners

Enrollments	670
Graduations	264

Degrees conferred
Baccalaureate

THE UNIVERSITY OF TEXAS - ARLINGTON — *Useful Facts**

411 S Nedderman Dr
Arlington, TX 76019
(817) 272-2776
Elizabeth Poster, PhD, RN, FAAN

www.uta.edu/nursing

Accreditation
Texas Board of Nurse Examiners, National League for Nursing Accrediting Commission (NLNAC)

Acceptance rate	20.3%

Tuition	
In state	$3,808
Out of state	$12,808
Enrollments	513
Graduations	313

Student Demographics	
Female	87.2%
Under age 25	54.2%
Minority	35.6%
Part-time	5.0%

Degrees conferred
Baccalaureate

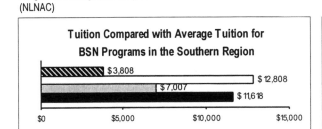

Tuition Compared with Average Tuition for BSN Programs in the Southern Region
$3,808 / $12,808 / $7,007 / $11,618

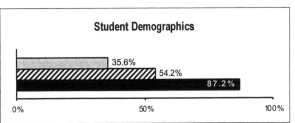

Student Demographics
35.6% / 54.2% / 87.2%

Demographics Chart	■ Female ⊠ Under age 25 ☐ Minority	Distance Learning 💻	¹The tuition reported for this program may be not be annualized. *Data reported between 2001 and 2004.

Texas

UNIVERSITY OF MARY HARDIN - BAYLOR

UMHB Box 8015, 900 College Street
Belton, TX 76513
(254) 295-4665
Linda Pehl, PhD, RNC

www.umhb.edu

Acceptance rate	97.5%

Tuition[1]		**Student Demographics**	
In state	$355	Female	95.7%
Out of state	$355	Under age 25	75.0%
Enrollments	140	Minority	18.1%
Graduations	47	Part-time	4.3%

Accreditation
Texas Board of Nurse Examiners, Commission on Collegiate Nursing Education (CCNE)

Degrees conferred
Baccalaureate

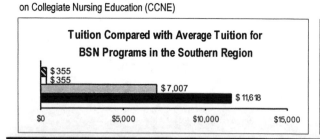

Tuition Compared with Average Tuition for BSN Programs in the Southern Region

$355
$355
$7,007
$11,618

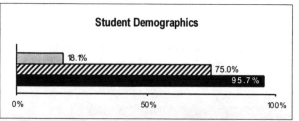

Student Demographics

18.1%
75.0%
95.7%

UNIVERSITY OF TEXAS - AUSTIN

1700 Red River
Austin, TX 78701
(512) 471-4100
Dolores Sands, RN, PhD, FAAN

www.utexas.edu/nursing

Acceptance rate		61.0%
Faculty-student ratio		1: 4
Faculty	Full time	63
	Part time	14

Tuition		**Student Demographics**	
In state	$7,304	Female	89.8%
Out of state	$16,460	Under age 25	100.0%
Enrollments	252	Minority	28.9%
Graduations	119	Part-time	2.5%

Accreditation
Texas Board of Nurse Examiners, Commission on Collegiate Nursing Education (CCNE)

Degrees conferred
Baccalaureate degree

Minimum degree required
High school diploma or GED

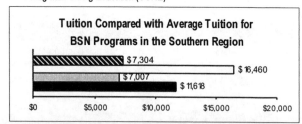

Tuition Compared with Average Tuition for BSN Programs in the Southern Region

$7,304
$16,460
$7,007
$11,618

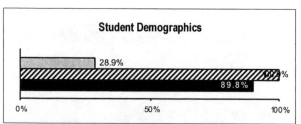

Student Demographics

28.9%
89.8%

UNIVERSITY OF TEXAS - EL PASO

1101 N Campbell
El Paso, TX 79902
(915) 747-8217
Leticia Lantican, PhD, RN

www.nurse.utep.edu/nurse/index.htm

Enrollments	296
Graduations	86

Accreditation
Texas Board of Nurse Examiners

Degrees conferred
Baccalaureate

Key | Tuition Chart | ▨ Program - in state ☐ Program - out of state ▢ Average - in state ■ Average - out of state

Texas

UNIVERSITY OF TEXAS - PAN AMERICAN
Useful Facts*

1201 W University Drive Edinburg, TX 78539 (956) 381-3491 Carolina Huerta, EdD, RN *panam.edu*	**Acceptance rate** 61.5%	**Tuition** In state $1,985 Out of state $7,145 **Enrollments** 127 **Graduations** 51	**Student Demographics** Female 66.7% Minority 89.9%

Accreditation
Texas Board of Nurse Examiners

Degrees conferred
Baccalaureate

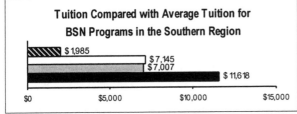

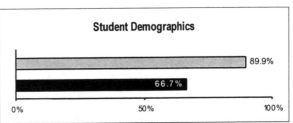

UNIVERSITY OF TEXAS - TYLER

3900 University Blvd
Tyler, TX 75799
(903) 566-7075
Linda Klotz, PhD, RN

www.uttyler.edu/nursing

Accreditation
Texas Board of Nurse Examiners, Commission
on Collegiate Nursing Education (CCNE)

At the request of this nursing school, publication has been witheld.
Please contact the school directly for more information.

UNIVERSITY OF TEXAS HEALTH SCIENCE CENTER - HOUSTON
Useful Facts*

6901 Bertner Houston, TX 77030 (713) 500-2002 Patricia Starck, DSN, RN, FAAN *www.uth.tmc.edu*	**Acceptance rate** 29.0%	**Tuition** In state $2,088 Out of state $9,864 **Enrollments** 185 **Graduations** 91

Accreditation
Texas Board of Nurse Examiners

Degrees conferred
Baccalaureate

Tuition Compared with Average Tuition for BSN Programs in the Southern Region

- $2,088
- $9,864
- $7,007
- $11,618

$0 — $5,000 — $10,000 — $15,000

UNIVERSITY OF TEXAS HEALTH SCIENCE CENTER - SAN ANTONIO

7703 Floyd Curl Drive - MSC 7942
San Antonio, TX 78229
(210) 567-5800
Robin Froman, PhD, RN, FAAN

www.nursing.uthscsa.edu

Accreditation
Texas Board of Nurse Examiners, Commission
on Collegiate Nursing Education (CCNE)

At the request of this nursing school, publication has been witheld.
Please contact the school directly for more information.

Demographics Chart	■Female ▨Under age 25 ☐Minority	Distance Learning	¹The tuition reported for this program may be not be annualized. *Data reported between 2001 and 2004.

Texas

UNIVERSITY OF TEXAS MEDICAL BRANCH - GALVESTON

Useful Facts*

1100 Mechanic, Mailing: 301 University Blvd
Galveston, TX 77555
(409) 772-1510
Pamela Watson, ScD, RN

www.son.utmb.edu

Acceptance rate	27.6%		

Tuition		**Student Demographics**
In state	$2,640	Female	84.4%
Out of state	$10,380	Under age 25	46.0%
Enrollments	397	Minority	36.6%
Graduations	187	Part-time	24.1%

Accreditation
Texas Board of Nurse Examiners

Degrees conferred
Baccalaureate

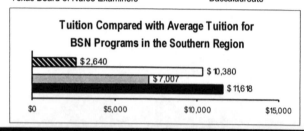
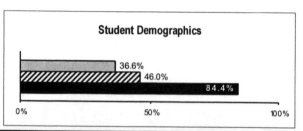

UNIVERSITY OF THE INCARNATE WORD

4301 Broadway, CPO 300
San Antonio, TX 78209
(210) 829-3982
Kathleen Light, EdD, RN

www.uiw.edu/nursing

At the request of this nursing school, publication has been withheld.
Please contact the school directly for more information.

Accreditation
Texas Board of Nurse Examiners

WEST TEXAS A&M UNIVERSITY

Useful Facts*

2501 Fourth Avenue, OM 313
Canyon, TX 79016
(806) 651-2631
Heidi Taylor, PhD, RN

www.wtamu.edu/nursing

Acceptance rate	90.6%		

Tuition		**Student Demographics**
In state	$2,445	Female	86.7%
Out of state	$9,525	Under age 25	51.0%
Enrollments	394	Minority	20.6%
Graduations	66	Part-time	16.2%

Accreditation
Texas Board of Nurse Examiners, Commission
on Collegiate Nursing Education (CCNE)

Degrees conferred
Baccalaureate

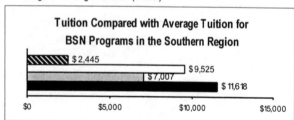
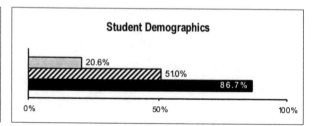

Key | Tuition Chart | ▨ Program - in state ☐ Program - out of state ☐ Average - in state ■ Average - out of state

Utah

BRIGHAM YOUNG UNIVERSITY — *Useful Facts*

500 SWKT
Provo, UT 84602
(801) 422-2747
Elaine Marshall, RN, PhD

nursing.byu.edu

Accreditation
Utah State Board of Nursing, Commission on Collegiate Nursing Education (CCNE), National League for Nursing Accrediting Commission (NLNAC)

Acceptance rate		52.0%
Faculty-student ratio		1:6
Faculty	Full time	40
	Part time	20

Degrees conferred
Baccalaureate degree

Tuition	
In state	$1,705
Out of state	$2,558
Enrollments	277
Graduations	89

Minimum degree required
N/A

Student Demographics	
Female	90.6%
Under age 25	87.0%
Minority	5.8%
Part-time	14.1%

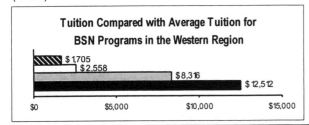

Tuition Compared with Average Tuition for BSN Programs in the Western Region

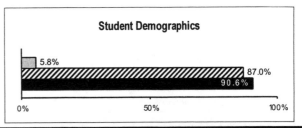

Student Demographics

SOUTHERN UTAH UNIVERSITY — *Useful Facts**

351 West University Blvd
Cedar City, UT 84720
(435) 586-1990
Donna Lister, APRN-C, MSN, PhD©

www.suu.edu/sci/nursing

Accreditation
Utah State Board of Nursing

Acceptance rate	52.6%

Degrees conferred
Baccalaureate

Tuition	
In state	$2,332
Out of state	$7,696
Enrollments	19
Graduations	0

Student Demographics	
Female	63.2%
Part-time	0.0%

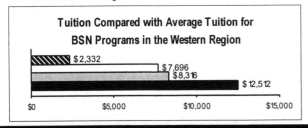

Tuition Compared with Average Tuition for BSN Programs in the Western Region

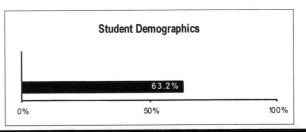

Student Demographics

UNIVERSITY OF UTAH — *Useful Facts**

10 South 2000 East
Salt Lake City, UT 84121
(801) 581-8262
Maureen Keefe, RN, PhD, FAAN

www.nurs.utah.edu

Accreditation
Utah State Board of Nursing, Commission on Collegiate Nursing Education (CCNE)

Acceptance rate	22.4%

Degrees conferred
Baccalaureate

Tuition	
In state	$3,364
Out of state	$11,774
Enrollments	216
Graduations	186

Student Demographics	
Female	92.7%
Under age 25	30.0%
Minority	10.5%
Part-time	0.0%

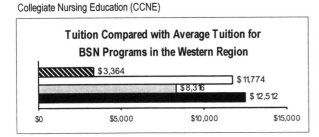

Tuition Compared with Average Tuition for BSN Programs in the Western Region

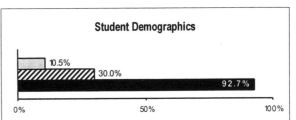

Student Demographics

Demographics Chart | ■ Female ▨ Under age 25 ☐ Minority

Distance Learning

¹The tuition reported for this program may be not be annualized.
*Data reported between 2001 and 2004.

Utah

UTAH CAREER COLLEGE

1902 W 7800 S
West Jordan, UT 84088
(801) 304-4224
Becky Richards, RN, MSN

www.utahcollege.com

Accreditation
Utah State Board of Nursing

Degrees conferred
Baccalaureate

UTAH VALLEY STATE COLLEGE
Useful Facts

800 West University Parkway
Orem, UT 84058
(801) 863-8192
Gary Measom, APRN, PhD

www.uvsc.edu/nurs

Faculty-student ratio		1: 14
Faculty	Full time	18
	Part time	4

Tuition	
In state	$2,580
Out of state	$9,030
Enrollments	48
Graduations	9

Accreditation
Utah State Board of Nursing, National League for
Nursing Accrediting Commission (NLNAC)

Degrees conferred
Baccalaureate degree

Minimum degree required
ADN

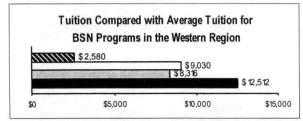

**Tuition Compared with Average Tuition for
BSN Programs in the Western Region**

- $2,580
- $9,030
- $8,316
- $12,512

WEBER STATE UNIVERSITY

3903 University Ave
Ogden, UT 84408
(801) 626-6833
Catherine Earl, postdoc, DPA, MSN, RN

www.weber.edu

Faculty-student ratio		1: 9
Faculty	Full time	37
	Part time	4

Accreditation
Utah State Board of Nursing, National League for
Nursing Accrediting Commission (NLNAC)

Degrees conferred
Baccalaureate

WESTMINSTER COLLEGE - ST MARKS
Useful Facts*

1840 South 1300 East
Salt Lake City, UT 84105
(801) 832-2150
Jean Dyer, PhD

www.westminstercollege.edu

Accreditation
Utah State Board of Nursing

Degrees conferred
Baccalaureate

Student Demographics

| **Enrollments** | 42 |
| Part-time | 7.5% |

Key | Tuition Chart | ▨ Program - in state ☐ Program - out of state ☐ Average - in state ■ Average - out of state

Vermont

NORWICH UNIVERSITY
*Useful Facts**

158 Harmon Drive
Northfield, VT 05663
(802) 485-2609
Marilyn Rinker, MSN, RN, OCN

www.norwich.edu

Acceptance rate	68.3%	

Tuition
In state	$16,710
Out of state	$16,710
Enrollments	119
Graduations	11

Student Demographics
Female	84.6%
Under age 25	84.0%
Minority	8.8%
Part-time	0.0%

Accreditation
Vermont State Board of Nursing, National
League for Nursing Accrediting Commission
(NLNAC)

Degrees conferred
Baccalaureate

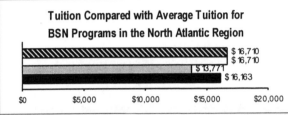

Tuition Compared with Average Tuition for BSN Programs in the North Atlantic Region
$16,710
$16,710
$13,771
$16,163

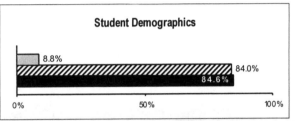

Student Demographics
8.8%
84.0%
84.6%

THE UNIVERSITY OF VERMONT
*Useful Facts**

106 Carrigan Dr, Rowell Bldg, Rm 216
Burlington, VT 05405
(802) 656-3830
Gregg Newschwander, PhD, RN

www.uvm.edu/nursing

Acceptance rate	51.9%	

Tuition
In state	$9,088
Out of state	$22,728
Enrollments	345
Graduations	66

Student Demographics
Female	91.4%
Under age 25	80.0%
Minority	3.8%
Part-time	3.8%

Accreditation
Vermont State Board of Nursing, National
League for Nursing Accrediting Commission
(NLNAC)

Degrees conferred
Baccalaureate

Tuition Compared with Average Tuition for BSN Programs in the North Atlantic Region
$9,088
$22,728
$13,771
$16,163

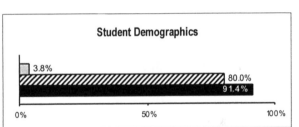

Student Demographics
3.8%
80.0%
91.4%

Virginia

EASTERN MENNONITE UNIVERSITY
*Useful Facts**

1200 Park Road
Harrisonburg, VA 22802
(540) 432-4186
Ann Hershberger, PhD, RN

www.emu.edu

Acceptance rate	100.0%	

Tuition
In state	$18,220
Out of state	$18,220
Enrollments	132
Graduations	47

Student Demographics
Female	93.8%
Under age 25	74.2%
Minority	4.7%
Part-time	0.0%

Accreditation
Virginia Board of Nursing, Commission on
Collegiate Nursing Education (CCNE)

Degrees conferred
Baccalaureate

Tuition Compared with Average Tuition for BSN Programs in the Southern Region
$18,220
$18,220
$7,007
$11,618

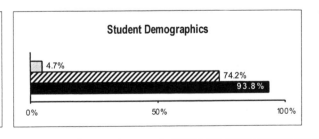

Student Demographics
4.7%
74.2%
93.8%

| Demographics Chart | ■Female ▨Under age 25 ▢Minority | Distance Learning | †The tuition reported for this program may be not be annualized.
*Data reported between 2001 and 2004. |
|---|---|---|---|

Virginia

GEORGE MASON UNIVERSITY
Useful Facts*

4400 University Drive
Fairfax, VA 22030
(703) 993-1918
Shirley Travis, PhD, APRN, FAN

cnhs.gmu.edu

Accreditation
Virginia Board of Nursing, Commission on
Collegiate Nursing Education (CCNE)

Acceptance rate		41.3%
Faculty-student ratio		1: 8
Faculty	Full time	50
	Part time	28

Tuition	
In state	$5,112
Out of state	$14,952
Enrollments	514
Graduations	168

Student Demographics	
Female	91.8%
Under age 25	20.0%
Minority	34.7%
Part-time	13.4%

Degrees conferred
Baccalaureate

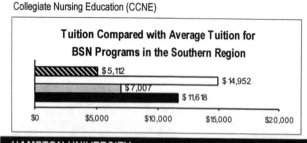

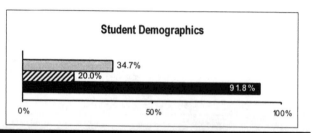

HAMPTON UNIVERSITY
Useful Facts*

William Freeman Hall, Rm 110
Hampton, VA 23668
(757) 727-5654
Constance Hendricks, PhD, RN

www.hamptonu.edu

Accreditation
Virginia Board of Nursing, Commission on
Collegiate Nursing Education (CCNE), National
League for Nursing Accrediting Commission
(NLNAC)

Acceptance rate	54.7%

Tuition	
In state	$12,116
Out of state	$12,116
Enrollments	565
Graduations	76

Student Demographics	
Female	92.9%
Minority	93.0%
Part-time	1.3%

Degrees conferred
Baccalaureate

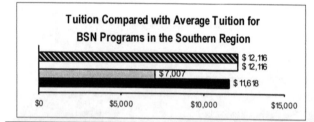

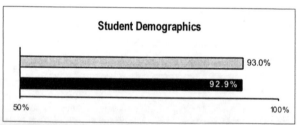

JAMES MADISON UNIVERSITY
Useful Facts

701 Carrier Drive, MSC 4305
Harrisonburg, VA 22807
(540) 568-6314
Merle Mast, PhD, RN

www.nursing.jmu.edu

Accreditation
Virginia Board of Nursing, Commission on
Collegiate Nursing Education (CCNE)

Acceptance rate		38.7%
Faculty-student ratio		1: 26
Faculty	Full time	17
	Part time	6

Tuition	
In state	$5,886
Out of state	$15,322
Enrollments	511
Graduations	56

Student Demographics	
Female	95.1%
Under age 25	99.8%
Minority	7.3%
Part-time	1.2%

Degrees conferred
Baccalaureate degree

Minimum degree required
High school diploma or GED

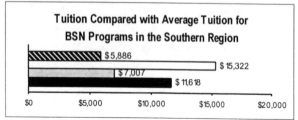

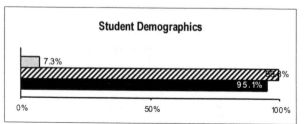

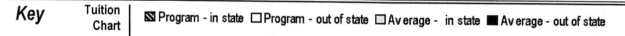

Virginia

LIBERTY UNIVERSITY | *Useful Facts**

1971 University Boulevard		**Student Demographics**	
Lynchburg, VA 24502		Female	92.7%
(804) 582-2521			
Deanna Britt, PhD, RN	**Enrollments** 132	Minority	8.1%
www.liberty.edu	**Graduations** 52		

Accreditation
Virginia Board of Nursing

Degrees conferred
Baccalaureate

LYNCHBURG COLLEGE | *Useful Facts**

1501 Lakeside Drive	**Acceptance rate**	100.0%	**Tuition**		**Student Demographics**
Lynchburg, VA 24501			In state	$20,040	Female 93.8%
(434) 544-8324			Out of state	$20,040	
Nancy Whitman, PhD, RN			**Enrollments**	96	Minority 16.1%
www.lynchburg.edu			**Graduations**	20	Part-time 8.3%

Accreditation
Virginia Board of Nursing

Degrees conferred
Baccalaureate

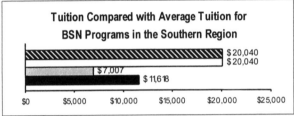

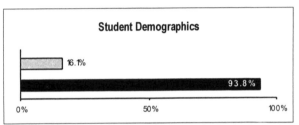

MARYMOUNT UNIVERSITY

2807 N Glebe Road
Arlington, VA 22207
(703) 284-1580
Theresa Cappello, PhD, RN

www.marymount.edu

Accreditation
Virginia Board of Nursing, Commission on
Collegiate Nursing Education (CCNE), National
League for Nursing Accrediting Commission
(NLNAC)

*At the request of this nursing school, publication has been witheld.
Please contact the school directly for more information.*

OLD DOMINION UNIVERSITY

One Hampton Boulevard
Norfolk, VA 23529
(757) 683-4297
Richardean Benjamin, RN, MPH, PhD

www.odu.edu/nursson

Accreditation
Virginia Board of Nursing, Commission on
Collegiate Nursing Education (CCNE)

*At the request of this nursing school, publication has been witheld.
Please contact the school directly for more information.*

RADFORD UNIVERSITY | *Useful Facts**

Box 6964, RM Station	**Acceptance rate**	80.4%	**Student Demographics**	
Radford, VA 24142			Female	95.8%
(540) 831-7700			Under age 25	75.0%
Janet Baettcher, PhD, CNAA, BC, FAAN, RN	**Enrollments**	324	Minority	3.3%
www.radford.edu	**Graduations**	43	Part-time	5.2%

Accreditation
Virginia Board of Nursing

Degrees conferred
Baccalaureate

Demographics Chart	■Female ☒Under age 25 ☐Minority	**Distance Learning**	†The tuition reported for this program may be not be annualized. *Data reported between 2001 and 2004.

Virginia

SHENANDOAH UNIVERSITY

Useful Facts*

1460 University Drive
Winchester, VA 22601
(540) 678-4381
Sheila Sparks, DNSs, RN, FAAN

www.su.edu

Acceptance rate	85.1%	

Tuition

In state	$18,310
Out of state	$18,310
Enrollments	136
Graduations	8

Student Demographics

Female	95.2%
Under age 25	73.0%
Minority	12.8%
Part-time	2.4%

Accreditation
Virginia Board of Nursing

Degrees conferred
Baccalaureate

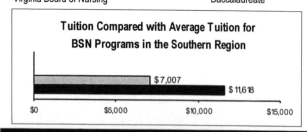
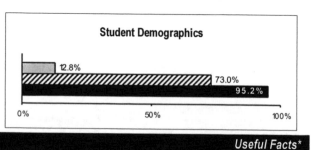

UNIVERSITY OF VIRGINIA

Useful Facts*

McLeod Hall, PO Box 800782
Charlottesville, VA 22908
(434) 924-0063
Jeanette Lancaster, PhD, RN, FAAN

www.nursing.virginia.edu

Acceptance rate	28.9%	
Faculty-student ratio	1: 5	
Faculty	Full time	52
	Part time	40

Tuition

In state	$7,133
Out of state	$24,053
Enrollments	339
Graduations	123

Student Demographics

Female	96.8%
Under age 25	89.3%
Minority	15.6%
Part-time	1.3%

Accreditation
Virginia Board of Nursing, Commission on
Collegiate Nursing Education (CCNE)

Degrees conferred
Baccalaureate degree

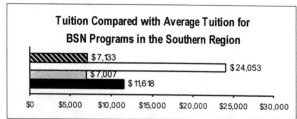
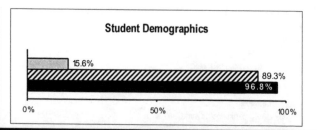

VIRGINIA COMMONWEALTH UNIVERSITY

1220 E Broad Street
Richmond, VA 23298
(804) 828-5174
Nancy Langston, PhD, RN

www.nursing.vcu.edu

Accreditation
Virginia Board of Nursing, National League for
Nursing Accrediting Commission (NLNAC)

*At the request of this nursing school, publication has been witheld.
Please contact the school directly for more information.*

Washington

GONZAGA UNIVERSITY

502 East Boone Avenue, AD Box 38
Spokane, WA 99258
(509) 323-6646
Suasan Norwood, EdD, ARNP

www.gonzaga.edu

Accreditation
Washington State Nursing Care Quality
Assurance Comm.

Degrees conferred
Baccalaureate

Key | Tuition Chart | ⬙ Program - in state ☐ Program - out of state ☐ Average - in state ■ Average - out of state

Washington

PACIFIC LUTHERAN UNIVERSITY

Ramstad Building #214
Tacoma, WA 98447-0029
(253) 535-7676
Terry Miller, PhD, RN

www.plu.edu/~nurs

Acceptance rate	24.0%

Tuition

In state	$20,790
Out of state	$20,790
Enrollments	231
Graduations	66

Student Demographics

Female	92.6%
Under age 25	34.0%
Minority	15.3%
Part-time	0.9%

Accreditation
Washington State Nursing Care Quality
Assurance Comm., Commission on Collegiate
Nursing Education (CCNE), National League for
Nursing Accrediting Commission (NLNAC)

Degrees conferred
Baccalaureate

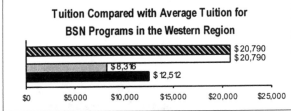

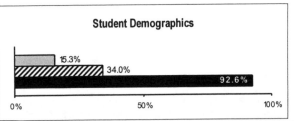

SEATTLE PACIFIC UNIVERSITY

3307 3rd Avenue West at Nickerson
Seattle, WA 98119
(206) 281-2608
Lucille Kelley, PhD, RN

www.spu.edu

Accreditation
Washington State Nursing Care Quality
Assurance Comm.

Degrees conferred
Baccalaureate

SEATTLE UNIVERSITY

900 Broadway and Madison
Seattle, WA 98122
(206) 296-5678
Mary Walker, PhD, RN, FAAN

www.seattleu.edu

Acceptance rate	70.9%

Tuition

In state	$17,010
Out of state	$17,010
Enrollments	281
Graduations	67

Student Demographics

Female	91.1%
Minority	40.7%

Accreditation
Washington State Nursing Care Quality
Assurance Comm.

Degrees conferred
Baccalaureate

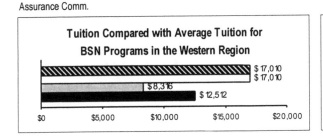

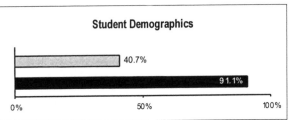

| Demographics Chart | ■Female ☑Under age 25 ☐Minority | Distance Learning | †The tuition reported for this program may be not be annualized.
*Data reported between 2001 and 2004. |

Washington

UNIVERSITY OF WASHINGTON

Useful Facts*

PO Box 357260
Seattle, WA 98195
(206) 543-8735
Susan Woods, PhD, RN, FAAN

www.washington.edu

Accreditation
Washington State Nursing Care Quality
Assurance Comm.

Acceptance rate	52.2%

Tuition
In state $3,639
Out of state $12,030

Graduations 187

Degrees conferred
Baccalaureate

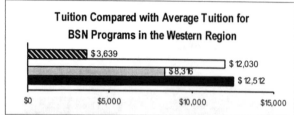

Tuition Compared with Average Tuition for BSN Programs in the Western Region
- $3,639
- $12,030
- $8,316
- $12,512

WASHINGTON STATE UNIVERSITY

Useful Facts*

2917 W Ft George Wright Drive
Spokane, WA 99224
(509) 324-7332
Dorothy Detlor, PhD, RN

nursing.wsu.edu

Accreditation
Washington State Nursing Care Quality
Assurance Comm., Commission on Collegiate
Nursing Education (CCNE)

Acceptance rate	41.1%	**Tuition**		**Student Demographics**
		In state	$5,146	Female	89.8%
		Out of state	$13,564	Under age 25	91.0%
		Enrollments	556	Minority	11.5%
		Graduations	171	Part-time	1.2%

Degrees conferred
Baccalaureate

Tuition Compared with Average Tuition for BSN Programs in the Western Region
- $5,146
- $13,564
- $8,316
- $12,512

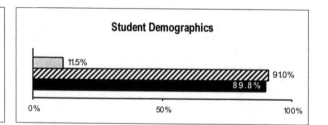

Student Demographics
- 11.5%
- 91.0%
- 89.8%

West Virginia

ALDERSON - BROADDUS COLLEGE

Useful Facts

Campus Box 2033
Philippi, WV 26416
(304) 457-6288
Threasia Witt, MSN, RN

www.ab.edu

Accreditation
West Virginia Board of Examiners for Registered
Professional Nurses, National League for
Nursing Accrediting Commission (NLNAC)

Acceptance rate	89.0%	**Tuition**		**Student Demographics**	
Faculty-student ratio	1:16	In state	$17,970	Female	92.4%
Faculty Full time	11	Out of state	$17,970	Under age 25	47.1%
Part time	3	Enrollments	194	Minority	1.2%
		Graduations	39	Part-time	0.0%

Minimum degree required
High school diploma or GED

Degrees conferred
Baccalaureate degree

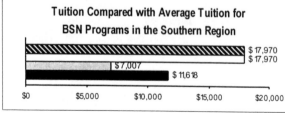

Tuition Compared with Average Tuition for BSN Programs in the Southern Region
- $17,970
- $17,970
- $7,007
- $11,618

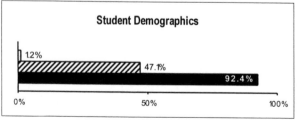

Student Demographics
- 1.2%
- 47.1%
- 92.4%

Key Tuition Chart | ▨ Program - in state ☐ Program - out of state ☐ Average - in state ■ Average - out of state

West Virginia

MARSHALL UNIVERSITY — *Useful Facts*

1 John Marshall Drive
Huntington, WV 25755
(304) 696-2639
Sandra Marra, EdD, NCC, RN

www.marshall.edu/cohp/nursing

Accreditation
West Virginia Board of Examiners for Registered
Professional Nurses, National League for
Nursing Accrediting Commission (NLNAC)

Acceptance rate	26.8%	
Faculty-student ratio	1: 14	
Faculty Full time	20	
Part time	16	

Tuition
In state $4,950
Out of state $14,400
Enrollments 382
Graduations 65

Degrees conferred
Baccalaureate degree

Minimum degree required
High school diploma or GED

Student Demographics
Female 83.7%
Under age 25 76.8%
Minority 1.9%
Part-time 0.0%

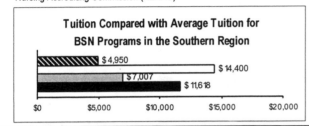

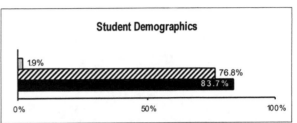

SHEPHERD COLLEGE

PO Box 3210
Shepherdstown, WV 25443
(304) 876-5341
Kathleen Gaberson, PhD, RN, CNOR, CNE

www.shepherd.edu

Accreditation
West Virginia Board of Examiners for Registered
Professional Nurses, National League for
Nursing Accrediting Commission (NLNAC)

At the request of this nursing school, publication has been witheld.
Please contact the school directly for more information.

THE MOUNTAIN STATE UNIVERSITY — *Useful Facts**

609 S Kanawha St
Beckley, WV 25802-2830
(304) 253-7351
Patsy Haslam, RN, BSN, MPH, EdD

www.cwv.edu

Accreditation
West Virginia Board of Examiners for Registered
Professional Nurses, National League for
Nursing Accrediting Commission (NLNAC)

Acceptance rate 28.2%

Tuition
In state $3,600
Out of state $3,600
Enrollments 166
Graduations 32

Degrees conferred
Baccalaureate

Student Demographics
Female 95.3%
Under age 25 30.0%
Minority 3.8%
Part-time 0.0%

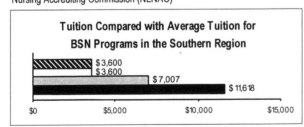

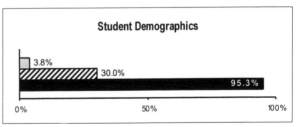

Demographics Chart | ■ Female ▨ Under age 25 ☐ Minority | **Distance Learning** | ¹The tuition reported for this program may be not be annualized.
*Data reported between 2001 and 2004.

West Virginia

UNIVERSITY OF CHARLESTON

2300 McCorkle Avenue, SE
Charleston, WV 25304
(304) 357-4835
Sandra Bowles, EdD, RN

www.ucwv.edu

Accreditation
West Virginia Board of Examiners for Registered
Professional Nurses, National League for
Nursing Accrediting Commission (NLNAC)

Acceptance rate   62.0%

Degrees conferred
Baccalaureate

Tuition		Student Demographics	
In state	$17,400	Female	90.2%
Out of state	$17,400		
Enrollments	103	Minority	4.9%
Graduations	31	Part-time	1.0%

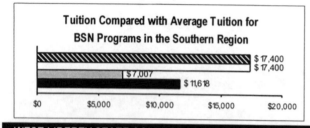

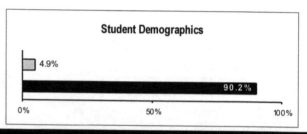

WEST LIBERTY STATE COLLEGE

PO Box 295, Route 88 N CMS #140
West Liberty, WV 26074
(304) 336-8108
Monica Kennison, EdD, RN

www.wlsc.edu

Accreditation
West Virginia Board of Examiners for Registered
Professional Nurses, National League for
Nursing Accrediting Commission (NLNAC)

Acceptance rate	57.1%
Faculty-student ratio	1: 12
Faculty Full time	6
Part time	6

Tuition		Student Demographics	
In state	$3,686	Female	78.7%
Out of state	$9,034	Under age 25	64.0%
Enrollments	106	Minority	1.3%
Graduations	23	Part-time	0.0%

Minimum degree required
High school diploma or GED

Degrees conferred
Baccalaureate degree

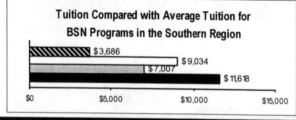

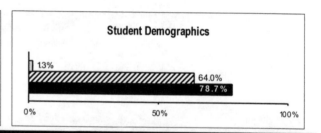

WEST VIRGINIA UNIVERSITY

6700 Health Sci Center S, PO Box 9600
Morgantown, WV 26506
(304) 293-4831
E Martin, PhD, RN, CS, FAAN

www.hsc.wvu.edu/son

Accreditation
West Virginia Board of Examiners for Registered
Professional Nurses

Degrees conferred
Baccalaureate

WEST VIRGINIA UNIVERSITY INSTITUTE OF TECHNOLOGY

405 Fayette Pike - Box 54
Montgomery, WV 25136
(304) 442-3109
Frances Snodgrass, RN, MS, MA, JD

www.wvutech.edu

Accreditation
West Virginia Board of Examiners for Registered
Professional Nurses

Degrees conferred
Baccalaureate

Key   Tuition Chart   ▨ Program - in state   ☐ Program - out of state   ☐ Average - in state   ■ Average - out of state

West Virginia

WEST VIRGINIA WESLEYAN COLLEGE
Useful Facts

59 College Avenue
Buckhannon, WV 26201
(304) 473-8224
Judith McKinney, EdD RN

www.wvwc.edu

Faculty-student ratio 1: 10
Faculty Full time 5
Part time 2

Tuition	
In state	$17,900
Out of state	$17,900
Enrollments	60
Graduations	19

Student Demographics	
Female	93.0%
Under age 25	96.5%
Minority	5.3%
Part-time	0.0%

Accreditation
West Virginia Board of Examiners for Registered
Professional Nurses, National League for
Nursing Accrediting Commission (NLNAC)

Degrees conferred
Baccalaureate degree

Minimum degree required
no students admitted program closing spring 2008

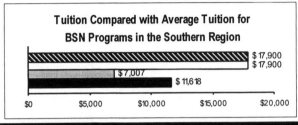

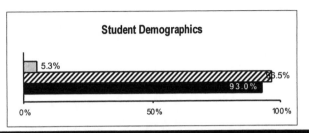

WHEELING JESUIT UNIVERSITY
Useful Facts*

316 Washington Avenue
Wheeling, WV 26003
(304) 243-2227
Rose Kutlenios, PhD, RN, CS

www.wju.edu/academics/departments/nursing

Acceptance rate 80.8%

Tuition	
In state	$16,000
Out of state	$16,000
Enrollments	124
Graduations	23

Student Demographics	
Female	85.7%
Part-time	0.0%

Accreditation
West Virginia Board of Examiners for Registered
Professional Nurses, Commission on Collegiate
Nursing Education (CCNE)

Degrees conferred
Baccalaureate

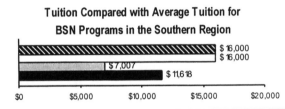

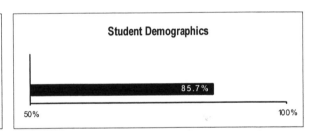

Wisconsin

ALVERNO COLLEGE

3400 South 43rd Street
Milwaukee, WI 53234
(414) 382-6284
Judeen Schulte, PhD, RN

www.alverno.edu/academics/nursing.html

Accreditation
Wisconsin Department of Regulation &
Licensing, Commission on Collegiate Nursing
Education (CCNE)

At the request of this nursing school, publication has been witheld.
Please contact the school directly for more information.

| Demographics Chart | ■Female ⊠Under age 25 ☐Minority | Distance Learning | †The tuition reported for this program may be not be annualized.
*Data reported between 2001 and 2004. |
| --- | --- | --- | --- |

Wisconsin

BELLIN HEALTH SYSTEM, INC

725 South Webster Avenue, PO Box 23400
Green Bay, WI 54305
(920) 433-7838
Patricia Swinford, PhD(c)

www.bcon.edu

At the request of this nursing school, publication has been witheld.
Please contact the school directly for more information.

Accreditation
Wisconsin Department of Regulation &
Licensing, Commission on Collegiate Nursing
Education (CCNE), National League for Nursing
Accrediting Commission (NLNAC)

CARDINAL STRITCH UNIVERSITY

6801 North Yates Road
Milwaukee, WI 53217
(414) 410-4390
Nancy Cervenansky, PhD, RN, NCC

www.stritch.edu

Tuition	
In state	$16,480
Out of state	$16,480

Accreditation
Wisconsin Department of Regulation & Licensing

Degrees conferred
Baccalaureate

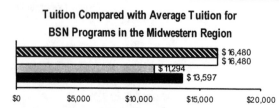

Tuition Compared with Average Tuition for BSN Programs in the Midwestern Region

- $16,480
- $16,480
- $11,294
- $13,597

CARROLL COLLEGE

100 Northeast Avenue
Waukesha, WI 53186
(262) 524-7381
Karen Gorton, RN, MSN

www.cc.edu

Accreditation
Wisconsin Department of Regulation & Licensing

Degrees conferred
Baccalaureate

COLUMBIA COLLEGE OF NURSING   *Useful Facts*

2121 East Newport Avenue
Milwaukee, WI 53211
(414) 961-4202
Katherine Dimmock, RN, MSN, EdD, JD

www.ccon.edu

Accreditation
Wisconsin Department of Regulation &
Licensing, National League for Nursing
Accrediting Commission (NLNAC)

Acceptance rate		50.6%
Faculty-student ratio		1: 14
Faculty	Full time	14
	Part time	7

Tuition	
In state	$7,988
Out of state	$7,988
Enrollments	240
Graduations	60

Minimum degree required
High school diploma or GED

Student Demographics	
Female	95.7%
Under age 25	60.8%
Minority	17.4%
Part-time	20.3%

Degrees conferred
Baccalaureate degree

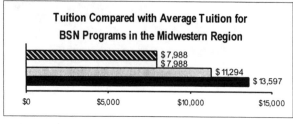

Tuition Compared with Average Tuition for BSN Programs in the Midwestern Region

- $7,988
- $7,988
- $11,294
- $13,597

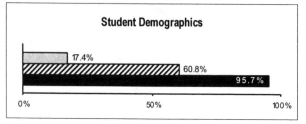

Student Demographics

- 17.4%
- 60.8%
- 95.7%

Key | Tuition Chart | ⬚ Program - in state ☐ Program - out of state ☐ Average - in state ■ Average - out of state

Wisconsin

CONCORDIA UNIVERSITY WISCONSIN/LUTHERAN CHURCH MISSOURI SYNOD *Useful Facts*

12800 North Lake Shore Drive
Mequon, WI 53097
(262) 243-4205
Grace Peterson, PhD, RN

www.cuw.edu

Acceptance rate	94.3%	
Faculty-student ratio	1: 19	
Faculty Full time	8	
Part time	8	

Tuition
In state $17,390
Out of state $17,390
Enrollments 228
Graduations 40

Student Demographics
Female 91.1%
Under age 25 77.8%
Minority 10.3%
Part-time 0.6%

Accreditation
Wisconsin Department of Regulation & Licensing, Commission on Collegiate Nursing Education (CCNE)

Degrees conferred
Baccalaureate degree

Minimum degree required
High school diploma or GED

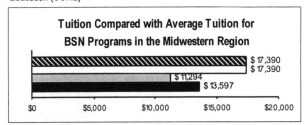
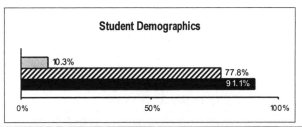

EDGEWOOD COLLEGE *Useful Facts*

1000 Edgewood College Drive
Madison, WI 53711
(608) 663-2292
Margaret Noreuil, PhD, RN

www.edgewood.edu

Acceptance rate	64.6%	
Faculty-student ratio	1: 10	
Faculty Full time	15	
Part time	11	

Tuition
In state $16,250
Out of state $16,250
Enrollments 206
Graduations 38

Student Demographics
Female 97.0%
Under age 25 62.5%
Minority 1.0%
Part-time 12.5%

Accreditation
Wisconsin Department of Regulation & Licensing, Commission on Collegiate Nursing Education (CCNE)

Degrees conferred
MSN, Baccalaureate degree

Minimum degree required
High school diploma or GED

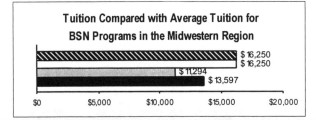
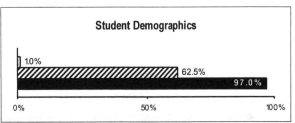

MARIAN COLLEGE OF FOND DU LAC *Useful Facts**

45 South National Avenue
Fond du Lac, WI 54935
(920) 923-8094
Elizabeth Parato, PhD, RN

www.mariancollege.edu

Tuition
In state $12,624
Out of state $12,624
Enrollments 348
Graduations 72

Student Demographics
Female 96.5%
Minority 2.8%
Part-time 4.2%

Accreditation
Wisconsin Department of Regulation & Licensing

Degrees conferred
Baccalaureate

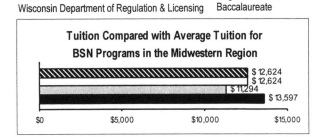
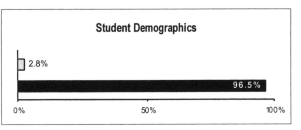

Demographics Chart	■Female ▨Under age 25 ▢Minority	**Distance Learning**	¹The tuition reported for this program may be not be annualized.
			*Data reported between 2001 and 2004.

Wisconsin

MARQUETTE UNIVERSITY
Useful Facts*

Clark Hall, PO Box 1881
Milwaukee, WI 53201
(414) 288-3812
Lea Acord, PhD, RN

www.marquette.edu/nursing

Accreditation
Wisconsin Department of Regulation &
Licensing, Commission on Collegiate Nursing
Education (CCNE), National League for Nursing
Accrediting Commission (NLNAC)

Acceptance rate	23.0%	**Tuition**		**Student Demographics**	
		In state	$20,350	Female	95.0%
		Out of state	$20,350	Under age 25	90.0%
		Enrollments	441	Minority	11.8%
		Graduations	77	Part-time	0.8%

Degrees conferred
Baccalaureate

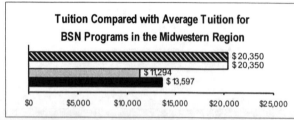

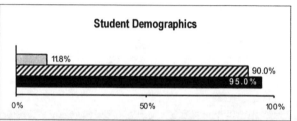

MILWAUKEE SCHOOL OF ENGINEERING
Useful Facts*

1025 N Broadway
Milwaukee, WI 53202
(414) 277-4516
Debra Jenks, BS, MS, PhD

www.msoe.edu

Accreditation
Wisconsin Department of Regulation & Licensing

Degrees conferred
Baccalaureate

Tuition	
In state	$19,845
Out of state	$19,845
Graduations	5

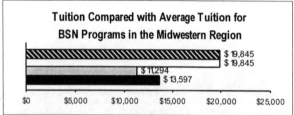

UNIVERSITY OF WISCONSIN - EAU CLAIRE
Useful Facts

105 Garfield Avenue, PO Box 4004
Eau Claire, WI 54702
(715) 836-5287
Linda Wendt, PhD, RN

www.uwec.edu/academic/nursing

Accreditation
Wisconsin Department of Regulation &
Licensing, Commission on Collegiate Nursing
Education (CCNE)

Acceptance rate	33.3%	**Tuition**		**Student Demographics**	
Faculty-student ratio	1:9	In state	$3,630	Female	91.6%
Faculty Full time	27	Out of state	$13,677	Under age 25	91.2%
Part time	16	Enrollments	303	Minority	4.3%
		Graduations	99	Part-time	0.0%

Degrees conferred
Baccalaureate degree

Minimum degree required
High school diploma or GED

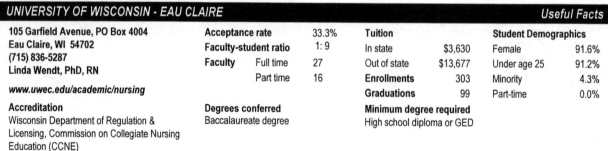

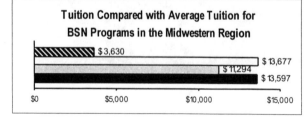

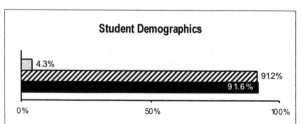

Key | Tuition Chart | ▨ Program - in state ☐ Program - out of state ☐ Average - in state ■ Average - out of state

Wisconsin

UNIVERSITY OF WISCONSIN - MADISON
Useful Facts*

600 Highland Avenue
Madison, WI 53792
(608) 263-5155
Katharyn May, DNSc, RN, FAAN

www.wisc.edu

Accreditation
Wisconsin Department of Regulation & Licensing

Degrees conferred
Baccalaureate

UNIVERSITY OF WISCONSIN - MILWAUKEE
Useful Facts*

1921 E Hartford Avenue
Milwaukee, WI 53211
(414) 229-4189
Sally Lundeen, PhD, RN, FAAN

www.nursing.uwm.edu

Accreditation
Wisconsin Department of Regulation &
Licensing, Commission on Collegiate Nursing
Education (CCNE)

Degrees conferred
Baccalaureate

Acceptance rate	83.0%	Tuition		Student Demographics	
		In state	$5,835	Female	87.6%
		Out of state	$18,587		
		Enrollments	1554	Minority	14.4%
		Graduations	209	Part-time	33.7%

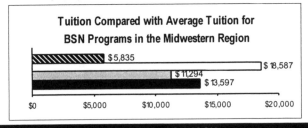

Tuition Compared with Average Tuition for BSN Programs in the Midwestern Region

$5,835
$18,587
$11,294
$13,597

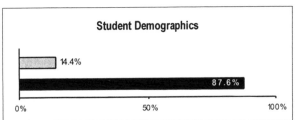

Student Demographics

14.4%
87.6%

UNIVERSITY OF WISCONSIN - OSHKOSH
Useful Facts*

800 Algoma Boulevard
Oshkosh, WI 54901
(920) 424-3089
Merritt Knox, PhD, RN

www.uwosh.edu

Accreditation
Wisconsin Department of Regulation & Licensing

Degrees conferred
Baccalaureate

Tuition		Student Demographics	
In state	$2,776		
Out of state	$9,920		
Enrollments	831		
Graduations	120	Part-time	19.3%

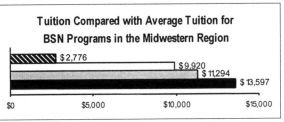

Tuition Compared with Average Tuition for BSN Programs in the Midwestern Region

$2,776
$9,920
$11,294
$13,597

Demographics Chart	■Female ☒Under age 25 ☐Minority	Distance Learning	┼The tuition reported for this program may be not be annualized. *Data reported between 2001 and 2004.

Wisconsin

VITERBO COLLEGE

815 South 9th Street
La Crosse, WI 54601
(608) 796-3687
Silvana Richardson, RN

www.viterbo.edu/academic

Tuition		Student Demographics	
In state	$12,220	Female	92.9%
Out of state	$12,220		
Enrollments	467	Minority	2.4%
Graduations	136		

Accreditation
Wisconsin Department of Regulation & Licensing

Degrees conferred
Baccalaureate

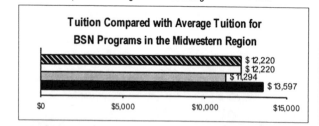

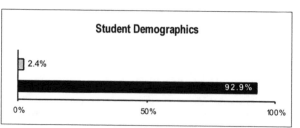

Wyoming

NORTHWEST COLLEGE (WASHINGTON)

5520-108th Ave, NE
Kirkland, WA 98033
(425) 889-7837
Carl Christensen, RN, PhD

nwcollege.edu

Accreditation
Washington State Nursing Care Quality
Assurance Comm., Commission on Collegiate
Nursing Education (CCNE)

Degrees conferred
Baccalaureate

UNIVERSITY OF WYOMING

Dept 3065, 1000 E University Ave
Laramie, WY 82071
(307) 766-6569
Pamela Clarke, PhD

www.uwyo.edu/nursing

			Tuition		Student Demographics	
Acceptance rate	40.5%		In state	$2,586	Female	89.8%
			Out of state	$7,266		
			Enrollments	435	Minority	9.1%
			Graduations	73	Part-time	9.6%

Accreditation
Wyoming State Board of Nursing, Commission
on Collegiate Nursing Education (CCNE)

Degrees conferred
Baccalaureate

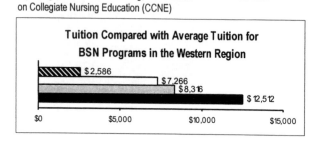

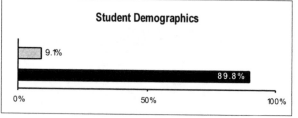

Key | Tuition Chart | ⊠ Program - in state ☐ Program - out of state ☐ Average - in state ■ Average - out of state

Arkansas

BAPTIST SCHOOL OF NURSING — *Useful Facts*

11900 Colonel Glenn Road
Little Rock, AR 72210
(501) 202-7433
Shirlene Harris, PhD, RN

www.baptist-health.org

Accreditation
Arkansas State Board of Nursing, National
League for Nursing Accrediting Commission
(NLNAC)

Acceptance rate		92.4%
Faculty-student ratio		1: 21
Faculty	Full time	35
	Part time	14

Degrees conferred
Diploma

Tuition	
In state	$7,450
Out of state	$7,450
Enrollments	876
Graduations	191

Minimum degree required
For the accelerated program, individual must be
LPN, LPTN or paramedic.

Student Demographics	
Female	87.3%
Under age 25	49.1%
Minority	17.7%
Part-time	5.0%

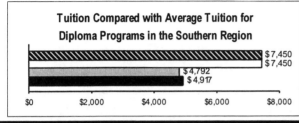

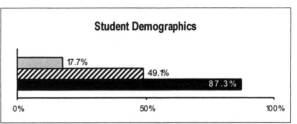

JEFFERSON REGIONAL MEDICAL CENTER — *Useful Facts*

1600 West 40th
Pine Bluff, AR 71603
(870) 541-7850
Jessie Clemmons, MNSC, RN, BSN

www.jrmc.org

Accreditation
Arkansas State Board of Nursing, National
League for Nursing Accrediting Commission
(NLNAC)

Acceptance rate	64.4%

Degrees conferred
Diploma

Tuition	
In state	$3,000
Out of state	$3,000
Enrollments	98
Graduations	26

Minimum degree required
High school diploma or GED

Student Demographics	
Female	86.7%
Under age 25	53.1%
Minority	17.3%
Part-time	0.0%

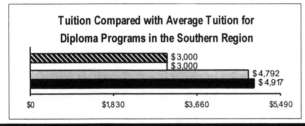

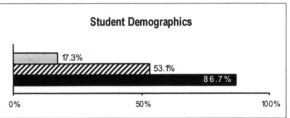

NORTHWEST HEALTH SYSTEM

610 East Emma
Springdale, AR 72764
(479) 750-6200
Linda Harwell, MNSc, MEd, RN

www.har-ber.org

Accreditation
Arkansas State Board of Nursing, National
League for Nursing Accrediting Commission
(NLNAC)

At the request of this nursing school, publication has been witheld.
Please contact the school directly for more information.

Demographics Chart	■Female ▨ Under age 25 ▢ Minority	Distance Learning	¹The tuition reported for this program may be not be annualized. *Data reported between 2001 and 2004.

Connecticut

BRIDGEPORT HOSPITAL

Useful Facts

200 Mill Hill Avenue
Bridgeport, CT 06610
(203) 384-3205
Carol DeBlois, RN, MA, CNOR

www.bhson.com

Accreditation
Connecticut Board of Examiners for Nursing, National League for Nursing Accrediting Commission (NLNAC)

Acceptance rate		32.2%
Faculty-student ratio		1: 16
Faculty	Full time	12
	Part time	7

Degrees conferred
Diploma

Tuition		
In state		$6,040
Out of state		$6,040
Enrollments		241
Graduations		102

Minimum degree required
High school diploma or GED

Student Demographics	
Female	89.2%
Under age 25	26.1%
Minority	28.7%
Part-time	45.6%

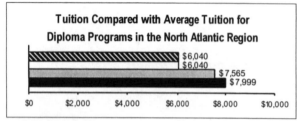

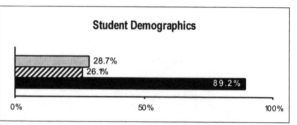

Delaware

BEEBE MEDICAL CENTER

Useful Facts

424 Savannah Road
Lewes, DE 19958
(302) 645-3251
Constance Bushey, MEd, BSN, RN

www.beebeschoolofnursing.org

Accreditation
Delaware Board of Nursing, National League for Nursing Accrediting Commission (NLNAC)

Acceptance rate		57.0%
Faculty-student ratio		1: 5
Faculty	Full time	10
	Part time	2

Degrees conferred
Diploma

Tuition		
In state		$3,700
Out of state		$3,700
Enrollments		52
Graduations		21

Minimum degree required
High school diploma or GED

Student Demographics	
Female	96.2%
Under age 25	65.4%
Minority	5.8%
Part-time	0.0%

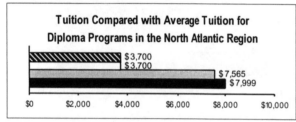

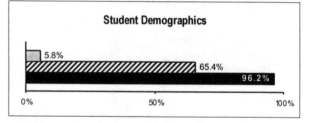

Key | Tuition Chart | ▨ Program - in state ☐ Program - out of state ☐ Average - in state ■ Average - out of state

Illinois

GRAHAM HOSPITAL | *Useful Facts*

210 West Walnut St
Canton, IL 61520
(309) 647-4086
Susan Livingston, RNC, MSN

www.grahamschoolofnursing.org

Accreditation
Illinois Department of Professional Regulation,
National League for Nursing Accrediting
Commission (NLNAC)

Acceptance rate	63.2%	
Faculty-student ratio	1 : 7	
Faculty Full time	9	
Part time	0	

Tuition
In state	$7,000
Out of state	$7,000
Enrollments	64
Graduations	15

Student Demographics
Female	85.9%
Under age 25	45.3%
Minority	7.8%
Part-time	23.4%

Degrees conferred
Diploma

Minimum degree required
High school diploma or GED

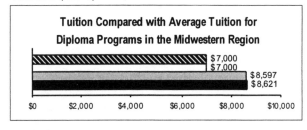

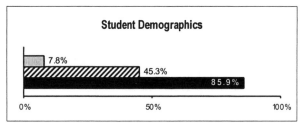

Indiana

GREATER LAFAYETTE HEALTH SERVICES | *Useful Facts*

1508 Tippecanoe Street
Lafayette, IN 47904
(765) 423-6408
John Jezierski, MSN, RN

www.ste.org

Accreditation
Indiana State Board of Nursing, National League
for Nursing Accrediting Commission (NLNAC)

Acceptance rate	52.9%	
Faculty-student ratio	1 : 9	
Faculty Full time	24	
Part time	2	

Tuition
In state	$12,060
Out of state	$12,060
Enrollments	229
Graduations	39

Student Demographics
Female	95.6%
Under age 25	59.0%
Minority	8.3%
Part-time	6.6%

Degrees conferred
Diploma

Minimum degree required
High school diploma or GED

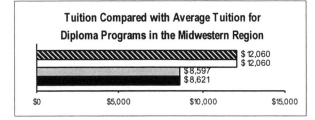

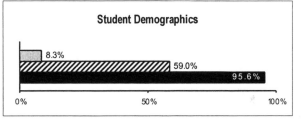

Demographics Chart	■Female ▨ Under age 25 ☐ Minority	**Distance Learning**	[1]The tuition reported for this program may be not be annualized. *Data reported between 2001 and 2004.

Louisiana

BATON ROUGE GENERAL MEDICAL CENTER *Useful Facts*

3616 North Boulevard
Baton Rouge, LA 70806
(225) 387-7623
Carol Tingle, MSN, RN

www.generalhealth.org

Acceptance rate		29.6%	**Tuition**			**Student Demographics**	
Faculty-student ratio		1: 8	In state	$6,900		Female	92.1%
Faculty	Full time	10	Out of state	$6,900		Under age 25	6.6%
	Part time	0	**Enrollments**	76		Minority	5.3%
			Graduations	20		Part-time	9.2%

Accreditation
Louisiana State Board of Nursing, National League for Nursing Accrediting Commission (NLNAC)

Degrees conferred
Diploma

Minimum degree required
High school diploma or GED

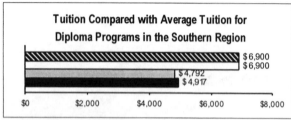

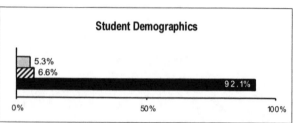

Massachusetts

BROCKTON HOSPITAL INC *Useful Facts**

680 Centre Street
Brockton, MA 02302
(508) 941-7056
Carol Bortman, EdD, RN, MSN, BSN

www.brocktonhospital.org

Acceptance rate	57.1%	**Tuition**			**Student Demographics**	
		In state	$14,371		Female	93.9%
		Out of state	$14,371		Minority	19.8%
		Enrollments	295		Part-time	49.2%
		Graduations	54			

Accreditation
Massachusetts Board of Registration in Nursing, National League for Nursing Accrediting Commission (NLNAC)

Degrees conferred
Diploma

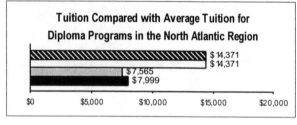

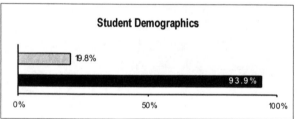

Key | Tuition Chart | ▨ Program - in state ☐ Program - out of state ☐ Average - in state ■ Average - out of state

Missouri

LUTHERAN SCHOOL OF NURSING
Useful Facts

3547 South Jefferson
St Louis, MO 63118
(314) 577-5855
Regina Cundall, MSN, BSN, RN

www.nursingschoollmc.com

Acceptance rate		56.3%
Faculty-student ratio		1: 7
Faculty	Full time	12
	Part time	1

Tuition	
In state	$6,750
Out of state	$6,750
Enrollments	84
Graduations	47

Student Demographics	
Female	89.3%
Under age 25	35.7%
Minority	45.7%
Part-time	38.1%

Accreditation
Missouri State Board of Nursing, National League for Nursing Accrediting Commission (NLNAC)

Degrees conferred
Diploma

Minimum degree required
HS Diploma + 9 college hours

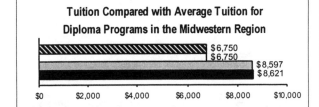

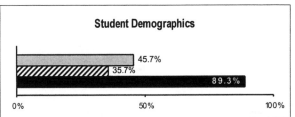

Nebraska

BRYAN LGH MEDICAL CENTER
Useful Facts*

5035 Everett
Lincoln, NE 68506
(402) 481-8602
Kay Maize, RN, MS, MSN, EdD

www.bryanlghcollege.org

Acceptance rate		58.0%
Faculty-student ratio		1: 11
Faculty	Full time	29
	Part time	4

Tuition	
In state	$7,940
Out of state	$7,940
Enrollments	194
Graduations	94

Student Demographics	
Female	92.3%
Under age 25	66.5%
Minority	2.6%
Part-time	0.0%

Accreditation
Nebraska Dept of Health & Human Services Regulation, National League for Nursing Accrediting Commission (NLNAC)

Degrees conferred
Diploma

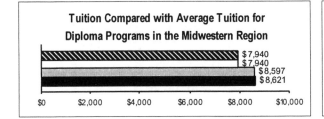

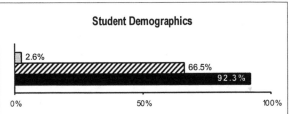

| **Demographics Chart** | ■Female ☒Under age 25 ☐Minority | **Distance Learning** | | ¹The tuition reported for this program may be not be annualized. *Data reported between 2001 and 2004. |

New Jersey

BAYONNE HOSPITAL

69-71 New Hook Road
Bayonne, NJ 07002
(201) 339-9656
Caroline Zall, RN, MSN

www.bayonnemedicalcenter.org

Acceptance rate	16.0%
Faculty-student ratio	1: 8
Faculty	Full time	7
	Part time	8

Tuition
In state	$2,625
Out of state	$7,700
Enrollments	89
Graduations	28

Student Demographics
Female	74.2%
Under age 25	40.4%
Minority	54.1%
Part-time	0.0%

Accreditation
New Jersey Board of Nursing, National League
for Nursing Accrediting Commission (NLNAC)

Degrees conferred
Diploma, Assoc in Science

Minimum degree required
High school diploma or GED

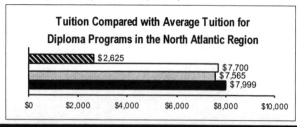
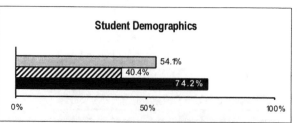

CAPITAL HEALTH SYSTEM

446 Bellevue Ave
Trenton, NJ 08618
(609) 394-4281
Sandra Quinn, MSN, RN, BC

www.capitalhealth.org

Acceptance rate	38.7%
Faculty-student ratio	1: 8
Faculty	Full time	11
	Part time	3

Tuition
In state	$3,130
Out of state	$3,130
Enrollments	106
Graduations	45

Student Demographics
Female	95.3%
Under age 25	32.1%
Minority	43.8%
Part-time	0.0%

Accreditation
New Jersey Board of Nursing, National League
for Nursing Accrediting Commission (NLNAC)

Degrees conferred
Diploma

Minimum degree required
High school diploma or GED

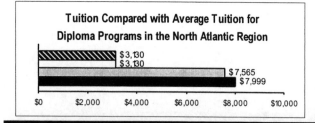
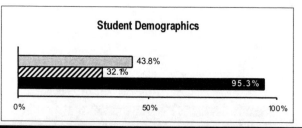

CHRIST HOSPITAL

176 Palisade Avenue
Jersey City, NJ 07306
(201) 795-8365
Carol Fasano, RN, BSN, MA, ANPC

www.christhospital.org

| Acceptance rate | 16.1% |

Tuition
In state	$2,760
Out of state	$2,760
Enrollments	190
Graduations	38

Student Demographics
Female	81.1%
Under age 25	38.0%
Minority	77.1%
Part-time	53.7%

Accreditation
New Jersey Board of Nursing, National League
for Nursing Accrediting Commission (NLNAC)

Degrees conferred
Diploma

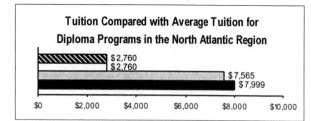
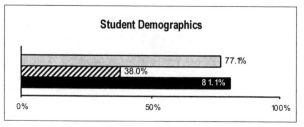

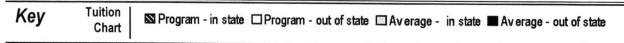

Key Tuition Chart | ⊠ Program - in state ☐ Program - out of state ☐ Average - in state ■ Average - out of state

New Jersey

HELENE FULD SCHOOL OF NURSING IN CAMDEN COUNTY — *Useful Facts*

Box 1669 College Drive
Blackwood, NJ 08012
(856) 374-0100
Rose Saunders, EdD, RN, MN, BSN

www.helenefuld.virtua.org

Accreditation
New Jersey Board of Nursing, National League
for Nursing Accrediting Commission (NLNAC)

Acceptance rate		47.8%
Faculty-student ratio		1: 20
Faculty	Full time	16
	Part time	7

Tuition
In state	$7,116
Out of state	$7,116
Enrollments	381
Graduations	121

Student Demographics
Female	89.0%
Under age 25	27.8%
Minority	23.6%
Part-time	0.0%

Degrees conferred
Diploma

Minimum degree required
High school diploma or GED

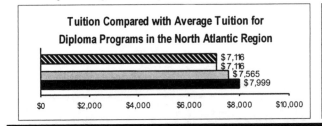

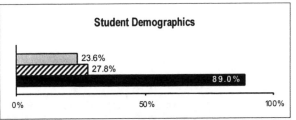

HOLY NAME HOSPITAL — *Useful Facts*

690 Teaneck Road
Teaneck, NJ 07666
(201) 833-3005
Claire Tynan, EdD, MEd, RN

www.schoolofnursing.info

Accreditation
New Jersey Board of Nursing, National League
for Nursing Accrediting Commission (NLNAC)

Acceptance rate		20.1%
Faculty-student ratio		1: 13
Faculty	Full time	9
	Part time	2

Tuition
In state	$11,760
Out of state	$11,760
Enrollments	130
Graduations	50

Student Demographics
Female	85.4%
Under age 25	55.4%
Minority	44.6%
Part-time	13.8%

Degrees conferred
Diploma, LPN or LVN

Minimum degree required
High school diploma or GED

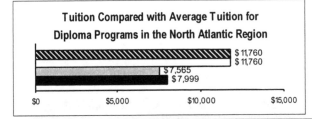

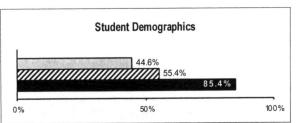

MOUNTAINSIDE HOSPITAL — *Useful Facts**

1 Bay Ave
Montclair, NJ 07042
(973) 429-6062
Louise DeBlois, RN

mhson.org

Accreditation
New Jersey Board of Nursing, National League
for Nursing Accrediting Commission (NLNAC)

Acceptance rate		50.0%
Faculty-student ratio		1: 10
Faculty	Full time	12
	Part time	6

Tuition
In state	$8,000
Out of state	$8,000
Enrollments	148
Graduations	47

Student Demographics
Female	82.4%
Under age 25	10.0%
Minority	30.4%
Part-time	0.0%

Degrees conferred
Diploma

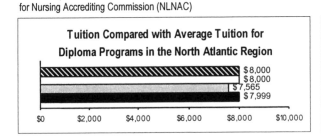

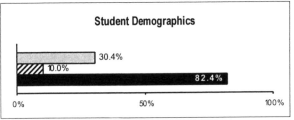

Demographics Chart	■Female ☒Under age 25 ☐Minority	Distance Learning 🖥	¹The tuition reported for this program may be not be annualized.
			*Data reported between 2001 and 2004.

New Jersey

MUHLENBERG REGIONAL MEDICAL CENTER

Useful Facts

Park Ave & Randolph Road
Plainfield, NJ 07061
(908) 668-2403
Judith Mathews, RN, PhD

solarishs.org

Accreditation
New Jersey Board of Nursing, National League
for Nursing Accrediting Commission (NLNAC)

Acceptance rate		36.5%
Faculty-student ratio		1: 17
Faculty	Full time	16
	Part time	13

Degrees conferred
Diploma

Tuition	
In state	$4,680
Out of state	$4,680
Enrollments	388
Graduations	72

Minimum degree required
High school diploma or GED

Student Demographics	
Female	90.5%
Under age 25	37.9%
Minority	58.2%
Part-time	84.0%

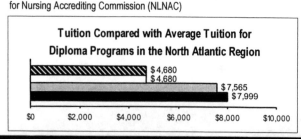

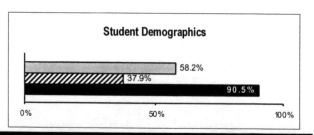

OUR LADY OF LOURDES SCHOOL OF NURSING

Useful Facts

1600 Haddon Ave
Camden, NJ 08103
(856) 757-3729
Dorothy Letizia, EdD, MSN, RN

ololnursing.com

Accreditation
New Jersey Board of Nursing, National League
for Nursing Accrediting Commission (NLNAC)

Acceptance rate		28.6%
Faculty-student ratio		1: 12
Faculty	Full time	11
	Part time	4

Degrees conferred
Diploma, In our cooperative
arrangement with Camden County
College, our graduates recieve an AS
from the coll

Tuition	
In state	$2,019
Out of state	$2,047
Enrollments	157
Graduations	45

Minimum degree required
BA or BS in a non-nursing field

Student Demographics	
Female	86.0%
Under age 25	31.2%
Minority	28.0%
Part-time	54.1%

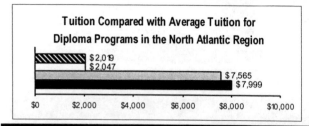

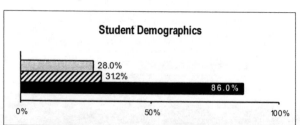

RARITAN BAY MEDICAL CENTER

Useful Facts

530 New Brunswick Avenue
Perth Amboy, NJ 08861
(732) 607-6500
Michelle Foley, RN, C, MA

www.rbmc.org

Accreditation
New Jersey Board of Nursing, National League
for Nursing Accrediting Commission (NLNAC)

Acceptance rate		42.5%
Faculty-student ratio		1: 13
Faculty	Full time	14
	Part time	0

Degrees conferred
Diploma

Tuition	
In state	$6,840
Out of state	$7,840
Enrollments	183
Graduations	39

Minimum degree required
High school diploma or GED

Student Demographics	
Female	83.6%
Under age 25	58.5%
Minority	52.8%
Part-time	0.0%

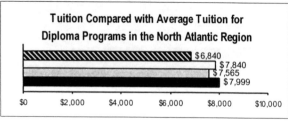

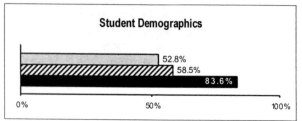

Key | Tuition Chart | ▨ Program - in state ☐ Program - out of state ☐ Average - in state ■ Average - out of state

New Jersey

ST FRANCIS MEDICAL CENTER - TRENTON
Useful Facts

601 Hamilton Ave
Trenton, NJ 08629
(609) 599-5192
Bonny Ross, RN, BSN, MA, EdD

stfrancismedical.com

Acceptance rate	24.6%	
Faculty-student ratio	1: 8	
Faculty	Full time	7
	Part time	2

Tuition
In state $4,067
Out of state $4,067
Enrollments 61
Graduations 41

Student Demographics
Female 86.9%
Under age 25 13.1%
Minority 23.0%
Part-time 0.0%

Accreditation
New Jersey Board of Nursing, National League
for Nursing Accrediting Commission (NLNAC)

Degrees conferred
Diploma

Minimum degree required
High school diploma or GED

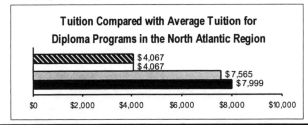

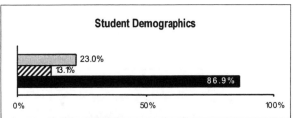

TRINITAS SCHOOL OF NURSING
Useful Facts

12 West Jersey Street
Elizabeth, NJ 07202
(908) 659-5200
Mary Kelley, RN, MSN, MEd, CNE

www.ucc.edu/go/trinitas

Acceptance rate	100.0%	
Faculty-student ratio	1: 62	
Faculty	Full time	12
	Part time	32

Tuition
In state $1,872
Out of state $1,872
Enrollments 1732
Graduations 53

Student Demographics
Female 83.5%
Under age 25 0.0%
Minority 81.7%
Part-time 68.8%

Accreditation
New Jersey Board of Nursing, National League
for Nursing Accrediting Commission (NLNAC)

Degrees conferred
Diploma

Minimum degree required
High school diploma or GED

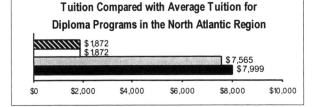

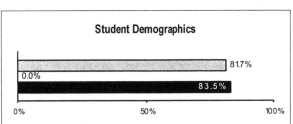

New York

ARNOT OGDEN MEDICAL CENTER
Useful Facts

600 Roe Ave
Elmira, NY 14905
(607) 737-4263
Linda MacAuslan, MS, RN

www.son.aomc.org

Acceptance rate	67.4%	
Faculty-student ratio	1: 6	
Faculty	Full time	9
	Part time	0

Tuition
In state $7,705
Out of state $7,705
Enrollments 51
Graduations 14

Student Demographics
Female 94.1%
Under age 25 56.9%
Minority 2.0%
Part-time 7.8%

Accreditation
New York State Board of Nursing, National
League for Nursing Accrediting Commission
(NLNAC)

Degrees conferred
Diploma

Minimum degree required
High school diploma or GED

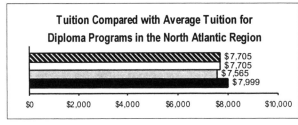

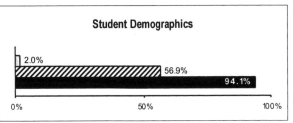

Demographics Chart	■Female ▨Under age 25 ☐Minority	Distance Learning 🖥	¹The tuition reported for this program may be not be annualized. *Data reported between 2001 and 2004.

North Carolina

DURHAM REGIONAL HOSPITAL
Useful Facts

3643 N Roxboro Road
Durham, NC 27704
(919) 470-7348
Peggy Baker, EdD, RN

wattsschoolofnursing.org

Acceptance rate	30.8%
Faculty-student ratio	1: 8
Faculty Full time	10
Part time	6

Tuition	
In state	$4,820
Out of state	$4,820
Enrollments	109
Graduations	46

Student Demographics	
Female	90.8%
Under age 25	45.9%
Minority	13.8%
Part-time	0.0%

Accreditation
North Carolina Board of Nursing, National
League for Nursing Accrediting Commission
(NLNAC)

Degrees conferred
Diploma

Minimum degree required
No waiting list, if admitted placed into the next
available class.

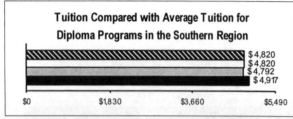
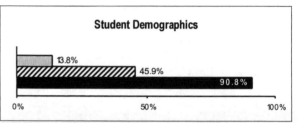

MERCY SCHOOL OF NURSING
Useful Facts

1921 Vail Avenue
Charlotte, NC 28207
(704) 379-5842
Deborah Blackwell, PhD, RNC, WHCNP,
APRN, BC

www.carolinashealthcare.org

Acceptance rate	14.3%
Faculty-student ratio	1: 10
Faculty Full time	12
Part time	2

Tuition	
In state	$4,950
Out of state	$4,950
Enrollments	127
Graduations	55

Student Demographics	
Female	91.3%
Under age 25	11.0%
Minority	20.0%
Part-time	83.5%

Accreditation
North Carolina Board of Nursing, National
League for Nursing Accrediting Commission
(NLNAC)

Degrees conferred
Diploma

Minimum degree required
High school diploma or GED

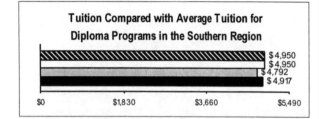
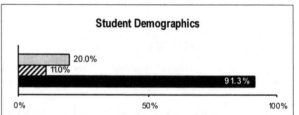

Ohio

AULTMAN HEALTH FOUNDATION
Useful Facts

2600 Sixth Street SW
Canton, OH 44710
(330) 363-3806
Joan Frey, EdD, MSN, RN, CNAA, BC

www.aultmanrn.com

Faculty-student ratio	1: 15
Faculty Full time	13
Part time	2

Tuition	
In state	$12,110
Out of state	$12,110
Enrollments	165
Graduations	118

Student Demographics	
Female	86.7%
Under age 25	41.8%
Minority	3.6%
Part-time	4.2%

Accreditation
Ohio Board of Nursing, National League for
Nursing Accrediting Commission (NLNAC)

Degrees conferred
Diploma

Minimum degree required
DK/NA

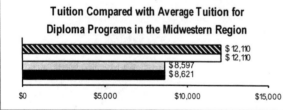
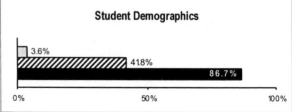

Key Tuition Chart | ▧ Program - in state ☐ Program - out of state ☐ Average - in state ■ Average - out of state

Ohio

CHRIST HOSPITAL - SCHOOL OF NURSING | *Useful Facts*

2139 Auburn Avenue
Cincinnati, OH 45219
(513) 585-2051
Teresa Goodwin, RN, BSN, MED

www.health-alliance.com/christ-control.html

Accreditation
Ohio Board of Nursing, National League for
Nursing Accrediting Commission (NLNAC)

Acceptance rate	37.3%	
Faculty-student ratio	1: 8	
Faculty Full time	32	
Part time	10	

Tuition
In state $5,250
Out of state $5,250
Enrollments 301
Graduations 97

Student Demographics
Female 86.4%
Under age 25 41.9%
Minority 6.8%
Part-time 24.9%

Degrees conferred
Diploma

Minimum degree required
High school diploma or GED

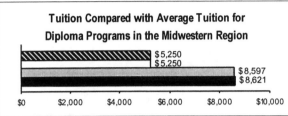
Tuition Compared with Average Tuition for Diploma Programs in the Midwestern Region
$5,250 / $5,250 / $8,597 / $8,621

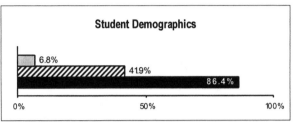
Student Demographics
6.8% / 41.9% / 86.4%

COMMUNITY HOSPITAL | *Useful Facts*

2615 East High Street
Springfield, OH 45505
(937) 328-8901
Dala DeWitt, MS, RN

www.chsn

Accreditation
Ohio Board of Nursing, National League for
Nursing Accrediting Commission (NLNAC)

Acceptance rate	28.1%	
Faculty-student ratio	1: 18	
Faculty Full time	12	
Part time	1	

Tuition
In state $6,510
Out of state $6,510
Enrollments 226
Graduations 47

Student Demographics
Female 91.2%
Under age 25 51.8%
Minority 8.5%
Part-time 43.4%

Degrees conferred
Diploma

Minimum degree required
High school diploma or GED

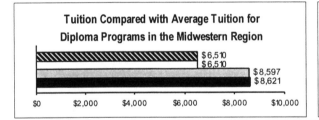
Tuition Compared with Average Tuition for Diploma Programs in the Midwestern Region
$6,510 / $6,510 / $8,597 / $8,621

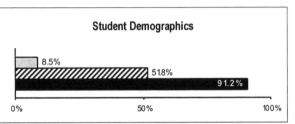
Student Demographics
8.5% / 51.8% / 91.2%

FIRELANDS REGIONAL MEDICAL CENTER | *Useful Facts*

1912 Hayes Avenue
Sandusky, OH 44870
(419) 557-7114
Holly Price, MSN, RN

www.firelands.com

Accreditation
Ohio Board of Nursing, National League for
Nursing Accrediting Commission (NLNAC)

Acceptance rate	59.4%	
Faculty-student ratio	1: 10	
Faculty Full time	10	
Part time	2	

Tuition
In state $12,304
Out of state $12,304
Enrollments 108
Graduations 28

Student Demographics
Female 94.4%
Under age 25 52.8%
Minority 8.3%
Part-time 26.9%

Degrees conferred
Diploma

Minimum degree required
High school diploma or GED

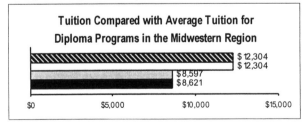
Tuition Compared with Average Tuition for Diploma Programs in the Midwestern Region
$12,304 / $12,304 / $8,597 / $8,621

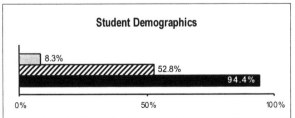
Student Demographics
8.3% / 52.8% / 94.4%

Demographics Chart	■ Female ▨ Under age 25 ☐ Minority	Distance Learning	¹The tuition reported for this program may be not be annualized. ²Data reported between 2001 and 2004.

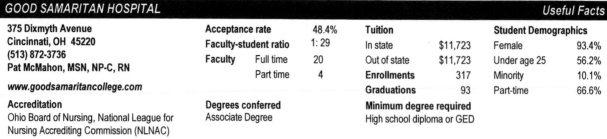

GOOD SAMARITAN HOSPITAL — *Useful Facts*

375 Dixmyth Avenue
Cincinnati, OH 45220
(513) 872-3736
Pat McMahon, MSN, NP-C, RN

www.goodsamaritancollege.com

Accreditation
Ohio Board of Nursing, National League for Nursing Accrediting Commission (NLNAC)

Acceptance rate		48.4%
Faculty-student ratio		1: 29
Faculty	Full time	20
	Part time	4

Degrees conferred
Associate Degree

Tuition	
In state	$11,723
Out of state	$11,723
Enrollments	317
Graduations	93

Minimum degree required
High school diploma or GED

Student Demographics	
Female	93.4%
Under age 25	56.2%
Minority	10.1%
Part-time	66.6%

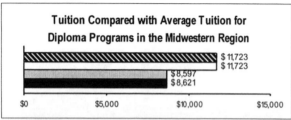

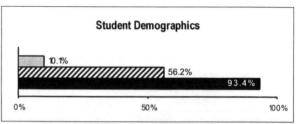

HURON SCHOOL OF NURSING — *Useful Facts*

Huron Hospital, 13951 Terrace Road
East Cleveland, OH 44112
(216) 761-6939
Kathleen Knittel, MSN, RN

www.cchseast.org/schools

Accreditation
Ohio Board of Nursing, National League for Nursing Accrediting Commission (NLNAC)

Acceptance rate		39.5%
Faculty-student ratio		1: 10
Faculty	Full time	15
	Part time	13

Degrees conferred
Diploma

Tuition	
In state	$6,030
Out of state	$6,030
Enrollments	221
Graduations	80

Minimum degree required
High school diploma or GED

Student Demographics	
Female	85.1%
Under age 25	12.2%
Minority	44.3%
Part-time	0.0%

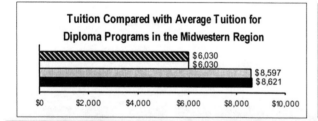

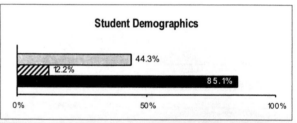

TRINITY HEALTH SYSTEMS — *Useful Facts*

380 Summit Avenue
Steubenville, OH 43952
(740) 283-7273
Patricia Gerlando, PhD, RN

www.trinityson.com

Accreditation
Ohio Board of Nursing, National League for Nursing Accrediting Commission (NLNAC)

Acceptance rate		55.6%
Faculty-student ratio		1: 17
Faculty	Full time	9
	Part time	2

Degrees conferred
Diploma

Tuition	
In state	$6,885
Out of state	$7,155
Enrollments	170
Graduations	46

Minimum degree required
High school diploma or GED

Student Demographics	
Female	85.3%
Under age 25	23.5%
Minority	2.4%
Part-time	0.0%

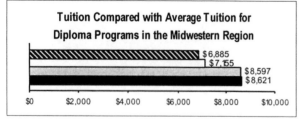

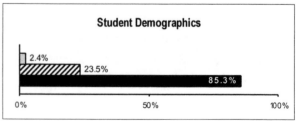

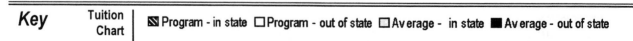

Key — Tuition Chart | ▨ Program - in state ☐ Program - out of state ☐ Average - in state ■ Average - out of state

Pennsylvania

ABINGTON MEMORIAL HOSPITAL — *Useful Facts*

2500 Maryland Rd Suite 200
Willow Grove, PA 19090
(215) 481-5514
Eileen Van Parys, RN, MSN, EdD

www.amhdixonson.org

Accreditation
Pennsylvania State Board of Nursing, National League for Nursing Accrediting Commission (NLNAC)

Acceptance rate	16.1%
Faculty-student ratio	1: 12
Faculty	Full time	15
	Part time	4

Degrees conferred
Diploma

Tuition	
In state	$6,000
Out of state	$6,000
Enrollments	207
Graduations	82

Minimum degree required
High school diploma or GED

Student Demographics	
Female	86.0%
Under age 25	33.8%
Minority	6.8%
Part-time	0.0%

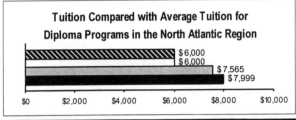

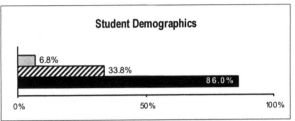

ALLE-KISKI MEDICAL CENTER — *Useful Facts*

651 Fourth Avenue
New Kensington, PA 15068
(724) 337-5090
Mary Lynne Rugh, MSN

www.wpahs.org/akmc

Accreditation
Pennsylvania State Board of Nursing, National League for Nursing Accrediting Commission (NLNAC)

Acceptance rate	56.9%
Faculty-student ratio	1: 7
Faculty	Full time	13
	Part time	1

Degrees conferred
Diploma

Tuition	
In state	$8,700
Out of state	$8,700
Enrollments	94
Graduations	39

Minimum degree required
High school diploma or GED

Student Demographics	
Female	80.9%
Under age 25	45.7%
Minority	7.4%
Part-time	0.0%

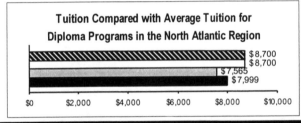

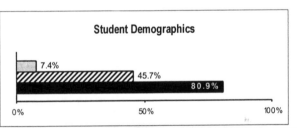

BRANDYWINE SCHOOL OF NURSING — *Useful Facts*

215 Reeceville Road
Coatesville, PA 19320
(610) 383-8216
Sharon Wolf, RN, MEd, MSN

www.brandywinehospital.com

Accreditation
Pennsylvania State Board of Nursing, National League for Nursing Accrediting Commission (NLNAC)

Acceptance rate	26.3%
Faculty-student ratio	1: 11
Faculty	Full time	7
	Part time	5

Degrees conferred
Diploma

Tuition	
In state	$9,196
Out of state	$9,196
Enrollments	104
Graduations	41

Minimum degree required
High school diploma or GED

Student Demographics	
Female	93.3%
Under age 25	42.3%
Minority	9.6%
Part-time	51.9%

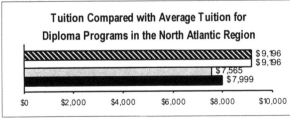

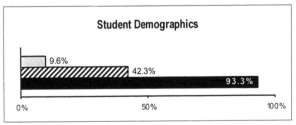

| Demographics Chart | ■ Female ⊠ Under age 25 ☐ Minority | Distance Learning | †The tuition reported for this program may be not be annualized.
*Data reported between 2001 and 2004. |

Pennsylvania

CONEMAUGH VALLEY MEMORIAL HOSPITAL

1086 Franklin Street
Johnstown, PA 15905
(814) 534-9477
Louise Pugliese, RN, MSN

conemaugh.org

Accreditation
Pennsylvania State Board of Nursing, National
League for Nursing Accrediting Commission
(NLNAC)

Acceptance rate		35.5%
Faculty-student ratio		1: 10
Faculty	Full time	14
	Part time	1

Degrees conferred
Diploma

Tuition	
In state	$10,590
Out of state	$13,630
Enrollments	138
Graduations	54

Minimum degree required
High school diploma or GED

Student Demographics	
Female	81.9%
Under age 25	59.4%
Minority	0.7%
Part-time	4.3%

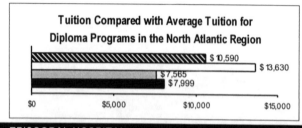

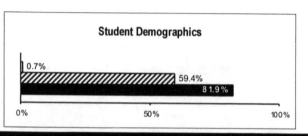

EPISCOPAL HOSPITAL

100 E Lehigh Ave
Philadelphia, PA 19125
(215) 707-1079
Dolores Alabrodzinski, MSN, RN

www.episcopal-hosp-nurse.com

Accreditation
Pennsylvania State Board of Nursing, National
League for Nursing Accrediting Commission
(NLNAC)

Faculty-student ratio		1: 6
Faculty	Full time	13
	Part time	11

Degrees conferred
Diploma

Tuition	
In state	$6,240
Out of state	$6,240
Enrollments	107
Graduations	14

Minimum degree required
29 college credits

Student Demographics	
Female	86.9%
Under age 25	6.5%
Minority	53.3%
Part-time	100.0%

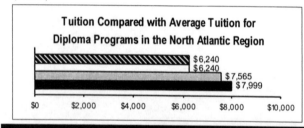

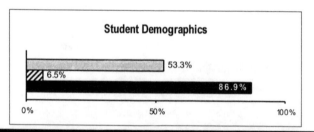

FRANKFORD HOSPITAL

4918 Penn Street
Philadelphia, PA 19124
(215) 831-6740
Jacquelyn Corcoran, EdD(c), RN

www.frankfordhospitals.org

Accreditation
Pennsylvania State Board of Nursing, National
League for Nursing Accrediting Commission
(NLNAC)

At the request of this nursing school, publication has been witheld.
Please contact the school directly for more information.

Key | Tuition Chart | ▨ Program - in state   ☐ Program - out of state   ☐ Average - in state   ■ Average - out of state

Pennsylvania

HERITAGE VALLEY HEALTH SYSTEM
Useful Facts

720 Blackburn Rd
Sewickley, PA 15143
(412) 749-7089
Marilu Piotrowski, MSN, RN

www.heritagevalley.org

Accreditation
Pennsylvania State Board of Nursing, National
League for Nursing Accrediting Commission
(NLNAC)

Acceptance rate	36.2%
Faculty-student ratio	1: 9
Faculty Full time	8
Part time	6

Degrees conferred
Diploma

Tuition	
In state	$7,200
Out of state	$7,200
Enrollments	103
Graduations	49

Minimum degree required
High school diploma or GED

Student Demographics	
Female	88.3%
Under age 25	57.3%
Minority	1.0%
Part-time	12.6%

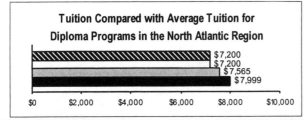

Tuition Compared with Average Tuition for Diploma Programs in the North Atlantic Region

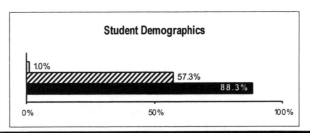

Student Demographics

JAMESON HEALTH SYSTEM
Useful Facts

1211 Wilmington Ave
New Castle, PA 16105
(724) 656-4052
Jayne Sheehan, RN, MSN, CRNP

www.jamesonhealthsystem.com

Accreditation
Pennsylvania State Board of Nursing, National
League for Nursing Accrediting Commission
(NLNAC)

Acceptance rate	58.8%
Faculty-student ratio	1: 7
Faculty Full time	13
Part time	3

Degrees conferred
Diploma

Tuition	
In state	$10,957
Out of state	$10,957
Enrollments	97
Graduations	45

Minimum degree required
High school diploma or GED

Student Demographics	
Female	87.6%
Under age 25	48.5%
Minority	4.1%
Part-time	43.3%

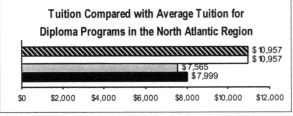

Tuition Compared with Average Tuition for Diploma Programs in the North Atlantic Region

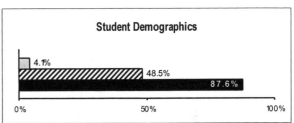

Student Demographics

LANCASTER INSTITUTE FOR HEALTH EDUCATION
*Useful Facts**

410 North Lime Street
Lancaster, PA 17602
(717) 544-4785
Alice Ahlfeld, MSN, RN

www.lihe.org

Accreditation
Pennsylvania State Board of Nursing, National
League for Nursing Accrediting Commission
(NLNAC)

Acceptance rate	26.1%
Faculty-student ratio	1: 6
Faculty Full time	16
Part time	17

Degrees conferred
Diploma

Tuition	
In state	$7,950
Out of state	$7,950
Enrollments	148
Graduations	89

Student Demographics	
Female	95.3%
Under age 25	57.4%
Part-time	39.2%

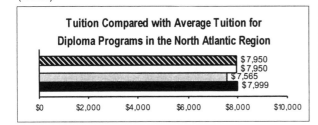

Tuition Compared with Average Tuition for Diploma Programs in the North Atlantic Region

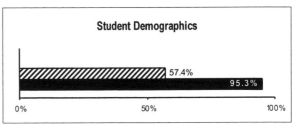

Student Demographics

| **Demographics Chart** | ■Female ▨Under age 25 □Minority | **Distance Learning** | ¹The tuition reported for this program may be not be annualized. *Data reported between 2001 and 2004. |

Pennsylvania

NORTHEASTERN HOSPITAL · *Useful Facts*

2301 East Allegheny Avenue
Philadelphia, PA 19134
(215) 291-3140
Eleanor Reinhardt, MSN, RN

www.nehson.templehealth.org

Accreditation
Pennsylvania State Board of Nursing, National
League for Nursing Accrediting Commission
(NLNAC)

Faculty-student ratio		1:8
Faculty	Full time	8
	Part time	5

Degrees conferred
Diploma

Tuition
In state	$6,579
Out of state	$6,579
Enrollments	83
Graduations	35

Minimum degree required
High school diploma or GED

Student Demographics
Female	86.7%
Under age 25	39.8%
Minority	36.1%
Part-time	0.0%

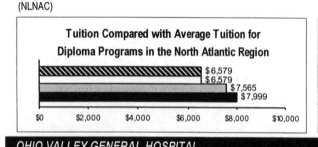

Tuition Compared with Average Tuition for Diploma Programs in the North Atlantic Region

$6,579
$6,579
$7,565
$7,999

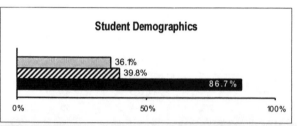

Student Demographics

36.1%
39.8%
86.7%

OHIO VALLEY GENERAL HOSPITAL · *Useful Facts*

25 Heckel Road
Mckees Rocks, PA 15136
(412) 777-6234
Gaye Falletta, MSN, RN

www.ohiovalleyhospital.org

Accreditation
Pennsylvania State Board of Nursing, National
League for Nursing Accrediting Commission
(NLNAC)

Acceptance rate		21.7%
Faculty-student ratio		1:9
Faculty	Full time	6
	Part time	1

Degrees conferred
Diploma

Tuition
In state	$24,735
Out of state	$24,735
Enrollments	57
Graduations	20

Minimum degree required
High school diploma or GED

Student Demographics
Female	91.2%
Under age 25	42.1%
Minority	3.5%
Part-time	0.0%

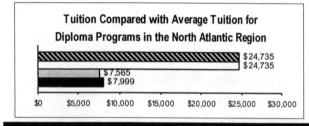

Tuition Compared with Average Tuition for Diploma Programs in the North Atlantic Region

$24,735
$24,735
$7,565
$7,999

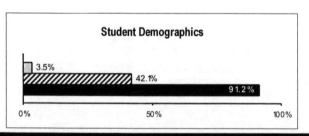

Student Demographics

3.5%
42.1%
91.2%

PITTSBURGH MERCY HEALTH SYSTEM · *Useful Facts*

1401 Boulevard of Allies
Pittsburgh, PA 15219
(412) 232-7964
Joanne Sperry, MN, RN

pmhs.org/schoolofmercy

Accreditation
Pennsylvania State Board of Nursing, National
League for Nursing Accrediting Commission
(NLNAC)

Acceptance rate		54.3%
Faculty-student ratio		1:9
Faculty	Full time	13
	Part time	0

Degrees conferred
Diploma

Tuition
In state	$7,800
Out of state	$7,800
Enrollments	112
Graduations	36

Minimum degree required
High school diploma or GED

Student Demographics
Female	88.4%
Under age 25	82.1%
Minority	5.4%
Part-time	0.0%

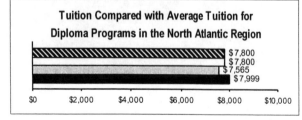

Tuition Compared with Average Tuition for Diploma Programs in the North Atlantic Region

$7,800
$7,800
$7,565
$7,999

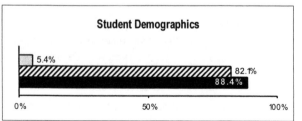

Student Demographics

5.4%
82.1%
88.4%

Key Tuition Chart | ▨ Program - in state ☐ Program - out of state ☐ Average - in state ■ Average - out of state

Pennsylvania

POTTSVILLE HOSPITAL AND WARNE CLINIC

420 South Jackson St
Pottsville, PA 17901
(570) 621-5032
Angela Pasco, RN, MSN

At the request of this nursing school, publication has been witheld.
Please contact the school directly for more information.

www.pottsvillehospitalschoolofnursing.com

Accreditation
Pennsylvania State Board of Nursing, National
League for Nursing Accrediting Commission
(NLNAC)

ROXBOROUGH MEMORIAL HOSPITAL   *Useful Facts**

5800 Ridge Ave
Philadelphia, PA 19128
(215) 487-4458
Margaret Judge, MSN

www.rnschool.org

Accreditation
Pennsylvania State Board of Nursing, National
League for Nursing Accrediting Commission
(NLNAC)

Acceptance rate	29.2%	

Tuition		Student Demographics	
In state	$8,562	Female	86.0%
Out of state	$8,680	Under age 25	30.0%
Enrollments	121	Minority	9.1%
Graduations	50	Part-time	0.0%

Degrees conferred
Diploma

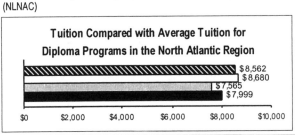

Tuition Compared with Average Tuition for Diploma Programs in the North Atlantic Region

$8,562
$8,680
$7,565
$7,999

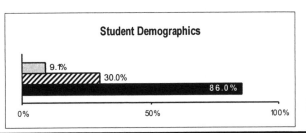

Student Demographics

9.1%
30.0%
86.0%

SAINT LUKE'S HOSPITAL   *Useful Facts*

801 Ostrum Street
Bethlehem, PA 18015
(610) 954-3449
Sandra Mesics, CNM, MSN, RN

www.sonstlukes.org

Accreditation
Pennsylvania State Board of Nursing, National
League for Nursing Accrediting Commission
(NLNAC)

Acceptance rate	29.7%	
Faculty-student ratio	1: 10	

Faculty	Full time	14
	Part time	4

Tuition		Student Demographics	
In state	$9,822	Female	91.0%
Out of state	$9,822	Under age 25	46.8%
Enrollments	156	Minority	11.5%
Graduations	50	Part-time	0.0%

Degrees conferred
Diploma

Minimum degree required
High school diploma or GED

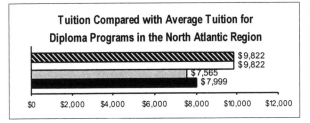

Tuition Compared with Average Tuition for Diploma Programs in the North Atlantic Region

$9,822
$9,822
$7,565
$7,999

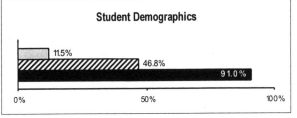

Student Demographics

11.5%
46.8%
91.0%

Demographics Chart	■Female ☒Under age 25 ☐Minority	Distance Learning	¹The tuition reported for this program may be not be annualized.
			*Data reported between 2001 and 2004.

Diploma Programs

Pennsylvania

SHARON REGIONAL HEALTH SYSTEM

Useful Facts

740 East State Street
Sharon, PA 16146
(724) 983-3971
Nora Bennett, MSN, RN

www.sharonregional.com

Accreditation
Pennsylvania State Board of Nursing, National
League for Nursing Accrediting Commission
(NLNAC)

Acceptance rate	44.4%	
Faculty-student ratio	1: 4	
Faculty	Full time	8
	Part time	1

Degrees conferred
Diploma

Tuition	
In state	$6,700
Out of state	$6,700
Enrollments	34
Graduations	24

Minimum degree required
26 college credits

Student Demographics	
Female	88.2%
Under age 25	32.4%
Minority	8.8%
Part-time	0.0%

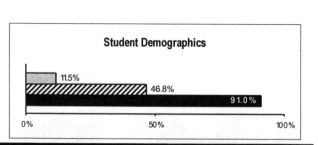

THE READING HOSPITAL

Useful Facts

Sixth Avenue and Spruce Street
West Reading, PA 19611
(610) 988-8331
Joanne Kovach, MEd, MSN, BS, RN

www.readinghospital.org

Accreditation
Pennsylvania State Board of Nursing, National
League for Nursing Accrediting Commission
(NLNAC)

Acceptance rate	39.6%	
Faculty-student ratio	1: 12	
Faculty	Full time	29
	Part time	4

Degrees conferred
Diploma

Tuition	
In state	$9,917
Out of state	$14,398
Enrollments	363
Graduations	135

Minimum degree required
High school diploma or GED

Student Demographics	
Female	90.9%
Under age 25	51.8%
Minority	7.6%
Part-time	34.7%

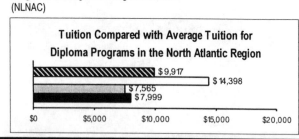
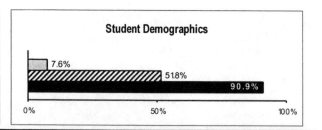

THE WASHINGTON HOSPITAL

155 Wilson Avenue
Washington, PA 15301
(724) 223-3172
Kathryn Yecko, RN, MSN

www.washingtonhospital.org

Accreditation
Pennsylvania State Board of Nursing, National
League for Nursing Accrediting Commission
(NLNAC)

At the request of this nursing school, publication has been withheld.
Please contact the school directly for more information.

Key | Tuition Chart | ▨ Program - in state ☐ Program - out of state ☐ Average - in state ■ Average - out of state

196　PA

Pennsylvania

THE WESTERN PENNSYLVANIA HOSPITAL · *Useful Facts*

4900 Friendship Avenue
Pittsburgh, PA 15224
(412) 578-5530
Nancy Cobb, RN, MSN

www.wpahs.org/education

Accreditation
Pennsylvania State Board of Nursing, National
League for Nursing Accrediting Commission
(NLNAC)

Acceptance rate	31.7%
Faculty-student ratio	1: 8
Faculty Full time	12
Part time	5

Degrees conferred
Diploma

Tuition	
In state	$4,544
Out of state	$4,544
Enrollments	122
Graduations	55

Minimum degree required
High school diploma or GED

Student Demographics	
Female	82.8%
Under age 25	63.1%
Minority	10.7%
Part-time	0.0%

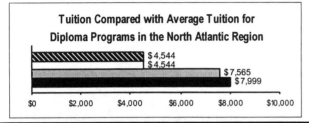

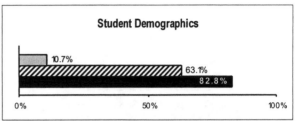

UPMC SHADYSIDE · *Useful Facts**

5230 Centre Avenue
Pittsburgh, PA 15232
(412) 623-2253
Tamra Merryman, RN, MSN, FACHE

www.upmc.edu/shadyside/schoolofnursing

Accreditation
Pennsylvania State Board of Nursing, National
League for Nursing Accrediting Commission
(NLNAC)

Acceptance rate	53.3%

Degrees conferred
Diploma

Tuition	
In state	$7,500
Out of state	$7,500
Enrollments	364
Graduations	73

Student Demographics	
Female	79.7%
Under age 25	25.0%
Minority	3.6%
Part-time	34.6%

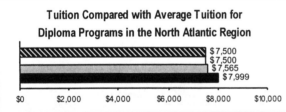

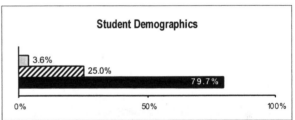

UPMC-ST MARGARET MEMORIAL HOSPITAL · *Useful Facts*

221 Seventh Street
Pittsburgh, PA 15238
(412) 784-4992
Ann Ciak, RN, PhD, MN, BSN

stmargaret.upmc.com

Accreditation
Pennsylvania State Board of Nursing, National
League for Nursing Accrediting Commission
(NLNAC)

Acceptance rate	52.2%
Faculty-student ratio	1: 6
Faculty Full time	15
Part time	7

Degrees conferred
Diploma

Tuition	
In state	$9,880
Out of state	$9,880
Enrollments	108
Graduations	52

Minimum degree required
High school diploma or GED

Student Demographics	
Female	85.2%
Under age 25	37.0%
Minority	3.7%
Part-time	0.0%

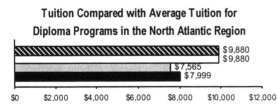

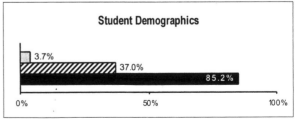

Demographics Chart	■Female ☒Under age 25 ☐Minority	Distance Learning	†The tuition reported for this program may be not be annualized. *Data reported between 2001 and 2004.

Rhode Island

ST JOSEPH HEALTH SERVICES OF RHODE ISLAND

*Useful Facts**

200 High Service Avenue
North Providence, RI 02904
(401) 456-3050
Marilyn Horan, MEd, RN

www.nursingri.com

Acceptance rate	51.6%	

Tuition		**Student Demographics**	
In state	$5,875	Female	85.2%
Out of state	$8,175	Under age 25	17.0%
Enrollments	88	Minority	11.4%
Graduations	11	Part-time	0.0%

Accreditation
Rhode Island Board of Nurse Registration &
Nursing Education, National League for Nursing
Accrediting Commission (NLNAC)

Degrees conferred
Diploma

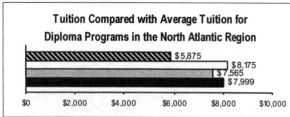

Tuition Compared with Average Tuition for Diploma Programs in the North Atlantic Region

- $5,875
- $8,175
- $7,565
- $7,999

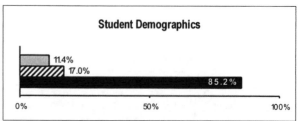

Student Demographics

- 11.4%
- 17.0%
- 85.2%

Texas

BAPTIST HEALTH SYSTEM

Useful Facts

730 North Main Avenue, Suite 212
San Antonio, TX 78205
(210) 297-9111
Diane Frazor, EdD, RN

www.baptistschools.com

Acceptance rate	43.2%		
Faculty-student ratio	1: 15		
Faculty	Full time	14	
	Part time	2	

Tuition		**Student Demographics**	
In state	$3,700	Female	85.8%
Out of state	$3,700	Under age 25	39.0%
Enrollments	218	Minority	52.7%
Graduations	43	Part-time	0.0%

Accreditation
Texas Board of Nurse Examiners, National
League for Nursing Accrediting Commission
(NLNAC)

Degrees conferred
Diploma

Minimum degree required
22 academic hrs for generic program; LVN
licensure + 28 academic hrs for LVN-to-RN
Mobility program

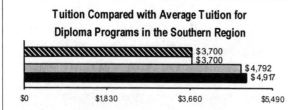

Tuition Compared with Average Tuition for Diploma Programs in the Southern Region

- $3,700
- $3,700
- $4,792
- $4,917

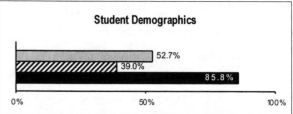

Student Demographics

- 52.7%
- 39.0%
- 85.8%

Key | Tuition Chart | ◩ Program - in state ☐ Program - out of state ▨ Average - in state ■ Average - out of state

Texas

COVENANT HEALTH SYSTEM | *Useful Facts*

2002 Miami Ave
Lubbock, TX 79410
(806) 797-0955
Annette Hallman, PhD

www.covenantson.com

Acceptance rate	32.9%	
Faculty-student ratio	1: 5	
Faculty Full time	34	
Part time	3	

Tuition	
In state	$6,600
Out of state	$6,600
Enrollments	179
Graduations	75

Student Demographics	
Female	86.6%
Under age 25	65.4%
Minority	16.9%
Part-time	0.0%

Accreditation
Texas Board of Nurse Examiners, National
League for Nursing Accrediting Commission
(NLNAC)

Degrees conferred
Diploma

Minimum degree required
High School/GED and 27 - 31 General Education
Semester Hours

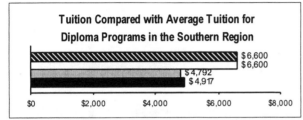

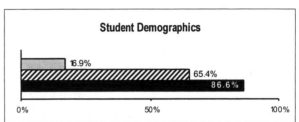

Virginia

BON SECOURS MEMORIAL | *Useful Facts*

8550 Magellan Parkway
Richmond, VA 23227
(804) 627-5352
Mary Fox, MSN, RN

www.bonsecours.com

Acceptance rate	63.7%	
Faculty-student ratio	1: 13	
Faculty Full time	32	
Part time	8	

Tuition	
In state	$4,900
Out of state	$4,900
Enrollments	466
Graduations	109

Student Demographics	
Female	94.6%
Under age 25	47.6%
Minority	18.8%
Part-time	6.2%

Accreditation
Virginia Board of Nursing, National League for
Nursing Accrediting Commission (NLNAC)

Degrees conferred
Diploma

Minimum degree required
Diploma

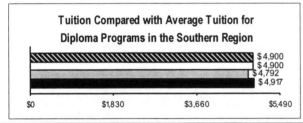

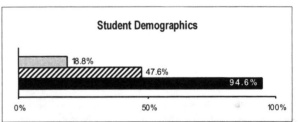

CENTRA HEALTH - LYNCHBURG GENERAL HOSPITAL | *Useful Facts*

1901 Tate Springs Road
Lynchburg, VA 24501
(434) 947-3070
Debra Patterson, RN, MSN, MBA

www.centrahealth.com

Acceptance rate	42.0%	
Faculty-student ratio	1: 8	
Faculty Full time	20	
Part time	4	

Tuition	
In state	$3,276
Out of state	$3,276
Enrollments	170
Graduations	47

Student Demographics	
Female	93.5%
Under age 25	52.4%
Minority	8.3%
Part-time	24.7%

Accreditation
Virginia Board of Nursing, National League for
Nursing Accrediting Commission (NLNAC)

Degrees conferred
Diploma

Minimum degree required
High school diploma or GED

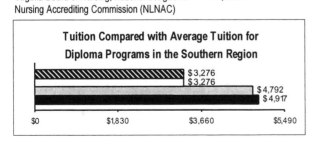

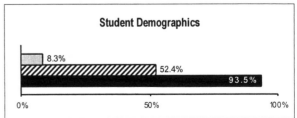

Demographics Chart	■ Female ⧄ Under age 25 ☐ Minority	**Distance Learning**	¹The tuition reported for this program may be not be annualized. *Data reported between 2001 and 2004.

Virginia

DANVILLE REGIONAL MEDICAL CENTER
Useful Facts

142 South Main Street
Danville, VA 24541
(434) 799-4510
Kamela Deel, RN, MSN, MED

www.danvilleregional.org/nursingschool

Accreditation
Virginia Board of Nursing, National League for
Nursing Accrediting Commission (NLNAC)

Acceptance rate	61.4%	
Faculty-student ratio	1: 10	
Faculty	Full time	6
	Part time	4

Degrees conferred
Diploma

Tuition		Student Demographics	
In state	$5,307	Female	93.5%
Out of state	$5,307	Under age 25	42.9%
Enrollments	77	Minority	19.5%
Graduations	45	Part-time	0.0%

Minimum degree required
for LPN-RN program, must have LPN

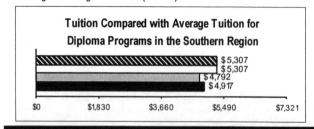
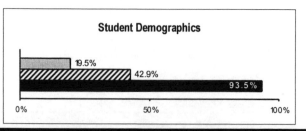

RIVERSIDE HEALTH SYSTEM
Useful Facts*

326 Main Street
Newport News, VA 23601
(757) 369-7410
Tracee Carmean, MSM, BSN, RN

www.riversideonline.com

Accreditation
Virginia Board of Nursing, National League for
Nursing Accrediting Commission (NLNAC)

Acceptance rate	98.1%

Degrees conferred
Diploma

Tuition		Student Demographics	
In state	$6,000	Female	96.3%
Out of state	$6,000	Under age 25	40.0%
Enrollments	164	Minority	15.3%
Graduations	45	Part-time	0.0%

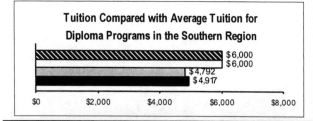
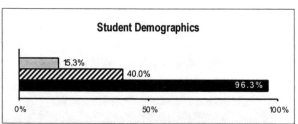

SENTARA NORFOLK GENERAL HOSPITAL
Useful Facts

1441 Crossways Blvd Suite 105
Chesapeake, VA 23320
(757) 388-2655
Shelly Cohen, MSN, MS, RN

www.sentara.com/healthprofessions

Accreditation
Virginia Board of Nursing, National League for
Nursing Accrediting Commission (NLNAC)

Acceptance rate	52.7%	
Faculty-student ratio	1: 9	
Faculty	Full time	19
	Part time	4

Degrees conferred
Diploma

Tuition		Student Demographics	
In state	$5,036	Female	98.4%
Out of state	$5,036	Under age 25	25.9%
Enrollments	189	Minority	18.5%
Graduations	61	Part-time	9.0%

Minimum degree required
High school diploma or GED

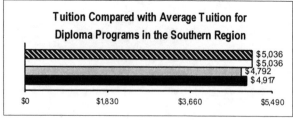
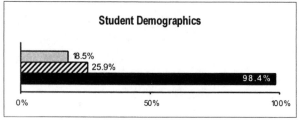

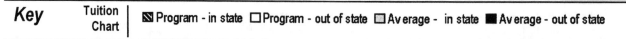

Key | Tuition Chart | ▨ Program - in state ☐ Program - out of state ☐ Average - in state ■ Average - out of state

Virginia

SOUTHSIDE REGIONAL MEDICAL CENTER *Useful Facts**

801 S Adams Street
Petersburg, VA 23803
(804) 862-5803
Rose Saunders, EdD, MN, RN

www.srmconline.com

Acceptance rate	26.5%

Tuition		**Student Demographics**	
In state	$2,976	Female	88.1%
Out of state	$4,716	Under age 25	48.0%
Enrollments	160	Minority	22.5%
Graduations	62	Part-time	41.3%

Accreditation
Virginia Board of Nursing, National League for
Nursing Accrediting Commission (NLNAC)

Degrees conferred
Diploma

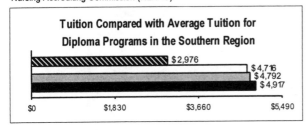

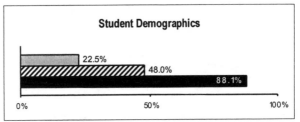

Demographics Chart | ■Female ☑Under age 25 □Minority | **Distance Learning** | ¹The tuition reported for this program may be not be annualized. *Data reported between 2001 and 2004.

Alabama

ALABAMA SOUTHERN COMMUNITY COLLEGE
Useful Facts*

PO Box 2000
Monroeville, AL 36461
(251) 575-3156
Phyllis Waits, MSN, EdD

www.ascc.edu

Accreditation
Alabama Board of Nursing

Degrees conferred
Associate Degree

Acceptance rate	78.9%

Tuition

In state	$2,100
Out of state	$4,200
Enrollments	31
Graduations	10

Student Demographics

Female	100.0%
Under age 25	61.0%
Minority	35.5%
Part-time	3.2%

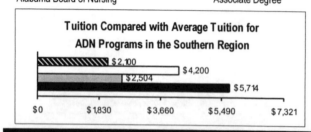

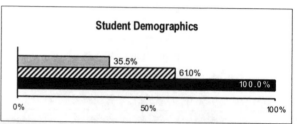

BEVILL STATE COMMUNITY COLLEGE
Useful Facts

1411 Indiana Avenue
Jasper, AL 35501
(205) 387-0511
Penne Mott, CRNP, MSN

www.bscc.edu

Accreditation
Alabama Board of Nursing, National League for
Nursing Accrediting Commission (NLNAC)

Degrees conferred
Associate Degree

Acceptance rate	42.8%
Faculty-student ratio	1: 21

Faculty	Full time	20
	Part time	2

Tuition

In state	$3,384
Out of state	$6,768
Enrollments	438
Graduations	153

Student Demographics

Female	79.5%
Under age 25	56.4%
Minority	6.5%
Part-time	50.7%

Minimum degree required
High school diploma or GED

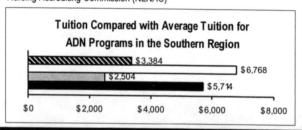

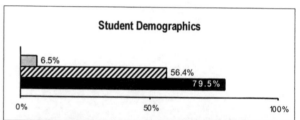

BISHOP STATE COMMUNITY COLLEGE
Useful Facts

1365 Dr ML King Jr Ave
Mobile, AL 36603
(251) 405-4497
Barbara Powe, MSN, RN

www.bishop.edu/health/nursing.htm

Accreditation
Alabama Board of Nursing, National League for
Nursing Accrediting Commission (NLNAC)

Degrees conferred
Associate Degree

Acceptance rate	19.4%
Faculty-student ratio	1: 10

Faculty	Full time	11
	Part time	11

Tuition

In state	$2,700
Out of state	$5,400
Enrollments	167
Graduations	19

Student Demographics

Female	85.0%
Under age 25	21.6%
Minority	36.8%
Part-time	0.0%

Minimum degree required
High school diploma or GED

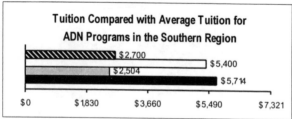

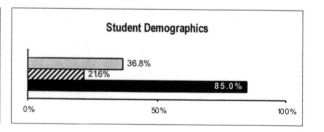

Key | Tuition Chart | ▨ Program - in state ☐ Program - out of state ☐ Average - in state ■ Average - out of state

Alabama

CENTRAL ALABAMA COMMUNITY COLLEGE

34091 US Hwy 280
Childersburg, AL 35044
(256) 378-2045
Melenie Bolton, PhD, MSN

www.cacc.cc.al.us

At the request of this nursing school, publication has been witheld.
Please contact the school directly for more information.

Accreditation
Alabama Board of Nursing, National League for
Nursing Accrediting Commission (NLNAC)

CHATTAHOOCHEE VALLEY COMMUNITY COLLEGE   *Useful Facts**

2602 College Drive
Phenix City, AL 36869
(334) 291-4925
Dixie Peterson, MSN, BSN, AS

www.cv.edu

			Tuition		**Student Demographics**	
Faculty-student ratio		1: 15	In state	$2,700	Female	92.3%
Faculty	Full time	3	Out of state	$4,830	Under age 25	19.0%
	Part time	1	**Enrollments**	52	Minority	62.2%
			Graduations	28	Part-time	0.0%

Accreditation
Alabama Board of Nursing, National League for
Nursing Accrediting Commission (NLNAC)

Degrees conferred
Associate Degree

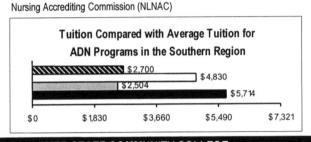

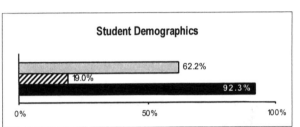

FAULKNER STATE COMMUNITY COLLEGE   *Useful Facts*

1900 Hwy 31 S
Bay Minette, AL 36507
(251) 580-2293
Jean Graham, MSN, NP-C, CNOR

faulknerstate.edu

			Tuition		**Student Demographics**	
Acceptance rate		14.2%	In state	$5,335	Female	90.1%
Faculty-student ratio		1: 7	Out of state	$9,020	Under age 25	31.0%
Faculty	Full time	4	**Enrollments**	71	Minority	12.9%
	Part time	11	**Graduations**	19	Part-time	0.0%

Accreditation
Alabama Board of Nursing

Degrees conferred
Associate Degree

Minimum degree required
High school diploma or GED

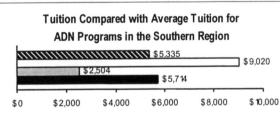

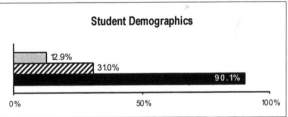

Demographics Chart	■ Female ▨ Under age 25 ☐ Minority	**Distance Learning** 🖥️	¹The tuition reported for this program may be not be annualized. *Data reported between 2001 and 2004.

Alabama

GADSDEN STATE COMMUNITY COLLEGE

Useful Facts*

PO Box 227
Gadsden, AL 35902
(256) 549-8321
Connie Meloun, RN, MSN

www.gadsdenst.cc.al.us

Accreditation
Alabama Board of Nursing, National League for
Nursing Accrediting Commission (NLNAC)

Degrees conferred
Associate Degree

Tuition		Student Demographics	
In state	$1,440	Female	86.4%
Out of state	$2,880	Under age 25	38.0%
Enrollments	169	Minority	5.9%
Graduations	48	Part-time	0.0%

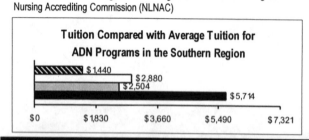

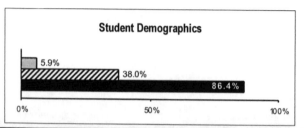

JEFFERSON DAVIS COMMUNITY COLLEGE

Useful Facts

PO Box 958
Brewton, AL 36427
(251) 809-1618
Ann Mantel

www.jdcc.edu

Accreditation
Alabama Board of Nursing, National League for
Nursing Accrediting Commission (NLNAC)

Degrees conferred
Associate Degree

Acceptance rate		22.5%
Faculty-student ratio		1: 11
Faculty	Full time	7
	Part time	5

Tuition		Student Demographics	
In state	$2,700	Female	78.0%
Out of state	$5,000	Under age 25	20.2%
Enrollments	109	Minority	16.5%
Graduations	91	Part-time	0.0%

Minimum degree required
High school diploma or GED

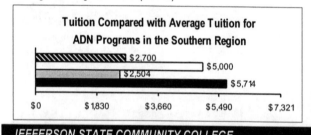

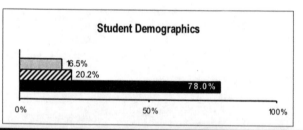

JEFFERSON STATE COMMUNITY COLLEGE

Useful Facts

2601 Carson Road
Birmingham, AL 35215
(205) 520-5990
Anita Norton, RN, BSN, MSN

www.jeffstateonline.com

Accreditation
Alabama Board of Nursing, National League for
Nursing Accrediting Commission (NLNAC)

Degrees conferred
Associate Degree

Acceptance rate		16.8%
Faculty-student ratio		1: 10
Faculty	Full time	17
	Part time	13

Tuition		Student Demographics	
In state	$2,130	Female	84.9%
Out of state	$4,260	Under age 25	41.2%
Enrollments	238	Minority	11.3%
Graduations	75	Part-time	0.0%

Minimum degree required
High school diploma or GED

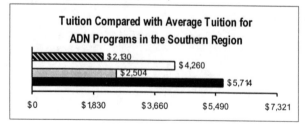

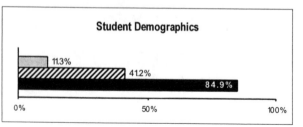

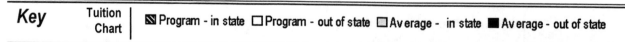

Key | Tuition Chart | ▨ Program - in state ☐ Program - out of state ☐ Average - in state ■ Average - out of state

Alabama

JOHN C CALHOUN COMMUNITY COLLEGE — *Useful Facts*

PO Box 2216
Decatur, AL 35609
(256) 306-2795
Jan Peek, RN, MSN

www.calhoun.edu

Acceptance rate		48.5%
Faculty-student ratio		1: 11
Faculty	Full time	20
	Part time	13

Tuition	
In state	$2,130
Out of state	$4,260
Enrollments	297
Graduations	115

Student Demographics	
Female	91.2%
Under age 25	33.0%
Minority	13.1%
Part-time	0.0%

Accreditation
Alabama Board of Nursing, National League for Nursing Accrediting Commission (NLNAC)

Degrees conferred
Associate Degree

Minimum degree required
High school diploma or GED

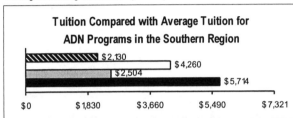

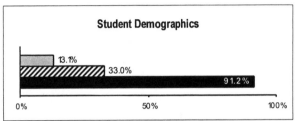

LAWSON STATE COMMUNITY COLLEGE — *Useful Facts*

3060 Wilson Road
Birmingham, AL 35221
(205) 929-6437
Shelia Marable, DSN, RN

www.lawsonstate.edu/programs/ctop/nur/health.htm

Acceptance rate		41.4%
Faculty-student ratio		1: 14
Faculty	Full time	8
	Part time	6

Tuition	
In state	$2,520
Out of state	$5,040
Enrollments	156
Graduations	24

Student Demographics	
Female	90.4%
Under age 25	31.4%
Minority	97.2%
Part-time	0.0%

Accreditation
Alabama Board of Nursing, National League for Nursing Accrediting Commission (NLNAC)

Degrees conferred
Associate Degree

Minimum degree required
High school diploma or GED

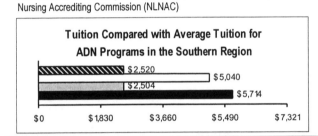

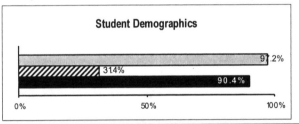

LURLEEN B WALLACE COMMUNITY COLLEGE

1708 North Main Street, PO Box 910
Opp, AL 36467
(334) 493-5373
Monica Cauley, MSN, BSN

www.lbwcc.edu

Accreditation
Alabama Board of Nursing

Degrees conferred
Associate Degree

Demographics Chart	■ Female ▨ Under age 25 ▢ Minority	Distance Learning	¹The tuition reported for this program may be not be annualized. *Data reported between 2001 and 2004.

Alabama

NORTHEAST ALABAMA COMMUNITY COLLEGE
Useful Facts

138 Highway 35 West
Rainsville, AL 35986
(256) 228-6001
Cindy Jones, EdD, RN

nacc.edu

Acceptance rate		31.9%
Faculty-student ratio		1: 14
Faculty	Full time	7
	Part time	3

Tuition	
In state	$3,240
Out of state	$5,796
Enrollments	121
Graduations	39

Student Demographics	
Female	87.6%
Under age 25	30.6%
Minority	11.6%
Part-time	0.0%

Accreditation
Alabama Board of Nursing, National League for
Nursing Accrediting Commission (NLNAC)

Degrees conferred
Associate Degree

Minimum degree required
High school diploma or GED

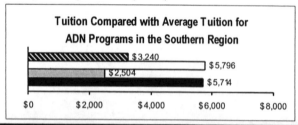
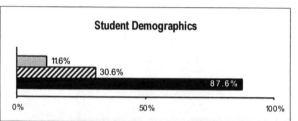

NORTHWEST SHOALS COMMUNITY COLLEGE
Useful Facts

2080 College Road
Phil Campbell, AL 35581
(256) 331-6207
Shelia Smith, RN, MSN

www.nwscc.cc.al.us/

Acceptance rate		32.4%
Faculty-student ratio		1: 17
Faculty	Full time	7
	Part time	6

Tuition	
In state	$2,130
Out of state	$4,260
Enrollments	174
Graduations	86

Student Demographics	
Female	88.5%
Under age 25	41.4%
Minority	5.7%
Part-time	9.8%

Accreditation
Alabama Board of Nursing, National League for
Nursing Accrediting Commission (NLNAC)

Degrees conferred
Associate Degree

Minimum degree required
High school diploma or GED

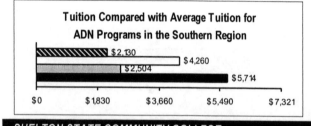
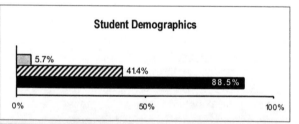

SHELTON STATE COMMUNITY COLLEGE
Useful Facts

9500 Old Greensboro Road
Tuscaloosa, AL 35405
(205) 391-2446
Kim Smith, MSN

www.sheltonstate.edu/nursing

Acceptance rate		37.1%
Faculty-student ratio		1: 7
Faculty	Full time	9
	Part time	11

Tuition	
In state	$2,700
Out of state	$4,830
Enrollments	107
Graduations	43

Student Demographics	
Female	91.6%
Under age 25	53.3%
Minority	28.8%
Part-time	0.0%

Accreditation
Alabama Board of Nursing, National League for
Nursing Accrediting Commission (NLNAC)

Degrees conferred
Associate Degree

Minimum degree required
High school diploma or GED

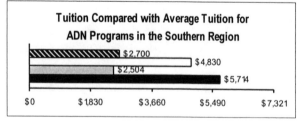
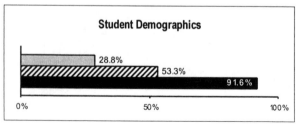

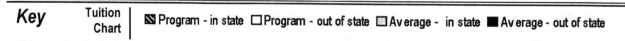

Key | Tuition Chart | ▨ Program - in state ▢ Program - out of state ▢ Average - in state ■ Average - out of state

Alabama

SOUTHERN UNION STATE COMMUNITY COLLEGE · *Useful Facts*

1701 LaFayette Parkway
Opelika, AL 36801
(334) 745-6437
Rhonda Davis, MSN

www.suscc.edu

Acceptance rate		10.2%
Faculty-student ratio		1: 10
Faculty	Full time	13
	Part time	21

Tuition	
In state	$2,640
Out of state	$5,280
Enrollments	230
Graduations	109

Student Demographics	
Female	87.0%
Under age 25	48.7%
Minority	12.3%
Part-time	6.5%

Accreditation
Alabama Board of Nursing, National League for Nursing Accrediting Commission (NLNAC)

Degrees conferred
Associate Degree

Minimum degree required
High school diploma or GED

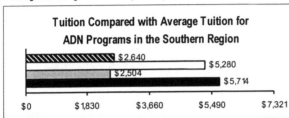

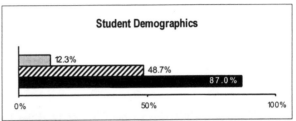

THE UNIVERSITY OF WEST ALABAMA · *Useful Facts**

Station 28
Livingston, AL 35470
(205) 652-3517
Sylvia Homan, MSN, RN, MSCE

www.uwa.edu

Acceptance rate	41.4%

Tuition	
In state	$1,392
Out of state	$2,784
Enrollments	112
Graduations	22

Student Demographics	
Female	95.5%
Under age 25	33.0%
Minority	23.2%
Part-time	0.0%

Accreditation
Alabama Board of Nursing, National League for Nursing Accrediting Commission (NLNAC)

Degrees conferred
Associate Degree

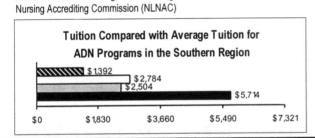

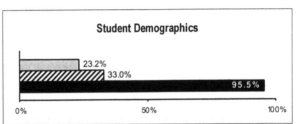

TROY STATE UNIVERSITY · *Useful Facts*

400 Pell Avenue
Troy, AL 36082
(334) 670-3428
Dr Bernita Hamilton, PhD, RN

www.spectrum.troy.edu/~nursing

Acceptance rate		37.1%
Faculty-student ratio		1: 10
Faculty	Full time	36
	Part time	19

Tuition	
In state	$4,004
Out of state	$8,008
Enrollments	320
Graduations	47

Student Demographics	
Female	93.1%
Under age 25	30.0%
Minority	45.9%
Part-time	70.3%

Accreditation
Alabama Board of Nursing, National League for Nursing Accrediting Commission (NLNAC)

Degrees conferred
Associate Degree

Minimum degree required
High school diploma or GED

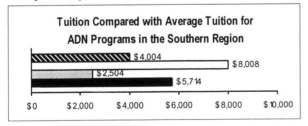

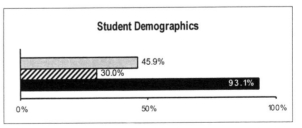

Demographics Chart	■ Female ▨ Under age 25 ▢ Minority	Distance Learning	†The tuition reported for this program may be not be annualized. *Data reported between 2001 and 2004.

Alabama

UNIVERSITY OF MOBILE
Useful Facts

5735 College Parkway
Mobile, AL 36663-0220
(251) 442-2227
Elizabeth Flanagan, EdD, RN

umobile.edu

Acceptance rate		44.4%
Faculty-student ratio		1: 9
Faculty	Full time	17
	Part time	5

Tuition	
In state	$10,230
Out of state	$10,230
Enrollments	87
Graduations	60

Student Demographics	
Female	89.7%
Under age 25	40.2%
Minority	23.0%
Part-time	0.0%

Accreditation
Alabama Board of Nursing

Degrees conferred
Associate Degree

Minimum degree required
High school diploma or GED

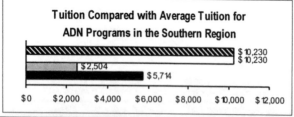

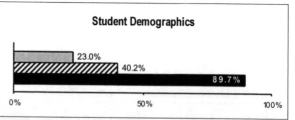

WALLACE COMMUNITY COLLEGE - DOTHAN
Useful Facts

1141 Wallace Drive
Dothan, AL 36303
(334) 556-2292
Kathy Buntin, MSN

www.wallace.edu

Acceptance rate		74.2%
Faculty-student ratio		1: 9
Faculty	Full time	28
	Part time	19

Tuition	
In state	$2,160
Out of state	$4,290
Enrollments	333
Graduations	85

Student Demographics	
Female	88.6%
Under age 25	42.3%
Minority	23.1%
Part-time	79.3%

Accreditation
Alabama Board of Nursing, National League for
Nursing Accrediting Commission (NLNAC)

Degrees conferred
Associate Degree

Minimum degree required
High school diploma or GED

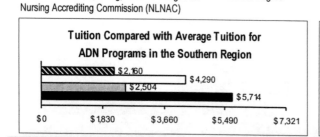

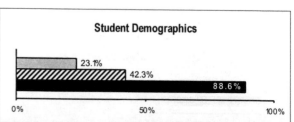

WALLACE COMMUNITY COLLEGE - SELMA
Useful Facts

3000 Earl Goodwin Parkway
Selma, AL 36701
(334) 876-9271
Becky Casey, MSN, RN

www.wccs.edu

Acceptance rate		17.0%
Faculty-student ratio		1: 9
Faculty	Full time	13
	Part time	6

Tuition	
In state	$2,160
Out of state	$4,320
Enrollments	139
Graduations	37

Student Demographics	
Female	93.5%
Under age 25	21.6%
Minority	56.8%
Part-time	0.0%

Accreditation
Alabama Board of Nursing, National League for
Nursing Accrediting Commission (NLNAC)

Degrees conferred
Associate Degree

Minimum degree required
High school diploma or GED

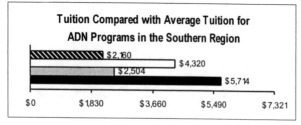

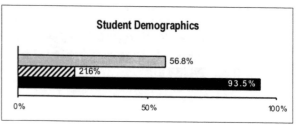

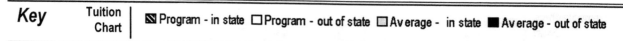

Key | Tuition Chart | ▨ Program - in state ▢ Program - out of state ▦ Average - in state ■ Average - out of state

Alabama

WALLACE STATE COMMUNITY COLLEGE - HANCEVILLE

Useful Facts*

PO Box 2000
Hanceville, AL 35077
(256) 352-8198
Denise Elliott, DSN, RN

www.wallacestate.edu

Acceptance rate		97.0%
Faculty-student ratio		1 : 5
Faculty	Full time	10
	Part time	45

Tuition
In state	$1,200
Out of state	$2,400
Enrollments	168
Graduations	67

Student Demographics
Female	88.1%
Minority	100.0%

Accreditation
Alabama Board of Nursing, National League for Nursing Accrediting Commission (NLNAC)

Degrees conferred
Associate Degree

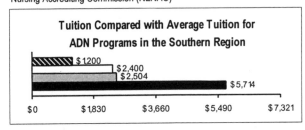

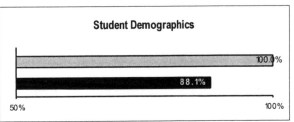

Alaska

UNIVERSITY OF ALASKA - ANCHORAGE

Useful Facts

3211 Providence Drive
Anchorage, AK 99508-8030
(907) 786-4571
Jean Ballantyne, PhD, RN

www.son.usaa.alaska.edu

Acceptance rate		29.6%
Faculty-student ratio		1 : 7
Faculty	Full time	38
	Part time	16

Tuition
In state	$3,270
Out of state	$10,890
Enrollments	110
Graduations	26

Student Demographics
Female	88.2%
Under age 25	17.3%
Minority	14.5%
Part-time	79.1%

Accreditation
Alaska Board of Nursing, National League for Nursing Accrediting Commission (NLNAC)

Degrees conferred
AAS Nursing

Minimum degree required
High school diploma or GED

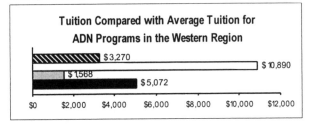

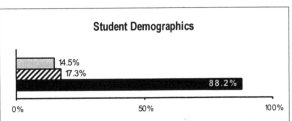

Arizona

ARIZONA WESTERN COLLEGE

Useful Facts

PO Box 929
Yuma, AZ 85366
(928) 344-7554
Mary Rhona Francoeur, RN, MSN

www.azwestern.edu/nursing

Acceptance rate		35.8%
Faculty-student ratio		1 : 8
Faculty	Full time	10
	Part time	10

Tuition
In state	$1,140
Out of state	$5,700
Enrollments	119
Graduations	30

Student Demographics
Female	89.1%
Under age 25	40.3%
Minority	46.2%
Part-time	0.0%

Accreditation
Arizona State Board of Nursing, National League for Nursing Accrediting Commission (NLNAC)

Degrees conferred
Associate Degree

Minimum degree required
High school diploma or GED

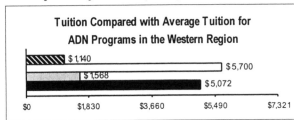

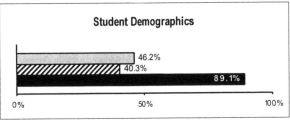

Demographics Chart	■Female ▨ Under age 25 ☐Minority	Distance Learning	¹The tuition reported for this program may be not be annualized. *Data reported between 2001 and 2004.

Arizona

CENTRAL ARIZONA COLLEGE

8470 N Overfield RD
Coolidge, AZ 85228
(520) 426-4330
Paula Calcaterra, MSN, RN

www.centralaz.edu/nursing

Acceptance rate		54.8%
Faculty-student ratio		1: 10
Faculty	Full time	3
	Part time	5

Tuition
In state	$1,200
Out of state	$2,400
Enrollments	54
Graduations	12

Student Demographics
Female	88.9%
Under age 25	20.0%
Minority	38.9%
Part-time	0.0%

Accreditation
Arizona State Board of Nursing, National League for Nursing Accrediting Commission (NLNAC)

Degrees conferred
Associate Degree

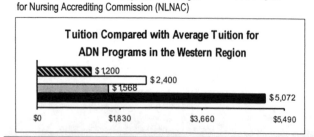

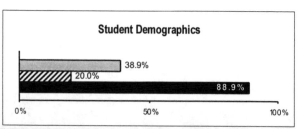

COCHISE COLLEGE

4190 West Highway 80
Douglas, AZ 84607
(520) 417-4110
Susan Macdonald, RN, MSN, MBA

www. cchise.org/nursing/index.htm

Accreditation
Arizona State Board of Nursing, National League for Nursing Accrediting Commission (NLNAC)

At the request of this nursing school, publication has been withheld. Please contact the school directly for more information.

COCONINO COMMUNITY COLLEGE

1800 S Lone Tree Road
Flagstaff, AZ 86004
(928) 526-7665
Donald Johnson, RN, MS

coconino.edu

Faculty	Full time	3
	Part time	5

Accreditation
Arizona State Board of Nursing

Degrees conferred
Associate Degree

EASTERN ARIZONA COLLEGE

615 S Stadium Ave
Thatcher, AZ 85552
(928) 428-8396
Mayuree Siripoon, DNSc, RN

www.eac.edu

Acceptance rate		71.4%
Faculty-student ratio		1: 9
Faculty	Full time	6
	Part time	4

Tuition
In state	$1,148
Out of state	$6,128
Enrollments	70
Graduations	26

Student Demographics
Female	91.4%
Under age 25	42.9%
Minority	17.1%
Part-time	0.0%

Accreditation
Arizona State Board of Nursing

Degrees conferred
Associate Degree

Minimum degree required
High school diploma or GED

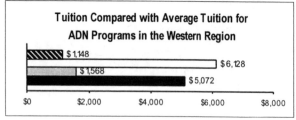

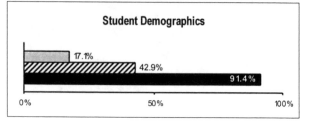

Key | Tuition Chart | ▨ Program - in state ☐ Program - out of state ☐ Average - in state ■ Average - out of state

Arizona

INTERNATIONAL INSTITUTE OF THE AMERICAS - Ethel Bauer School of Nursing

6049 N 43rd Ave
Phoenix, AZ 85019
(602) 589-1323
Ann Nichols, RN

www.iaa-online.com

Accreditation
Arizona State Board of Nursing

Degrees conferred
Associate Degree

MARICOPA COMMUNITY COLLEGE - Chandler-Gilbert Community College

2411 W 14th St
Tempe, AZ 85281
(602) 286-8567
Cathy Lucius, RN, MS

www.maricopa.edu

Accreditation
Arizona State Board of Nursing, National League
for Nursing Accrediting Commission (NLNAC)

Acceptance rate		8.9%
Faculty-student ratio		1: 11
Faculty	Full time	89
	Part time	99

Degrees conferred
Associate Degree

Tuition	
In state	$1,800
Out of state	$7,740
Enrollments	37
Graduations	0

Minimum degree required
High school diploma or GED

Student Demographics	
Female	94.6%
Under age 25	40.5%
Minority	32.4%
Part-time	0.0%

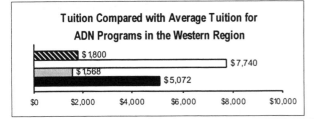

Tuition Compared with Average Tuition for ADN Programs in the Western Region

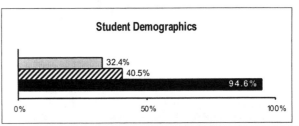

Student Demographics

MARICOPA COMMUNITY COLLEGE - Mesa Community College - Boswell Center

2411 W 14th St
Tempe, AZ 85281
(602) 286-8567
Cathy Lucius, RN, MS

www.maricopa.edu

Accreditation
Arizona State Board of Nursing, National League
for Nursing Accrediting Commission (NLNAC)

Acceptance rate		13.6%
Faculty-student ratio		1: 11
Faculty	Full time	89
	Part time	99

Degrees conferred
Associate Degree

Tuition	
In state	$1,800
Out of state	$7,740
Enrollments	187
Graduations	64

Minimum degree required
High school diploma or GED

Student Demographics	
Female	86.1%
Under age 25	36.4%
Minority	21.0%
Part-time	0.0%

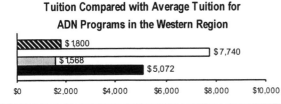

Tuition Compared with Average Tuition for ADN Programs in the Western Region

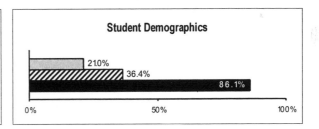

Student Demographics

| Demographics Chart | ■Female ▨Under age 25 □Minority | Distance Learning 🖥 | ¹The tuition reported for this program may be not be annualized. *Data reported between 2001 and 2004. |

Arizona

MARICOPA COMMUNITY COLLEGE - Paradise Valley Community College - JC Lincoln

2411 W 14th St
Tempe, AZ 85281
(602) 286-8567
Cathy Lucius, RN, MS

www.maricopa.edu

Accreditation
Arizona State Board of Nursing, National League for Nursing Accrediting Commission (NLNAC)

Faculty-student ratio		1: 11
Faculty	Full time	89
	Part time	99

Degrees conferred
Associate Degree

Tuition
In state	$1,800
Out of state	$7,740
Enrollments	63
Graduations	0

Minimum degree required
High school diploma or GED

Student Demographics
Female	92.1%
Under age 25	27.0%
Minority	21.0%
Part-time	0.0%

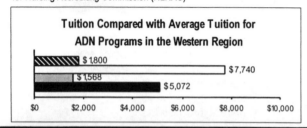

Tuition Compared with Average Tuition for ADN Programs in the Western Region

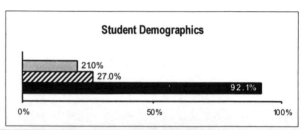

Student Demographics

MARICOPA COMMUNITY COLLEGE - Glendale Community College

2411 W 14th St
Tempe, AZ 85281
(602) 286-8567
Cathy Lucius, RN, MS

www.maricopa.edu

Accreditation
Arizona State Board of Nursing, National League for Nursing Accrediting Commission (NLNAC)

Acceptance rate		27.6%
Faculty-student ratio		1: 11
Faculty	Full time	89
	Part time	99

Degrees conferred
Associate Degree

Tuition
In state	$1,800
Out of state	$7,740
Enrollments	221
Graduations	93

Minimum degree required
High school diploma or GED

Student Demographics
Female	86.9%
Under age 25	31.2%
Minority	28.7%
Part-time	32.6%

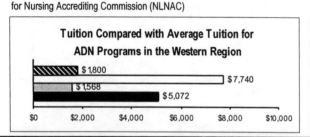

Tuition Compared with Average Tuition for ADN Programs in the Western Region

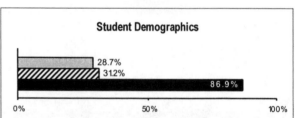

Student Demographics

MARICOPA COMMUNITY COLLEGE - Mesa Community College

2411 W 14th St
Tempe, AZ 85281
(602) 286-8567
Cathy Lucius, RN, MS

www.maricopa.edu

Accreditation
Arizona State Board of Nursing, National League for Nursing Accrediting Commission (NLNAC)

Acceptance rate		17.3%
Faculty-student ratio		1: 11
Faculty	Full time	89
	Part time	99

Degrees conferred
Associate Degree

Tuition
In state	$1,800
Out of state	$7,740
Enrollments	242
Graduations	107

Minimum degree required
High school diploma or GED

Student Demographics
Female	87.6%
Under age 25	44.2%
Minority	24.0%
Part-time	0.0%

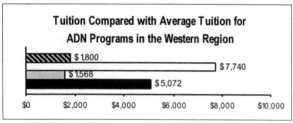

Tuition Compared with Average Tuition for ADN Programs in the Western Region

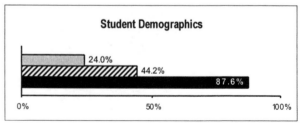

Student Demographics

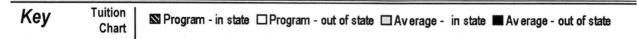

Key | Tuition Chart | ▧ Program - in state ☐ Program - out of state ☐ Average - in state ■ Average - out of state

Arizona

MARICOPA COMMUNITY COLLEGE - Gateway Community College

2411 W 14th St
Tempe, AZ 85281
(602) 286-8567
Cathy Lucius, RN, MS

www.maricopa.edu

Accreditation
Arizona State Board of Nursing, National League for Nursing Accrediting Commission (NLNAC)

Acceptance rate		26.2%
Faculty-student ratio		1: 11
Faculty	Full time	89
	Part time	99

Degrees conferred
Associate Degree

Tuition	
In state	$1,800
Out of state	$7,740
Enrollments	347
Graduations	150

Minimum degree required
High school diploma or GED

Student Demographics	
Female	84.4%
Under age 25	33.7%
Minority	28.4%
Part-time	32.3%

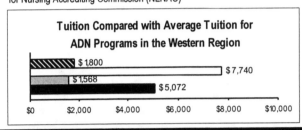

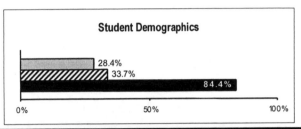

MARICOPA COMMUNITY COLLEGE - Scottsdale Community College

2411 W 14th St
Tempe, AZ 85281
(602) 286-8567
Cathy Lucius, RN, MS

www.maricopa.edu

Accreditation
Arizona State Board of Nursing, National League for Nursing Accrediting Commission (NLNAC)

Acceptance rate		11.1%
Faculty-student ratio		1: 11
Faculty	Full time	89
	Part time	99

Degrees conferred
Associate Degree

Tuition	
In state	$1,800
Out of state	$7,740
Enrollments	191
Graduations	76

Minimum degree required
High school diploma or GED

Student Demographics	
Female	85.3%
Under age 25	34.0%
Minority	16.1%
Part-time	0.0%

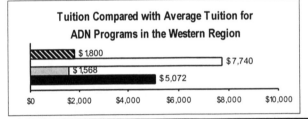

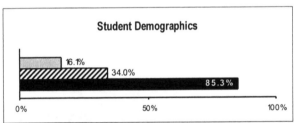

MARICOPA COMMUNITY COLLEGE - Phoenix College

2411 W 14th St
Tempe, AZ 85281
(602) 286-8567
Cathy Lucius, RN, MS

www.maricopa.edu

Accreditation
Arizona State Board of Nursing, National League for Nursing Accrediting Commission (NLNAC)

Acceptance rate		12.4%
Faculty-student ratio		1: 11
Faculty	Full time	89
	Part time	99

Degrees conferred
Associate Degree

Tuition	
In state	$1,800
Out of state	$7,740
Enrollments	162
Graduations	89

Minimum degree required
High school diploma or GED

Student Demographics	
Female	84.6%
Under age 25	34.6%
Minority	39.5%
Part-time	0.0%

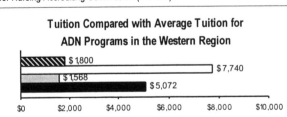

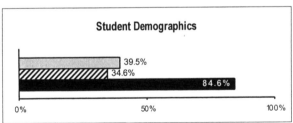

Demographics Chart	■Female ▨ Under age 25 □ Minority	Distance Learning	¹The tuition reported for this program may be not be annualized. *Data reported between 2001 and 2004.

Arizona

MARICOPA COMMUNITY COLLEGE - *Rio Salgado College*

2411 W 14th St
Tempe, AZ 85281
(602) 286-8567
Cathy Lucius, RN, MS

www.maricopa.edu

Accreditation
Arizona State Board of Nursing, National League
for Nursing Accrediting Commission (NLNAC)

Acceptance rate		9.6%
Faculty-student ratio		1: 11
Faculty	Full time	89
	Part time	99

Degrees conferred
Associate Degree

Tuition	
In state	$1,800
Out of state	$7,740
Enrollments	60
Graduations	12

Minimum degree required
High school diploma or GED

Student Demographics	
Female	81.7%
Under age 25	18.3%
Minority	15.0%
Part-time	0.0%

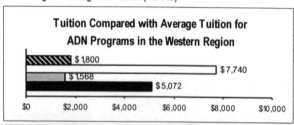

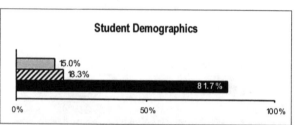

MOHAVE COMMUNITY COLLEGE

1977 West Acoma Blvd
Lake Havasu City, AZ 86403
(928) 505-3378
Linda Riesdorph, RN, MSN

www.mohave.edu

Accreditation
Arizona State Board of Nursing, National League
for Nursing Accrediting Commission (NLNAC)

At the request of this nursing school, publication has been withheld.
Please contact the school directly for more information.

NORTHLAND PIONEER COLLEGE   *Useful Facts**

PO Box 610
Holbrook, AZ 86025
(928) 532-6132
Penny Fairman, RN, MS, EdD

www.northland.cc.az.us

Accreditation
Arizona State Board of Nursing

Degrees conferred
Associate Degree

Acceptance rate	41.7%

Tuition	
In state	$800
Out of state	$3,210
Enrollments	56
Graduations	28

Student Demographics	
Female	92.9%
Minority	12.5%
Part-time	0.0%

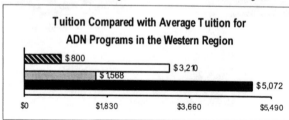

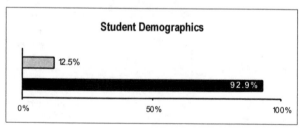

Arizona

PIMA COMMUNITY COLLEGE   *Useful Facts*

2202 West Anklam Road
Tucson, AZ 85709-1010
(520) 206-6785
Marie Barrentine, MSN, MRC, BSN

www.pima.edu

Acceptance rate	50.0%	**Tuition**		**Student Demographics**	
Faculty-student ratio	1: 12	In state	$850	Female	88.7%
Faculty Full time	16	Out of state	$2,538	Under age 25	5.9%
Part time	28	**Enrollments**	353	Minority	34.5%
		Graduations	153	Part-time	5.7%

Accreditation
Arizona State Board of Nursing, National League
for Nursing Accrediting Commission (NLNAC)

Degrees conferred
Associate Degree

Minimum degree required
High school diploma or GED

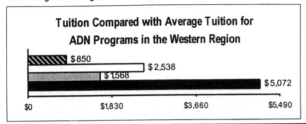

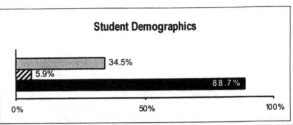

YAVAPAI COLLEGE   *Useful Facts*

1100 East Sheldon Street
Prescott, AZ 86301
(928) 776-2246
Barbara Nubile, RN, MSN

www.yc.edu/divnursing.nsf

Acceptance rate	37.5%	**Tuition**		**Student Demographics**	
Faculty-student ratio	1: 10	In state	$1,320	Female	87.6%
Faculty Full time	15	Out of state	$7,120	Under age 25	32.1%
Part time	11	**Enrollments**	209	Minority	7.5%
		Graduations	46	Part-time	67.9%

Accreditation
Arizona State Board of Nursing, National League
for Nursing Accrediting Commission (NLNAC)

Degrees conferred
Associate Degree

Minimum degree required
High school diploma or GED

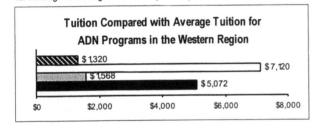

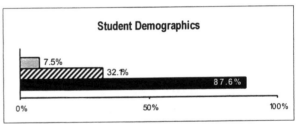

Arkansas

ARKANSAS NORTHEASTERN COLLEGE

PO Box 1109, 2501 S Division St
Blytheville, AR 72315
(870) 763-1486
Sharon Fulling, MSN, BSN, RN

www.anc.edu

Accreditation
Arkansas State Board of Nursing, National
League for Nursing Accrediting Commission
(NLNAC)

At the request of this nursing school, publication has been witheld.
Please contact the school directly for more information.

Demographics Chart	■ Female ▨ Under age 25 ▢ Minority	Distance Learning	¹The tuition reported for this program may be not be annualized. *Data reported between 2001 and 2004.

Arkansas

ARKANSAS STATE UNIVERSITY

Useful Facts

PO Box 910
State University, AR 72467
(870) 972-3074
Sue McLarry, PhD, RN

www.conhp.astate.edu/nursing/index.html

Accreditation
Arkansas State Board of Nursing, National
League for Nursing Accrediting Commission
(NLNAC)

Acceptance rate		90.7%
Faculty-student ratio		1 : 9
Faculty	Full time	35
	Part time	33

Degrees conferred
Associate Degree

Tuition		Student Demographics	
In state	$4,260	Female	90.5%
Out of state	$10,950	Under age 25	19.0%
Enrollments	189	Minority	11.6%
Graduations	77	Part-time	14.3%

Minimum degree required
Fall 2005 admission LPN, Spring admission HS
graduation or GED

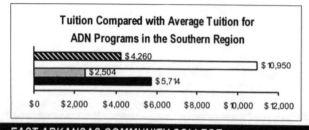

Tuition Compared with Average Tuition for
ADN Programs in the Southern Region

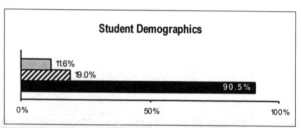

Student Demographics

EAST ARKANSAS COMMUNITY COLLEGE

Useful Facts

1700 Newcastle Road
Forrest City, AR 72335
(870) 633-4480
Janie Bailey, RN, MSN

www.eacc.edu

Accreditation
Arkansas State Board of Nursing, National
League for Nursing Accrediting Commission
(NLNAC)

Acceptance rate		50.0%
Faculty-student ratio		1 : 11
Faculty	Full time	4
	Part time	2

Degrees conferred
Associate Degree

Tuition		Student Demographics	
In state	$1,620	Female	90.6%
Out of state	$2,220	Under age 25	28.3%
Enrollments	53	Minority	18.9%
Graduations	27	Part-time	0.0%

Minimum degree required
High school diploma or GED

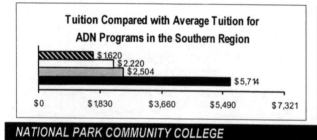

Tuition Compared with Average Tuition for
ADN Programs in the Southern Region

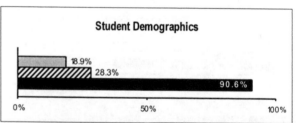

Student Demographics

NATIONAL PARK COMMUNITY COLLEGE

Useful Facts

101 College Drive
Hot Springs, AR 71913
(501) 760-4288
Linda Castaldi, MNSc, RN

www.npcc.edu

Accreditation
Arkansas State Board of Nursing, National
League for Nursing Accrediting Commission
(NLNAC)

Acceptance rate		60.2%
Faculty-student ratio		1 : 7
Faculty	Full time	13
	Part time	7

Degrees conferred
Associate Degree

Tuition		Student Demographics	
In state	$1,200	Female	86.8%
Out of state	$2,976	Under age 25	26.4%
Enrollments	121	Minority	13.2%
Graduations	52	Part-time	68.6%

Minimum degree required
High school diploma or GED

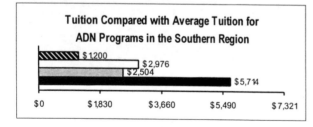

Tuition Compared with Average Tuition for
ADN Programs in the Southern Region

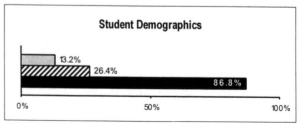

Student Demographics

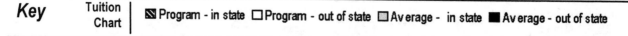

Key | Tuition Chart | ▧ Program - in state ☐ Program - out of state ☐ Average - in state ■ Average - out of state

Arkansas

NORTH ARKANSAS COLLEGE | Useful Facts

1515 Pioneer Ridge Drive
Harrison, AR 72601
(870) 391-3262
Elizabeth Robinson, MSN, RN, CNS

www.northark.edu

Acceptance rate		44.1%	**Tuition**		**Student Demographics**	
Faculty-student ratio		1: 11	In state	$1,320	Female	85.6%
Faculty	Full time	6	Out of state	$3,390	Under age 25	12.2%
	Part time	4	**Enrollments**	90	Minority	4.4%
			Graduations	37	Part-time	34.4%

Accreditation
Arkansas State Board of Nursing, National League for Nursing Accrediting Commission (NLNAC)

Degrees conferred
Associate Degree

Minimum degree required
High school diploma or GED

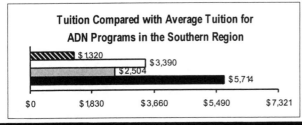

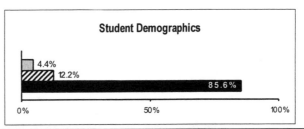

NORTHWEST ARKANSAS COMMUNITY COLLEGE | Useful Facts*

One College Drive
Bentonville, AR 72712
(479) 619-4255
Elaine Holloway, MSN, RN

www.nwacc.edu

Acceptance rate	32.7%	**Tuition**		**Student Demographics**	
		In state	$2,610	Female	82.9%
		Out of state	$3,690	Under age 25	50.0%
		Enrollments	70	Minority	4.3%
		Graduations	27	Part-time	0.0%

Accreditation
Arkansas State Board of Nursing

Degrees conferred
Associate Degree

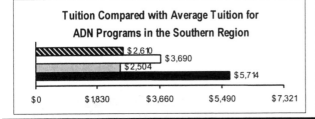

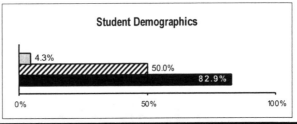

PHILLIPS COMMUNITY COLLEGE OF UNIVERSITY OF ARKANSAS | Useful Facts

PO Box 785
Helena, AR 72342
(870) 338-6474
Amy Hudson, MSN, RN

www.pccua.edu

Acceptance rate		92.9%	**Tuition**		**Student Demographics**	
Faculty-student ratio		1: 8	In state	$1,760	Female	82.7%
Faculty	Full time	12	Out of state	$3,170	Under age 25	56.1%
	Part time	1	**Enrollments**	98	Minority	27.6%
			Graduations	16	Part-time	8.2%

Accreditation
Arkansas State Board of Nursing, National League for Nursing Accrediting Commission (NLNAC)

Degrees conferred
Associate Degree

Minimum degree required
High school diploma or GED

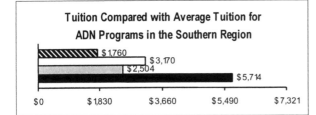

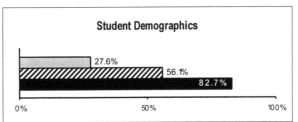

Demographics Chart	■ Female ▨ Under age 25 ☐ Minority	Distance Learning	¹The tuition reported for this program may be not be annualized. *Data reported between 2001 and 2004.

Arkansas

SOUTHEAST ARKANSAS COLLEGE

*Useful Facts**

1900 Hazel St
Pine Bluff, AR 71603
(870) 543-5927
Diann Williams, RN, MSN

www.seark.edu

Acceptance rate	57.1%	**Tuition**		**Student Demographics**
		In state	$600	Female	95.8%
		Out of state	$1,200	Under age 25	29.0%
		Enrollments	24	Minority	66.7%
		Graduations	19	Part-time	0.0%

Accreditation
Arkansas State Board of Nursing, National
League for Nursing Accrediting Commission
(NLNAC)

Degrees conferred
Associate Degree

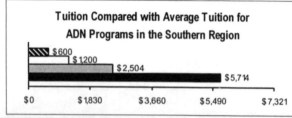

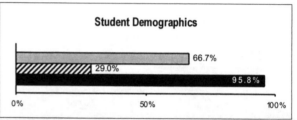

SOUTHERN ARKANSAS UNIVERSITY

*Useful Facts**

PO Box 9406
Magnolia, AR 71754
(870) 235-4330
Golden Tradewell, PhD, RN

www.saumag.edu.nursing

Acceptance rate	85.0%	**Tuition**		**Student Demographics**
Faculty-student ratio	1: 15	In state	$1,248	Female	85.6%
Faculty Full time	12	Out of state	$1,920	Under age 25	56.9%
Part time	0	**Enrollments**	181	Minority	43.3%
		Graduations	39	Part-time	55.8%

Accreditation
Arkansas State Board of Nursing, National
League for Nursing Accrediting Commission
(NLNAC)

Degrees conferred
Associate Degree

Minimum degree required
0

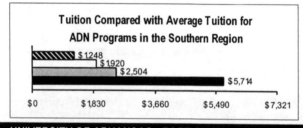

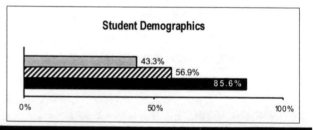

UNIVERSITY OF ARKANSAS - FORT SMITH

PO Box 3649
Fort Smith, AR 72913
(479) 788-7840
Brenda Mitchell, DSN, MS, RN

www.uafortsmith.edu

Accreditation
Arkansas State Board of Nursing, National
League for Nursing Accrediting Commission
(NLNAC)

*At the request of this nursing school, publication has been witheld.
Please contact the school directly for more information.*

Key | Tuition Chart | ▪ Program - in state □ Program - out of state □ Average - in state ■ Average - out of state

Arkansas

UNIVERSITY OF ARKANSAS - LITTLE ROCK
Useful Facts*

2801South University
Little Rock, AR 72204
(501) 569-8081
Ann Schlumberger, MSN, EdD

www.ualr.edu

Accreditation
Arkansas State Board of Nursing, National
League for Nursing Accrediting Commission
(NLNAC)

Acceptance rate		52.5%
Faculty-student ratio		1: 14
Faculty	Full time	15
	Part time	8

Degrees conferred
Associate Degree

Tuition[1]	
In state	$141
Out of state	$370
Enrollments	265
Graduations	65

Minimum degree required
High school diploma or GED

Student Demographics	
Female	81.5%
Under age 25	43.4%
Minority	28.7%
Part-time	47.9%

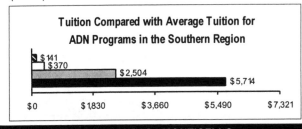

Tuition Compared with Average Tuition for ADN Programs in the Southern Region

$141
$370
$2,504
$5,714

$0 $1,830 $3,660 $5,490 $7,321

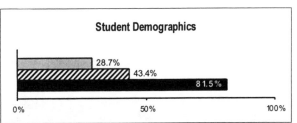

Student Demographics

28.7%
43.4%
81.5%

0%   50%   100%

UNIVERSITY OF ARKANSAS - MONTICELLO
Useful Facts

358 University Drive, PO Box 3606
Monticello, AR 71656
(870) 460-1069
Larry Eustace, AASN, BSN, MSN, DSN, RN, CNE

www.uamont.edu/nursing

Accreditation
Arkansas State Board of Nursing

Acceptance rate		80.0%
Faculty-student ratio		1: 10
Faculty	Full time	9
	Part time	1

Degrees conferred
AASN

Tuition	
In state	$3,000
Out of state	$3,750
Enrollments	14
Graduations	8

Minimum degree required
LPN

Student Demographics	
Female	85.7%
Under age 25	14.3%
Minority	35.7%
Part-time	0.0%

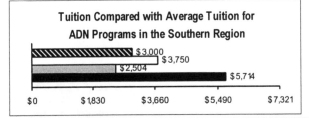

Tuition Compared with Average Tuition for ADN Programs in the Southern Region

$3,000
$3,750
$2,504
$5,714

$0 $1,830 $3,660 $5,490 $7,321

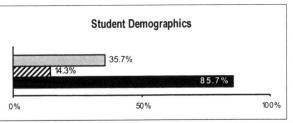

Student Demographics

35.7%
14.3%
85.7%

0%   50%   100%

UNIVERSITY OF ARKANSAS COMMUNITY COLLEGE - BATESVILLE
Useful Facts

2005 White Drive
Batesville, AR 72503
(870) 793-7581
Dianne Plemmons, MSN, RN

www.uaccb.edu

Accreditation
Arkansas State Board of Nursing, National
League for Nursing Accrediting Commission
(NLNAC)

Acceptance rate		92.7%
Faculty-student ratio		1: 7
Faculty	Full time	3
	Part time	3

Degrees conferred
Associate Degree

Tuition	
In state	$810
Out of state	$2,052
Enrollments	30
Graduations	31

Minimum degree required
Licensed Practical Nurse

Student Demographics	
Female	93.3%
Under age 25	26.7%
Part-time	0.0%

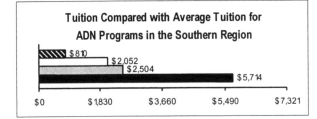

Tuition Compared with Average Tuition for ADN Programs in the Southern Region

$810
$2,052
$2,504
$5,714

$0 $1,830 $3,660 $5,490 $7,321

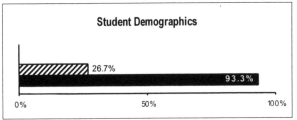

Student Demographics

26.7%
93.3%

0%   50%   100%

Demographics Chart	■Female ▨ Under age 25 ☐Minority	**Distance Learning**	[1]The tuition reported for this program may be not be annualized. *Data reported between 2001 and 2004.

California

ALLAN HANCOCK COLLEGE

800 South College Drive
Santa Maria, CA 93454
(805) 922-6966
Holly Stromberg, RN, MSN, CCRN

www.hancockcollege.edu

Accreditation
California Board of Registered Nursing

Faculty-student ratio		1: 3
Faculty	Full time	6
	Part time	4

Degrees conferred
Associate Degree

Tuition[1]	
In state	$11
Enrollments	21
Graduations	19

Student Demographics	
Female	85.7%
Under age 25	19.0%
Minority	52.4%
Part-time	0.0%

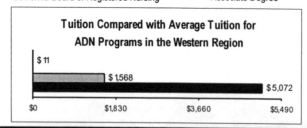

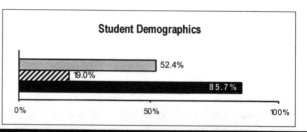

AMERICAN RIVER COLLEGE

4700 College Oak Dr
Sacramento, CA 95841
(916) 484-8254
Victoria Maryatt, MSN, RN

www.arc.losrios.edu

Accreditation
California Board of Registered Nursing

Acceptance rate	30.0%

Degrees conferred
Associate Degree

Tuition[1]	
In state	$360
Out of state	$4,500
Enrollments	60
Graduations	60

Student Demographics	
Female	91.7%
Under age 25	0.0%
Minority	13.8%
Part-time	0.0%

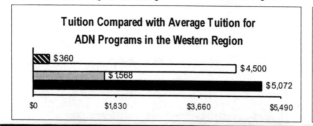

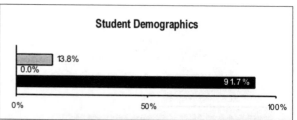

ANTELOPE VALLEY COLLEGE

3041 West Avenue K
Lancaster, CA 93536
(661) 722-6402
Karen Cowell, PhD, RN

www.avc.edu

Accreditation
California Board of Registered Nursing

Acceptance rate		47.1%
Faculty-student ratio		1: 13
Faculty	Full time	11
	Part time	16

Degrees conferred
Associate Degree

Tuition	
In state	$780
Out of state	$4,800
Enrollments	243
Graduations	100

Minimum degree required
High school diploma or GED

Student Demographics	
Female	81.5%
Under age 25	29.6%
Minority	50.6%
Part-time	81.5%

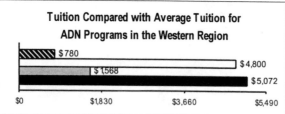

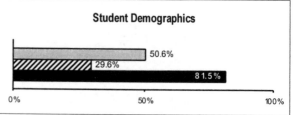

Key | Tuition Chart | ⊠ Program - in state ☐ Program - out of state ▨ Average - in state ■ Average - out of state

California

BAKERSFIELD COLLEGE
*Useful Facts**

1801 Panorama Drive
Bakersfield, CA 93305
(661) 395-4282
Cindy Collier, BSN, MSN

www.bakersfieldcollege.org

Accreditation
California Board of Registered Nursing

Degrees conferred
Associate Degree

Student Demographics

Female	90.0%

Enrollments 210

Minority	45.6%
Part-time	0.0%

BUTTE COLLEGE

3536 Butte Campus
Oroville, CA 95965
(508) 895-2329
Macy Kelly

www.butte.edu

Accreditation
California Board of Registered Nursing

Degrees conferred
Associate Degree

CABRILLO COLLEGE
*Useful Facts**

6500 Soquel Drive
Aptos, CA 95003
(831) 479-6389
Kathleen Welch, PhD, RN

cabrillo.cc.ca.us

Accreditation
California Board of Registered Nursing

Degrees conferred
Associate Degree

Acceptance rate 65.0%

Tuition	
In state	$780
Out of state	$2,400
Enrollments	95
Graduations	45

Student Demographics	
Female	90.5%
Under age 25	33.0%
Minority	29.5%
Part-time	0.0%

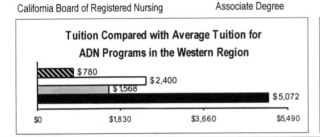

Tuition Compared with Average Tuition for ADN Programs in the Western Region

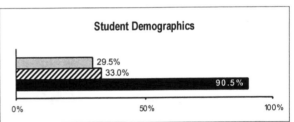

Student Demographics

CERRITOS COLLEGE

1110 East Alondra Blvd
Norwalk, CA 90650
(562) 860-2451
Charlene Fobi, RN, MN, EdD

www.cerritos.edu/nursing

Accreditation
California Board of Registered Nursing, National League for Nursing Accrediting Commission (NLNAC)

At the request of this nursing school, publication has been witheld. Please contact the school directly for more information.

CHABOT COLLEGE

25555 Hesperian Boulevard
Hayward, CA 94545
(510) 723-6871
Nancy Cowan, MSN, EdD, RN

www.chabotcollege.edu

Accreditation
California Board of Registered Nursing

At the request of this nursing school, publication has been witheld. Please contact the school directly for more information.

Demographics Chart	■ Female ▨ Under age 25 ☐ Minority	Distance Learning	†The tuition reported for this program may be not be annualized. *Data reported between 2001 and 2004.

California

CHAFFEY COLLEGE
Useful Facts

5885 Haven Avenue
Rancho Cucamonga, CA 91737
(909) 941-2619
Barbara Hindman, MN

www.chaffey.edu

Acceptance rate	34.0%
Faculty-student ratio	1: 11
Faculty Full time	10
Part time	12

Tuition	
In state	$780
Out of state	$5,250
Enrollments	169
Graduations	62

Student Demographics	
Female	85.8%
Under age 25	26.6%
Minority	54.8%
Part-time	23.1%

Accreditation
California Board of Registered Nursing, National
League for Nursing Accrediting Commission
(NLNAC)

Degrees conferred
Associate Degree

Minimum degree required
High school diploma or GED

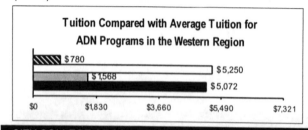

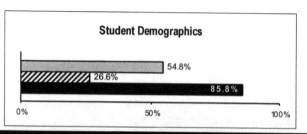

CITY COLLEGE OF SAN FRANCISCO
Useful Facts*

1860 Hayes Street
San Francisco, CA 94117
(415) 561-1908
Linda Squire-Grohee

www.ccsf.cc.ca.us

Acceptance rate	14.8%

Tuition[1]	
In state	$284
Out of state	$3,888
Enrollments	169
Graduations	70

Student Demographics	
Female	88.2%
Under age 25	5.0%
Minority	55.0%
Part-time	0.0%

Accreditation
California Board of Registered Nursing

Degrees conferred
Associate Degree

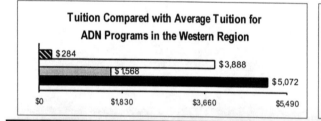

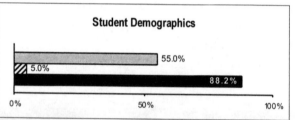

COLLEGE OF MARIN
Useful Facts

835 College Avenue
Kentfield, CA 94904
(415) 485-9326
Rosalind Hartman, MSN, RN

www.marin.cc.ca.us

Acceptance rate	23.7%
Faculty-student ratio	1: 8
Faculty Full time	6
Part time	7

Tuition[1]	
In state	$26
Out of state	$166
Enrollments	79
Graduations	45

Student Demographics	
Female	83.5%
Under age 25	20.3%
Minority	23.3%
Part-time	1.3%

Accreditation
California Board of Registered Nursing, National
League for Nursing Accrediting Commission
(NLNAC)

Degrees conferred
Associate Degree

Minimum degree required
High school diploma or GED

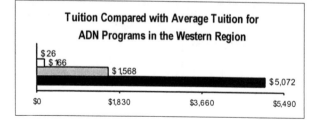

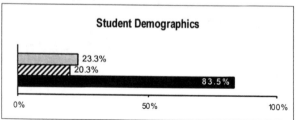

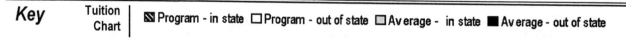

Key Tuition Chart | ▨ Program - in state ☐ Program - out of state ☐ Average - in state ■ Average - out of state

California

COLLEGE OF SAN MATEO

1700 West Hillsdale Boulevard
San Mateo, CA 94402
(650) 574-6218
Ruth McCracken, MSNEd, RN

gocsm.net

Accreditation
California Board of Registered Nursing

*At the request of this nursing school, publication has been withheld.
Please contact the school directly for more information.*

COLLEGE OF THE CANYONS   *Useful Facts*

26455 Rockwell Canyon Road
Santa Clarita, CA 91355
(661) 362-3366
Sue Albert, RN, MN, MHA

www.canyons.edu/nursing

Accreditation
California Board of Registered Nursing, National
League for Nursing Accrediting Commission
(NLNAC)

Acceptance rate	9.6%	
Faculty-student ratio	1: 6	
Faculty Full time	11	
Part time	31	

Tuition	
In state	$780
Out of state	$925
Enrollments	158
Graduations	63

Student Demographics	
Female	83.5%
Under age 25	60.1%
Minority	55.7%
Part-time	0.0%

Degrees conferred
Associate Degree

Minimum degree required
High school diploma or GED

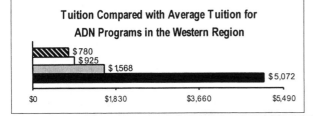

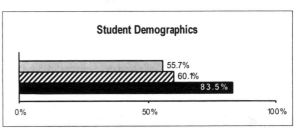

COLLEGE OF THE DESERT   *Useful Facts*

43-500 Monterey Avenue
Palm Desert, CA 92260
(760) 346-8041
Sandi Emerson, MSN, RN

www.collegeofthedesert.edu

Accreditation
California Board of Registered Nursing, National
League for Nursing Accrediting Commission
(NLNAC)

Acceptance rate	19.0%	
Faculty-student ratio	1: 13	
Faculty Full time	7	
Part time	21	

Tuition	
In state	$795
Out of state	$5,318
Enrollments	224
Graduations	81

Student Demographics	
Female	81.7%
Under age 25	28.1%
Minority	48.1%
Part-time	0.0%

Degrees conferred
Associate Degree

Minimum degree required
High school diploma or GED

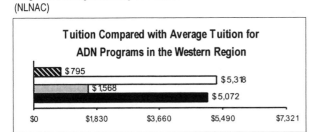

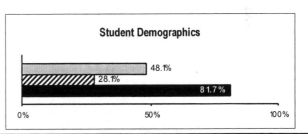

COLLEGE OF THE SEQUOIAS   *Useful Facts**

915 South Mooney Road
Visalia, CA 93277
(559) 730-3732
Cynthia DeLain, RN, MSN

www.cos.edu

Accreditation
California Board of Registered Nursing

Acceptance rate	25.0%
Enrollments	137
Graduations	50

Student Demographics	
Female	84.7%
Minority	33.3%

Degrees conferred
Associate Degree

Demographics Chart | ■Female ▨Under age 25 ▥Minority | Distance Learning | †The tuition reported for this program may be not be annualized.
*Data reported between 2001 and 2004.

California

COMPTON COMMUNITY COLLEGE

1111 East Artesia Boulevard
Compton, CA 90221
(310) 900-1600
Robert West, EdD

www.compton.edu

Accreditation
California Board of Registered Nursing

At the request of this nursing school, publication has been witheld.
Please contact the school directly for more information.

CONTRA COSTA COLLEGE

2600 Mission Bell Drive
San Pablo, CA 94806
(510) 235-7800
Roseanne Packard, MS, JD, RN

contracosta.edu

Accreditation
California Board of Registered Nursing

At the request of this nursing school, publication has been witheld.
Please contact the school directly for more information.

COPPER MOUNTAIN COMMUNITY COLLEGE

6162 Rotary Way
Joshua Tree, CA 92252
(818) 325-7743
Judy Holton, RN, EdD

www.cmccd.cc.ca.us/index.shtml

Accreditation
California Board of Registered Nursing

Degrees conferred
Associate Degree

CUESTA COLLEGE | Useful Facts

PO Box 8106
San Luis Obispo, CA 93403
(805) 546-3119
Mary Parker, EdD, RN

www.cuestanursing.org

Accreditation
California Board of Registered Nursing

Faculty-student ratio		1 : 7
Faculty	Full time	7
	Part time	12

Degrees conferred
Associate Degree

Tuition	
In state	$672
Out of state	$3,840
Enrollments	96
Graduations	35

Minimum degree required
High school diploma or GED

Student Demographics	
Female	91.7%
Under age 25	27.1%
Minority	7.4%
Part-time	0.0%

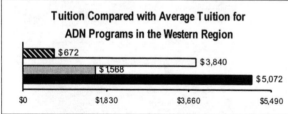

Tuition Compared with Average Tuition for ADN Programs in the Western Region
- $672
- $3,840
- $1,568
- $5,072

$0 — $1,830 — $3,660 — $5,490

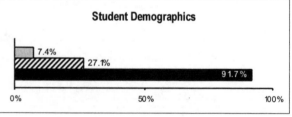

Student Demographics
- 7.4%
- 27.1%
- 91.7%

0% — 50% — 100%

Key | Tuition Chart | ▨ Program - in state ☐ Program - out of state ▤ Average - in state ■ Average - out of state

California

CYPRESS COLLEGE
Useful Facts*

9200 Valley View
Cypress, CA 90630
(714) 484-7283
Darlene Fishman, MSN, RN

www.cypresscollege.edu

Accreditation
California Board of Registered Nursing, National
League for Nursing Accrediting Commission
(NLNAC)

Degrees conferred
Associate Degree

Acceptance rate	29.8%

Tuition[1]		Student Demographics	
In state	$264	Female	81.4%
Out of state	$3,120	Under age 25	40.0%
Enrollments	156	Minority	57.4%
Graduations	61	Part-time	0.0%

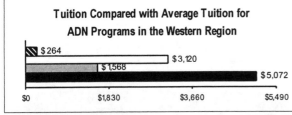

Tuition Compared with Average Tuition for ADN Programs in the Western Region

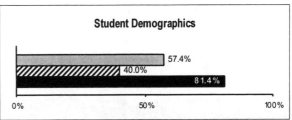

Student Demographics

DE ANZA COLLEGE
Useful Facts*

21250 Stevens Creek Boulevard
Cupertino, CA 95014
(408) 864-8908
Georgeanne Adamy, RN

www.deanza.fhda.edu

Accreditation
California Board of Registered Nursing

Degrees conferred
Associate Degree

		Student Demographics	
Enrollments	154		
Graduations	125	Part-time	0.0%

EAST LOS ANGELES COLLEGE
Useful Facts*

1301 Avenida Cesar Chavez
Monterey Park, CA 91754
(323) 265-8896
Lurelean Gaines

www.elac.edu

Accreditation
California Board of Registered Nursing

Degrees conferred
Associate Degree

		Student Demographics	
		Female	87.3%
		Under age 25	11.0%
Enrollments	165	Minority	98.2%
Graduations	60	Part-time	0.0%

EL CAMINO COMMUNITY COLLEGE
Useful Facts*

16007 Crenshaw Boulevard
Torrance, CA 90506
(310) 660-3282
Katherine Townsend, EdD, MS, BSN

www.elcamino.edu/nursing

Accreditation
California Board of Registered Nursing, National
League for Nursing Accrediting Commission
(NLNAC)

Degrees conferred
Associate Degree

Acceptance rate	32.3%

Tuition		Student Demographics	
In state	$780	Female	83.5%
Out of state	$4,470	Under age 25	30.0%
Enrollments	237	Minority	75.1%
Graduations	48	Part-time	0.0%

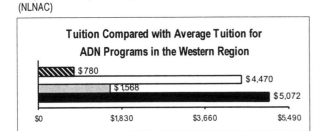

Tuition Compared with Average Tuition for ADN Programs in the Western Region

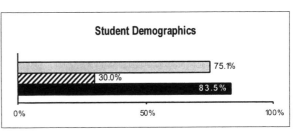

Student Demographics

Demographics Chart	■ Female ▨ Under age 25 ☐ Minority	Distance Learning	[1]The tuition reported for this program may be not be annualized. *Data reported between 2001 and 2004.

California

FRESNO CITY COLLEGE

1101 East University Avenue
Fresno, CA 93741
(559) 244-2685
Dianne Moore, PhD, RN, CNM, MPH

www.fresnocitycolleg.com

Tuition[1]		Student Demographics	
In state	$330	Female	84.5%
Out of state	$330	Under age 25	18.0%
Enrollments	252	Minority	50.7%
Graduations	127	Part-time	0.0%

Accreditation
California Board of Registered Nursing

Degrees conferred
Associate Degree

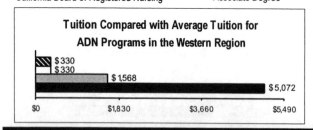
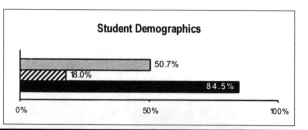

GAVILAN COLLEGE

5055 Santa Theresa Blvd
Gilroy, CA 95020
(408) 848-4883
Kaye Bedell, RN, MSN

www.gavilan.edu

		Tuition		Student Demographics	
Acceptance rate	46.7%	In state	$780	Female	78.6%
		Out of state	$5,790		
		Enrollments	14		
		Graduations	10		

Accreditation
California Board of Registered Nursing

Degrees conferred
Associate Degree

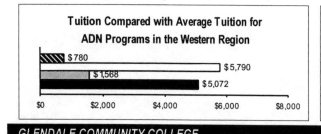
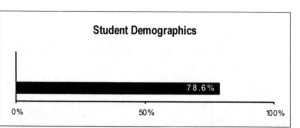

GLENDALE COMMUNITY COLLEGE

1500 North Verdugo Road
Glendale, CA 91208
(818) 551-5270
Sharon Hall, RN, MN, EdD

www.glendale.edu/nursing

		Tuition		Student Demographics	
Acceptance rate	9.7%	In state	$780	Female	75.9%
		Out of state	$4,200	Under age 25	32.0%
		Enrollments	112	Minority	67.9%
		Graduations	60	Part-time	4.5%

Accreditation
California Board of Registered Nursing

Degrees conferred
Associate Degree

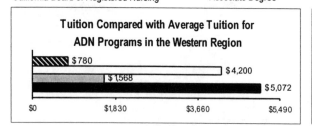
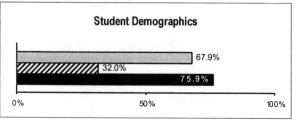

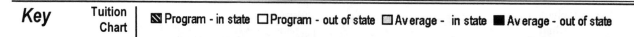

Key | Tuition Chart | ⬚ Program - in state ☐ Program - out of state ⬜ Average - in state ■ Average - out of state

California

GOLDEN WEST COLLEGE   *Useful Facts*

15744 Golden West Street, PO Box 2748
Huntington Beach, CA 92647
(714) 895-8157
Lois Miller, PhD

www.gwc.info

Accreditation
California Board of Registered Nursing, National
League for Nursing Accrediting Commission
(NLNAC)

Acceptance rate	17.4%
Faculty-student ratio	1: 10
Faculty Full time	19
Part time	3

Degrees conferred
Associate Degree

Tuition	
In state	$780
Out of state	$4,560
Enrollments	209
Graduations	114

Minimum degree required
High school diploma or GED

Student Demographics	
Female	85.2%
Under age 25	36.4%
Minority	39.7%
Part-time	0.0%

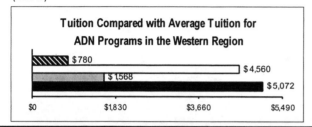

Tuition Compared with Average Tuition for ADN Programs in the Western Region

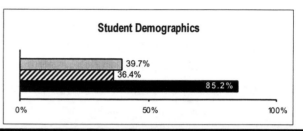

Student Demographics

GROSSMONT COLLEGE

8800 Grossmont College Drive
El Cajon, CA 92020
(619) 644-7301
Mary Callahan, EdD, RN

www.grossmont.net/nursing

Accreditation
California Board of Registered Nursing, National
League for Nursing Accrediting Commission
(NLNAC)

*At the request of this nursing school, publication has been witheld.
Please contact the school directly for more information.*

HARTNELL COLLEGE

156 Homestead Avenue
Salinas, CA 93901
(831) 755-6771
Thomas McKay, PhD, RN

www.hartnell.edu

Accreditation
California Board of Registered Nursing

*At the request of this nursing school, publication has been witheld.
Please contact the school directly for more information.*

IMPERIAL VALLEY COLLEGE   *Useful Facts**

PO Box 158
Imperial, CA 92251
(760) 355-6347
Kathy Berry, MSN, RN

imperial.cc.ca.us

Accreditation
California Board of Registered Nursing

Degrees conferred
Associate Degree

Student Demographics

Enrollments	72		
Graduations	35	Part-time	0.0%

Demographics Chart	■ Female ▨ Under age 25 ☐ Minority	Distance Learning 🖥	†The tuition reported for this program may be not be annualized. *Data reported between 2001 and 2004.

California

LONG BEACH CITY COLLEGE

4901 East Carson Street
Long Beach, CA 90808
(562) 938-4172
Brenda McCane-Harrell, MSN, RN, EdD

www.lbcc.edu

Acceptance rate	64.0%

Tuition[1]	
In state	$198
Out of state	$2,556
Enrollments	240
Graduations	83

Student Demographics	
Female	87.5%
Under age 25	51.0%
Minority	56.9%
Part-time	0.0%

Accreditation
California Board of Registered Nursing, National League for Nursing Accrediting Commission (NLNAC)

Degrees conferred
Associate Degree

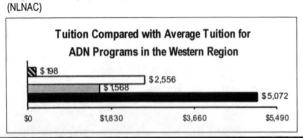

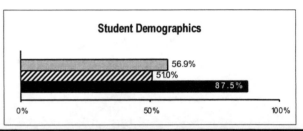

LOS ANGELES COMMUNITY COLLEGE OF NURSING AND ALLIED HEALTH

1237 N Mission Rd
Los Angeles, CA 90033
(323) 226-6509
Nancy Miller, EdD, RN

ladhs.org/lacusc/lacnah

Acceptance rate		62.6%
Faculty-student ratio		1: 10
Faculty	Full time	26
	Part time	0

Tuition	
In state	$2,400
Out of state	$2,400
Enrollments	272
Graduations	112

Student Demographics	
Female	76.5%
Under age 25	23.9%
Minority	72.6%
Part-time	100.0%

Accreditation
California Board of Registered Nursing

Degrees conferred
Associate Degree

Minimum degree required
High school diploma or GED

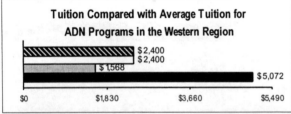

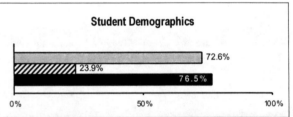

LOS ANGELES HARBOR COLLEGE

1111 Figueroa Place
Wilmington, CA 90744
(310) 233-4361
Wendy Hollis, MN, RN

www.lahc.edu

Acceptance rate		31.2%
Faculty-student ratio		1: 11
Faculty	Full time	10
	Part time	17

Tuition	
In state	$780
Out of state	$4,620
Enrollments	211
Graduations	64

Student Demographics	
Female	79.6%
Under age 25	44.1%
Minority	74.5%
Part-time	0.0%

Accreditation
California Board of Registered Nursing, National League for Nursing Accrediting Commission (NLNAC)

Degrees conferred
Associate Degree

Minimum degree required
High school diploma or GED

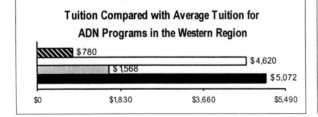

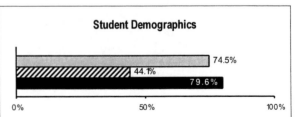

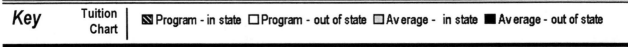

Key | Tuition Chart | ▨ Program - in state ☐ Program - out of state ▧ Average - in state ■ Average - out of state

California

LOS ANGELES PIERCE COLLEGE

6201 Winnetka Avenue
Woodland Hills, CA 91371
(818) 710-2963
Marica Solomon, MED, RN, EdD

www.piercecollege.edu

Acceptance rate 25.8%

Tuition		Student Demographics	
In state	$780	Female	95.6%
Out of state	$5,400	Under age 25	15.0%
Enrollments	136	Minority	57.0%
Graduations	60	Part-time	0.0%

Accreditation
California Board of Registered Nursing, National League for Nursing Accrediting Commission (NLNAC)

Degrees conferred
Associate Degree

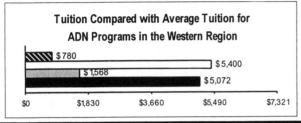

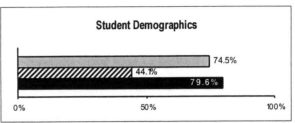

LOS ANGELES SOUTHWEST COLLEGE

1600 West Imperial Highway
Los Angeles, CA 90047
(323) 241-5405
Vincent Jackson, MS

www.lasc.cc.ca.us/nursing

Acceptance rate 50.6%

Tuition[1]		Student Demographics	
In state	$264	Female	89.4%
Out of state	$282		
Enrollments	180	Minority	100.0%
Graduations	24	Part-time	0.0%

Accreditation
California Board of Registered Nursing

Degrees conferred
Associate Degree

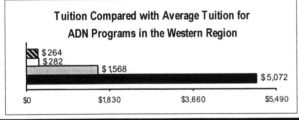

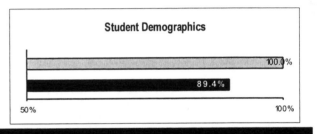

LOS ANGELES TRADE - TECHNICAL COLLEGE

400 West Washington Boulevard
Los Angeles, CA 90015
(213) 763-7182
Pat Merrill, RN, BSN

www.wellness.lattc.edu/nursing

Accreditation
California Board of Registered Nursing, National League for Nursing Accrediting Commission (NLNAC)

At the request of this nursing school, publication has been witheld. Please contact the school directly for more information.

Demographics Chart	■Female ☒Under age 25 ☐Minority	Distance Learning		[1]The tuition reported for this program may be not be annualized. *Data reported between 2001 and 2004.

California

LOS ANGELES VALLEY COLLEGE

5800 Fulton Avenue
Valley Glen, CA 91401
(818) 947-2847
Carole Rosales, MSN, RN

www.lavc.cc.ca.us/nursing/index.html

Accreditation
California Board of Registered Nursing, National League for Nursing Accrediting Commission (NLNAC)

Acceptance rate		18.8%

Tuition[1]

In state	$432
Out of state	$3,120
Enrollments	172
Graduations	84

Student Demographics

Female	86.6%
Under age 25	26.0%
Minority	76.8%
Part-time	0.0%

Degrees conferred
Associate Degree

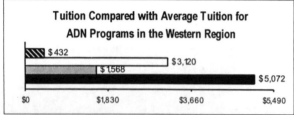

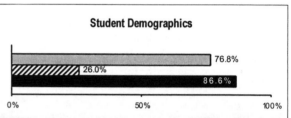

LOS MEDANOS COLLEGE

2700 East Leland Road
Pittsburg, CA 94565
(925) 439-2181
Elisabeth Coats, MSN, RN

www.losmedanos.net

Accreditation
California Board of Registered Nursing

Acceptance rate		58.6%

Tuition[1]

In state	$330
Out of state	$4,020
Enrollments	81
Graduations	39

Student Demographics

Female	87.7%
Under age 25	30.0%
Minority	37.5%
Part-time	0.0%

Degrees conferred
Associate Degree

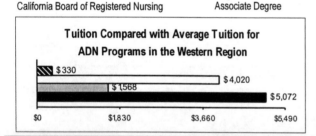

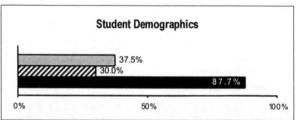

MENDOCINO COLLEGE

100 Hensley Creek Road
Ukiah, CA 95482
(707) 468-3111
Barbara French, RN, PhD

www.mendocino.edu

Accreditation
California Board of Registered Nursing

Degrees conferred
Associate Degree

Key | Tuition Chart | ▨ Program - in state ☐ Program - out of state ▦ Average - in state ■ Average - out of state

California

MERCED COLLEGE
Useful Facts*

3600 M Street
Merced, CA 94548
(209) 384-6133
Mary Ann Dunan, MSN, RN

www.merced.cc.ca.us

Acceptance rate	68.2%	

Tuition¹
In state	$242
Out of state	$2,750
Enrollments	46
Graduations	17

Student Demographics
Female	91.3%
Under age 25	39.0%
Minority	47.8%
Part-time	0.0%

Accreditation
California Board of Registered Nursing

Degrees conferred
Associate Degree

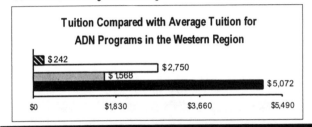

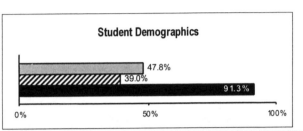

MERRITT COLLEGE

12500 Campus Drive
Oakland, CA 94619
(510) 436-2506
Carol Lee, MSN, RN

www.merritt.edu

Accreditation
California Board of Registered Nursing

Degrees conferred
Associate Degree

MODESTO JUNIOR COLLEGE
Useful Facts*

435 College Avenue
Modesto, CA 95350
(209) 575-6550
Teryl Ward, RN, MSN

mjc.yosemite.cc.ca.us

Acceptance rate	24.0%	

Tuition¹
In state	$330
Out of state	$4,020
Enrollments	147
Graduations	84

Student Demographics
Female	83.7%
Under age 25	30.0%
Minority	43.2%
Part-time	0.0%

Accreditation
California Board of Registered Nursing

Degrees conferred
Associate Degree

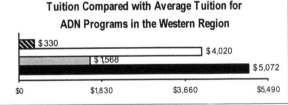

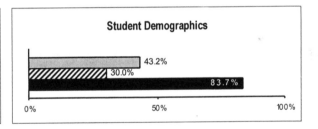

Demographics Chart	■ Female ▨ Under age 25 ☐ Minority	Distance Learning 💻	¹The tuition reported for this program may be not be annualized. *Data reported between 2001 and 2004.

California

MONTEREY PENINSULA COLLEGE
Useful Facts

980 Fremont Street
Monterey, CA 93940
(831) 646-4258
Debra Hacker, RN, EdD

www.mpc.edu

Acceptance rate 24.4%
Faculty-student ratio 1: 9
Faculty Full time 8
Part time 3

Tuition
In state $780
Out of state $5,310
Enrollments 88
Graduations 35

Student Demographics
Female 89.8%
Under age 25 17.0%
Minority 43.2%
Part-time 0.0%

Accreditation
California Board of Registered Nursing, National League for Nursing Accrediting Commission (NLNAC)

Degrees conferred
Associate Degree

Minimum degree required
High school diploma or GED

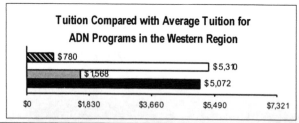

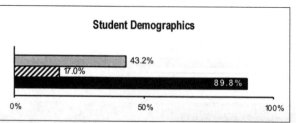

MOORPARK COLLEGE
Useful Facts

7075 Campus Road
Moorpark, CA 93021
(805) 378-1400
Karen Jensen, PhD, RN

vcccd.net/health sciences institute

Acceptance rate 36.7%
Faculty-student ratio 1: 10
Faculty Full time 9
Part time 14

Tuition[1]
In state $26
Out of state $155
Enrollments 159
Graduations 66

Student Demographics
Female 91.8%
Under age 25 34.6%
Minority 31.5%
Part-time 0.0%

Accreditation
California Board of Registered Nursing, National League for Nursing Accrediting Commission (NLNAC)

Degrees conferred
Associate Degree

Minimum degree required
High school diploma or GED

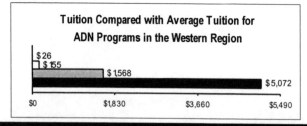

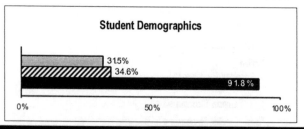

MOUNT SAINT MARY COLLEGE (CALIFORNIA)

12001 Chalon Road
Los Angeles, CA 90049
(310) 954-4230
Mary Wickman, RN, PhD

www.msmc.la.edu

Accreditation
California Board of Registered Nursing

Degrees conferred
Associate Degree

Key | Tuition Chart | ▨ Program - in state ▢ Program - out of state ▨ Average - in state ▪ Average - out of state

California

MOUNT SAN ANTONIO COLLEGE

1100 North Grand Avenue, Building 5-14
Walnut, CA 91765
(909) 594-5611
Genene Arvidson-Perfkins, MSN, RN, PHN

www.mtsac.edu

Accreditation
California Board of Registered Nursing

Acceptance rate	35.6%	

Tuition¹
In state	$144
Out of state	$1,500
Enrollments	117
Graduations	38

Student Demographics
Female	88.0%
Under age 25	43.0%
Minority	60.0%
Part-time	0.0%

Degrees conferred
Associate Degree

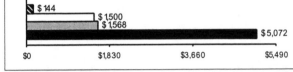

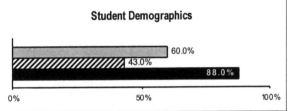

MOUNT SAN JACINTO COLLEGE

28237 La Piedra Road
Menifee, CA 92584
(909) 672-6752
Wayne Boyer, MSN, RN

msjc.cc.ca.us

Accreditation
California Board of Registered Nursing

Degrees conferred
Associate Degree

NAPA VALLEY COLLEGE

2277 Napa/Vallejo Highway
Napa, CA 94558
(707) 253-2121
Patty Vail, MA

www.campus.nvc.cc.ca.us/vn

Accreditation
California Board of Registered Nursing

Acceptance rate	30.0%	

Tuition¹
In state	$330
Out of state	$3,960
Enrollments	115
Graduations	53

Student Demographics
Female	91.3%
Minority	64.5%
Part-time	0.9%

Degrees conferred
Associate Degree

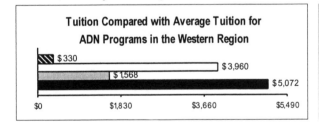

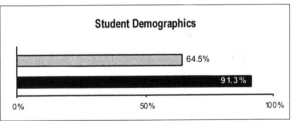

Demographics Chart	■Female ▨Under age 25 ▢Minority	Distance Learning	¹The tuition reported for this program may be not be annualized. *Data reported between 2001 and 2004.

California

NATIONAL UNIVERSITY

11355 North Torrey Pines Road
La Jolla, CA 92037
(858) 642-8344
Nancy Saks, DNSc, RN

www.nu.edu/academics/schools/sohhs/nursing.html

Acceptance rate	48.2%
Faculty-student ratio	1: 4
Faculty Full time	6
Part time	52

Tuition
In state $10,440
Out of state $10,440
Enrollments 62
Graduations 0

Student Demographics
Female 72.6%
Under age 25 25.8%
Minority 60.7%
Part-time 0.0%

Accreditation
California Board of Registered Nursing

Degrees conferred
NEW PROGRAM...NO GRADS YE

Minimum degree required
High school diploma or GED

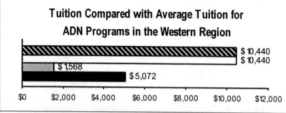
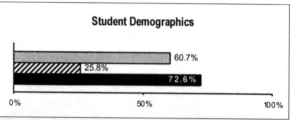

OHLONE COLLEGE

43600 Mission Boulevard
Fremont, CA 94539
(510) 979-7542
Gale Carli, EdD, RN

ohlone.edu

Acceptance rate	20.4%
Faculty-student ratio	1: 7
Faculty Full time	10
Part time	9

Tuition
In state $780
Out of state $4,680
Enrollments 104
Graduations 39

Student Demographics
Female 90.4%
Under age 25 36.5%
Minority 38.9%
Part-time 0.0%

Accreditation
California Board of Registered Nursing, National
League for Nursing Accrediting Commission
(NLNAC)

Degrees conferred
Associate Degree

Minimum degree required
High school diploma or GED

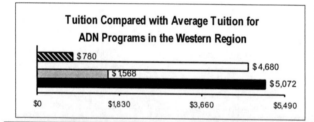
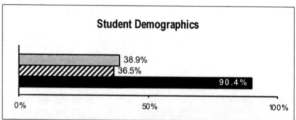

PACIFIC UNION COLLEGE

One Angwin Avenue
Angwin, CA 94508
(707) 965-7262
Nancy Tucker, PhD, RN

www.puc.edu/puc/academics/academic_departments/nursing_dept

Acceptance rate	73.9%
Faculty-student ratio	1: 9
Faculty Full time	15
Part time	19

Tuition
In state $18,990
Out of state $18,990
Enrollments 220
Graduations 78

Student Demographics
Female 77.7%
Under age 25 55.5%
Minority 37.7%
Part-time 0.0%

Accreditation
California Board of Registered Nursing, National
League for Nursing Accrediting Commission
(NLNAC)

Degrees conferred
Associate Degree

Minimum degree required
High school diploma or GED

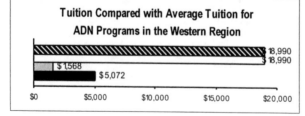

Key Tuition Chart ⊠ Program - in state ☐ Program - out of state ☐ Average - in state ■ Average - out of state

California

PALOMAR COLLEGE — *Useful Facts*

1140 West Mission Road
San Marcos, CA 92069
(760) 744-1150
Judith Eckhart, DNSc, BSN

www.palomar.edu/health

Faculty-student ratio		1: 10
Faculty	Full time	9
	Part time	8

Tuition
In state	$520
Out of state	$3,540
Enrollments	131
Graduations	55

Student Demographics
Female	89.3%
Under age 25	41.2%
Minority	20.6%
Part-time	0.0%

Accreditation
California Board of Registered Nursing, National League for Nursing Accrediting Commission (NLNAC)

Degrees conferred
Associate Degree

Minimum degree required
High school diploma or GED

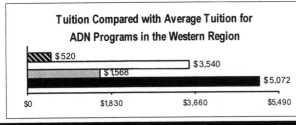

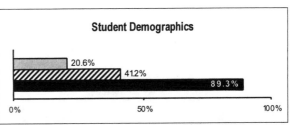

PASADENA CITY COLLEGE — *Useful Facts**

1570 East Colorado Blvd
Pasadena, CA 91106
(626) 585-7326
Kathleen Winston, MSN, RN

www.pasadena.edu

Acceptance rate	35.0%

Tuition[1]
In state	$264
Out of state	$1,608
Enrollments	227
Graduations	67

Student Demographics
Female	87.2%
Under age 25	37.0%
Minority	82.5%
Part-time	100.0%

Accreditation
California Board of Registered Nursing, National League for Nursing Accrediting Commission (NLNAC)

Degrees conferred
Associate Degree

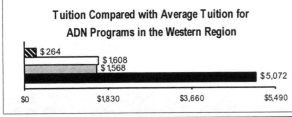

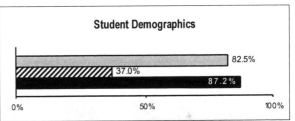

RIO HONDO COLLEGE — *Useful Facts**

3600 Workman Mill Road
Whittier, CA 90601
(562) 692-0921
Marcia McCormick, MSN, RN, MEd

www.rh.cc.ca.us/department/academic/healthscience/nursing/toc.htm

Acceptance rate	29.1%

Tuition
In state	$780
Out of state	$3,720
Enrollments	154
Graduations	69

Student Demographics
Female	79.2%
Under age 25	22.0%
Minority	83.7%
Part-time	0.0%

Accreditation
California Board of Registered Nursing

Degrees conferred
Associate Degree

Demographics Chart	■ Female ▨ Under age 25 ▢ Minority	Distance Learning	[1]The tuition reported for this program may be not be annualized. *Data reported between 2001 and 2004.

Associate Degree Programs

California

RIVERSIDE COMMUNITY COLLEGE — *Useful Facts*

**4800 Magnolia Avenue
Riverside, CA 92506
(951) 222-8408
Sandra Baker, MSN, RN**

www.academic.rccd.cc.ca.us/nursing

Accreditation
California Board of Registered Nursing, National League for Nursing Accrediting Commission (NLNAC)

Acceptance rate	14.4%
Faculty-student ratio	1: 6
Faculty Full time	20
Part time	59

Degrees conferred
LPN or LVN, Associate Degree

Tuition	
In state	$780
Out of state	$5,310
Enrollments	278
Graduations	98

Minimum degree required
High school diploma or GED

Student Demographics	
Female	84.5%
Under age 25	38.5%
Minority	54.3%
Part-time	0.0%

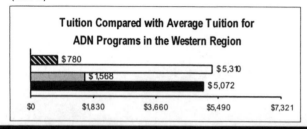

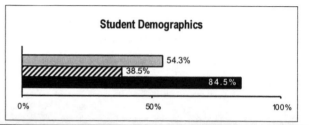

SACRAMENTO CITY COLLEGE — *Useful Facts**

**3835 Freeport Boulevard
Sacramento, CA 95822
(916) 558-2225
Diane Welch, MSN, RN**

www.scc.losrios.edu

Accreditation
California Board of Registered Nursing

Acceptance rate	14.2%

Degrees conferred
Associate Degree

Tuition[1]	
In state	$121
Out of state	$1,375
Enrollments	214
Graduations	46

Student Demographics	
Female	85.5%
Under age 25	21.0%
Minority	44.6%
Part-time	9.3%

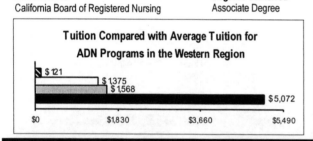

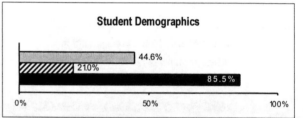

SADDLEBACK COLLEGE — *Useful Facts*

**28000 Marguerite Parkway
Mission Viejo, CA 92692
(949) 582-4787
Tamera Rice, MSN, RN**

iserver.saddleback.cc.ca.us/div/hs/nursing.htm

Accreditation
California Board of Registered Nursing, National League for Nursing Accrediting Commission (NLNAC)

Acceptance rate	12.6%
Faculty-student ratio	1: 12
Faculty Full time	16
Part time	4

Degrees conferred
Associate Degree

Tuition[1]	
In state	$26
Out of state	$148
Enrollments	223
Graduations	113

Minimum degree required
None

Student Demographics	
Female	94.6%
Under age 25	13.5%
Minority	40.6%
Part-time	0.0%

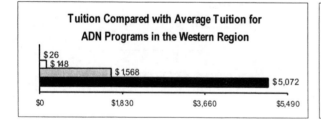

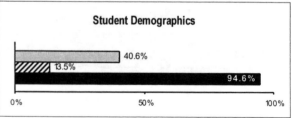

Key | Tuition Chart | ▨ Program - in state ☐ Program - out of state ☐ Average - in state ■ Average - out of state

California

SAN BERNARDINO COMMUNITY COLLEGE DISTRICT | *Useful Facts*

701 S Mt Vernon Avenue
San Bernardino, CA 92410
(909) 384-8575
Marilyn Johnson, MN

www.valleycollege.net

Accreditation
California Board of Registered Nursing, National
League for Nursing Accrediting Commission
(NLNAC)

Acceptance rate		16.3%
Faculty-student ratio		1: 9
Faculty	Full time	13
	Part time	19

Tuition	
In state	$780
Out of state	$5,580
Enrollments	197
Graduations	84

Degrees conferred
Associate Degree

Minimum degree required
High school diploma or GED

Student Demographics	
Female	76.1%
Under age 25	5.6%
Minority	60.5%
Part-time	6.1%

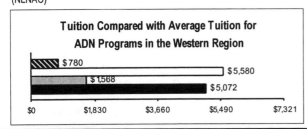

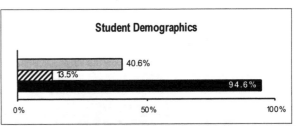

SAN DIEGO CITY COLLEGE | *Useful Facts*

1313 Park Boulevard
San Diego, CA 92101
(619) 388-3439
Jo-Ann Rossitto, DNSc, RN

www.sdcity.edu/nursing

Accreditation
California Board of Registered Nursing, National
League for Nursing Accrediting Commission
(NLNAC)

Acceptance rate		35.6%
Faculty-student ratio		1: 12
Faculty	Full time	9
	Part time	5

Tuition	
In state	$624
Out of state	$3,840
Enrollments	138
Graduations	62

Degrees conferred
Associate Degree

Minimum degree required
High school diploma or GED

Student Demographics	
Female	84.1%
Under age 25	26.8%
Minority	56.7%
Part-time	0.0%

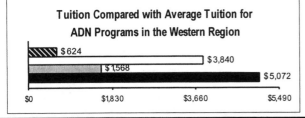

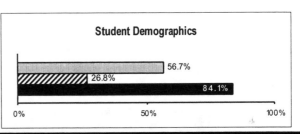

SAN JOAQUIN DELTA COLLEGE | *Useful Facts**

5151 Pacific Avenue
Stockton, CA 95207
(209) 954-5516
Debra Lewis, MSN, RN

www.deltacollege.org/div/fchs/adn.html

Accreditation
California Board of Registered Nursing, National
League for Nursing Accrediting Commission
(NLNAC)

| Acceptance rate | 29.6% |

Tuition	
In state	$1,278
Out of state	$11,968
Enrollments	235
Graduations	88

Degrees conferred
Associate Degree

Student Demographics	
Female	87.2%
Under age 25	32.5%
Minority	52.1%
Part-time	0.0%

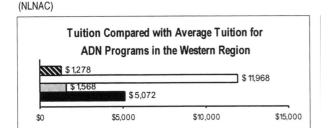

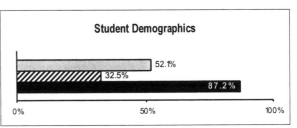

| Demographics Chart | ■Female ☒Under age 25 ☐Minority | Distance Learning | †The tuition reported for this program may be not be annualized. *Data reported between 2001 and 2004. |

California

SAN JOSE/EVERGREEN COMMUNITY COLLEGE DISTRICT | *Useful Facts*

3095 Yerba Buena Road
San Jose, CA 95135
(408) 270-6448
Dianne Helmer, MPH, PhD, RN

www.evc.edu

Accreditation
California Board of Registered Nursing, National
League for Nursing Accrediting Commission
(NLNAC)

Acceptance rate		15.2%
Faculty-student ratio		1: 11
Faculty	Full time	7
	Part time	9

Tuition[1]
In state	$446
Out of state	$2,734
Enrollments	121
Graduations	54

Degrees conferred
Associate Degree

Minimum degree required
High school diploma or GED

Student Demographics
Female	80.2%
Under age 25	24.8%
Minority	73.0%
Part-time	0.0%

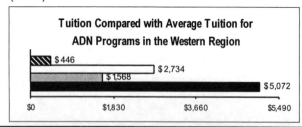

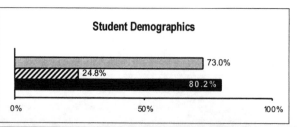

SANTA ANA COLLEGE | *Useful Facts*

1530 West 17th Street
Santa Ana, CA 92706
(714) 564-6839
Rebecca Miller, MSN, RN

www.sac.edu

Accreditation
California Board of Registered Nursing, National
League for Nursing Accrediting Commission
(NLNAC)

Acceptance rate		24.1%
Faculty-student ratio		1: 13
Faculty	Full time	12
	Part time	7

Tuition
In state	$780
Out of state	$4,770
Enrollments	198
Graduations	101

Degrees conferred
Associate Degree

Minimum degree required
High school diploma or GED

Student Demographics
Female	83.3%
Under age 25	19.7%
Minority	65.6%
Part-time	23.2%

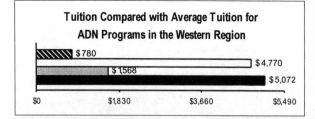

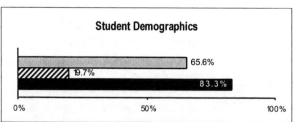

SANTA BARBARA CITY COLLEGE | *Useful Facts**

721 Cliff Drive
Santa Barbara, CA 93109
(805) 965-0581
Jan Anderson, MSN, RN, BSN

www.sbcc.edu/nursing/website

Accreditation
California Board of Registered Nursing, National
League for Nursing Accrediting Commission
(NLNAC)

Acceptance rate		23.0%
Faculty-student ratio		1: 9
Faculty	Full time	11
	Part time	5

Tuition
In state	$624
Out of state	$3,624
Enrollments	118
Graduations	42

Degrees conferred
Associate Degree

Minimum degree required
High school diploma or GED

Student Demographics
Female	86.4%
Under age 25	36.4%
Minority	34.5%
Part-time	0.0%

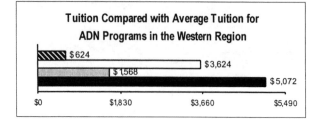

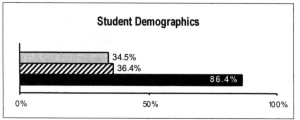

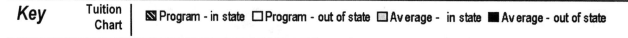

Key Tuition Chart | ▨ Program - in state ☐ Program - out of state ▧ Average - in state ■ Average - out of state

California

SANTA MONICA COLLEGE — *Useful Facts*

1900 Pico Boulevard
Santa Monica, CA 90405
(310) 434-3458
Ida Danzey, MSN

www.smc.edu/nursing

Acceptance rate		29.1%
Faculty-student ratio		1: 14
Faculty	Full time	6
	Part time	9

Tuition[1]	
In state	$350
Out of state	$1,860
Enrollments	151
Graduations	51

Student Demographics	
Female	83.4%
Under age 25	22.5%
Minority	69.0%
Part-time	0.0%

Accreditation
California Board of Registered Nursing, National League for Nursing Accrediting Commission (NLNAC)

Degrees conferred
Associate Degree

Minimum degree required
High school diploma or GED

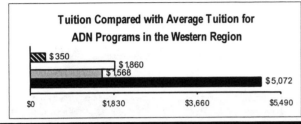

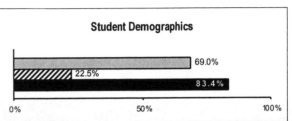

SANTA ROSA JUNIOR COLLEGE

1501 Mendocino Avenue
Santa Rosa, CA 95401
(707) 522-4529
Joan Scarborough, MSN

santarosa.edu

Accreditation
California Board of Registered Nursing

Degrees conferred
Associate Degree

SHASTA COLLEGE — *Useful Facts**

PO Box 496006
Redding, CA 96049
(530) 225-4725
J Dinkel, MSN, RN

www.shastacollege.edu

Acceptance rate	100.0%

Tuition[1]	
In state	$330
Out of state	$4,230
Enrollments	50
Graduations	50

Student Demographics	
Female	70.0%
Under age 25	10.0%
Minority	20.0%
Part-time	0.0%

Accreditation
California Board of Registered Nursing

Degrees conferred
Associate Degree

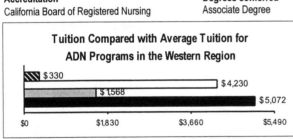

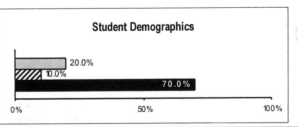

SIERRA COLLEGE — *Useful Facts**

5000 Rocklin Road
Rocklin, CA 95677
(916) 781-6221
Margaret White, MSN, RN

www.sierra.cc.ca.us

Enrollments	85

Student Demographics	
Female	87.1%
Under age 25	17.0%
Minority	10.5%
Part-time	21.2%

Accreditation
California Board of Registered Nursing

Degrees conferred
Associate Degree

Demographics Chart	■Female ▨Under age 25 ▢Minority	Distance Learning	[1]The tuition reported for this program may be not be annualized. *Data reported between 2001 and 2004.

California

SOLANO COMMUNITY COLLEGE
Useful Facts*

4000 Suisun Valley Road
Fairfield, CA 94534
(707) 864-7000
Francesca Brown, RN, MSN

www.solano.edu

Acceptance rate	33.3%	**Tuition**		**Student Demographics**	
				Female	87.6%
				Under age 25	25.0%
		Out of state	$3,432	Minority	45.7%
		Enrollments	97	Part-time	0.0%
		Graduations	37		

Accreditation
California Board of Registered Nursing

Degrees conferred
Associate Degree

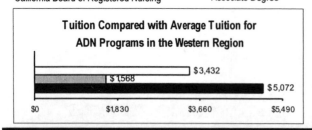
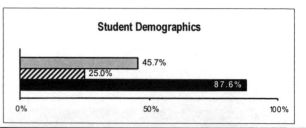

SOUTHWESTERN COLLEGE
Useful Facts

900 Otay Lakes Road, 560J
Chula Vista, CA 91910
(619) 421-6700
Sandra Comstock, MSN, RNP, CNM

www.swccd.edu~nursing

Acceptance rate	32.8%	**Tuition[1]**		**Student Demographics**	
Faculty-student ratio	1: 10	In state	$312	Female	85.3%
Faculty Full time	6	Out of state	$2,100	Under age 25	25.3%
Part time	8	**Enrollments**	95	Minority	66.3%
		Graduations	39	Part-time	100.0%

Accreditation
California Board of Registered Nursing, National
League for Nursing Accrediting Commission
(NLNAC)

Degrees conferred
Associate Degree

Minimum degree required
High school diploma or GED

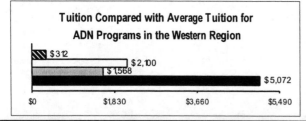
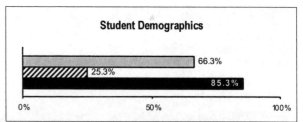

VENTURA COLLEGE
Useful Facts*

4667 Telegraph Road
Ventura, CA 93003
(805) 654-6400
Joan Beem, RN, MSN

venturacollege.edu

Acceptance rate	23.0%	**Tuition**		**Student Demographics**	
		In state	$780	Female	91.5%
		Out of state	$3,969	Under age 25	29.0%
		Enrollments	164	Minority	49.4%
		Graduations	79	Part-time	0.0%

Accreditation
California Board of Registered Nursing

Degrees conferred
Associate Degree

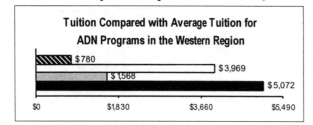
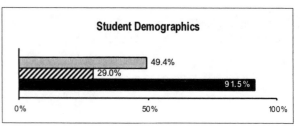

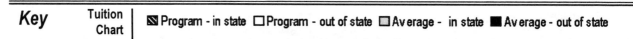

Key | Tuition Chart | ▨ Program - in state ☐ Program - out of state ▤ Average - in state ■ Average - out of state

California

VICTOR VALLEY COLLEGE
Useful Facts*

18422 Bear Valley Road
Victorville, CA 92392
(760) 245-4271
Patricia Green, MSN, MA, RN

vvcconline.com/nursing

Accreditation
California Board of Registered Nursing

Degrees conferred
Associate Degree

Acceptance rate		44.4%

Tuition[1]		Student Demographics	
In state	$330	Female	86.4%
Out of state	$3,900	Under age 25	33.0%
Enrollments	110	Minority	31.2%
Graduations	49	Part-time	0.0%

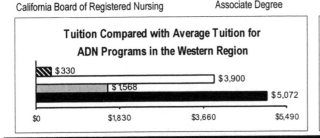

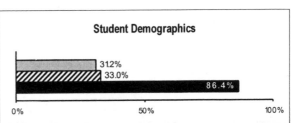

YUBA COLLEGE
Useful Facts*

2088 North Beale Road
Marysville, CA 95901
(530) 741-6785
Betty Bonner, MSN, RN

www.yccd.edu/nursing

Accreditation
California Board of Registered Nursing

Degrees conferred
Associate Degree

Acceptance rate		55.6%

Tuition[1]		Student Demographics	
In state	$264	Female	89.5%
Out of state	$3,816	Under age 25	10.0%
Enrollments	86	Minority	38.6%
Graduations	37	Part-time	0.0%

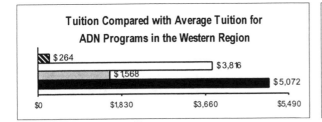

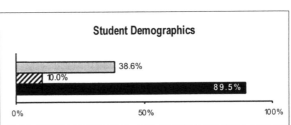

Colorado

ARAPAHOE COMMUNITY COLLEGE
Useful Facts*

5900 South Santa Fe Drive
Littleton, CO 80160
(303) 797-5896
Linda Stroup, MSN

www.arapahoe.edu

Accreditation
Colorado State Board of Nursing

Degrees conferred
Associate Degree

Acceptance rate		14.8%

Tuition		Student Demographics	
In state	$1,585	Female	95.0%
Out of state	$8,283		
Enrollments	161		
Graduations	54	Part-time	0.0%

Tuition Compared with Average Tuition for ADN Programs in the Western Region

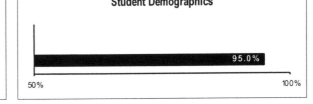

Student Demographics

Demographics Chart	■Female ▨Under age 25 ☐Minority	Distance Learning		[1]The tuition reported for this program may be not be annualized. *Data reported between 2001 and 2004.

Colorado

COLORADO MOUNTAIN COLLEGE

3000 County Road 114
Glenwood Springs, CO 81601
(970) 947-8257
Nancy Kuhrick, BSN, MSN, PhD

coloradomtn.edu

Acceptance rate	100.0%	**Tuition[1]**		**Student Demographics**
		In state	$69	Female	100.0%
		Out of state	$220	
		Enrollments	17	Minority	17.6%
		Graduations	15	Part-time	0.0%

Accreditation
Colorado State Board of Nursing

Degrees conferred
Associate Degree

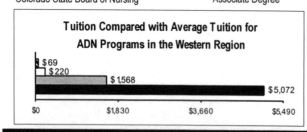

Tuition Compared with Average Tuition for ADN Programs in the Western Region

- $69
- $220
- $1,568
- $5,072

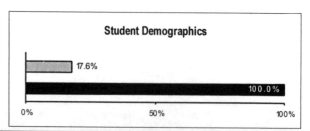

Student Demographics

- 17.6%
- 100.0%

COMMUNITY COLLEGE OF DENVER

1070 Alton Way, Bldg 849
Denver, CO 80230
(303) 365-8367
Janet Dionne, MS, RN, CNS

www.ccdrightchoice.edu

Acceptance rate	36.4%	**Tuition**		**Student Demographics**
		In state	$1,200	Female	83.3%
		Out of state	$5,000	Under age 25	10.0%
		Enrollments	240	Minority	19.2%
		Graduations	70	Part-time	0.0%

Accreditation
Colorado State Board of Nursing

Degrees conferred
Associate Degree

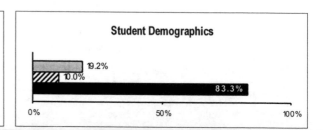

Tuition Compared with Average Tuition for ADN Programs in the Western Region

- $1,200
- $5,000
- $1,568
- $5,072

Student Demographics

- 19.2%
- 10.0%
- 83.3%

CONCORDE CAREER INSTITUTE - DENVER

111 N Havana
Aurora, CO 80010
(720) 207-0496
Mary Johnson, RN, MSN

www.concorde.edu

Acceptance rate	50.0%		
Faculty-student ratio	1:0		
Faculty	Full time	17	
	Part time	4	**Enrollments** 0

Accreditation
Colorado State Board of Nursing

Degrees conferred
Associate Degree

Minimum degree required
High school diploma or GED

DENVER SCHOOL OF NURSING

1401 19th Street
Denver, CO 80202
(303) 292-0015
Rebekah Lynch, PhD, RN, CNS

www.denverschoolofnursing.org

Accreditation
Colorado State Board of Nursing

Degrees conferred
Associate Degree

Key | Tuition Chart | ◪ Program - in state ☐ Program - out of state ☐ Average - in state ■ Average - out of state

Colorado

FRONT RANGE COMMUNITY COLLEGE - LARIMER COUNTY CENTER

4616 South Shields
Ft. Collins, CO 80522
(970) 204-8217
Marty Bachman, PhD, RN

www.frontrange.edu

Accreditation
Colorado State Board of Nursing

Degrees conferred
Associate Degree

FRONT RANGE COMMUNITY COLLEGE - LONGMONT (BOULDER)

2255 Main Street, Suite 118
Longmont, CO 80501
(303) 516-8917
Merrilee McDuffie, BSN, MPH

www.frontrange.edu

Accreditation
Colorado State Board of Nursing

Degrees conferred
Associate Degree

FRONT RANGE COMMUNITY COLLEGE - WESTMINSTER

3645 West 112th Avenue
Westminster, CO 80031
(303) 404-5207
Nancy Walters, BSN, MSN

Faculty	Full time	10
	Part time	35

www.frontrange.edu

Accreditation
Colorado State Board of Nursing

Degrees conferred
Associate Degree

LAMAR COMMUNITY COLLEGE — *Useful Facts**

2401 S Main Street
Lamar, CO 81052
(719) 336-1598
Sandy Summers, BSN, RN, MSN, FNP

www.lamarcc.edu

Accreditation
Colorado State Board of Nursing

Degrees conferred
Associate Degree

Acceptance rate	70.8%

Tuition		Student Demographics	
In state	$2,004	Female	91.9%
Out of state	$8,283		
Enrollments	62	Minority	17.7%
Graduations	29	Part-time	0.0%

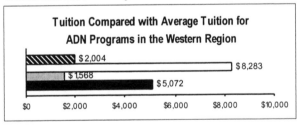

Tuition Compared with Average Tuition for ADN Programs in the Western Region

$2,004
$8,283
$1,568
$5,072

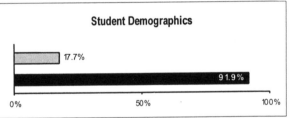

Student Demographics

17.7%
91.9%

Demographics Chart ■Female ⊠Under age 25 ☐Minority | **Distance Learning** | 'The tuition reported for this program may be not be annualized. *Data reported between 2001 and 2004.

CO — 243

Colorado

MESA STATE COLLEGE
Useful Facts

1100 North Avenue
Grand Junction, CO 81502
(970) 248-1398
Kristine Reuss, PhD, RN

mesastate.edu

Accreditation
Colorado State Board of Nursing

Acceptance rate		100.0%
Faculty-student ratio		1: 7
Faculty	Full time	14
	Part time	23

Degrees conferred
Associate Degree

Tuition	
In state	$2,359
Out of state	$9,546
Enrollments	12
Graduations	0

Minimum degree required
LPN

Student Demographics	
Female	66.7%
Under age 25	16.7%
Part-time	8.3%

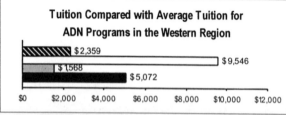

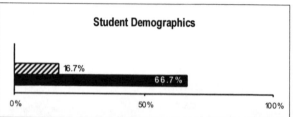

MORGAN COMMUNITY COLLEGE - NORTHEASTERN JUNIOR COLLEGE
Useful Facts*

17800 Road 20 South
Fort Morgan, CO 80701
(970) 542-3235
Sheryl George, MSN, RN

www.mcc.cccoes.edu

Accreditation
Colorado State Board of Nursing

Acceptance rate	100.0%

Degrees conferred
Associate Degree

Tuition	
In state	$1,650
Out of state	$7,830
Enrollments	11
Graduations	13

Student Demographics	
Female	81.8%
Under age 25	10.0%
Minority	9.1%
Part-time	0.0%

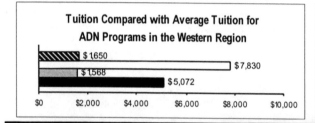

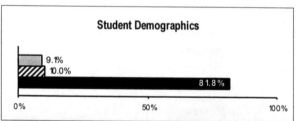

OTERO JUNIOR COLLEGE
Useful Facts

1802 Colorado Avenue
La Junta, CO 81050
(719) 384-6894
Denise Root, MSN, BSN, ADN

www.ojc.cccoes.edu

Accreditation
Colorado State Board of Nursing, National
League for Nursing Accrediting Commission
(NLNAC)

Acceptance rate		47.0%
Faculty-student ratio		1: 11
Faculty	Full time	9
	Part time	3

Degrees conferred
Associate Degree

Tuition	
In state	$2,247
Out of state	$7,940
Enrollments	117
Graduations	21

Minimum degree required
High school diploma or GED

Student Demographics	
Female	88.0%
Under age 25	26.5%
Minority	27.2%
Part-time	41.9%

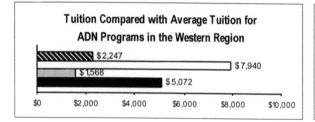

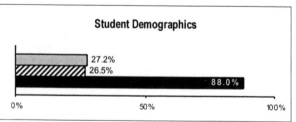

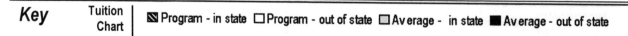

Key | Tuition Chart | ▨ Program - in state ☐ Program - out of state ☐ Average - in state ■ Average - out of state

Colorado

PIKES PEAK COMMUNITY COLLEGE

11195 State Highway 83 RR-13
Colorado Springs, CO 80921
(719) 538-5400
Mary Wermers, MSN, BSN, RN, CNAA, CNS

www.ppcc.edu

			Student Demographics	
Acceptance rate	100.0%	Tuition[1]		
		In state	$67	Female	87.8%
		Out of state	$345	Under age 25	22.0%
		Enrollments	131	Minority	22.8%
		Graduations	62	Part-time	0.0%

Accreditation
Colorado State Board of Nursing

Degrees conferred
Associate Degree

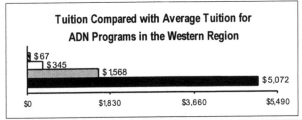

Tuition Compared with Average Tuition for ADN Programs in the Western Region

$67
$345
$1,568
$5,072

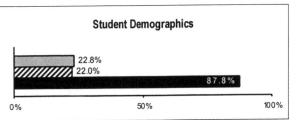

Student Demographics

22.8%
22.0%
87.8%

PUEBLO COMMUNITY COLLEGE - Pueblo

415 Harrison
Pueblo, CO 81004
(719) 549-3409
Eva Tapia, MSN, RN, NNP

www.pcc.cccoes.edu

			Student Demographics	
Acceptance rate	61.4%	Tuition		
		In state	$2,105	Female	91.6%
		Out of state	$9,630	Under age 25	3.0%
		Enrollments	95	Minority	27.4%
		Graduations	74	Part-time	28.4%

Accreditation
Colorado State Board of Nursing, National
League for Nursing Accrediting Commission
(NLNAC)

Degrees conferred
Associate Degree

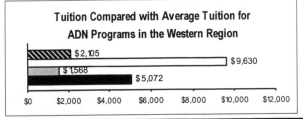

Tuition Compared with Average Tuition for ADN Programs in the Western Region

$2,105
$9,630
$1,568
$5,072

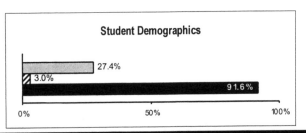

Student Demographics

27.4%
3.0%
91.6%

TRINIDAD STATE JUNIOR COLLEGE

600 Prospect Street
Trinidad, CO 81082
(719) 846-5524
Vicki Brownrigg, NP, PhD(c)

www.trinidadstate.edu

			Student Demographics	
Acceptance rate	100.0%	Tuition		
		In state	$2,535	Female	100.0%
		Enrollments	14	Minority	57.1%
		Graduations	59	Part-time	100.0%

Accreditation
Colorado State Board of Nursing

Degrees conferred
Associate Degree

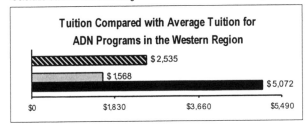

Tuition Compared with Average Tuition for ADN Programs in the Western Region

$2,535
$1,568
$5,072

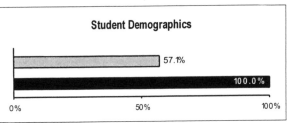

Student Demographics

57.1%
100.0%

Demographics Chart	■Female ▨Under age 25 ☐Minority	Distance Learning		[1]The tuition reported for this program may be not be annualized. *Data reported between 2001 and 2004.

Connecticut

CAPITAL COMMUNITY - TECHNICAL COLLEGE

61 Woodland Street
Hartford, CT 06105
(860) 520-7835
Judith Patrizzi, MSN, MEd, RN

cctc.commnet.edu

Accreditation
Connecticut Board of Examiners for Nursing,
National League for Nursing Accrediting
Commission (NLNAC)

Degrees conferred
Associate Degree

GATEWAY COMMUNITY COLLEGE

88 Bassett Rd
North Haven, CT 06473
(203) 285-2393
Sheila Solernou, RN, MSN

www.gwcc.commnet.edu

Accreditation
Connecticut Board of Examiners for Nursing,
National League for Nursing Accrediting
Commission (NLNAC)

At the request of this nursing school, publication has been witheld.
Please contact the school directly for more information.

GOODWIN COLLEGE

745 Burnside Avenue
East Hartford, CT 06108
(860) 528-4111
Lois Daniels, MSN, RN, CNM

www.goodwin.edu

Accreditation
Connecticut Board of Examiners for Nursing

Degrees conferred
Associate Degree

NAUGATUCK VALLEY COMMUNITY COLLEGE

Useful Facts

750 Chase Parkway
Waterbury, CT 06708
(203) 575-8057
Joanne Ottman, MSN, RN

www.nvctc.commnet.edu

Accreditation
Connecticut Board of Examiners for Nursing,
National League for Nursing Accrediting
Commission (NLNAC)

Degrees conferred
Associate Degree

Acceptance rate		36.4%
Faculty-student ratio		1:9
Faculty	Full time	13
	Part time	22
Enrollments		206
Graduations		84

Tuition
In state	$2,536
Out of state	$7,568

Minimum degree required
High school diploma or GED

Student Demographics
Female	92.7%
Under age 25	24.3%
Minority	13.8%
Part-time	0.0%

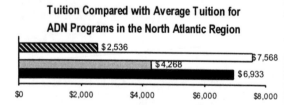

Tuition Compared with Average Tuition for ADN Programs in the North Atlantic Region

$2,536
$7,568
$4,268
$6,933

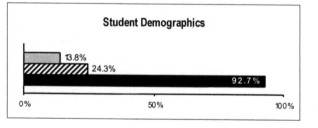

Student Demographics

13.8%
24.3%
92.7%

Key | Tuition Chart | ▨ Program - in state ☐ Program - out of state ▨ Average - in state ■ Average - out of state

Connecticut

NORWALK COMMUNITY COLLEGE
Useful Facts*

188 Richards Ave
Norwalk, CT 06854
(203) 857-7123
Mary Schuler, RN, EdD

www.ncc.commnet.edu

Acceptance rate		43.3%
Faculty-student ratio		1: 10
Faculty	Full time	10
	Part time	4

Tuition	
In state	$2,028
Out of state	$6,890
Enrollments	124
Graduations	27

Student Demographics	
Female	85.5%
Under age 25	22.0%
Minority	45.4%
Part-time	0.0%

Accreditation
Connecticut Board of Examiners for Nursing,
National League for Nursing Accrediting
Commission (NLNAC)

Degrees conferred
Associate Degree

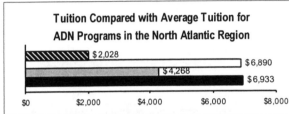

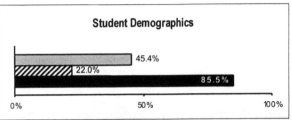

SAINT VINCENT'S COLLEGE

2800 Main Street
Bridgeport, CT 06606
(203) 576-5556
Susan Abbe, PhD, RN

www.stvincentscollege.edu

At the request of this nursing school, publication has been witheld.
Please contact the school directly for more information.

Accreditation
Connecticut Board of Examiners for Nursing,
National League for Nursing Accrediting
Commission (NLNAC)

THREE RIVERS COMMUNITY COLLEGE
Useful Facts*

7 Mahan Drive
Norwich, CT 06360
(860) 383-5241
Linda Perfetto, MSN, RN

www.trcc.commnet.edu/acad_depts/nurse_all_hlth

Acceptance rate		44.9%

Tuition	
In state	$2,112
Out of state	$6,336
Enrollments	150
Graduations	35

Student Demographics	
Female	88.7%
Under age 25	23.0%
Minority	6.9%
Part-time	0.0%

Accreditation
Connecticut Board of Examiners for Nursing,
National League for Nursing Accrediting
Commission (NLNAC)

Degrees conferred
Associate Degree

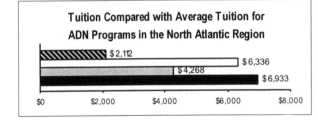

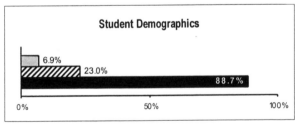

Demographics Chart	■ Female ▨ Under age 25 ☐ Minority	Distance Learning 💻	¹The tuition reported for this program may be not be annualized. *Data reported between 2001 and 2004.

Delaware

DELAWARE TECHNICAL & COMMUNITY COLLEGE - OWENS CAMPUS
Useful Facts

PO Box 610
Georgetown, DE 19947
(302) 855-1691
Daryl Berryman, MSN, RN

www.dtcc.edu/owens

Accreditation
Delaware Board of Nursing, National League for
Nursing Accrediting Commission (NLNAC)

Acceptance rate	45.0%
Faculty-student ratio	1: 7
Faculty Full time	20
Part time	3

Degrees conferred
Associate Degree

Tuition	
In state	$1,956
Out of state	$4,890
Enrollments	144
Graduations	42

Minimum degree required
High school diploma or GED

Student Demographics	
Female	91.0%
Under age 25	25.0%
Minority	18.8%
Part-time	0.0%

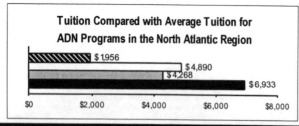

Tuition Compared with Average Tuition for
ADN Programs in the North Atlantic Region

$1,956
$4,890
$4,268
$6,933

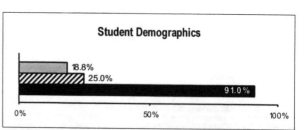

Student Demographics

18.8%
25.0%
91.0%

DELAWARE TECHNICAL & COMMUNITY COLLEGE - STANTON CAMPUS

400 Stanton-Christiana Road
Newark, DE 19713
(302) 454-3948
Kathy Janvier, PhD, RN

www.dtcc.edu

Accreditation
Delaware Board of Nursing, National League for
Nursing Accrediting Commission (NLNAC)

*At the request of this nursing school, publication has been witheld.
Please contact the school directly for more information.*

DELAWARE TECHNICAL & COMMUNITY COLLEGE - TERRY CAMPUS
Useful Facts*

100 Campus Drive
Dover, DE 19904
(302) 857-1300
JoAnn Baker, MSN, RN, FNP

www.dtcc.edu/terry/nurse

Accreditation
Delaware Board of Nursing, National League for
Nursing Accrediting Commission (NLNAC)

Acceptance rate	47.9%
Faculty-student ratio	1: 5
Faculty Full time	14
Part time	7

Degrees conferred
Associate Degree

Tuition	
In state	$1,848
Out of state	$4,620
Enrollments	95
Graduations	15

Student Demographics	
Female	94.7%
Under age 25	30.0%
Minority	27.4%
Part-time	0.0%

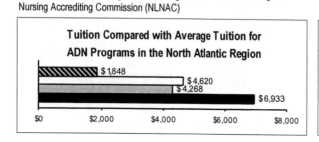

Tuition Compared with Average Tuition for
ADN Programs in the North Atlantic Region

$1,848
$4,620
$4,268
$6,933

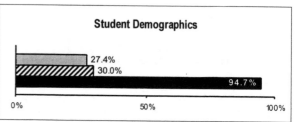

Student Demographics

27.4%
30.0%
94.7%

Key Tuition Chart | ▨ Program - in state □ Program - out of state ▤ Average - in state ■ Average - out of state

District of Columbia

UNIVERSITY OF THE DISTRICT OF COLUMBIA | *Useful Facts**

4200 Connecticut Avenue, NW, Building 44	Acceptance rate	30.8%
Washington, DC 20008		
(202) 274-5940		
Susie Cato, MSN, MA, RN		

www.udc.edu

Tuition
In state	$2,070
Out of state	$4,710
Enrollments	178
Graduations	72

Student Demographics
Female	92.1%
Under age 25	20.0%
Minority	96.1%
Part-time	40.4%

Accreditation
District of Columbia Board of Nursing, National
League for Nursing Accrediting Commission
(NLNAC)

Degrees conferred
Associate Degree

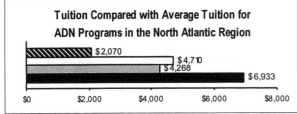

Tuition Compared with Average Tuition for ADN Programs in the North Atlantic Region

$2,070
$4,710
$4,268
$6,933

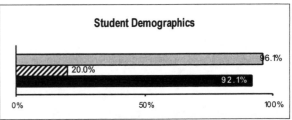

Student Demographics

96.1%
20.0%
92.1%

Florida

BREVARD COMMUNITY COLLEGE

1519 Clearlake Road
Cocoa, FL 32922
(321) 433-7584
Constance Bobik, MSN, BSN, RN

www.brevardcc.edu

Accreditation
Florida Board of Nursing

*At the request of this nursing school, publication has been witheld.
Please contact the school directly for more information.*

BROWARD COMMUNITY COLLEGE - *Central Campus*

3501 SW Davie Road	Acceptance rate	39.5%
Davie, FL 33314		
(954) 201-6851		
Diane Whitehead, EdD, RN		

www.broward.edu

Tuition
In state	$1,449
Out of state	$5,796
Enrollments	858
Graduations	358

Student Demographics
Female	88.7%
Under age 25	4.0%
Minority	52.8%
Part-time	0.0%

Accreditation
Florida Board of Nursing, National League for
Nursing Accrediting Commission (NLNAC)

Degrees conferred
Associate Degree

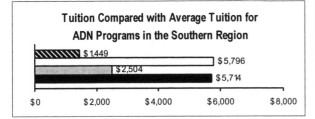

Tuition Compared with Average Tuition for ADN Programs in the Southern Region

$1449
$5,796
$2,504
$5,714

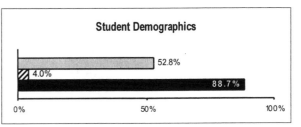

Student Demographics

52.8%
4.0%
88.7%

Demographics Chart	■ Female ▨ Under age 25 ▢ Minority	Distance Learning	†The tuition reported for this program may be not be annualized.
			*Data reported between 2001 and 2004.

Florida

CENTRAL FLORIDA COMMUNITY COLLEGE *Useful Facts*

PO Box 1388
Ocala, FL 34478
(352) 237-2111
Gwen Lapham-Alcorn, PhD, RN

www.cfcc.cc.fl.us

Acceptance rate		57.9%
Faculty-student ratio		1: 11
Faculty	Full time	14
	Part time	5

Tuition	
In state	$2,354
Out of state	$8,613
Enrollments	174
Graduations	77

Student Demographics	
Female	90.2%
Under age 25	43.1%
Minority	15.0%
Part-time	19.5%

Accreditation
Florida Board of Nursing, National League for
Nursing Accrediting Commission (NLNAC)

Degrees conferred
Associate Degree

Minimum degree required
High school diploma or GED

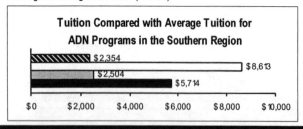

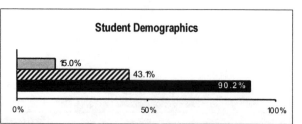

CHIPOLA JUNIOR COLLEGE *Useful Facts**

3094 Indian Circle
Marianna, FL 32446
(850) 718-2278
Kathy Wheeler, MSN, ARNP

www.chipola.edu

Student Demographics

Enrollments	70		
Graduations	29	Part-time	0.0%

Accreditation
Florida Board of Nursing

Degrees conferred
Associate Degree

DAYTONA BEACH COMMUNITY COLLEGE - *Daytona Beach*

1200 West International Speedway Blvd
Daytona Beach, FL 32120
(386) 255-8131
Linda Miles, MS

www.dbcc.edu

Acceptance rate		51.4%
Faculty-student ratio		1: 8
Faculty	Full time	25
	Part time	36

Tuition[1]	
In state	$58
Out of state	$218
Enrollments	356
Graduations	140

Student Demographics	
Female	84.3%
Under age 25	100.0%
Part-time	0.0%

Accreditation
Florida Board of Nursing, National League for
Nursing Accrediting Commission (NLNAC)

Degrees conferred
Associate Degree

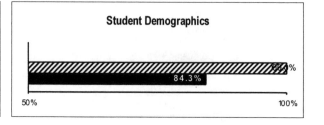

Key Tuition Chart | ▨ Program - in state ☐ Program - out of state ▦ Average - in state ■ Average - out of state

Florida

EDISON COMMUNITY COLLEGE - Lee Center

8099 College Parkway
Fort Myers, FL 33919
(941) 489-9239
Shirley Ruder, MS, MSN, EdD, RN

www.edison.edu

Accreditation
Florida Board of Nursing, National League for
Nursing Accrediting Commission (NLNAC)

Acceptance rate	61.7%

Degrees conferred
Associate Degree

Tuition		Student Demographics	
In state	$1,449	Female	93.2%
Out of state	$5,370		
Enrollments	220	Minority	25.4%
Graduations	86	Part-time	36.4%

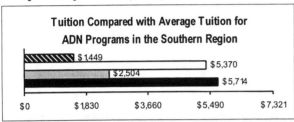

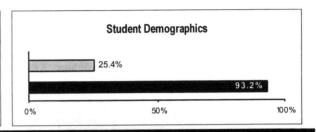

FLORIDA COMMUNITY COLLEGE AT JACKSONVILLE

4501 Capper Road
Jacksonville, FL 32218
(904) 766-6550
June Chandler, MSN, EdD, BSN

www.fccj.org

Accreditation
Florida Board of Nursing, National League for
Nursing Accrediting Commission (NLNAC)

Acceptance rate	35.5%

Degrees conferred
Associate Degree

Tuition[1]		Student Demographics	
In state	$58	Female	89.1%
Out of state	$217	Under age 25	45.0%
Enrollments	349	Minority	25.1%
Graduations	302	Part-time	0.0%

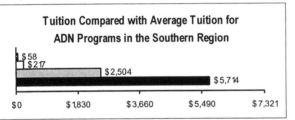

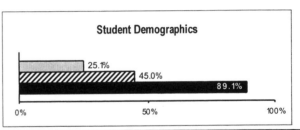

FLORIDA HOSPITAL COLLEGE OF HEALTH SCIENCES

795 Lake Estelle Drive
Orlando, FL 32803
(407) 303-7893
Nancy Haugen, PhD, RN

www.fhchs.edu

Accreditation
Florida Board of Nursing, National League for
Nursing Accrediting Commission (NLNAC)

Acceptance rate		51.1%
Faculty-student ratio		1: 10
Faculty	Full time	22
	Part time	4

Degrees conferred
Associate Degree

Tuition		Student Demographics	
In state	$6,600	Female	85.4%
Out of state	$6,600	Under age 25	57.0%
Enrollments	240	Minority	48.0%
Graduations	67	Part-time	42.5%

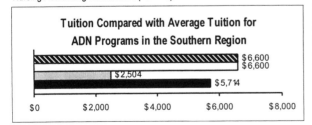

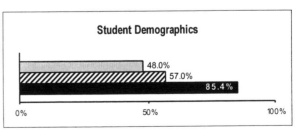

Demographics Chart	■Female ☑Under age 25 ☐Minority	Distance Learning		[1]The tuition reported for this program may be not be annualized. *Data reported between 2001 and 2004.

Florida

FLORIDA KEYS COMMUNITY COLLEGE - Key West

5901 College Road
Key West, FL 33042
(305) 296-9081
Coleen Dooley, MSN, ARNP, CS

www.fkcc.cc

Acceptance rate		48.0%

Tuition[1]

In state	$55
Out of state	$205
Enrollments	69
Graduations	17

Student Demographics

Female	97.1%
Under age 25	10.0%
Minority	31.9%
Part-time	0.0%

Accreditation
Florida Board of Nursing

Degrees conferred
Associate Degree

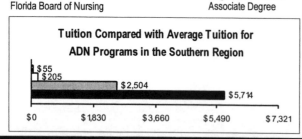

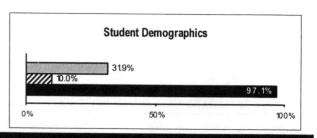

GALEN HEALTH INSTITUTES INC

9549 Koger Blvd, Suite 100
St. Petersburg, FL 33702
(727) 577-1497
Sharon Roberts, MSN

www.galened.com

Accreditation
Florida Board of Nursing

Degrees conferred
Associate Degree

GULF COAST COMMUNITY COLLEGE   *Useful Facts*

5230 West US Highway 98
Panama City, FL 32401
(850) 913-3317
Christine Bottkol, CNS, MSN, RN

gulfcoast.edu/nursing

Acceptance rate		61.2%
Faculty-student ratio		1: 11
Faculty	Full time	11
	Part time	13

Tuition

In state	$1,870
Out of state	$6,893
Enrollments	195
Graduations	79

Student Demographics

Female	85.6%
Under age 25	38.5%
Minority	13.6%
Part-time	44.6%

Accreditation
Florida Board of Nursing, National League for
Nursing Accrediting Commission (NLNAC)

Degrees conferred
Associate Degree

Minimum degree required
High school diploma or GED

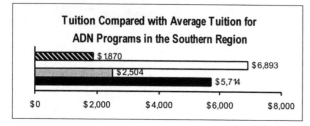

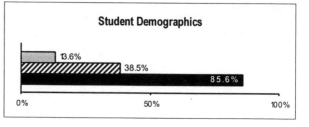

Key | Tuition Chart | ⊠ Program - in state ☐ Program - out of state ▦ Average - in state ■ Average - out of state

Florida

HILLSBOROUGH COMMUNITY COLLEGE - Tampa

PO Box 30030
Tampa, FL 33630
(813) 253-7268
Kathy DiSanto, MSN

www.hccfl.edu

Acceptance rate	100.0%	

Tuition		**Student Demographics**	
In state	$1,440	Female	90.4%
Out of state	$5,310	Under age 25	34.0%
Enrollments	512	Minority	37.3%
Graduations	165	Part-time	81.3%

Accreditation
Florida Board of Nursing, National League for
Nursing Accrediting Commission (NLNAC)

Degrees conferred
Associate Degree

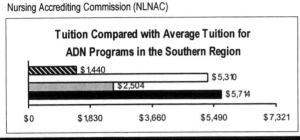

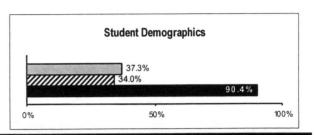

INDIAN RIVER COMMUNITY COLLEGE - Fort Pierce

3209 Virginia Avenue
Fort Pierce, FL 34981
(772) 462-7570
Ann Hubbard, MSN, EdD

www.ircc.edu

Accreditation
Florida Board of Nursing, National League for
Nursing Accrediting Commission (NLNAC)

*At the request of this nursing school, publication has been withheld.
Please contact the school directly for more information.*

KEISER COLLEGE - Fort Lauderdale

1500 NW 49th Street
Fort Lauderdale, FL 33309
(954) 776-4456
Kenneth Hazell, PhD, ARNP

www.keisercollege.edu

Accreditation
Florida Board of Nursing

Degrees conferred
Associate Degree

LAKE CITY COMMUNITY COLLEGE   *Useful Facts*

149 SE College Place
Lake City, FL 32025
(386) 754-4304
Robbie Carson, RN, MEd, MSN

www.lakecitycc.edu

Acceptance rate		39.0%
Faculty-student ratio		1: 11
Faculty	Full time	7
	Part time	6.5

Tuition		**Student Demographics**	
In state	$2,250	Female	88.2%
Out of state	$2,034	Under age 25	57.3%
Enrollments	110	Minority	11.2%
Graduations	45	Part-time	86.4%

Accreditation
Florida Board of Nursing, National League for
Nursing Accrediting Commission (NLNAC)

Degrees conferred
Associate Degree

Minimum degree required
13 college credit hours required prerequsites

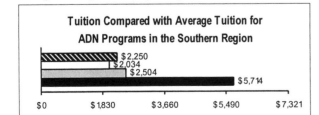

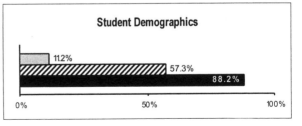

Demographics Chart | ■Female ⊠Under age 25 □Minority | **Distance Learning** | ¹The tuition reported for this program may be not be annualized.
*Data reported between 2001 and 2004.

FL   **253**

Florida

LAKE-SUMTER COMMUNITY COLLEGE
*Useful Facts**

9501 US Highway 441
Leesburg, FL 34788
(352) 365-3519
Susan Pennacchia, MSN, MEd, ARNP

www.lscc.cc.fl.us

Acceptance rate	62.9%	

Tuition¹

In state	$58
Out of state	$213
Enrollments	144
Graduations	66

Student Demographics

Female	93.1%
Under age 25	47.0%
Minority	7.6%
Part-time	0.0%

Accreditation
Florida Board of Nursing

Degrees conferred
Associate Degree

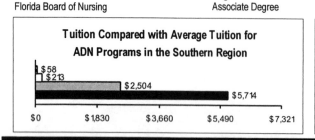
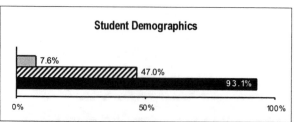

MANATEE COMMUNITY COLLEGE - Bradenton

5840 26th Street West
Bradenton, FL 34207
(941) 752-5526
Bonnie Hesselberg, EdD, ARNP

www.mccfl.edu

Acceptance rate	40.0%	
Faculty-student ratio	1: 14	
Faculty	Full time	15
	Part time	12

Tuition

In state	$1,983
Out of state	$6,834
Enrollments	209
Graduations	75

Student Demographics

Female	82.3%
Under age 25	38.3%
Minority	22.5%
Part-time	62.7%

Accreditation
Florida Board of Nursing, National League for
Nursing Accrediting Commission (NLNAC)

Degrees conferred
Associate Degree

Minimum degree required
High school diploma or GED

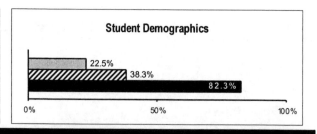

MANATEE COMMUNITY COLLEGE - Venice

5840 26th Street West
Bradenton, FL 34207
(941) 752-5526
Bonnie Hesselberg, EdD, ARNP

www.mccfl.edu

Acceptance rate	36.5%	
Faculty-student ratio	1: 14	
Faculty	Full time	15
	Part time	12

Tuition

In state	$1,983
Out of state	$6,834
Enrollments	81
Graduations	23

Student Demographics

Female	85.2%
Under age 25	27.2%
Minority	12.7%
Part-time	71.6%

Accreditation
Florida Board of Nursing, National League for
Nursing Accrediting Commission (NLNAC)

Degrees conferred
Associate Degree

Minimum degree required
High school diploma or GED

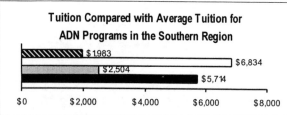
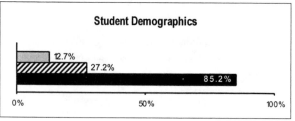

Key | Tuition Chart | ▨ Program - in state ▢ Program - out of state ▨ Average - in state ■ Average - out of state

Florida

MIAMI-DADE COLLEGE

950 North West 20th Street
Miami, FL 33127
(305) 237-4039
Frances Aronovitz, PhD, ARNP

www.mdcc.edu/medical

				Student Demographics	
Acceptance rate	22.1%	**Tuition**			
		In state	$4,400	Female	78.5%
		Out of state	$13,300	Under age 25	24.0%
		Enrollments	717	Minority	85.9%
		Graduations	457	Part-time	27.1%

Accreditation
Florida Board of Nursing, National League for Nursing Accrediting Commission (NLNAC)

Degrees conferred
Associate Degree

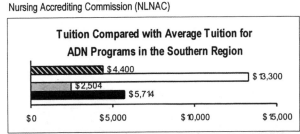

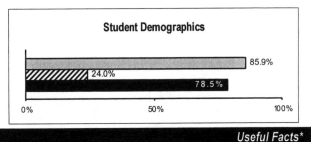

OKALOOSA-WALTON COMMUNITY COLLEGE

100 College Boulevard
Niceville, FL 32578
(850) 729-4928
Linda Whitentan, RN, MSN, CS

www.owcc.cc.fl.us

				Student Demographics	
Acceptance rate	14.7%	**Tuition**			
		In state	$1,744	Female	90.1%
		Out of state	$6,728	Under age 25	50.0%
		Enrollments	91	Minority	18.9%
		Graduations	41	Part-time	0.0%

Accreditation
Florida Board of Nursing

Degrees conferred
Associate Degree

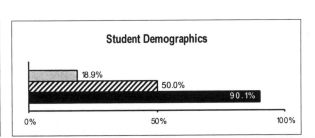

PALM BEACH COMMUNITY COLLEGE - Lake Worth

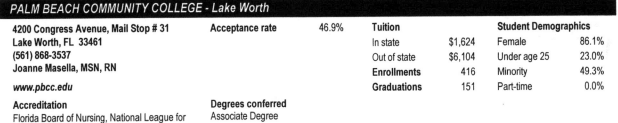

4200 Congress Avenue, Mail Stop # 31
Lake Worth, FL 33461
(561) 868-3537
Joanne Masella, MSN, RN

www.pbcc.edu

				Student Demographics	
Acceptance rate	46.9%	**Tuition**			
		In state	$1,624	Female	86.1%
		Out of state	$6,104	Under age 25	23.0%
		Enrollments	416	Minority	49.3%
		Graduations	151	Part-time	0.0%

Accreditation
Florida Board of Nursing, National League for Nursing Accrediting Commission (NLNAC)

Degrees conferred
Associate Degree

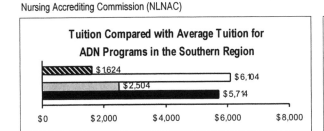

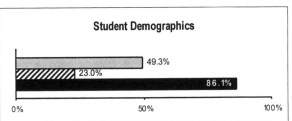

Demographics Chart	■ Female ▨ Under age 25 □ Minority	Distance Learning		†The tuition reported for this program may be not be annualized.
				*Data reported between 2001 and 2004.

Florida

PASCO-HERNANDO COMMUNITY COLLEGE - *West Campus*

10230 Ridge Road
New Port Richey, FL 34654
(727) 816-3230
Karen Richardson, MS, ARNP

www.pasco-hernandocc.com

Accreditation
Florida Board of Nursing, National League for
Nursing Accrediting Commission (NLNAC)

Acceptance rate	100.0%

Degrees conferred
Associate Degree

Tuition[1]	
In state	$52
Out of state	$193
Enrollments	211
Graduations	83

Student Demographics	
Female	89.6%
Minority	13.0%
Part-time	0.0%

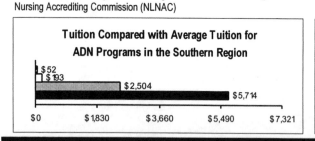

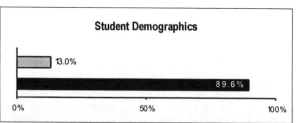

PENSACOLA JUNIOR COLLEGE *Useful Facts*

5555 West Highway 98
Pensacola, FL 32507
(850) 484-2253
Janice Ingle, DSN, RN

pjc.cc.fl.us

Accreditation
Florida Board of Nursing

Acceptance rate	25.4%
Faculty-student ratio	1 : 8
Faculty Full time	16
Part time	6

Degrees conferred
Associate Degree

Tuition	
In state	$5,734
Out of state	$17,765
Enrollments	148
Graduations	131

Minimum degree required
High school diploma or GED

Student Demographics	
Female	85.8%
Under age 25	26.4%
Minority	20.9%
Part-time	0.0%

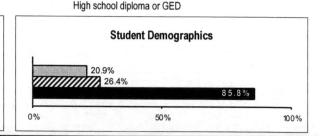

POLK COMMUNITY COLLEGE

999 Avenue "H" NE
Winter Haven, FL 33881
(863) 297-1039
Sharon Davis, PhD, RN

www.polk.edu

Accreditation
Florida Board of Nursing, National League for
Nursing Accrediting Commission (NLNAC)

Degrees conferred
Associate Degree

Key Tuition Chart | ▧ Program - in state ☐ Program - out of state ▨ Average - in state ■ Average - out of state

Florida

SAINT JOHNS RIVER COMMUNITY COLLEGE - Palatka

5001 Saint Johns Avenue
Palatka, FL 32177
(386) 312-4176
Virginia McColm, MSN, RN

www.sjrcc.fl.us

Accreditation
Florida Board of Nursing

Acceptance rate	26.9%

Degrees conferred
Associate Degree

Tuition	
In state	$1,374
Out of state	$5,149
Enrollments	78
Graduations	28

Student Demographics	
Female	91.0%
Under age 25	17.0%
Minority	9.0%
Part-time	0.0%

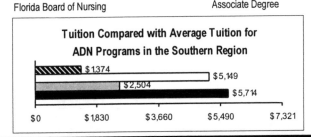

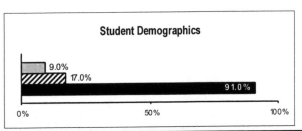

SAINT PETERSBURG COLLEGE

7200 66th Street North
Pinellas Park, FL 33781
(727) 341-3640
Jean Wortock, PhD, RN

www.spcollege.edu/hec/nursing

Accreditation
Florida Board of Nursing, National League for
Nursing Accrediting Commission (NLNAC)

*At the request of this nursing school, publication has been withheld.
Please contact the school directly for more information.*

SANTA FE COMMUNITY COLLEGE   *Useful Facts**

3000 NW 83 Street, W-201
Gainesville, FL 32606
(352) 395-5731
Rita Sutherland, PhD, ARNP

inst.sfcc.edu

Accreditation
Florida Board of Nursing, National League for
Nursing Accrediting Commission (NLNAC)

Acceptance rate	35.0%

Degrees conferred
Associate Degree

Tuition	
In state	$2,457
Out of state	$9,156
Enrollments	248
Graduations	114

Student Demographics	
Female	83.1%
Under age 25	47.0%
Minority	12.5%
Part-time	0.0%

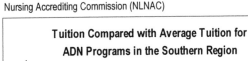
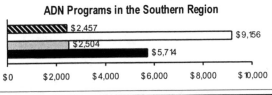

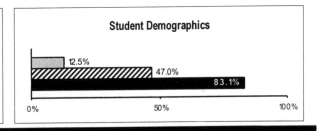

SEMINOLE COMMUNITY COLLEGE

100 Weldon Boulevard
Sanford, FL 32773
(407) 708-2013
Virginia Corey, MS, BSN, RN

seminole.cc.fl.us

Accreditation
Florida Board of Nursing, National League for
Nursing Accrediting Commission (NLNAC)

*At the request of this nursing school, publication has been withheld.
Please contact the school directly for more information.*

Demographics Chart	■ Female ▨ Under age 25 ☐ Minority	Distance Learning	¹The tuition reported for this program may be not be annualized.
			*Data reported between 2001 and 2004.

Florida

SOUTH FLORIDA COMMUNITY COLLEGE
Useful Facts*

600 West College Drive
Avon Park, FL 33825
(863) 784-7118
Mary Ann Fritz, PhD

www.southflorida.edu

Acceptance rate	40.0%

Tuition		**Student Demographics**	
In state	$1,400	Female	90.0%
Out of state	$5,000	Under age 25	27.0%
Enrollments	30	Minority	23.3%
Graduations	18	Part-time	0.0%

Accreditation
Florida Board of Nursing

Degrees conferred
Associate Degree

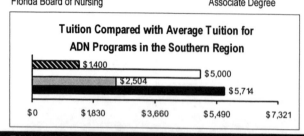

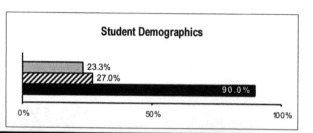

TALLAHASSEE COMMUNITY COLLEGE
Useful Facts*

444 Appleyard Drive
Tallahassee, FL 32304
(850) 922-8155
Patricia Muar, PhD, RN

www.tcc.cc.fl.us

		Student Demographics	
		Female	85.9%
Enrollments	71	Minority	21.1%
Graduations	29	Part-time	0.0%

Accreditation
Florida Board of Nursing

Degrees conferred
Associate Degree

VALENCIA COMMUNITY COLLEGE
Useful Facts

1800 Kirkman Road
Orlando, FL 32801
(407) 582-1555
Patricia Woodbery, MSN, ARNP, BC

www.valenciacc.edu/departments/west/health/nursing

Acceptance rate	51.3%
Faculty-student ratio	1: 11

Faculty	Full time	25
	Part time	39

Tuition		**Student Demographics**	
In state	$1,983	Female	91.8%
Out of state	$7,442	Under age 25	11.8%
Enrollments	490	Minority	45.9%
Graduations	242	Part-time	0.0%

Accreditation
Florida Board of Nursing, National League for
Nursing Accrediting Commission (NLNAC)

Degrees conferred
Associate Degree

Minimum degree required
High school diploma or GED

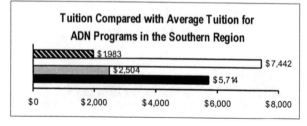

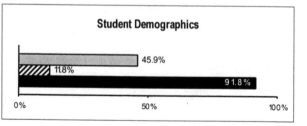

Key | Tuition Chart | ⧄ Program - in state ☐ Program - out of state ▦ Average - in state ▪ Average - out of state

Georgia

ABRAHAM BALDWIN AGRICULTURAL COLLEGE

Useful Facts

2802 Moore Highway
Tifton, GA 31793
(229) 391-5020
Wanda Golden, MSN, CCRN

www.abac.edu/nursing

Acceptance rate	20.0%	
Faculty-student ratio	1: 19	
Faculty	Full time	12
	Part time	1

Tuition	
In state	$1,398
Out of state	$5,592
Enrollments	238
Graduations	128

Student Demographics	
Female	93.7%
Under age 25	29.8%
Minority	19.3%
Part-time	0.0%

Accreditation
Georgia Board of Nursing, National League for Nursing Accrediting Commission (NLNAC)

Degrees conferred
Associate Degree

Minimum degree required
High school diploma or GED

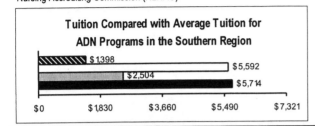

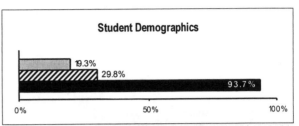

ATHENS TECHNICAL COLLEGE - Athens

800 US Hwy 29 North
Athens, GA 30601
(706) 355-5047
Gloria Buck, PhD, RN

www.athen.tec.ga.us/programs.html

Acceptance rate	22.5%

Tuition	
In state	$1,152
Out of state	$2,304
Enrollments	92
Graduations	47

Student Demographics	
Female	81.5%
Under age 25	13.0%
Minority	11.1%
Part-time	64.1%

Accreditation
Georgia Board of Nursing, National League for Nursing Accrediting Commission (NLNAC)

Degrees conferred
Associate Degree

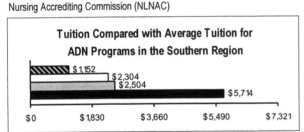

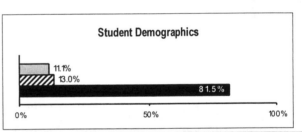

AUGUSTA STATE UNIVERSITY

Useful Facts

2500 Walton Way
Augusta, GA 30304
(706) 737-1725
Charlotte Price, EdD, RN

www.aug.edu

Acceptance rate	16.7%	
Faculty-student ratio	1: 10	
Faculty	Full time	10
	Part time	6

Tuition	
In state	$5,118
Out of state	$6,093
Enrollments	126
Graduations	59

Student Demographics	
Female	91.3%
Under age 25	28.6%
Minority	36.5%
Part-time	0.0%

Accreditation
Georgia Board of Nursing, National League for Nursing Accrediting Commission (NLNAC)

Degrees conferred
Associate Degree

Minimum degree required
High school diploma or GED

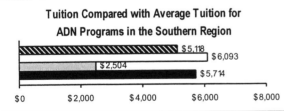

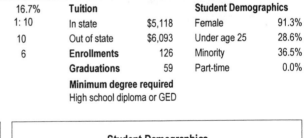

Demographics Chart	■Female ▨Under age 25 ☐Minority	Distance Learning	¹The tuition reported for this program may be not be annualized. *Data reported between 2001 and 2004.

Georgia

CLAYTON COLLEGE AND STATE UNIVERSITY

2000 Clayton State Blvd
Morrow, GA 30260
(770) 961-3481
Sue Odom, DSN, RN

www.healthsci.clayton.edu

Faculty-student ratio		1: 18
Faculty	Full time	6
	Part time	5
Enrollments		0
Graduations		0

Student Demographics

Under age 25	0.0%

Accreditation
Georgia Board of Nursing

Degrees conferred
Associate Degree

COASTAL GEORGIA COMMUNITY COLLEGE

3700 Altama Avenue
Brunswick, GA 31520
(912) 262-3340
Judith Gift, MSN, RN

www.cgcc.edu

Acceptance rate		31.9%
Faculty-student ratio		1: 10
Faculty	Full time	14
	Part time	7

Tuition	
In state	$2,284
Out of state	$9,061
Enrollments	175
Graduations	56

Minimum degree required
High school diploma or GED

Student Demographics	
Female	93.1%
Under age 25	34.3%
Minority	25.6%
Part-time	0.0%

Accreditation
Georgia Board of Nursing, National League for
Nursing Accrediting Commission (NLNAC)

Degrees conferred
Associate Degree

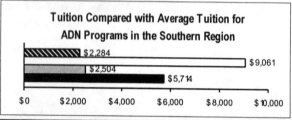

Tuition Compared with Average Tuition for ADN Programs in the Southern Region

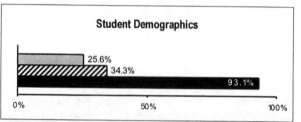

Student Demographics

COLUMBUS TECHNICAL COLLEGE - Columbus

928 Manchester Expressway
Columbus, GA 31904
(706) 649-1588
Linn Storey, BSN, MPA, ABD

www.columbustech.org

Acceptance rate		44.4%

Tuition	
In state	$1,674
Out of state	$1,674
Enrollments	66
Graduations	26

Student Demographics	
Female	69.7%
Under age 25	21.0%
Minority	30.3%
Part-time	0.0%

Accreditation
Georgia Board of Nursing, National League for
Nursing Accrediting Commission (NLNAC)

Degrees conferred
Associate Degree

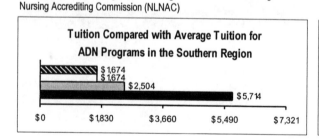

Tuition Compared with Average Tuition for ADN Programs in the Southern Region

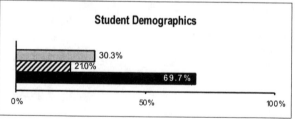

Student Demographics

Key | Tuition Chart | ▧ Program - in state ☐ Program - out of state ▨ Average - in state ■ Average - out of state

Georgia

DALTON STATE COLLEGE — *Useful Facts*

650 College Drive
Dalton, GA 30720
(706) 272-4453
Cordia Starling, BSN, MS, EdD

www.daltonstate.edu

Accreditation
Georgia Board of Nursing, National League for
Nursing Accrediting Commission (NLNAC)

Acceptance rate		21.4%
Faculty-student ratio		1: 12
Faculty	Full time	9
	Part time	1

Degrees conferred
Associate Degree

Tuition	
In state	$1,542
Out of state	$5,986
Enrollments	118
Graduations	51

Minimum degree required
High school diploma or GED

Student Demographics	
Female	88.1%
Under age 25	42.4%
Minority	7.0%
Part-time	54.2%

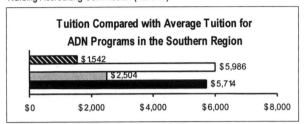

Tuition Compared with Average Tuition for ADN Programs in the Southern Region

$1,542
$5,986
$2,504
$5,714

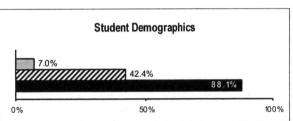

Student Demographics

7.0%
42.4%
88.1%

DARTON COLLEGE

2400 Gillionville Rd
Albany, GA 31707
(229) 430-6820
Kimberly Cribb, EdD, MSN, RN, CEN

www.darton.edu

Accreditation
Georgia Board of Nursing, National League for
Nursing Accrediting Commission (NLNAC)

At the request of this nursing school, publication has been witheld.
Please contact the school directly for more information.

FLOYD COLLEGE — *Useful Facts**

415 E 3rd Ave
Rome, GA 30161
(706) 295-6321
Barbara Rees, DSN, RN

www.floyd.edu/nursingdept

Accreditation
Georgia Board of Nursing, National League for
Nursing Accrediting Commission (NLNAC)

Degrees conferred
Associate Degree

Acceptance rate	36.1%

Tuition	
In state	$1,398
Out of state	$5,594
Enrollments	184
Graduations	85

Student Demographics	
Female	85.9%
Under age 25	40.0%
Minority	12.6%
Part-time	85.9%

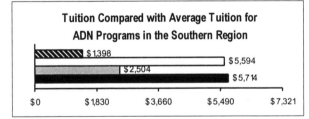

Tuition Compared with Average Tuition for ADN Programs in the Southern Region

$1,398
$5,594
$2,504
$5,714

$0 $1,830 $3,660 $5,490 $7,321

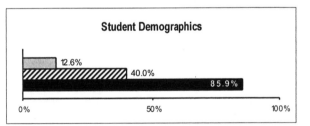

Student Demographics

12.6%
40.0%
85.9%

Demographics Chart | ■Female ⊠Under age 25 ▢Minority | **Distance Learning**

¹The tuition reported for this program may be not be annualized.
*Data reported between 2001 and 2004.

GA   261

Georgia

GEORGIA PERIMETER COLLEGE

555 N Indian Creek Drive
Clarkston, GA 30021
(678) 891-3857
Verna Rauschenberg, MN, RN

www.gpc.edu/~nursing

Acceptance rate		16.0%
Faculty-student ratio		1: 6
Faculty	Full time	22
	Part time	12

Tuition		
In state	$1,950
Out of state	$7,710
Enrollments	175
Graduations	70

Student Demographics	
Female	96.0%
Under age 25	24.0%
Minority	36.9%
Part-time	0.0%

Accreditation
Georgia Board of Nursing, National League for
Nursing Accrediting Commission (NLNAC)

Degrees conferred
Associate Degree

Minimum degree required
High school diploma or GED

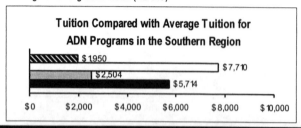

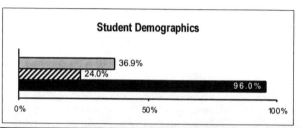

GORDON COLLEGE

419 College Drive
Barnesville, GA 30204
(770) 358-5085
Patsy Brown, RN, MSN

www.gdn.edu

Acceptance rate		36.1%
Faculty-student ratio		1: 10
Faculty	Full time	15
	Part time	6

Tuition		
In state	$871
Out of state	$3,444
Enrollments	176
Graduations	66

Student Demographics	
Female	89.8%
Under age 25	38.6%
Minority	31.6%
Part-time	0.0%

Accreditation
Georgia Board of Nursing, National League for
Nursing Accrediting Commission (NLNAC)

Degrees conferred
Associate Degree

Minimum degree required
High school diploma or GED

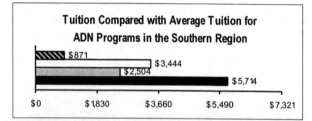

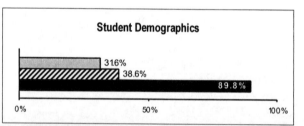

MACON STATE COLLEGE

100 College Station Drive
Macon, GA 31206
(478) 471-2979
Victoria Brown, PhD

www.maconstate.edu/nursing

Acceptance rate		20.7%
Faculty-student ratio		1: 5
Faculty	Full time	19
	Part time	10

Tuition		
In state	$2,313
Out of state	$9,249
Enrollments	123
Graduations	68

Student Demographics	
Female	82.9%
Under age 25	39.8%
Minority	27.0%
Part-time	100.0%

Accreditation
Georgia Board of Nursing, National League for
Nursing Accrediting Commission (NLNAC)

Degrees conferred
Associate Degree

Minimum degree required
None

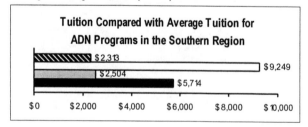

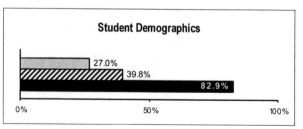

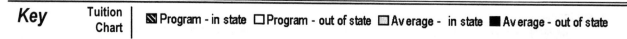

Key   Tuition Chart | ▨ Program - in state   ☐ Program - out of state   ▨ Average - in state   ■ Average - out of state

Georgia

MIDDLE GEORGIA COLLEGE
Useful Facts

1100 Second St SE
Cochran, GA 31014
(478) 934-3414
Debbie Greene, RN, MSN

www.mgc.edu

Acceptance rate		25.7%
Faculty-student ratio		1: 7
Faculty	Full time	10
	Part time	9

Tuition	
In state	$1,542
Out of state	$6,166
Enrollments	106
Graduations	67

Student Demographics	
Female	92.5%
Under age 25	45.3%
Minority	20.8%
Part-time	0.0%

Accreditation
Georgia Board of Nursing, National League for
Nursing Accrediting Commission (NLNAC)

Degrees conferred
Associate Degree

Minimum degree required
None

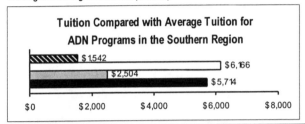

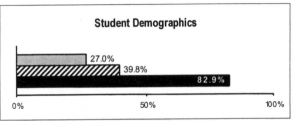

NORTH GEORGIA COLLEGE AND STATE UNIVERSITY
Useful Facts

155 Sunset Drive
Dahlonega, GA 30597
(706) 864-1930
Toni Barnett, PhD, RN

www.ngcsu.edu

Acceptance rate		16.7%
Faculty-student ratio		1: 8
Faculty	Full time	22
	Part time	9

Tuition	
In state	$2,438
Out of state	$9,754
Enrollments	209
Graduations	100

Student Demographics	
Female	89.0%
Under age 25	38.8%
Minority	23.1%
Part-time	29.7%

Accreditation
Georgia Board of Nursing, National League for
Nursing Accrediting Commission (NLNAC)

Degrees conferred
Associate Degree

Minimum degree required
High school diploma or GED

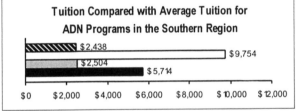

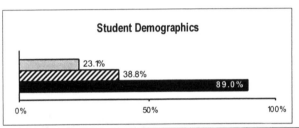

NORTHWESTERN TECHNICAL COLLEGE
Useful Facts

265 Bicentennial Trail
Rock Spring, GA 30739
(706) 764-3854
Cheryl Miller, MSN, RN

www.northwesterntech.edu

Acceptance rate	15.3%

Tuition	
In state	$1,000
Out of state	$1,000
Enrollments	78
Graduations	26

Student Demographics	
Female	87.2%
Under age 25	38.5%
Minority	3.8%
Part-time	94.9%

Accreditation
Georgia Board of Nursing, National League for
Nursing Accrediting Commission (NLNAC)

Degrees conferred
Associate Degree

Minimum degree required
High school diploma or GED

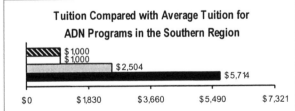

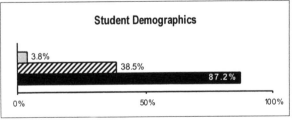

Demographics Chart	■Female ▨Under age 25 ☐Minority	Distance Learning	¹The tuition reported for this program may be not be annualized. *Data reported between 2001 and 2004.

Georgia

SOUTH GEORGIA COLLEGE

100 W College Park Drive
Douglas, GA 31533
(912) 389-4503
Linda Osban, RN, MSN

www.sga.edu

Acceptance rate	47.6%

Tuition

In state	$1,468
Out of state	$5,872
Enrollments	144
Graduations	58

Student Demographics

Female	88.9%
Under age 25	41.0%
Minority	9.1%
Part-time	3.5%

Accreditation
Georgia Board of Nursing, National League for Nursing Accrediting Commission (NLNAC)

Degrees conferred
Associate Degree

Minimum degree required
High school diploma or GED

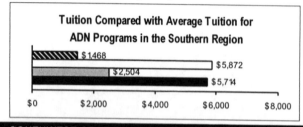

Tuition Compared with Average Tuition for ADN Programs in the Southern Region

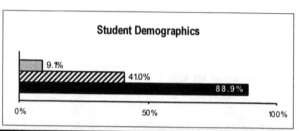

Student Demographics

SOUTHWEST GEORGIA TECHNICAL COLLEGE - *Thomasville*

15689 US Highway 19 North
Thomasville, GA 31792
(229) 225-5201
Tammy Bryant, RN

www.southwest.gatech.edu

Accreditation
Georgia Board of Nursing, National League for Nursing Accrediting Commission (NLNAC)

Degrees conferred
Associate Degree

WEST CENTRAL TECHNICAL COLLEGE - *Waco*

176 Murphy Campus Blvd
Waco, GA 30182
(770) 537-6034
Lisa Robinson, MSN, FNP-C

westcentral.org

Accreditation
Georgia Board of Nursing

Degrees conferred
Associate Degree

Hawaii

HAWAII COMMUNITY COLLEGE

200 West Kawili Street
Hilo, HI 96720
(808) 974-7560
Elizabeth Ojala, PhD, RN

www.hawcc.hawaii.edu/nursing

Acceptance rate		37.5%
Faculty-student ratio		1:4
Faculty	Full time	8
	Part time	3

Tuition

In state	$1,176
Out of state	$5,808
Enrollments	42
Graduations	22

Student Demographics

Female	95.2%
Under age 25	11.9%
Part-time	2.4%

Accreditation
Hawaii Board of Nursing, National League for Nursing Accrediting Commission (NLNAC)

Degrees conferred
Associate Degree

Minimum degree required
High school diploma or GED

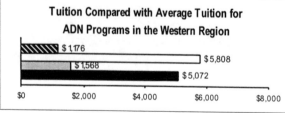

Tuition Compared with Average Tuition for ADN Programs in the Western Region

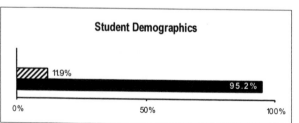

Student Demographics

Key | Tuition Chart | ▨ Program - in state ☐ Program - out of state ▨ Average - in state ■ Average - out of state

Hawaii

KAPIOLANI COMMUNITY COLLEGE
Useful Facts*

4303 Diamond Head Road
Honolulu, HI 96816
(808) 734-9301
May Kanemoto, BSN, MPH, MSN

programs.kcc.hawaii.edu/~nursing

Acceptance rate	18.9%

Enrollments	180

Student Demographics
Female	70.0%
Under age 25	6.7%
Minority	69.0%
Part-time	0.0%

Accreditation
Hawaii Board of Nursing, National League for Nursing Accrediting Commission (NLNAC)

Degrees conferred
Associate Degree

Minimum degree required
High school diploma or GED

KAUAI COMMUNITY COLLEGE
Useful Facts

3-1901 Kaumualii Highway
Lihue, HI 96766
(808) 245-8255
Richard Carmichael, MS, MPH, APRN

www.kauaicc.hawaii.edu

Acceptance rate		29.2%
Faculty-student ratio		1: 5
Faculty	Full time	9
	Part time	0

Tuition
In state	$1,176
Out of state	$5,808
Enrollments	49
Graduations	18

Student Demographics
Female	85.7%
Under age 25	51.0%
Minority	57.1%
Part-time	55.1%

Accreditation
Hawaii Board of Nursing, National League for Nursing Accrediting Commission (NLNAC)

Degrees conferred
Associate Degree

Minimum degree required
High school diploma or GED

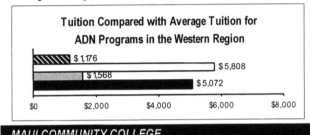

Tuition Compared with Average Tuition for ADN Programs in the Western Region
$1,176 / $5,808 / $1,568 / $5,072

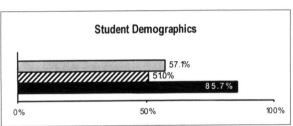

Student Demographics
57.1% / 51.0% / 85.7%

MAUI COMMUNITY COLLEGE
Useful Facts

310 Kaahumanu Avenue
Kahului, HI 96732
(808) 984-3250
Nancy Johnson, MSN, FNP, RN

mauicc.hawaii.edu/unit/nursing/welcome.html

Acceptance rate		14.4%
Faculty-student ratio		1: 7
Faculty	Full time	12.5
	Part time	2

Tuition
In state	$1,575
Enrollments	94
Graduations	82

Student Demographics
Female	81.9%
Under age 25	25.5%
Minority	57.4%
Part-time	0.0%

Accreditation
Hawaii Board of Nursing, National League for Nursing Accrediting Commission (NLNAC)

Degrees conferred
LPN or LVN, Associate Degree

Minimum degree required
High school diploma or GED

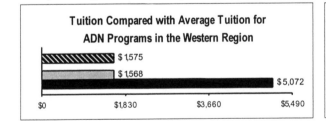

Tuition Compared with Average Tuition for ADN Programs in the Western Region
$1,575 / $1,568 / $5,072

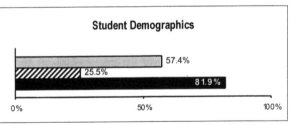

Student Demographics
57.4% / 25.5% / 81.9%

Demographics Chart	■Female ☒Under age 25 ☐Minority	Distance Learning 🖥	⁺The tuition reported for this program may be not be annualized. *Data reported between 2001 and 2004.

Idaho

BOISE STATE UNIVERSITY
Useful Facts

1910 University Drive
Boise, ID 83725
(208) 426-3600
Pam Springer, PhD, RN

nursing.boisestate.edu

Acceptance rate		13.2%
Faculty-student ratio		1: 10
Faculty	Full time	37
	Part time	5

Tuition	
Out of state	$7,056
Enrollments	125
Graduations	97

Student Demographics	
Female	78.4%
Under age 25	29.6%
Minority	9.2%
Part-time	0.0%

Accreditation
Idaho Board of Nursing, National League for
Nursing Accrediting Commission (NLNAC)

Degrees conferred
AS

Minimum degree required
High school diploma or GED

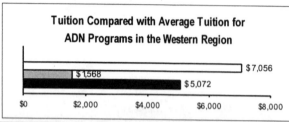
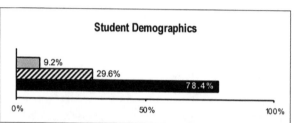

BRIGHAM YOUNG UNIVERSITY - IDAHO
Useful Facts*

175 Clarke Building
Rexburg, ID 83460
(208) 496-1325
Kathy Barnhill, MSN, RN, PhD

www.byui.edu

Acceptance rate	35.9%

Tuition	
In state	$2,640
Out of state	$3,960
Enrollments	169
Graduations	62

Student Demographics	
Female	88.8%
Under age 25	90.0%
Minority	1.8%
Part-time	24.3%

Accreditation
Idaho Board of Nursing, National League for
Nursing Accrediting Commission (NLNAC)

Degrees conferred
Associate Degree

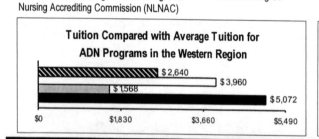
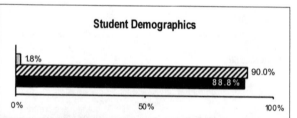

COLLEGE OF SOUTHERN IDAHO
Useful Facts

PO Box 1238
Twin Falls, ID 83303
(208) 732-6720
Pam Holloway, PhD, RN

www.csi.edu/nsg

Acceptance rate		17.5%
Faculty-student ratio		1: 13
Faculty	Full time	9
	Part time	7

Tuition	
In state	$1,900
Out of state	$5,300
Enrollments	160
Graduations	51

Student Demographics	
Female	87.5%
Under age 25	16.9%
Minority	3.8%
Part-time	0.0%

Accreditation
Idaho Board of Nursing, National League for
Nursing Accrediting Commission (NLNAC)

Degrees conferred
Associate Degree

Minimum degree required
High school diploma or GED

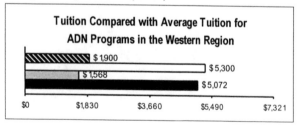
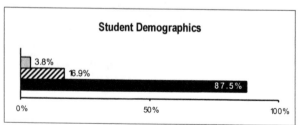

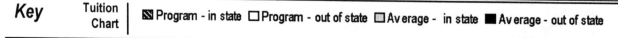

Key | Tuition Chart | ▨ Program - in state ☐ Program - out of state ▥ Average - in state ■ Average - out of state

Idaho

IDAHO STATE UNIVERSITY

650 Memorial Drive, Building 66
Pocatello, ID 83201
(208) 282-2185
Carla Dando, MSN, RN

nursing.isu.edu

Accreditation
Idaho Board of Nursing

Degrees conferred
Associate Degree

NORTH IDAHO COLLEGE — *Useful Facts*

1000 West Garden
Coeur d'Alene, ID 83814
(208) 769-3481
Manuelita Burns, MS

nic.edu/program/transfer/nurr.htm

Accreditation
Idaho Board of Nursing, National League for Nursing Accrediting Commission (NLNAC)

Degrees conferred
Associate Degree

Minimum degree required
High school diploma or GED

Acceptance rate	36.2%
Faculty-student ratio	1:7
Faculty Full time	12
Part time	6

Tuition	
In state	$1,068
Out of state	$5,620
Enrollments	109
Graduations	45

Student Demographics	
Female	88.1%
Under age 25	27.5%
Minority	2.2%
Part-time	0.0%

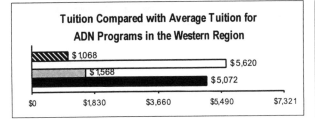

Tuition Compared with Average Tuition for ADN Programs in the Western Region
$1,068 / $5,620 / $1,568 / $5,072

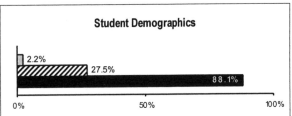

Student Demographics
2.2% / 27.5% / 88.1%

Illinois

BLACK HAWK COLLEGE — *Useful Facts*

6600 34th Ave
Moline, IL 61265
(309) 796-5361
Stephanie Valdes, MS, RN

www.bhc.edu

Accreditation
Illinois Department of Professional Regulation, National League for Nursing Accrediting Commission (NLNAC)

Degrees conferred
Associate Degree

Minimum degree required
High school diploma or GED

Acceptance rate	32.5%
Faculty-student ratio	1:9
Faculty Full time	11
Part time	13

Tuition	
In state	$1,620
Out of state	$7,770
Enrollments	164
Graduations	70

Student Demographics	
Female	87.2%
Under age 25	30.5%
Minority	6.5%
Part-time	0.0%

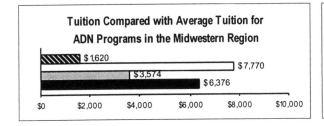

Tuition Compared with Average Tuition for ADN Programs in the Midwestern Region
$1,620 / $7,770 / $3,574 / $6,376

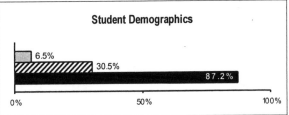

Student Demographics
6.5% / 30.5% / 87.2%

Demographics Chart	■ Female ▨ Under age 25 ▢ Minority	Distance Learning	†The tuition reported for this program may be not be annualized. *Data reported between 2001 and 2004.

Illinois

CARL SANDBURG COLLEGE

2400 Tom L Wilson Blvd
Galesburg, IL 61401
(309) 341-5318
Sally Day, MSN, RN

www.sandburg.edu

Accreditation
Illinois Department of Professional Regulation,
National League for Nursing Accrediting
Commission (NLNAC)

Acceptance rate		52.9%
Faculty-student ratio		1:5
Faculty	Full time	8
	Part time	10

Degrees conferred
Associate Degree

Tuition	
In state	$2,145
Out of state	$3,885
Enrollments	68
Graduations	31

Minimum degree required
High school diploma or GED

Student Demographics	
Female	92.6%
Under age 25	32.4%
Minority	1.5%
Part-time	19.1%

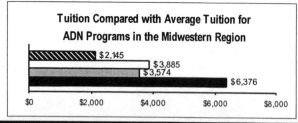

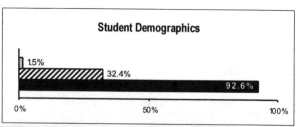

CITY COLLEGES OF CHICAGO - TRUMAN COLLEGE

1145 W Wilson Ave
Chicago, IL 60640
(773) 907-4641
Deborah Terrell, MS, DNSc, BSN

www.ccc.edu/truman

Accreditation
Illinois Department of Professional Regulation,
National League for Nursing Accrediting
Commission (NLNAC)

Acceptance rate	22.2%

Degrees conferred
Associate Degree

Tuition	
In state	$1,250
Out of state	$6,100
Enrollments	180
Graduations	60

Student Demographics	
Female	81.7%
Under age 25	30.0%
Minority	63.3%
Part-time	0.0%

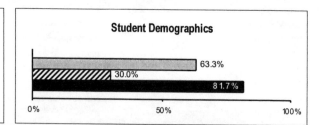

COLLEGE OF DUPAGE

425 22nd St
Glen Ellyn, IL 60137
(630) 942-2652
Ellen Davel, EdD, RN

www.cod.edu

Accreditation
Illinois Department of Professional Regulation

Acceptance rate		25.7%
Faculty-student ratio		1:8
Faculty	Full time	12
	Part time	36

Degrees conferred
Associate Degree

Tuition	
In state	$2,610
Out of state	$8,580
Enrollments	239
Graduations	89

Minimum degree required
Illinois Certified Nursing Assistant

Student Demographics	
Female	84.1%
Under age 25	15.5%
Minority	22.2%
Part-time	57.7%

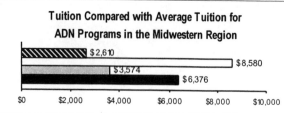

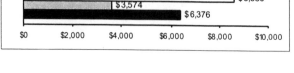

Illinois

COLLEGE OF LAKE COUNTY

19351 West Washington St
Grayslake, IL 60030
(847) 543-2339
Deborah Jezuit, DNSc, RN

www.clcillinois.edu/index.asp

Accreditation
Illinois Department of Professional Regulation,
National League for Nursing Accrediting
Commission (NLNAC)

*At the request of this nursing school, publication has been withheld.
Please contact the school directly for more information.*

DANVILLE AREA COMMUNITY COLLEGE

2000 E Main St
Danville, IL 61832
(217) 443-8814
Ann Wogle, PhD(c), RN

www.dacc.cc.il.us

Accreditation
Illinois Department of Professional Regulation

Degrees conferred
Associate Degree

ELGIN COMMUNITY COLLEGE   *Useful Facts*

1700 Spartan Dr
Elgin, IL 60123
(847) 214-7326
Phyllis Thomson, MS, RN

www.elgin.edu

Accreditation
Illinois Department of Professional Regulation,
National League for Nursing Accrediting
Commission (NLNAC)

Acceptance rate		28.7%
Faculty-student ratio		1: 13
Faculty	Full time	15
	Part time	8

Tuition	
In state	$2,260
Out of state	$9,948
Enrollments	238
Graduations	64

Student Demographics	
Female	86.1%
Under age 25	27.7%
Minority	25.6%
Part-time	8.4%

Degrees conferred
AAS

Minimum degree required
High school diploma or GED

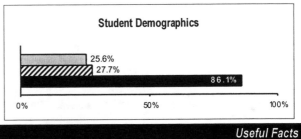

HEARTLAND COMMUNITY COLLEGE   *Useful Facts*

1500 West Raab Rd
Normal, IL 61761
(309) 268-8754
H Miller, MSN, RN

www.heartland.edu/divisions/hs/nurs/adn/index.html

Accreditation
Illinois Department of Professional Regulation,
National League for Nursing Accrediting
Commission (NLNAC)

Acceptance rate		23.6%
Faculty-student ratio		1: 8
Faculty	Full time	6
	Part time	4

Tuition	
In state	$1,890
Out of state	$5,670
Enrollments	67
Graduations	24

Student Demographics	
Female	89.6%
Under age 25	37.3%
Minority	7.6%
Part-time	76.1%

Degrees conferred
Associate Degree

Minimum degree required
High school diploma or GED

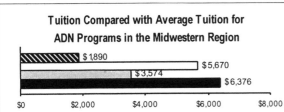
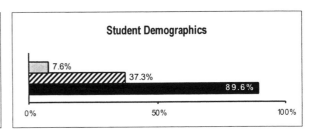

Demographics Chart	■Female ☒Under age 25 □Minority	Distance Learning	¹The tuition reported for this program may be not be annualized. *Data reported between 2001 and 2004.

Illinois

HIGHLAND COMMUNITY COLLEGE — *Useful Facts**

2998 Pearl City Road	Acceptance rate	38.6%	**Tuition[1]**		**Student Demographics**
Freeport, IL 61032			In state	$53	Female	92.0%
(815) 599-3516			Out of state	$81	Under age 25	28.0%
Alice Nied, RN, MSN			**Enrollments**	50	Minority	6.0%
www.highland.cc.il.us			**Graduations**	14		

Accreditation
Illinois Department of Professional Regulation

Degrees conferred
Associate Degree

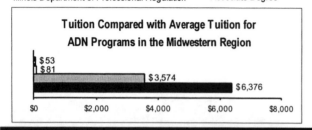

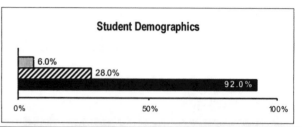

ILLINOIS CENTRAL COLLEGE — *Useful Facts*

201 SW Adams Street	Acceptance rate	30.0%	**Tuition[1]**		**Student Demographics**
East Peoria, IL 61635	Faculty-student ratio	1: 10	In state	$64	Female	90.8%
(309) 999-4655	Faculty Full time	11	Out of state	$110	Under age 25	26.3%
Mary Kiefner, RN, MS	Part time	8	**Enrollments**	152	Minority	12.5%
icc.edu			**Graduations**	56	Part-time	48.0%

Accreditation
Illinois Department of Professional Regulation,
National League for Nursing Accrediting
Commission (NLNAC)

Degrees conferred
Associate Degree

Minimum degree required
High school diploma or GED

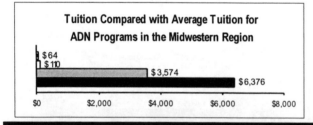

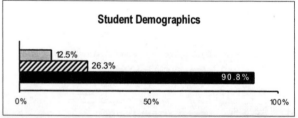

ILLINOIS EASTERN COMMUNITY COLLEGES — *Useful Facts*

305 N West St	Acceptance rate	71.7%	**Tuition**		**Student Demographics**
Olney, IL 62450	Faculty-student ratio	1: 16	In state	$1,961	Female	92.1%
(618) 395-7777	Faculty Full time	19	Out of state	$8,456	Under age 25	40.0%
Donna Henry, RN, MS, CHTP	Part time	2	**Enrollments**	315	Minority	1.6%
www.iecc.edu			**Graduations**	100	Part-time	37.5%

Accreditation
Illinois Department of Professional Regulation,
National League for Nursing Accrediting
Commission (NLNAC)

Degrees conferred
LPN or LVN

Minimum degree required
LPN

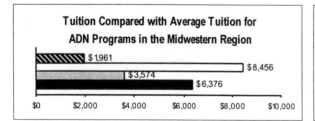

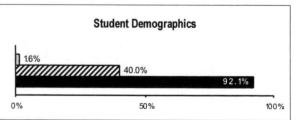

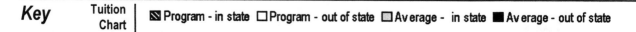

Key	Tuition Chart	▨ Program - in state ☐ Program - out of state ▢ Average - in state ■ Average - out of state

Illinois

ILLINOIS VALLEY COMMUNITY COLLEGE — *Useful Facts*

815 N Orlando Smith Rd
Oglesby, IL 61348
(815) 224-0485
Gloria Bouxsein, RN, MSN

www.iucc.edu

Accreditation
Illinois Department of Professional Regulation,
National League for Nursing Accrediting
Commission (NLNAC)

Acceptance rate	34.3%

Degrees conferred
Associate Degree

Tuition
In state	$1,838
Out of state	$6,360
Enrollments	139
Graduations	77

Minimum degree required
High school diploma or GED

Student Demographics
Female	97.1%
Under age 25	41.7%
Minority	14.4%
Part-time	0.0%

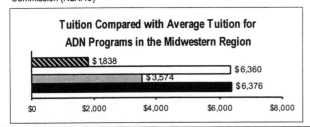

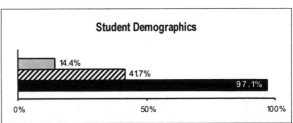

JOHN A LOGAN COLLEGE

700 Logan College Rd
Carterville, IL 62918
(618) 985-2828
Marilyn Murphy, MSN, RN, CNA

www.jal.cc.il.us

Accreditation
Illinois Department of Professional Regulation

At the request of this nursing school, publication has been withheld.
Please contact the school directly for more information.

JOHN WOOD COMMUNITY COLLEGE — *Useful Facts*

1301 South 48th St
Quincy, IL 62305
(217) 224-6564
Julie Barry, RNC, PhD

www.jwcc.edu

Accreditation
Illinois Department of Professional Regulation

Acceptance rate		13.3%
Faculty-student ratio		1: 6
Faculty	Full time	11
	Part time	3

Degrees conferred
Associate Degree

Tuition
In state	$2,430
Out of state	$5,310
Enrollments	76
Graduations	25

Minimum degree required
High school diploma or GED

Student Demographics
Female	92.1%
Under age 25	36.8%
Minority	2.6%
Part-time	34.2%

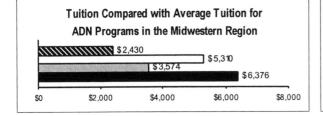

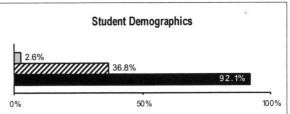

Demographics Chart	■ Female ▨ Under age 25 ☐ Minority	Distance Learning	¹The tuition reported for this program may be not be annualized. *Data reported between 2001 and 2004.

Illinois

JOLIET JUNIOR COLLEGE

1215 Houbolt Rd
Joliet, IL 60431
(815) 280-6648
Michaelene Nash, MS, RN

jjc.cc.il.us

Acceptance rate	78.6%

Tuition
In state	$1,176
Out of state	$5,328
Enrollments	229
Graduations	97

Student Demographics
Female	95.2%
Under age 25	20.0%
Minority	27.8%
Part-time	0.0%

Accreditation
Illinois Department of Professional Regulation,
National League for Nursing Accrediting
Commission (NLNAC)

Degrees conferred
Associate Degree

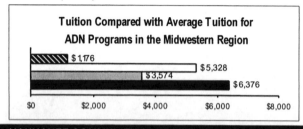
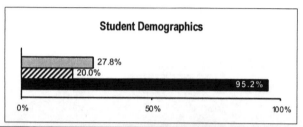

KANKAKEE COMMUNITY COLLEGE

Box 888 River Rd
Kankakee, IL 60901
(815) 802-8802
Phyllis Nichols, RN, MS

kankakee.edu

Acceptance rate	60.4%

Tuition
In state	$1,650
Out of state	$9,697
Enrollments	133
Graduations	43

Student Demographics
Female	94.0%
Under age 25	41.0%
Minority	7.5%
Part-time	54.9%

Accreditation
Illinois Department of Professional Regulation

Degrees conferred
Associate Degree

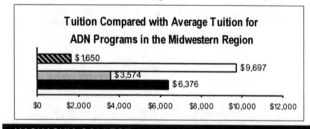
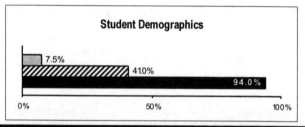

KASKASKIA COLLEGE

27210 College Rd
Centralia, IL 62801
(618) 545-3331
Mary Whitten, RN, MSN

www.kaskaskia.edu

Acceptance rate	52.6%
Faculty-student ratio	1: 14

Faculty	Full time	10
	Part time	5

Tuition[1]
In state	$53
Out of state	$235
Enrollments	175
Graduations	88

Student Demographics
Female	93.1%
Under age 25	38.9%
Minority	3.4%
Part-time	42.9%

Accreditation
Illinois Department of Professional Regulation,
National League for Nursing Accrediting
Commission (NLNAC)

Degrees conferred
Associate Degree

Minimum degree required
High school diploma or GED

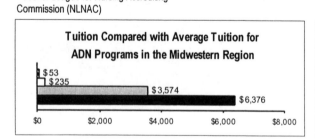
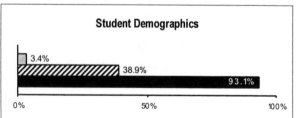

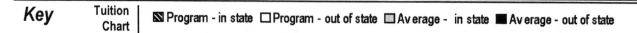

Key | Tuition Chart | ▨ Program - in state ☐ Program - out of state ▥ Average - in state ■ Average - out of state

Illinois

KENNEDY-KING COLLEGE - CHICAGO CITY COLLEGES
Useful Facts*

6800 South Wentworth Ave
Chcago, IL 60621
(773) 602-5183
Mickle Ward-Ellison, RN, MSN

www.ccc.edu

Acceptance rate	39.7%	**Tuition**		**Student Demographics**	
		In state	$1,860	Female	86.0%
		Out of state	$9,449	Under age 25	16.0%
		Enrollments	107	Minority	100.0%
		Graduations	24	Part-time	0.0%

Accreditation
Illinois Department of Professional Regulation, National League for Nursing Accrediting Commission (NLNAC)

Degrees conferred
Associate Degree

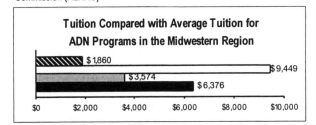

Tuition Compared with Average Tuition for ADN Programs in the Midwestern Region

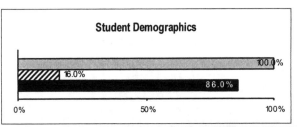

Student Demographics

KISHWAUKEE COLLEGE

21193 Malta Rd
Malta, IL 60150
(815) 825-2086
Heather Peters, RN, MS, MBA

kish.cc.il.us

Accreditation
Illinois Department of Professional Regulation

Degrees conferred
Associate Degree

LAKE LAND COLLEGE
Useful Facts

5001 Lake Land Blvd
Mattoon, IL 61938
(217) 234-5452
Kathleen Doehring, RN, BS, MS

www.lakeland.cc.il.us

Acceptance rate	44.9%	**Tuition**		**Student Demographics**	
Faculty-student ratio	1: 10	In state	$2,016	Female	93.5%
Faculty Full time	8	Out of state	$9,000	Under age 25	41.3%
Part time	2	**Enrollments**	92	Minority	3.3%
		Graduations	34	Part-time	10.9%

Accreditation
Illinois Department of Professional Regulation, National League for Nursing Accrediting Commission (NLNAC)

Degrees conferred
Associate Degree

Minimum degree required
None

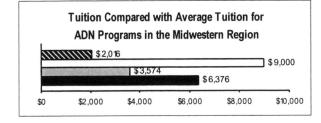

Tuition Compared with Average Tuition for ADN Programs in the Midwestern Region

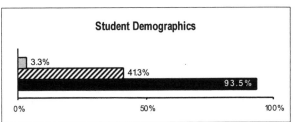

Student Demographics

Demographics Chart	■Female ▨Under age 25 ▢Minority	Distance Learning		⁺The tuition reported for this program may be not be annualized. *Data reported between 2001 and 2004.

Illinois

LEWIS & CLARK COMMUNITY COLLEGE
Useful Facts*

5800 Godfrey Rd
Godfrey, IL 62035
(618) 468-4400
Donna Meyer, RN, MSN

www.lc.edu

Accreditation
Illinois Department of Professional Regulation,
National League for Nursing Accrediting
Commission (NLNAC)

Acceptance rate 45.9%

Degrees conferred
Associate Degree

Tuition		Student Demographics	
In state	$1,368	Female	89.0%
Out of state	$2,052	Under age 25	46.0%
Enrollments	146	Minority	7.5%
Graduations	43	Part-time	15.8%

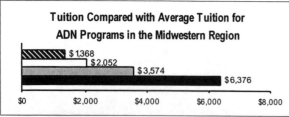

Tuition Compared with Average Tuition for ADN Programs in the Midwestern Region

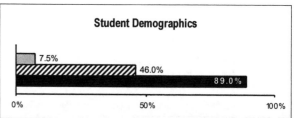

Student Demographics

LINCOLN LAND COMMUNITY COLLEGE
Useful Facts*

5250 Shepherd Road, PO Box 19256
Springfield, IL 62794
(217) 786-2436
Joan Lewis, MSN, CFNP

llcc.edu

Accreditation
Illinois Department of Professional Regulation,
National League for Nursing Accrediting
Commission (NLNAC)

Acceptance rate 62.5%

Degrees conferred
Associate Degree

Tuition[1]		Student Demographics	
In state	$50	Female	93.3%
Out of state	$300	Under age 25	15.0%
Enrollments	135	Minority	7.4%
Graduations	66	Part-time	0.0%

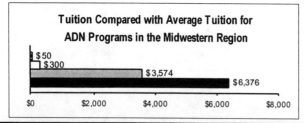

Tuition Compared with Average Tuition for ADN Programs in the Midwestern Region

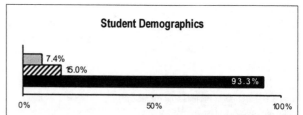

Student Demographics

MALCOLM X COLLEGE
Useful Facts

1900 West Van Buren, RM 3204
Chicago, IL 60612
(312) 850-7145
Betty Gammon, MSN, RN

www.ccc.edu

Accreditation
Illinois Department of Professional Regulation,
National League for Nursing Accrediting
Commission (NLNAC)

Acceptance rate		100.0%
Faculty-student ratio		1: 13
Faculty	Full time	4
	Part time	10

Degrees conferred
Associate Degree

Minimum degree required
High school diploma or GED

Tuition		Student Demographics	
In state	$1,140	Female	83.3%
Out of state	$5,050	Under age 25	12.5%
Enrollments	120	Minority	90.9%
Graduations	40	Part-time	29.2%

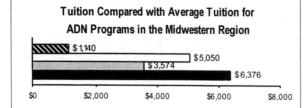

Tuition Compared with Average Tuition for ADN Programs in the Midwestern Region

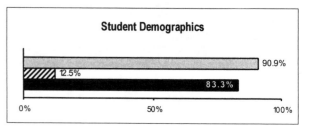

Student Demographics

Key Tuition Chart | ▨ Program - in state ☐ Program - out of state ▨ Average - in state ■ Average - out of state

Illinois

MORAINE VALLEY COMMUNITY COLLEGE
Useful Facts

9000 West College Pkwy
Palos Hills, IL 60465
(708) 974-5303
Gloria Victoria, MSN

www.morainevalley.edu/healthsciences

Acceptance rate		14.3%
Faculty-student ratio		1: 9
Faculty	Full time	13
	Part time	14

Tuition	
In state	$1,920
Out of state	$7,260
Enrollments	182
Graduations	85

Student Demographics	
Female	93.4%
Under age 25	11.5%
Minority	17.6%
Part-time	0.0%

Accreditation
Illinois Department of Professional Regulation,
National League for Nursing Accrediting
Commission (NLNAC)

Degrees conferred
Associate Degree

Minimum degree required
High school diploma or GED

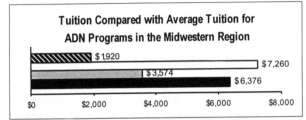
Tuition Compared with Average Tuition for ADN Programs in the Midwestern Region

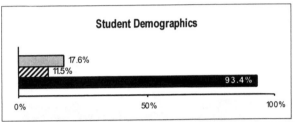
Student Demographics

MORTON COLLEGE
Useful Facts*

3801 S Central Ave
Cicero, IL 60804
(708) 656-8000
Aline Turpa, RN, MSN, ED

www.morton.edu

| Acceptance rate | 19.8% |

Tuition	
In state	$1,650
Out of state	$6,600
Enrollments	133
Graduations	42

Student Demographics	
Female	97.0%
Under age 25	30.0%
Minority	67.2%
Part-time	0.0%

Accreditation
Illinois Department of Professional Regulation

Degrees conferred
Associate Degree

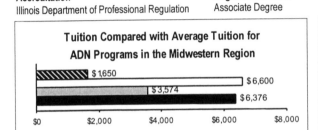
Tuition Compared with Average Tuition for ADN Programs in the Midwestern Region

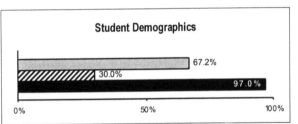
Student Demographics

OAKTON COMMUNITY COLLEGE
Useful Facts

1600 E Golf Rd
Des Plaines, IL 60016
(847) 635-1720
Sandra Kubala, MSN, RN

www.oakton.edu

Acceptance rate		22.9%
Faculty-student ratio		1: 9
Faculty	Full time	12
	Part time	25

Tuition	
In state	$2,380
Out of state	$9,090
Enrollments	217
Graduations	71

Student Demographics	
Female	80.2%
Under age 25	37.3%
Minority	48.4%
Part-time	0.0%

Accreditation
Illinois Department of Professional Regulation,
National League for Nursing Accrediting
Commission (NLNAC)

Degrees conferred
LPN or LVN, Associate Degree

Minimum degree required
High school diploma or GED

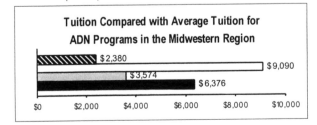
Tuition Compared with Average Tuition for ADN Programs in the Midwestern Region

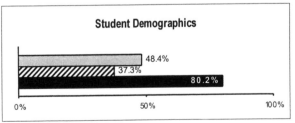
Student Demographics

| Demographics Chart | ■Female ⊠Under age 25 ☐Minority | Distance Learning | †The tuition reported for this program may be not be annualized. |
| | | | *Data reported between 2001 and 2004. |

OLIVE-HARVEY COLLEGE — *Useful Facts**

1001 S Woodlawn
Chicago, IL 60628
(773) 291-6100

oliveharvey.ccc.edu

Accreditation
Illinois Department of Professional Regulation

Acceptance rate 80.0%

Tuition[1]
In state $62
Out of state $315
Enrollments 135
Graduations 25

Degrees conferred
Associate Degree

Student Demographics
Female 88.9%
Under age 25 15.0%
Minority 100.0%
Part-time 48.1%

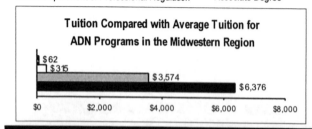
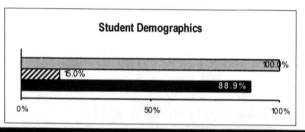

PARKLAND COLLEGE — *Useful Facts*

2400 West Bradley
Champaign, IL 61821
(217) 403-4570
Susan Caneva, MS, RN

www.parkland.edu

Accreditation
Illinois Department of Professional Regulation,
National League for Nursing Accrediting
Commission (NLNAC)

Acceptance rate 12.9%
Faculty-student ratio 1: 15
Faculty Full time 8
Part time 10

Tuition
In state $2,160
Out of state $8,940
Enrollments 201
Graduations 48

Student Demographics
Female 91.0%
Under age 25 20.9%
Minority 18.5%
Part-time 74.1%

Degrees conferred
Associate Degree

Minimum degree required
Associate degree in a non-nursing field

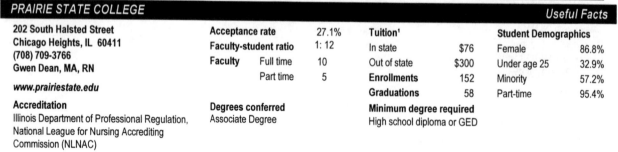

PRAIRIE STATE COLLEGE — *Useful Facts*

202 South Halsted Street
Chicago Heights, IL 60411
(708) 709-3766
Gwen Dean, MA, RN

www.prairiestate.edu

Accreditation
Illinois Department of Professional Regulation,
National League for Nursing Accrediting
Commission (NLNAC)

Acceptance rate 27.1%
Faculty-student ratio 1: 12
Faculty Full time 10
Part time 5

Tuition[1]
In state $76
Out of state $300
Enrollments 152
Graduations 58

Student Demographics
Female 86.8%
Under age 25 32.9%
Minority 57.2%
Part-time 95.4%

Degrees conferred
Associate Degree

Minimum degree required
High school diploma or GED

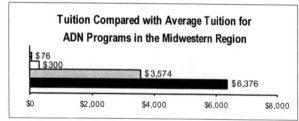
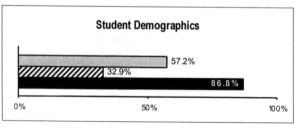

Key Tuition Chart | ▨ Program - in state ☐ Program - out of state ☐ Average - in state ■ Average - out of state

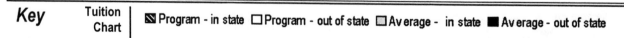

Illinois

REND LAKE COLLEGE
*Useful Facts**

468 North Ken Gray Parkway
Ina, IL 62846
(618) 437-5321
Sharon Beasley, PhD, RN, MSN

www.rlc.cc.il.us

Enrollments	45	

Student Demographics
Female 97.8%
Under age 25 100.0%
Minority 100.0%
Part-time 0.0%

Accreditation
Illinois Department of Professional Regulation

Degrees conferred
Associate Degree

RICHARD J DALEY COLLEGE
*Useful Facts**

7500 S Pulaski
Chicago, IL 60652
(773) 838-7681
Sheila Bouie, RN, MSN, APRN-BC

daley.ccc.edu

Acceptance rate	25.8%

Tuition	
In state	$1,488
Out of state	$6,071
Enrollments	112
Graduations	41

Student Demographics
Female 90.2%

Minority 66.1%
Part-time 15.2%

Accreditation
Illinois Department of Professional Regulation,
National League for Nursing Accrediting
Commission (NLNAC)

Degrees conferred
Associate Degree

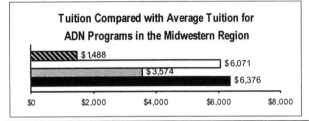

Tuition Compared with Average Tuition for ADN Programs in the Midwestern Region
$1,488
$6,071
$3,574
$6,376

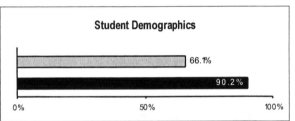

Student Demographics
66.1%
90.2%

RICHLAND COMMUNITY COLLEGE
Useful Facts

One College Park Dr
Decatur, IL 62521
(217) 875-7211
Roberta Scholze, RN, MSN

www.richland.edu

Acceptance rate	100.0%	
Faculty-student ratio	1:9	
Faculty	Full time	7
	Part time	2

Tuition[1]	
In state	$62
Out of state	$345
Enrollments	69
Graduations	20

Student Demographics
Female 85.5%
Under age 25 49.3%
Minority 22.1%
Part-time 56.5%

Accreditation
Illinois Department of Professional Regulation,
National League for Nursing Accrediting
Commission (NLNAC)

Degrees conferred
Associate Degree

Minimum degree required
High school diploma or GED

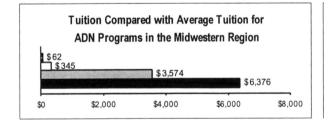

Tuition Compared with Average Tuition for ADN Programs in the Midwestern Region
$62
$345
$3,574
$6,376

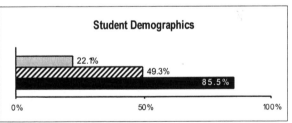

Student Demographics
22.1%
49.3%
85.5%

Demographics Chart | ■Female ⊠Under age 25 ☐Minority | **Distance Learning** | [1]The tuition reported for this program may be not be annualized.
*Data reported between 2001 and 2004.

Illinois

ROCK VALLEY COLLEGE

3301 North Mulford Rd
Rockford, IL 61114
(815) 654-4410
Cynthia Luxton, MS, RN

www.rvc.cc.il.us

Acceptance rate	31.4%	**Tuition**		**Student Demographics**
		In state	$1,312	Female	97.2%
		Out of state	$4,972	
		Enrollments	71	Minority	9.9%
		Graduations	31	Part-time	0.0%

Accreditation
Illinois Department of Professional Regulation

Degrees conferred
Associate Degree

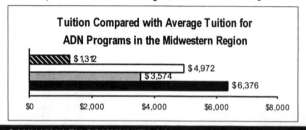

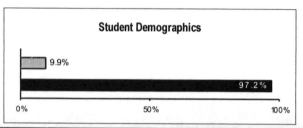

SAUK VALLEY COMMUNITY COLLEGE

173 Illinois Route #2
Dixon, IL 61021
(815) 288-5511
Janet Lynch, RN, MS

svcc.edu

Acceptance rate	35.7%	**Tuition**		**Student Demographics**
		In state	$1,980	Female	96.7%
		Out of state	$8,550	
		Enrollments	61	
		Graduations	11	Part-time	0.0%

Accreditation
Illinois Department of Professional Regulation

Degrees conferred
Associate Degree

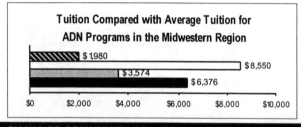

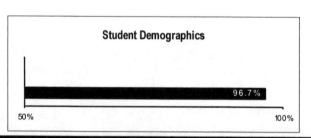

SHAWNEE COMMUNITY COLLEGE

8364 Shawnee College Rd
Ullin, IL 62992
(618) 634-3200
Carol Belt, MSN

www.shawnee.cc.il.us

Accreditation
Illinois Department of Professional Regulation

Degrees conferred
Associate Degree

Key | Tuition Chart | ▧ Program - in state ☐ Program - out of state ▨ Average - in state ■ Average - out of state

Illinois

SOUTH SUBURBAN COLLEGE | *Useful Facts**

15800 State St
South Holland, IL 60473
(708) 596-2000
Marjorie Roache, MS, RN

www.southsuburbancollege.edu/acad/career/depts/alliedhealth/nursing/index.htm

Acceptance rate	36.4%	

Tuition			Student Demographics	
In state	$1,920		Female	92.3%
Out of state	$8,250		Under age 25	20.0%
Enrollments	182		Minority	67.2%
Graduations	73		Part-time	0.0%

Accreditation
Illinois Department of Professional Regulation,
National League for Nursing Accrediting
Commission (NLNAC)

Degrees conferred
Associate Degree

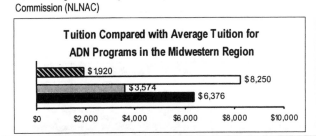

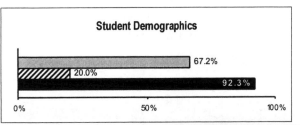

SOUTHEASTERN ILLINOIS COLLEGE

Alumni Hall, RM 2332, Box 1066
Edwardsville, IL 62026
(618) 650-3959
Felissa Lashley, RN, PhD, ACRN, FAAN

www.siue.edu/nursing

Accreditation
Illinois Department of Professional Regulation

Degrees conferred
Associate Degree

SOUTHWESTERN ILLINOIS COLLEGE | *Useful Facts*

2500 Carlyle
Belleville, IL 62221
(618) 235-2700
Carol Eckert, RN, MSN

www.southwestern.cc.il.us

Acceptance rate		33.6%
Faculty-student ratio		1: 14
Faculty	Full time	10
	Part time	5

Tuition[1]			Student Demographics	
In state	$58		Female	92.2%
Out of state	$249		Under age 25	50.0%
Enrollments	180		Minority	7.8%
Graduations	69		Part-time	97.2%

Accreditation
Illinois Department of Professional Regulation,
National League for Nursing Accrediting
Commission (NLNAC)

Degrees conferred
Associate Degree

Minimum degree required
High school diploma or GED

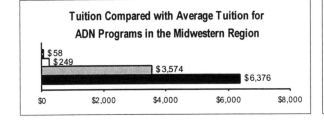

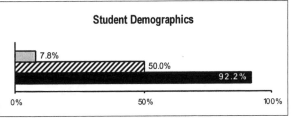

Demographics Chart	■ Female ▨ Under age 25 ☐ Minority	Distance Learning	[1]The tuition reported for this program may be not be annualized.
			*Data reported between 2001 and 2004.

Illinois

SPOON RIVER COLLEGE
Useful Facts*

23235 N Co Rd 22
Canton, IL 61520
(309) 649-6227
Katherine Walls, RN, MS

www.spoonrivercollege.net/prog/nur-cur.html

Acceptance rate	19.2%	

Tuition

		Student Demographics	
In state	$4,030	Female	93.3%
		Under age 25	48.0%
Enrollments	60	Minority	1.7%
Graduations	12	Part-time	5.0%

Accreditation
Illinois Department of Professional Regulation

Degrees conferred
Associate Degree

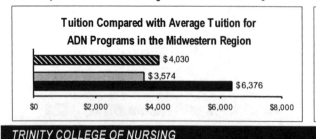

Tuition Compared with Average Tuition for ADN Programs in the Midwestern Region

$4,030
$3,574
$6,376

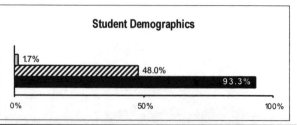

Student Demographics

1.7%
48.0%
93.3%

TRINITY COLLEGE OF NURSING
Useful Facts*

2122 25th Avenue
Rock Island, IL 61201
(309) 779-7710
Beth Cameron, ND, FNP

www.trinitycollege

Acceptance rate	34.6%	

Tuition

		Student Demographics	
In state	$5,675	Female	89.3%
Out of state	$5,675	Under age 25	46.0%
Enrollments	84	Minority	2.4%
Graduations	33	Part-time	77.4%

Accreditation
Illinois Department of Professional Regulation

Degrees conferred
Associate Degree

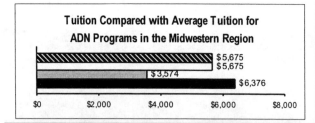

Tuition Compared with Average Tuition for ADN Programs in the Midwestern Region

$5,675
$5,675
$3,574
$6,376

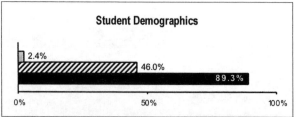

Student Demographics

2.4%
46.0%
89.3%

TRITON COLLEGE
Useful Facts

2000 North 5th Ave
River Grove, IL 60171
(708) 456-0300
Joan Libner, MSN, RN, BC

www.triton.edu/adacepts/health

Acceptance rate	14.6%		
Faculty-student ratio	1: 11		
Faculty	Full time	9	
	Part time	4	

Tuition

		Student Demographics	
In state	$1,680	Female	89.3%
Out of state	$6,670	Under age 25	42.6%
Enrollments	122	Minority	54.1%
Graduations	32	Part-time	77.9%

Accreditation
Illinois Department of Professional Regulation,
National League for Nursing Accrediting
Commission (NLNAC)

Degrees conferred
Associate Degree

Minimum degree required
High school diploma or GED

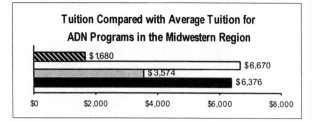

Tuition Compared with Average Tuition for ADN Programs in the Midwestern Region

$1,680
$6,670
$3,574
$6,376

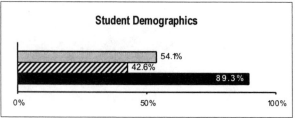

Student Demographics

54.1%
42.6%
89.3%

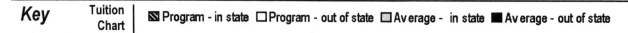

Key | Tuition Chart | ▧ Program - in state ☐ Program - out of state ▨ Average - in state ■ Average - out of state

Illinois

WAUBONSEE COMMUNITY COLLEGE

Route 47 at Wabonsee Dr
Suger Grove, IL 60554
(630) 466-2467
Patricia Brown, MS, RN, CCRN

www.wcc.cc.il.us

Accreditation
Illinois Department of Professional Regulation

*At the request of this nursing school, publication has been withheld.
Please contact the school directly for more information.*

WILLIAM RAINEY HARPER COLLEGE   *Useful Facts*

1200 W Algonquin Road
Palatine, IL 60067
(847) 925-6523
Peggy Gallagher, EdD, MSN, RN

www.harpercollege.edu

Accreditation
Illinois Department of Professional Regulation,
National League for Nursing Accrediting
Commission (NLNAC)

Acceptance rate	30.0%	
Faculty-student ratio	1: 13	
Faculty Full time	13	
Part time	13	

Degrees conferred
LPN or LVN, Associate Degree

Tuition	
In state	$2,625
Out of state	$12,040
Enrollments	250
Graduations	88

Minimum degree required
High school diploma or GED

Student Demographics	
Female	93.2%
Under age 25	30.0%
Minority	24.5%
Part-time	54.4%

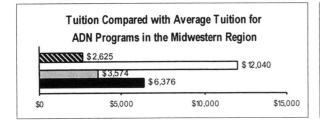

Tuition Compared with Average Tuition for ADN Programs in the Midwestern Region

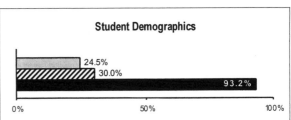

Student Demographics

Indiana

BALL STATE UNIVERSITY

2000 University Ave
Muncie, IN 47306
(765) 285-5571
Linda Siktberg, PhD, RN

www.bsu.edu/nursing

Accreditation
Indiana State Board of Nursing

Faculty-student ratio	1: 9	
Faculty Full time	29	
Part time	8	

Degrees conferred
Associate Degree

BETHEL COLLEGE - Mishawaka

1001 West McKinley
Mishawaka, IN 46545
(574) 257-2594
Ruth Davidhizar, RN, DNS, ARNP, BC, FAAN

www.bethelcollege.edu

Accreditation
Indiana State Board of Nursing, National League
for Nursing Accrediting Commission (NLNAC)

Acceptance rate	81.4%	
Faculty-student ratio	1: 8	
Faculty Full time	14	
Part time	20	

Degrees conferred
Associate Degree

Tuition	
In state	$15,800
Out of state	$15,800
Enrollments	88
Graduations	50

Minimum degree required
High school diploma or GED

Student Demographics	
Female	93.2%
Under age 25	45.5%
Minority	16.1%
Part-time	20.5%

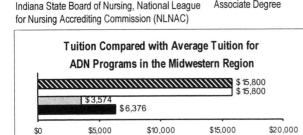

Tuition Compared with Average Tuition for ADN Programs in the Midwestern Region

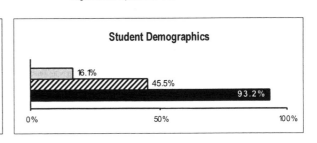

Student Demographics

| Demographics Chart | ■ Female ▨ Under age 25 ☐ Minority | Distance Learning | †The tuition reported for this program may be not be annualized.
*Data reported between 2001 and 2004. |
|---|---|---|---|

Indiana

INDIANA STATE UNIVERSITY

749 Chestnut
Terre Haute, IN 47809
(812) 237-3683
Esther Acree, MSN, FNP

www.indstate.edu/site/nurs

Faculty-student ratio		1: 22
Faculty	Full time	21
	Part time	0

Tuition	
In state	$7,114
Out of state	$16,004
Enrollments	2
Graduations	43

Student Demographics	
Female	100.0%
Under age 25	50.0%
Part-time	100.0%

Accreditation
Indiana State Board of Nursing

Degrees conferred
Associate Degree

Minimum degree required
High school diploma or GED

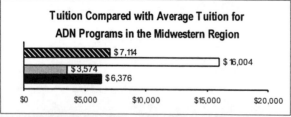

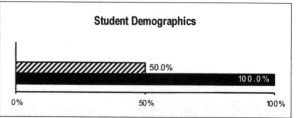

INDIANA UNIVERSITY - EAST

2325 Chester Boulevard
Richmond, IN 47374
(765) 973-8242
Karen Clark, EdD, RN

www.iue.edu/departments/nursing

Acceptance rate		31.3%
Faculty-student ratio		1: 11
Faculty	Full time	15
	Part time	0

Tuition	
In state	$4,475
Out of state	$11,153
Enrollments	40
Graduations	22

Student Demographics	
Female	92.5%
Under age 25	22.5%
Part-time	0.0%

Accreditation
Indiana State Board of Nursing, National League
for Nursing Accrediting Commission (NLNAC)

Degrees conferred
Associate Degree

Minimum degree required
High school diploma or GED

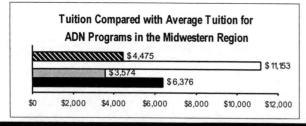

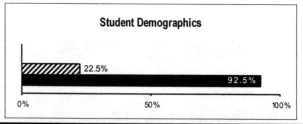

INDIANA UNIVERSITY - KOKOMO

PO Box 9003
Kokomo, IN 46904
(765) 455-9288
Penny Cass, PhD, RN

www.iuk.edu/~konurse

Acceptance rate		41.2%
Faculty-student ratio		1: 14
Faculty	Full time	15
	Part time	25

Tuition[1]	
In state	$131
Out of state	$353
Enrollments	213
Graduations	116

Student Demographics	
Female	93.9%
Under age 25	30.5%
Minority	8.0%
Part-time	68.1%

Accreditation
Indiana State Board of Nursing, National League
for Nursing Accrediting Commission (NLNAC)

Degrees conferred
Associate Degree

Minimum degree required
11 credits of general education courses

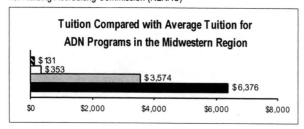

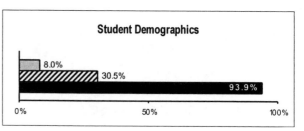

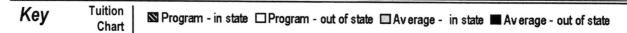

Key | Tuition Chart | ⬛ Program - in state ☐ Program - out of state ▨ Average - in state ■ Average - out of state

Indiana

INDIANA UNIVERSITY - NORTHWEST
Useful Facts

3400 Broadway
Gary, IN 46408
(219) 980-6604
Linda Rooda, PhD, RN

www.iun.edu/~nurse

Acceptance rate		20.1%
Faculty-student ratio		1: 12
Faculty	Full time	15
	Part time	9

Tuition		
In state	$3,932
Out of state	$10,599
Enrollments	70
Graduations	43

Student Demographics	
Female	88.6%
Under age 25	34.3%
Minority	27.1%
Part-time	0.0%

Accreditation
Indiana State Board of Nursing, National League for Nursing Accrediting Commission (NLNAC)

Degrees conferred
Associate Degree

Minimum degree required
High school diploma or GED

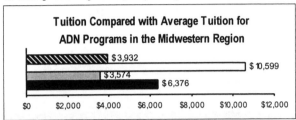

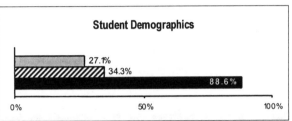

INDIANA UNIVERSITY - PURDUE UNIVERSITY - FORT WAYNE
Useful Facts*

2101 East Coliseum Blvd
Fort Wayne, IN 46805
(260) 481-5798
Carol Sternberger, PhD, RNC

www.ipfw.edu/nursing

Acceptance rate		76.2%
Faculty-student ratio		1: 9
Faculty	Full time	17
	Part time	25

Tuition		
In state	$5,025
Out of state	$12,380
Enrollments	278
Graduations	135

Student Demographics	
Female	89.6%
Under age 25	38.5%
Minority	6.0%
Part-time	58.3%

Accreditation
Indiana State Board of Nursing, National League for Nursing Accrediting Commission (NLNAC)

Degrees conferred
AS

Minimum degree required
18 hours of prenursing credit hours

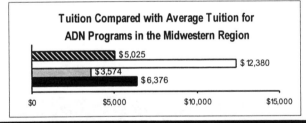

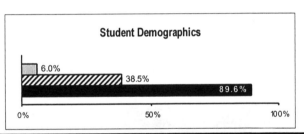

INDIANA UNIVERSITY - PURDUE UNIVERSITY - INDIANAPOLIS
Useful Facts

1111 Middle Drive
Indianapolis, IN 46202
(317) 274-1486
Marion Broome, PhD, RN, FAAN

nursing.iupui.edu

Acceptance rate		90.9%
Faculty-student ratio		1: 6
Faculty	Full time	99
	Part time	95

Tuition[1]		
In state	$158
Out of state	$205
Enrollments	60
Graduations	76

Student Demographics	
Female	96.7%
Under age 25	6.7%
Minority	5.0%
Part-time	58.3%

Accreditation
Indiana State Board of Nursing, National League for Nursing Accrediting Commission (NLNAC)

Degrees conferred
ASN

Minimum degree required
High school diploma or GED

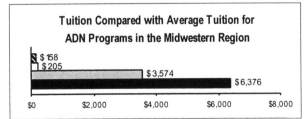

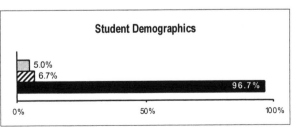

| Demographics Chart | ■ Female ▨ Under age 25 ▢ Minority | Distance Learning | [1]The tuition reported for this program may be not be annualized.
*Data reported between 2001 and 2004. |

Indiana

IVY TECH STATE COLLEGE - BLOOMINGTON
Useful Facts*

200 Daniels Way
Bloomington, IN 47403
(317) 917-5903
Jan Kramer, MSN

www.ivytech.edu

Accreditation
Indiana State Board of Nursing

Acceptance rate	41.5%

Tuition
In state	$1,771
Out of state	$3,570
Enrollments	76
Graduations	39

Student Demographics
Female	89.5%
Under age 25	32.0%
Minority	2.6%

Degrees conferred
Associate Degree

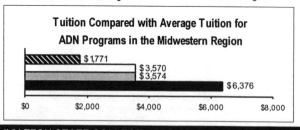
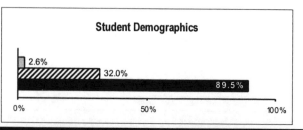

IVY TECH STATE COLLEGE - REGION 1 (MADISON)
Useful Facts*

590 Ivy Tech Drive
Madison, IN 47250
(812) 273-0105
Gene Shapinsky, MSN

www.ivytech.edu

Accreditation
Indiana State Board of Nursing

Acceptance rate	80.0%

Tuition
In state	$2,016
Out of state	$4,032
Enrollments	32
Graduations	28

Student Demographics
Female	90.6%
Under age 25	0.0%
Part-time	0.0%

Degrees conferred
Associate Degree

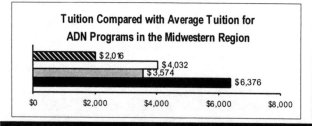
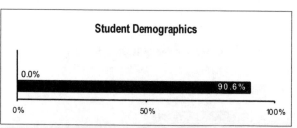

IVY TECH STATE COLLEGE - REGION 12 (EVANSVILLE)
Useful Facts*

3501 First Avenue
Evansville, IN 47710
(812) 429-1496
Judith McCutchan, RN, MSN, ASN

www.ivytech.edu

Accreditation
Indiana State Board of Nursing

Acceptance rate	26.7%

Tuition
In state	$2,618
Out of state	$5,100
Enrollments	81
Graduations	33

Student Demographics
Female	90.1%
Under age 25	27.0%
Minority	2.5%
Part-time	0.0%

Degrees conferred
Associate Degree

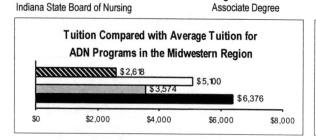
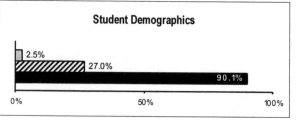

Key | Tuition Chart | ▨ Program - in state ☐ Program - out of state ▨ Average - in state ■ Average - out of state

Indiana

IVY TECH STATE COLLEGE - REGION 13 (SELLERSBURG) — *Useful Facts**

8204 Highway 311
Sellersburg, IN 47172
(812) 246-3301
Susan Jewell, MSEd, RN, BSN

www.ivytech.edu

Acceptance rate	20.0%

Tuition
In state $2,509
Out of state $5,058
Enrollments 100
Graduations 52

Student Demographics
Female 88.0%
Under age 25 37.0%
Minority 3.0%
Part-time 42.0%

Accreditation
Indiana State Board of Nursing

Degrees conferred
Associate Degree

Tuition Compared with Average Tuition for ADN Programs in the Midwestern Region

$2,509
$5,058
$3,574
$6,376

$0 $2,000 $4,000 $6,000 $8,000

Student Demographics

3.0%
37.0%
88.0%

0% 50% 100%

IVY TECH STATE COLLEGE - REGION 4 (LAFAYETTE) — *Useful Facts**

3101 S Creasy Lane, PO Box 6299
Lafayette, IN 47903
(765) 772-9237
Karen Dolk, RN, MSN

www.ivytech.edu

Acceptance rate	28.3%

Tuition
In state $2,952
Out of state $5,950
Enrollments 73
Graduations 31

Student Demographics
Female 89.0%
Under age 25 33.0%
Minority 2.8%
Part-time 0.0%

Accreditation
Indiana State Board of Nursing

Degrees conferred
Associate Degree

Tuition Compared with Average Tuition for ADN Programs in the Midwestern Region

$2,952
$5,950
$3,574
$6,376

$0 $2,000 $4,000 $6,000 $8,000

Student Demographics

2.8%
33.0%
89.0%

0% 50% 100%

IVY TECH STATE COLLEGE - REGION 6 (MUNCIE)

4301 S Cowan Road
Muncie, IN 47302
(765) 289-2291
Mary Hiday, RN, BSN, MA

www.ivytech.edu

Accreditation
Indiana State Board of Nursing

Degrees conferred
Associate Degree

Demographics Chart	■ Female ▨ Under age 25 ▢ Minority	Distance Learning	¹The tuition reported for this program may be not be annualized. *Data reported between 2001 and 2004.

Indiana

IVY TECH STATE COLLEGE - REGION 8 (INDIANAPOLIS)

One West 26th Street
Indianapolis, IN 46208
(317) 927-7176
Janet Kramer, RN, MSN

www.ivy.tec.in.us/indianapolis/pdf/asn.pdf

Accreditation
Indiana State Board of Nursing, National League
for Nursing Accrediting Commission (NLNAC)

Acceptance rate	31.0%

Degrees conferred
Associate Degree

Tuition
In state	$1,932
Out of state	$3,862
Enrollments	135
Graduations	51

Student Demographics
Female	95.6%
Under age 25	9.0%
Minority	8.1%
Part-time	0.0%

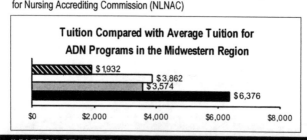

Tuition Compared with Average Tuition for ADN Programs in the Midwestern Region

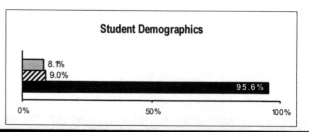

Student Demographics

IVY TECH STATE COLLEGE - REGION 9 (RICHMOND)

2325 Chester Blvd
Richmond, IN 47374
(765) 966-2656
Jillene Anderson, RN, MSN

www.ivytech.edu

Accreditation
Indiana State Board of Nursing

Acceptance rate		50.0%
Faculty-student ratio		1: 11
Faculty	Full time	4
	Part time	3

Degrees conferred
Associate Degree

Tuition
In state	$3,000
Out of state	$5,800
Enrollments	58
Graduations	27

Minimum degree required
High school diploma or GED

Student Demographics
Female	93.1%
Under age 25	8.6%
Minority	1.7%
Part-time	0.0%

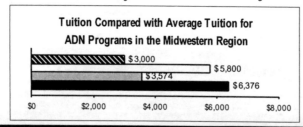

Tuition Compared with Average Tuition for ADN Programs in the Midwestern Region

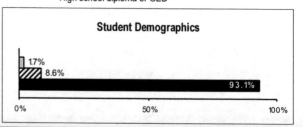

Student Demographics

MARIAN COLLEGE

3200 Cold Spring Rd
Indianapolis, IN 46222
(317) 955-6155
Marian Pettengill, PhD, RN

www.marian.edu

Accreditation
Indiana State Board of Nursing

At the request of this nursing school, publication has been witheld.
Please contact the school directly for more information.

Key	Tuition Chart	▨ Program - in state ☐ Program - out of state ▥ Average - in state ■ Average - out of state

Indiana

PURDUE UNIVERSITY - CALUMET CAMPUS | Useful Facts

2200 169th
Hammond, IN 46323
(219) 989-2818
Peggy Gerard, DNSc, RN

nursing.calumet.purdue.edu

Accreditation
Indiana State Board of Nursing, National League
for Nursing Accrediting Commission (NLNAC)

Acceptance rate	20.3%	
Faculty-student ratio	1: 10	
Faculty	Full time	25
	Part time	10

Tuition
In state	$5,825
Out of state	$12,545
Enrollments	134
Graduations	94

Student Demographics
Female	87.3%
Under age 25	26.1%
Minority	36.2%
Part-time	36.6%

Degrees conferred
Associate Degree

Minimum degree required
High school diploma or GED

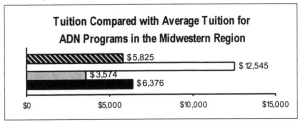

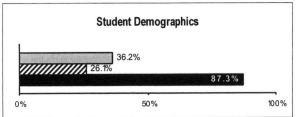

PURDUE UNIVERSITY - NORTH CENTRAL | Useful Facts*

1401 S US 421
Westville, IN 46391
(219) 785-5324
Elizabeth Hayes, MS, RN

www.pnc.edu

Accreditation
Indiana State Board of Nursing, National League
for Nursing Accrediting Commission (NLNAC)

Acceptance rate	47.3%

Tuition
In state	$4,518
Out of state	$11,140
Enrollments	183
Graduations	60

Student Demographics
Female	92.9%
Under age 25	56.0%
Minority	9.5%
Part-time	66.7%

Degrees conferred
Associate Degree

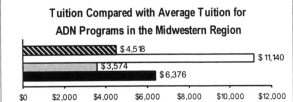

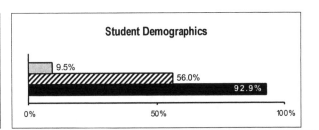

UNIVERSITY OF INDIANAPOLIS | Useful Facts

1400 E Hanna Avenue
Indianapolis, IN 46220
(317) 788-3206
Sharon Isaac, EdD, RN, MSN, BSN

www.uindy.edu

Accreditation
Indiana State Board of Nursing

Acceptance rate	60.6%	
Faculty-student ratio	1: 9	
Faculty	Full time	22
	Part time	28

Tuition
In state	$17,980
Out of state	$17,980
Enrollments	100
Graduations	40

Student Demographics
Female	94.0%
Under age 25	18.0%
Minority	11.1%
Part-time	88.0%

Degrees conferred
Associate Degree

Minimum degree required
High school diploma or GED

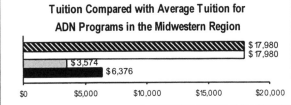

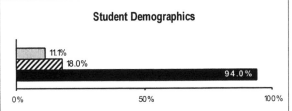

Demographics Chart	■Female ☒Under age 25 ☐Minority	Distance Learning 🖥️	¹The tuition reported for this program may be not be annualized. *Data reported between 2001 and 2004.

Indiana

UNIVERSITY OF SAINT FRANCIS (INDIANA)

Useful Facts

2701 Spring Street
Fort Wayne, IN 46808
(260) 434-7644
Lorene Arnold, WHNP, MSN, RNC

www.sf.edu

Accreditation
Indiana State Board of Nursing, National League
for Nursing Accrediting Commission (NLNAC)

Acceptance rate		95.4%
Faculty-student ratio		1: 14
Faculty	Full time	28
	Part time	32

Degrees conferred
ASN

Tuition	
In state	$16,750
Out of state	$16,750
Enrollments	330
Graduations	68

Minimum degree required
High school diploma or GED

Student Demographics	
Female	94.2%
Under age 25	39.7%
Minority	8.2%
Part-time	58.2%

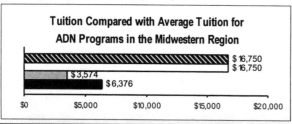

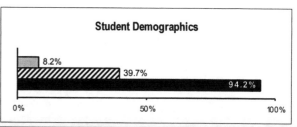

VINCENNES UNIVERSITY

Useful Facts

1002 North First Street
Vincennes, IN 47591
(812) 888-5372
Jana Vieck, MSN, RN

www.vinu.edu

Accreditation
Indiana State Board of Nursing, National League
for Nursing Accrediting Commission (NLNAC)

Acceptance rate		43.7%
Faculty-student ratio		1: 13
Faculty	Full time	19
	Part time	0

Degrees conferred
Associate Degree

Tuition	
In state	$3,380
Out of state	$8,200
Enrollments	245
Graduations	72

Minimum degree required
High school diploma or GED

Student Demographics	
Female	95.1%
Under age 25	58.0%
Minority	0.8%
Part-time	35.9%

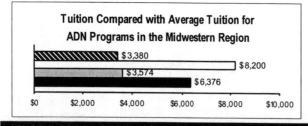

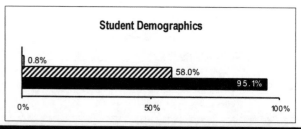

VINCENNES UNIVERSITY - JASPER CAMPUS

850 College Blvd
Jasper, IN 47546
(812) 481-5951
Judy Dahl, RN, MSN

vinu.edu

Accreditation
Indiana State Board of Nursing

Degrees conferred
Associate Degree

| **Key** | Tuition Chart | ▨ Program - in state ☐ Program - out of state ☐ Average - in state ■ Average - out of state |

Iowa

DES MOINES AREA COMMUNITY COLLEGE - Boone

2006 South Ankeny
Ankeny, IA 50023
(515) 964-6466
Virginia (Ginny) Wangerin, RN, MSN, PhD(c)

www.dmacc.edu/programs/nursing

Accreditation
Iowa Board of Nursing, National League for
Nursing Accrediting Commission (NLNAC)

Acceptance rate		7.8%
Faculty-student ratio		1: 11
Faculty	Full time	25
	Part time	17

Degrees conferred
Associate Degree

Tuition	
In state	$2,850
Out of state	$5,700
Enrollments	178
Graduations	117

Minimum degree required
High school diploma or GED

Student Demographics	
Female	96.1%
Under age 25	41.0%
Minority	13.1%
Part-time	12.9%

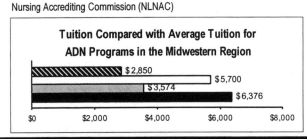

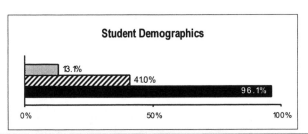

DES MOINES AREA COMMUNITY COLLEGE - Ankeny

2006 South Ankeny
Ankeny, IA 50023
(515) 964-6466
Virginia (Ginny) Wangerin, RN, MSN, PhD(c)

www.dmacc.edu/programs/nursing

Accreditation
Iowa Board of Nursing, National League for
Nursing Accrediting Commission (NLNAC)

Acceptance rate		7.8%
Faculty-student ratio		1: 11
Faculty	Full time	25
	Part time	17

Degrees conferred
Associate Degree

Tuition	
In state	$2,850
Out of state	$5,800
Enrollments	178
Graduations	117

Minimum degree required
High school diploma or GED

Student Demographics	
Female	96.1%
Under age 25	41.0%
Minority	13.1%
Part-time	12.9%

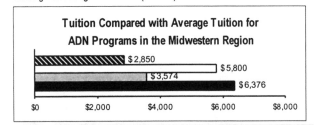

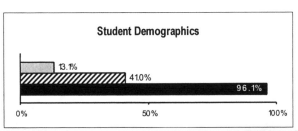

EASTERN IOWA COMMUNITY COLLEGE - CLINTON COMMUNITY COLLEGE - Clinton CC

500 Belmont Road
Bettendorf, IA 52722
(563) 441-4256
Ruth Sueverkruber, RN, MS

www.eicc.edu

Accreditation
Iowa Board of Nursing

| Acceptance rate | 26.1% |

Degrees conferred
Associate Degree

Tuition¹	
In state	$75
Out of state	$113
Enrollments	260
Graduations	65

Student Demographics	
Female	94.6%
Under age 25	9.0%
Minority	8.5%
Part-time	0.0%

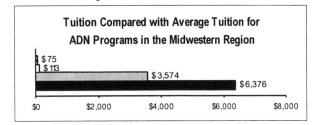

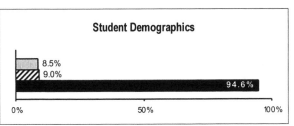

| Demographics Chart | ■Female ⊠Under age 25 ☐Minority | Distance Learning | ¹The tuition reported for this program may be not be annualized.
*Data reported between 2001 and 2004. |

Iowa

HAWKEYE COMMUNITY COLLEGE

Useful Facts*

1501 East Orange Rd
Waterloo, IA 50701
(319) 296-2320
Brenda Hempen, RN

www.hawkeye.cc.ia.us

		Student Demographics	
		Female	95.7%
Enrollments	69		
Graduations	69	Part-time	13.0%

Accreditation	**Degrees conferred**
Iowa Board of Nursing	Associate Degree

INDIAN HILLS COMMUNITY COLLEGE - Ottumwa

525 Grandview
Ottuma, IA 52501
(515) 683-5165
Ann Aulwes, RN

www.ihcc.cc.ia.us

Accreditation	**Degrees conferred**
Iowa Board of Nursing	Associate Degree

IOWA CENTRAL COMMUNITY COLLEGE - Fort Dodge

330 Ave M
Fort Dodge, IA 50501
(515) 576-7201
Connie Boyd, RN, MSN

www.iowacentral.com

				Tuition		**Student Demographics**	
Acceptance rate		43.6%		In state	$2,790	Female	96.6%
Faculty-student ratio		1: 14		Out of state	$4,185	Under age 25	56.2%
Faculty	Full time	11				Minority	2.3%
	Part time	15		**Enrollments**	267		
				Graduations	97	Part-time	23.2%

Accreditation	**Degrees conferred**	**Minimum degree required**
Iowa Board of Nursing, National League for Nursing Accrediting Commission (NLNAC)	Associate Degree	High school diploma or GED

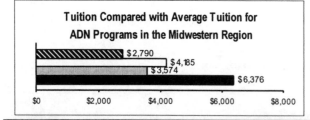

Tuition Compared with Average Tuition for ADN Programs in the Midwestern Region

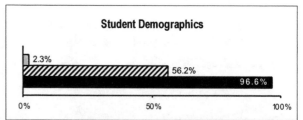

Student Demographics

IOWA LAKES COMMUNITY COLLEGE

Useful Facts*

3200 College Dr
Emmetsburg, IA 50536
(712) 852-5285
Judith Donahue, RN, MSN

iowalakes.edu

		Tuition[1]		**Student Demographics**	
Acceptance rate	100.0%	In state	$82	Female	96.9%
		Out of state	$84	Under age 25	42.0%
		Enrollments	32	Minority	6.3%
		Graduations	27		

Accreditation	**Degrees conferred**
Iowa Board of Nursing	Associate Degree

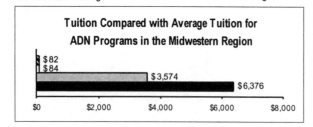

Tuition Compared with Average Tuition for ADN Programs in the Midwestern Region

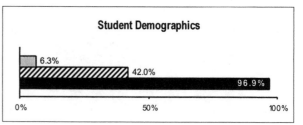

Student Demographics

Key | Tuition Chart | ▨ Program - in state ☐ Program - out of state ▨ Average - in state ■ Average - out of state

Iowa

IOWA VALLEY COMMUNITY COLLEGE - ELLSWORTH COMMUNITY COLLEGE - Iowa Valley Community College District - Marshalltown

3700 South Center Street
Marshalltown, IA 50158
(641) 752-7106
Kathy Deibert, MSN

www.iowavalleycommunitycollege.com

Acceptance rate	76.5%

Tuition[1]	
In state	$81
Out of state	$81
Enrollments	36
Graduations	35

Student Demographics	
Female	94.4%
Minority	2.8%

Accreditation
Iowa Board of Nursing

Degrees conferred
Associate Degree

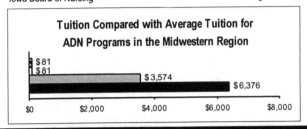

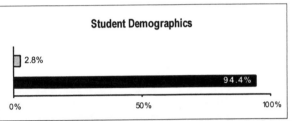

KIRKWOOD COMMUNITY COLLEGE — *Useful Facts**

6301 Kirkwood Blvd
SW Cedar Rapids, IA 52406
(319) 398-5566
Linda Kalb, RN, MSN

kirkwoodcollege.com

Acceptance rate	19.2%

Tuition	
In state	$1,560
Out of state	$3,120
Enrollments	156
Graduations	64

Student Demographics	
Female	82.7%
Under age 25	25.0%
Minority	7.1%
Part-time	0.0%

Accreditation
Iowa Board of Nursing

Degrees conferred
Associate Degree

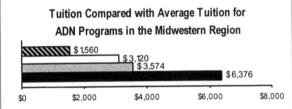

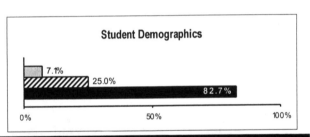

MERCY COLLEGE OF HEALTH SCIENCES — *Useful Facts*

928 6th Ave
Des Moines, IA 50309
(515) 643-6615
Shirley Beaver, RN, MN, CNAA

www.mchs.edu

Acceptance rate	35.1%
Faculty-student ratio	1: 19

Faculty	
Full time	16
Part time	4

Tuition	
In state	$11,700
Out of state	$11,700
Enrollments	347
Graduations	153

Student Demographics	
Female	93.1%
Under age 25	16.1%
Minority	4.1%
Part-time	23.3%

Accreditation
Iowa Board of Nursing, National League for
Nursing Accrediting Commission (NLNAC)

Degrees conferred
Associate Degree

Minimum degree required
High school diploma or GED

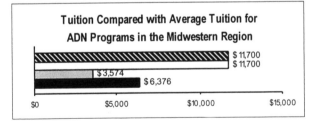

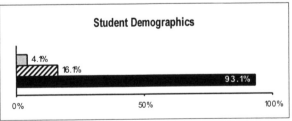

Demographics Chart	■ Female ▨ Under age 25 ▢ Minority	Distance Learning		[1]The tuition reported for this program may be not be annualized. *Data reported between 2001 and 2004.

Iowa

NORTH IOWA AREA COMMUNITY COLLEGE

Useful Facts*

500 College Dr
Mason City, IA 50401
(641) 422-4216
Donna Orton, MSN, RN

niacc.edu

Acceptance rate		14.0%
Faculty-student ratio		1: 14
Faculty	Full time	6
	Part time	7

Tuition[1]	
In state	$83
Out of state	$125
Enrollments	133
Graduations	34

Student Demographics	
Female	93.2%
Under age 25	62.0%
Minority	4.5%
Part-time	36.8%

Accreditation
Iowa Board of Nursing, National League for
Nursing Accrediting Commission (NLNAC)

Degrees conferred
Associate Degree

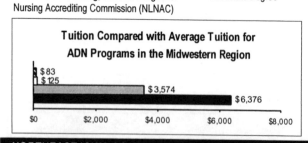
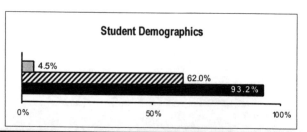

NORTHEAST IOWA COMMUNITY COLLEGE

Useful Facts*

10250 Sundown Rd
Peosta, IA 52068
(563) 556-5110
Nancy Glab, MSN

www.nicc.edu

Acceptance rate	100.0%

Enrollments	18
Graduations	28

Student Demographics	
Female	72.2%
Minority	11.1%
Part-time	0.0%

Accreditation
Iowa Board of Nursing

Degrees conferred
Associate Degree

NORTHEAST IOWA COMMUNITY COLLEGE - CALMAR

Useful Facts*

Hwy 150 South
Calmar, IA 52162
(800) 728-2256
Cindy O'Bryon, RN, MSN

www.nicc.edu

Acceptance rate	36.0%

Tuition[1]	
In state	$86
Out of state	$86
Enrollments	262
Graduations	50

Student Demographics	
Female	91.6%
Part-time	45.8%

Accreditation
Iowa Board of Nursing

Degrees conferred
Associate Degree

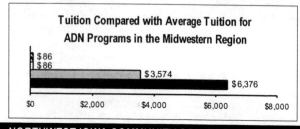
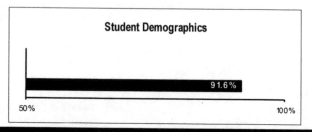

NORTHWEST IOWA COMMUNITY COLLEGE

603 W Park
Sheldon, IA 51201
(712) 324-5061
Mary Mohni, RN, MPH

www.nwicc.ia.edu

Accreditation
Iowa Board of Nursing

Degrees conferred
Associate Degree

Key | Tuition Chart | ▨ Program - in state ☐ Program - out of state ▦ Average - in state ■ Average - out of state

Iowa

SOUTHEASTERN COMMUNITY COLLEGE

1500 West Agency Road
West Burlington, ID 52655-0180
(910) 642-7142
Pamela Bradley, MS, RN

www.secc.cc.ia.us

Accreditation
Iowa Board of Nursing

Degrees conferred
Associate Degree

SOUTHEASTERN COMMUNITY COLLEGE - Keokuk

1500 West Agency Road
West Burlington, ID 52655-0180
(910) 642-7142
Pamela Bradley, MS, RN

www.secc.cc.ia.us

Accreditation
Iowa Board of Nursing

Degrees conferred
Associate Degree

SOUTHWESTERN COMMUNITY COLLEGE - Creston

1501 W Townline St
Creston, IA 50801
(641) 782-3312
Loretta Eckels, RN, BS, MS

At the request of this nursing school, publication has been witheld.
Please contact the school directly for more information.

www.swcc.cc.ia.us

Accreditation
Iowa Board of Nursing

ST LUKE'S COLLEGE - IOWA HEALTH SYSTEM   *Useful Facts**

2720 Stone Park Blvd
Sioux City, IA 51104
(712) 279-7969
JoAnn Breyfogle, RN, MS

www.stlukes.org/college

Accreditation
Iowa Board of Nursing, National League for
Nursing Accrediting Commission (NLNAC)

Degrees conferred
Associate Degree

			Student Demographics	
Acceptance rate	62.4%	**Tuition**		
		In state	$9,800	Female	92.3%
		Out of state	$9,800	Under age 25	73.0%
		Enrollments	91	Minority	3.3%
		Graduations	36	Part-time	35.2%

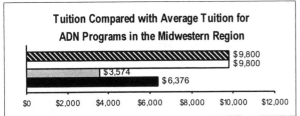

Tuition Compared with Average Tuition for ADN Programs in the Midwestern Region
$9,800
$9,800
$3,574
$6,376

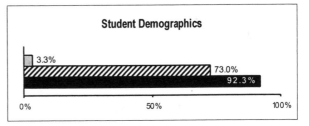

Student Demographics
3.3%
73.0%
92.3%

Demographics Chart	■ Female ▨ Under age 25 ☐ Minority	Distance Learning	†The tuition reported for this program may be not be annualized. *Data reported between 2001 and 2004.

Iowa

WESTERN IOWA TECH
Useful Facts

4647 Stone Ave, PO Box 5199
Sioux City, IA 51102
(712) 274-8733
Gloria Stewart, RN, MSN, EdD

www.witcc.edu

Acceptance rate		33.1%
Faculty-student ratio		1: 4
Faculty	Full time	11
	Part time	16

Tuition	
In state	$3,441
Out of state	$4,921
Enrollments	85
Graduations	71

Student Demographics	
Female	95.3%
Under age 25	28.2%
Minority	4.7%
Part-time	0.0%

Accreditation
Iowa Board of Nursing, National League for
Nursing Accrediting Commission (NLNAC)

Degrees conferred
Associate Degree

Minimum degree required
LPN or completion our practical nursing program

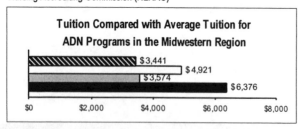

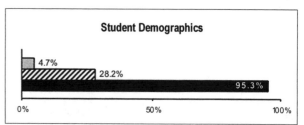

Kansas

BAKER UNIVERSITY
*Useful Facts**

1500 South West Tenth Street
Topeka, KS 66604
(785) 354-5853
Kathleen Harr, DNSc, RN

www.bakeru.edu

Enrollments	0
Graduations	0

Accreditation
Kansas State Board of Nursing

Degrees conferred
Associate Degree

BARTON COUNTY COMMUNITY COLLEGE
*Useful Facts**

245 NE 30th Road
Great Bend, KS 67530
(620) 792-9355
Cheryl Berg, MSN, RN

www.bartonccc.edu/nursing

Acceptance rate	60.3%

Tuition	
In state	$1,598
Out of state	$2,414
Enrollments	80
Graduations	21

Student Demographics	
Female	88.8%
Under age 25	42.0%
Minority	10.0%
Part-time	0.0%

Accreditation
Kansas State Board of Nursing, National League
for Nursing Accrediting Commission (NLNAC)

Degrees conferred
Associate Degree

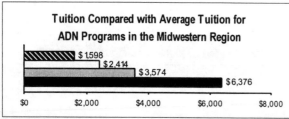

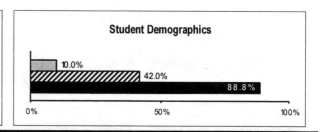

BETHEL COLLEGE (KANSAS)

300 East 27th Street
North Newton, KS 67117
(316) 284-5377
Gregg Schroeder, MSN, ARNP

www.bethelks.edu

Accreditation
Kansas State Board of Nursing

Degrees conferred
Associate Degree

Kansas

BUTLER COUNTY COMMUNITY COLLEGE - EL DORADO
Useful Facts*

901 S Haverhill Rd
El Dorado, KS 67042
(316) 322-3146
Patricia Hutchinson, RN, BSN, MS, Ed

www.butlercc.edu/nursing

Accreditation
Kansas State Board of Nursing, National League
for Nursing Accrediting Commission (NLNAC)

Acceptance rate	15.6%

Degrees conferred
Associate Degree

Tuition	
In state	$1,575
Out of state	$2,845
Enrollments	182
Graduations	92

Student Demographics	
Female	87.4%
Under age 25	36.0%
Minority	15.1%
Part-time	0.0%

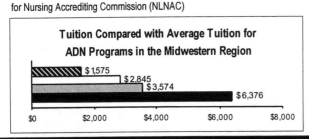

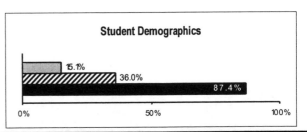

CLOUD COUNTY COMMUNITY COLLEGE
Useful Facts

PO Box 507
Beloit, KS 67420
(785) 738-9025
Vera Streit, MN, RN

cloud.edu

Accreditation
Kansas State Board of Nursing, National League
for Nursing Accrediting Commission (NLNAC)

Acceptance rate		53.3%
Faculty-student ratio		1: 9
Faculty	Full time	3
	Part time	1

Degrees conferred
Associate Degree

Tuition	
In state	$792
Out of state	$792
Enrollments	32
Graduations	31

Minimum degree required
practical nursing

Student Demographics	
Female	93.8%
Under age 25	15.6%
Minority	3.1%
Part-time	0.0%

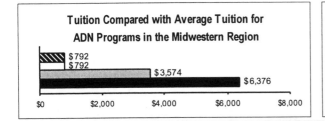

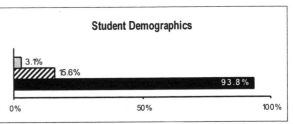

COLBY COMMUNITY COLLEGE
Useful Facts

1255 South Range
Colby, KS 67701
(785) 462-3984
Kerri Schippers, MSN, ARNP

www.colby.cc.edu/nursing

Accreditation
Kansas State Board of Nursing, National League
for Nursing Accrediting Commission (NLNAC)

Acceptance rate		93.8%
Faculty-student ratio		1: 4
Faculty	Full time	7
	Part time	1

Degrees conferred
Associate Degree

Tuition[1]	
In state	$43
Out of state	$83
Enrollments	29
Graduations	29

Minimum degree required
PN program completion certificate

Student Demographics	
Female	96.6%
Under age 25	34.5%
Minority	10.3%
Part-time	37.9%

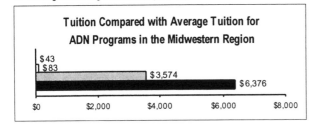

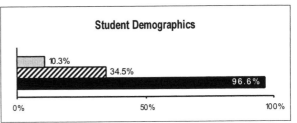

Demographics Chart	■Female ▨Under age 25 ▢Minority	**Distance Learning**		[1]The tuition reported for this program may be not be annualized. *Data reported between 2001 and 2004.

Kansas

DODGE CITY COMMUNITY COLLEGE — *Useful Facts*

2501 North 14th Avenue
Dodge City, KS 67801
(620) 227-9240
Rebecca Bredfeldt, RN, MS

www.dccc.cc.ks.us

Acceptance rate		78.9%	Tuition			Student Demographics	
Faculty-student ratio		1: 3	In state		$875	Female	92.6%
Faculty	Full time	7	Out of state		$875	Under age 25	40.7%
	Part time	2	Enrollments		27	Minority	7.4%
			Graduations		25	Part-time	55.6%

Accreditation
Kansas State Board of Nursing, National League for Nursing Accrediting Commission (NLNAC)

Degrees conferred
Associate Degree

Minimum degree required
High school diploma or GED

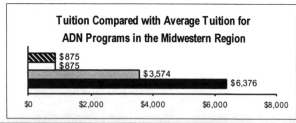

Tuition Compared with Average Tuition for ADN Programs in the Midwestern Region

- $875
- $875
- $3,574
- $6,376

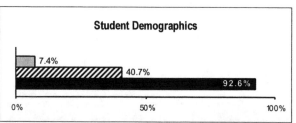

Student Demographics

- 7.4%
- 40.7%
- 92.6%

FORT SCOTT COMMUNITY COLLEGE

2108 South Horton
Fort Scott, KS 66701
(620) 768-2909
Elizabeth Meyer, BSN, MSN

www.fortscott.edu

Accreditation
Kansas State Board of Nursing, National League for Nursing Accrediting Commission (NLNAC)

At the request of this nursing school, publication has been witheld. Please contact the school directly for more information.

GARDEN CITY COMMUNITY COLLEGE

801 Campus Dr
Garden City, KS 67846
(620) 276-9562
Lenora Cook, RN, MSN

www.gcccks.edu

Accreditation
Kansas State Board of Nursing, National League for Nursing Accrediting Commission (NLNAC)

At the request of this nursing school, publication has been witheld. Please contact the school directly for more information.

HESSTON COLLEGE — *Useful Facts*

PO Box 3000
Hesston, KS 67062
(620) 327-8140
Bonnie Sowers, MS, RN

www.hesston.edu

Acceptance rate		62.9%	Tuition			Student Demographics	
Faculty-student ratio		1: 12	In state		$15,150	Female	92.4%
Faculty	Full time	7	Out of state		$15,150	Under age 25	50.0%
	Part time	2	Enrollments		92	Minority	5.4%
			Graduations		46	Part-time	38.0%

Accreditation
Kansas State Board of Nursing, National League for Nursing Accrediting Commission (NLNAC)

Degrees conferred
Associate Degree

Minimum degree required
High school diploma or GED

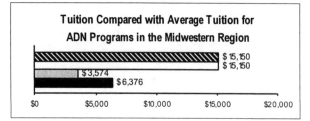

Tuition Compared with Average Tuition for ADN Programs in the Midwestern Region

- $15,150
- $15,150
- $3,574
- $6,376

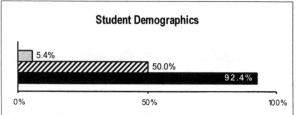

Student Demographics

- 5.4%
- 50.0%
- 92.4%

Key | Tuition Chart | ▨ Program - in state ☐ Program - out of state ☐ Average - in state ■ Average - out of state

Kansas

HUTCHINSON COMMUNITY COLLEGE

815 N Walnut-Davis Hall
Hutchinson, KS 67501
(620) 665-4930
Debra Hackler, RN, MSN

www.hutchcc.edu

Accreditation
Kansas State Board of Nursing, National League
for Nursing Accrediting Commission (NLNAC)

*At the request of this nursing school, publication has been witheld.
Please contact the school directly for more information.*

JOHNSON COUNTY COMMUNITY COLLEGE - OVERLAND PARK   *Useful Facts*

12345 College Blvd
Overland Park, KS 66210
(913) 469-8500
Jeanne Walsh, RN, MSN

www.johnco.cc.ks.us/acad/nurs

Accreditation
Kansas State Board of Nursing, National League
for Nursing Accrediting Commission (NLNAC)

Acceptance rate		32.9%
Faculty-student ratio		1:7
Faculty	Full time	12
	Part time	8

Degrees conferred
Associate Degree

Tuition[1]	
In state	$64
Out of state	$142
Enrollments	118
Graduations	68

Minimum degree required
High school diploma or GED

Student Demographics	
Female	92.4%
Under age 25	15.3%
Minority	6.8%
Part-time	29.7%

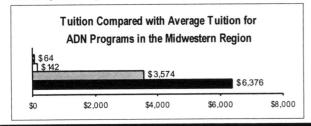

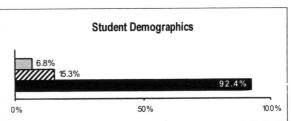

KANSAS CITY KANSAS COMMUNITY COLLEGE   *Useful Facts**

7250 State Ave
Kansas City, KS 66112
(913) 288-7126
Shirley Wendel, PhD

www.kckcc.cc.ks.us

Accreditation
Kansas State Board of Nursing, National League
for Nursing Accrediting Commission (NLNAC)

| Acceptance rate | 51.2% |

Degrees conferred
Associate Degree

Tuition	
In state	$1,080
Out of state	$2,760
Enrollments	153
Graduations	76

Student Demographics	
Female	92.8%
Under age 25	33.0%
Minority	30.7%

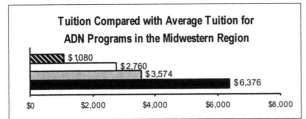

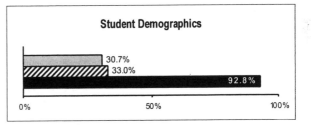

| **Demographics Chart** | ■ Female ▨ Under age 25 ▢ Minority | **Distance Learning** | | [1]The tuition reported for this program may be not be annualized.
*Data reported between 2001 and 2004. |

Kansas

KANSAS WESLEYAN UNIVERSITY

100 East Claflin Avenue
Salina, KS 67401
(785) 827-5541
Patricia Brown, RN, PhD

www.kwu.edu

Acceptance rate		100.0%
Faculty-student ratio		1: 9
Faculty	Full time	5
	Part time	4

Tuition	
In state	$15,800
Out of state	$15,800
Enrollments	39
Graduations	27

Student Demographics	
Female	94.9%
Under age 25	43.6%
Minority	10.5%
Part-time	23.1%

Accreditation
Kansas State Board of Nursing, National League
for Nursing Accrediting Commission (NLNAC)

Degrees conferred
Associate Degree

Minimum degree required
High school diploma or GED

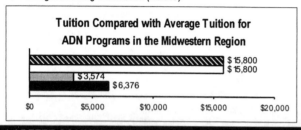

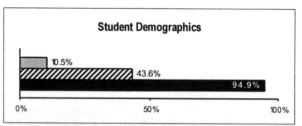

LABETTE COMMUNITY COLLEGE

200 S 14th
Parsons, KS 67357
(620) 820-1263
Patricia Thompson, RN, MSN

www.labette.edu/dept/nursing/nursing.htm

Acceptance rate		50.6%
Faculty-student ratio		1: 11
Faculty	Full time	6
	Part time	10

Tuition	
In state	$615
Out of state	$1,425
Enrollments	125
Graduations	33

Student Demographics	
Female	84.8%
Under age 25	21.6%
Minority	8.0%
Part-time	68.8%

Accreditation
Kansas State Board of Nursing, National League
for Nursing Accrediting Commission (NLNAC)

Degrees conferred
Associate Degree

Minimum degree required
High school diploma or GED

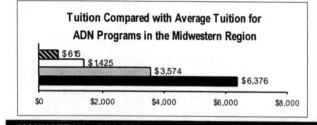

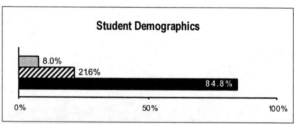

MANHATTAN AREA TECHNICAL COLLEGE

3136 Dickens Avenue
Manhattan, KS 66503
(785) 587-2800
Rebecca Claus, MSN, RN

matc.net

Acceptance rate		39.0%
Faculty-student ratio		1: 4
Faculty	Full time	6
	Part time	4

Tuition	
In state	$2,000
Out of state	$2,000
Enrollments	30
Graduations	27

Student Demographics	
Female	93.3%
Under age 25	36.7%
Minority	16.7%
Part-time	0.0%

Accreditation
Kansas State Board of Nursing, National League
for Nursing Accrediting Commission (NLNAC)

Degrees conferred
Associate Degree

Minimum degree required
LPN/LVN licensed in Kansas

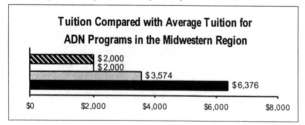

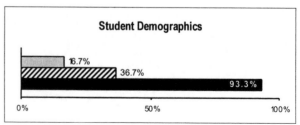

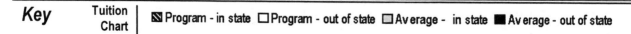

Key Tuition Chart | ▨ Program - in state ☐ Program - out of state ▥ Average - in state ■ Average - out of state

Kansas

NEOSHO COUNTY COMMUNITY COLLEGE - Ottawa

800 W 14th Street
Chanute, KS 66720
(620) 431-2820
Karen Gilpin, RN, MSN, CNAA

www.neosho.edu

Faculty-student ratio		1: 9
Faculty	Full time	11
	Part time	18

Tuition	
In state	$1,110
Out of state	$1,110
Enrollments	87
Graduations	37

Student Demographics	
Female	93.1%
Under age 25	29.9%
Minority	6.9%
Part-time	44.8%

Accreditation
Kansas State Board of Nursing, National League
for Nursing Accrediting Commission (NLNAC)

Degrees conferred
Associate Degree

Minimum degree required
High school diploma or GED

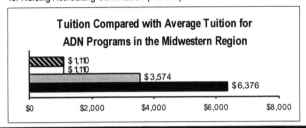

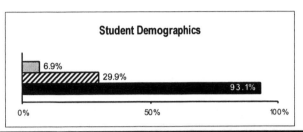

NEOSHO COUNTY COMMUNITY COLLEGE - Chanute

800 W 14th Street
Chanute, KS 66720
(620) 431-2820
Karen Gilpin, RN, MSN, CNAA

www.neosho.edu

Acceptance rate		49.5%
Faculty-student ratio		1: 9
Faculty	Full time	11
	Part time	18

Tuition	
In state	$1,110
Out of state	$1,110
Enrollments	87
Graduations	37

Student Demographics	
Female	94.3%
Under age 25	41.4%
Minority	8.0%
Part-time	51.7%

Accreditation
Kansas State Board of Nursing, National League
for Nursing Accrediting Commission (NLNAC)

Degrees conferred
Associate Degree

Minimum degree required
High school diploma or GED

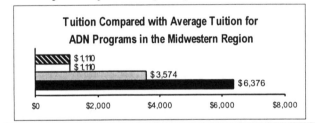

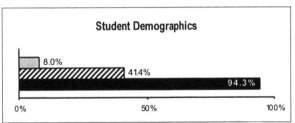

NEWMAN UNIVERSITY

3100 McCormick Ave
Wichita, KS 67213
(316) 942-4291
Anthony Chipas, PhD

www.newmanu.edu

Accreditation
Kansas State Board of Nursing

Degrees conferred
Associate Degree

Demographics Chart	■Female ▨Under age 25 ▢Minority	Distance Learning		¹The tuition reported for this program may be not be annualized.
				*Data reported between 2001 and 2004.

Kansas

NORTH CENTRAL KANSAS TECHNICAL COLLEGE
Useful Facts

2205 Wheatland
Hays, KS 67601
(785) 623-6155
Sandra Gottschalk, MSN, RN

ncktc.tec.ks.us

Acceptance rate		66.7%
Faculty-student ratio		1: 4
Faculty	Full time	5
	Part time	0

Tuition	
In state	$1,250
Enrollments	20
Graduations	17

Student Demographics	
Female	90.0%
Under age 25	35.0%
Part-time	0.0%

Accreditation
Kansas State Board of Nursing, National League for Nursing Accrediting Commission (NLNAC)

Degrees conferred
Associate Degree

Minimum degree required
High school diploma or GED

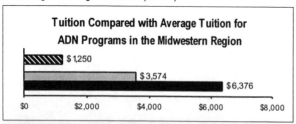

Tuition Compared with Average Tuition for ADN Programs in the Midwestern Region

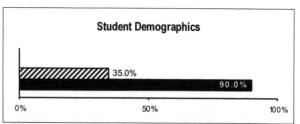

Student Demographics

PRATT COMMUNITY COLLEGE
Useful Facts

348 NE SR 61
Pratt, KS 67124
(620) 450-2232
Gail Withers, RN, MSN, ARNP-CNS

www.prattcc.edu

Acceptance rate		37.2%
Faculty-student ratio		1: 9
Faculty	Full time	8
	Part time	4

Tuition	
In state	$1,200
Out of state	$1,400
Enrollments	88
Graduations	26

Student Demographics	
Female	81.8%
Under age 25	60.2%
Minority	12.9%
Part-time	37.5%

Accreditation
Kansas State Board of Nursing, National League for Nursing Accrediting Commission (NLNAC)

Degrees conferred
Associate Degree

Minimum degree required
High school diploma or GED

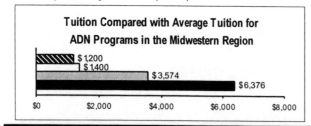

Tuition Compared with Average Tuition for ADN Programs in the Midwestern Region

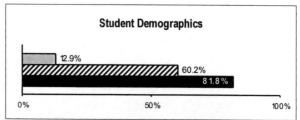

Student Demographics

SEWARD COUNTY COMMUNITY COLLEGE
Useful Facts

520 North Washington
Liberal, KS 67901
(620) 626-3026
Steve Hecox, RN, MSN

www.sccc.edu

Acceptance rate		93.9%
Faculty-student ratio		1: 3
Faculty	Full time	6
	Part time	6

Tuition	
In state	$1,280
Out of state	$2,016
Enrollments	27
Graduations	24

Student Demographics	
Female	85.2%
Under age 25	37.0%
Minority	29.6%
Part-time	37.0%

Accreditation
Kansas State Board of Nursing, National League for Nursing Accrediting Commission (NLNAC)

Degrees conferred
Associate Degree

Minimum degree required
High school diploma or GED

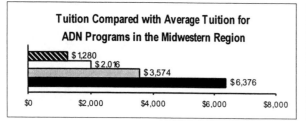

Tuition Compared with Average Tuition for ADN Programs in the Midwestern Region

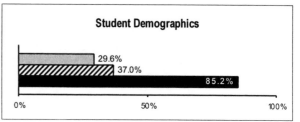

Student Demographics

Key | Tuition Chart |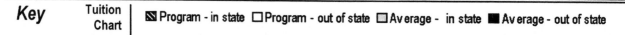

Kentucky

ASHLAND COMMUNITY COLLEGE *Useful Facts*

1400 College Drive
Ashland, KY 41101
(606) 326-2087
Janie Kitchen, RN, BSN, MSN, MHEd

www.ashland.kctcs.edu/degrees/associatenursing

Acceptance rate		31.9%
Faculty-student ratio		1: 10
Faculty	Full time	9
	Part time	9

Tuition	
In state	$2,940
Out of state	$8,820
Enrollments	132
Graduations	55

Student Demographics	
Female	85.6%
Under age 25	34.1%
Minority	1.5%
Part-time	78.8%

Accreditation
Kentucky Board of Nursing, National League for Nursing Accrediting Commission (NLNAC)

Degrees conferred
Associate Degree

Minimum degree required
High school diploma or GED

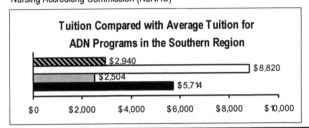

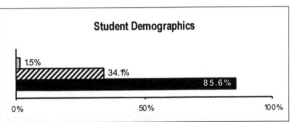

BECKFIELD COLLEGE

16 Spiral Drive
Florence, KY 41042
(859) 371-9393
Tim Curl, RN

www.beckfield.org

Accreditation
Kentucky Board of Nursing

Degrees conferred
Associate Degree

BIG SANDY COMMUNITY & TECHNICAL COLLEGE

One Bert T Combs Drive
Prestonsburg, KY 41653
(606) 886-3863
Myrat Elliot

www.bigsandy.kctcs.edu

Accreditation
Kentucky Board of Nursing

Degrees conferred
Associate Degree

EASTERN KENTUCKY UNIVERSITY *Useful Facts*

521 Lancaster, 220 Rowlett
Richmond, KY 40475
(859) 626-1942
Peggy Tudor, RN, MSN

www.adn.eku.edu

Acceptance rate		32.9%
Faculty-student ratio		1: 27
Faculty	Full time	18
	Part time	15

Tuition	
In state	$2,330
Out of state	$6,535
Enrollments	334
Graduations	104

Student Demographics	
Female	91.3%
Under age 25	41.6%
Minority	7.6%
Part-time	0.0%

Accreditation
Kentucky Board of Nursing, National League for Nursing Accrediting Commission (NLNAC)

Degrees conferred
Associate Degree

Minimum degree required
High school diploma or GED

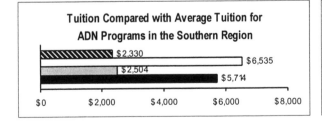

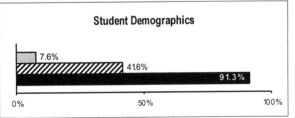

Demographics Chart	■Female ▨Under age 25 ☐Minority	Distance Learning	¹The tuition reported for this program may be not be annualized. ²Data reported between 2001 and 2004.

Kentucky

ELIZABETHTOWN COMMUNITY AND TECHNICAL COLLEGE

Useful Facts*

600 College Street Road
Elizabethtown, KY 42701
(270) 769-2371
Susan Mudd, RN, BSN, MSN

www.elizabethtowncc.com

Acceptance rate	38.9%	

Tuition		**Student Demographics**	
In state	$725	Female	97.4%
Out of state	$2,175	Under age 25	49.0%
Enrollments	116	Minority	9.6%
Graduations	36	Part-time	35.3%

Accreditation
Kentucky Board of Nursing

Degrees conferred
Associate Degree

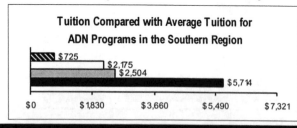

Tuition Compared with Average Tuition for ADN Programs in the Southern Region

$725
$2,175
$2,504
$5,714

$0 $1,830 $3,660 $5,490 $7,321

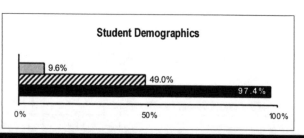

Student Demographics

9.6%
49.0%
97.4%

0%   50%   100%

GALEN COLLEGE OF NURSING

612 S 4th Street
Louisville, KY 40202
(502) 582-2305
Margaret Stutyenberger, MS, RN, BSN

nursingcareer.com

Accreditation
Kentucky Board of Nursing

Degrees conferred
Associate Degree

GATEWAY COMMUNITY & TECHNICAL COLLEGE

790 Thomas More Parkway
Edgewood, KY 41017
(859) 442-4150
Terry Mayo

www.gateway.kctcs.edu

Accreditation
Kentucky Board of Nursing

Degrees conferred
Associate Degree

HAZARD COMMUNITY COLLEGE

One Community College Drive
Hazard, KY 41701
(606) 487-3298
Janie Richie, MSN, RN

www.hazard.kctcs.edu

Accreditation
Kentucky Board of Nursing

At the request of this nursing school, publication has been witheld. Please contact the school directly for more information.

Key | Tuition Chart | ▧ Program - in state ▫ Program - out of state ▨ Average - in state ■ Average - out of state

Kentucky

HENDERSON COMMUNITY COLLEGE

2660 South Green Street
Henderson, KY 42420
(270) 831-9737
Mary Wilder, RN, DSN

www.hencc.kctcs.edu/nursing

Acceptance rate	39.6%

Tuition[1]

In state	$64
Out of state	$192
Enrollments	107
Graduations	33

Student Demographics

Female	91.6%
Under age 25	44.0%
Minority	4.7%
Part-time	57.0%

Accreditation
Kentucky Board of Nursing, National League for Nursing Accrediting Commission (NLNAC)

Degrees conferred
Associate Degree

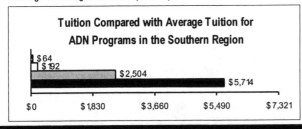

Tuition Compared with Average Tuition for ADN Programs in the Southern Region

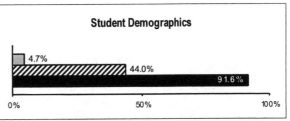

Student Demographics

HOPKINSVILLE COMMUNITY COLLEGE

720 North Drive
Hopkinsville, KY 42240
(270) 707-3840
Elwanda Adams, RN, MSN

www.hopkinsville.kctcs.edu

Acceptance rate	90.4%
Faculty-student ratio	1: 12

Faculty	Full time	11
	Part time	0

Tuition[1]

In state	$98
Out of state	$294
Enrollments	132
Graduations	43

Student Demographics

Female	93.2%
Under age 25	43.2%
Minority	14.4%
Part-time	52.3%

Accreditation
Kentucky Board of Nursing, National League for Nursing Accrediting Commission (NLNAC)

Degrees conferred
Associate Degree

Minimum degree required
High school diploma or GED

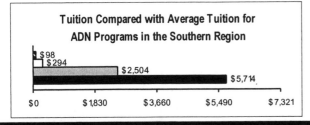

Tuition Compared with Average Tuition for ADN Programs in the Southern Region

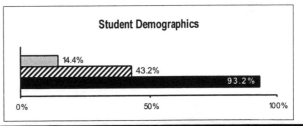

Student Demographics

JEFFERSON COMMUNITY AND TECHNICAL COLLEGE (KENTUCKY)

109 East Broadway
Louisville, KY 40202
(502) 213-2292
Margie Charasika, EdD, MSN, CNE, RN

www.kctcs.edu

Acceptance rate	26.0%
Faculty-student ratio	1: 10

Faculty	Full time	22
	Part time	20

Tuition[1]

In state	$98
Out of state	$118
Enrollments	325
Graduations	122

Student Demographics

Female	88.0%
Under age 25	7.7%
Minority	5.3%
Part-time	0.0%

Accreditation
Kentucky Board of Nursing, National League for Nursing Accrediting Commission (NLNAC)

Degrees conferred
Associate Degree

Minimum degree required
High school diploma or GED

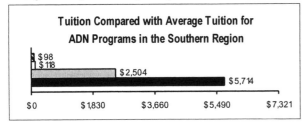

Tuition Compared with Average Tuition for ADN Programs in the Southern Region

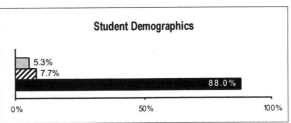

Student Demographics

Demographics Chart | ■Female ▨Under age 25 ▢Minority | **Distance Learning** | [1]The tuition reported for this program may be not be annualized.
*Data reported between 2001 and 2004.

Kentucky

KENTUCKY STATE UNIVERSITY

400 East Main Street
Frankfort, KY 40601
(502) 597-5957
Betty Olinger, EdD, RN
www.kysu.edu

Acceptance rate		40.9%
Faculty-student ratio		1: 8
Faculty	Full time	10
	Part time	5

Tuition			**Student Demographics**	
In state	$4,440		Female	91.8%
Out of state	$12,570		Under age 25	44.3%
Enrollments	97		Minority	24.7%
Graduations	36		Part-time	21.6%

Accreditation
Kentucky Board of Nursing, National League for
Nursing Accrediting Commission (NLNAC)

Degrees conferred
Associate Degree

Minimum degree required
HS GPA 2.3; College GPA 2.7; ACT 21 or above

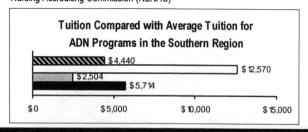

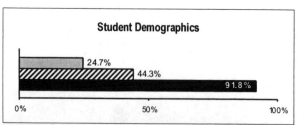

LEXINGTON COMMUNITY COLLEGE

Oswald Bldg, Copper Drive
Lexington, KY 40506-0235
(859) 257-4872
Erla Mowbray, PhD, RN
uky.edu/lcc/nsg

Acceptance rate		50.1%

Tuition			**Student Demographics**	
In state	$2,771		Female	89.2%
Out of state	$7,187		Under age 25	39.0%
Enrollments	195		Minority	4.6%
Graduations	68		Part-time	44.1%

Accreditation
Kentucky Board of Nursing, National League for
Nursing Accrediting Commission (NLNAC)

Degrees conferred
Associate Degree

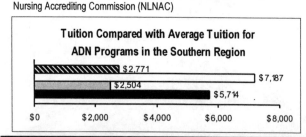

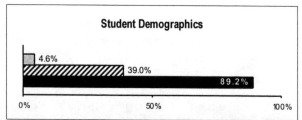

LINCOLN MEMORIAL UNIVERSITY - Harrogate

Cumberland Gap Parkway
Harrogate, TN 37752
(423) 869-6326
Elisa Barr, PhD
inetlmu.lmunet.edu

Acceptance rate		72.0%

Tuition			**Student Demographics**	
In state	$6,300		Female	91.3%
Out of state	$6,300		Under age 25	39.0%
Enrollments	368		Minority	5.0%
Graduations	102		Part-time	38.9%

Accreditation
Kentucky Board of Nursing, National League for
Nursing Accrediting Commission (NLNAC)

Degrees conferred
Associate Degree

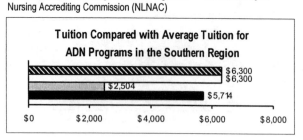

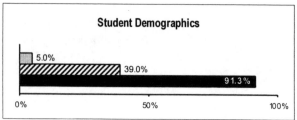

Key | Tuition Chart

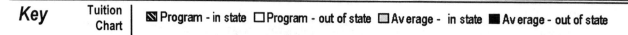

Program - in state ☐ Program - out of state ☐ Average - in state ■ Average - out of state

Kentucky

MADISONVILLE COMMUNITY COLLEGE
Useful Facts

750 North Laffoon Street
Madisonville, KY 42431
(270) 824-1784
Linda Thomas, MSN

www.madcc.kctcs.edu

| Acceptance rate | 47.7% |
| Faculty-student ratio | 1: 13 |

| Faculty | Full time | 13 |
| | Part time | 3 |

Tuition

In state	$2,352
Out of state	$7,056
Enrollments	182
Graduations	78

Student Demographics

Female	84.6%
Under age 25	37.4%
Minority	2.7%
Part-time	57.1%

Accreditation
Kentucky Board of Nursing, National League for
Nursing Accrediting Commission (NLNAC)

Degrees conferred
Associate Degree

Minimum degree required
High school diploma or GED

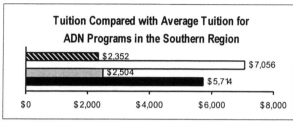

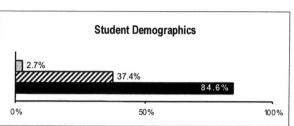

MAYSVILLE COMMUNITY COLLEGE - MAYSVILLE
Useful Facts

1755 US 68
Maysville, KY 41056
(606) 759-7141
Linda Dunaway, MSN, RN

www.maysville.kctcs.edu

| Acceptance rate | 30.0% |
| Faculty-student ratio | 1: 50 |

| Faculty | Full time | 1 |
| | Part time | 0 |

Tuition

In state	$2,940
Out of state	$8,820
Enrollments	50
Graduations	24

Student Demographics

Female	96.0%
Under age 25	28.0%
Part-time	0.0%

Accreditation
Kentucky Board of Nursing

Degrees conferred
Associate Degree

Minimum degree required
High school diploma or GED

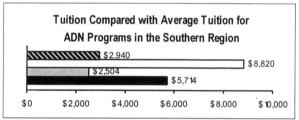

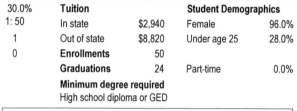

MIDWAY COLLEGE
Useful Facts

512 E Stephens St
Midway, KY 40347
(859) 846-5335
Barbara Kitchen, RN, DNP

www.midway.edu

| Acceptance rate | 67.5% |
| Faculty-student ratio | 1: 11 |

| Faculty | Full time | 8 |
| | Part time | 5 |

Tuition

In state	$13,800
Out of state	$13,800
Enrollments	117
Graduations	47

Student Demographics

Female	95.7%
Under age 25	30.8%
Minority	7.7%
Part-time	14.5%

Accreditation
Kentucky Board of Nursing, National League for
Nursing Accrediting Commission (NLNAC)

Degrees conferred
Associate Degree

Minimum degree required
High school diploma or GED

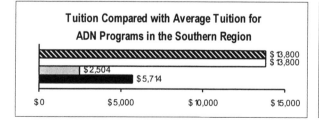

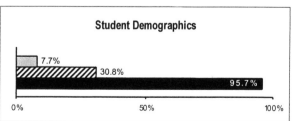

| Demographics Chart | ■Female ☑Under age 25 ☐Minority | Distance Learning | ¹The tuition reported for this program may be not be annualized.
²Data reported between 2001 and 2004. |

Kentucky

MOREHEAD STATE UNIVERSITY — *Useful Facts*

Reed Hall 234
Morehead, KY 40351
(606) 783-2296
Erla Mowbray, PhD, RN

www.moreheadstate.edu/nursing/index.aspx?id=5178

Acceptance rate	36.1%	
Faculty-student ratio	1 : 9	
Faculty	Full time	18
	Part time	6

Tuition	
In state	$4,320
Out of state	$11,480
Enrollments	70
Graduations	26

Student Demographics	
Female	85.7%
Under age 25	40.0%
Minority	2.9%
Part-time	48.6%

Accreditation
Kentucky Board of Nursing, National League for
Nursing Accrediting Commission (NLNAC)

Degrees conferred
Associate Degree

Minimum degree required
High school diploma or GED

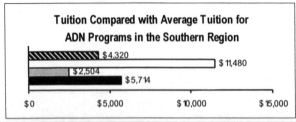

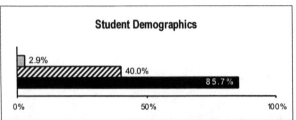

NORTHERN KENTUCKY UNIVERSITY — *Useful Facts**

Nunn Drive, HC 303
Highland Heights, KY 41099
(859) 572-5248
Margaret Anderson, EdD, RN, CNAA

www.nku.edu/nursing

Tuition	
In state	$4,690
Out of state	$5,970
Enrollments	0
Graduations	21

Student Demographics	
Under age 25	100.0%

Accreditation
Kentucky Board of Nursing

Degrees conferred
Associate Degree

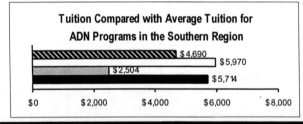

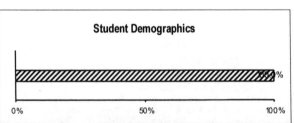

OWENSBORO COMMUNITY COLLEGE

4800 New Hartford Road
Owensboro, KY 42303
(270) 686-4546
Kelly Morris, MSN, RN

www.owecc.net

Accreditation
Kentucky Board of Nursing

*At the request of this nursing school, publication has been witheld.
Please contact the school directly for more information.*

Key | Tuition Chart | ▨ Program - in state   ☐ Program - out of state   ☐ Average - in state   ■ Average - out of state

Kentucky

PIKEVILLE COLLEGE

147 Sycamore Street
Pikeville, KY 41501
(606) 218-5750
Mary Simpson, RN, PhD

www.pc.edu

Accreditation
Kentucky Board of Nursing

Acceptance rate	34.5%	
Faculty-student ratio	1 : 9	
Faculty Full time	6	
Part time	5	

Tuition	
In state	$13,500
Out of state	$13,500
Enrollments	73
Graduations	24

Student Demographics	
Female	89.0%
Under age 25	45.2%
Minority	1.4%
Part-time	21.9%

Degrees conferred
Associate Degree

Minimum degree required
High school diploma or GED

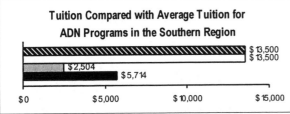

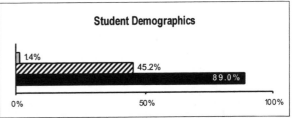

SOMERSET COMMUNITY COLLEGE - Somerset

808 Monticello Street
Somerset, KY 42501
(606) 451-6737
Linda Ballard, RN, MSN

www.somcc.kctcs.edu

Accreditation
Kentucky Board of Nursing, National League for
Nursing Accrediting Commission (NLNAC)

Acceptance rate	37.8%	
Faculty-student ratio	1 : 7	
Faculty Full time	11	
Part time	4	

Tuition	
In state	$2,940
Out of state	$8,820
Enrollments	96
Graduations	37

Student Demographics	
Female	86.5%
Under age 25	34.4%
Minority	2.1%
Part-time	49.0%

Degrees conferred
Associate Degree

Minimum degree required
High school diploma or GED

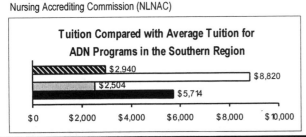

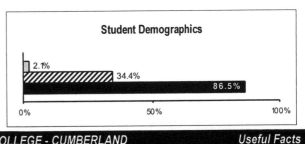

SOUTHEAST KENTUCKY COMMUNITY AND TECHNICAL COLLEGE - CUMBERLAND

700 College Road
Cumberland, KY 40823
(606) 589-2145
Milton Borntrager, MSN

www.secc.kctcs.net/academicaffairs/alliedhealth/nursing.htm

Accreditation
Kentucky Board of Nursing, National League for
Nursing Accrediting Commission (NLNAC)

Acceptance rate	53.3%	
Faculty-student ratio	1 : 4	
Faculty Full time	11	
Part time	8	

Tuition	
In state	$1,176
Out of state	$3,528
Enrollments	67
Graduations	38

Student Demographics	
Female	91.0%
Under age 25	23.9%
Part-time	65.7%

Degrees conferred
Associate Degree

Minimum degree required
High school diploma or GED

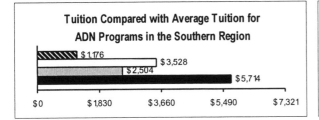

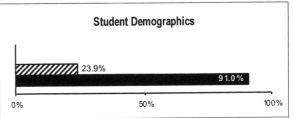

Demographics Chart	■ Female ▨ Under age 25 ▢ Minority	**Distance Learning**	¹The tuition reported for this program may be not be annualized. *Data reported between 2001 and 2004.

Kentucky

SPENCERIAN COLLEGE *Useful Facts**

4627 Dixie Highway
Louisville, KY 40216
(502) 449-7850
Gail Finney, RN, MSN

www.spencerian.edu

Acceptance rate	100.0%	

Accreditation
Kentucky Board of Nursing

Degrees conferred
Associate Degree

Tuition		Student Demographics	
In state	$15,980	Female	92.2%
Out of state	$15,980	Under age 25	13.0%
Enrollments	166	Minority	16.9%
Graduations	117	Part-time	32.5%

Tuition Compared with Average Tuition for ADN Programs in the Southern Region

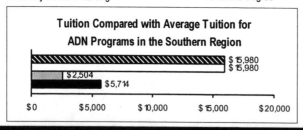

Student Demographics

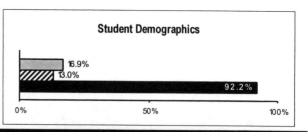

ST CATHARINE COLLEGE *Useful Facts**

2735 Bardstown Road
St Catharine, KY 40061
(859) 336-5082
Jeanette Jeffers, RN, MN, PhD

www.sccky.edu

Acceptance rate	100.0%		
Faculty-student ratio	1: 3		
Faculty	Full time	4	
	Part time	4	

Accreditation
Kentucky Board of Nursing

Degrees conferred
Associate Degree

Tuition		Student Demographics	
In state	$9,716	Female	90.0%
Out of state	$9,716	Under age 25	20.0%
Enrollments	20	Minority	10.0%
Graduations	17	Part-time	0.0%

Tuition Compared with Average Tuition for ADN Programs in the Southern Region

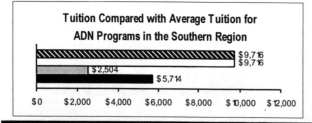

Student Demographics

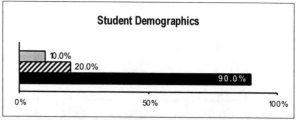

WEST KENTUCKY COMMUNITY AND TECHNICAL COLLEGE - PADUCAH *Useful Facts*

PO Box 7380
Paducah, KY 42002
(270) 534-3342
Tena Payne, RN, EdD

nursing.westkentucky.kctcs.edu

Acceptance rate	31.6%		
Faculty-student ratio	1: 14		
Faculty	Full time	13	
	Part time	1.5	

Accreditation
Kentucky Board of Nursing, National League for Nursing Accrediting Commission (NLNAC)

Degrees conferred
Associate Degree

Minimum degree required
High school diploma or GED

Tuition		Student Demographics	
In state	$2,940	Female	86.3%
Out of state	$8,820	Under age 25	33.0%
Enrollments	197	Minority	3.4%
Graduations	72	Part-time	46.7%

Tuition Compared with Average Tuition for ADN Programs in the Southern Region

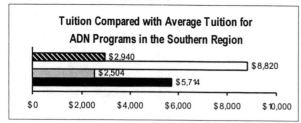

Student Demographics

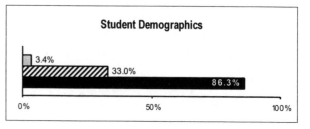

Key | Tuition Chart | ▨ Program - in state ▢ Program - out of state ▢ Average - in state ▪ Average - out of state

Kentucky

WESTERN KENTUCKY UNIVERSITY
Useful Facts

1906 College Heights Blvd - #11036
Bowling Green, KY 42101
(270) 745-3579
Donna Blackburn, PhD, RN

www.wku.edu/dept/academic/chhs/nursing

Acceptance rate		38.8%
Faculty-student ratio		1: 10
Faculty	Full time	40
	Part time	16

Tuition	
In state	$5,160
Out of state	$12,576
Enrollments	252
Graduations	98

Student Demographics	
Female	88.5%
Under age 25	37.7%
Minority	2.4%
Part-time	34.9%

Accreditation
Kentucky Board of Nursing

Degrees conferred
Associate Degree

Minimum degree required
2.75 GPA, on 10 or more credit hours, completion of pre-requisite courses, 60 on DET

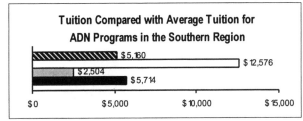

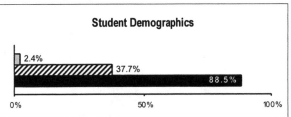

Louisiana

DELGADO COMMUNITY COLLEGE
Useful Facts

450 South Claiborne Avenue
New Orleans, LA 70112
(504) 568-6466
Patricia Egers, MS, RN

www.dcc.edu

Acceptance rate		68.4%
Faculty-student ratio		1: 1
Faculty	Full time	79
	Part time	17

Tuition	
In state	$1,536
Out of state	$4,516
Enrollments	129
Graduations	251

Student Demographics	
Female	88.4%
Under age 25	28.7%
Minority	23.9%
Part-time	100.0%

Accreditation
Louisiana State Board of Nursing, National League for Nursing Accrediting Commission (NLNAC)

Degrees conferred
Associate Degree

Minimum degree required
High school diploma or GED

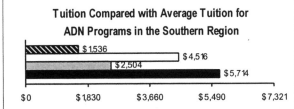

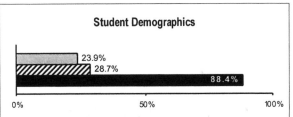

LOUISIANA STATE UNIVERSITY - ALEXANDRIA
Useful Facts

8100 Highway 71 South
Alexandria, LA 71303
(318) 473-6459
Dorothy Lary, RN, MSN

www.lsua.edu

Acceptance rate		46.4%
Faculty-student ratio		1: 14
Faculty	Full time	15
	Part time	5

Tuition	
In state	$2,816
Out of state	$5,276
Enrollments	252
Graduations	94

Student Demographics	
Female	86.9%
Under age 25	42.9%
Minority	14.8%
Part-time	82.9%

Accreditation
Louisiana State Board of Nursing, National League for Nursing Accrediting Commission (NLNAC)

Degrees conferred
Associate Degree

Minimum degree required
High school diploma or GED

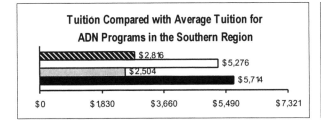

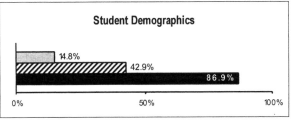

Demographics Chart	■Female ☑Under age 25 ☐Minority	Distance Learning	¹The tuition reported for this program may be not be annualized. *Data reported between 2001 and 2004.

Louisiana

LOUISIANA STATE UNIVERSITY - EUNICE
Useful Facts

PO Box 1129
Eunice, LA 70535
(337) 550-1363
Bonnie Johnson, MSN, RN

www.lsue.edu

Acceptance rate		49.6%
Faculty-student ratio		1 : 9
Faculty	Full time	12
	Part time	2

Tuition
In state	$2,096
Out of state	$5,096
Enrollments	117
Graduations	46

Student Demographics
Female	83.8%
Under age 25	29.9%
Minority	14.5%
Part-time	89.7%

Accreditation
Louisiana State Board of Nursing, National League for Nursing Accrediting Commission (NLNAC)

Degrees conferred
Associate Degree

Minimum degree required
High school diploma or GED

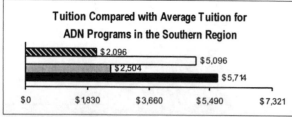

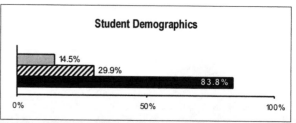

LOUISIANA STATE UNIVERSITY HEALTH SCIENCES CENTER
*Useful Facts**

1900 Gravier Street
New Orleans, LA 70072
(504) 568-4106
Elizabeth Humphrey, EdD, RN

lsuhsc.edu/school/nursing

Enrollments	0
Graduations	0

Accreditation
Louisiana State Board of Nursing

Degrees conferred
Associate Degree

LOUISIANA TECHNICAL UNIVERSITY
Useful Facts

PO Box 3152
Ruston, LA 71272
(318) 257-3101
Pamela Moore, RN, C, BSN, MSN, CNS

www.ans.latech.edu

Acceptance rate		43.0%
Faculty-student ratio		1 : 26
Faculty	Full time	14
	Part time	1

Tuition
In state	$1,291
Out of state	$2,556
Enrollments	374
Graduations	66

Student Demographics
Female	80.2%
Under age 25	59.1%
Minority	11.8%
Part-time	30.5%

Accreditation
Louisiana State Board of Nursing, National League for Nursing Accrediting Commission (NLNAC)

Degrees conferred
Associate Degree

Minimum degree required
High school diploma or GED

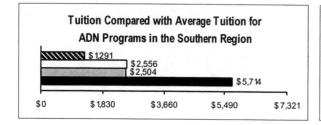

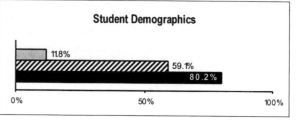

Key | Tuition Chart | ▨ Program - in state ☐ Program - out of state ☐ Average - in state ■ Average - out of state

Louisiana

MCNEESE STATE UNIVERSITY
Useful Facts

PO Box 90415
Lake Charles, LA 70609
(337) 475-5822
Peggy Wolfe, PhD

www.mcneese.edu/colleges/nursing

Accreditation
Louisiana State Board of Nursing

Acceptance rate		68.6%
Faculty-student ratio		1: 35
Faculty	Full time	29
	Part time	9

Tuition	
In state	$1,113
Out of state	$3,033
Enrollments	186
Graduations	13

Student Demographics	
Female	81.7%
Under age 25	28.5%
Minority	18.1%
Part-time	61.8%

Degrees conferred
Associate Degree

Minimum degree required
High school diploma or GED

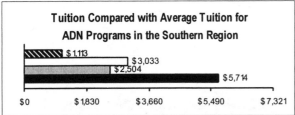

Tuition Compared with Average Tuition for ADN Programs in the Southern Region

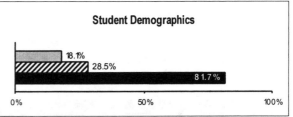

Student Demographics

NICHOLLS STATE UNIVERSITY
Useful Facts

College Station, PO Box 2057
Thibodaux, LA 70310
(985) 448-4687
Velma Westbrook, DNS, RN

www.nicholls.edu/nursing

Accreditation
Louisiana State Board of Nursing, National
League for Nursing Accrediting Commission
(NLNAC)

Acceptance rate		32.3%
Faculty-student ratio		1: 12
Faculty	Full time	25
	Part time	0

Tuition	
In state	$3,390
Out of state	$8,838
Enrollments	28
Graduations	13

Student Demographics	
Female	78.6%
Under age 25	17.9%
Minority	10.7%
Part-time	0.0%

Degrees conferred
Associate Degree

Minimum degree required
DK/NA

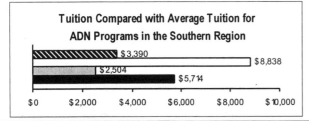

Tuition Compared with Average Tuition for ADN Programs in the Southern Region

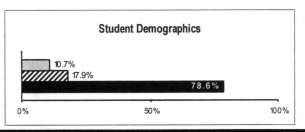

Student Demographics

NORTHWESTERN STATE UNIVERSITY

1800 Line Avenue
Shreveport, LA 71101
(318) 677-3100
Norann Planchock, PhD, APRN, BC, FNP

www.nsula.edu/nursing

Accreditation
Louisiana State Board of Nursing

*At the request of this nursing school, publication has been witheld.
Please contact the school directly for more information.*

Demographics Chart | ■ Female ▨ Under age 25 ▢ Minority | **Distance Learning** | ¹The tuition reported for this program may be not be annualized.
*Data reported between 2001 and 2004.

Louisiana

OUR LADY OF THE LAKE COLLEGE   *Useful Facts*

7434 Perkins Road
Baton Rouge, LA 70808
(225) 768-1753
Melanie Green, MN, RNC

www.ololcollege.edu

Acceptance rate		51.1%
Faculty-student ratio		1: 15
Faculty	Full time	26
	Part time	9

Tuition	
In state	$4,500
Out of state	$4,500
Enrollments	454
Graduations	198

Student Demographics	
Female	81.7%
Under age 25	42.5%
Minority	33.0%
Part-time	10.1%

Accreditation
Louisiana State Board of Nursing, National
League for Nursing Accrediting Commission
(NLNAC)

Degrees conferred
Associate Degree

Minimum degree required
High school diploma or GED

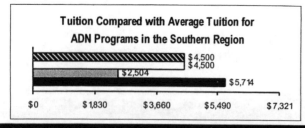

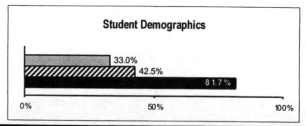

SOUTHERN UNIVERSITY AT SHREVEPORT   *Useful Facts**

610 Texas St
Shreveport, LA 71101
(318) 678-4641
Sandra Tucker, BSN, MSN, PhD, JD

www.susla.edu

Faculty-student ratio		1: 7
Faculty	Full time	9
	Part time	3

Enrollments	70

Student Demographics	
Female	84.3%
Under age 25	4.3%
Minority	58.6%
Part-time	0.0%

Accreditation
Louisiana State Board of Nursing

Degrees conferred
Associate Degree

Maine

CENTRAL MAINE COMMUNITY COLLEGE   *Useful Facts*

1250 Turner Street
Auburn, ME 04210
(207) 755-5408
Anne Schuettinger, RN, MS

www.cmcc.edu

Acceptance rate		15.2%
Faculty-student ratio		1: 7
Faculty	Full time	6
	Part time	3

Tuition	
In state	$2,220
Out of state	$4,650
Enrollments	53
Graduations	23

Student Demographics	
Female	86.8%
Under age 25	24.5%
Minority	12.5%
Part-time	73.6%

Accreditation
Maine State Board of Nursing, National League
for Nursing Accrediting Commission (NLNAC)

Degrees conferred
Associate Degree

Minimum degree required
High school diploma or GED

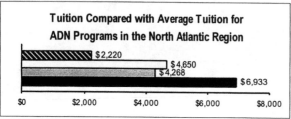

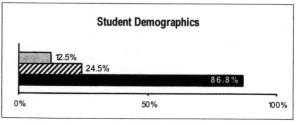

Key | Tuition Chart | ▨ Program - in state ☐ Program - out of state ▤ Average - in state ■ Average - out of state

Maine

CENTRAL MAINE MEDICAL CENTER
*Useful Facts**

70 Middle Street
Lewiston, ME 04240
(207) 795-2841
Sharon Kuhrt, RN,MSN

www.cmmcson.edu

Accreditation
Maine State Board of Nursing, National League
for Nursing Accrediting Commission (NLNAC)

Acceptance rate	33.3%	

Tuition
In state	$4,443
Out of state	$4,443
Enrollments	116
Graduations	47

Student Demographics
Female	86.2%
Under age 25	20.0%
Minority	0.9%
Part-time	1.7%

Degrees conferred
Associate Degree

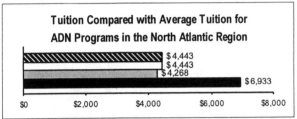

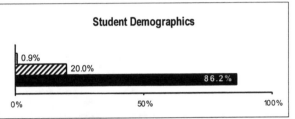

EASTERN MAINE COMMUNITY COLLEGE
*Useful Facts**

354 Hogan Road
Bangor, ME 04401
(207) 974-4657
Suzanne Brunner, RN, MS

www.emcc.edu

Accreditation
Maine State Board of Nursing, National League
for Nursing Accrediting Commission (NLNAC)

Acceptance rate	15.5%	

Tuition
In state	$2,312
Out of state	$5,066
Enrollments	55
Graduations	29

Student Demographics
Female	85.5%
Under age 25	16.4%
Part-time	81.8%

Degrees conferred
Associate Degree

**Tuition Compared with Average Tuition for
ADN Programs in the North Atlantic Region**

$2,312
$5,066
$4,268
$6,933

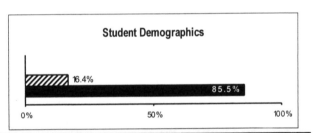

KENNEBEC VALLEY COMMUNITY COLLEGE
*Useful Facts**

92 Western Ave
Fairfield, ME 04937
(207) 453-5000
Marcia Parker, RN, MS

www.kvcc.me.edu

Accreditation
Maine State Board of Nursing, National League
for Nursing Accrediting Commission (NLNAC)

Acceptance rate	17.1%	

Tuition[1]
In state	$68
Out of state	$149
Enrollments	80
Graduations	41

Student Demographics
Female	91.3%
Under age 25	23.0%
Minority	1.3%
Part-time	86.3%

Degrees conferred
Associate Degree

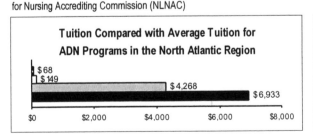

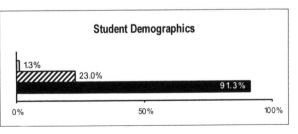

Demographics Chart	■ Female ▨ Under age 25 ☐ Minority	Distance Learning	[1]The tuition reported for this program may be not be annualized. *Data reported between 2001 and 2004.

Maine

NORTHERN MAINE COMMUNITY COLLEGE
Useful Facts

33 Edgemont Drive
Presque Isle, ME 04769
(207) 768-2749
Betty Kent-Conant, MSN, RN

www.nmcc.edu

Accreditation
Maine State Board of Nursing, National League
for Nursing Accrediting Commission (NLNAC)

Acceptance rate		39.0%
Faculty-student ratio		1: 8
Faculty	Full time	9
	Part time	2

Degrees conferred
Associate Degree

Tuition			Student Demographics	
In state	$2,664		Female	92.2%
Out of state	$5,580		Under age 25	31.2%
Enrollments	77		Minority	6.7%
Graduations	36		Part-time	5.2%

Minimum degree required
High school diploma or GED

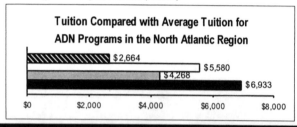

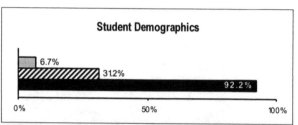

SOUTHERN MAINE COMMUNITY COLLEGE
Useful Facts*

2 Fort Road
South Portland, ME 04106
(207) 767-9588
Nancy Smith, RN, MS

www.smtc.net

Accreditation
Maine State Board of Nursing, National League
for Nursing Accrediting Commission (NLNAC)

Acceptance rate	13.0%

Degrees conferred
Associate Degree

Tuition			Student Demographics	
In state	$1,140		Female	84.5%
Out of state	$2,020			
Enrollments	116		Minority	6.0%
Graduations	32		Part-time	0.0%

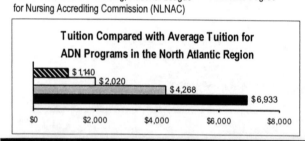

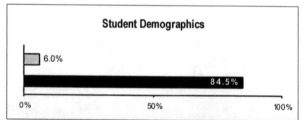

UNIVERSITY OF MAINE - AUGUSTA
Useful Facts

46 University Dr
Augusta, ME 04330
(207) 621-3469
Nancy Cooley, RN, MSN, CS-FNP

www.uma.maine.edu

Accreditation
Maine State Board of Nursing, National League
for Nursing Accrediting Commission (NLNAC)

Faculty-student ratio		1: 10
Faculty	Full time	9
	Part time	9

Degrees conferred
Associate Degree

Tuition			Student Demographics	
In state	$4,290		Female	92.8%
Out of state	$10,380		Under age 25	3.6%
Enrollments	138		Minority	0.7%
Graduations	50		Part-time	0.0%

Minimum degree required
High school diploma or GED

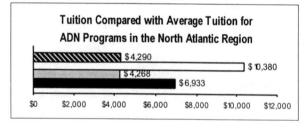

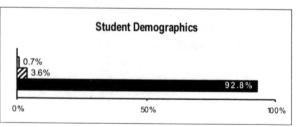

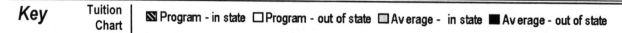

Key | Tuition Chart | ▨ Program - in state ☐ Program - out of state ☐ Average - in state ■ Average - out of state

Maine

UNIVERSITY OF NEW ENGLAND

716 Stevens Avenue
Portland, ME 04103
(207) 221-4476
Karen Pardue, MS, BSN, RN, BC

At the request of this nursing school, publication has been witheld.
Please contact the school directly for more information.

www.une.edu

Accreditation
Maine State Board of Nursing, National League
for Nursing Accrediting Commission (NLNAC)

Maryland

ALLEGANY COLLEGE OF MARYLAND   *Useful Facts**

12401 Willowbrook Rd
Cumberland, MD 21502
(301) 784-5567
Fran Leibfreid, MEd, BSN, RN

www.ac.cc.md.us/careers/health/nurse

			Tuition		Student Demographics	
Acceptance rate	26.5%		In state	$5,010	Female	86.9%
			Out of state	$5,910	Under age 25	39.0%
			Enrollments	222	Minority	0.5%
			Graduations	68	Part-time	0.0%

Accreditation
Maryland Board of Nursing, National League for
Nursing Accrediting Commission (NLNAC)

Degrees conferred
Associate Degree

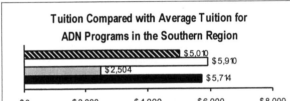

Tuition Compared with Average Tuition for
ADN Programs in the Southern Region

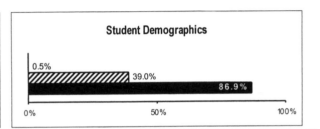

Student Demographics

ANNE ARUNDEL COMMUNITY COLLEGE   *Useful Facts*

101 College Parkway
Arnold, MD 21012
(410) 777-7352
Beth Anne Batturs, MSN, RN

www.aacc.edu

			Tuition[1]		Student Demographics	
Acceptance rate	27.5%		In state	$83	Female	93.1%
Faculty-student ratio	1:7		Out of state	$282	Under age 25	46.9%
Faculty	Full time	16	**Enrollments**	160	Minority	18.4%
	Part time	13	**Graduations**	94	Part-time	0.0%

Accreditation
Maryland Board of Nursing, National League for
Nursing Accrediting Commission (NLNAC)

Degrees conferred
Associate Degree

Minimum degree required
High school diploma or GED

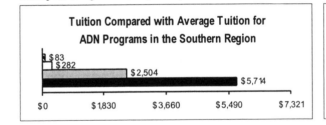

Tuition Compared with Average Tuition for
ADN Programs in the Southern Region

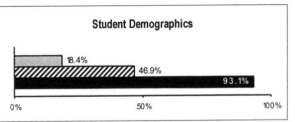

Student Demographics

Demographics Chart	■ Female ▨ Under age 25 ▢ Minority	Distance Learning 🖥	[1]The tuition reported for this program may be not be annualized. *Data reported between 2001 and 2004.

Maryland

BALTIMORE CITY COMMUNITY COLLEGE

2901 Liberty Hts Ave
Baltimore, MD 21215
(410) 462-7786
Dorothy Holley, RN, MS

www.bccc.state.md.us

Accreditation
Maryland Board of Nursing, National League for Nursing Accrediting Commission (NLNAC)

Degrees conferred
Associate Degree

Useful Facts*

Tuition		Student Demographics	
In state	$828	Female	90.9%
Out of state	$1,908		
Enrollments	143	Minority	94.4%
Graduations	35	Part-time	8.4%

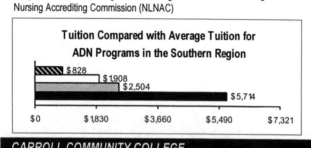

Tuition Compared with Average Tuition for ADN Programs in the Southern Region

$828
$1908
$2,504
$5,714

$0 $1,830 $3,660 $5,490 $7,321

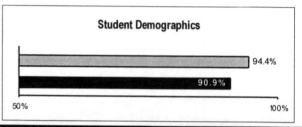

Student Demographics

94.4%
90.9%

50%   100%

CARROLL COMMUNITY COLLEGE

1601 Washington Road
Westminster, MD 21157
(410) 386-8231
Nancy Perry, RN, BSN, MS

www.carrollcc.edu/courses/credit/academic/nursing/default.asp

Accreditation
Maryland Board of Nursing

Degrees conferred
Associate Degree

Minimum degree required
High school diploma or GED

Useful Facts

		Tuition		Student Demographics	
Acceptance rate	55.0%	In state	$2,760	Female	96.6%
Faculty-student ratio	1: 8	Out of state	$6,314	Under age 25	31.0%
Faculty Full time	7	Enrollments	87	Minority	6.9%
Part time	7	Graduations	19	Part-time	100.0%

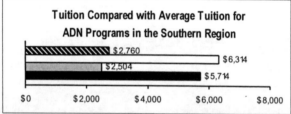

Tuition Compared with Average Tuition for ADN Programs in the Southern Region

$2,760
$6,314
$2,504
$5,714

$0 $2,000 $4,000 $6,000 $8,000

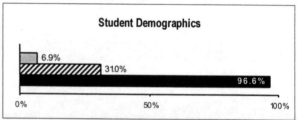

Student Demographics

6.9%
31.0%
96.6%

0%   50%   100%

CECIL COMMUNITY COLLEGE

One Seahawk Drive
North East, MD 21901
(410) 287-6060
Carol Roane, MS, RN

www.cecil.cc.edu

Accreditation
Maryland Board of Nursing, National League for Nursing Accrediting Commission (NLNAC)

Degrees conferred
LPN or LVN, Associate Degree

Minimum degree required
High school diploma or GED

Useful Facts

		Tuition		Student Demographics	
Acceptance rate	39.7%	In state	$2,400	Female	87.6%
Faculty-student ratio	1: 11	Out of state	$6,450	Under age 25	34.7%
Faculty Full time	7	Enrollments	121	Minority	6.7%
Part time	9	Graduations	51	Part-time	90.1%

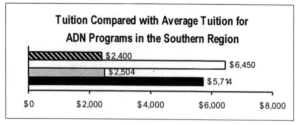

Tuition Compared with Average Tuition for ADN Programs in the Southern Region

$2,400
$6,450
$2,504
$5,714

$0 $2,000 $4,000 $6,000 $8,000

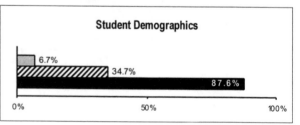

Student Demographics

6.7%
34.7%
87.6%

0%   50%   100%

Key Tuition Chart | ▨ Program - in state ☐ Program - out of state ▨ Average - in state ■ Average - out of state

Maryland

CHESAPEAKE COLLEGE — Useful Facts

PO Box 8
Wye Mills, MD 21679
(410) 827-5935
Judith Stetson, PhD, RN

www.chesapeake.edu

Accreditation
Maryland Board of Nursing, National League for
Nursing Accrediting Commission (NLNAC)

Acceptance rate		47.8%
Faculty-student ratio		1: 9
Faculty	Full time	8
	Part time	8

Tuition
In state	$1,944
Out of state	$5,256
Enrollments	104
Graduations	36

Degrees conferred
Associate Degree, LPN or LVN

Minimum degree required
High school diploma or GED

Student Demographics
Female	91.3%
Under age 25	13.5%
Minority	9.6%
Part-time	0.0%

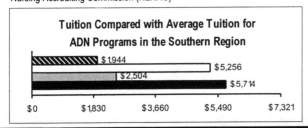

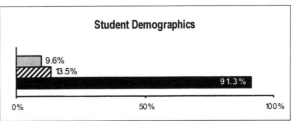

COLLEGE OF SOUTHERN MARYLAND — Useful Facts

PO Box 910
La Plata, MD 20646
(301) 934-7535
Sandra Genrich, RN, PhD

www.csmd.edu

Accreditation
Maryland Board of Nursing, National League for
Nursing Accrediting Commission (NLNAC)

Acceptance rate		25.4%
Faculty-student ratio		1: 11
Faculty	Full time	15
	Part time	11

Tuition
In state	$3,312
Out of state	$7,236
Enrollments	223
Graduations	72

Degrees conferred
Associate Degree

Minimum degree required
High school diploma or GED

Student Demographics
Female	92.4%
Under age 25	33.6%
Minority	30.2%
Part-time	90.1%

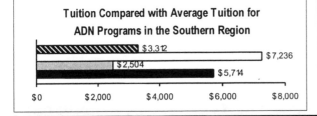

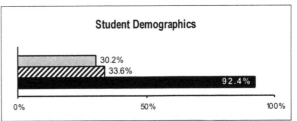

FREDERICK COMMUNITY COLLEGE — Useful Facts

7932 Opossumtown Pike
Frederick, MD 21702
(301) 846-2525
Jane Garvin, RN, MS, APRN-PMH, BC

www.frederick.edu

Accreditation
Maryland Board of Nursing, National League for
Nursing Accrediting Commission (NLNAC)

Acceptance rate		30.6%
Faculty-student ratio		1: 8
Faculty	Full time	9
	Part time	18

Tuition
In state	$2,550
Out of state	$7,620
Enrollments	142
Graduations	50

Degrees conferred
LPN or LVN, Associate Degree

Minimum degree required
ADN

Student Demographics
Female	92.3%
Under age 25	12.0%
Minority	14.5%
Part-time	100.0%

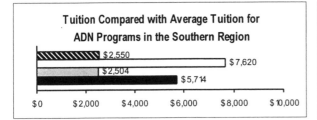

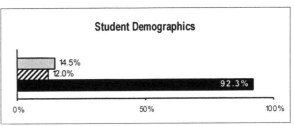

Demographics Chart	■ Female ▨ Under age 25 ▢ Minority	Distance Learning	¹The tuition reported for this program may be not be annualized. *Data reported between 2001 and 2004.

Maryland

HAGERSTOWN COMMUNITY COLLEGE

11400 Robinwood Dr
Hagerstown, MD 21742
(301) 790-2800
Diana Foley, RN, MSN, EdD

www.hcc.cc.md.us

Acceptance rate	60.0%		

Tuition		**Student Demographics**	
In state	$1,944	Female	91.9%
Out of state	$4,104	Under age 25	37.0%
Enrollments	86	Minority	5.9%
Graduations	36	Part-time	81.4%

Accreditation
Maryland Board of Nursing

Degrees conferred
Associate Degree

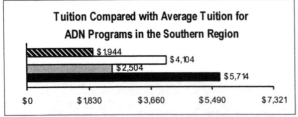

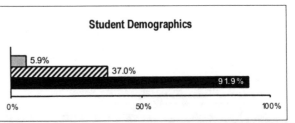

HARFORD COMMUNITY COLLEGE

401 Thomas Run Rd
Bel Air, MD 21015
(410) 836-4438
Laura Putland, RN, MS

www.harford.edu

Acceptance rate	23.2%		
Faculty-student ratio	1:9		
Faculty	Full time	11	
	Part time	15	

Tuition		**Student Demographics**	
In state	$2,250	Female	89.7%
Out of state	$4,500	Under age 25	25.1%
Enrollments	175	Minority	14.5%
Graduations	81	Part-time	0.0%

Accreditation
Maryland Board of Nursing, National League for Nursing Accrediting Commission (NLNAC)

Degrees conferred
LPN or LVN, Associate Degree

Minimum degree required
High school diploma or GED

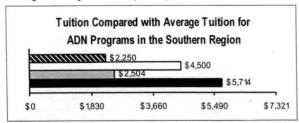

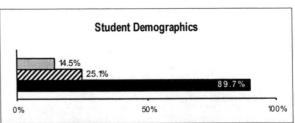

HOWARD COMMUNITY COLLEGE

10901 Little Patuxent Parkway
Columbia, MD 21044
(410) 772-4949
Sharon Pierce, EdD, MSN

www.howardcc.edu/health/hshp.htm

Acceptance rate	36.8%		
Faculty-student ratio	1:10		
Faculty	Full time	11	
	Part time	17	

Tuition		**Student Demographics**	
In state	$3,150	Female	86.0%
Out of state	$6,990	Under age 25	25.8%
Enrollments	186	Minority	55.8%
Graduations	76	Part-time	71.0%

Accreditation
Maryland Board of Nursing, National League for Nursing Accrediting Commission (NLNAC)

Degrees conferred
Associate Degree

Minimum degree required
High school diploma or GED

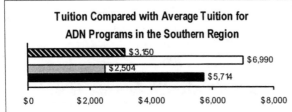

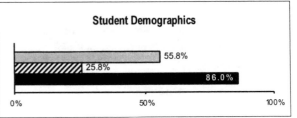

Key	Tuition Chart	▨ Program - in state ☐ Program - out of state ▤ Average - in state ■ Average - out of state

Maryland

MONTGOMERY COLLEGE | Useful Facts

7600 Takoma Avenue
Takoma Park, MD 20912
(301) 562-5532
Molly Clay, MS, CRNP

montgomerycollege.edu/nursing

Accreditation
Maryland Board of Nursing, National League for Nursing Accrediting Commission (NLNAC)

Acceptance rate		24.0%
Faculty-student ratio		1: 8
Faculty	Full time	22
	Part time	15

Degrees conferred
Associate Degree

Tuition	
In state	$2,790
Out of state	$5,730
Enrollments	239
Graduations	91

Minimum degree required
High school diploma or GED

Student Demographics	
Female	84.1%
Under age 25	23.8%
Minority	69.6%
Part-time	2.9%

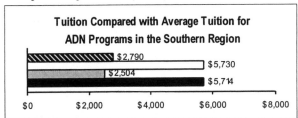

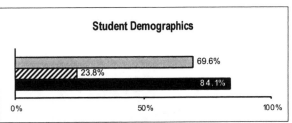

PRINCE GEORGES COMMUNITY COLLEGE | Useful Facts

301 Largo Rd, L-312
Largo, MD 20774
(301) 322-0734
Cheryl Dee Dover, MS, RN, CNA, BC

www.pgweb.pg.cc.md.us

Accreditation
Maryland Board of Nursing, National League for Nursing Accrediting Commission (NLNAC)

Acceptance rate		77.3%
Faculty-student ratio		1: 8
Faculty	Full time	15
	Part time	21

Degrees conferred
LPN or LVN, Associate Degree

Tuition	
In state	$2,820
Out of state	$7,590
Enrollments	205
Graduations	92

Minimum degree required
High school diploma or GED

Student Demographics	
Female	89.3%
Under age 25	10.2%
Minority	85.9%
Part-time	0.0%

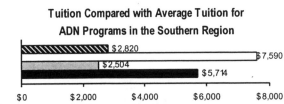

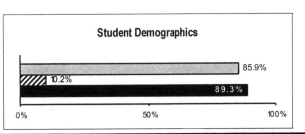

THE COMMUNITY COLLEGE OF BALTIMORE COUNTY | Useful Facts

7201 Rossville Blvd
Baltimore, MD 21237
(410) 780-6807
Roberta Raymond, PhD, RN

www.ccbcmd.edu

Accreditation
Maryland Board of Nursing, National League for Nursing Accrediting Commission (NLNAC)

Acceptance rate		26.7%
Faculty-student ratio		1: 21
Faculty	Full time	26
	Part time	0

Degrees conferred
Associate Degree

Tuition	
In state	$2,700
Out of state	$6,150
Enrollments	539
Graduations	196

Minimum degree required
High school diploma or GED

Student Demographics	
Female	85.3%
Under age 25	28.2%
Minority	31.9%
Part-time	95.5%

Tuition Compared with Average Tuition for ADN Programs in the Southern Region

$2,700
$6,150
$2,504
$5,714

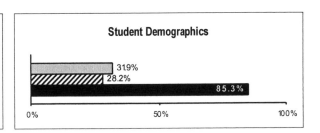

| Demographics Chart | ■Female ▨ Under age 25 ☐Minority | Distance Learning | †The tuition reported for this program may be not be annualized. *Data reported between 2001 and 2004. |

Maryland

WOR-WIC COMMUNITY COLLEGE

32000 Campus Dr
Salisbury, MD 21804
(410) 572-8700
Denise Marshall, MEd, RN

www.worwic.edu

Accreditation
Maryland Board of Nursing

At the request of this nursing school, publication has been witheld.
Please contact the school directly for more information.

Massachusetts

ANNA MARIA COLLEGE

50 Sunset Lane
Paxton, MA 01612
(508) 849-3316
Audrey Silveri, MS, MA, RN, EdD

www.annamaria.edu

Accreditation
Massachusetts Board of Registration in Nursing

Faculty	Full time	2
	Part time	4

Degrees conferred
Associate Degree

ATLANTIC UNION COLLEGE

Useful Facts

338 Main Street, Box 1000
South Lancaster, MA 01561
(978) 368-2401
Kristal Imperio, PhD(c), RN, CS, ANP, GNP

www.atlanticuc.edu

Accreditation
Massachusetts Board of Registration in Nursing,
National League for Nursing Accrediting
Commission (NLNAC)

Acceptance rate	36.5%
Faculty-student ratio	1:8

Faculty	Full time	6
	Part time	6

Tuition	
In state	$12,600
Out of state	$12,600
Enrollments	73
Graduations	10

Minimum degree required
High school diploma or GED

Degrees conferred
Associate Degree

Student Demographics	
Female	86.3%
Under age 25	67.1%
Minority	64.1%
Part-time	4.1%

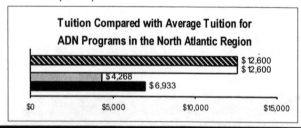

Tuition Compared with Average Tuition for ADN Programs in the North Atlantic Region

- $12,600
- $12,600
- $4,268
- $6,933

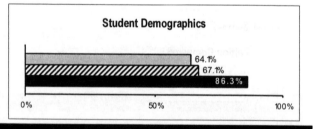

Student Demographics

- 64.1%
- 67.1%
- 86.3%

BECKER COLLEGE

61 Sever Street
Worchester, MA 01615
(508) 791-9241
Judith Tuori, MS, MSN, APRN, BC

www.beckercollege.edu

Accreditation
Massachusetts Board of Registration in Nursing,
National League for Nursing Accrediting
Commission (NLNAC)

At the request of this nursing school, publication has been witheld.
Please contact the school directly for more information.

Key	Tuition Chart	▨ Program - in state ☐ Program - out of state ▨ Average - in state ■ Average - out of state

Massachusetts

BERKSHIRE COMMUNITY COLLEGE

1350 West Street
Pittsfield, MA 01201
(413) 499-4660
Patricia Brien, RN, MEd, MSN

At the request of this nursing school, publication has been witheld.
Please contact the school directly for more information.

www.berkshirecc.edu

Accreditation
Massachusetts Board of Registration in Nursing,
National League for Nursing Accrediting
Commission (NLNAC)

BRISTOL COMMUNITY COLLEGE

777 Elsbree St
Fall River, MA 02720
(508) 678-2811
Gail MacDonald, DNSc, RN

At the request of this nursing school, publication has been witheld.
Please contact the school directly for more information.

www.bristol.mass.edu

Accreditation
Massachusetts Board of Registration in Nursing,
National League for Nursing Accrediting
Commission (NLNAC)

BUNKER HILL COMMUNITY COLLEGE   *Useful Facts**

250 New Rutherford Ave
Charlestown, MA 02129
(617) 228-2318
Deborah Westaway, MS, RN

www.bhcc.mass.edu/newsite

Accreditation
Massachusetts Board of Registration in Nursing,
National League for Nursing Accrediting
Commission (NLNAC)

Acceptance rate	46.5%	

Degrees conferred
Associate Degree

Tuition[1]		**Student Demographics**	
In state	$135	Female	81.3%
Out of state	$306	Under age 25	18.0%
Enrollments	160	Minority	53.9%
Graduations	31	Part-time	4.4%

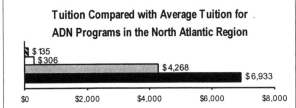

Tuition Compared with Average Tuition for ADN Programs in the North Atlantic Region

$135
$306
$4,268
$6,933

$0 $2,000 $4,000 $6,000 $8,000

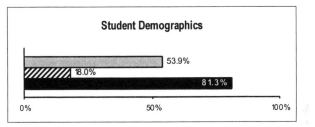

Student Demographics

53.9%
18.0%
81.3%

0%   50%   100%

Demographics Chart	■ Female ▨ Under age 25 ▢ Minority	**Distance Learning** 🖥	[1]The tuition reported for this program may be not be annualized. *Data reported between 2001 and 2004.

Massachusetts

CAPE COD COMMUNITY COLLEGE   *Useful Facts*

2240 Iyanough Rd
West Barnstable, MA 02668
(508) 362-2131
Luise Speakman, PhD, RN

www.capecod.edu

Acceptance rate	28.8%	
Faculty-student ratio	1: 11	
Faculty Full time	8	
Part time	12	

Tuition	
In state	$3,660
Out of state	$9,840
Enrollments	155
Graduations	73

Student Demographics	
Female	90.3%
Under age 25	17.4%
Minority	8.8%
Part-time	0.0%

Accreditation
Massachusetts Board of Registration in Nursing,
National League for Nursing Accrediting
Commission (NLNAC)

Degrees conferred
Associate Degree

Minimum degree required
High school diploma or GED

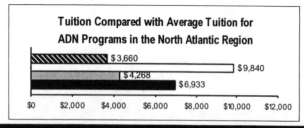

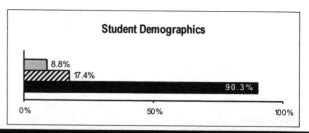

GREENFIELD COMMUNITY COLLEGE

270 Main Street
Greenfield, MA 01301
(413) 775-1630
Teresa Mariani, MS, RN

www.gcc.mass.edu

Accreditation
Massachusetts Board of Registration in Nursing,
National League for Nursing Accrediting
Commission (NLNAC)

At the request of this nursing school, publication has been withheld.
Please contact the school directly for more information.

HOLYOKE COMMUNITY COLLEGE   *Useful Facts**

303 Homestead
Holyoke, MA 01040
(413) 552-2458
Ninon Amertil, PhD, RN

hcc.mass.edu

Acceptance rate	12.8%	
Faculty-student ratio	1: 7	
Faculty Full time	7	
Part time	16	

Tuition	
In state	$1,152
Out of state	$5,520
Enrollments	101
Graduations	48

Student Demographics	
Female	89.1%
Minority	14.9%
Part-time	0.0%

Accreditation
Massachusetts Board of Registration in Nursing,
National League for Nursing Accrediting
Commission (NLNAC)

Degrees conferred
Associate Degree

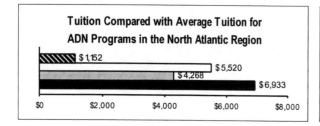

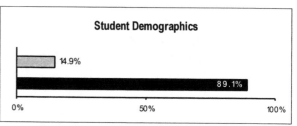

Key | Tuition Chart | ▧ Program - in state ☐ Program - out of state ☐ Average - in state ■ Average - out of state

Massachusetts

LABOURÉ COLLEGE

2120 Dorchester Ave
Boston, MA 02124
(617) 296-8300
Nancy Pedranti, MSN

www.laboure.edu

Accreditation
Massachusetts Board of Registration in Nursing,
National League for Nursing Accrediting
Commission (NLNAC)

*At the request of this nursing school, publication has been witheld.
Please contact the school directly for more information.*

LAWRENCE MEMORIAL/REGIS COLLEGE — Useful Facts

170 Governors Avenue
Medford, MA 02155
(781) 768-7091
Antoinette Hays, PhD

www.regiscollege.edu

Accreditation
Massachusetts Board of Registration in Nursing,
National League for Nursing Accrediting
Commission (NLNAC)

Acceptance rate		30.3%
Faculty-student ratio		1: 9
Faculty	Full time	30
	Part time	8

Tuition	
In state	$12,415
Out of state	$12,415
Enrollments	317
Graduations	100

Student Demographics	
Female	88.3%
Under age 25	20.8%
Minority	11.0%
Part-time	24.6%

Degrees conferred
Associate Degree

Minimum degree required
High school diploma or GED

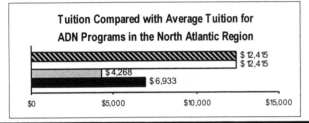

Tuition Compared with Average Tuition for ADN Programs in the North Atlantic Region

$12,415
$12,415
$4,268
$6,933

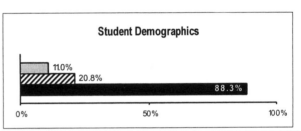

Student Demographics

11.0%
20.8%
88.3%

MASSACHUSETTS BAY COMMUNITY COLLEGE — Useful Facts

19 Flagg Drive
Framingham, MA 01702
(508) 270-4025
Claire MacDonald, RN, MSN

www.mbcc.mass.edu

Accreditation
Massachusetts Board of Registration in Nursing,
National League for Nursing Accrediting
Commission (NLNAC)

Acceptance rate		18.3%
Faculty-student ratio		1: 9
Faculty	Full time	12
	Part time	40

Tuition[1]	
In state	$119
Out of state	$325
Enrollments	287
Graduations	104

Student Demographics	
Female	87.1%
Under age 25	14.6%
Minority	19.8%
Part-time	58.9%

Degrees conferred
Associate Degree

Minimum degree required
High school diploma or GED

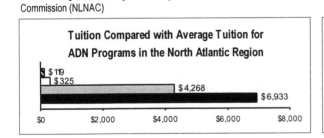

Tuition Compared with Average Tuition for ADN Programs in the North Atlantic Region

$119
$325
$4,268
$6,933

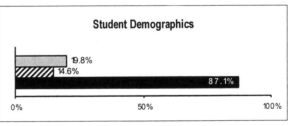

Student Demographics

19.8%
14.6%
87.1%

Demographics Chart	■Female ▨Under age 25 ▢Minority	Distance Learning	[1]The tuition reported for this program may be not be annualized. *Data reported between 2001 and 2004.

Massachusetts

MASSASOIT COMMUNITY COLLEGE

1 Massasoit Blvd
Brockton, MA 02302
(508) 588-9100
Barbara Waible, MSN, RN

www.massasoit.mass.edu

Accreditation
Massachusetts Board of Registration in Nursing,
National League for Nursing Accrediting
Commission (NLNAC)

At the request of this nursing school, publication has been witheld.
Please contact the school directly for more information.

MIDDLESEX COMMUNITY COLLEGE   *Useful Facts*

Derby Bldg, 33 Kearney Sq
Lowell, MA 01852
(978) 656-3047
Katherine Gehly, MSN, RN, CPNP

www.mymcc.middlesex.mass.edu

Accreditation
Massachusetts Board of Registration in Nursing,
National League for Nursing Accrediting
Commission (NLNAC)

Acceptance rate	15.4%	
Faculty-student ratio	1: 8	
Faculty Full time	10	
Part time	25	

Tuition		**Student Demographics**	
In state	$4,140	Female	88.9%
Out of state	$4,554	Under age 25	29.4%
Enrollments	180	Minority	23.0%
Graduations	48	Part-time	34.4%

Degrees conferred
Associate Degree

Minimum degree required
High school diploma or GED

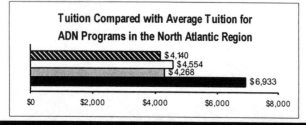

**Tuition Compared with Average Tuition for
ADN Programs in the North Atlantic Region**

$4,140
$4,554
$4,268
$6,933

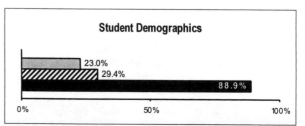

Student Demographics

23.0%
29.4%
88.9%

MOUNT WACHUSETT COMMUNITY COLLEGE   *Useful Facts*

444 Green Street
Gardner, MA 01440
(978) 632-6600
Eileen Costello, MS, RN

mwcc.mass.edu/html/nursing/index.html

Accreditation
Massachusetts Board of Registration in Nursing,
National League for Nursing Accrediting
Commission (NLNAC)

Acceptance rate	19.8%	
Faculty-student ratio	1: 7	
Faculty Full time	15	
Part time	23	

Tuition		**Student Demographics**	
In state	$900	Female	82.3%
Out of state	$1,350	Under age 25	18.2%
Enrollments	198	Minority	11.8%
Graduations	85	Part-time	89.4%

Degrees conferred
Associate Degree

Minimum degree required
High school diploma or GED

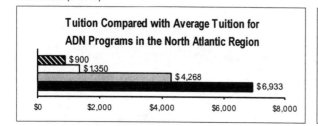

**Tuition Compared with Average Tuition for
ADN Programs in the North Atlantic Region**

$900
$1,350
$4,268
$6,933

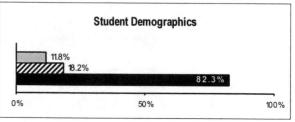

Student Demographics

11.8%
18.2%
82.3%

Key | Tuition Chart | ▨ Program - in state ▢ Program - out of state ▢ Average - in state ■ Average - out of state

Massachusetts

NORTHERN ESSEX COMMUNITY COLLEGE | *Useful Facts*

45 Franklin Street
Lawrence, MA 01840
(978) 738-7446
Anne Zabriskie, RN, MS

www.nec.mass.edu

Acceptance rate	16.8%
Faculty-student ratio	1: 9
Faculty Full time	8
Part time	23

Tuition¹

In state	$105
Out of state	$346
Enrollments	167
Graduations	80

Student Demographics

Female	87.4%
Under age 25	17.4%
Minority	17.0%
Part-time	0.0%

Accreditation
Massachusetts Board of Registration in Nursing,
National League for Nursing Accrediting
Commission (NLNAC)

Degrees conferred
Associate Degree

Minimum degree required
High school diploma or GED

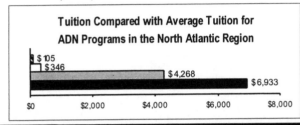
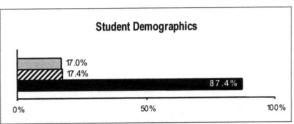

QUINCY COLLEGE | *Useful Facts*

34 Coddington St
Quincy, MA 02169
(617) 984-1614
Kristin Parks, MSN, RN, C

www.quincycollege.edu

Acceptance rate	74.5%
Faculty-student ratio	1: 11
Faculty Full time	6
Part time	38

Tuition

In state	$10,552
Out of state	$10,552
Enrollments	270
Graduations	114

Student Demographics

Female	87.8%
Under age 25	18.9%
Minority	16.6%
Part-time	43.3%

Accreditation
Massachusetts Board of Registration in Nursing,
National League for Nursing Accrediting
Commission (NLNAC)

Degrees conferred
Associate Degree

Minimum degree required
High school diploma or GED

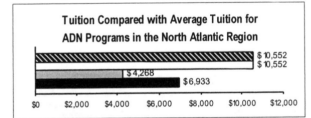
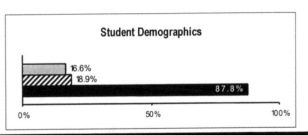

QUINSIGAMOND COMMUNITY COLLEGE | *Useful Facts*

670 W Boylston St
Worcester, MA 01606
(508) 854-2735
Patricia Creelman, RN, MS

www.qcc.mass.edu/nursing

Acceptance rate	8.5%
Faculty-student ratio	1: 7
Faculty Full time	17
Part time	16

Tuition

In state	$720
Out of state	$6,900
Enrollments	187
Graduations	87

Student Demographics

Female	89.3%
Under age 25	17.1%
Minority	34.6%
Part-time	0.0%

Accreditation
Massachusetts Board of Registration in Nursing,
National League for Nursing Accrediting
Commission (NLNAC)

Degrees conferred
Associate Degree

Minimum degree required
High school diploma or GED

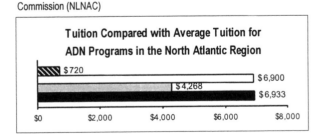
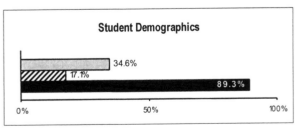

Demographics Chart	■ Female ▨ Under age 25 ☐ Minority	Distance Learning	¹The tuition reported for this program may be not be annualized. *Data reported between 2001 and 2004.

Massachusetts

ROXBURY COMMUNITY COLLEGE
Useful Facts

1234 Columbus Avenue
Boston, MA 02120
(617) 427-0060
JoAnn Mulready-Shick, MS, RN

www.rcc.mass.edu/nursing

Accreditation
Massachusetts Board of Registration in Nursing,
National League for Nursing Accrediting
Commission (NLNAC)

Acceptance rate		34.0%
Faculty-student ratio		1: 7
Faculty	Full time	8
	Part time	24

Degrees conferred
Associate Degree

Tuition	
In state	$1,070
Out of state	$2,000
Enrollments	134
Graduations	43

Minimum degree required
High school diploma or GED

Student Demographics	
Female	89.6%
Under age 25	11.2%
Minority	90.3%
Part-time	0.0%

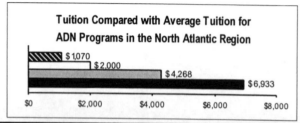

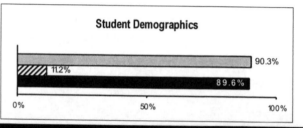

SPRINGFIELD TECHNICAL COMMUNITY COLLEGE
Useful Facts

One Armory Sq
Springfield, MA 01102
(413) 755-4855
Mary Tarbell, MS, RN

www.stcc.edu

Accreditation
Massachusetts Board of Registration in Nursing,
National League for Nursing Accrediting
Commission (NLNAC)

Acceptance rate		13.8%
Faculty-student ratio		1: 11
Faculty	Full time	10
	Part time	17

Degrees conferred
Associate Degree

Tuition	
In state	$600
Out of state	$5,520
Enrollments	198
Graduations	83

Minimum degree required
High school diploma or GED

Student Demographics	
Female	86.4%
Under age 25	11.6%
Minority	7.4%
Part-time	100.0%

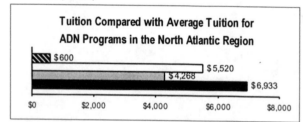

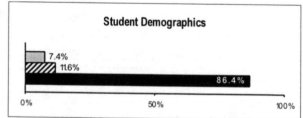

Michigan

ALPENA COMMUNITY COLLEGE
Useful Facts*

666 Johnson
Alpena, MI 49707
(989) 358-7333
Kathleen Gouin, MSN, RN

www.alpena.cc.mi.us

Accreditation
Michigan/DCH/Bureau of Health Professions

Acceptance rate	100.0%

Degrees conferred
Associate Degree

Tuition¹	
In state	$63
Out of state	$93
Enrollments	18
Graduations	13

Student Demographics	
Female	83.3%

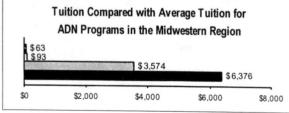

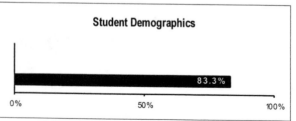

Key Tuition Chart | ▨ Program - in state □ Program - out of state ▤ Average - in state ■ Average - out of state

Michigan

BAKER COLLEGE - CLINTON TOWNSHIP

34950 Little Mack Avenue
Clinton Township, MI 48035
(586) 790-9680
Anna Czubatyi

www.baker.edu

Accreditation
Michigan/DCH/Bureau of Health Professions

Degrees conferred
Associate Degree

BAKER COLLEGE - FLINT

1050 West Bristol Road
Flint, MI 48507
(810) 766-4325
Bonnie Whaite

www.baker.edu

Accreditation
Michigan/DCH/Bureau of Health Professions

Degrees conferred
Associate Degree

BAKER COLLEGE - OWOSSO

1020 S Washington
Owosso, MI 48867
(989) 729-3388
Mary Slingerland

www.baker.edu

Accreditation
Michigan/DCH/Bureau of Health Professions

Degrees conferred
Associate Degree

BAY DE NOC COMMUNITY COLLEGE   Useful Facts

2001 North Lincoln Road
Escabana, MI 49829
(906) 786-5802
Linda Lewandowski, MSN, RN

www.baycollege.edu

Accreditation
Michigan/DCH/Bureau of Health Professions,
National League for Nursing Accrediting
Commission (NLNAC)

Acceptance rate		40.3%
Faculty-student ratio		1: 5
Faculty	Full time	6
	Part time	19

Tuition

In state	$1,977
Out of state	$4,470
Enrollments	75
Graduations	62

Student Demographics

Female	92.0%
Under age 25	29.3%
Minority	5.3%
Part-time	60.0%

Degrees conferred
Associate Degree

Minimum degree required
PN certificate if generic student or LPN if non-generic

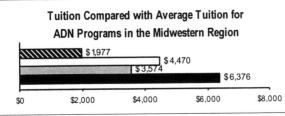

Tuition Compared with Average Tuition for ADN Programs in the Midwestern Region

$1,977
$4,470
$3,574
$6,376

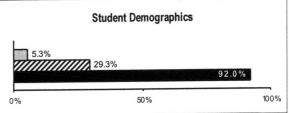

Student Demographics

5.3%
29.3%
92.0%

Demographics Chart | ■Female ▨Under age 25 ☐Minority | **Distance Learning** | ⌨ | ¹The tuition reported for this program may be not be annualized.
*Data reported between 2001 and 2004.

Michigan

DAVENPORT UNIVERSITY SYSTEM
Useful Facts*

3555 East Patrick Road
Midland, MI 48642
(517) 367-8219
Barbara Carter, MSN

www.davenport.edu

Accreditation
Michigan/DCH/Bureau of Health Professions

Acceptance rate	50.0%	

Degrees conferred
Associate Degree

Tuition[1]
In state	$253
Out of state	$253
Enrollments	50
Graduations	37

Student Demographics
Female	90.0%
Under age 25	10.0%
Minority	10.0%
Part-time	60.0%

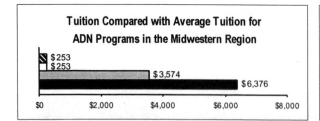

Tuition Compared with Average Tuition for ADN Programs in the Midwestern Region

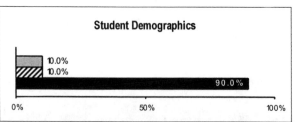

Student Demographics

DELTA COLLEGE
Useful Facts

1961 Delta Road
University Center, MI 48710
(989) 686-9274
David Peruski, RN, MSA, MSN

www.delta.edu/nursing

Accreditation
Michigan/DCH/Bureau of Health Professions,
National League for Nursing Accrediting
Commission (NLNAC)

Acceptance rate	50.4%	
Faculty-student ratio	1: 8	
Faculty	Full time	13
	Part time	22

Degrees conferred
Associate Degree

Tuition
In state	$2,175
Out of state	$3,120
Enrollments	190
Graduations	99

Student Demographics
Female	87.9%
Under age 25	27.4%
Minority	6.9%
Part-time	33.2%

Minimum degree required
High school diploma or GED

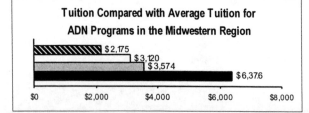

Tuition Compared with Average Tuition for ADN Programs in the Midwestern Region

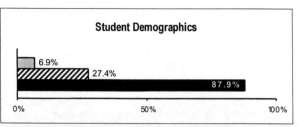

Student Demographics

FERRIS STATE UNIVERSITY
Useful Facts

200 Ferris Drive
Big Rapids, MI 49307
(231) 591-2267
Julie Coon, MSN, EdD

www.ferris.edu

Accreditation
Michigan/DCH/Bureau of Health Professions

Acceptance rate	21.7%	
Faculty-student ratio	1: 9	
Faculty	Full time	6
	Part time	4

Degrees conferred
Associate Degree

Tuition
In state	$6,740
Out of state	$13,480
Enrollments	72
Graduations	55

Student Demographics
Female	94.4%
Under age 25	86.1%
Minority	7.1%
Part-time	16.7%

Minimum degree required
High school diploma or GED

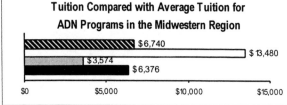

Tuition Compared with Average Tuition for ADN Programs in the Midwestern Region

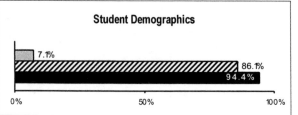

Student Demographics

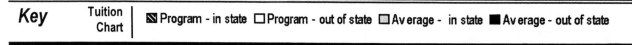

Key | Tuition Chart | ◩ Program - in state ☐ Program - out of state ☐ Average - in state ■ Average - out of state

Michigan

FINLANDIA UNIVERSITY
*Useful Facts**

601 Quincy Street
Hancock, MI 49930
(906) 487-7305
Frederika De Yampert, MSN, RN

www.finlandia.edu

Accreditation
Michigan/DCH/Bureau of Health Professions

Acceptance rate	70.4%

Degrees conferred
Associate Degree

Tuition		Student Demographics	
In state	$13,750	Female	91.7%
Out of state	$13,750	Under age 25	39.0%
Enrollments	108	Minority	4.6%
Graduations	17	Part-time	0.0%

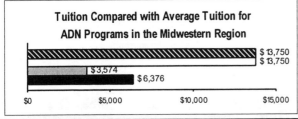

Tuition Compared with Average Tuition for ADN Programs in the Midwestern Region

$13,750
$13,750
$3,574
$6,376

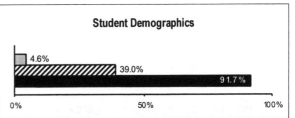

Student Demographics

4.6%
39.0%
91.7%

GLEN OAKS COMMUNITY COLLEGE

62249 Shimmel Road
Centreville, MI 49032
(616) 467-9945
Karen Ganger, ADN, BSN, MED, MS, RN, CS, CARN

www.glenoaks.cc.mi.us

Accreditation
Michigan/DCH/Bureau of Health Professions

Degrees conferred
Associate Degree

GOGEBIC COMMUNITY COLLEGE
Useful Facts

East 4946 Jackson Road
Ironwood, MI 49938
(906) 932-4231
Kari Luoma, RN, MSN

www.gogebic.cc.mi.us

Accreditation
Michigan/DCH/Bureau of Health Professions

Acceptance rate		63.6%
Faculty-student ratio		1:4
Faculty	Full time	2
	Part time	7

Degrees conferred
Associate Degree

Tuition		Student Demographics	
In state	$1,998	Female	100.0%
Out of state	$3,240	Under age 25	30.0%
Enrollments	20		
Graduations	20	Part-time	0.0%

Minimum degree required
Diploma

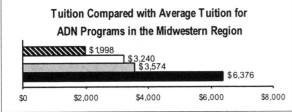

Tuition Compared with Average Tuition for ADN Programs in the Midwestern Region

$1,998
$3,240
$3,574
$6,376

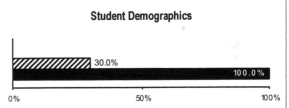

Student Demographics

30.0%
100.0%

Demographics Chart	■Female ☑Under age 25 ☐Minority	Distance Learning	†The tuition reported for this program may be not be annualized. *Data reported between 2001 and 2004.

MI   **329**

Michigan

GRAND RAPIDS COMMUNITY COLLEGE

143 Bostwick, North East
Grand Rapids, MI 49503
(616) 234-3902
Juan Olivarez, PhD

www.grcc.edu

Accreditation
Michigan/DCH/Bureau of Health Professions,
National League for Nursing Accrediting
Commission (NLNAC)

Acceptance rate	8.0%	
Faculty-student ratio	1: 7	
Faculty	Full time	20
	Part time	18

Degrees conferred
Associate Degree

Tuition	
In state	$2,085
Out of state	$3,750
Enrollments	210
Graduations	48

Minimum degree required
High school diploma or GED

Student Demographics	
Female	90.5%
Under age 25	36.7%
Minority	23.3%
Part-time	50.0%

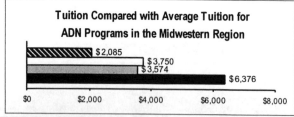

Tuition Compared with Average Tuition for ADN Programs in the Midwestern Region

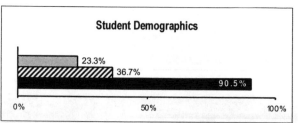

Student Demographics

HENRY FORD COMMUNITY COLLEGE

5101 Evergreen Road
Dearborn, MI 48128
(313) 845-9661
Katherine Bradley, PhD, RN

hfcc.edu

Accreditation
Michigan/DCH/Bureau of Health Professions,
National League for Nursing Accrediting
Commission (NLNAC)

Acceptance rate	49.9%	
Faculty-student ratio	1: 13	
Faculty	Full time	17
	Part time	35

Degrees conferred
Associate Degree

Tuition[1]	
In state	$57
Out of state	$120
Enrollments	440
Graduations	166

Minimum degree required
High school diploma or GED

Student Demographics	
Female	89.5%
Under age 25	36.8%
Minority	32.0%
Part-time	0.0%

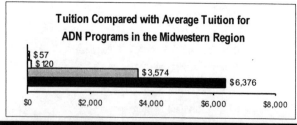

Tuition Compared with Average Tuition for ADN Programs in the Midwestern Region

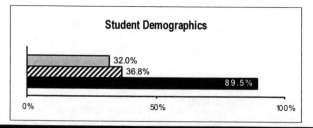

Student Demographics

JACKSON COMMUNITY COLLEGE

2111 Emmons Road
Jackson, MI 49201
(517) 796-8515
Kathleen Walsh, RN, MS, BSN

www.jackson.cc.mi.us

Accreditation
Michigan/DCH/Bureau of Health Professions

Degrees conferred
Associate Degree

Key | Tuition Chart | ▨ Program - in state ☐ Program - out of state ▧ Average - in state ■ Average - out of state

Michigan

KALAMAZOO VALLEY COMMUNITY COLLEGE
*Useful Facts**

6767 West O Avenue
Kalamazoo, MI 49009
(616) 488-4108
Dennis Bertch, RN, MSN

www.kvcc.edu

Acceptance rate	29.6%	

Tuition		
In state	$1,449
Out of state	$3,576
Enrollments	159
Graduations	62

Student Demographics	
Female	88.7%
Minority	9.8%
Part-time	15.1%

Accreditation
Michigan/DCH/Bureau of Health Professions

Degrees conferred
Associate Degree

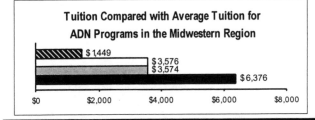

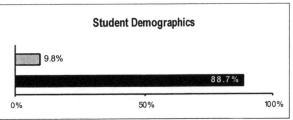

KELLOGG COMMUNITY COLLEGE
*Useful Facts**

450 North Avenue
Battle Creek, MI 49017
(616) 965-3931
Cynthia Sublett, DNSc, RN

www.kellogg.edu

Acceptance rate	34.5%	

Tuition		
In state	$8,500
Out of state	$10,500
Enrollments	187
Graduations	82

Student Demographics	
Female	91.4%
Under age 25	25.0%
Minority	5.3%
Part-time	27.8%

Accreditation
Michigan/DCH/Bureau of Health Professions

Degrees conferred
Associate Degree

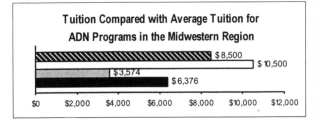

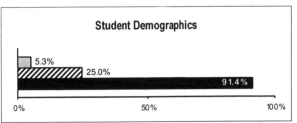

KIRTLAND COMMUNITY COLLEGE
*Useful Facts**

10775 North St Helen Road
Roscommon, MI 48653
(989) 275-5000
Karen Brown, RN, BC, EdD

www.kirtland.edu/health/nursing.htm

Faculty-student ratio	1: 4	
Faculty	Full time	6
	Part time	25
Enrollments		37

Student Demographics	
Female	81.1%
Under age 25	27.0%
Part-time	45.9%

Accreditation
Michigan/DCH/Bureau of Health Professions

Degrees conferred
Associate Degree

| Demographics Chart | ■Female ☒Under age 25 ☐Minority | Distance Learning | †The tuition reported for this program may be not be annualized.
*Data reported between 2001 and 2004. |
|---|---|---|---|

Michigan

KIRTLAND COMMUNITY COLLEGE - RN from LPN Online Program

10775 North St Helen Road
Roscommon, MI 48653
(989) 275-5000
Karen Brown, RN, BC, EdD

www.kirtland.edu/health/nursing.htm

Accreditation
Michigan/DCH/Bureau of Health Professions

Acceptance rate		100.0%
Faculty-student ratio		1:4
Faculty	Full time	6
	Part time	25

Degrees conferred
Associate Degree

Tuition[1]	
In state	$63
Out of state	$142
Enrollments	38
Graduations	41

Minimum degree required
LPN

Student Demographics	
Female	81.6%
Under age 25	21.1%
Part-time	42.1%

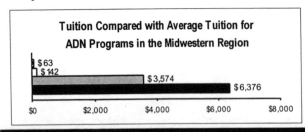

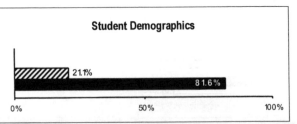

LAKE MICHIGAN COLLEGE

2755 East Napier
Benton Harbor, MI 49022
(269) 927-8100
Delores Jackson, RN, ASN, BSN, MSN

lakemichigancollege.edu/occu/healthsci/nursing.html

Accreditation
Michigan/DCH/Bureau of Health Professions,
National League for Nursing Accrediting
Commission (NLNAC)

At the request of this nursing school, publication has been witheld.
Please contact the school directly for more information.

LANSING COMMUNITY COLLEGE — Useful Facts

3100 - Nursing Careers Dept, PO Box 40010
Lansing, MI 48901
(517) 483-1461
Margie Clark, MSN, RN, CS, CCRN, GNP

www.lcc.edu/nursing

Accreditation
Michigan/DCH/Bureau of Health Professions,
National League for Nursing Accrediting
Commission (NLNAC)

Acceptance rate		9.1%
Faculty-student ratio		1:8
Faculty	Full time	11
	Part time	60

Degrees conferred
LPN or LVN, Associate Degree

Tuition	
In state	$2,681
Out of state	$5,981
Enrollments	346
Graduations	111

Minimum degree required
High school diploma or GED

Student Demographics	
Female	87.9%
Under age 25	32.4%
Minority	13.8%
Part-time	23.7%

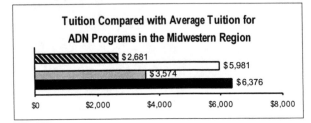

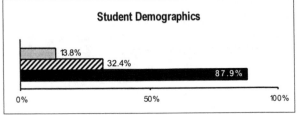

Key | Tuition Chart | ⬛ Program - in state ☐ Program - out of state ▦ Average - in state ■ Average - out of state

Michigan

MACOMB COMMUNITY COLLEGE — *Useful Facts*

44575 Garfield Road
Clinton Township, MI 48038
(586) 286-2074
Bernadette Pieczynski, MSN, APRN, BC

www.macomb.edu

Accreditation
Michigan/DCH/Bureau of Health Professions,
National League for Nursing Accrediting
Commission (NLNAC)

Acceptance rate	18.5%	
Faculty-student ratio	1: 13	
Faculty	Full time	12
	Part time	12

Degrees conferred
Associate Degree

Tuition	
In state	$1,950
Out of state	$2,970
Enrollments	229
Graduations	94

Minimum degree required
None

Student Demographics	
Female	85.2%
Under age 25	22.3%
Minority	3.1%
Part-time	0.0%

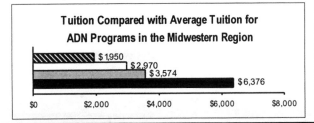

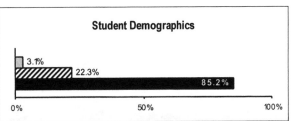

MID-MICHIGAN COMMUNITY COLLEGE — *Useful Facts**

1375 South Clare Avenue
Harrison, MI 48625
(989) 386-6645
Beth Sendre, MSN, RN

www.midmich.cc.mi.us

Accreditation
Michigan/DCH/Bureau of Health Professions

Acceptance rate	100.0%

Degrees conferred
Associate Degree

Tuition	
In state	$1,736
Out of state	$2,816
Enrollments	30

Student Demographics	
Female	96.7%
Part-time	33.3%

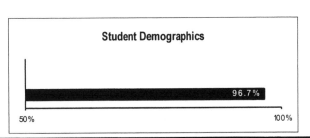

MONROE COUNTY COMMUNITY COLLEGE — *Useful Facts*

1555 S Raisinville Road
Monroe, MI 48161
(734) 384-4102
Gail Odneal, MSN, RN

www.monroe.ccc.edu

Accreditation
Michigan/DCH/Bureau of Health Professions,
National League for Nursing Accrediting
Commission (NLNAC)

Acceptance rate	41.2%	
Faculty-student ratio	1: 10	
Faculty	Full time	4
	Part time	8

Degrees conferred
Associate Degree

Tuition	
In state	$2,232
Out of state	$4,032
Enrollments	82
Graduations	33

Minimum degree required
High school diploma or GED

Student Demographics	
Female	92.7%
Under age 25	39.0%
Minority	7.3%
Part-time	65.9%

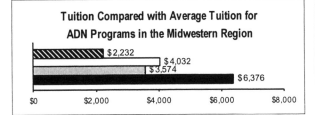

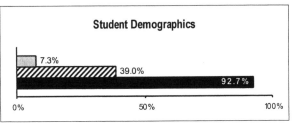

Demographics Chart	■ Female ▨ Under age 25 ☐ Minority	Distance Learning	¹The tuition reported for this program may be not be annualized.
			*Data reported between 2001 and 2004.

Michigan

MONTCALM COMMUNITY COLLEGE
Useful Facts*

2800 College Drive
Sidney, MI 48885
(989) 328-1217
Bertha Mowatt, MSN, RN

www.montcalm.edu

Accreditation
Michigan/DCH/Bureau of Health Professions

Degrees conferred
Associate Degree

Acceptance rate	100.0%	

Tuition		Student Demographics	
In state	$2,640	Female	92.8%
Out of state	$5,148	Under age 25	45.0%
Enrollments	97	Minority	2.1%
Graduations	37	Part-time	16.5%

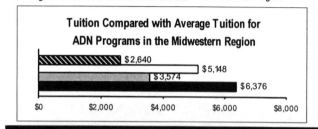

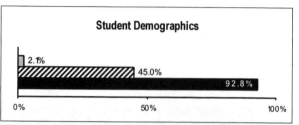

MOTT COMMUNITY COLLEGE
Useful Facts

1401 East Court Street
Flint, MI 48503
(810) 232-3271
Patricia Markowicz, BSN, MSN, RN

mcc.edu

Accreditation
Michigan/DCH/Bureau of Health Professions,
National League for Nursing Accrediting
Commission (NLNAC)

Degrees conferred
Associate Degree

Faculty-student ratio		1: 8	
Faculty	Full time	18	
	Part time	31	

Tuition		Student Demographics	
In state	$3,790	Female	93.2%
Out of state	$7,570	Under age 25	37.6%
Enrollments	266	Minority	24.8%
Graduations	93	Part-time	0.0%

Minimum degree required
High school diploma or GED

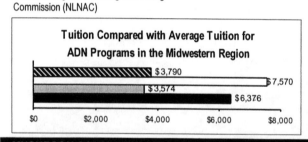

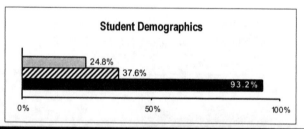

MUSKEGON COMMUNITY COLLEGE
Useful Facts*

221 South Quarterline Road
Muskegon, MI 49442
(231) 777-0281
Pamela Brown, MSN, RNCS

www.muskegoncc.edu

Accreditation
Michigan/DCH/Bureau of Health Professions

Degrees conferred
Associate Degree

Acceptance rate	100.0%	

		Student Demographics	
		Female	97.9%
		Under age 25	10.0%
Enrollments	140	Minority	3.6%
Graduations	47	Part-time	0.0%

NORTH CENTRAL MICHIGAN COLLEGE
Useful Facts*

1515 Howard Street
Petoskey, MI 49770
(231) 348-6681
Polly Flippo, MSN, RN

www.ncmc.cc.mi.us

Accreditation
Michigan/DCH/Bureau of Health Professions

Degrees conferred
Associate Degree

Acceptance rate	27.0%	

		Student Demographics	
		Female	87.7%
		Under age 25	25.0%
Enrollments	57	Minority	8.8%
Graduations	31	Part-time	0.0%

Key | Tuition Chart | ⧄ Program - in state ☐ Program - out of state ▨ Average - in state ■ Average - out of state

Michigan

NORTHWESTERN MICHIGAN COLLEGE — *Useful Facts**

1701 East Front St, Les Biederman Bldg
Traverse City, MI 49686
(231) 995-1245
Laura Schmidt, MSN, RN

www.nmc.edu/healthoccupations

Acceptance rate	85.1%

Tuition	
In state	$3,378
Out of state	$4,215
Enrollments	148
Graduations	47

Student Demographics	
Female	85.8%
Under age 25	39.9%
Minority	2.1%
Part-time	23.6%

Accreditation
Michigan/DCH/Bureau of Health Professions

Degrees conferred
Associate Degree

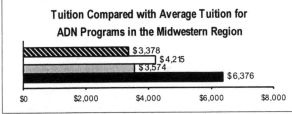

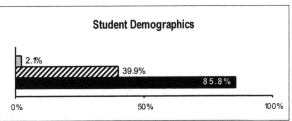

OAKLAND COMMUNITY COLLEGE — *Useful Facts*

7350 Cooley Lake Road
Waterford, MI 48327
(248) 942-3337
Nadia Boulos, PhD, RN

www.oaklandcc.edu

Acceptance rate	52.9%
Faculty-student ratio	1: 10

Faculty	Full time	13
	Part time	63

Tuition	
In state	$3,216
Out of state	$6,170
Enrollments	462
Graduations	212

Student Demographics	
Female	90.5%
Under age 25	25.5%
Minority	39.8%
Part-time	100.0%

Minimum degree required
High school diploma or GED

Accreditation
Michigan/DCH/Bureau of Health Professions,
National League for Nursing Accrediting
Commission (NLNAC)

Degrees conferred
Associate Degree

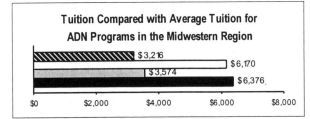

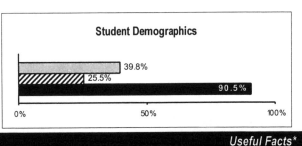

SAINT CLAIR COUNTY COMMUNITY COLLEGE — *Useful Facts**

323 Erie Street, PO Box 5015
Port Huron, MI 48060
(810) 989-5680
Susan Meeker, BSN, MSN, RN

stclair.cc.mi.us

Acceptance rate	79.2%

Tuition	
In state	$1,458
Out of state	$2,136
Enrollments	151
Graduations	80

Student Demographics	
Female	92.7%
Minority	5.3%
Part-time	0.0%

Accreditation
Michigan/DCH/Bureau of Health Professions

Degrees conferred
Associate Degree

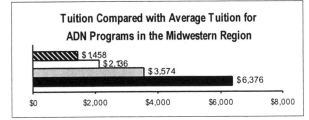

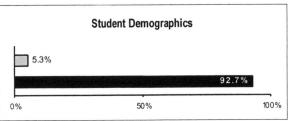

Demographics Chart	■ Female ▨ Under age 25 ▢ Minority	Distance Learning	†The tuition reported for this program may be not be annualized. *Data reported between 2001 and 2004.

Michigan

SCHOOLCRAFT COLLEGE
Useful Facts*

18600 Haggerty Road
Livonia, MI 48152
(734) 462-4528
Midge Carleton, RN, MS

www.lv.schoolcraft.cc.mi.us

Acceptance rate	100.0%	**Tuition**		**Student Demographics**	
		In state	$4,015	Female	93.8%
		Out of state	$5,986	Under age 25	30.0%
		Enrollments	160	Minority	17.9%
		Graduations	40	Part-time	0.0%

Accreditation
Michigan/DCH/Bureau of Health Professions

Degrees conferred
Associate Degree

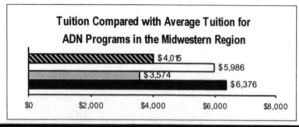

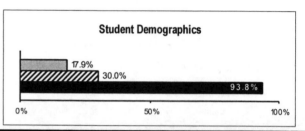

SOUTHWESTERN MICHIGAN COLLEGE
Useful Facts*

58900 Cherry Grove Road
Dowagiac, MI 49047
(616) 782-1237
Elaine Foster, MSN, RN

www.smc.cc.mi.us

Accreditation
Michigan/DCH/Bureau of Health Professions

Degrees conferred
Associate Degree

WASHTENAW COMMUNITY COLLEGE
Useful Facts*

4800 E Huron River Drive
Ann Arbor, MI 48106
(734) 677-5110
Gloria Velarde, MSN, BSN

www.wccnet.org/dept/health/nurs

Acceptance rate	32.1%	**Tuition¹**		**Student Demographics**	
		In state	$81	Female	87.8%
		Out of state	$104	Under age 25	34.1%
		Enrollments	246	Minority	21.5%
		Graduations	80	Part-time	11.0%

Accreditation
Michigan/DCH/Bureau of Health Professions,
National League for Nursing Accrediting
Commission (NLNAC)

Degrees conferred
Associate Degree

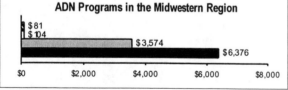

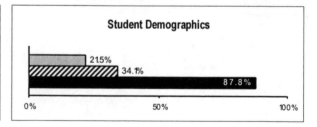

Key | Tuition Chart | ⊠ Program - in state ☐ Program - out of state ▨ Average - in state ■ Average - out of state

Michigan

WAYNE COUNTY COMMUNITY COLLEGE — *Useful Facts*

8551 Greenfield
Detroit, MI 48228
(313) 943-4478
Rosellen Burkart, MSN, RNC

wcccd.edu

Acceptance rate	68.6%	
Faculty-student ratio	1: 14	
Faculty Full time	14	
Part time	32	

Tuition	
In state	$1,620
Out of state	$2,670
Enrollments	420
Graduations	116

Student Demographics	
Female	86.9%
Under age 25	22.1%
Minority	62.1%
Part-time	0.0%

Accreditation
Michigan/DCH/Bureau of Health Professions

Degrees conferred
Associate Degree

Minimum degree required
High school diploma or GED

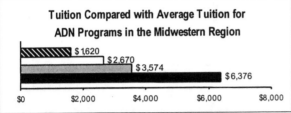
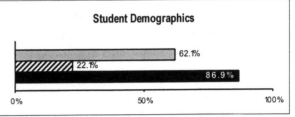

WEST SHORE COMMUNITY COLLEGE — *Useful Facts**

3000 North Stiles Road
Scottville, MI 49454
(231) 845-6211
Patricia Collins, BSN, MSN, MEd, EdD

www.westshore.edu

Acceptance rate	14.2%	
Faculty-student ratio	1: 10	
Faculty Full time	4	
Part time	3	

Tuition	
In state	$1,875
Out of state	$4,050
Enrollments	56
Graduations	30

Student Demographics	
Female	89.3%
Under age 25	15.0%
Minority	8.9%
Part-time	7.1%

Accreditation
Michigan/DCH/Bureau of Health Professions

Degrees conferred
Associate Degree

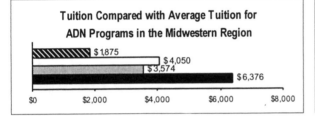
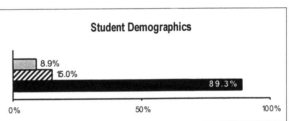

Minnesota

ANOKA-RAMSEY COMMUNITY COLLEGE — *Useful Facts*

11200 Mississippi Boulevard North West
Coon Rapids, MN 55433
(763) 433-1113
Ann Holland, MA, RN

www.anokaramsey.edu

Acceptance rate	39.5%	
Faculty-student ratio	1: 15	
Faculty Full time	14	
Part time	17	

Tuition	
In state	$3,198
Out of state	$6,396
Enrollments	334
Graduations	162

Student Demographics	
Female	88.0%
Under age 25	41.0%
Minority	8.8%
Part-time	91.6%

Accreditation
Minnesota Board of Nursing, National League for
Nursing Accrediting Commission (NLNAC)

Degrees conferred
Associate Degree

Minimum degree required
None

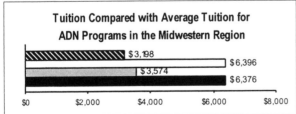
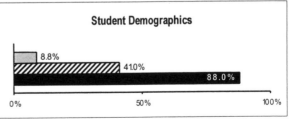

Demographics Chart	■Female ☒Under age 25 ☐Minority	Distance Learning	†The tuition reported for this program may be not be annualized. *Data reported between 2001 and 2004.

Minnesota

CENTRAL LAKES COLLEGE

501 West College Drive
Brainerd, MN 56401
(218) 855-8195
Linda Anderson, RN, MA

www.clcmn.edu

Acceptance rate		53.6%
Faculty-student ratio		1: 18
Faculty	Full time	2
	Part time	1

Tuition	
In state	$7,815
Out of state	$15,630
Enrollments	45
Graduations	36

Student Demographics	
Female	88.9%
Under age 25	33.3%
Part-time	0.0%

Accreditation
Minnesota Board of Nursing

Degrees conferred
Associate Degree

Minimum degree required
Diploma

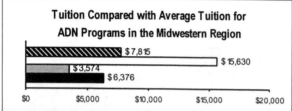

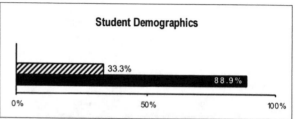

COLLEGE OF SAINT CATHERINE

2004 Randolph Ave
St Paul, MN 55105
(651) 690-6583
Alice Swan, DNSc, RN

minerva.stkate.edu/offices/academic/nursing.nsf

Acceptance rate		17.3%
Faculty-student ratio		1: 9
Faculty	Full time	50
	Part time	18

Tuition	
In state	$13,800
Out of state	$13,800
Enrollments	290
Graduations	142

Student Demographics	
Female	95.9%
Under age 25	34.8%
Minority	23.5%
Part-time	83.8%

Accreditation
Minnesota Board of Nursing, National League for
Nursing Accrediting Commission (NLNAC)

Degrees conferred
Associate Degree

Minimum degree required
High school diploma or GED

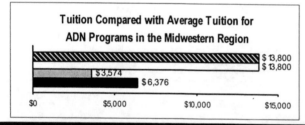

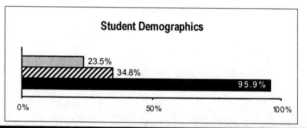

FOND DU LAC TRIBAL AND COMMUNITY COLLEGE - LAKE SUPERIOR COLLEGE

2101 14th Street
Cloquet, MN 55720
(218) 879-0800
Diane Kostrzewski

fdltcc.edu

Accreditation
Minnesota Board of Nursing

Degrees conferred
Associate Degree

Key | Tuition Chart | ◩ Program - in state ☐ Program - out of state ▢ Average - in state ■ Average - out of state

Minnesota

HIBBING COMMUNITY COLLEGE
Useful Facts*

1515 East 25th St
Hibbing, MN 55746
(218) 262-6743
Susan Hyndman, RN, EdD

www.hcc.mnscu.edu

Acceptance rate		51.0%

Tuition[1]			**Student Demographics**	
In state	$96		Female	92.6%
Out of state	$96		Under age 25	44.0%
Enrollments	176		Minority	8.0%
Graduations	48		Part-time	0.0%

Accreditation
Minnesota Board of Nursing

Degrees conferred
Associate Degree

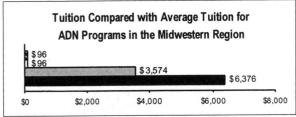

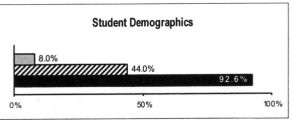

INVER HILLS COMMUNITY COLLEGE
Useful Facts

2500 80th Street East
Inver Grove Heights, MN 55076
(651) 450-8372
Lee Ann Joy, MSN

century.mnscu.edu/icnursing

Acceptance rate		20.2%
Faculty-student ratio		1: 16
Faculty	Full time	22
	Part time	7

Tuition[1]			**Student Demographics**	
In state	$126		Female	85.0%
Out of state	$252		Under age 25	26.0%
Enrollments	407		Minority	21.6%
Graduations	172		Part-time	96.6%

Accreditation
Minnesota Board of Nursing, National League for
Nursing Accrediting Commission (NLNAC)

Degrees conferred
Associate Degree

Minimum degree required
High school diploma or GED

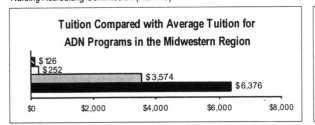

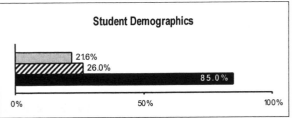

LAKE SUPERIOR COLLEGE

2101 Trinity Road
Duluth, MN 55811
(218) 723-5911
Kris Wagner, MA, RN

www.lsc.mnscu.edu

Accreditation
Minnesota Board of Nursing

Degrees conferred
Associate Degree

Demographics Chart	■Female ☑Under age 25 ☐Minority	Distance Learning	[1]The tuition reported for this program may be not be annualized. *Data reported between 2001 and 2004.

Minnesota

MINNEAPOLIS COMMUNITY AND TECHNICAL COLLEGE
Useful Facts

1501 Hennepin Ave
Minneapolis, MN 55403
(612) 659-6437
Faye Uppman, RN, BSN, MS

www.minneapolis.edu

Acceptance rate	25.4%
Faculty-student ratio	1: 10
Faculty Full time	20
Part time	3

Tuition[1]	
In state	$134
Out of state	$256
Enrollments	207
Graduations	115

Student Demographics	
Female	77.3%
Under age 25	25.1%
Minority	43.1%
Part-time	91.3%

Accreditation
Minnesota Board of Nursing, National League for Nursing Accrediting Commission (NLNAC)

Degrees conferred
LPN or LVN, Associate Degree

Minimum degree required
High school diploma or GED

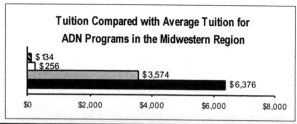

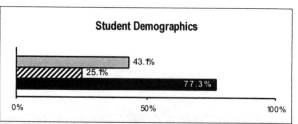

MINNESOTA STATE COLLEGE - SOUTHEAST TECHNICAL

110 Galewski Drive
Winona, MN 55987
(507) 453-2635
Laurie Becker, RN, MSN, DON

www.southeastmn.edu

Accreditation
Minnesota Board of Nursing

Degrees conferred
Associate Degree

MINNESOTA STATE COMMUNITY AND TECHNICAL COLLEGE - DETROIT LAKES

900 Hwy 34 E
Detroit Lakes, MN 56501
(218) 846-3769
Kathy Burlingame, MS

www.minnesota.edu

Accreditation
Minnesota Board of Nursing

Degrees conferred
Associate Degree

MINNESOTA WEST COMMUNITY & TECHNICAL COLLEGE - WORTHINGTON
Useful Facts*

1450 Collegeway
Worthington, MN 56187
(507) 372-3443
Joan Kuemper, RN, MS

www.mnwest.mnscu.edu/worthington/nursing

Acceptance rate	39.1%

Tuition	
In state	$3,900
Out of state	$3,900
Enrollments	68
Graduations	27

Student Demographics	
Female	91.2%
Under age 25	22.0%
Part-time	44.1%

Accreditation
Minnesota Board of Nursing, National League for Nursing Accrediting Commission (NLNAC)

Degrees conferred
Associate Degree

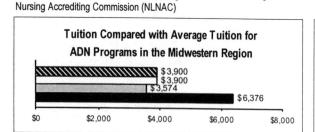

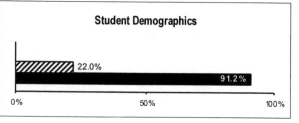

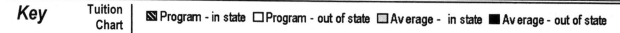

Key | Tuition Chart | ▨ Program - in state ▢ Program - out of state ▤ Average - in state ■ Average - out of state

Minnesota

NORMANDALE COMMUNITY COLLEGE — *Useful Facts*

9700 France Ave South
Bloomington, MN 55431
(952) 487-8158
Kathleen Manahan, EdD, RN

www.normandale.edu

Acceptance rate	57.5%
Faculty-student ratio	1: 16
Faculty Full time	12
Part time	0

Tuition[1]	
In state	$133
Out of state	$253
Enrollments	193
Graduations	79

Student Demographics	
Female	85.5%
Under age 25	24.9%
Minority	16.2%
Part-time	96.9%

Accreditation
Minnesota Board of Nursing, National League for
Nursing Accrediting Commission (NLNAC)

Degrees conferred
Associate Degree

Minimum degree required
High school diploma or GED

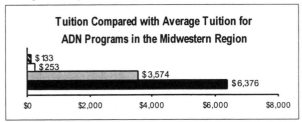

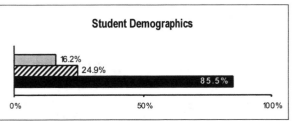

NORTH HENNEPIN COMMUNITY COLLEGE — *Useful Facts**

7411 85th Ave North
Brooklyn Park, MN 55445
(763) 424-0759
Mary Reuland, EdD, RN

www.nh.cc.us

Acceptance rate	42.9%

Tuition[1]	
In state	$105
Out of state	$208
Enrollments	260
Graduations	104

Student Demographics	
Female	86.2%
Under age 25	0.0%
Part-time	0.0%

Accreditation
Minnesota Board of Nursing, National League for
Nursing Accrediting Commission (NLNAC)

Degrees conferred
Associate Degree

Minimum degree required
High school diploma or GED

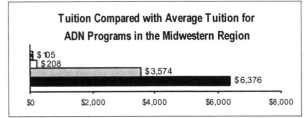

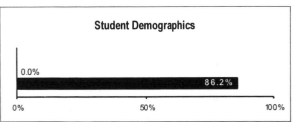

NORTHLAND COMMUNITY AND TECHNICAL COLLEGE - *Thief River Falls*

1101 Hwy 1 East
Thief River Falls, MN 56701
(218) 681-0841
Sue Field, RN, MS

www.northlandcollege.edu

Acceptance rate	57.7%

Enrollments	58
Graduations	51

Student Demographics	
Female	96.6%
Under age 25	33.0%
Minority	1.7%

Accreditation
Minnesota Board of Nursing

Degrees conferred
Associate Degree

Demographics Chart | ■ Female ▨ Under age 25 ▢ Minority | **Distance Learning** | [1]The tuition reported for this program may be not be annualized.
*Data reported between 2001 and 2004.

Minnesota

RIDGEWATER COLLEGE
Useful Facts

2101 15th Ave NW
Willmar, MN 56201
(320) 231-6034
Lynn Johnson, MSN, RN

www.ridgewater.edu

Accreditation
Minnesota Board of Nursing, National League for
Nursing Accrediting Commission (NLNAC)

Acceptance rate	62.5%
Faculty-student ratio	1: 3
Faculty Full time	5
Part time	6

Tuition	
In state	$3,675
Out of state	$7,350
Enrollments	25
Graduations	65

Student Demographics	
Female	100.0%
Under age 25	20.0%
Part-time	80.0%

Degrees conferred
Associate Degree

Minimum degree required
Diploma

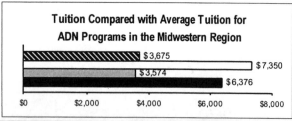

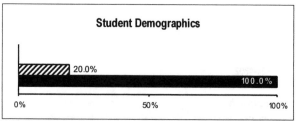

RIVERLAND COMMUNITY COLLEGE
Useful Facts

1900 8th Avenue NW
Austin, MN 55912
(507) 433-0826
Patricia Parsons, MSN

www.riverland.cc.mn.us

Accreditation
Minnesota Board of Nursing, National League for
Nursing Accrediting Commission (NLNAC)

Acceptance rate	35.0%
Faculty-student ratio	1: 18
Faculty Full time	7
Part time	3

Tuition	
In state	$3,390
Out of state	$6,780
Enrollments	150
Graduations	63

Student Demographics	
Female	86.0%
Under age 25	36.0%
Minority	5.4%
Part-time	87.3%

Degrees conferred
Associate Degree

Minimum degree required
High school diploma or GED

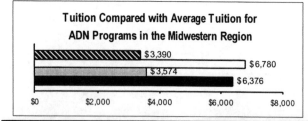

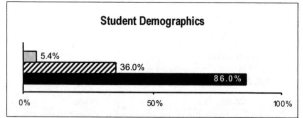

ROCHESTER COMMUNITY & TECHNICAL COLLEGE
Useful Facts

851 30th Ave SE
Rochester, MN 55904
(507) 285-7143
Merry Gay, MSN, RN

www.rctc.edu/program/nurs

Accreditation
Minnesota Board of Nursing, National League for
Nursing Accrediting Commission (NLNAC)

Acceptance rate	29.5%
Faculty-student ratio	1: 12
Faculty Full time	12
Part time	14

Tuition	
In state	$3,498
Out of state	$6,996
Enrollments	233
Graduations	109

Student Demographics	
Female	90.1%
Under age 25	42.9%
Minority	5.4%
Part-time	73.4%

Degrees conferred
Associate Degree

Minimum degree required
High school diploma or GED

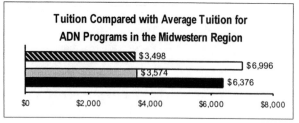

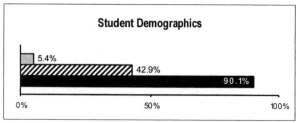

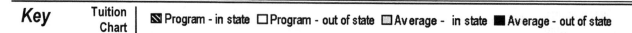

Key | Tuition Chart | ▨ Program - in state ☐ Program - out of state ▧ Average - in state ■ Average - out of state

Minnesota

SOUTH CENTRAL TECHNICAL COLLEGE - MANKATO

1920 Lee Blvd
Mankato, MN 56003
(507) 389-7200
Gail Westphal, MS

At the request of this nursing school, publication has been withheld.
Please contact the school directly for more information.

southcentral.edu

Accreditation
Minnesota Board of Nursing

Mississippi

ALCORN STATE UNIVERSITY   *Useful Facts*

15 Campus Drive	**Acceptance rate**	31.9%	**Tuition**		**Student Demographics**	
Natchez, MS 39120	**Faculty-student ratio**	1: 12	In state	$4,417	Female	85.5%
(601) 304-4302	**Faculty** Full time	15	Out of state	$6,902	Under age 25	51.6%
Mary Hill, DSN, RN	Part time	5	**Enrollments**	124	Minority	63.7%
www.alcorn.edu			**Graduations**	28	Part-time	33.1%

Accreditation
Mississippi Board of Nursing, National League
for Nursing Accrediting Commission (NLNAC)

Degrees conferred
Associate Degree

Minimum degree required
High school diploma or GED

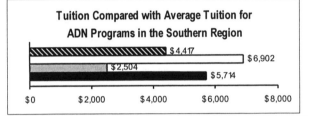

Tuition Compared with Average Tuition for ADN Programs in the Southern Region

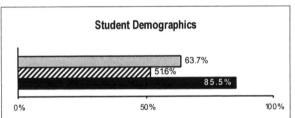

Student Demographics

COAHOMA COMMUNITY COLLEGE

3240 Friars Point Rd
Clarksdale, MS 38614
(662) 621-8898
Paula Bell, AAN, BSN, CCRN

www.ccc.cc.ms.us

Accreditation
Mississippi Board of Nursing

Degrees conferred
Associate Degree

COPIAH - LINCOLN COMMUNITY COLLEGE - Wesson

PO Box 649	**Acceptance rate**	28.7%	**Tuition**		**Student Demographics**	
Wesson, MS 39191			In state	$1,700	Female	82.7%
(601) 643-8413			Out of state	$3,500	Under age 25	51.0%
Mary Canterbury, MSN, RN			**Enrollments**	81	Minority	18.5%
www.colin.edu/nursing			**Graduations**	28	Part-time	0.0%

Accreditation
Mississippi Board of Nursing, National League
for Nursing Accrediting Commission (NLNAC)

Degrees conferred
Associate Degree

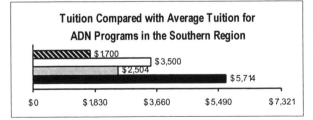

Tuition Compared with Average Tuition for ADN Programs in the Southern Region

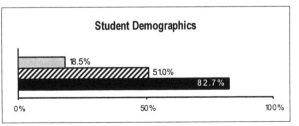

Student Demographics

Demographics Chart	■Female ☑Under age 25 ▢Minority	Distance Learning	¹The tuition reported for this program may be not be annualized. *Data reported between 2001 and 2004.

Mississippi

EAST CENTRAL COMMUNITY COLLEGE

275 West Broad Street, PO Box 129
Decatur, MS 39327
(601) 635-2111
Melanie Gilmore, MSN, RN

www.eccc.edu

Acceptance rate	38.5%	
Faculty-student ratio	1: 12	
Faculty	Full time	8
	Part time	2

Tuition
In state $1,400
Out of state $2,100
Enrollments 104
Graduations 50

Student Demographics
Female 82.7%
Under age 25 58.7%
Minority 16.3%
Part-time 0.0%

Accreditation
Mississippi Board of Nursing, National League
for Nursing Accrediting Commission (NLNAC)

Degrees conferred
AAS

Minimum degree required
High school diploma or GED

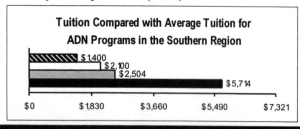
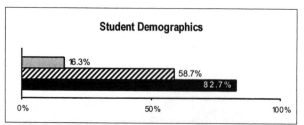

HINDS COMMUNITY COLLEGE - Jackson

1750 Chadwick Drive
Jackson, MS 39204
(601) 371-3503
Debra Spring, BS, MS

www. hindscc.edu/departments/nursing/ad_nursing/

Acceptance rate	39.2%	
Faculty-student ratio	1: 10	
Faculty	Full time	36
	Part time	13

Tuition
In state $1,660
Out of state $3,866
Enrollments 443
Graduations 136

Student Demographics
Female 85.6%
Under age 25 45.8%
Minority 23.5%
Part-time 9.9%

Accreditation
Mississippi Board of Nursing, National League
for Nursing Accrediting Commission (NLNAC)

Degrees conferred
Associate Degree

Minimum degree required
High school diploma or GED

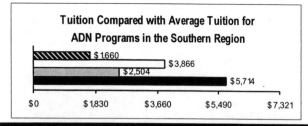
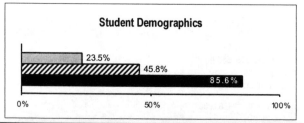

HOLMES COMMUNITY COLLEGE

1060 Avent Drive
Grenada, MS 38901
(662) 227-2305
Joyce Vaughn, MSN, RN

www.holmescc.edu

Acceptance rate	91.7%	
Faculty-student ratio	1: 11	
Faculty	Full time	16
	Part time	5

Tuition
In state $712
Out of state $1,562
Enrollments 202
Graduations 51

Student Demographics
Female 88.6%
Under age 25 44.1%
Minority 23.8%
Part-time 0.0%

Accreditation
Mississippi Board of Nursing, National League
for Nursing Accrediting Commission (NLNAC)

Degrees conferred
Associate Degree

Minimum degree required
High school diploma or GED

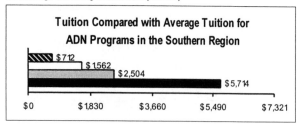
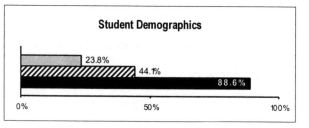

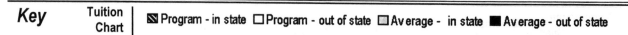

Key | Tuition Chart | ▨ Program - in state ☐ Program - out of state ☐ Average - in state ■ Average - out of state

Mississippi

ITAWAMBA COMMUNITY COLLEGE

602 West Hill
Fulton, MS 38843
(662) 862-8328
Melisa Lepard, MSN, RN

www.iccms.edu

| Acceptance rate | 25.3% |
| Faculty-student ratio | 1: 12 |

| Faculty | Full time | 17 |
| | Part time | 0 |

Tuition
In state	$700
Out of state	$1,575
Enrollments	198
Graduations	46

Student Demographics
Female	82.8%
Under age 25	44.0%
Minority	12.8%
Part-time	4.5%

Accreditation
Mississippi Board of Nursing, National League for Nursing Accrediting Commission (NLNAC)

Degrees conferred
Associate Degree

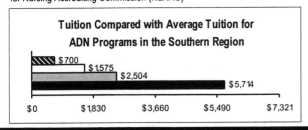

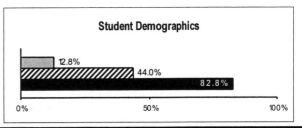

JONES COUNTY JUNIOR COLLEGE

900 South Court Street
Ellisville, MS 39437
(601) 477-4019
Linda Suttle, RN, MS

www.jcjc.edu/depts/adn

| Acceptance rate | 21.7% |
| Faculty-student ratio | 1: 9 |

| Faculty | Full time | 16 |
| | Part time | 0 |

Tuition
In state	$1,588
Out of state	$1,588
Enrollments	144
Graduations	50

Student Demographics
Female	84.0%
Under age 25	59.7%
Minority	11.1%
Part-time	0.0%

Accreditation
Mississippi Board of Nursing, National League for Nursing Accrediting Commission (NLNAC)

Degrees conferred
Associate Degree

Minimum degree required
High school diploma or GED

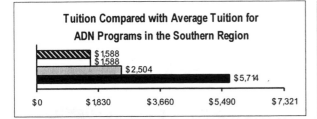

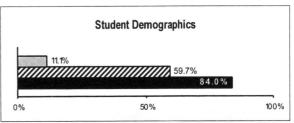

MERIDIAN COMMUNITY COLLEGE

910 Highway 19 North
Meridian, MS 39307
(601) 484-8745
Betty Davis, MSN, RN

meridiancc.edu

| Acceptance rate | 40.8% |
| Faculty-student ratio | 1: 10 |

| Faculty | Full time | 30 |
| | Part time | 4 |

Tuition
In state	$1,450
Out of state	$2,740
Enrollments	313
Graduations	124

Student Demographics
Female	89.5%
Under age 25	47.6%
Minority	27.8%
Part-time	0.0%

Accreditation
Mississippi Board of Nursing, National League for Nursing Accrediting Commission (NLNAC)

Degrees conferred
Associate Degree, LPN to RN

Minimum degree required
High school diploma or GED

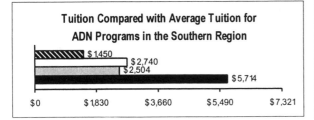

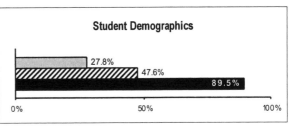

| Demographics Chart | ■ Female ▨ Under age 25 ▢ Minority | Distance Learning | | †The tuition reported for this program may be not be annualized. |
| | | | | *Data reported between 2001 and 2004. |

Mississippi

MISSISSIPPI DELTA COMMUNITY COLLEGE *Useful Facts*

PO Box 668
Moorhead, MS 38761
(662) 246-6407
Patricia Livingston, MSN, RN

www.mdcc.cc.ms.us

Acceptance rate	56.9%	
Faculty-student ratio	1: 11	
Faculty	Full time	9
	Part time	1

Tuition		
In state	$1,920
Out of state	$3,528
Enrollments	100
Graduations	37

Student Demographics	
Female	85.0%
Under age 25	48.0%
Minority	32.0%
Part-time	1.0%

Accreditation
Mississippi Board of Nursing, National League
for Nursing Accrediting Commission (NLNAC)

Degrees conferred
Associate Degree

Minimum degree required
High school diploma or GED

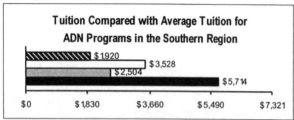

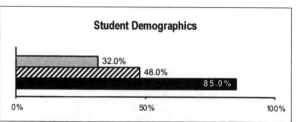

MISSISSIPPI GULF COAST COMMUNITY COLLEGE - ADN PROGRAMS - *Perkinston*

PO Box 548
Perkinston, MS 39573
(601) 528-8406
Nica Cason, MS, RN

www.mgccc.edu

Acceptance rate	55.1%	
Faculty-student ratio	1: 12	
Faculty	Full time	37
	Part time	11

Tuition		
In state	$1,490
Out of state	$3,336
Enrollments	378
Graduations	157

Student Demographics	
Female	86.0%
Under age 25	29.1%
Minority	16.4%
Part-time	0.0%

Accreditation
Mississippi Board of Nursing

Degrees conferred
Associate Degree

Minimum degree required
High school diploma or GED

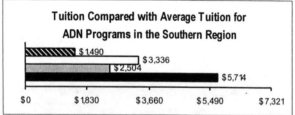

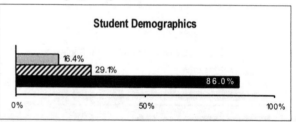

MISSISSIPPI GULF COAST COMMUNITY COLLEGE - ADN PROGRAMS - *Jefferson Davis*

PO Box 548
Perkinston, MS 39573
(601) 528-8406
Nica Cason, MS, RN

www.mgccc.edu

Acceptance rate	51.0%	
Faculty-student ratio	1: 12	
Faculty	Full time	37
	Part time	11

Tuition		
In state	$1,290
Out of state	$3,136
Enrollments	148
Graduations	41

Student Demographics	
Female	87.8%
Under age 25	20.0%
Minority	18.9%
Part-time	0.0%

Accreditation
Mississippi Board of Nursing

Degrees conferred
Associate Degree

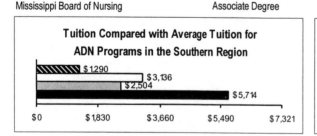

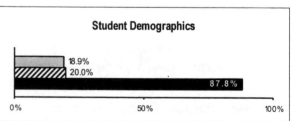

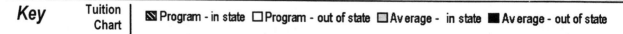

Key Tuition Chart ▨ Program - in state ☐ Program - out of state ▢ Average - in state ■ Average - out of state

Mississippi

MISSISSIPPI UNIVERSITY FOR WOMEN - *Columbus*

1100 College Street MUW-910
Columbus, MS 39701
(662) 329-7299
Sheila Adams, EdD

www.muw.edu/nursing

Accreditation
Mississippi Board of Nursing, National League
for Nursing Accrediting Commission (NLNAC)

Acceptance rate	16.7%	
Faculty-student ratio	1: 6	
Faculty Full time	32	
Part time	3	

Tuition
In state $3,690
Out of state $8,914
Enrollments 96
Graduations 38

Student Demographics
Female 91.7%
Under age 25 52.1%
Minority 26.0%
Part-time 0.0%

Degrees conferred
Associate Degree

Minimum degree required
High school diploma or GED

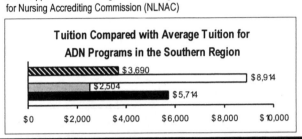
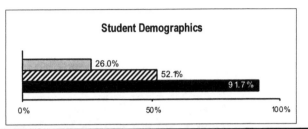

NORTHEAST MISSISSIPPI COMMUNITY COLLEGE *Useful Facts*

101 Cunningham Blvd
Booneville, MS 38829
(662) 720-7236
Rebecca West, MSN, RN-BC

www.nemcc.edu

Accreditation
Mississippi Board of Nursing, National League
for Nursing Accrediting Commission (NLNAC)

Acceptance rate	23.0%	
Faculty-student ratio	1: 11	
Faculty Full time	20	
Part time	0	

Tuition
In state $1,700
Out of state $3,420
Enrollments 211
Graduations 90

Student Demographics
Female 86.7%
Under age 25 57.3%
Minority 6.2%
Part-time 0.0%

Degrees conferred
Associate Degree

Minimum degree required
High school diploma or GED

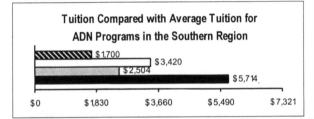
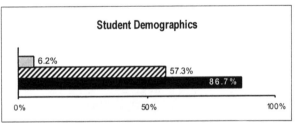

NORTHWEST MISSISSIPPI COMMUNITY COLLEGE - *Senatobia*

4975 Highway 51 North
Senatobia, MS 38668
(662) 562-3283
Vicki Hale, RN

www.northwestms.edu

Accreditation
Mississippi Board of Nursing, National League
for Nursing Accrediting Commission (NLNAC)

Acceptance rate	21.1%	
Faculty-student ratio	1: 13	
Faculty Full time	13	
Part time	3	

Tuition
In state $1,300
Out of state $2,000
Enrollments 186
Graduations 58

Student Demographics
Female 96.2%
Under age 25 43.5%
Minority 16.7%
Part-time 0.5%

Degrees conferred
Associate Degree

Minimum degree required
High school diploma or GED

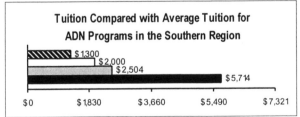
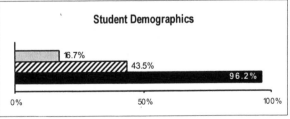

Demographics Chart	■ Female ☒ Under age 25 ☐ Minority	Distance Learning	¹The tuition reported for this program may be not be annualized. *Data reported between 2001 and 2004.

Mississippi

PEARL RIVER COMMUNITY COLLEGE - *Poplarville*

Box 5760
Poplarville, MS 39470
(601) 403-1017
Peggy Dease, MS, RN

www.prcc.edu/dphpages/adn/index.html

Accreditation
Mississippi Board of Nursing, National League
for Nursing Accrediting Commission (NLNAC)

Acceptance rate	34.0%	
Faculty-student ratio	1: 10	
Faculty	Full time	20
	Part time	4

Tuition	
In state	$1,620
Out of state	$2,398
Enrollments	213
Graduations	57

Degrees conferred
Associate Degree

Minimum degree required
High school diploma or GED

Student Demographics	
Female	81.2%
Under age 25	46.0%
Minority	15.2%
Part-time	0.0%

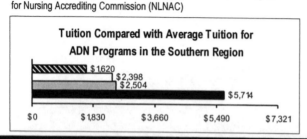

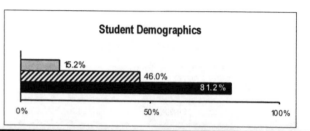

SOUTHWEST MISSISSIPPI COMMUNITY COLLEGE

Useful Facts

2000 College Drive
Summit, MS 39666
(601) 276-3850
Truda Mcgrew, MN

www.smcc.cc.ms.us

Accreditation
Mississippi Board of Nursing, National League
for Nursing Accrediting Commission (NLNAC)

Acceptance rate	27.1%	
Faculty-student ratio	1: 97	
Faculty	Full time	2
	Part time	0

Tuition	
In state	$1,700
Out of state	$3,900
Enrollments	194
Graduations	48

Degrees conferred
Associate Degree

Minimum degree required
High school diploma or GED

Student Demographics	
Female	85.6%
Under age 25	37.6%
Minority	20.6%
Part-time	0.0%

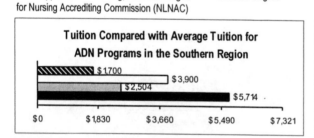

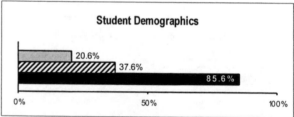

Missouri

COLUMBIA COLLEGE - *Columbia*

1001 Rogers Street
Columbia, MO 65216
(573) 875-7220
Mary Kennish

www.ccis.edu

Accreditation
Missouri State Board of Nursing, National
League for Nursing Accrediting Commission
(NLNAC)

Degrees conferred
Associate Degree

CROWDER COLLEGE

Useful Facts*

601 Laclede
Neosho, MO 64850
(417) 451-3223
Karen Vinyard, MS, RN

www.crowder.edu

Accreditation
Missouri State Board of Nursing

Degrees conferred
Associate Degree

Enrollments	29
Graduations	27

Student Demographics	
Female	96.6%

Key | Tuition Chart | ▧ Program - in state ☐ Program - out of state ▨ Average - in state ■ Average - out of state

Missouri

DEACONESS COLLEGE OF NURSING - *Traditional ADN Program*

6150 Oakland Avenue
Saint Louis, MO 63139
(314) 768-3861
Julia Raithel, PhD, RN

www.deaconess.edu

Accreditation
Missouri State Board of Nursing, National
League for Nursing Accrediting Commission
(NLNAC)

Acceptance rate		59.5%
Faculty-student ratio		1: 28
Faculty	Full time	12
	Part time	14

Degrees conferred
ASN

Tuition	
In state	$5,915
Out of state	$5,915
Enrollments	226
Graduations	37

Minimum degree required
High school diploma or GED

Student Demographics	
Female	89.8%
Under age 25	11.5%
Minority	35.8%
Part-time	99.1%

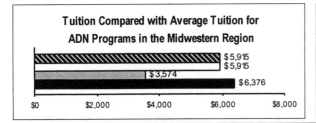

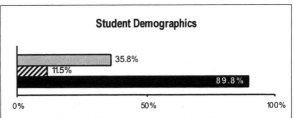

EAST CENTRAL COLLEGE *Useful Facts**

500 Forum
Rolla, MO 65401
(636) 583-5195
Mary O'Connor, PhD(c)

www.eastcentral.edu

Accreditation
Missouri State Board of Nursing

Degrees conferred
Associate Degree

Acceptance rate	50.0%

Tuition	
In state	$3,000
Out of state	$3,000
Enrollments	11
Graduations	10

Student Demographics	
Female	100.0%
Part-time	0.0%

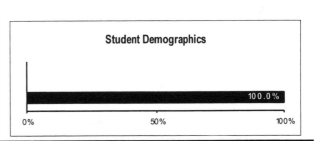

EAST CENTRAL COLLEGE - UNION *Useful Facts**

1964 Prairie Dell Road
Union, MO 63084
(636) 583-5193
Patrice O'Connor, PhD(c), RN

www.eastcentral.edu

Accreditation
Missouri State Board of Nursing

Degrees conferred
Associate Degree

Tuition	
In state	$7,500
Out of state	$9,000
Enrollments	30

Student Demographics	
Female	86.7%
Part-time	0.0%

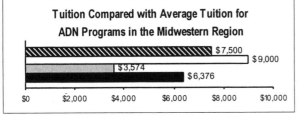

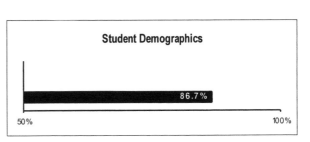

Demographics Chart	■ Female ▨ Under age 25 ▢ Minority	Distance Learning	¹The tuition reported for this program may be not be annualized. *Data reported between 2001 and 2004.

Missouri

HANNIBAL LAGRANGE COLLEGE

2800 Palmyra Road
Hannibal, MO 63401
(573) 221-3675
Jan Akright, MSN, RN

www.hlg.edu

Acceptance rate	93.3%
Faculty-student ratio	1: 6
Faculty Full time	5
Part time	2

Tuition
In state	$11,420
Out of state	$11,420
Enrollments	33
Graduations	9

Student Demographics
Female	100.0%
Under age 25	72.7%
Minority	3.0%
Part-time	15.2%

Accreditation
Missouri State Board of Nursing, National League for Nursing Accrediting Commission (NLNAC)

Degrees conferred
Associate Degree, RN to BSN

Minimum degree required
High school diploma or GED

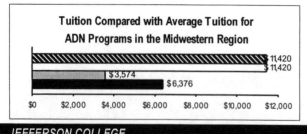

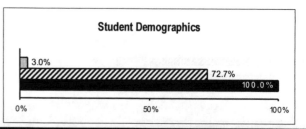

JEFFERSON COLLEGE

1000 Viking Drive
Hillsboro, MO 63050
(636) 789-3000
Michele Soest, MSN, ANP, BC, RN

www.jeffco.edu

Acceptance rate	100.0%

Tuition
In state	$3,685
Out of state	$5,623
Enrollments	41
Graduations	23

Student Demographics
Female	87.8%
Under age 25	54.0%
Minority	2.6%
Part-time	0.0%

Accreditation
Missouri State Board of Nursing

Degrees conferred
Associate Degree

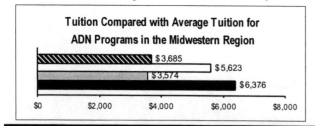

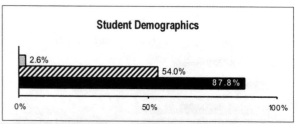

JEWISH HOSPITAL COLLEGE OF NURSING & ALLIED HEALTH

306 South Kingshighway Blvd
St Louis, MO 63110
(314) 362-6119
Coreen Vlodarchyk, MSA, BSN, RN

www.bjconah.edu

Acceptance rate	34.3%
Faculty-student ratio	1: 19
Faculty Full time	26
Part time	1

Tuition
In state	$11,400
Out of state	$11,400
Enrollments	504
Graduations	137

Student Demographics
Female	90.7%
Under age 25	40.7%
Minority	24.7%
Part-time	83.3%

Accreditation
Missouri State Board of Nursing, National League for Nursing Accrediting Commission (NLNAC)

Degrees conferred
Associate Degree

Minimum degree required
High school diploma or GED

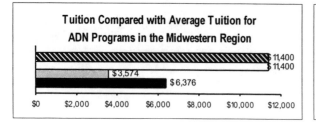

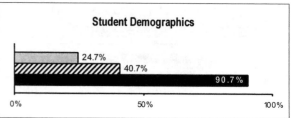

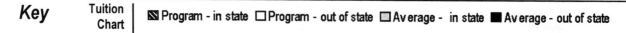

Key | Tuition Chart | ⬛ Program - in state ☐ Program - out of state ▥ Average - in state ■ Average - out of state

Missouri

LESTER L COX COLLEGE — *Useful Facts**

1423 North Jefferson
Springfield, MO 65802
(417) 269-3401
Julie Luetschwager, DNSc, RN

www.coxcollege.edu

Accreditation
Missouri State Board of Nursing, National League for Nursing Accrediting Commission (NLNAC)

Acceptance rate 33.5%

Degrees conferred
Associate Degree

Tuition	
In state	$8,910
Out of state	$8,910
Enrollments	374
Graduations	79

Student Demographics	
Female	92.0%
Under age 25	42.0%
Minority	4.0%
Part-time	69.0%

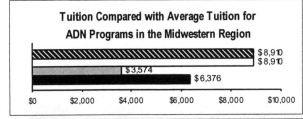
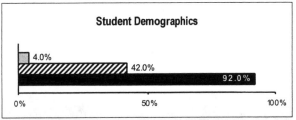

LINCOLN UNIVERSITY - Jefferson City

820 Chestnut Room 100 Eliff
Jefferson City, MO 65102
(573) 681-5421
Connie Hamacher, PhD

www.lincolnu.edu/pages/555.asp

Accreditation
Missouri State Board of Nursing, National League for Nursing Accrediting Commission (NLNAC)

Acceptance rate 68.0%
Faculty-student ratio 1:7
Faculty Full time 17 / Part time 5

Degrees conferred
Associate Degree

Minimum degree required
High school diploma or GED

Tuition	
In state	$4,512
Out of state	$8,059
Enrollments	135
Graduations	47

Student Demographics	
Female	90.4%
Under age 25	15.6%
Minority	9.0%
Part-time	86.7%

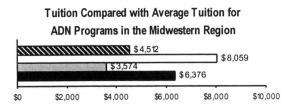
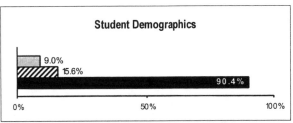

METROPOLITAN COMMUNITY COLLEGE - PENN VALLEY — *Useful Facts*

3201 Southwest Trafficway
Kansas City, MO 64111
(816) 759-4174
Karen Komoroski, RN, EdS, PhD

kcmetro.edu

Accreditation
Missouri State Board of Nursing, National League for Nursing Accrediting Commission (NLNAC)

Faculty-student ratio 1:7
Faculty Full time 28 / Part time 27

Degrees conferred
Associate Degree

Minimum degree required
High school diploma or GED

Tuition	
In state	$2,280
Out of state	$5,400
Enrollments	292
Graduations	120

Student Demographics	
Female	91.8%
Under age 25	27.4%
Minority	9.3%
Part-time	25.0%

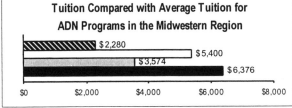
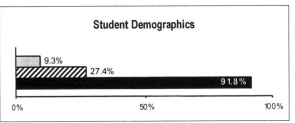

Demographics Chart: ■Female ▨Under age 25 ☐Minority | Distance Learning | †The tuition reported for this program may be not be annualized. *Data reported between 2001 and 2004.

Missouri

MINERAL AREA COLLEGE

Useful Facts*

PO Box 1000, 5270 Flat River Road
Park Hills, MO 63601
(573) 518-2103
Teri Douglas, MSN, RN

mineralarea.org

Acceptance rate	61.7%	

Student Demographics

Female		91.7%

Enrollments	72		
Graduations	43	Part-time	0.0%

Accreditation
Missouri State Board of Nursing

Degrees conferred
Associate Degree

MOBERLY AREA COMMUNITY COLLEGE - *Moberly*

101 College Avenue
Moberly, MO 65270
(660) 263-4110
Ruth Jones, MN, RN

www.macc.cc.mo.us

Student Demographics

Enrollments	72		
Graduations	28	Part-time	0.0%

Accreditation
Missouri State Board of Nursing

Degrees conferred
Associate Degree

NORTH CENTRAL MISSOURI COLLEGE - *Outreach One-Plus-One*

1301 Main
Trenton, MO 64683
(660) 359-3948
Janet Vanderpool, BSN, RN

www.ncmc.cc.mo.us

Tuition

In state	$1,582
Out of state	$1,782

Enrollments	31		
Graduations	29	Part-time	0.0%

Student Demographics

Accreditation
Missouri State Board of Nursing

Degrees conferred
Associate Degree

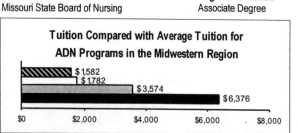

Tuition Compared with Average Tuition for ADN Programs in the Midwestern Region

- $1,582
- $1,782
- $3,574
- $6,376

$0 — $2,000 — $4,000 — $6,000 — $8,000

PARK UNIVERSITY

8700 NW River Park Drive
Parkville, MO 64152
(816) 584-6256
Margaret Monahan, MS

www.park.edu

Accreditation
Missouri State Board of Nursing, National
League for Nursing Accrediting Commission
(NLNAC)

Degrees conferred
Associate Degree

Key | Tuition Chart | ⊠ Program - in state ☐ Program - out of state ▨ Average - in state ■ Average - out of state

Missouri

SAINT LOUIS COMMUNITY COLLEGE - *Meramec*

3400 Pershall Road
St Louis, MO 63135
(314) 513-4810
Karen Mayes, MSN, RN

www.stlcc.edu/nursing

Accreditation
Missouri State Board of Nursing, National League for Nursing Accrediting Commission (NLNAC)

Acceptance rate	59.7%	
Faculty-student ratio	1: 10	
Faculty Full time	32	
Part time	18	

Degrees conferred
Associate Degree

Tuition	
In state	$2,340
Out of state	$4,140
Enrollments	415
Graduations	144

Minimum degree required
High school diploma or GED

Student Demographics	
Female	90.1%
Under age 25	32.5%
Minority	28.2%
Part-time	86.7%

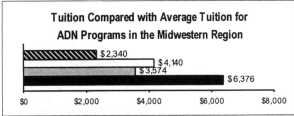

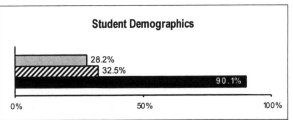

SANFORD BROWN COLLEGE

3555 Franks Drive
St. Charles, MO 63301
(636) 949-2620
Vanessa Loyd

www.sanford-brown.edu

Accreditation
Missouri State Board of Nursing

Degrees conferred
Associate Degree

SOUTHEAST MISSOURI HOSPITAL   *Useful Facts**

1819 Broadway
Cape Girardeau, MO 63701
(573) 334-6825
Tonya Buttry, MSN, RNC

www.southeastmissourihospital.com/college

Accreditation
Missouri State Board of Nursing

Acceptance rate	37.1%

Degrees conferred
Associate Degree

Tuition	
In state	$14,960
Out of state	$14,960
Enrollments	52
Graduations	25

Student Demographics	
Female	80.8%
Under age 25	27.0%
Part-time	0.0%

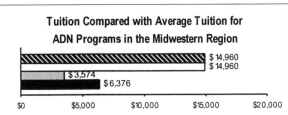

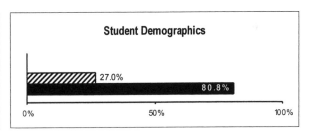

Demographics Chart	■ Female ▨ Under age 25 ▢ Minority	**Distance Learning** 🖥	†The tuition reported for this program may be not be annualized. *Data reported between 2001 and 2004.

Missouri

SOUTHWEST BAPTIST UNIVERSITY

4431 South Fremont
Springfield, MO 65804
(417) 820-2069
Jennifer Wilson, EdD, RN

www.sbuniv.edu/collegeofnursing

Accreditation
Missouri State Board of Nursing, National
League for Nursing Accrediting Commission
(NLNAC)

Acceptance rate	35.8%
Faculty-student ratio	1: 9
Faculty Full time	16
Part time	17

Degrees conferred
Associate Degree

Tuition	
In state	$9,000
Out of state	$9,000
Enrollments	227
Graduations	91

Minimum degree required
High school diploma or GED

Student Demographics	
Female	88.1%
Under age 25	45.4%
Minority	3.3%
Part-time	70.9%

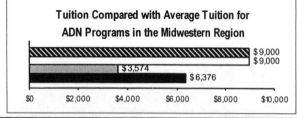

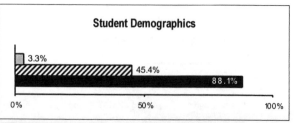

SOUTHWEST MISSOURI STATE UNIVERSITY - WEST PLAINS

128 Garfield Avenue
West Plains, MO 65775
(417) 255-7247
Donna Jones, MPH, MSN

www.wp.missouristate.edu/nursing

Accreditation
Missouri State Board of Nursing, National
League for Nursing Accrediting Commission
(NLNAC)

Acceptance rate	24.5%
Faculty-student ratio	1: 12
Faculty Full time	3
Part time	7

Degrees conferred
Associate Degree

Tuition	
In state	$3,360
Out of state	$6,720
Enrollments	78
Graduations	33

Minimum degree required
High school diploma or GED

Student Demographics	
Female	89.7%
Under age 25	35.9%
Minority	2.6%
Part-time	6.4%

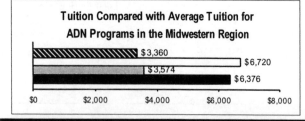

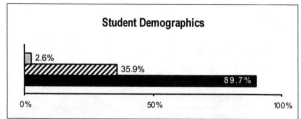

ST CHARLES COUNTY COMMUNITY COLLEGE

4601 Mid Rivers Mall Drive
St Peters, MO 63376
(636) 922-8280
Patricia Porterfield, EdD, MSN, RN

www.stchas.edu

Accreditation
Missouri State Board of Nursing, National
League for Nursing Accrediting Commission
(NLNAC)

Acceptance rate	72.7%
Faculty-student ratio	1: 13
Faculty Full time	6
Part time	10

Degrees conferred
Associate Degree

Tuition	
In state	$2,130
Out of state	$4,590
Enrollments	147
Graduations	68

Minimum degree required
High school diploma or GED

Student Demographics	
Female	93.2%
Under age 25	31.3%
Minority	7.5%
Part-time	55.8%

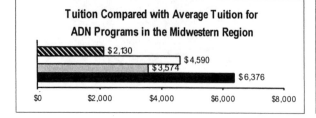

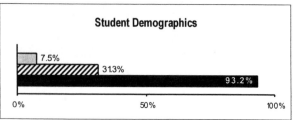

Key | Tuition Chart

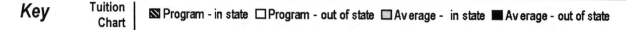

☒ Program - in state ☐ Program - out of state ☐ Average - in state ■ Average - out of state

Missouri

STATE FAIR COMMUNITY COLLEGE
*Useful Facts**

3201 West 16th Street
Sedalia, MO 65301
(660) 530-5800
Beverly Wilkerson, MSN

www.sfcc.cc.mo.us/staff/heocc

Accreditation
Missouri State Board of Nursing

Acceptance rate	40.9%

Tuition¹	
In state	$56
Out of state	$83
Enrollments	24
Graduations	33

Student Demographics	
Female	95.8%
Minority	8.3%
Part-time	0.0%

Degrees conferred
Associate Degree

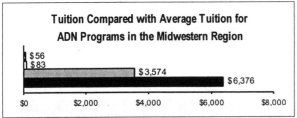

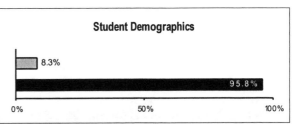

TEXAS TECHNICAL INSTITUTE

6915 South Highway 63
Houston, MO 65483
(417) 967-5466
Nancy Stubbs, RN, MSN

www.texascountytech.edu

Accreditation
Missouri State Board of Nursing

At the request of this nursing school, publication has been witheld.
Please contact the school directly for more information.

THREE RIVERS COMMUNITY COLLEGE - *Poplar Bluff*

2080 Three Rivers Blvd
Poplar Bluff, MO 63901
(573) 840-9680
Catherine Wampler, MN, BSN, RN

www.trcc.edu

Accreditation
Missouri State Board of Nursing, National
League for Nursing Accrediting Commission
(NLNAC)

Acceptance rate		33.5%
Faculty-student ratio		1: 11
Faculty	Full time	10
	Part time	0

Tuition	
In state	$1,770
Out of state	$3,480
Enrollments	86
Graduations	31

Student Demographics	
Female	89.5%
Under age 25	46.5%
Minority	2.3%
Part-time	33.7%

Degrees conferred
Associate Degree

Minimum degree required
High school diploma or GED

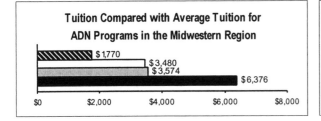

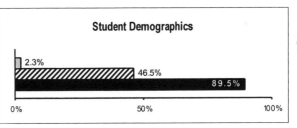

Demographics Chart	■ Female ▨ Under age 25 ▢ Minority	**Distance Learning**	¹The tuition reported for this program may be not be annualized.
			*Data reported between 2001 and 2004.

Missouri

THREE RIVERS COMMUNITY COLLEGE - *Sikeston*

2080 Three Rivers Blvd
Poplar Bluff, MO 63901
(573) 840-9680
Catherine Wampler, MN, BSN, RN

www.trcc.edu

Acceptance rate		83.9%
Faculty-student ratio		1: 11
Faculty	Full time	10
	Part time	0

Tuition	
In state	$1,770
Out of state	$3,480
Enrollments	22
Graduations	23

Student Demographics	
Female	100.0%
Under age 25	27.3%
Minority	27.8%
Part-time	77.3%

Accreditation
Missouri State Board of Nursing, National
League for Nursing Accrediting Commission
(NLNAC)

Degrees conferred
Associate Degree

Minimum degree required
Licensed Practical Nurse

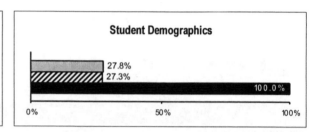

Montana

MILES COMMUNITY COLLEGE *Useful Facts*

2715 Dickinson Street
Miles City, MT 59301
(406) 874-6188
Kathleen Wankel, MN, RN

www.milescc.edu

Acceptance rate		46.5%
Faculty-student ratio		1: 8
Faculty	Full time	6
	Part time	7

Tuition	
In state	$1,680
Out of state	$4,740
Enrollments	79
Graduations	42

Student Demographics	
Female	91.1%
Under age 25	29.1%
Minority	2.5%
Part-time	0.0%

Accreditation
Montana State Board of Nursing, National
League for Nursing Accrediting Commission
(NLNAC)

Degrees conferred
Associate Degree

Minimum degree required
High school diploma or GED

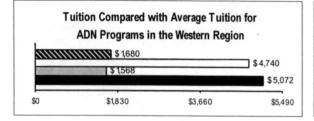

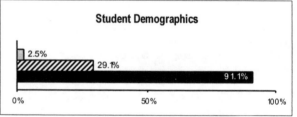

Key | Tuition Chart | ▨ Program - in state ☐ Program - out of state ▥ Average - in state ■ Average - out of state

Montana

MONTANA STATE UNIVERSITY - NORTHERN
Useful Facts

PO Box 7751
Havre, MT 59501
(406) 265-3748
Mary Pappas, EdDc, MSN, APRN

www.msun.edu

Accreditation
Montana State Board of Nursing, National
League for Nursing Accrediting Commission
(NLNAC)

Acceptance rate	78.7%	
Faculty-student ratio	1: 16	
Faculty Full time	8	
Part time	1	

Degrees conferred
ASN

Tuition	
In state	$5,101
Out of state	$15,000
Enrollments	135
Graduations	58

Minimum degree required
High school diploma or GED

Student Demographics	
Female	87.4%
Under age 25	35.6%
Minority	3.7%
Part-time	5.2%

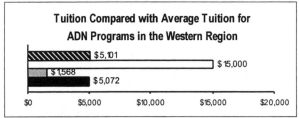

Tuition Compared with Average Tuition for ADN Programs in the Western Region
$5,101
$15,000
$1,568
$5,072

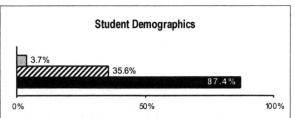

Student Demographics
3.7%
35.6%
87.4%

MONTANA TECH

1300 West Park
Butte, MT 59701
(406) 496-3722
Karen VanDaveer, MN, RN

www.mtech.edu

Accreditation
Montana State Board of Nursing

Degrees conferred
Associate Degree

SALISH KOOTENAI COLLEGE
Useful Facts

PO Box 70, 52000 Highway 93
Pablo, MT 59855
(406) 275-4921
Jacque Dolberry, MS, RN

www.skc.edu

Accreditation
Montana State Board of Nursing, National
League for Nursing Accrediting Commission
(NLNAC)

Acceptance rate	37.6%	
Faculty-student ratio	1: 9	
Faculty Full time	8	
Part time	2	

Degrees conferred
Associate Degree

Tuition	
In state	$3,201
Out of state	$11,592
Enrollments	81
Graduations	31

Minimum degree required
CNA

Student Demographics	
Female	87.7%
Under age 25	38.3%
Minority	63.0%
Part-time	0.0%

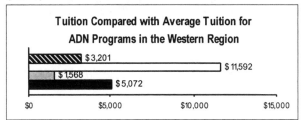

Tuition Compared with Average Tuition for ADN Programs in the Western Region
$3,201
$11,592
$1,568
$5,072

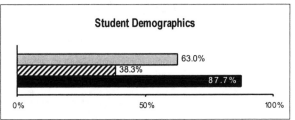

Student Demographics
63.0%
38.3%
87.7%

Demographics Chart	■Female ☒Under age 25 ☐Minority	Distance Learning	¹The tuition reported for this program may be not be annualized. *Data reported between 2001 and 2004.

Nebraska

CENTRAL COMMUNITY COLLEGE - *Grand Island*

PO Box 4903, 3134 W Hwy 34
Grand Island, NE 68802
(308) 398-7455
Patricia Karsk, RN, MSN

cccneb.edu

Acceptance rate		12.0%
Faculty-student ratio		1: 9
Faculty	Full time	12
	Part time	4

Tuition	
In state	$2,494
Out of state	$3,741
Enrollments	121
Graduations	47

Student Demographics	
Female	90.9%
Under age 25	43.8%
Minority	3.3%
Part-time	24.0%

Accreditation
Nebraska Dept of Health & Human Services
Regulation, National League for Nursing
Accrediting Commission (NLNAC)

Degrees conferred
Associate Degree

Minimum degree required
High school diploma or GED

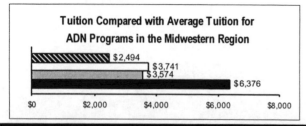

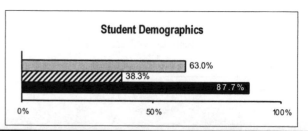

COLLEGE OF SAINT MARY
Useful Facts

7000 Mercy Road
Omaha, NE 68106
(402) 399-2658
Peggy Hawkins, RN, BC, PhD

www.csm.edu

Acceptance rate		59.2%
Faculty-student ratio		1: 9
Faculty	Full time	16
	Part time	15

Tuition	
In state	$17,750
Out of state	$17,750
Enrollments	223
Graduations	84

Student Demographics	
Female	100.0%
Under age 25	55.2%
Minority	13.0%
Part-time	16.1%

Accreditation
Nebraska Dept of Health & Human Services
Regulation, National League for Nursing
Accrediting Commission (NLNAC)

Degrees conferred
Associate Degree

Minimum degree required
High school diploma or GED

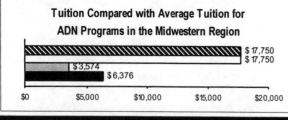

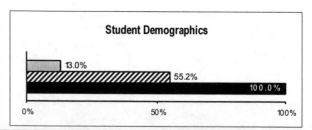

METROPOLITAN COMMUNITY COLLEGE
Useful Facts

30th and Fort Streets
Omaha, NE 68103
(402) 457-2467
Diane Hughes, MSN, RN

www.mccneb.edu/healthcareers

Acceptance rate		32.0%
Faculty-student ratio		1: 10
Faculty	Full time	6
	Part time	2.5

Tuition	
In state	$1,155
Out of state	$1,740
Enrollments	70
Graduations	23

Student Demographics	
Female	88.6%
Under age 25	31.4%
Minority	24.2%
Part-time	45.7%

Accreditation
Nebraska Dept of Health & Human Services
Regulation, National League for Nursing
Accrediting Commission (NLNAC)

Degrees conferred
Associate Degree

Minimum degree required
High school diploma or GED

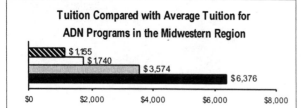

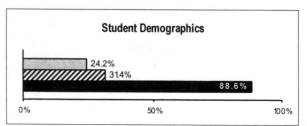

Key | Tuition Chart | ▨ Program - in state ☐ Program - out of state ☐ Average - in state ■ Average - out of state

Nebraska

MID-PLAINS COMMUNITY COLLEGE AREA | Useful Facts

1101 Halligan Drive
North Platte, NE 69101
(308) 535-3623
Diane Hoffman, MSN

www.mpcc.edu

Accreditation
Nebraska Dept of Health & Human Services
Regulation, National League for Nursing
Accrediting Commission (NLNAC)

Acceptance rate	18.2%	
Faculty-student ratio	1: 6	
Faculty Full time	8	
Part time	3	

Degrees conferred
Associate Degree

Tuition[1]		Student Demographics	
In state	$65	Female	98.2%
Out of state	$76	Under age 25	20.0%
Enrollments	55		
Graduations	29	Part-time	0.0%

Minimum degree required
Diploma

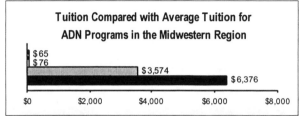

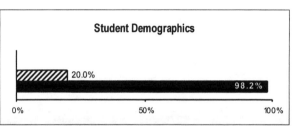

NORTHEAST COMMUNITY COLLEGE | Useful Facts*

PO Box 469
Norfolk, NE 68701
(402) 844-7321
Anita Brenneman, BSN

www.northeastcollege.com

Accreditation
Nebraska Dept of Health & Human Services
Regulation, National League for Nursing
Accrediting Commission (NLNAC)

Acceptance rate	19.3%

Degrees conferred
Associate Degree

Tuition		Student Demographics	
In state	$1,008	Female	92.3%
Out of state	$1,056	Under age 25	30.0%
Enrollments	195	Minority	2.1%
Graduations	24	Part-time	76.9%

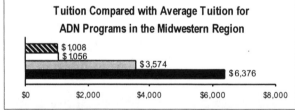

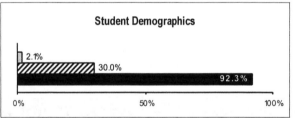

SOUTHEAST COMMUNITY COLLEGE - Lincoln

8800 O Street
Lincoln, NE 68520
(402) 437-2730
Virginia Hess, RN, BS, MSN

www.southeast.edu

Accreditation
Nebraska Dept of Health & Human Services
Regulation, National League for Nursing
Accrediting Commission (NLNAC)

Acceptance rate	42.9%	
Faculty-student ratio	1: 3	
Faculty Full time	24	
Part time	2	

Degrees conferred
Associate Degree

Tuition		Student Demographics	
In state	$1,755	Female	90.5%
Out of state	$2,257	Under age 25	25.0%
Enrollments	84	Minority	7.1%
Graduations	53	Part-time	61.9%

Minimum degree required
High school diploma or GED

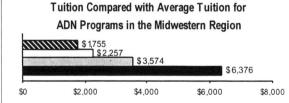

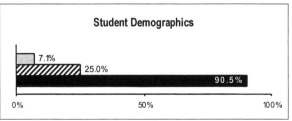

Demographics Chart	■Female ▨Under age 25 ☐Minority	Distance Learning	[1]The tuition reported for this program may be not be annualized.
			*Data reported between 2001 and 2004.

Nevada

COMMUNITY COLLEGE OF SOUTHERN NEVADA

Useful Facts*

6375 W Charleston Blvd, W1B
Las Vegas, NV 89146
(702) 651-5674
Lisa Kless-Kern, MSN, RN

www.ccsn.nevada.edu

Acceptance rate	41.2%	

Tuition

In state	$1,470
Out of state	$3,816
Enrollments	337
Graduations	131

Student Demographics

Female	84.0%
Under age 25	19.0%
Minority	40.7%
Part-time	4.7%

Accreditation
Nevada State Board of Nursing, National League for Nursing Accrediting Commission (NLNAC)

Degrees conferred
Associate Degree

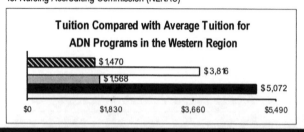

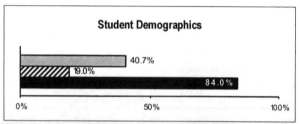

GREAT BASIN COLLEGE

Useful Facts*

1500 College Pkwy
Elko, NV 89801
(775) 753-2135
Margaret Puccinelli, RN, PhD

gbcnv.edu

Acceptance rate	50.0%	

Tuition

In state	$2,700
Out of state	$4,700
Enrollments	26
Graduations	14

Student Demographics

Female	96.2%
Under age 25	27.0%
Minority	15.4%
Part-time	69.2%

Accreditation
Nevada State Board of Nursing, National League for Nursing Accrediting Commission (NLNAC)

Degrees conferred
Associate Degree

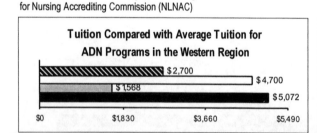

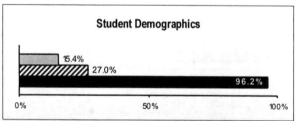

TRUCKEE MEADOWS COMMUNITY COLLEGE

Useful Facts*

209 Basil O'Connor Hall
Tuskegee University, AL 36088
(334) 727-8382
Doris Holeman, PhD, RN

www.tuskegee.edu

Acceptance rate	41.5%	

Tuition

In state	$636
Out of state	$2,982
Enrollments	752
Graduations	44

Student Demographics

Female	89.1%
Under age 25	44.6%
Minority	30.0%
Part-time	60.1%

Accreditation
Nevada State Board of Nursing, National League for Nursing Accrediting Commission (NLNAC)

Degrees conferred
Associate Degree

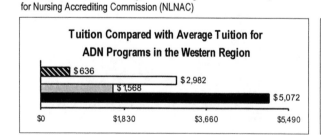

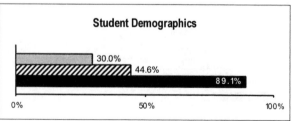

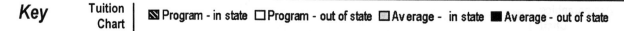

Key | Tuition Chart | ▨ Program - in state ▢ Program - out of state ▨ Average - in state ■ Average - out of state

Nevada

WESTERN NEVADA COMMUNITY COLLEGE — *Useful Facts**

2201 W College Pkwy
Carson City, NV 89703
(775) 445-3295
Judith Cordia, EdD, MS, RN

www.wncc.edu

Accreditation
Nevada State Board of Nursing

Acceptance rate	38.7%
Faculty-student ratio	1: 9

Faculty	Full time	9
	Part time	2

Degrees conferred
Associate Degree

Tuition	
In state	$1,590
Out of state	$3,936
Enrollments	94
Graduations	30

Student Demographics	
Female	86.2%
Under age 25	29.0%
Minority	13.3%
Part-time	40.4%

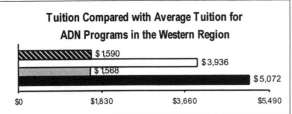

Tuition Compared with Average Tuition for ADN Programs in the Western Region
$1,590 / $3,936 / $1,568 / $5,072

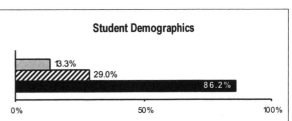

Student Demographics
13.3% / 29.0% / 86.2%

New Hampshire

NEW HAMPSHIRE COMMUNITY TECHNICAL COLLEGE - BERLIN — *Useful Facts**

2020 Riverside Dr
Berlin, NH 03570
(603) 752-1113
John Colbath, MSN, MBA, RN-C

www.berl.nhctc.edu

Accreditation
New Hampshire Board of Nursing

Acceptance rate	22.9%

Degrees conferred
Associate Degree

Tuition	
In state	$4,032
Out of state	$7,896
Enrollments	64
Graduations	19

Student Demographics	
Female	81.3%
Under age 25	12.0%
Minority	1.6%
Part-time	21.9%

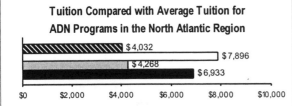

Tuition Compared with Average Tuition for ADN Programs in the North Atlantic Region
$4,032 / $7,896 / $4,268 / $6,933

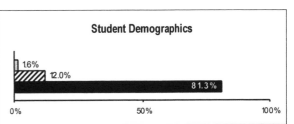

Student Demographics
1.6% / 12.0% / 81.3%

NEW HAMPSHIRE COMMUNITY TECHNICAL COLLEGE - CLAREMONT — *Useful Facts**

One College Dr
Claremont, NH 03743
(603) 542-7744
Dianna Scherlin, RN, BS, MS, CA, GS

www.claremont.tec.nh.us

Accreditation
New Hampshire Board of Nursing, National
League for Nursing Accrediting Commission
(NLNAC)

Acceptance rate	14.9%

Degrees conferred
Associate Degree

Tuition	
In state	$4,522
Out of state	$10,404
Enrollments	100
Graduations	36

Student Demographics	
Female	86.0%
Under age 25	24.0%
Part-time	76.0%

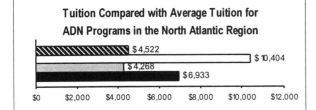

Tuition Compared with Average Tuition for ADN Programs in the North Atlantic Region
$4,522 / $10,404 / $4,268 / $6,933

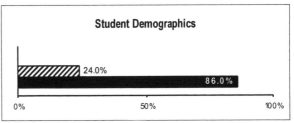

Student Demographics
24.0% / 86.0%

Demographics Chart	■ Female ☒ Under age 25 ☐ Minority	Distance Learning	¹The tuition reported for this program may be not be annualized. *Data reported between 2001 and 2004.

New Hampshire

NEW HAMPSHIRE COMMUNITY TECHNICAL COLLEGE - LACONIA

379 Belmont Road
Laconia, NH 03246
(603) 524-3207
Harriet Redmond, MSN, ARNP

www.nhtc.edu

Accreditation
New Hampshire Board of Nursing

Degrees conferred
Associate Degree

NEW HAMPSHIRE COMMUNITY TECHNICAL COLLEGE - MANCHESTER   Useful Facts*

1066 Front St
Manchester, NH 03102
(603) 668-6706
Lisa McCurley, RN, MS, CS-ANP

www.ms.nhctc.edu

Accreditation
New Hampshire Board of Nursing, National
League for Nursing Accrediting Commission
(NLNAC)

Degrees conferred
Associate Degree

Acceptance rate	26.7%	**Tuition**		**Student Demographics**	
Faculty-student ratio	1:7	In state	$4,920	Female	91.5%
Faculty	Full time	16	Out of state	$11,280	Under age 25	5.0%
	Part time	7	**Enrollments**	141	Minority	5.0%
			Graduations	49	Part-time	54.6%

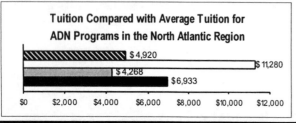

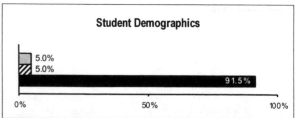

NEW HAMPSHIRE TECHNICAL INSTITUTE   Useful Facts

31 College Drive
Concord, NH 03301
(603) 271-7177
Anita Pavlidis, MS, RN, BC

nhti.edu

Accreditation
New Hampshire Board of Nursing, National
League for Nursing Accrediting Commission
(NLNAC)

Degrees conferred
Associate Degree

Minimum degree required
High school diploma or GED

Acceptance rate	40.7%	**Tuition**		**Student Demographics**	
Faculty-student ratio	1:11	In state	$6,068	Female	88.7%
Faculty	Full time	16	Out of state	$9,102	Under age 25	25.1%
	Part time	5	**Enrollments**	195	Minority	3.7%
			Graduations	75	Part-time	96.4%

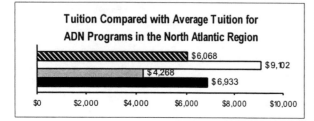

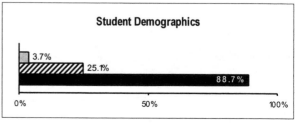

Key	Tuition Chart	▨ Program - in state ☐ Program - out of state ☐ Average - in state ■ Average - out of state

New Hampshire

RIVIER COLLEGE — *Useful Facts**

420 Main St
Nashua, NH 03060
(603) 897-8628
Paula Williams, RN, MS, CAGS, EdD(c)

www.rivier.edu

Accreditation
New Hampshire Board of Nursing, National
League for Nursing Accrediting Commission
(NLNAC)

Acceptance rate		83.5%
Faculty-student ratio		1: 12
Faculty	Full time	20
	Part time	1

Degrees conferred
Associate Degree

Tuition	
In state	$19,200
Out of state	$19,200
Enrollments	247
Graduations	107

Student Demographics	
Female	93.5%
Part-time	40.1%

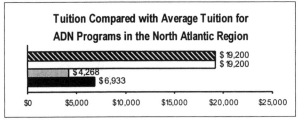

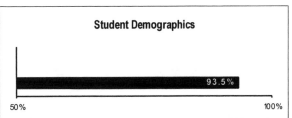

New Jersey

ATLANTIC CAPE COMMUNITY COLLEGE — *Useful Facts**

5100 Black Horse Pike
Mays Landing, NJ 08330
(609) 343-5035
Barbara Warner, PhD

www.atlantic.edu

Accreditation
New Jersey Board of Nursing, National League
for Nursing Accrediting Commission (NLNAC)

Acceptance rate	85.0%

Degrees conferred
Associate Degree

Tuition	
In state	$2,100
Out of state	$2,310
Enrollments	77
Graduations	44

Student Demographics	
Female	96.1%
Under age 25	0.0%
Minority	19.5%
Part-time	0.0%

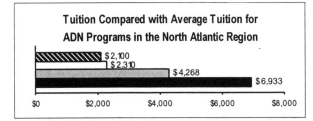

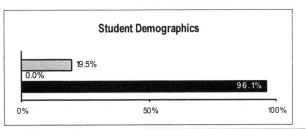

BERGEN COMMUNITY COLLEGE — *Useful Facts*

400 Paramus Road
Paramus, NJ 07652
(201) 447-7181
Janet Rubino, RN, MA

www.bergen.edu

Accreditation
New Jersey Board of Nursing, National League
for Nursing Accrediting Commission (NLNAC)

Acceptance rate		26.3%
Faculty-student ratio		1: 11
Faculty	Full time	23
	Part time	9

Degrees conferred
Associate Degree

Tuition[1]	
In state	$87
Out of state	$189
Enrollments	314
Graduations	105

Minimum degree required
High school diploma or GED

Student Demographics	
Female	79.9%
Under age 25	36.9%
Minority	48.6%
Part-time	86.0%

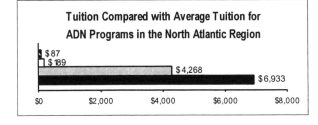

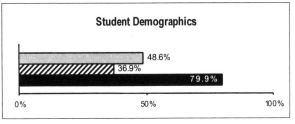

Demographics Chart	■ Female ▨ Under age 25 ▢ Minority	Distance Learning	[1]The tuition reported for this program may be not be annualized. *Data reported between 2001 and 2004.

New Jersey

BROOKDALE COMMUNITY COLLEGE
Useful Facts*

765 Newman Springs Rd
Lincroft, NJ 07738
(732) 224-2418
Maris Lown, MSN, RN

www.brookdalecc.edu

Acceptance rate	43.3%	

Tuition[1]		**Student Demographics**	
In state	$84	Female	88.0%
Out of state	$168	Under age 25	23.0%
Enrollments	300	Minority	50.0%
Graduations	88	Part-time	82.3%

Accreditation
New Jersey Board of Nursing, National League
for Nursing Accrediting Commission (NLNAC)

Degrees conferred
Associate Degree

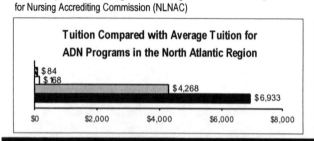

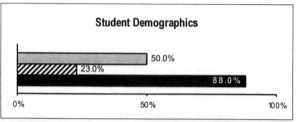

BURLINGTON COUNTY COLLEGE
Useful Facts

601 Pemberton Browns Mills Road
Pemberton, NJ 08068
(609) 894-9311
Charlotte McCarraher, MSN, RN

www.bcc.edu

Acceptance rate	24.2%	
Faculty-student ratio	1: 13	
Faculty	Full time	6
	Part time	22

Tuition		**Student Demographics**	
In state	$1,716	Female	87.6%
Out of state	$4,500	Under age 25	20.8%
Enrollments	226	Minority	23.4%
Graduations	89	Part-time	89.4%

Accreditation
New Jersey Board of Nursing, National League
for Nursing Accrediting Commission (NLNAC)

Degrees conferred
Associate Degree

Minimum degree required
High school diploma or GED

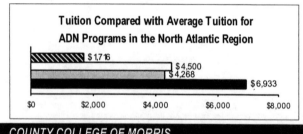

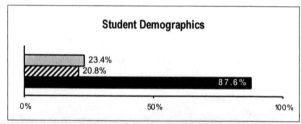

COUNTY COLLEGE OF MORRIS
Useful Facts

214 Center Grove Road
Randolph, NJ 07869
(973) 328-5352
Joan Cunningham, RN, MA

www.ccm.edu/hns/nursing

Acceptance rate	49.4%	
Faculty-student ratio	1: 13	
Faculty	Full time	17
	Part time	11

Tuition		**Student Demographics**	
In state	$2,485	Female	82.9%
Out of state	$6,870	Under age 25	29.8%
Enrollments	299	Minority	25.5%
Graduations	134	Part-time	85.3%

Accreditation
New Jersey Board of Nursing, National League
for Nursing Accrediting Commission (NLNAC)

Degrees conferred
Associate Degree

Minimum degree required
High school diploma or GED

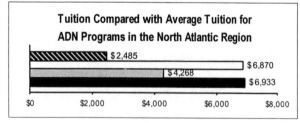

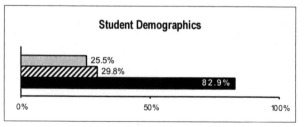

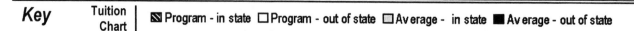

Key | Tuition Chart | ▧ Program - in state ☐ Program - out of state ☐ Average - in state ■ Average - out of state

New Jersey

CUMBERLAND COUNTY COLLEGE · Useful Facts*

PO Box 1500
Vineland, NJ 08362
(856) 691-8600
Martha Pollick, EdD, MSN, RN, CNAAC

www.ccnj.net/snmay/ahs/pages/nursingaa.html

Accreditation
New Jersey Board of Nursing, National League
for Nursing Accrediting Commission (NLNAC)

			Student Demographics	
Acceptance rate	47.3%	**Tuition**		
		In state	$2,220	Female	88.1%
		Out of state	$8,880	Under age 25	35.0%
		Enrollments	135	Minority	27.8%
		Graduations	47	Part-time	74.1%

Degrees conferred
Associate Degree

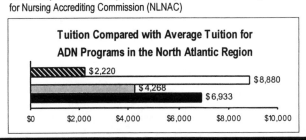

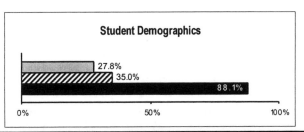

ESSEX COUNTY COLLEGE

303 University Avenue
Newark, NJ 07102
(973) 877-1885
Marlene Dey, RN, APN-C, MSN

www.essex.edu

Accreditation
New Jersey Board of Nursing, National League
for Nursing Accrediting Commission (NLNAC)

*At the request of this nursing school, publication has been witheld.
Please contact the school directly for more information.*

GLOUCESTER COUNTY COLLEGE · Useful Facts*

1400 Tanyard Road
Sewell, NJ 08080
(856) 415-2178
Yvonne Burgess, MSN, APRN, BC

gccnj.edu

Accreditation
New Jersey Board of Nursing, National League
for Nursing Accrediting Commission (NLNAC)

			Student Demographics	
Acceptance rate	54.4%	**Tuition**		
		In state	$2,130	Female	91.8%
		Out of state	$4,260	Under age 25	24.0%
		Enrollments	159	Minority	20.1%
		Graduations	67	Part-time	65.4%

Degrees conferred
Associate Degree

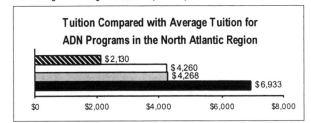

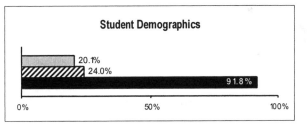

Demographics Chart	■ Female ☑ Under age 25 ☐ Minority	Distance Learning	¹The tuition reported for this program may be not be annualized. *Data reported between 2001 and 2004.

New Jersey

MERCER COUNTY COMMUNITY COLLEGE
Useful Facts

PO Box B
Trenton, NJ 08608
(609) 586-4800
Linda Martin, MSN, APRN, BC

www.mccc.edu

Accreditation
New Jersey Board of Nursing, National League
for Nursing Accrediting Commission (NLNAC)

Acceptance rate	65.9%

Tuition

In state	$2,730
Out of state	$3,645
Enrollments	175
Graduations	33

Degrees conferred
Associate Degree

Minimum degree required
High school diploma or GED

Student Demographics

Female	88.0%
Under age 25	21.1%
Minority	37.3%
Part-time	88.6%

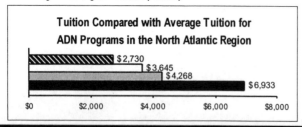

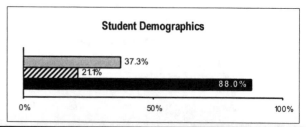

OCEAN COUNTY COLLEGE
Useful Facts*

College Dr, PO Box 2001
Toms River, NJ 08754
(732) 255-0395
Sandra Kearns, MSN, RN

www.ocean.edu

Accreditation
New Jersey Board of Nursing, National League
for Nursing Accrediting Commission (NLNAC)

Acceptance rate	45.0%

Tuition[1]

In state	$67
Out of state	$77
Enrollments	300
Graduations	112

Degrees conferred
Associate Degree

Student Demographics

Female	83.3%
Minority	88.2%
Part-time	60.0%

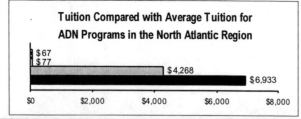

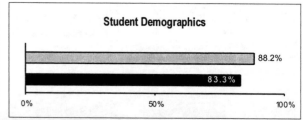

PASSAIC COUNTY COMMUNITY COLLEGE
Useful Facts

One College Blvd
Paterson, NJ 07505
(973) 684-5221
Donna Stankiewicz, MSN, RN

pccc.cc.nj.us

Accreditation
New Jersey Board of Nursing, National League
for Nursing Accrediting Commission (NLNAC)

Acceptance rate		37.3%
Faculty-student ratio		1: 10
Faculty	Full time	13
	Part time	18

Tuition[1]

In state	$73
Out of state	$146
Enrollments	226
Graduations	69

Degrees conferred
Associate Degree

Minimum degree required
ADN

Student Demographics

Female	87.6%
Under age 25	16.4%
Minority	60.6%
Part-time	0.0%

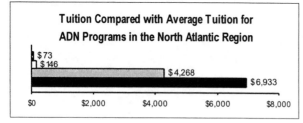

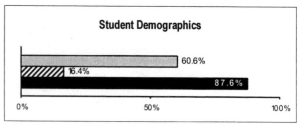

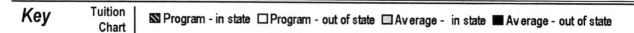

Key Tuition Chart | ▨ Program - in state ☐ Program - out of state ▨ Average - in state ■ Average - out of state

New Jersey

PASSAIC COUNTY TECHNICAL INSTITUTE

1006 Hamburg Turnpike
Wayne, NJ 07470
(973) 628-9208
Janice Kilgallon, RNC, MSN, CS

www.pcti.tec.nj.us

Accreditation
New Jersey Board of Nursing

Degrees conferred
Associate Degree

RARITAN VALLEY COMMUNITY COLLEGE

PO Box 3300
Somerville, NJ 08876
(908) 218-8877
Helen jones, RN, APN, C, PhD

*At the request of this nursing school, publication has been witheld.
Please contact the school directly for more information.*

www.raritanval.edu

Accreditation
New Jersey Board of Nursing, National League
for Nursing Accrediting Commission (NLNAC)

UNIVERSITY OF MEDICINE AND DENTISTRY OF NEW JERSEY - NEWARK - *Edison*

65 Bergen Street, Suite 1143
Newark, NJ 07101
(973) 972-4322
Sara Torres, PhD, RN, FAAN

sn.umdnj.edu

Acceptance rate		8.8%	**Tuition**		**Student Demographics**	
Faculty-student ratio		1: 9	In state	$2,378	Female	77.7%
Faculty	Full time	54	Out of state	$4,755	Under age 25	31.1%
	Part time	25	**Enrollments**	148	Minority	44.9%
			Graduations	70	Part-time	0.0%

Accreditation
New Jersey Board of Nursing, National League
for Nursing Accrediting Commission (NLNAC)

Degrees conferred
Associate Degree

Minimum degree required
High school diploma or GED

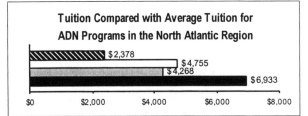

Tuition Compared with Average Tuition for ADN Programs in the North Atlantic Region

- $2,378
- $4,755
- $4,268
- $6,933

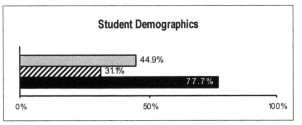

Student Demographics

- 44.9%
- 31.1%
- 77.7%

New Mexico

ALBUQUERQUE TECHNICAL VOCATIONAL INSTITUTE

Useful Facts

525 Buena Vista SE
Albuquerque, NM 87106
(505) 224-4143
Deborah Cassady, MSN, RN

www.tvi/hod

Acceptance rate		40.0%	**Tuition**		**Student Demographics**	
Faculty-student ratio		1: 12	In state	$965	Female	86.6%
Faculty	Full time	17	Out of state	$5,143	Under age 25	19.3%
	Part time	25	**Enrollments**	367	Minority	57.1%
			Graduations	105	Part-time	25.9%

Accreditation
New Mexico Board of Nursing, National League
for Nursing Accrediting Commission (NLNAC)

Degrees conferred
LPN or LVN, Associate Degree

Minimum degree required
High school diploma or GED

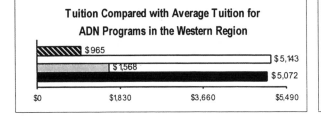

Tuition Compared with Average Tuition for ADN Programs in the Western Region

- $965
- $5,143
- $1,568
- $5,072

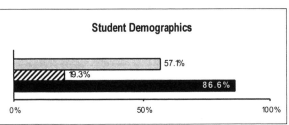

Student Demographics

- 57.1%
- 19.3%
- 86.6%

Demographics Chart	■Female ☒Under age 25 ☐Minority	**Distance Learning**	¹The tuition reported for this program may be not be annualized.
			*Data reported between 2001 and 2004.

New Mexico

CLOVIS COMMUNITY COLLEGE
Useful Facts

417 Schepps Bulevard
Clovis, NM 88101
(505) 769-4954
Robin Jones, EdD, MSN, RN

www.clovis.edu

Acceptance rate	54.9%	
Faculty-student ratio	1: 9	
Faculty Full time	11	
Part time	4	

Tuition
In state $712
Out of state $1,432
Enrollments 120
Graduations 57

Student Demographics
Female 90.0%
Under age 25 41.7%
Minority 38.3%
Part-time 0.0%

Accreditation
New Mexico Board of Nursing, National League
for Nursing Accrediting Commission (NLNAC)

Degrees conferred
LPN or LVN, Associate Degree

Minimum degree required
High school diploma or GED

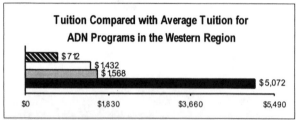

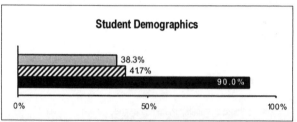

DOÑA ANA BRANCH COMMUNITY COLLEGE
Useful Facts*

3400 South Espina
Las Cruces, NM 88003
(505) 527-7514
M Ford, MSN, BSN, RN

dabc-www.nmsu.edu/hps

Acceptance rate 41.7%

Tuition
In state $1,008
Out of state $2,952
Enrollments 95
Graduations 37

Student Demographics
Female 88.4%
Under age 25 29.0%
Minority 57.0%
Part-time 0.0%

Accreditation
New Mexico Board of Nursing, National League
for Nursing Accrediting Commission (NLNAC)

Degrees conferred
Associate Degree

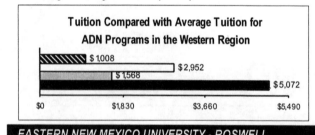

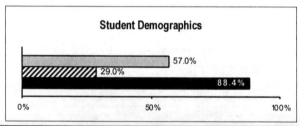

EASTERN NEW MEXICO UNIVERSITY - ROSWELL
Useful Facts

PO Box 6000
Roswell, NM 88202
(505) 624-7237
Tamaliah Lueras, MSN, RN

www.roswell.enmu.edu

Acceptance rate	47.7%	
Faculty-student ratio	1: 11	
Faculty Full time	5	
Part time	1	

Tuition
In state $882
Out of state $4,148
Enrollments 62
Graduations 27

Student Demographics
Female 93.5%
Under age 25 45.2%
Minority 51.6%
Part-time 56.5%

Accreditation
New Mexico Board of Nursing, National League
for Nursing Accrediting Commission (NLNAC)

Degrees conferred
Associate Degree

Minimum degree required
High school diploma or GED

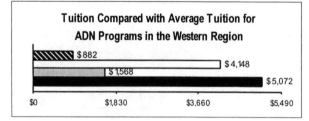

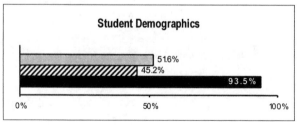

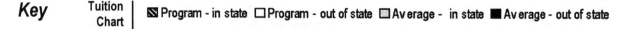

Key | Tuition Chart | ▨ Program - in state ☐ Program - out of state ☐ Average - in state ■ Average - out of state

New Mexico

LUNA COMMUNITY COLLEGE

1510 Hot Springs Blvd
Las Vegas, NM 87701
(505) 454-2527
Dolores Whitaker, MS, RN, CS

www.luna.com

Accreditation
New Mexico Board of Nursing

At the request of this nursing school, publication has been witheld.
Please contact the school directly for more information.

NEW MEXICO JUNIOR COLLEGE   *Useful Facts*

5317 Lovington Highway
Hobbs, NM 88240
(505) 492-2519
Karen Cummings, MSN, RN

www.nmjc.edu

Accreditation
New Mexico Board of Nursing, National League
for Nursing Accrediting Commission (NLNAC)

Acceptance rate	73.2%	
Faculty-student ratio	1: 10	
Faculty Full time	7	
Part time	1	

Degrees conferred
Associate Degree

Tuition[1]	
In state	$264
Out of state	$528
Enrollments	73
Graduations	27

Minimum degree required
High school diploma or GED

Student Demographics	
Female	86.3%
Under age 25	27.4%
Minority	33.8%
Part-time	4.1%

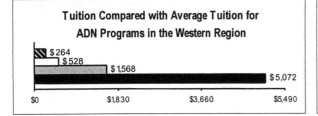

Tuition Compared with Average Tuition for ADN Programs in the Western Region

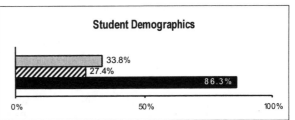

Student Demographics

NEW MEXICO STATE UNIVERSITY - ALAMOGORDO   *Useful Facts*

2400 North Scenic Drive
Alamogordo, NM 88310
(505) 439-3662
Jeanette Little, BSN, MSN, RN

www.alamo.nmsu.edu

Accreditation
New Mexico Board of Nursing, National League
for Nursing Accrediting Commission (NLNAC)

Acceptance rate	50.7%	
Faculty-student ratio	1: 7	
Faculty Full time	6	
Part time	7	

Degrees conferred
Associate Degree

Tuition	
In state	$1,200
Out of state	$3,960
Enrollments	62
Graduations	22

Minimum degree required
High school diploma or GED

Student Demographics	
Female	90.3%
Under age 25	21.0%
Minority	19.4%
Part-time	0.0%

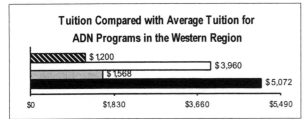

Tuition Compared with Average Tuition for ADN Programs in the Western Region

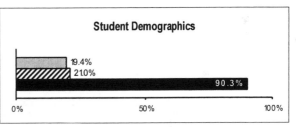

Student Demographics

Demographics Chart	■Female ▨Under age 25 ▢Minority	Distance Learning	[1]The tuition reported for this program may be not be annualized. *Data reported between 2001 and 2004.

New Mexico

NEW MEXICO STATE UNIVERSITY - CARLSBAD

1500 University Drive
Carlsbad, NM 88220
(505) 234-9301
Deanna Suggs, RN, MSN, FNP-C

www.cavern.nmsu.edu

Acceptance rate	90.0%
Faculty-student ratio	1: 8
Faculty Full time	8
Part time	4

Tuition	
In state	$1,080
Out of state	$2,496
Enrollments	75
Graduations	18

Student Demographics	
Female	92.0%
Under age 25	52.0%
Minority	34.7%
Part-time	0.0%

Accreditation
New Mexico Board of Nursing, National League
for Nursing Accrediting Commission (NLNAC)

Degrees conferred
LPN or LVN, Associate Degree

Minimum degree required
HS diploma or GED, successful completion of
CNA

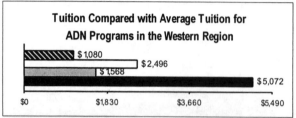

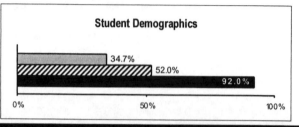

NORTHERN NEW MEXICO COMMUNITY COLLEGE

921 Paseo de Onate
Espanola, NM 87532
(505) 747-2207
Nancy Schlapper, MSN, BSN, RN

www.nnmcc.edu

Acceptance rate	76.4%
Faculty-student ratio	1: 6
Faculty Full time	6
Part time	4

Tuition	
In state	$990
Out of state	$2,550
Enrollments	51
Graduations	20

Student Demographics	
Female	88.2%
Under age 25	37.3%
Minority	74.5%
Part-time	29.4%

Accreditation
New Mexico Board of Nursing

Degrees conferred
LPN or LVN, Associate Degree

Minimum degree required
High school diploma or GED

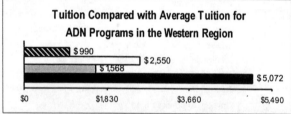

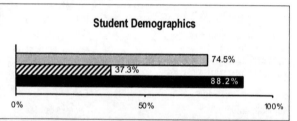

SAN JUAN COLLEGE

4601 College Boulevard
Farmington, NM 87402
(505) 556-3226
Ann Clark, RN, MSN

www.sanjuancollege.edu/nursing

Acceptance rate	22.5%
Faculty-student ratio	1: 7
Faculty Full time	6
Part time	17

Tuition	
In state	$600
Out of state	$840
Enrollments	97
Graduations	33

Student Demographics	
Female	81.4%
Under age 25	27.8%
Minority	23.3%
Part-time	2.1%

Accreditation
New Mexico Board of Nursing, National League
for Nursing Accrediting Commission (NLNAC)

Degrees conferred
Associate Degree

Minimum degree required
High school diploma or GED

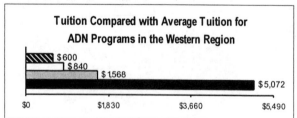

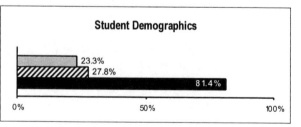

Key | Tuition Chart | ▨ Program - in state ☐ Program - out of state ☐ Average - in state ■ Average - out of state

New Mexico

SANTA FE COMMUNITY COLLEGE - SANTA FE — *Useful Facts*

6401 Richards Avenue
Santa Fe, NM 87508
(505) 428-1324
Margaret Glass, MSN, RN

www.sfccnm.edu

Accreditation
New Mexico Board of Nursing, National League
for Nursing Accrediting Commission (NLNAC)

Acceptance rate	46.2%
Faculty-student ratio	1: 6
Faculty Full time	6
Part time	20

Tuition
In state $768
Out of state $984
Enrollments 95
Graduations 41

Student Demographics
Female 85.3%
Under age 25 12.6%
Minority 40.2%
Part-time 0.0%

Degrees conferred
Associate Degree

Minimum degree required
High school diploma or GED

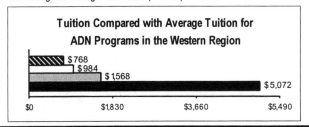
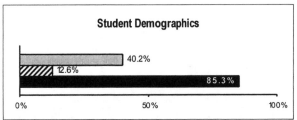

UNIVERSITY OF NEW MEXICO - GALLUP — *Useful Facts**

200 College Road
Gallup, NM 87301
(505) 863-7516
Kathleen Head, RN, MSN

www.gallup.unm.edu

Accreditation
New Mexico Board of Nursing

Acceptance rate	40.0%

Tuition
In state $552
Out of state $1,128
Enrollments 69
Graduations 28

Student Demographics
Female 97.1%
Under age 25 14.0%
Minority 66.7%
Part-time 0.0%

Degrees conferred
Associate Degree

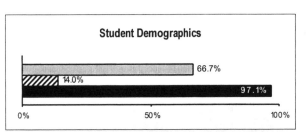

WESTERN NEW MEXICO UNIVERSITY — *Useful Facts**

PO Box 680
Silver City, NM 88062
(505) 574-5140
Patricia McIntire, CFNP, MS

wnmu.edu

Accreditation
New Mexico Board of Nursing, National League
for Nursing Accrediting Commission (NLNAC)

Acceptance rate	41.6%

Tuition
In state $2,557
Out of state $9,565
Enrollments 48
Graduations 13

Student Demographics
Female 83.3%
Under age 25 18.7%
Minority 45.8%
Part-time 14.6%

Degrees conferred
Associate Degree

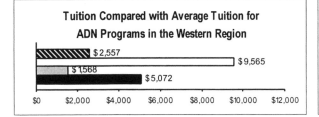
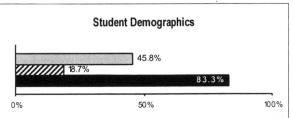

Demographics Chart ■Female ▨Under age 25 ☐Minority **Distance Learning**

†The tuition reported for this program may be not be annualized.
*Data reported between 2001 and 2004.

New York

ADIRONDACK COMMUNITY COLLEGE
Useful Facts

640 Bay Rd
Queensbury, NY 12804
(518) 743-2300
Cynthia Schenone, RN, MSN

www.sunyacc.edu

Acceptance rate		61.8%
Faculty-student ratio		1: 13
Faculty	Full time	7
	Part time	17

Tuition	
In state	$2,730
Out of state	$5,460
Enrollments	209
Graduations	87

Student Demographics	
Female	85.2%
Under age 25	30.1%
Minority	4.8%
Part-time	49.8%

Accreditation
New York State Board of Nursing, National League for Nursing Accrediting Commission (NLNAC)

Degrees conferred
Associate Degree

Minimum degree required
High school diploma or GED

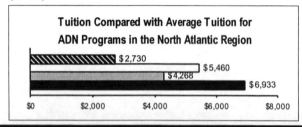

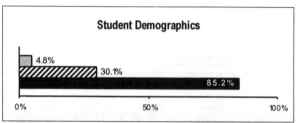

BOROUGH OF MANHATTAN COMMUNITY COLLEGE
Useful Facts

199 Chambers St
New York, NY 10007
(212) 220-8230
Barbara Tacinelli, RN, MA

www.bmcc.cuny.edu

Acceptance rate		49.6%
Faculty-student ratio		1: 13
Faculty	Full time	18
	Part time	40

Tuition	
In state	$2,800
Out of state	$4,560
Enrollments	491
Graduations	199

Student Demographics	
Female	76.8%
Under age 25	16.3%
Minority	80.8%
Part-time	33.8%

Accreditation
New York State Board of Nursing, National League for Nursing Accrediting Commission (NLNAC)

Degrees conferred
Associate Degree

Minimum degree required
High school diploma or GED

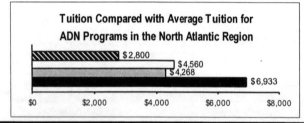

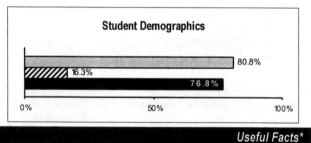

BRONX COMMUNITY COLLEGE
Useful Facts*

West 181 St and University Ave
Bronx, NY 10453
(718) 289-5426
Lois Augustug, MA, RN

www.bcc.cuny.edu

Tuition	
In state	$2,500
Out of state	$3,076
Enrollments	173
Graduations	40

Student Demographics	
Under age 25	25.0%

Accreditation
New York State Board of Nursing, National League for Nursing Accrediting Commission (NLNAC)

Degrees conferred
Associate Degree

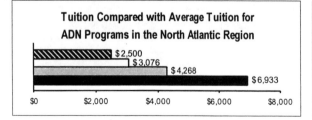

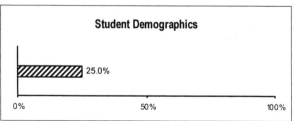

Key | Tuition Chart | ▨ Program - in state ☐ Program - out of state ☐ Average - in state ■ Average - out of state

New York

BROOME COMMUNITY COLLEGE — *Useful Facts*

Front Street
Binghamton, NY 13902
(607) 778-5059
Claire Ligeikis-Clayton, RN, MS, EdD

www.sunybroome.edu

Acceptance rate		38.9%
Faculty-student ratio		1: 18
Faculty	Full time	7
	Part time	10

Tuition	
In state	$2,814
Out of state	$5,628
Enrollments	219
Graduations	67

Student Demographics	
Female	91.8%
Under age 25	32.0%
Minority	6.4%
Part-time	34.2%

Accreditation
New York State Board of Nursing, National League for Nursing Accrediting Commission (NLNAC)

Degrees conferred
Associate Degree

Minimum degree required
High school diploma or GED

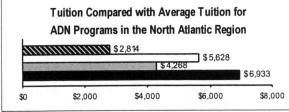

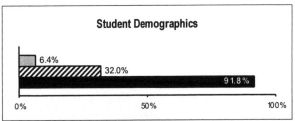

CAYUGA COMMUNITY COLLEGE — *Useful Facts**

197 Franklin St
Auburn, NY 13021
(315) 255-1743
Vicki Condie, MSN, RN, CAS

www.cayuga-cc.edu

Acceptance rate	21.5%

Tuition	
In state	$2,900
Out of state	$5,800
Enrollments	118
Graduations	40

Student Demographics	
Female	94.1%
Under age 25	0.0%
Minority	6.8%
Part-time	63.6%

Accreditation
New York State Board of Nursing, National League for Nursing Accrediting Commission (NLNAC)

Degrees conferred
Associate Degree

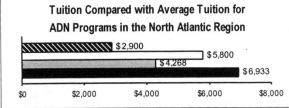

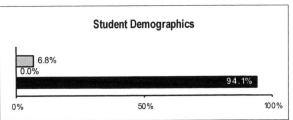

CLINTON COMMUNITY COLLEGE — *Useful Facts**

136 Clinton Point Dr
Plattsburgh, NY 12901
(518) 562-4162
Patricia Shinn, MS

www.clintoncc.edu

Acceptance rate	42.4%

Tuition	
In state	$2,940
Out of state	$7,350
Enrollments	114
Graduations	38

Student Demographics	
Female	87.7%
Under age 25	47.4%
Minority	6.1%
Part-time	32.5%

Accreditation
New York State Board of Nursing, National League for Nursing Accrediting Commission (NLNAC)

Degrees conferred
Associate Degree

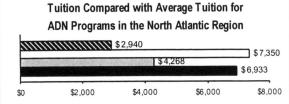

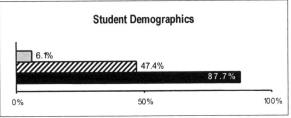

Demographics Chart	■ Female ▨ Under age 25 ☐ Minority	Distance Learning	†The tuition reported for this program may be not be annualized. *Data reported between 2001 and 2004.

New York

COCHRAN SCHOOL OF NURSING
Useful Facts*

967 North Broadway
Yonkers, NY 10701
(914) 964-4282
Kathleen Dirschel, PhD, RN

www.riversidehealth.org

Accreditation
New York State Board of Nursing

Degrees conferred
Associate Degree

Acceptance rate		27.3%
Faculty-student ratio		1: 7
Faculty	Full time	15
	Part time	42

Tuition		Student Demographics	
In state	$5,742	Female	85.3%
Out of state	$5,742	Under age 25	22.7%
Enrollments	245	Minority	60.7%
Graduations	61	Part-time	57.1%

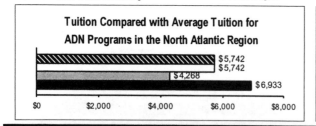

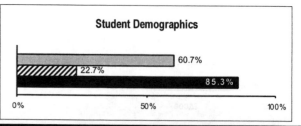

COLUMBIA GREENE COMMUNITY COLLEGE
Useful Facts

4400 Route 23
Hudson, NY 12534
(518) 828-4181
Dawn Wrigley, RN, MS

www.sunycgcc.edu

Accreditation
New York State Board of Nursing, National
League for Nursing Accrediting Commission
(NLNAC)

Degrees conferred
Associate Degree

Minimum degree required
High school diploma or GED

Acceptance rate		18.4%
Faculty-student ratio		1: 18
Faculty	Full time	6
	Part time	3

Tuition		Student Demographics	
In state	$2,832	Female	90.9%
Out of state	$5,664	Under age 25	31.1%
Enrollments	132	Minority	7.6%
Graduations	40	Part-time	77.3%

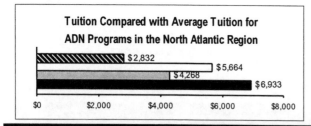

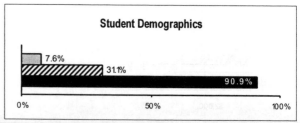

CORNING COMMUNITY COLLEGE
Useful Facts

1 Academic Dr
Corning, NY 14830
(607) 962-9241
Gail Ropelewski, RN

www.corning-cc.edu/academic_divisions/nursing

Accreditation
New York State Board of Nursing, National
League for Nursing Accrediting Commission
(NLNAC)

Degrees conferred
Associate Degree

Minimum degree required
High school diploma or GED

Acceptance rate	69.5%

Tuition		Student Demographics	
In state	$2,864	Female	92.3%
Out of state	$5,728	Under age 25	35.6%
Enrollments	194	Minority	6.3%
Graduations	62	Part-time	20.1%

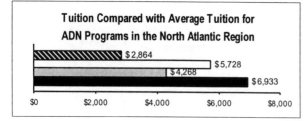

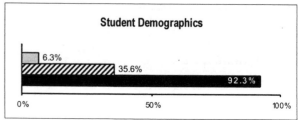

Key | Tuition Chart | ▨ Program - in state ☐ Program - out of state ▧ Average - in state ■ Average - out of state

New York

CROUSE HOSPITAL SCHOOL OF NURSING — Useful Facts

736 Irving Ave
Syracuse, NY 13210
(315) 470-7481
JoAnn Herne, MS, APRN, BC

www.crouse.org/nursing

Accreditation
New York State Board of Nursing

Acceptance rate		45.7%
Faculty-student ratio		1: 12
Faculty	Full time	19
	Part time	8

Degrees conferred
Associate Degree

Tuition	
In state	$7,352
Out of state	$11,568
Enrollments	279
Graduations	71

Minimum degree required
High school diploma or GED

Student Demographics	
Female	87.8%
Under age 25	49.1%
Minority	10.5%
Part-time	51.3%

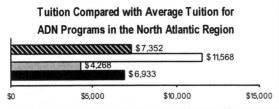

Tuition Compared with Average Tuition for ADN Programs in the North Atlantic Region

$7,352 / $11,568 / $4,268 / $6,933

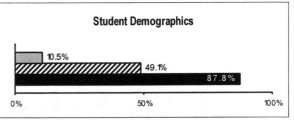

Student Demographics

10.5% / 49.1% / 87.8%

DUTCHESS COMMUNITY COLLEGE — Useful Facts*

53 Pendell Rd
Poughkeepsie, NY 12601
(845) 431-8571
Toni Doherty, RN, MSN

www.sunydutchess.edu/nursing

Accreditation
New York State Board of Nursing, National
League for Nursing Accrediting Commission
(NLNAC)

Acceptance rate	100.0%

Degrees conferred
Associate Degree

Tuition	
In state	$2,350
Out of state	$4,700
Enrollments	751
Graduations	74

Student Demographics	
Female	89.5%
Under age 25	36.0%
Minority	34.8%
Part-time	70.7%

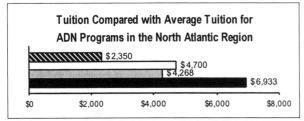

Tuition Compared with Average Tuition for ADN Programs in the North Atlantic Region

$2,350 / $4,700 / $4,268 / $6,933

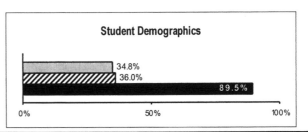

Student Demographics

34.8% / 36.0% / 89.5%

ELLIS HOSPITAL — Useful Facts

1101 Nott St
Schnectady, NY 12308
(518) 243-4471
Mary Lee Pollard, RNCS, PhD

www.ehson.org

Accreditation
New York State Board of Nursing, National
League for Nursing Accrediting Commission
(NLNAC)

Acceptance rate		53.1%
Faculty-student ratio		1: 11
Faculty	Full time	11
	Part time	1

Degrees conferred
Associate Degree

Tuition	
In state	$4,676
Out of state	$6,692
Enrollments	130
Graduations	29

Minimum degree required
ADN

Student Demographics	
Female	89.2%
Under age 25	45.4%
Minority	15.4%
Part-time	61.5%

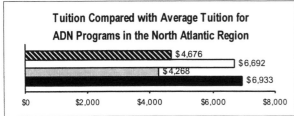

Tuition Compared with Average Tuition for ADN Programs in the North Atlantic Region

$4,676 / $6,692 / $4,268 / $6,933

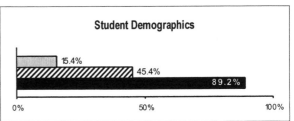

Student Demographics

15.4% / 45.4% / 89.2%

Demographics Chart | ■ Female ▨ Under age 25 ▢ Minority | **Distance Learning**

†The tuition reported for this program may be not be annualized.
*Data reported between 2001 and 2004.

New York

ERIE COMMUNITY COLLEGE
Useful Facts*

6805 Main St
Williamsville, NY 14221
(716) 851-1357
Theresa Ranne, RN

www.ecc.edu

Acceptance rate	73.2%

Tuition		Student Demographics	
In state	$1,350	Female	87.5%
Out of state	$2,700	Under age 25	23.0%
Enrollments	368	Minority	29.3%
Graduations	81	Part-time	56.5%

Accreditation
New York State Board of Nursing, National League for Nursing Accrediting Commission (NLNAC)

Degrees conferred
Associate Degree

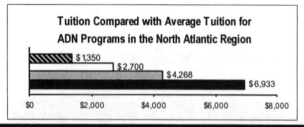

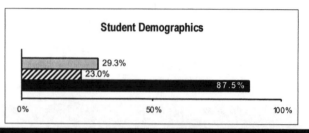

ERIE COMMUNITY COLLEGE CITY CAMPUS

121 Ellicott St
Buffalo, NY 14203
(716) 851-1066
Theresa Ranne

www.ecc.edu

Accreditation
New York State Board of Nursing

Degrees conferred
Associate Degree

EXCELSIOR COLLEGE
Useful Facts

7 Columbia Circle
Albany, NY 12203
(518) 464-8661
Bridget Nettleton, PhD, RN

www.excelsior.edu

Acceptance rate	100.0%
Faculty-student ratio	: 1155

Faculty	Full time	12
	Part time	4

Tuition		Student Demographics	
In state	$2,700	Female	76.2%
Out of state	$2,700	Under age 25	4.0%
Enrollments	15002	Minority	35.2%
Graduations	1433	Part-time	100.0%

Accreditation
New York State Board of Nursing, National League for Nursing Accrediting Commission (NLNAC)

Degrees conferred
Associate Degree

Minimum degree required
open to individuals w/clinically oriented healthcare bkgd

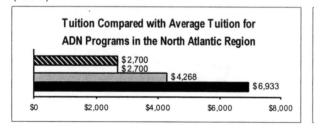

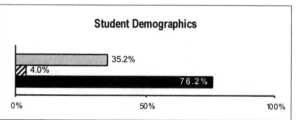

Key	Tuition Chart	⬚ Program - in state ☐ Program - out of state ☐ Average - in state ■ Average - out of state

New York

FINGER LAKES COMMUNITY COLLEGE — *Useful Facts*

4355 Lakeshore Dr
Canandaigua, NY 14424
(585) 394-3500
Nancy Robinson, MEd, RNBC

www.flcc.edu/nursing

Accreditation
New York State Board of Nursing, National League for Nursing Accrediting Commission (NLNAC)

Acceptance rate	12.2%
Faculty-student ratio	1: 11
Faculty Full time	10
Part time	3

Degrees conferred
Associate Degree

Tuition	
In state	$2,900
Out of state	$5,800
Enrollments	126
Graduations	49

Minimum degree required
High school diploma or GED

Student Demographics	
Female	89.7%
Under age 25	36.5%
Minority	8.7%
Part-time	53.2%

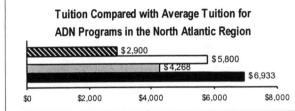

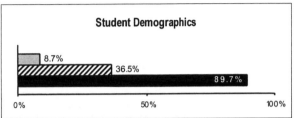

FULTON - MONTGOMERY COMMUNITY COLLEGE — *Useful Facts*

2805 St Hwy 67
Johnstown, NY 12095
(518) 762-4651
Robert Warner, MS, RN

w2.fmcc.suny.edu/nursing/nursing.html

Accreditation
New York State Board of Nursing

Acceptance rate	46.2%
Faculty-student ratio	1: 11
Faculty Full time	5
Part time	6

Degrees conferred
Associate Degree

Tuition	
In state	$2,975
Out of state	$5,950
Enrollments	85
Graduations	30

Minimum degree required
High school diploma or GED

Student Demographics	
Female	88.2%
Under age 25	35.3%
Minority	6.0%
Part-time	55.3%

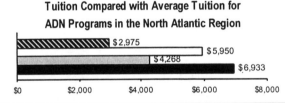

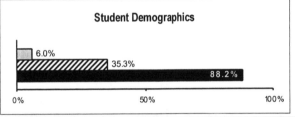

GENESEE COMMUNITY COLLEGE — *Useful Facts**

1 College Rd
Batavia, NY 14020
(585) 343-0055
Kathleen Hankel, RN, MS

www.genesee.edu

Accreditation
New York State Board of Nursing, National League for Nursing Accrediting Commission (NLNAC)

Acceptance rate	23.7%
Faculty-student ratio	1: 13
Faculty Full time	7
Part time	6

Degrees conferred
Associate Degree

Tuition	
In state	$2,900
Out of state	$3,250
Enrollments	128
Graduations	48

Student Demographics	
Female	93.0%
Under age 25	44.0%
Minority	9.4%
Part-time	21.9%

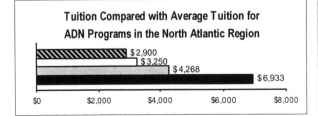

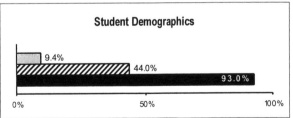

Demographics Chart	■Female ☑Under age 25 ☐Minority	Distance Learning	¹The tuition reported for this program may be not be annualized. *Data reported between 2001 and 2004.

New York

HELENE FULD COLLEGE OF NURSING
Useful Facts*

1879 Madison Ave
New York, NY 10035
(212) 423-2700
Margaret Wines, RN, PhD

helenefuld.edu

Acceptance rate	66.2%	**Tuition**		**Student Demographics**	
		In state	$12,096	Female	89.7%
		Out of state	$12,096	Under age 25	6.0%
		Enrollments	377	Minority	95.2%
		Graduations	221	Part-time	61.8%

Accreditation
New York State Board of Nursing, National
League for Nursing Accrediting Commission
(NLNAC)

Degrees conferred
Associate Degree

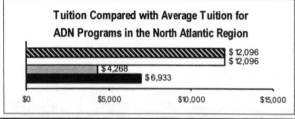

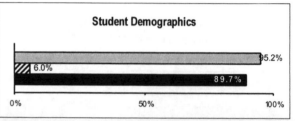

HOSTOS COMMUNITY COLLEGE

475 Grand Concourse
Bronx, NY 10451
(718) 518-4121
Christine O'Reilly

www.hostos.cuny.edu

Accreditation
New York State Board of Nursing

Degrees conferred
Associate Degree

HUDSON VALLEY COMMUNITY COLLEGE
Useful Facts

80 Vandenburgh Ave
Troy, NY 12180
(518) 629-7469
Dicey O'Malley, PhD, RN

hvcc.edu/academ/catalog/programs/hsc/nuscur.html

Acceptance rate	38.2%	**Tuition**		**Student Demographics**	
Faculty-student ratio	1: 14	In state	$2,700	Female	87.9%
Faculty	Full time	14	Out of state	$8,100	Under age 25	4.5%
	Part time	4	**Enrollments**	223	Minority	20.2%
			Graduations	61	Part-time	27.8%

Accreditation
New York State Board of Nursing, National
League for Nursing Accrediting Commission
(NLNAC)

Degrees conferred
Associate Degree

Minimum degree required
High school diploma or GED

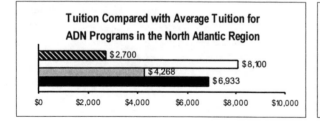

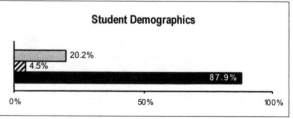

Key | Tuition Chart | ▨ Program - in state ☐ Program - out of state ▢ Average - in state ■ Average - out of state

New York

JAMESTOWN COMMUNITY COLLEGE — *Useful Facts*

525 Falconer St
Jamestown, NY 14701
(716) 665-5220
Dawn Columbare, MS, RN

www.sunyjcc.edu/jamestown/nursing/index.html

Accreditation
New York State Board of Nursing, National League for Nursing Accrediting Commission (NLNAC)

Acceptance rate	34.1%	
Faculty-student ratio	1: 8	
Faculty Full time	10	
Part time	29	

Tuition		**Student Demographics**	
In state	$3,150	Female	87.5%
Out of state	$6,300	Under age 25	33.2%
Enrollments	208	Minority	2.9%
Graduations	70	Part-time	56.7%

Degrees conferred
Associate Degree

Minimum degree required
High School top 33% and 85% average, if GED must take college course work first

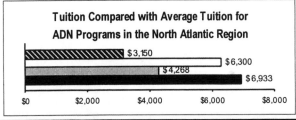

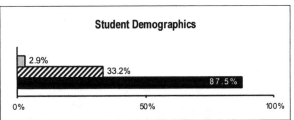

JEFFERSON COMMUNITY COLLEGE (NEW YORK) — *Useful Facts*

1220 Coffeen St
Watertown, NY 13601
(315) 786-2340
Debra Marsala, MS, RN, ANP

www.sunyjefferson.edu

Accreditation
New York State Board of Nursing, National League for Nursing Accrediting Commission (NLNAC)

Acceptance rate	59.8%	
Faculty-student ratio	1: 11	
Faculty Full time	6	
Part time	5	

Tuition		**Student Demographics**	
In state	$2,928	Female	92.3%
Out of state	$4,358	Under age 25	45.1%
Enrollments	91	Minority	10.0%
Graduations	26	Part-time	39.6%

Degrees conferred
Associate Degree

Minimum degree required
High school diploma or GED

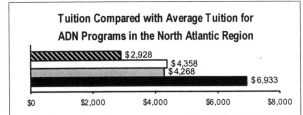

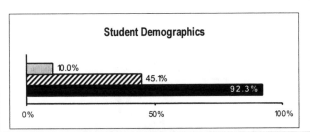

KINGSBOROUGH COMMUNITY COLLEGE - CUNY — *Useful Facts*

2001 Oriental Blvd
Brooklyn, NY 11235
(718) 368-5522
Dolores Shrimpton, RN, MA

www.kbcc.cuny.edu

Accreditation
New York State Board of Nursing, National League for Nursing Accrediting Commission (NLNAC)

Acceptance rate	74.6%	
Faculty-student ratio	1: 13	
Faculty Full time	12	
Part time	18	

Tuition		**Student Demographics**	
In state	$3,100	Female	82.6%
Out of state	$5,700	Under age 25	28.6%
Enrollments	276	Minority	47.8%
Graduations	72	Part-time	77.5%

Degrees conferred
Associate Degree

Minimum degree required
High school diploma or GED

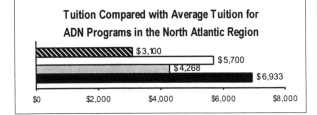

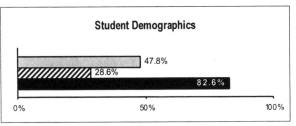

Demographics Chart	■ Female ▨ Under age 25 ▢ Minority	Distance Learning	¹The tuition reported for this program may be not be annualized. *Data reported between 2001 and 2004.

New York

LAGUARDIA COMMUNITY COLLEGE · *Useful Facts*

31-10 Thomson Ave
Long Island City, NY 11101
(718) 482-5497
Patricia Dillon, MA, RN

www.lagcc.cuny.edu

Accreditation
New York State Board of Nursing, National
League for Nursing Accrediting Commission
(NLNAC)

Acceptance rate	31.4%	
Faculty-student ratio	1: 78	
Faculty Full time	10	
Part time	10	

Degrees conferred
Associate Degree

Tuition		
In state	$2,800
Out of state	$4,560
Enrollments	1171
Graduations	46

Minimum degree required
High school diploma or GED

Student Demographics	
Female	80.5%
Under age 25	49.6%
Minority	80.3%
Part-time	55.5%

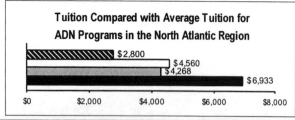

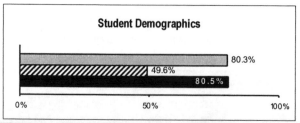

LONG ISLAND COLLEGE HOSPITAL · *Useful Facts*

340 Court Street
Brooklyn, NY 11231
(718) 780-1998
Janet Mackin, EdD, RN

www.lich.org

Accreditation
New York State Board of Nursing, National
League for Nursing Accrediting Commission
(NLNAC)

Acceptance rate	17.1%	
Faculty-student ratio	1: 15	
Faculty Full time	6	
Part time	7	

Degrees conferred
Associate Degree

Tuition		
In state	$11,235
Out of state	$11,235
Enrollments	147
Graduations	41

Minimum degree required
High school diploma or GED

Student Demographics	
Female	80.3%
Under age 25	46.3%
Minority	66.0%
Part-time	50.3%

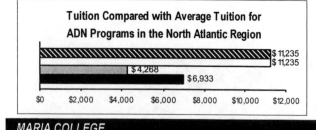

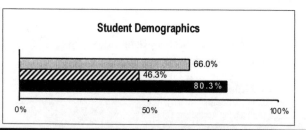

MARIA COLLEGE · *Useful Facts**

700 New Scotland Ave
Albany, NY 12208
(518) 438-3111
Linda Millenbach, RN, PhD

www.mariacollege.edu

Accreditation
New York State Board of Nursing, National
League for Nursing Accrediting Commission
(NLNAC)

Acceptance rate	68.8%	
Faculty-student ratio	1: 13	
Faculty Full time	11	
Part time	22	

Degrees conferred
Associate Degree

Tuition		
In state	$7,100
Out of state	$7,100
Enrollments	280
Graduations	78

Student Demographics	
Female	89.3%
Under age 25	30.4%
Minority	18.9%
Part-time	70.0%

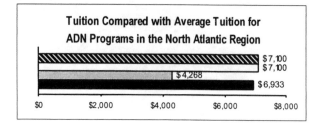

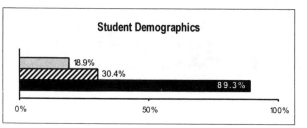

Key | Tuition Chart | ◩ Program - in state ▢ Program - out of state ▨ Average - in state ■ Average - out of state

New York

MEDGAR EVERS COLLEGE - CUNY   *Useful Facts**

1150 Carroll Street
Brooklyn, NY 11225
(718) 270-6222
Georgia McDuffie, PhD

www.mec.cuny.edu/academic_affairs/science_tech_school/nursing/nurse_home.htm

Acceptance rate	19.0%

Tuition		Student Demographics	
In state	$3,200	Female	88.9%
Out of state	$6,800	Under age 25	3.0%
Enrollments	54	Minority	94.0%
Graduations	26	Part-time	44.4%

Accreditation
New York State Board of Nursing, National
League for Nursing Accrediting Commission
(NLNAC)

Degrees conferred
Associate Degree

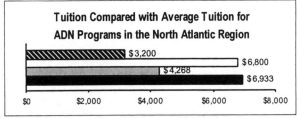

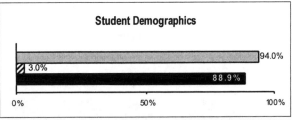

MERCY COLLEGE

555 Broadway
Dobbs Ferry, NY 10522
9146747865
Mary McGuinness, PhD, RN

www.mercy.edu

Accreditation
New York State Board of Nursing

Degrees conferred
Associate Degree

MOHAWK VALLEY COMMUNITY COLLEGE   *Useful Facts**

1101 Sherman Dr
Utica, NY 13501
(315) 792-5499
Nancy Caputo, MSN

mvcc.edu

Acceptance rate	100.0%

Tuition		Student Demographics	
In state	$2,500	Female	74.3%
Out of state	$3,750	Under age 25	20.0%
Enrollments	269	Minority	12.3%
Graduations	56	Part-time	44.2%

Accreditation
New York State Board of Nursing, National
League for Nursing Accrediting Commission
(NLNAC)

Degrees conferred
Associate Degree

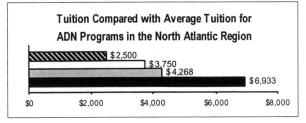

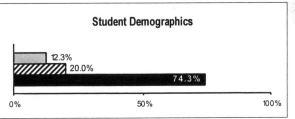

Demographics Chart	■Female ▨Under age 25 ☐Minority	Distance Learning	'The tuition reported for this program may be not be annualized. *Data reported between 2001 and 2004.

New York

MONROE COMMUNITY COLLEGE

1000 E Henrietta Rd
Rochester, NY 14623
(585) 292-2453
Laurel Sanger, RN, MS, MPA

monroecc.edu/go/nursing

Acceptance rate		28.6%
Faculty-student ratio		1: 12
Faculty	Full time	17
	Part time	21

Tuition
In state	$1,300
Out of state	$2,600
Enrollments	340
Graduations	135

Student Demographics
Female	87.9%
Under age 25	25.3%
Minority	17.9%
Part-time	79.7%

Accreditation
New York State Board of Nursing, National League for Nursing Accrediting Commission (NLNAC)

Degrees conferred
Associate Degree

Minimum degree required
Completion of HS level bio, chem, algebra and enough earned points

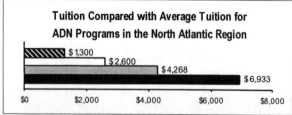

Tuition Compared with Average Tuition for ADN Programs in the North Atlantic Region

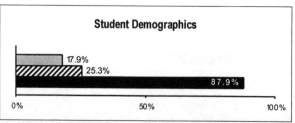

Student Demographics

NASSAU COMMUNITY COLLEGE

1 Education Dr
Garden City, NY 11530
(516) 572-9630
Carol Mottola, PhD, RN

ncc.edu

Acceptance rate		15.9%
Faculty-student ratio		1: 8
Faculty	Full time	41
	Part time	14

Tuition
In state	$3,140
Out of state	$6,280
Enrollments	368
Graduations	145

Student Demographics
Female	84.0%
Under age 25	21.7%
Minority	46.9%
Part-time	81.0%

Accreditation
New York State Board of Nursing, National League for Nursing Accrediting Commission (NLNAC)

Degrees conferred
Associate Degree

Minimum degree required
High school diploma or GED

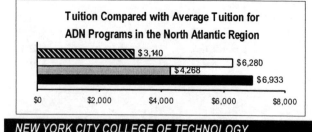

Tuition Compared with Average Tuition for ADN Programs in the North Atlantic Region

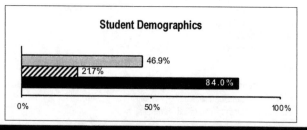

Student Demographics

NEW YORK CITY COLLEGE OF TECHNOLOGY

300 Jay Street
Brooklyn, NY 11201
(718) 260-5660
Kathryn Richardson, MSN

www.citytech.cuny.edu

Acceptance rate	95.1%

Tuition
In state	$3,200
Out of state	$6,400
Enrollments	601
Graduations	40

Student Demographics
Female	92.5%
Under age 25	51.4%
Minority	94.0%
Part-time	52.9%

Accreditation
New York State Board of Nursing, National League for Nursing Accrediting Commission (NLNAC)

Degrees conferred
Associate Degree

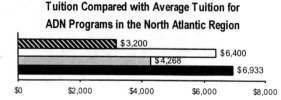

Tuition Compared with Average Tuition for ADN Programs in the North Atlantic Region

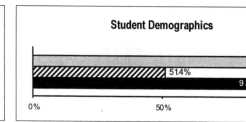

Student Demographics

Key | Tuition Chart | ▨ Program - in state ☐ Program - out of state ▥ Average - in state ■ Average - out of state

New York

NIAGARA COUNTY COMMUNITY COLLEGE - Sanborn

3111 Saunders Settlement Rd
Sanborn, NY 14132
(716) 614-5941
Katherine Collard, MS, RN

www.niagaracc.suny.edu/nursing/index.html

Accreditation
New York State Board of Nursing, National
League for Nursing Accrediting Commission
(NLNAC)

Acceptance rate		55.9%
Faculty-student ratio		1: 18
Faculty	Full time	14
	Part time	29

Degrees conferred
Associate Degree

Tuition	
In state	$3,096
Out of state	$4,644
Enrollments	516
Graduations	101

Minimum degree required
High school diploma or GED

Student Demographics	
Female	87.8%
Under age 25	38.6%
Minority	19.1%
Part-time	31.8%

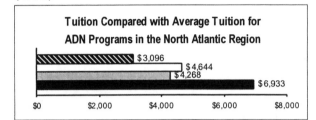

Tuition Compared with Average Tuition for ADN Programs in the North Atlantic Region

$3,096
$4,644
$4,268
$6,933

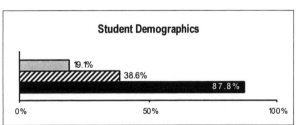

Student Demographics

19.1%
38.6%
87.8%

NORTH COUNTRY COMMUNITY COLLEGE - Saranac Lake

20 Winona Ave
Saranac Lake, NY 12983
(518) 891-2915
Peggy LaFrance, RN, MS

www.nccc.edu

Accreditation
New York State Board of Nursing

Degrees conferred
Associate Degree

ONONDAGA COMMUNITY COLLEGE   *Useful Facts*

4941 Onondaga Rd
Syracuse, NY 13215
(315) 498-2360
Pamela Ryan, MS, RNC

www.sunyocc.edu/programs/nursing

Accreditation
New York State Board of Nursing, National
League for Nursing Accrediting Commission
(NLNAC)

Acceptance rate		10.1%
Faculty-student ratio		1: 11
Faculty	Full time	9
	Part time	17

Degrees conferred
Associate Degree

Tuition	
In state	$3,180
Out of state	$9,540
Enrollments	197
Graduations	43

Minimum degree required
High school diploma or GED

Student Demographics	
Female	80.2%
Under age 25	26.4%
Minority	19.3%
Part-time	37.6%

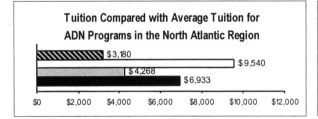

Tuition Compared with Average Tuition for ADN Programs in the North Atlantic Region

$3,180
$9,540
$4,268
$6,933

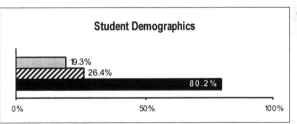

Student Demographics

19.3%
26.4%
80.2%

Demographics Chart	■Female ☑Under age 25 ▢Minority	Distance Learning	¹The tuition reported for this program may be not be annualized. ²Data reported between 2001 and 2004.

New York

ORANGE COUNTY COMMUNITY COLLEGE

Useful Facts*

115 South St
Middletown, NY 10940
(845) 341-4108
Margaret Scribner, RN, MS

www.sunyorange.edu

Accreditation
New York State Board of Nursing, National
League for Nursing Accrediting Commission
(NLNAC)

Acceptance rate	33.0%

Degrees conferred
Associate Degree

Tuition
In state	$2,700
Out of state	$5,400
Enrollments	192
Graduations	80

Student Demographics
Female	92.2%
Under age 25	34.0%
Minority	29.2%
Part-time	59.9%

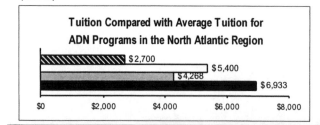

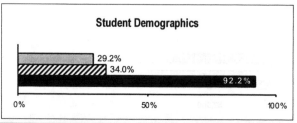

PHILLIPS BETH ISRAEL MEDICAL CENTER

Useful Facts

776 6th Avenue
New York, NY 10001
(212) 614-6107
Janet Mackin, EdD, RN

www.futurenursebi.org

Accreditation
New York State Board of Nursing, National
League for Nursing Accrediting Commission
(NLNAC)

Acceptance rate	15.0%
Faculty-student ratio	1: 13
Faculty Full time	11
Part time	8

Degrees conferred
Associate Degree

Tuition
In state	$8,700
Out of state	$8,700
Enrollments	194
Graduations	71

Minimum degree required
High school diploma or GED

Student Demographics
Female	72.2%
Under age 25	36.6%
Minority	49.0%
Part-time	80.4%

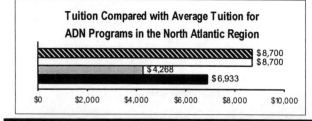

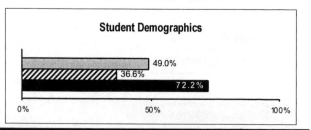

QUEENSBOROUGH COMMUNITY COLLEGE - CUNY

Useful Facts*

222-05 56th Ave
Bayside, NY 11364
(718) 631-6080
Maureen Wallace, EdD, RN

www.qcc.cuny.edu/nursing

Accreditation
New York State Board of Nursing, National
League for Nursing Accrediting Commission
(NLNAC)

Acceptance rate	60.1%
Faculty-student ratio	1: 56
Faculty Full time	21
Part time	18

Degrees conferred
Associate Degree

Tuition
In state	$2,500
Out of state	$3,076
Enrollments	1688
Graduations	107

Student Demographics
Female	84.5%
Under age 25	45.0%
Minority	81.8%
Part-time	71.1%

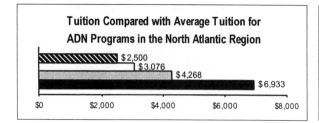

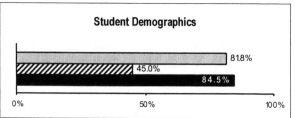

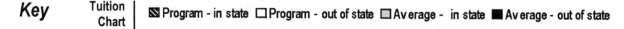

Key | Tuition Chart | ▨ Program - in state   ☐ Program - out of state   ☐ Average - in state   ■ Average - out of state

New York

SAINT ELIZABETH MEDICAL CENTER — *Useful Facts**

2215 Genesee St
Utica, NY 13501
(315) 798-8125
Marianne Monahan, MS, RN

www.stemc.org

Accreditation
New York State Board of Nursing, National League for Nursing Accrediting Commission (NLNAC)

Degrees conferred
Associate Degree

Tuition		Student Demographics	
In state	$6,094	Female	88.1%
Out of state	$6,094	Under age 25	10.0%
Enrollments	160	Minority	1.9%
		Part-time	37.5%

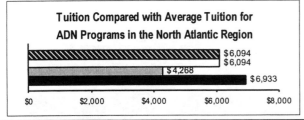

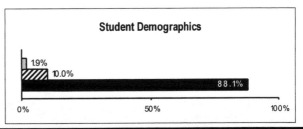

SAINT JOSEPH'S HOSPITAL HEALTH CENTER — *Useful Facts**

206 Prospect Ave
Syracuse, RI 13203
(315) 448-5040
Marianne Markowitz, RN, MS

www.sjhsyr.org/nursing

Accreditation
New York State Board of Nursing

Degrees conferred
Associate Degree

Tuition		Student Demographics	
In state	$5,907	Female	94.8%
Out of state	$9,142	Under age 25	61.0%
Enrollments	191	Minority	6.3%
Graduations	47	Part-time	30.9%

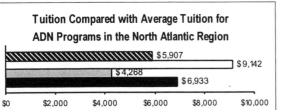

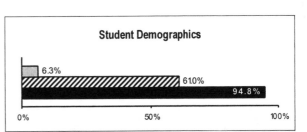

SAINT VINCENT CATHOLIC MEDICAL CENTER OF NY - *Queens*

175-05 Horace Harding Expy
Fresh Meadows, NY 11365
(718) 357-0500
Genevieve Jensen, MS, RN

www.svcmc.org

Accreditation
New York State Board of Nursing

Degrees conferred
Associate Degree

Acceptance rate		11.1%
Faculty-student ratio		1: 19
Faculty	Full time	8
	Part time	7

Tuition		Student Demographics	
In state	$5,682	Female	79.6%
Out of state	$5,682	Under age 25	37.0%
Enrollments	108	Minority	45.4%
Graduations	54	Part-time	52.8%

Minimum degree required
High school diploma or GED

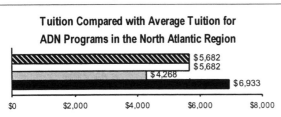

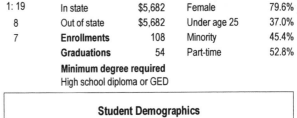

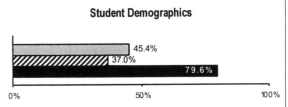

Demographics Chart	■Female ☒Under age 25 ▢Minority	Distance Learning	¹The tuition reported for this program may be not be annualized. *Data reported between 2001 and 2004.

New York

SAINT VINCENT CATHOLIC MEDICAL CENTER OF NY - Staten Island

175-05 Horace Harding Expy
Fresh Meadows, NY 11365
(718) 357-0500
Genevieve Jensen, MS, RN

www.svcmc.org

Acceptance rate			26.1%
Faculty-student ratio			1: 19
Faculty	Full time		8
	Part time		7

Tuition	
In state	$6,240
Out of state	$6,240
Enrollments	112
Graduations	36

Student Demographics	
Female	83.9%
Under age 25	50.0%
Minority	27.4%
Part-time	59.8%

Accreditation
New York State Board of Nursing

Degrees conferred
Associate Degree

Minimum degree required
High school diploma or GED

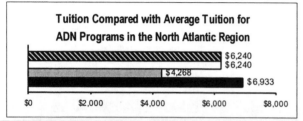

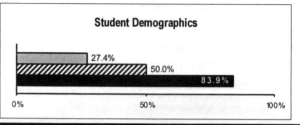

SAMARITAN HOSPITAL

2215 Burdett Avenue
Troy, NY 12180
(518) 271-3285
Mary Harknett-Martin

www.nehealth.com

Accreditation
New York State Board of Nursing

Degrees conferred
Associate Degree

STATE UNIVERSITY OF NEW YORK - CANTON
Useful Facts

Cook Hall 113
Canton, NY 13617
(315) 386-7419
John Conklin, MSN

www.canton.edu

Acceptance rate			18.9%
Faculty-student ratio			1: 14
Faculty	Full time		7
	Part time		9

Tuition	
In state	$4,350
Out of state	$7,000
Enrollments	157
Graduations	40

Student Demographics	
Female	87.3%
Under age 25	50.3%
Minority	13.9%
Part-time	8.9%

Accreditation
New York State Board of Nursing, National
League for Nursing Accrediting Commission
(NLNAC)

Degrees conferred
Associate Degree

Minimum degree required
High school diploma or GED

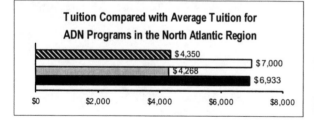

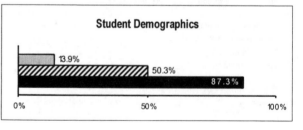

Key | Tuition Chart | ▨ Program - in state ☐ Program - out of state ☐ Average - in state ■ Average - out of state

New York

STATE UNIVERSITY OF NEW YORK - FARMINGDALE — *Useful Facts*

2350 Broadhollow Road
Farmingdale, NY 11735
(631) 420-2229
Kathleen Walsh, EdD, RN-C

www.farmingdale.edu

Accreditation
New York State Board of Nursing, National
League for Nursing Accrediting Commission
(NLNAC)

Acceptance rate	16.1%	
Faculty-student ratio	1: 9	
Faculty Full time	14	
Part time	42	

Degrees conferred
Associate Degree

Tuition		Student Demographics	
In state	$4,350	Female	87.7%
Out of state	$10,610	Under age 25	18.4%
Enrollments	326	Minority	42.6%
Graduations	104	Part-time	81.3%

Minimum degree required
High school diploma or GED

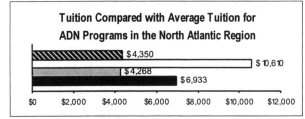

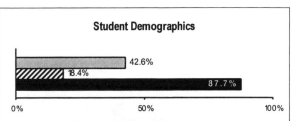

STATE UNIVERSITY OF NEW YORK - MORRISVILLE — *Useful Facts*

PO Box 901
Morrisville, NY 13408
(315) 684-6049
Margaret Golden, MS, RN

www.morrisville.edu

Accreditation
New York State Board of Nursing, National
League for Nursing Accrediting Commission
(NLNAC)

Acceptance rate	39.6%	
Faculty-student ratio	1: 12	
Faculty Full time	12	
Part time	2	

Degrees conferred
Associate Degree

Tuition		Student Demographics	
In state	$4,350	Female	89.0%
Out of state	$7,210	Under age 25	46.8%
Enrollments	154	Minority	10.4%
Graduations	26	Part-time	20.1%

Minimum degree required
High school diploma or GED

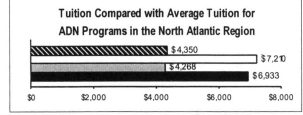

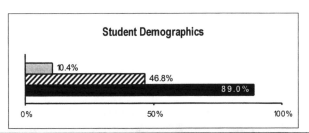

STATE UNIVERSITY OF NEW YORK COLLEGE OF TECHNOLOGY AT ALFRED — *Useful Facts*

Allied Health Building, SUNY Alfred
Alfred, NY 14802
(607) 587-3680
Cynthie Luehman, RN, BS, MS

www.alfredstate.edu

Accreditation
New York State Board of Nursing, National
League for Nursing Accrediting Commission
(NLNAC)

Acceptance rate	46.5%	
Faculty-student ratio	1: 19	
Faculty Full time	6	
Part time	6	

Degrees conferred
Associate Degree, AAS

Tuition		Student Demographics	
In state	$4,350	Female	84.6%
Out of state	$7,210	Under age 25	60.4%
Enrollments	169	Minority	8.3%
Graduations	38	Part-time	4.7%

Minimum degree required
High school diploma or GED

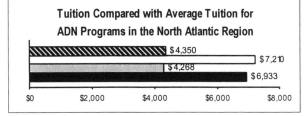

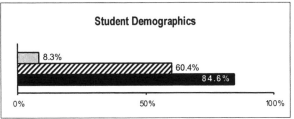

Demographics Chart	■ Female ▨ Under age 25 ▢ Minority	Distance Learning	¹The tuition reported for this program may be not be annualized. *Data reported between 2001 and 2004.

New York

STATE UNIVERSITY OF NEW YORK COLLEGE OF TECHNOLOGY AT DELHI | *Useful Facts*

2 Main Street
Delhi, NY 13753
(607) 746-4492
Mary Pat Lewis, PhD, RN

www.delhi.edu/academics/nursing

Acceptance rate		47.5%
Faculty-student ratio		1: 10
Faculty	Full time	10
	Part time	9

Tuition	
In state	$4,350
Out of state	$7,210
Enrollments	144
Graduations	42

Student Demographics	
Female	86.1%
Under age 25	51.4%
Minority	21.9%
Part-time	10.4%

Accreditation
New York State Board of Nursing, National
League for Nursing Accrediting Commission
(NLNAC)

Degrees conferred
Associate Degree

Minimum degree required
High school diploma or GED

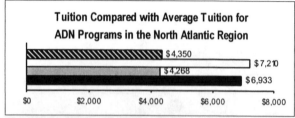
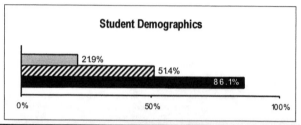

SUFFOLK COUNTY COMMUNITY COLLEGE - *Selden*

533 College Rd, Riverhead Bldg, Rm 106
Selden, NY 11784
(631) 451-4268
Frances La Fauci, MS RN

www.sunysuffolk.edu

Acceptance rate	42.3%

Tuition	
In state	$2,330
Out of state	$4,660
Enrollments	303
Graduations	130

Student Demographics	
Female	87.5%
Under age 25	20.0%
Minority	16.9%
Part-time	35.0%

Accreditation
New York State Board of Nursing, National
League for Nursing Accrediting Commission
(NLNAC)

Degrees conferred
Associate Degree

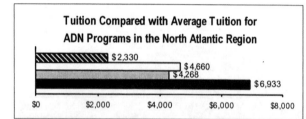
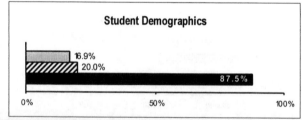

SULLIVAN COUNTY COMMUNITY COLLEGE | *Useful Facts**

112 College Rd
Loch Sheldrake, NY 12759
(845) 434-5750
Donna Kleister, MS, RN

www.sullivan.suny.edu

Acceptance rate	100.0%

Tuition	
In state	$2,500
Out of state	$5,000
Enrollments	61

Student Demographics	
Female	88.5%
Minority	23.0%
Part-time	42.6%

Accreditation
New York State Board of Nursing, National
League for Nursing Accrediting Commission
(NLNAC)

Degrees conferred
Associate Degree

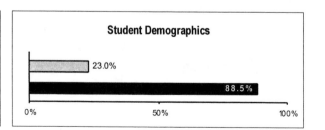

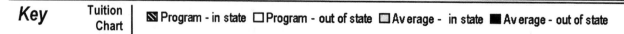

Key | Tuition Chart | ▨ Program - in state ☐ Program - out of state ☐ Average - in state ■ Average - out of state

New York

SUNY ROCKLAND COMMUNITY COLLEGE

145 College Rd
Suffern, NY 10901
(845) 574-4777
Frances Monahan, RN

www.sunyrockland.edu

Accreditation
New York State Board of Nursing, National
League for Nursing Accrediting Commission
(NLNAC)

Acceptance rate	77.1%	

Degrees conferred
Associate Degree

Tuition		**Student Demographics**	
In state	$2,325	Female	88.9%
Out of state	$4,650	Under age 25	15.0%
Enrollments	441		
Graduations	68	Part-time	61.5%

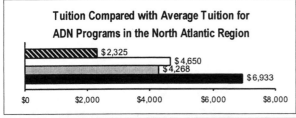

Tuition Compared with Average Tuition for ADN Programs in the North Atlantic Region
$2,325 / $4,650 / $4,268 / $6,933

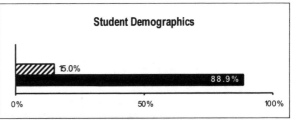

Student Demographics
15.0% / 88.9%

THE COLLEGE OF STATEN ISLAND

2800 Victory Blvd, Marcus Hall
Staten Island, NY 10314
(718) 982-3810
Mary O'Donnell, RN, PhD

www.csi.cuny.edu/nursing

Accreditation
New York State Board of Nursing, National
League for Nursing Accrediting Commission
(NLNAC)

Acceptance rate	63.7%	
Faculty-student ratio	1: 11	
Faculty	Full time	17
	Part time	33

Degrees conferred
Associate Degree

Tuition		**Student Demographics**	
In state	$4,000	Female	84.1%
Out of state	$6,800	Under age 25	35.2%
Enrollments	352	Minority	40.5%
Graduations	97	Part-time	69.3%

Minimum degree required
High school diploma or GED

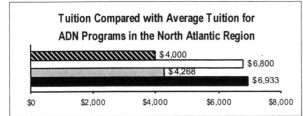

Tuition Compared with Average Tuition for ADN Programs in the North Atlantic Region
$4,000 / $6,800 / $4,268 / $6,933

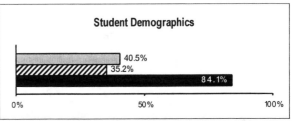

Student Demographics
40.5% / 35.2% / 84.1%

THE MOUNT VERNON HOSPITAL

53 Valentine St
Mount Vernon, NY 10550
(914) 664-8000
Joanna Scalabrini, MS, MA, RN

hopfer.org

Accreditation
New York State Board of Nursing

Acceptance rate	15.9%	
Faculty-student ratio	1: 9	
Faculty	Full time	8
	Part time	14

Degrees conferred
Associate Degree

Tuition		**Student Demographics**	
In state	$6,858	Female	84.8%
Out of state	$6,895	Under age 25	16.7%
Enrollments	138	Minority	77.4%
Graduations	57	Part-time	71.0%

Minimum degree required
High school diploma or GED

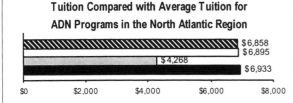

Tuition Compared with Average Tuition for ADN Programs in the North Atlantic Region
$6,858 / $6,895 / $4,268 / $6,933

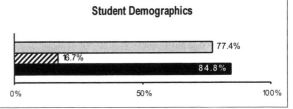

Student Demographics
77.4% / 16.7% / 84.8%

Demographics Chart	■ Female ☑ Under age 25 ☐ Minority	Distance Learning	†The tuition reported for this program may be not be annualized. *Data reported between 2001 and 2004.

New York

TOMPKINS CORTLAND

170 North St, PO Box 139
Dryden, NY 13053
(607) 844-8211
Janet Morgan, PhD, RN

www.tc3.edu

Accreditation
New York State Board of Nursing, National
League for Nursing Accrediting Commission
(NLNAC)

Acceptance rate		18.2%
Faculty-student ratio		1: 9
Faculty	Full time	10
	Part time	7

Tuition
In state	$3,100
Out of state	$6,500
Enrollments	125
Graduations	40

Student Demographics
Female	90.4%
Under age 25	32.0%
Minority	4.2%
Part-time	41.6%

Degrees conferred
Associate Degree

Minimum degree required
High school diploma or GED

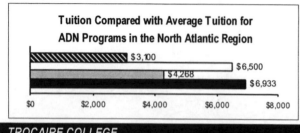
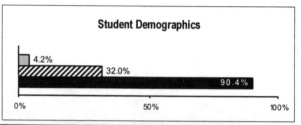

TROCAIRE COLLEGE

360 Choate Ave
Buffalo, NY 14220
(716) 827-2462
Carol Fanutti, EdD, RN

www.trocaire.edu

Accreditation
New York State Board of Nursing, National
League for Nursing Accrediting Commission
(NLNAC)

Acceptance rate		97.1%
Faculty-student ratio		1: 14
Faculty	Full time	15
	Part time	14

Tuition
In state	$8,980
Out of state	$8,980
Enrollments	305
Graduations	81

Student Demographics
Female	92.1%
Under age 25	37.7%
Minority	20.7%
Part-time	48.9%

Degrees conferred
Associate Degree

Minimum degree required
High school diploma or GED

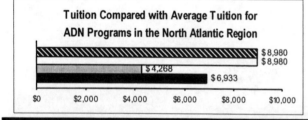
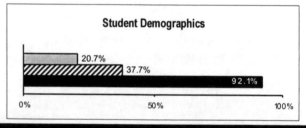

ULSTER COUNTY COMMUNITY COLLEGE

Cottekill Rd
Stone Ridge, NY 12484
(845) 687-5235
Joan Gilbert, RN, MA

www.sunyulster.edu

Accreditation
New York State Board of Nursing

Acceptance rate	75.1%

Tuition
In state	$3,000
Out of state	$6,000
Enrollments	332
Graduations	42

Student Demographics
Female	82.2%
Under age 25	33.0%
Minority	19.0%
Part-time	65.1%

Degrees conferred
Associate Degree

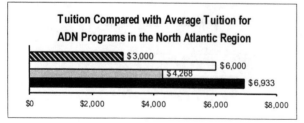
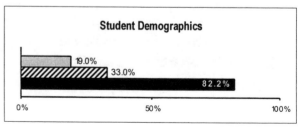

Key Tuition Chart | ⬚ Program - in state ☐ Program - out of state ⬛ Average - in state ■ Average - out of state

New York

WESTCHESTER COMMUNITY COLLEGE   *Useful Facts**

75 Grasslands Rd
Valhalla, NY 10595
(914) 785-6891
Joanna Scahabrini, MSN, MHED, RN, C

www.sunywcc.edu

Acceptance rate	16.1%	**Tuition**	**Student Demographics**
		In state $2,200	Female 94.2%
		Out of state $4,400	Under age 25 8.0%
		Enrollments 86	Minority 33.7%
		Graduations 35	Part-time 0.0%

Accreditation
New York State Board of Nursing

Degrees conferred
Associate Degree

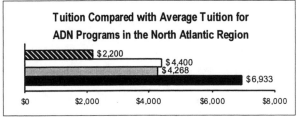
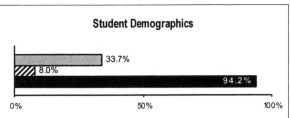

North Carolina

ALAMANCE COMMUNITY COLLEGE   *Useful Facts*

PO Box 8000
Graham, NC 27253
(336) 506-4162
Susan Holt, MSN, RN

www.alamance.cc.nc.us

Acceptance rate	6.9%	**Tuition**	**Student Demographics**
Faculty-student ratio	1: 8	In state $1,200	Female 90.0%
Faculty Full time	6	Out of state $7,500	Under age 25 28.2%
Part time	15	**Enrollments** 110	Minority 19.4%
		Graduations 46	Part-time 0.0%

Accreditation
North Carolina Board of Nursing

Degrees conferred
Associate Degree

Minimum degree required
High school diploma or GED

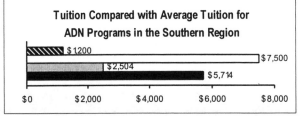
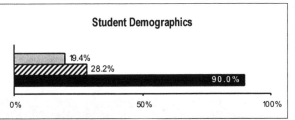

ASHEVILLE-BUNCOMBE TECHNICAL COMMUNITY COLLEGE   *Useful Facts**

340 Victoria Road
Asheville, NC 28801
(828) 254-1921
Brenda Causey, MSN, RN

www.asheville.cc.nc.us

Acceptance rate	34.6%	**Tuition**	**Student Demographics**
		In state $1,182	Female 78.2%
		Out of state $7,299	Under age 25 31.0%
		Enrollments 147	
		Graduations 57	

Accreditation
North Carolina Board of Nursing

Degrees conferred
Associate Degree

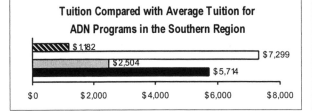
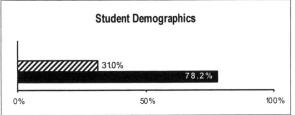

Demographics Chart	■Female ▨Under age 25 ▢Minority	Distance Learning 🖥	¹The tuition reported for this program may be not be annualized.
			*Data reported between 2001 and 2004.

North Carolina

BEAUFORT COUNTY COMMUNITY COLLEGE

5337 Highway 264 East
Washington, NC 27889
(252) 940-6266
Laura Bliley, MSN

www.beaufort.cc.nc.us

Acceptance rate		11.1%
Faculty-student ratio		1: 10
Faculty	Full time	5
	Part time	3

Tuition	
In state	$1,245
Out of state	$6,645
Enrollments	68
Graduations	27

Student Demographics	
Female	89.7%
Under age 25	30.9%
Minority	14.7%
Part-time	0.0%

Accreditation
North Carolina Board of Nursing

Degrees conferred
Associate Degree

Minimum degree required
High school diploma or GED

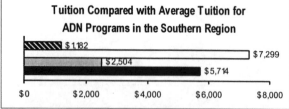

Tuition Compared with Average Tuition for ADN Programs in the Southern Region

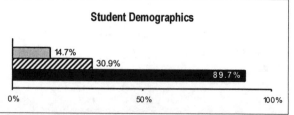

Student Demographics

BLADEN COMMUNITY COLLEGE

PO Box 266
Dublin, NC 28332
(910) 879-5509
Anne-Marie Goff, MSN, RN

www.bladen.cc.nc.us

Acceptance rate	26.0%

Tuition	
In state	$608
Out of state	$3,152
Enrollments	20
Graduations	0

Student Demographics	
Female	90.0%
Under age 25	55.0%
Minority	40.0%
Part-time	0.0%

Accreditation
North Carolina Board of Nursing

Degrees conferred
Associate Degree

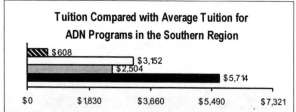

Tuition Compared with Average Tuition for ADN Programs in the Southern Region

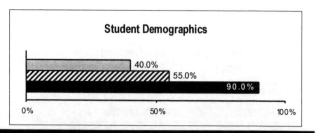

Student Demographics

BLUE RIDGE COMMUNITY COLLEGE - NORTH CAROLINA

180 West Campus Drive
Flat Rock, NC 28731
(828) 694-1825
Rita Conner, MSN, RN

blueridge.edu

Acceptance rate		36.1%
Faculty-student ratio		1: 7
Faculty	Full time	4
	Part time	8

Tuition	
In state	$1,264
Out of state	$7,024
Enrollments	55
Graduations	21

Student Demographics	
Female	89.1%
Under age 25	29.1%
Minority	7.3%
Part-time	76.4%

Accreditation
North Carolina Board of Nursing

Degrees conferred
Associate Degree

Minimum degree required
High school diploma or GED

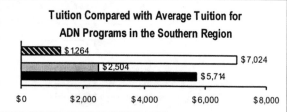

Tuition Compared with Average Tuition for ADN Programs in the Southern Region

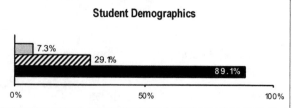

Student Demographics

Key | Tuition Chart | ▨ Program - in state ☐ Program - out of state ▨ Average - in state ■ Average - out of state

North Carolina

BRUNSWICK COMMUNITY COLLEGE

PO Box 30
Supply, NC 28462
(910) 755-7350
Connie Milliken, MEd, BSN

www.brunswick.cc.nc.us

Accreditation
North Carolina Board of Nursing

Degrees conferred
Associate Degree

CABARRUS COLLEGE OF HEALTH SCIENCES   *Useful Facts**

401 Medical Park Drive
Concord, NC 28025
(704) 783-1629
Elizabeth Baucom, MSN, RN

www.cabarruscollege.edu

			Tuition		Student Demographics	
Acceptance rate	23.7%		In state	$7,340	Female	92.1%
			Out of state	$7,340	Under age 25	70.0%
			Enrollments	165	Minority	4.3%
			Graduations	29	Part-time	24.8%

Accreditation
North Carolina Board of Nursing, National
League for Nursing Accrediting Commission
(NLNAC)

Degrees conferred
Associate Degree

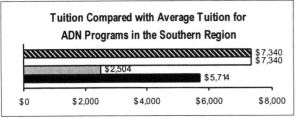

Tuition Compared with Average Tuition for
ADN Programs in the Southern Region

$7,340
$7,340
$2,504
$5,714

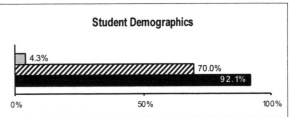

Student Demographics

4.3%
70.0%
92.1%

CALDWELL COMMUNITY COLLEGE & TECHNICAL INSTITUTE   *Useful Facts**

2855 Hickory Blvd
Hudson, NC 28638
(828) 726-2343
Jan Overman, MSN, RN

cccti.com

Tuition		Student Demographics	
In state	$1,108	Female	92.4%
Out of state	$9,506		
Enrollments	92		
Graduations	28	Part-time	0.0%

Accreditation
North Carolina Board of Nursing

Degrees conferred
Associate Degree

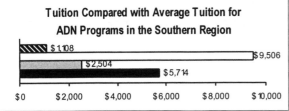

Tuition Compared with Average Tuition for
ADN Programs in the Southern Region

$1,108
$9,506
$2,504
$5,714

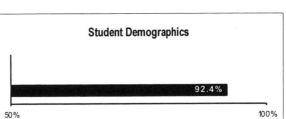

Student Demographics

92.4%

Demographics Chart	■Female ◪Under age 25 ▢Minority	**Distance Learning**	†The tuition reported for this program may be not be annualized.
			*Data reported between 2001 and 2004.

North Carolina

CAPE FEAR COMMUNITY COLLEGE — *Useful Facts*

411 N Front Street
Wilmington, NC 28401
(910) 362-7082
Regina McBarron, MSN

cfcc.edu

Acceptance rate	25.1%
Faculty-student ratio	1: 8
Faculty Full time	11
Part time	13

Tuition	
In state	$1,185
Out of state	$6,585
Enrollments	135
Graduations	59

Student Demographics	
Female	85.9%
Under age 25	38.5%
Minority	8.2%
Part-time	0.0%

Accreditation
North Carolina Board of Nursing, National League for Nursing Accrediting Commission (NLNAC)

Degrees conferred
Associate Degree

Minimum degree required
High school diploma or GED

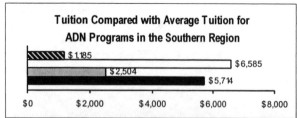

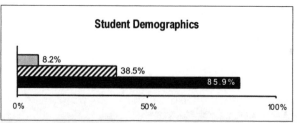

CAROLINAS COLLEGE OF HEALTH SCIENCES — *Useful Facts*

1200 Blythe Blvd
Charlotte, NC 28232
(704) 355-5970
Deborah Blackwell, PhD, RNC, WHCNP, APRN, BC

www.carolinascollege.edu

Acceptance rate	36.4%
Faculty-student ratio	1: 10
Faculty Full time	19
Part time	11

Tuition	
In state	$5,250
Out of state	$5,250
Enrollments	239
Graduations	106

Student Demographics	
Female	90.8%
Under age 25	47.7%
Minority	17.1%
Part-time	58.6%

Accreditation
North Carolina Board of Nursing, National League for Nursing Accrediting Commission (NLNAC)

Degrees conferred
Associate Degree

Minimum degree required
High school diploma or GED

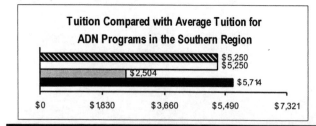

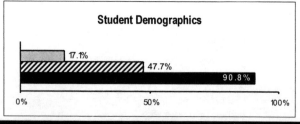

CARTERET COMMUNITY COLLEGE

3505 Arendell Street
Morehead City, NC 28557
(252) 247-6000
Nancy McBride

www.carteret.cc.nc.us.edu

Accreditation
North Carolina Board of Nursing

Degrees conferred
Associate Degree

Key | Tuition Chart | ▧ Program - in state ☐ Program - out of state ☐ Average - in state ■ Average - out of state

North Carolina

CATAWBA VALLEY COMMUNITY COLLEGE   *Useful Facts*

2550 Highway, 70 SE
Hickory, NC 28602
(828) 327-7000
Colleen Burgess, MSN, RN

www.cvcc.cc.nc.us/programs/health/adnprogram.htm

Acceptance rate	6.6%	
Faculty-student ratio	1: 8	
Faculty Full time	8	
Part time	15	

Tuition		
In state	$608
Out of state	$3,376
Enrollments	128
Graduations	55

Student Demographics	
Female	89.8%
Under age 25	33.6%
Minority	6.3%
Part-time	0.0%

Accreditation
North Carolina Board of Nursing, National
League for Nursing Accrediting Commission
(NLNAC)

Degrees conferred
Associate Degree

Minimum degree required
High school diploma or GED

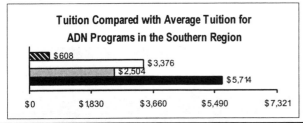

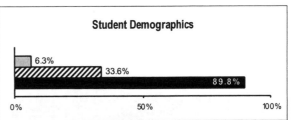

CENTRAL CAROLINA COMMUNITY COLLEGE

1105 Kelly Drive
Sanford, NC 27330
(919) 775-5401
Rhonda Evans, MSN, RN

www.ccarolina.cc.nc.us

Accreditation
North Carolina Board of Nursing

Degrees conferred
Associate Degree

CENTRAL PIEDMONT COMMUNITY COLLEGE   *Useful Facts*

PO Box 35009
Charlotte, NC 28235
(704) 330-6716
Joan Eudy, RNCS, PhD

www.cpcc.edu

Acceptance rate	56.0%	
Faculty-student ratio	1: 12	
Faculty Full time	6	
Part time	8	

Tuition		
In state	$992
Out of state	$5,544
Enrollments	115
Graduations	33

Student Demographics	
Female	77.4%
Under age 25	29.6%
Minority	54.5%
Part-time	77.4%

Accreditation
North Carolina Board of Nursing

Degrees conferred
Associate Degree

Minimum degree required
High school diploma or GED

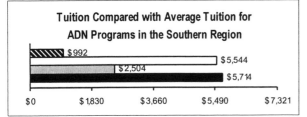

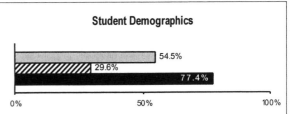

Demographics Chart	■ Female ▨ Under age 25 ▢ Minority	**Distance Learning**	¹The tuition reported for this program may be not be annualized. *Data reported between 2001 and 2004.

North Carolina

COASTAL CAROLINA COMMUNITY COLLEGE
Useful Facts

444 Western Boulevard
Jacksonville, NC 28546
(910) 938-6269
Paula Gribble, MSAS, BSN, RN

www.coastal.cc.nc.us

Acceptance rate		39.4%
Faculty-student ratio		1:8
Faculty	Full time	6
	Part time	2

Tuition	
In state	$1,896
Out of state	$10,536
Enrollments	58
Graduations	23

Student Demographics	
Female	93.1%
Under age 25	36.2%
Minority	9.3%
Part-time	0.0%

Accreditation
North Carolina Board of Nursing

Degrees conferred
Associate Degree

Minimum degree required
High school diploma or GED

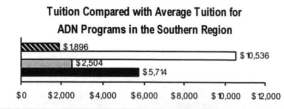

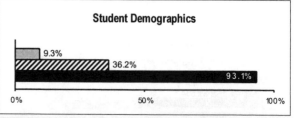

COLLEGE OF THE ALBEMARLE
Useful Facts*

PO Box 2327
Elizabeth City, NC 27906
(252) 335-0821
Mary Omer, MS, RN

www.albemarle.edu

Acceptance rate	26.3%

Tuition	
In state	$880
Out of state	$5,432
Enrollments	56
Graduations	21

Student Demographics	
Female	96.4%
Under age 25	11.0%
Minority	8.9%
Part-time	69.6%

Accreditation
North Carolina Board of Nursing, National
League for Nursing Accrediting Commission
(NLNAC)

Degrees conferred
Associate Degree

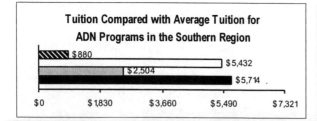

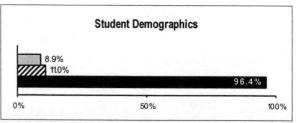

CRAVEN COMMUNITY COLLEGE
Useful Facts

800 College Court
New Bern, NC 28562
(252) 638-7342
Carolyn Jones, MSN, MAED, RN

www.cravencc.edu

Acceptance rate		34.4%
Faculty-student ratio		1:7
Faculty	Full time	9
	Part time	15

Tuition	
In state	$1,896
Out of state	$10,536
Enrollments	114
Graduations	67

Student Demographics	
Female	91.2%
Under age 25	35.1%
Minority	16.8%
Part-time	29.8%

Accreditation
North Carolina Board of Nursing

Degrees conferred
Associate Degree

Minimum degree required
High school diploma or GED

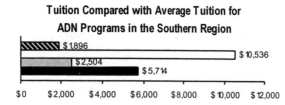

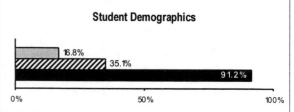

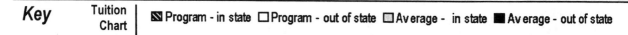

Key | Tuition Chart | ▨ Program - in state ☐ Program - out of state ▥ Average - in state ■ Average - out of state

North Carolina

DAVIDSON COUNTY COMMUNITY COLLEGE — Useful Facts

PO Box 1287
Lexington, NC 27293
(336) 249-8186
Jeannine Woody, MSN, BSN, RN

www.davidsonccc.edu/nurs

Accreditation
North Carolina Board of Nursing, National League for Nursing Accrediting Commission (NLNAC)

Acceptance rate	9.6%
Faculty-student ratio	1: 9
Faculty Full time	8
Part time	5

Degrees conferred
Associate Degree

Tuition
In state $1,185
Out of state $6,585
Enrollments 95
Graduations 47

Minimum degree required
High school diploma or GED

Student Demographics
Female 87.4%
Under age 25 37.9%
Minority 4.4%
Part-time 0.0%

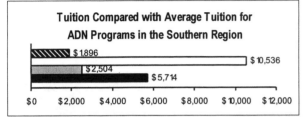
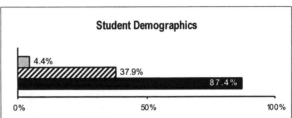

DURHAM TECHNICAL COMMUNITY COLLEGE — Useful Facts*

1637 Lawson Street
Durham, NC 27707
(919) 686-3416
Helen Ayres, MSN, EdD

www.durhamtech.org

Accreditation
North Carolina Board of Nursing

Acceptance rate	10.1%
Faculty-student ratio	1: 10
Faculty Full time	10
Part time	8

Degrees conferred
Associate Degree

Tuition
In state $1,216
Out of state $6,752
Enrollments 139
Graduations 40

Student Demographics
Female 89.9%
Under age 25 16.0%
Minority 56.3%
Part-time 89.2%

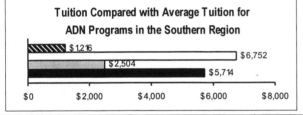
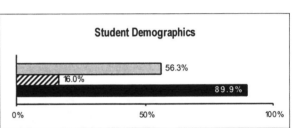

EDGECOMBE COMMUNITY COLLEGE — Useful Facts*

225 Tarboro St
Rocky Mount, NC 27801
(252) 446-0436
Katherine Williford, RN, MSN

www.edgecombe.cc.nc.us

Accreditation
North Carolina Board of Nursing

Acceptance rate	25.7%
Faculty-student ratio	1: 8
Faculty Full time	28
Part time	11

Degrees conferred
Associate Degree

Enrollments 260
Graduations 60

Student Demographics
Female 90.0%
Under age 25 35.0%
Minority 32.0%
Part-time 0.0%

Demographics Chart: ■Female ▨Under age 25 ☐Minority | Distance Learning | ¹The tuition reported for this program may be not be annualized. *Data reported between 2001 and 2004.

North Carolina

FAYETTEVILLE TECHNICAL COMMUNITY COLLEGE

2201 Hull Road
Fayetteville, NC 28303
(910) 678-8482
Kathy Weeks, MSN, RN

www.faytechcc.edu

Accreditation
North Carolina Board of Nursing, National
League for Nursing Accrediting Commission
(NLNAC)

Acceptance rate	42.9%
Faculty-student ratio	1:8
Faculty Full time	17
Part time	14

Degrees conferred
Associate Degree

Tuition	
In state	$1,185
Out of state	$8,670
Enrollments	187
Graduations	63

Minimum degree required
High school diploma or GED

Student Demographics	
Female	92.5%
Under age 25	29.9%
Minority	32.6%
Part-time	64.2%

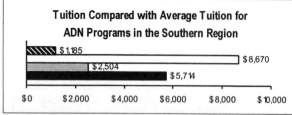

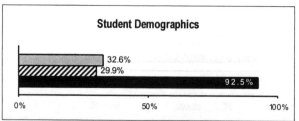

FOOTHILLS NURSING CONSORTIUM

PO Box 804 Isothermal Loop Rd
Spindale, NC 28160
(828) 286-3636
Jeanette Cheshire, MPH, RN

cleveland.cc.nc.us/staff/mckibbin.foothills.htm

Accreditation
North Carolina Board of Nursing

Acceptance rate	9.1%

Degrees conferred
Associate Degree

Tuition	
In state	$744
Out of state	$4,158
Enrollments	65
Graduations	26

Student Demographics	
Female	89.2%
Under age 25	5.0%
Minority	9.5%
Part-time	21.5%

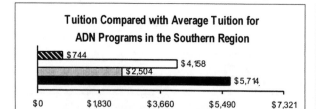

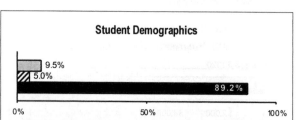

FORSYTH TECHNICAL COMMUNITY COLLEGE

2100 Silas Creek Parkway
Winston-Salem, NC 27103
(336) 734-7428
Phyllis Sample, MS, BSN, RN

www.forsyth.tec.nc.us

Accreditation
North Carolina Board of Nursing

Acceptance rate	15.4%

Degrees conferred
Associate Degree

Tuition	
In state	$744
Out of state	$4,158
Enrollments	206
Graduations	80

Student Demographics	
Female	90.8%
Under age 25	30.0%
Minority	18.0%
Part-time	0.0%

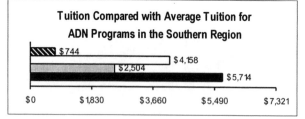

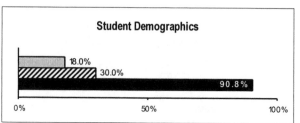

Key | Tuition Chart | ▨ Program - in state ☐ Program - out of state ☐ Average - in state ■ Average - out of state

North Carolina

GARDNER-WEBB UNIVERSITY
Useful Facts*

PO Box 997
Boiling Springs, NC 28017
(704) 406-4366
Shirley Toney, PhD, RN

www.gardner-webb.edu

Acceptance rate		55.8%
Faculty-student ratio		1: 6
Faculty	Full time	17
	Part time	8

Tuition	
In state	$14,160
Out of state	$14,160
Enrollments	133
Graduations	47

Student Demographics	
Female	92.5%
Under age 25	69.2%
Minority	14.5%
Part-time	24.8%

Accreditation
North Carolina Board of Nursing, National League for Nursing Accrediting Commission (NLNAC)

Degrees conferred
Associate Degree

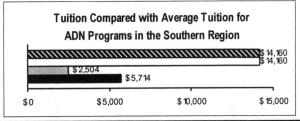
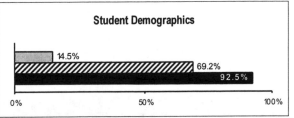

GASTON COLLEGE
Useful Facts*

201 Highway, 321 South
Dallas, NC 28034
(704) 922-6367
Lois Bradley, MeD, BSN, RN

www.gaston.cc.nc.us

Acceptance rate	71.3%

Tuition	
In state	$1,320
Out of state	$8,148
Enrollments	109
Graduations	28

Student Demographics	
Female	97.2%
Under age 25	13.0%
Minority	8.3%
Part-time	0.0%

Accreditation
North Carolina Board of Nursing

Degrees conferred
Associate Degree

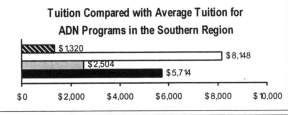
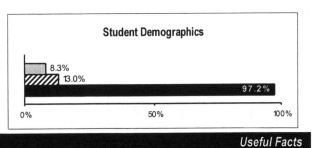

GUILFORD TECHNICAL COMMUNITY COLLEGE
Useful Facts

PO Box 309
Jamestown, NC 27282
(336) 334-4822
Katherine Phillips, RN, MSN

www.gtcc.edu

Acceptance rate	6.0%

Tuition	
In state	$1,200
Out of state	$6,600
Enrollments	214
Graduations	54

Student Demographics	
Female	93.5%
Under age 25	30.4%
Minority	25.2%
Part-time	2.8%

Accreditation
North Carolina Board of Nursing

Degrees conferred
Associate Degree

Minimum degree required
High school diploma or GED

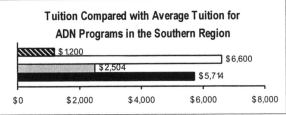
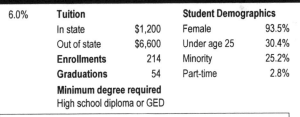
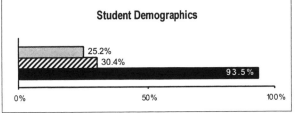

Demographics Chart	■ Female ▨ Under age 25 ▢ Minority	Distance Learning	¹The tuition reported for this program may be not be annualized. *Data reported between 2001 and 2004.

North Carolina

JAMES SPRUNT COMMUNITY COLLEGE

PO Box 398
Kenansville, NC 28349
(910) 296-2450
Rhonda Ferrell, MSN, BSN, RN

www.sprunt.com

Accreditation
North Carolina Board of Nursing

Acceptance rate	35.7%

Tuition[1]

In state	$496
Out of state	$2,772
Enrollments	77
Graduations	32

Student Demographics

Female	96.1%
Under age 25	40.0%
Minority	13.0%
Part-time	0.0%

Degrees conferred
Associate Degree

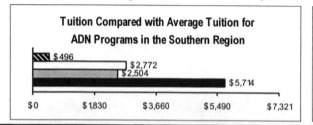

Tuition Compared with Average Tuition for ADN Programs in the Southern Region

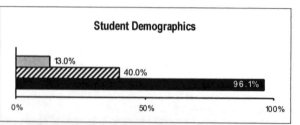

Student Demographics

JOHNSTON COMMUNITY COLLEGE

245 College Road
Smithfield, NC 27577
(919) 209-2024
Linda Smith, RN, MSN

www.johnston.cc.nc.us

Accreditation
North Carolina Board of Nursing

Tuition

In state	$740
Out of state	$4,536
Enrollments	52
Graduations	25

Degrees conferred
Associate Degree

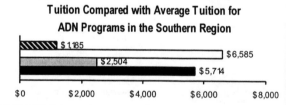

Tuition Compared with Average Tuition for ADN Programs in the Southern Region

LENOIR COMMUNITY COLLEGE

PO Box 188
Kinston, NC 28502
(252) 527-6223
Alexis Welch, RN, EdD

lenoircc.edu

Accreditation
North Carolina Board of Nursing

Acceptance rate		91.5%
Faculty-student ratio		1: 9
Faculty	Full time	8
	Part time	1

Tuition

In state	$1,185
Out of state	$6,585
Enrollments	77
Graduations	26

Student Demographics

Female	85.7%
Under age 25	42.9%
Minority	21.1%
Part-time	0.0%

Minimum degree required
High school diploma or GED

Degrees conferred
Associate Degree

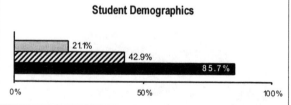

Tuition Compared with Average Tuition for ADN Programs in the Southern Region

Student Demographics

Key	Tuition Chart	▨ Program - in state ☐ Program - out of state ▨ Average - in state ■ Average - out of state

North Carolina

MAYLAND COMMUNITY COLLEGE   *Useful Facts**

PO Box 547
Spruce Pine, NC 28777
(828) 765-7351
Fredel Reighard, MSN, MA, RN

mayland.edu

Accreditation
North Carolina Board of Nursing

Acceptance rate	47.8%	

Degrees conferred
Associate Degree

Tuition		**Student Demographics**	
In state	$1,128	Female	87.5%
Out of state	$6,960		
Enrollments	48		
Graduations	19	Part-time	0.0%

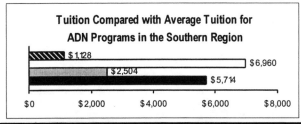

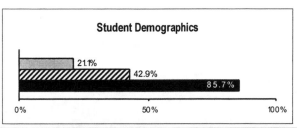

MITCHELL COMMUNITY COLLEGE

500 W Broad Street
Statesville, NC 28677
(704) 878-4261
Camille Reese, EdD, MSN, RNC

www.mitchell.cc.nc.us

Accreditation
North Carolina Board of Nursing, National
League for Nursing Accrediting Commission
(NLNAC)

At the request of this nursing school, publication has been withheld.
Please contact the school directly for more information.

PIEDMONT COMMUNITY COLLEGE   *Useful Facts**

PO Box 1197
Roxboro, NC 27573
(336) 599-1181
James Bevill, MSN, RN

www.piedmont.cc.nc.us

Accreditation
North Carolina Board of Nursing

Acceptance rate	88.0%	

Degrees conferred
Associate Degree

Tuition		**Student Demographics**	
In state	$913	Female	90.3%
Out of state	$5,465	Under age 25	44.0%
Enrollments	31	Minority	16.1%
Graduations	13	Part-time	0.0%

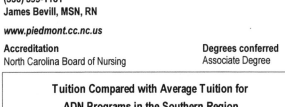

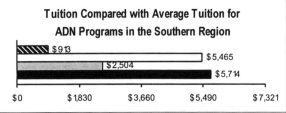

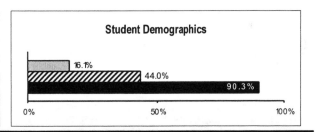

PITT COMMUNITY COLLEGE

PO Drawer 7007
Greenville, NC 27858
(252) 493-7474
Elizabeth Toderick, MSN

www.pittcc.edu

Accreditation
North Carolina Board of Nursing

At the request of this nursing school, publication has been withheld.
Please contact the school directly for more information.

Demographics Chart	■ Female ▨ Under age 25 ☐ Minority	Distance Learning	'The tuition reported for this program may be not be annualized. *Data reported between 2001 and 2004.

North Carolina

PRESBYTERIAN HOSPITAL
Useful Facts

1901 East 5th Street
Charlotte, NC 28204
(704) 384-4143
Kay Smith, RN, EdD

www.presbyterian.org

Acceptance rate	58.3%	

Tuition[1]

		Student Demographics	
In state	$290	Female	92.7%
Out of state	$290	Under age 25	52.6%
Enrollments	287	Minority	18.9%
Graduations	102	Part-time	0.0%

Accreditation
North Carolina Board of Nursing

Degrees conferred
Associate Degree, Diploma

Minimum degree required
High school diploma or GED

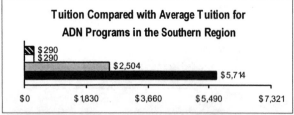

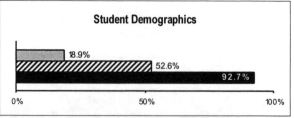

RANDOLPH COMMUNITY COLLEGE
Useful Facts

629 Industrial Park Avenue, PO Box 1009
Asheboro, NC 27205
(336) 633-0315
Patricia Tesh, MSN, RN

www.randolph.edu

Acceptance rate	19.7%	
Faculty-student ratio	1: 9	

Faculty	Full time	6
	Part time	4

Tuition

		Student Demographics	
In state	$1,786	Female	93.3%
Out of state	$9,817	Under age 25	30.7%
Enrollments	75	Minority	8.0%
Graduations	21	Part-time	0.0%

Accreditation
North Carolina Board of Nursing, National
League for Nursing Accrediting Commission
(NLNAC)

Degrees conferred
Associate Degree

Minimum degree required
High school diploma or GED

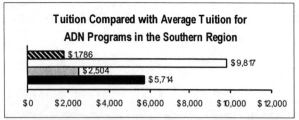

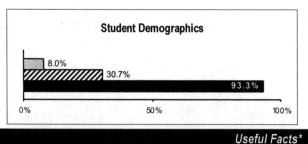

REGION A NURSING CONSORTIUM
Useful Facts*

185 Freelander Drive
Clyde, NC 28721
(828) 627-4650
Blake Rogers, MSN, RN

www.haywood.edu

Acceptance rate	30.0%	

Tuition[1]

		Student Demographics	
In state	$34	Female	92.3%
Out of state	$191	Under age 25	38.0%
Enrollments	78		
Graduations	37	Part-time	0.0%

Accreditation
North Carolina Board of Nursing

Degrees conferred
Associate Degree

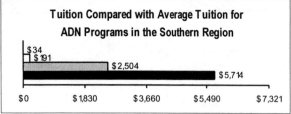

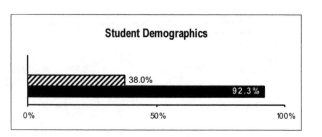

Key	Tuition Chart	▨ Program - in state ☐ Program - out of state ▤ Average - in state ■ Average - out of state

North Carolina

RICHMOND COMMUNITY COLLEGE — Useful Facts

PO Box 1189
Hamlet, NC 28345
(910) 582-7061
Carole Gibson, MSN

richmondcc.edu

Accreditation
North Carolina Board of Nursing

Degrees conferred
Associate Degree

Acceptance rate	27.7%
Faculty-student ratio	1: 12
Faculty Full time	7
Part time	5

Tuition
In state	$1,738
Out of state	$9,658
Enrollments	113
Graduations	37

Minimum degree required
High school diploma or GED

Student Demographics
Female	91.2%
Under age 25	44.2%
Minority	38.9%
Part-time	0.0%

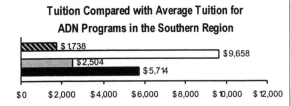

Tuition Compared with Average Tuition for ADN Programs in the Southern Region

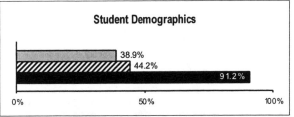

Student Demographics

ROANOKE-CHOWAN COMMUNITY COLLEGE — Useful Facts

109 Community College Road
Ahoskie, NC 27910
(252) 862-1295
Virginia Crocker, RN, MSN

www.roanoke.cc.nc.us/adnweb/homepage.htm

Accreditation
North Carolina Board of Nursing

Degrees conferred
Associate Degree

Acceptance rate	53.3%
Faculty-student ratio	1: 7
Faculty Full time	5
Part time	5

Tuition
In state	$660
Out of state	$4,074
Enrollments	51
Graduations	16

Minimum degree required
High school diploma or GED

Student Demographics
Female	92.2%
Under age 25	37.3%
Minority	31.4%
Part-time	51.0%

Tuition Compared with Average Tuition for ADN Programs in the Southern Region

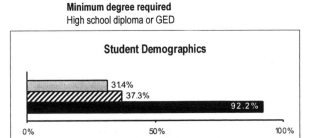

Student Demographics

ROBESON COMMUNITY COLLEGE — Useful Facts

PO Box 1420
Lumberton, NC 28359
(910) 618-5680
Cheryl Ermini, RN, BSN, MBA

www.robeson.cc.nc.us

Accreditation
North Carolina Board of Nursing

Degrees conferred
Associate Degree

Acceptance rate	5.3%
Faculty-student ratio	1: 16
Faculty Full time	3
Part time	3

Tuition
In state	$1,185
Out of state	$6,585
Enrollments	70
Graduations	30

Minimum degree required
High school diploma or GED

Student Demographics
Female	88.6%
Under age 25	31.4%
Minority	43.9%
Part-time	0.0%

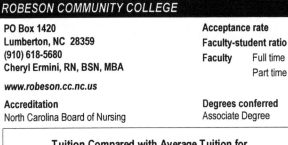
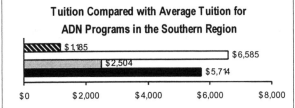

Tuition Compared with Average Tuition for ADN Programs in the Southern Region

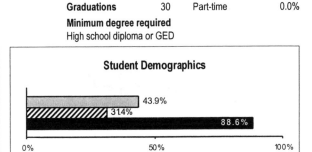

Student Demographics

Demographics Chart | ■Female ☒Under age 25 ☐Minority | **Distance Learning** | ¹The tuition reported for this program may be not be annualized.
*Data reported between 2001 and 2004.

North Carolina

ROCKINGHAM COMMUNITY COLLEGE

*Useful Facts**

PO Box 38
Wentworth, NC 27375
(336) 342-4261
Nettie Guy, MSN, RN

www.rockinghamcc.edu

Accreditation
North Carolina Board of Nursing

Acceptance rate	32.2%

Tuition
In state	$1,185
Out of state	$6,585
Enrollments	59
Graduations	24

Student Demographics
Female	96.6%
Under age 25	24.0%
Minority	8.5%
Part-time	0.0%

Degrees conferred
Associate Degree

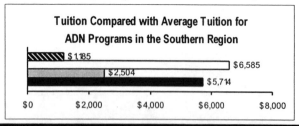

Tuition Compared with Average Tuition for ADN Programs in the Southern Region

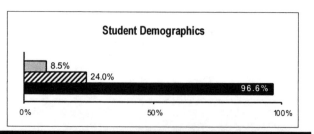

Student Demographics

ROWAN-CABARRUS COMMUNITY COLLEGE

Useful Facts

PO Box 1595
Salisbury, NC 28145
(704) 637-0760
Cathy Norris, MSN, RN

www.rowancabarrus.edu

Accreditation
North Carolina Board of Nursing, National
League for Nursing Accrediting Commission
(NLNAC)

Acceptance rate		10.8%
Faculty-student ratio		1:9
Faculty	Full time	7
	Part time	6

Tuition
In state	$1,216
Out of state	$6,752
Enrollments	89
Graduations	21

Student Demographics
Female	96.6%
Under age 25	51.7%
Minority	12.4%
Part-time	49.4%

Degrees conferred
Associate Degree

Minimum degree required
High school diploma or GED

Tuition Compared with Average Tuition for ADN Programs in the Southern Region

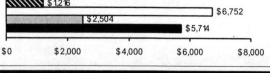

Student Demographics

SAMPSON COMMUNITY COLLEGE

PO Box 318
Clinton, NC 28329
(910) 592-8081
Lucinda Gurley, MSN, BSN, RN

www.sampson.cc.nc.us

Accreditation
North Carolina Board of Nursing

*At the request of this nursing school, publication has been witheld.
Please contact the school directly for more information.*

SANDHILLS COMMUNITY COLLEGE

*Useful Facts**

3395 Airport Road
Pinehurst, NC 28374
(910) 695-3843
Star Mitchelle, RN, MSN

www.sandhills.cc.nc.us

Accreditation
North Carolina Board of Nursing

Enrollments	115
Graduations	60

Degrees conferred
Associate Degree

Key	Tuition Chart	▨ Program - in state ☐ Program - out of state ▨ Average - in state ■ Average - out of state

North Carolina

SOUTHEASTERN COMMUNITY COLLEGE - *Whiteville*

4564 Chadbourn Highway
Whiteville, NC 28472
(910) 642-7141
Peggy Blackmon, MSN, RN

www.southeastern.cc.nc.us

Accreditation
North Carolina Board of Nursing

Acceptance rate	35.5%	

Degrees conferred
Associate Degree

Tuition		Student Demographics	
In state	$1,233	Female	92.4%
Out of state	$6,867	Under age 25	49.0%
Enrollments	131	Minority	17.7%
Graduations	23	Part-time	0.0%

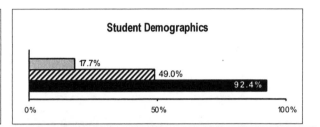

Tuition Compared with Average Tuition for ADN Programs in the Southern Region
$1,233 / $6,867 / $2,504 / $5,714

Student Demographics
17.7% / 49.0% / 92.4%

STANLY COMMUNITY COLLEGE   *Useful Facts*

141 College Drive
Albermarle, NC 28001
(704) 991-0270
Susan Spence, RN, MSN

stanly.edu

Accreditation
North Carolina Board of Nursing

Acceptance rate	11.9%
Faculty-student ratio	1: 8
Faculty Full time	6
Part time	12

Degrees conferred
Associate Degree

Tuition		Student Demographics	
In state	$632	Female	94.8%
Out of state	$3,512	Under age 25	34.4%
Enrollments	96	Minority	9.5%
Graduations	33	Part-time	9.4%

Minimum degree required
High school diploma or GED

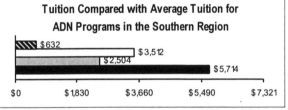
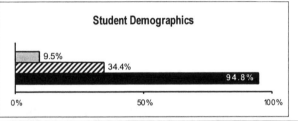

Tuition Compared with Average Tuition for ADN Programs in the Southern Region
$632 / $3,512 / $2,504 / $5,714

Student Demographics
9.5% / 34.4% / 94.8%

SURRY COMMUNITY COLLEGE   *Useful Facts**

PO Box 304
Dobson, NC 27017
(336) 386-8121
Sharon Kallam, MSN, BSN, RN

www.surry.cc.nc.us/

Accreditation
North Carolina Board of Nursing

Acceptance rate	25.6%	

Degrees conferred
Associate Degree

Tuition		Student Demographics	
In state	$512	Female	97.5%
Out of state	$2,788	Under age 25	48.0%
Enrollments	119	Minority	2.5%
Graduations	44	Part-time	16.8%

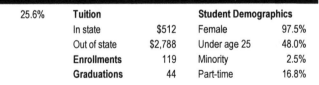
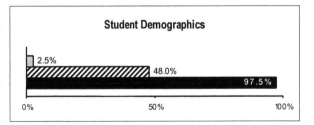

Tuition Compared with Average Tuition for ADN Programs in the Southern Region
$512 / $2,788 / $2,504 / $5,714

Student Demographics
2.5% / 48.0% / 97.5%

Demographics Chart	■Female ▨Under age 25 ▢Minority	Distance Learning	¹The tuition reported for this program may be not be annualized. *Data reported between 2001 and 2004.

North Carolina

VANCE GRANVILLE COMMUNITY COLLEGE

PO Box 917
Henderson, NC 27536
(252) 738-3222
Renee Hill, RN, MA

www.vgcc.edu

Acceptance rate		7.7%
Faculty-student ratio		1: 6
Faculty	Full time	12
	Part time	6

Tuition	
In state	$1,264
Out of state	$7,024
Enrollments	94
Graduations	43

Student Demographics	
Female	86.2%
Under age 25	33.0%
Minority	20.2%
Part-time	0.0%

Accreditation
North Carolina Board of Nursing

Degrees conferred
Associate Degree

Minimum degree required
High school diploma or GED

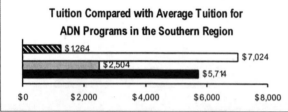

Tuition Compared with Average Tuition for ADN Programs in the Southern Region

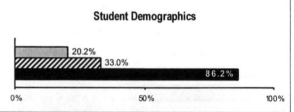

Student Demographics

WAKE TECHNICAL COMMUNITY COLLEGE

9101 Fayetteville Road
Raleigh, NC 27603
(919) 212-3828
Judith Rahm, MS

www.wake.tec.nc.us

Acceptance rate		4.2%
Faculty-student ratio		1: 12
Faculty	Full time	19
	Part time	12

Tuition	
In state	$1,140
Out of state	$6,330
Enrollments	292
Graduations	123

Student Demographics	
Female	89.0%
Under age 25	15.8%
Minority	18.5%
Part-time	0.0%

Accreditation
North Carolina Board of Nursing

Degrees conferred
Associate Degree

Minimum degree required
High school diploma or GED

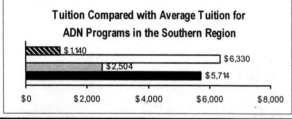

Tuition Compared with Average Tuition for ADN Programs in the Southern Region

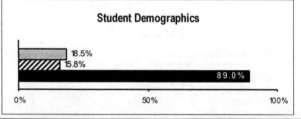

Student Demographics

WAYNE COMMUNITY COLLEGE

PO Box 8002
Goldsboro, NC 27533
(919) 735-5151
Rachel Hall, MSN, BSN, RN

www.waynecc.edu

At the request of this nursing school, publication has been withheld. Please contact the school directly for more information.

Accreditation
North Carolina Board of Nursing

Key | Tuition Chart | ▨ Program - in state ▢ Program - out of state ▢ Average - in state ■ Average - out of state

North Carolina

WESTERN PIEDMONT COMMUNITY COLLEGE — Useful Facts

1001 Burkemont Ave
Morganton, NC 28655
(828) 438-6000
Cynthia Davis, MSN, RN

www.wpcc.edu

Acceptance rate		10.6%
Faculty-student ratio		1: 7
Faculty	Full time	7
	Part time	16

Tuition	
In state	$1,216
Out of state	$6,752
Enrollments	102
Graduations	39

Student Demographics	
Female	88.2%
Under age 25	33.3%
Minority	10.8%
Part-time	0.0%

Accreditation
North Carolina Board of Nursing, National
League for Nursing Accrediting Commission
(NLNAC)

Degrees conferred
Associate Degree

Minimum degree required
High school diploma or GED

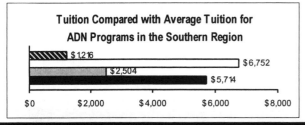

Tuition Compared with Average Tuition for ADN Programs in the Southern Region
$1,216 / $6,752 / $2,504 / $5,714

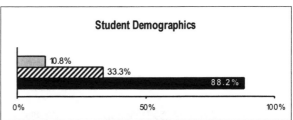

Student Demographics
10.8% / 33.3% / 88.2%

WILKES COMMUNITY COLLEGE

PO Box 120, 1328 Collegiate Drive
Wilkesboro, NC 28697
(336) 838-6257
Larry Taylor, RN, BS, MA

www.wilkes.cc.nc.us

Accreditation
North Carolina Board of Nursing

Degrees conferred
Associate Degree

North Dakota

DAKOTA NURSE PROGRAM - Bismark State College

500 E Front Ave, Suite 2
Bismarck, ND 58504
(701) 224-5783
April Hall, MSN

www.bismarckstate.edu

Accreditation
North Dakota Board of Nursing

Degrees conferred
Associate Degree

DAKOTA NURSE PROGRAM - Lake Region State College

1801 N College Drive
Devils Lake, ND 58301
(701) 662-1569

www.lrsc.nodak.edu

Accreditation
North Dakota Board of Nursing

Degrees conferred
Associate Degree

DAKOTA NURSE PROGRAM - Minot State University - Bottineau

105 Simrall Blvd
Bottineau, ND 58318
(800) 542-6866

www.misu-b.nodak.edu

Accreditation
North Dakota Board of Nursing

Degrees conferred
Associate Degree

Demographics Chart	■Female ▨Under age 25 ▢Minority	Distance Learning	'The tuition reported for this program may be not be annualized. *Data reported between 2001 and 2004.

North Dakota

DAKOTA NURSE PROGRAM - Williston State College

PO Box 1326
Williston, ND 58801
(701) 774-4290

www.wsc.nodak.edu

Accreditation
North Dakota Board of Nursing

Degrees conferred
Associate Degree

JAMESTOWN COLLEGE

6010 College Lane
Jamestown, ND 58405
(701) 252-3467
Jacqueline Mangnall, PhD(c), RN

www.jc.edu

Faculty-student ratio		1: 8
Faculty	Full time	5
	Part time	7

Accreditation
North Dakota Board of Nursing

Degrees conferred
Associate Degree

NORTH DAKOTA STATE COLLEGE OF SCIENCE

800 Sixth Street North
Wahpeton, ND 58076
(701) 671-2968
Marsha Trom, MS, RN

www.ndscs.nodak.edu

Accreditation
North Dakota Board of Nursing

Degrees conferred
Associate Degree

Ohio

AULTMAN HEALTH FOUNDATION   *Useful Facts*

2600 Sixth Street SW
Canton, OH 44710
(330) 363-3806
Joan Frey, EdD, MSN, RN, CNAA, BC

www.aultmanrn.com

Accreditation
Ohio Board of Nursing

Degrees conferred
Associate Degree

Acceptance rate		12.6%
Faculty-student ratio		1: 15
Faculty	Full time	13
	Part time	2

Tuition	
In state	$12,045
Out of state	$12,045
Enrollments	47
Graduations	0

Minimum degree required
High school diploma or GED

Student Demographics	
Female	100.0%
Under age 25	57.4%
Part-time	59.6%

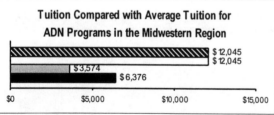

Tuition Compared with Average Tuition for ADN Programs in the Midwestern Region

$12,045
$12,045
$3,574
$6,376

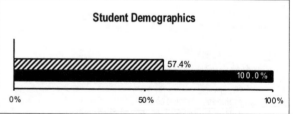

Student Demographics

57.4%
100.0%

BELMONT TECHNICAL COLLEGE

120 Fox-Shannon Place
St Craisville, OH 43950
(740) 695-9500
Brenda Lohri-Posey, EdD, RN

www.btc.edu

Accreditation
Ohio Board of Nursing

*At the request of this nursing school, publication has been witheld.
Please contact the school directly for more information.*

Key | Tuition Chart | ▨ Program - in state ☐ Program - out of state ▧ Average - in state ■ Average - out of state

Ohio

CENTRAL OHIO TECHNICAL COLLEGE

1179 University Drive
Newark, OH 43055
(740) 366-9383
Rose Saliba, MSN

www.newarkcampus.org

Accreditation
Ohio Board of Nursing, National League for
Nursing Accrediting Commission (NLNAC)

Acceptance rate	100.0%
Faculty-student ratio	1: 12
Faculty Full time	14
Part time	25

Degrees conferred
Associate Degree

Tuition	
In state	$4,512
Out of state	$8,112
Enrollments	321
Graduations	147

Minimum degree required
Licensed Practical Nurse

Student Demographics	
Female	86.3%
Under age 25	31.2%
Minority	19.6%
Part-time	68.5%

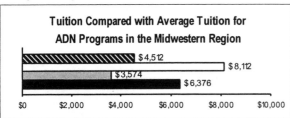

Tuition Compared with Average Tuition for ADN Programs in the Midwestern Region

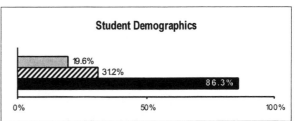

Student Demographics

CINCINNATI STATE TECHNICAL & COMMUNITY COLLEGE

3520 Central Parkway
Cincinnati, OH 45223
(513) 569-1476
Alice Palmer, MS, RN

www.cincinnatistate.edu

Accreditation
Ohio Board of Nursing, National League for
Nursing Accrediting Commission (NLNAC)

Acceptance rate	31.0%
Faculty-student ratio	1: 8
Faculty Full time	20
Part time	10

Degrees conferred
Associate Degree

Tuition	
In state	$4,160
Out of state	$8,320
Enrollments	202
Graduations	99

Minimum degree required
High school diploma or GED

Student Demographics	
Female	93.1%
Under age 25	39.1%
Minority	31.3%
Part-time	85.6%

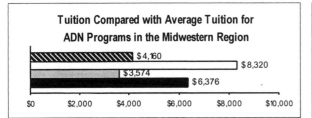

Tuition Compared with Average Tuition for ADN Programs in the Midwestern Region

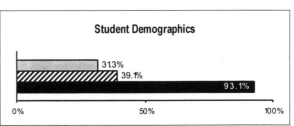

Student Demographics

CLARK STATE COMMUNITY COLLEGE

570 East Leffel Lane
Springfield, OH 45505
(937) 328-6060
Kathleen Wilcox, BSN, MSN

www.clarkstate.edu

Accreditation
Ohio Board of Nursing, National League for
Nursing Accrediting Commission (NLNAC)

Acceptance rate	27.6%
Faculty-student ratio	1: 13
Faculty Full time	8
Part time	13

Degrees conferred
Associate Degree

Tuition	
In state	$3,308
Out of state	$6,120
Enrollments	194
Graduations	87

Minimum degree required
DK/NA

Student Demographics	
Female	92.3%
Under age 25	26.8%
Minority	10.6%
Part-time	91.2%

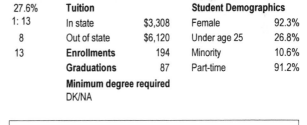

Tuition Compared with Average Tuition for ADN Programs in the Midwestern Region

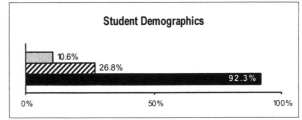

Student Demographics

| Demographics Chart | ■ Female ▨ Under age 25 ▢ Minority | Distance Learning | †The tuition reported for this program may be not be annualized. *Data reported between 2001 and 2004. |

Ohio

COLUMBUS STATE COMMUNITY COLLEGE - COLUMBUS
Useful Facts

550 E Spring Street, PO Box 1609
Columbus, OH 43216
(614) 287-2507
Polly Owen, PhD, RN

www.cscc.edu/nursing

Accreditation
Ohio Board of Nursing, National League for
Nursing Accrediting Commission (NLNAC)

Acceptance rate	32.9%
Faculty-student ratio	1: 12
Faculty Full time	17
Part time	48

Degrees conferred
Associate Degree

Tuition		Student Demographics	
In state	$4,352	Female	88.8%
Out of state	$9,860	Under age 25	23.9%
Enrollments	481	Minority	19.9%
Graduations	131	Part-time	86.3%

Minimum degree required
Bachelor's for Online Track.

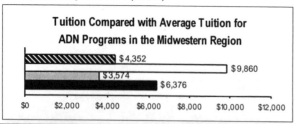
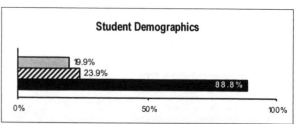

CUYAHOGA COMMUNITY COLLEGE
Useful Facts

2900 Community College Avenue
Cleveland, OH 44115
(216) 987-4106
Elizabeth Berrey, PhD, RN

www.tri-c.cc.oh.us/health/nursing/defaultalt.htm

Accreditation
Ohio Board of Nursing, National League for
Nursing Accrediting Commission (NLNAC)

Acceptance rate	33.3%

Degrees conferred
Associate Degree

Tuition		Student Demographics	
In state	$5,369	Female	82.9%
Out of state	$7,098	Under age 25	26.7%
Enrollments	409	Minority	23.0%
Graduations	154	Part-time	0.0%

Minimum degree required
0

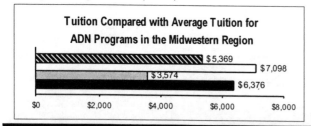
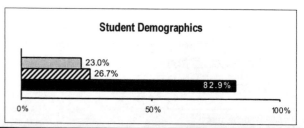

EDISON COMMUNITY COLLEGE - PIQUA
Useful Facts

1973 Edison Drive
Piqua, OH 45356
(937) 778-8600
Sharon Brown, MSN, BSN, RN

www.edisonohio.edu

Accreditation
Ohio Board of Nursing, National League for
Nursing Accrediting Commission (NLNAC)

Acceptance rate	35.1%
Faculty-student ratio	1: 14
Faculty Full time	5
Part time	7

Degrees conferred
Associate Degree

Tuition		Student Demographics	
In state	$3,270	Female	87.8%
Out of state	$5,880	Under age 25	38.2%
Enrollments	123	Minority	1.6%
Graduations	41	Part-time	50.4%

Minimum degree required
High school diploma or GED

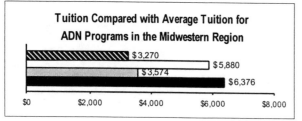
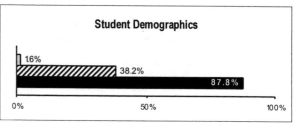

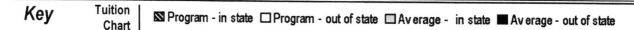

Key   Tuition Chart | ▨ Program - in state ☐ Program - out of state ☐ Average - in state ■ Average - out of state

Ohio

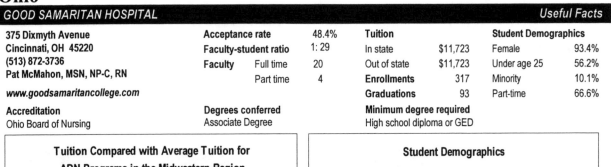

GOOD SAMARITAN HOSPITAL · *Useful Facts*

375 Dixmyth Avenue
Cincinnati, OH 45220
(513) 872-3736
Pat McMahon, MSN, NP-C, RN

www.goodsamaritancollege.com

Acceptance rate	48.4%	
Faculty-student ratio	1: 29	
Faculty	Full time	20
	Part time	4

Tuition	
In state	$11,723
Out of state	$11,723
Enrollments	317
Graduations	93

Student Demographics	
Female	93.4%
Under age 25	56.2%
Minority	10.1%
Part-time	66.6%

Accreditation
Ohio Board of Nursing

Degrees conferred
Associate Degree

Minimum degree required
High school diploma or GED

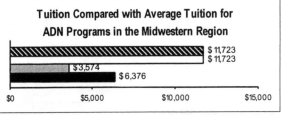
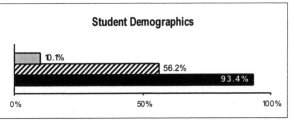

HOCKING TECHNICAL COLLEGE · *Useful Facts*

3301 Hocking Parkway
Nelsonville, OH 45764
(740) 753-6355
Mary (Molly) Weiland, PhD, MSN, RN

www.hocking.edu

Acceptance rate	10.4%	
Faculty-student ratio	1: 11	
Faculty	Full time	22
	Part time	25

Tuition	
In state	$3,072
Out of state	$6,144
Enrollments	383
Graduations	138

Student Demographics	
Female	86.4%
Under age 25	0.0%
Minority	6.8%
Part-time	7.8%

Accreditation
Ohio Board of Nursing, National League for
Nursing Accrediting Commission (NLNAC)

Degrees conferred
Associate Degree, LPN or LVN

Minimum degree required
High school diploma or GED

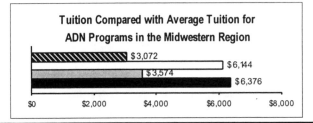
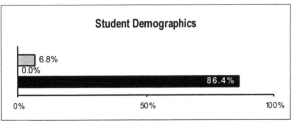

JAMES A RHODES STATE COLLEGE · *Useful Facts*

4240 Campus Drive
Lima, OH 45804
(419) 995-8218
Marjorie Walker, RN, CNA, BC, MSN

www.rodesstate.edu

Acceptance rate	29.2%	
Faculty-student ratio	1: 19	
Faculty	Full time	18
	Part time	4

Tuition	
In state	$3,757
Out of state	$7,515
Enrollments	370
Graduations	89

Student Demographics	
Female	92.7%
Under age 25	18.9%
Minority	6.5%
Part-time	50.0%

Accreditation
Ohio Board of Nursing, National League for
Nursing Accrediting Commission (NLNAC)

Degrees conferred
Associate Degree

Minimum degree required
Diploma

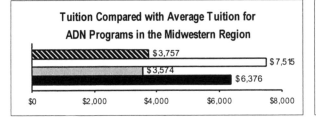
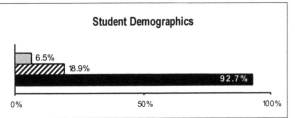

Demographics Chart	■Female ☒Under age 25 ☐Minority	Distance Learning 🖥	¹The tuition reported for this program may be not be annualized. *Data reported between 2001 and 2004.

Ohio

KENT STATE UNIVERSITY

113 Henderson Hall
Kent, OH 44242
(330) 672-3777
Julie Johnson, PhD, RN, FAAN

www.kent.edu/nursing

At the request of this nursing school, publication has been witheld.
Please contact the school directly for more information.

Accreditation
Ohio Board of Nursing, National League for
Nursing Accrediting Commission (NLNAC)

KENT STATE UNIVERSITY - Ashtabula

113 Henderson Hall
Kent, OH 44242
(330) 672-3777
Julie Johnson, PhD, RN, FAAN

www.kent.edu/nursing

At the request of this nursing school, publication has been witheld.
Please contact the school directly for more information.

Accreditation
Ohio Board of Nursing, National League for
Nursing Accrediting Commission (NLNAC)

KENT STATE UNIVERSITY - Tuscarawas Campus

113 Henderson Hall
Kent, OH 44242
(330) 672-3777
Julie Johnson, PhD, RN, FAAN

www.kent.edu/nursing

At the request of this nursing school, publication has been witheld.
Please contact the school directly for more information.

Accreditation
Ohio Board of Nursing, National League for
Nursing Accrediting Commission (NLNAC)

KENT STATE UNIVERSITY - East Liverpool

113 Henderson Hall
Kent, OH 44242
(330) 672-3777
Julie Johnson, PhD, RN, FAAN

www.kent.edu/nursing

At the request of this nursing school, publication has been witheld.
Please contact the school directly for more information.

Accreditation
Ohio Board of Nursing, National League for
Nursing Accrediting Commission (NLNAC)

KETTERING COLLEGE OF MEDICAL ARTS

Useful Facts

3737 Southern Boulevard
Kettering, OH 45429
(937) 395-8619
Brenda Stevenson, PhD, RN

www.kcma.edu

| Acceptance rate | 34.5% |
| Faculty-student ratio | 1: 9 |

Faculty		
	Full time	15
	Part time	29

Tuition	
In state	$7,800
Out of state	$7,800
Enrollments	260
Graduations	65

Student Demographics	
Female	90.4%
Under age 25	51.9%
Minority	8.7%
Part-time	51.5%

Accreditation
Ohio Board of Nursing, National League for
Nursing Accrediting Commission (NLNAC)

Degrees conferred
Associate Degree

Minimum degree required
High school diploma or GED

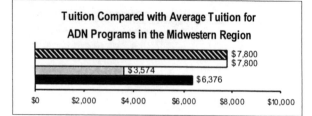

Tuition Compared with Average Tuition for ADN Programs in the Midwestern Region

$7,800
$7,800
$3,574
$6,376

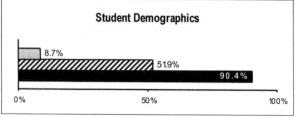

Student Demographics

8.7%
51.9%
90.4%

Ohio

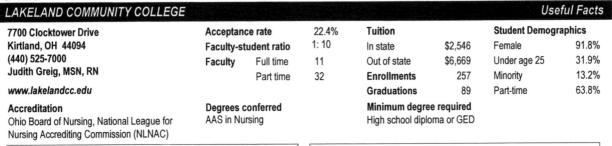

LAKELAND COMMUNITY COLLEGE · Useful Facts

7700 Clocktower Drive
Kirtland, OH 44094
(440) 525-7000
Judith Greig, MSN, RN

www.lakelandcc.edu

Acceptance rate		22.4%
Faculty-student ratio		1: 10
Faculty	Full time	11
	Part time	32

Tuition	
In state	$2,546
Out of state	$6,669
Enrollments	257
Graduations	89

Student Demographics	
Female	91.8%
Under age 25	31.9%
Minority	13.2%
Part-time	63.8%

Accreditation
Ohio Board of Nursing, National League for
Nursing Accrediting Commission (NLNAC)

Degrees conferred
AAS in Nursing

Minimum degree required
High school diploma or GED

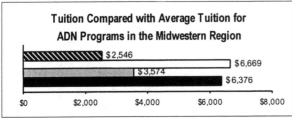

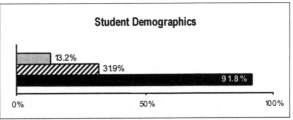

LORAIN COUNTY COMMUNITY COLLEGE · Useful Facts

1005 North Abbe Road
Elyria, OH 44035
(440) 366-7183
Hope Moon, MSN, CNS, RN

www.lorainccc.edu/divisions/ahn

Faculty-student ratio		1: 12
Faculty	Full time	13
	Part time	62

Tuition	
In state	$2,662
Out of state	$6,480
Enrollments	529
Graduations	179

Student Demographics	
Female	88.3%
Under age 25	21.6%
Minority	12.0%
Part-time	100.0%

Accreditation
Ohio Board of Nursing, National League for
Nursing Accrediting Commission (NLNAC)

Degrees conferred
Associate Degree

Minimum degree required
High school diploma or GED

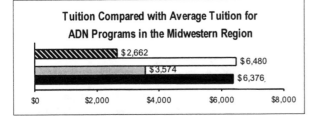

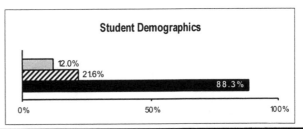

MARION TECHNICAL COLLEGE · Useful Facts

1467 Mount Vernon Avenue
Marion, OH 43302
(740) 389-4636
Carol Hoffman, MS, RN, BSN

www.mtc.edu

Acceptance rate		71.1%
Faculty-student ratio		1: 10
Faculty	Full time	10
	Part time	15

Tuition	
In state	$4,032
Out of state	$6,258
Enrollments	180
Graduations	46

Student Demographics	
Female	93.3%
Under age 25	38.3%
Minority	3.4%
Part-time	76.1%

Accreditation
Ohio Board of Nursing, National League for
Nursing Accrediting Commission (NLNAC)

Degrees conferred
Associate Degree

Minimum degree required
High school diploma or GED

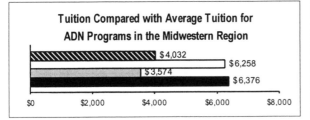

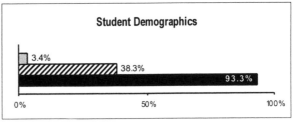

| Demographics Chart | ■Female ☒Under age 25 ☐Minority | Distance Learning | 'The tuition reported for this program may be not be annualized. |
| | | | *Data reported between 2001 and 2004. |

Ohio

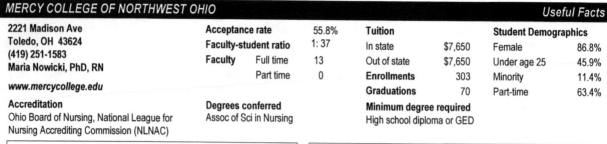

MERCY COLLEGE OF NORTHWEST OHIO · *Useful Facts*

2221 Madison Ave
Toledo, OH 43624
(419) 251-1583
Maria Nowicki, PhD, RN

www.mercycollege.edu

Accreditation
Ohio Board of Nursing, National League for
Nursing Accrediting Commission (NLNAC)

Acceptance rate	55.8%
Faculty-student ratio	1: 37
Faculty Full time	13
Part time	0

Degrees conferred
Assoc of Sci in Nursing

Tuition
In state	$7,650
Out of state	$7,650
Enrollments	303
Graduations	70

Minimum degree required
High school diploma or GED

Student Demographics
Female	86.8%
Under age 25	45.9%
Minority	11.4%
Part-time	63.4%

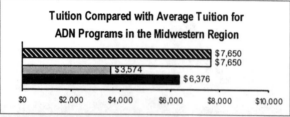

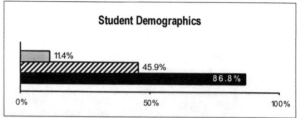

MIAMI UNIVERSITY · *Useful Facts*

1601 University Boulevard
Hamilton, OH 45011
(513) 785-7751
Paulette Worcester, DNS, CFNP, RN

www.ham.muohio.edu/nsg

Accreditation
Ohio Board of Nursing, National League for
Nursing Accrediting Commission (NLNAC)

Acceptance rate	35.6%
Faculty-student ratio	1: 6
Faculty Full time	24
Part time	12

Degrees conferred
Associate Degree

Tuition
In state	$6,216
Out of state	$17,748
Enrollments	172
Graduations	78

Minimum degree required
High school diploma or GED

Student Demographics
Female	90.7%
Under age 25	46.5%
Minority	8.7%
Part-time	31.4%

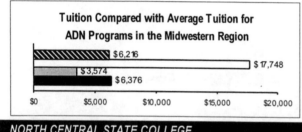

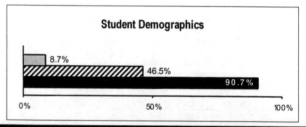

NORTH CENTRAL STATE COLLEGE · *Useful Facts*

2441 Kenwood Circle, Box 698
Mansfield, OH 44901
(419) 755-4823
Janet Boeckman, MSN, CPNP, RN

ncstatecollege.edu

Accreditation
Ohio Board of Nursing, National League for
Nursing Accrediting Commission (NLNAC)

Acceptance rate	31.1%
Faculty-student ratio	1: 15
Faculty Full time	10
Part time	5

Degrees conferred
Associate Degree

Tuition
In state	$3,431
Out of state	$6,750
Enrollments	187
Graduations	62

Minimum degree required
High school diploma or GED

Student Demographics
Female	93.0%
Under age 25	41.2%
Minority	1.6%
Part-time	0.0%

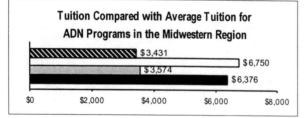

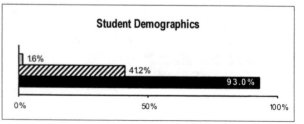

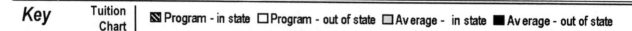

Key Tuition Chart | ⬚ Program - in state ☐ Program - out of state ☐ Average - in state ■ Average - out of state

Ohio

NORTHWEST STATE COMMUNITY COLLEGE   *Useful Facts*

22600 State Route 34
Archbold, OH 43502
(419) 267-1233
Cindy Krueger, MSN, RN

www.northweststate.edu

Acceptance rate	11.0%	
Faculty-student ratio	1: 5	
Faculty Full time	9	
Part time	34	

Tuition	
In state	$4,392
Out of state	$8,100
Enrollments	118
Graduations	42

Student Demographics	
Female	93.2%
Under age 25	50.0%
Minority	6.3%
Part-time	70.3%

Accreditation
Ohio Board of Nursing, National League for
Nursing Accrediting Commission (NLNAC)

Degrees conferred
Associate Degree

Minimum degree required
High school diploma or GED

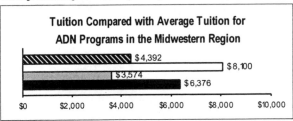

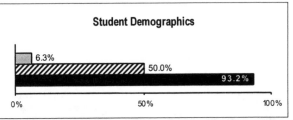

OHIO UNIVERSITY - Chillicothe

101 University Drive
Chillicothe, OH 45601
(740) 588-1514
Sally Fusner, PhD, RNC

oucweb.chillicothe.ohiou.edu

Tuition	
In state	$1,188
Out of state	$2,776
Enrollments	247
Graduations	75

Student Demographics	
Minority	2.0%

Accreditation
Ohio Board of Nursing

Degrees conferred
Associate Degree

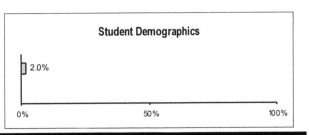

OWENS STATE COMMUNITY COLLEGE   *Useful Facts*

Oregon Road, PO Box 10000
Toledo, OH 43699
(419) 661-7338
Dawn Wetmore, RN

www.owens.cc.oh.us

Acceptance rate	18.9%

Tuition	
In state	$2,280
Out of state	$4,560
Enrollments	623
Graduations	163

Student Demographics	
Female	89.7%
Under age 25	58.7%
Minority	11.6%
Part-time	68.2%

Accreditation
Ohio Board of Nursing, National League for
Nursing Accrediting Commission (NLNAC)

Degrees conferred
Associate Degree

Minimum degree required
High school diploma or GED

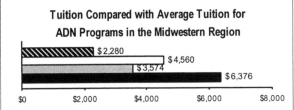

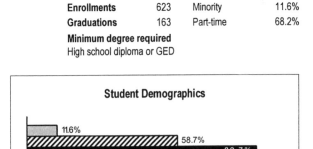

Demographics Chart	■ Female ▨ Under age 25 ☐ Minority	**Distance Learning**	¹The tuition reported for this program may be not be annualized. *Data reported between 2001 and 2004.

Ohio

RETS TECH CENTER PRACTICAL NURSE PROGRAM

555 E Alex-Bell Road
Centerville, OH 45459
(937) 433-3410
Donna Siegrist, BSN, MsEd

www.retstechcenter.com

Accreditation
Ohio Board of Nursing

Degrees conferred
Associate Degree

SHAWNEE STATE UNIVERSITY   *Useful Facts**

940 Second Street
Portsmouth, OH 45662
(740) 351-3210
Mattie Burton, PhD(c), RN, APRN, BC

www.shawnee.edu

Accreditation
Ohio Board of Nursing, National League for
Nursing Accrediting Commission (NLNAC)

Degrees conferred
Associate Degree

Acceptance rate	46.7%

Tuition		**Student Demographics**	
In state	$1,449	Female	80.0%
Out of state	$2,481	Under age 25	60.0%
Enrollments	125	Minority	100.0%
Graduations	36	Part-time	20.0%

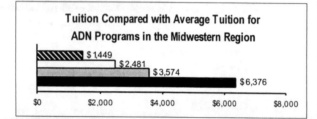

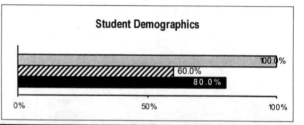

SINCLAIR COMMUNITY COLLEGE   *Useful Facts*

444 West Third Street
Dayton, OH 45402
(937) 512-2424
Gloria Goldman, PhD, RN

www.sinclair.edu

Accreditation
Ohio Board of Nursing, National League for
Nursing Accrediting Commission (NLNAC)

Degrees conferred
Associate Degree

Acceptance rate		32.8%
Faculty-student ratio		1: 11
Faculty	Full time	34
	Part time	7

Tuition		**Student Demographics**	
In state	$1,658	Female	89.7%
Out of state	$2,818	Under age 25	28.9%
Enrollments	408	Minority	15.7%
Graduations	101	Part-time	78.4%

Minimum degree required
High school diploma or GED

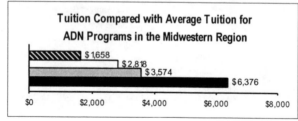

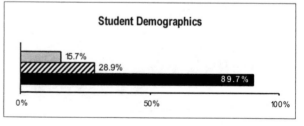

Ohio

SOUTHERN STATE COMMUNITY COLLEGE — *Useful Facts*

100 Hobart Drive
Hillsboro, OH 45133
(937) 393-3431
Marsha Snyder, MS, RN

www.sscc.edu

Acceptance rate	66.7%
Faculty-student ratio	1: 13
Faculty Full time	7
Part time	3

Tuition
In state	$3,690
Out of state	$7,155
Enrollments	109
Graduations	36

Student Demographics
Female	97.2%
Under age 25	38.5%
Minority	0.9%
Part-time	0.0%

Accreditation
Ohio Board of Nursing, National League for Nursing Accrediting Commission (NLNAC)

Degrees conferred
Associate Degree

Minimum degree required
High school diploma or GED

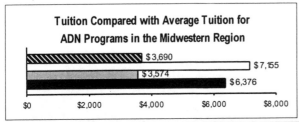
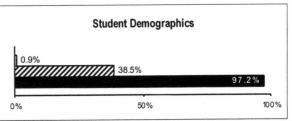

STARK STATE COLLEGE OF TECHNOLOGY — *Useful Facts**

6200 Frank Aveune NW
Massillon, OH 44720
(330) 966-5458
Gloria Kline, RN, MSN, CS

www.starkstate.edu

Tuition
In state	$1,830
Out of state	$2,550
Enrollments	126
Graduations	47

Student Demographics
Female	95.2%
Under age 25	25.0%
Minority	5.6%
Part-time	89.7%

Accreditation
Ohio Board of Nursing, National League for Nursing Accrediting Commission (NLNAC)

Degrees conferred
Associate Degree

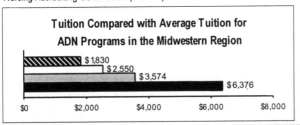
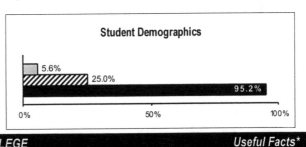

UNIVERSITY OF CINCINNATTI - RAYMOND WALTERS COLLEGE — *Useful Facts**

9555 Plainfield Road
Cincinnati, OH 45208
(513) 745-5603
Marisue Naber, PhD, RN

www.rwc.uc.edu

| Acceptance rate | 17.7% |

Tuition
In state	$4,659
Out of state	$12,135
Enrollments	191
Graduations	72

Student Demographics
Female	93.7%
Under age 25	44.5%
Minority	15.1%
Part-time	58.6%

Accreditation
Ohio Board of Nursing, National League for Nursing Accrediting Commission (NLNAC)

Degrees conferred
Associate Degree

Minimum degree required
Adm criteria: 2.5 GPA; eligib for college level Math and English; HS Biol. and Chem. with C or bette

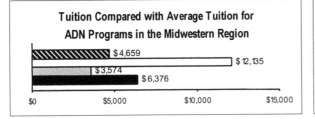
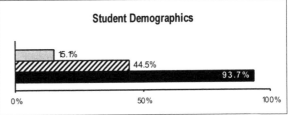

| Demographics Chart | ■Female ▨Under age 25 ☐Minority | Distance Learning | | †The tuition reported for this program may be not be annualized.
*Data reported between 2001 and 2004. |

Ohio

UNIVERSITY OF RIO GRANDE - *Holzer School of Nursing*

218 North College Avenue
Rio Grande, OH 45685
(740) 245-7302
Janet Byers, PhD, RN

www.rio.edu/nursing

Acceptance rate	40.5%

Tuition

In state	$3,150
Out of state	$4,859
Enrollments	156
Graduations	61

Student Demographics

Female	87.2%
Under age 25	45.0%
Minority	1.3%
Part-time	0.0%

Accreditation
Ohio Board of Nursing, National League for Nursing Accrediting Commission (NLNAC)

Degrees conferred
Associate Degree

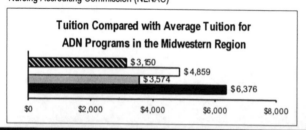
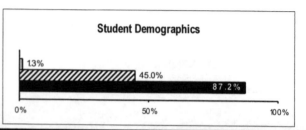

UNIVERSITY OF TOLEDO

2801 Bancroft Street, Mail stop # 400
Toledo, OH 43606
(419) 530-4586
Ruth Baldwin, MSN, RN

www.hhs.utoledo.edu/nursing/nursing_home.html

Acceptance rate		97.1%
Faculty-student ratio		1:5
Faculty	Full time	9
	Part time	28

Tuition

In state	$6,430
Out of state	$15,241
Enrollments	106
Graduations	43

Student Demographics

Female	84.0%
Under age 25	66.0%
Minority	15.5%
Part-time	21.7%

Accreditation
Ohio Board of Nursing, National League for Nursing Accrediting Commission (NLNAC)

Degrees conferred
Associate Degree

Minimum degree required
High school diploma or GED

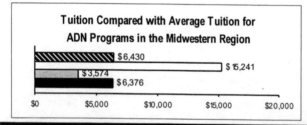
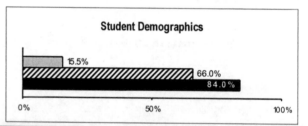

WASHINGTON STATE COMMUNITY COLLEGE

710 Colegate Drive
Marietta, OH 45750
(740) 374-8716
Joyce Joy, RN

www.wscc.edu

Accreditation
Ohio Board of Nursing

Degrees conferred
Associate Degree

Key | Tuition Chart | ▨ Program - in state ☐ Program - out of state ☐ Average - in state ■ Average - out of state

Oklahoma

BACONE COLLEGE

2299 Old Bacone Road
Muskogee, OK 74403
(918) 781-7325
Jackie Swanson, RN, CNS, WHNP, PhD

www.bacone.edu

Acceptance rate	52.0%	**Tuition**	
Faculty-student ratio	1: 5	In state	$7,900
Faculty Full time	7	Out of state	$7,900
Part time	9	**Enrollments**	59
		Graduations	21

Student Demographics

Female	89.8%
Under age 25	49.2%
Minority	62.7%
Part-time	0.0%

Accreditation
Oklahoma Board of Nursing, National League for Nursing Accrediting Commission (NLNAC)

Degrees conferred
Associate Degree

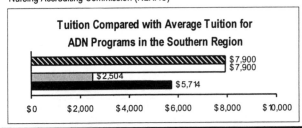
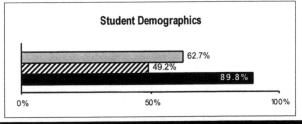

CARL ALBERT STATE COLLEGE

1507 S McKenna
Poteau, OK 74953
(918) 647-1350
Donnell Richison, RN, MSN

www.carlalbert.edu

Acceptance rate	35.2%	**Tuition**	
Faculty-student ratio	1: 9	In state	$816
Faculty Full time	6	Out of state	$2,004
Part time	6	**Enrollments**	82
		Graduations	20

Student Demographics

Female	93.9%
Under age 25	36.6%
Minority	28.0%
Part-time	32.9%

Accreditation
Oklahoma Board of Nursing, National League for Nursing Accrediting Commission (NLNAC)

Degrees conferred
Associate Degree

Minimum degree required
High school diploma or GED

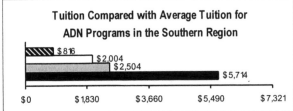
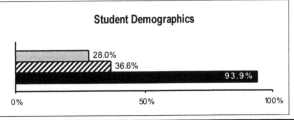

CONNORS STATE COLLEGE

Rt 1, Box 1000
Warner, OK 74469
(918) 463-2931
Glenda Shockley, RN, MS

www.connorsstate.edu/nursing

Acceptance rate	27.0%	**Tuition**	
Faculty-student ratio	1: 12	In state	$1,592
Faculty Full time	9	Out of state	$4,502
Part time	5	**Enrollments**	141
		Graduations	62

Student Demographics

Female	89.4%
Under age 25	31.9%
Minority	26.2%
Part-time	11.3%

Accreditation
Oklahoma Board of Nursing, National League for Nursing Accrediting Commission (NLNAC)

Degrees conferred
Associate Degree

Minimum degree required
None

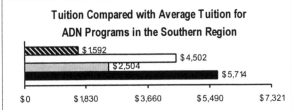
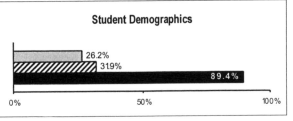

Demographics Chart	■ Female ▨ Under age 25 ☐ Minority	Distance Learning	⁺The tuition reported for this program may be not be annualized. *Data reported between 2001 and 2004.

Oklahoma

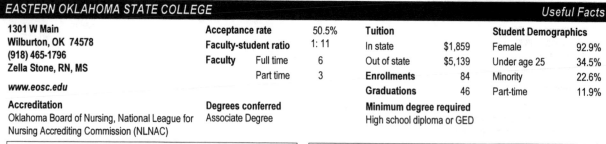

EASTERN OKLAHOMA STATE COLLEGE · *Useful Facts*

1301 W Main
Wilburton, OK 74578
(918) 465-1796
Zella Stone, RN, MS

www.eosc.edu

Acceptance rate		50.5%
Faculty-student ratio		1: 11
Faculty	Full time	6
	Part time	3

Tuition	
In state	$1,859
Out of state	$5,139
Enrollments	84
Graduations	46

Student Demographics	
Female	92.9%
Under age 25	34.5%
Minority	22.6%
Part-time	11.9%

Accreditation
Oklahoma Board of Nursing, National League for
Nursing Accrediting Commission (NLNAC)

Degrees conferred
Associate Degree

Minimum degree required
High school diploma or GED

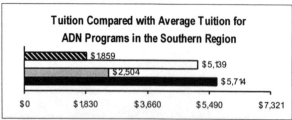

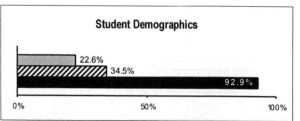

MURRAY STATE COLLEGE · *Useful Facts*

One Murray Campus Suite N/AH 105
Tishomingo, OK 73460
(580) 371-2371
Joni Jeter, RN, MS

mscok.edu

Acceptance rate		56.6%
Faculty-student ratio		1: 12
Faculty	Full time	7
	Part time	3

Tuition	
In state	$2,250
Out of state	$5,250
Enrollments	106
Graduations	32

Student Demographics	
Female	90.6%
Under age 25	31.1%
Minority	18.9%
Part-time	0.0%

Accreditation
Oklahoma Board of Nursing, National League for
Nursing Accrediting Commission (NLNAC)

Degrees conferred
Associate Degree

Minimum degree required
High school diploma or GED

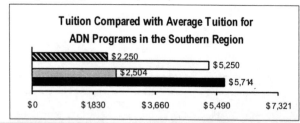

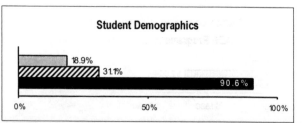

NORTHEASTERN OKLAHOMA A&M COLLEGE · *Useful Facts*

200 I Street NE
Miami, OK 74354
(918) 540-6312
Deborah Morgan, MS, RN

www.neoam.edu

Acceptance rate		49.3%
Faculty-student ratio		1: 10
Faculty	Full time	8
	Part time	4

Tuition	
In state	$1,234
Out of state	$2,883
Enrollments	99
Graduations	40

Student Demographics	
Female	85.9%
Under age 25	32.3%
Minority	15.5%
Part-time	0.0%

Accreditation
Oklahoma Board of Nursing, National League for
Nursing Accrediting Commission (NLNAC)

Degrees conferred
Associate Degree

Minimum degree required
High school diploma or GED

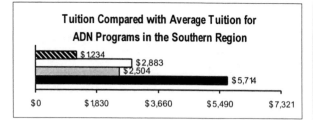

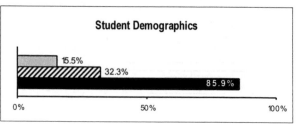

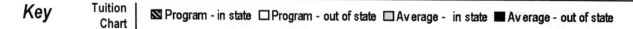

Key | Tuition Chart | ▨ Program - in state ☐ Program - out of state ▨ Average - in state ■ Average - out of state

Oklahoma

NORTHERN OKLAHOMA COLLEGE *Useful Facts*

1220 E Grand Box 310
Tonkawa, OK 74653
(580) 628-6649
Kim Webb, RN, MN

www.north-ok.edu

Acceptance rate		37.7%
Faculty-student ratio		1: 15
Faculty	Full time	10
	Part time	3

Tuition	
In state	$1,860
Out of state	$4,710
Enrollments	173
Graduations	65

Student Demographics	
Female	93.1%
Under age 25	12.1%
Minority	6.9%
Part-time	32.4%

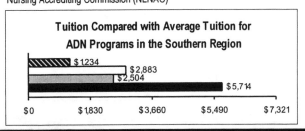

Accreditation
Oklahoma Board of Nursing, National League for Nursing Accrediting Commission (NLNAC)

Degrees conferred
Associate Degree

Minimum degree required
High school diploma or GED

Tuition Compared with Average Tuition for ADN Programs in the Southern Region

$1234
$2,883
$2,504
$5,714

$0 $1,830 $3,660 $5,490 $7,321

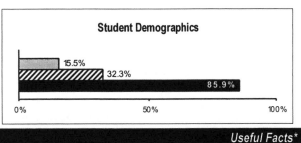

Student Demographics

15.5%
32.3%
85.9%

0%   50%   100%

OKLAHOMA CITY COMMUNITY COLLEGE *Useful Facts**

7777 S May Ave
Oklahoma City, OK 73159
(405) 682-1611
Rosemary Klepper, MS, RN

okccc.edu

Tuition[1]	
In state	$53
Out of state	$133
Enrollments	233
Graduations	113

Student Demographics	
Female	87.1%
Under age 25	25.0%
Minority	15.2%
Part-time	71.7%

Accreditation
Oklahoma Board of Nursing, National League for Nursing Accrediting Commission (NLNAC)

Degrees conferred
Associate Degree

Tuition Compared with Average Tuition for ADN Programs in the Southern Region

$53
$133
$2,504
$5,714

$0 $1,830 $3,660 $5,490 $7,321

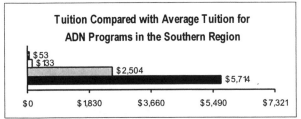

Student Demographics

15.2%
25.0%
87.1%

0%   50%   100%

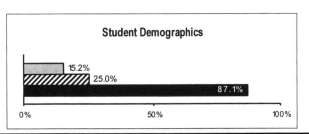

OKLAHOMA STATE UNIVERSITY - OKLAHOMA CITY *Useful Facts*

900 North Portland
Oklahoma City, OK 73107
(405) 945-3305
DeAnne Parrott, MEd, MS, RN

www.osuokc.edu

Acceptance rate	21.5%

Tuition	
In state	$2,424
Out of state	$6,264
Enrollments	228
Graduations	110

Student Demographics	
Female	86.0%
Under age 25	0.0%
Minority	17.5%
Part-time	100.0%

Accreditation
Oklahoma Board of Nursing, National League for Nursing Accrediting Commission (NLNAC)

Degrees conferred
Associate Degree

Minimum degree required
High school diploma or GED

Tuition Compared with Average Tuition for ADN Programs in the Southern Region

$2,424
$6,264
$2,504
$5,714

$0 $2,000 $4,000 $6,000 $8,000

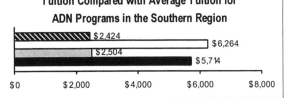

Student Demographics

17.5%
0.0%
86.0%

0%   50%   100%

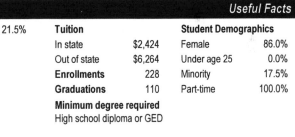
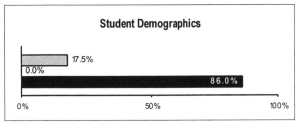

Demographics Chart	■Female ☒Under age 25 ☐Minority	Distance Learning	[1]The tuition reported for this program may be not be annualized. *Data reported between 2001 and 2004.

Oklahoma

OKLAHOMA STATE UNIVERSITY - OKMULGEE
Useful Facts

1801 E 4th St
Okmulgee, OK 74447
(918) 293-5339
Pam Price-Hoskins, PhD, RN, C

www.osu-okmulgee.edu

Acceptance rate	44.8%	
Faculty-student ratio	1: 6	
Faculty	Full time	4
	Part time	4

Tuition		
In state	$4,050	
Out of state	$8,316	
Enrollments	38	
Graduations	22	

Student Demographics	
Female	89.5%
Under age 25	21.1%
Minority	44.4%
Part-time	10.5%

Accreditation
Oklahoma Board of Nursing

Degrees conferred
Associate Degree

Minimum degree required
High school diploma or GED

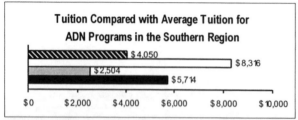

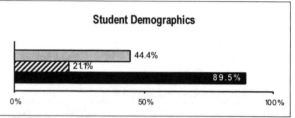

PLATT COLLEGE - OKLAHOMA CITY

2727 W Memorial Road
Oklahoma City, OK 73134
(405) 749-2433
Linda Fly, MPA, MSN

www.plattcollege.org

Accreditation
Oklahoma Board of Nursing

Degrees conferred
Associate Degree

PLATT COLLEGE - TULSA

3801 S Sheridan
Tulsa, OK 74145
(918) 663-9000
Brenda Boesch, RN, MSN

www.plattcollege.org

Accreditation
Oklahoma Board of Nursing

Degrees conferred
Associate Degree

REDLANDS COMMUNITY COLLEGE
Useful Facts

1300 South Country Club
El Reno, OK 73036
(405) 262-2552
Rose Marie Smith, MS, RN

www.redlandscc.edu

Acceptance rate	20.1%	
Faculty-student ratio	1: 12	
Faculty	Full time	8
	Part time	4

Tuition		
In state	$2,190	
Out of state	$4,440	
Enrollments	122	
Graduations	60	

Student Demographics	
Female	91.8%
Under age 25	60.7%
Minority	5.8%
Part-time	59.8%

Accreditation
Oklahoma Board of Nursing, National League for
Nursing Accrediting Commission (NLNAC)

Degrees conferred
Associate Degree

Minimum degree required
High school diploma or GED

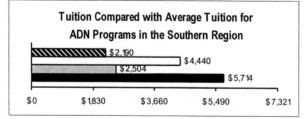

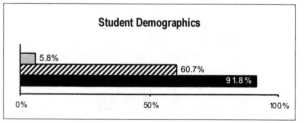

Key	Tuition Chart	⊠ Program - in state ☐ Program - out of state ☐ Average - in state ■ Average - out of state

Oklahoma

ROGERS STATE UNIVERSITY · *Useful Facts*

1701 West Will Rogers Boulevard
Claremore, OK 74017
(918) 343-7635
Linda Andrews, RN, MS

www.rsu.edu

Acceptance rate		48.3%
Faculty-student ratio		1: 12
Faculty	Full time	8
	Part time	9

Tuition
In state	$3,030
Out of state	$7,230
Enrollments	146
Graduations	60

Student Demographics
Female	89.0%
Under age 25	31.5%
Minority	31.5%
Part-time	65.8%

Accreditation
Oklahoma Board of Nursing, National League for Nursing Accrediting Commission (NLNAC)

Degrees conferred
Associate Degree

Minimum degree required
High school diploma or GED

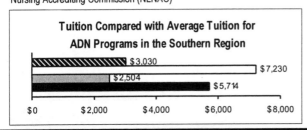
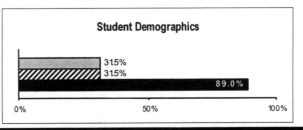

ROSE STATE COLLEGE · *Useful Facts*

6420 SE 15th Street
Midwest City, OK 73110
(405) 733-7546
Rebekah Ray, MS, RN

www.rose.edu

Acceptance rate		29.3%
Faculty-student ratio		1: 11
Faculty	Full time	9
	Part time	11

Tuition
In state	$1,422
Out of state	$4,711
Enrollments	165
Graduations	92

Student Demographics
Female	81.8%
Under age 25	20.0%
Minority	19.9%
Part-time	0.0%

Accreditation
Oklahoma Board of Nursing, National League for Nursing Accrediting Commission (NLNAC)

Degrees conferred
Associate Degree

Minimum degree required
High school diploma or GED

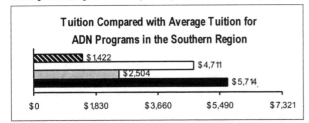
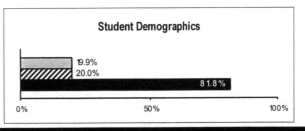

SEMINOLE STATE COLLEGE · *Useful Facts*

2701 Boren Blvd, PO Box 351
Seminole, OK 74868
(405) 382-9268
Nina Kirk, MS, RN

www.sscok.edu

Acceptance rate		32.0%
Faculty-student ratio		1: 8
Faculty	Full time	7
	Part time	1

Tuition
In state	$1,395
Out of state	$4,487
Enrollments	63
Graduations	20

Student Demographics
Female	93.7%
Under age 25	39.7%
Minority	12.7%
Part-time	0.0%

Accreditation
Oklahoma Board of Nursing, National League for Nursing Accrediting Commission (NLNAC)

Degrees conferred
Associate Degree

Minimum degree required
None

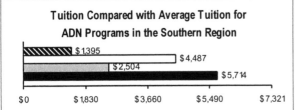
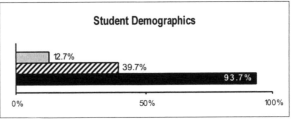

Demographics Chart	■ Female ▨ Under age 25 ▢ Minority	Distance Learning	¹The tuition reported for this program may be not be annualized. *Data reported between 2001 and 2004.

Oklahoma

TULSA COMMUNITY COLLEGE

Useful Facts*

909 S Boston
Tulsa, OK 74119
(918) 595-7188
Ann Strong Anthony, RN, MSN

www.tulsa.cc.ok.us/nursing

Accreditation
Oklahoma Board of Nursing, National League for
Nursing Accrediting Commission (NLNAC)

Acceptance rate	74.8%

Degrees conferred
Associate Degree

Tuition		Student Demographics	
In state	$1,328	Female	88.6%
Out of state	$4,784	Under age 25	27.8%
Enrollments	281	Minority	14.3%
Graduations	88	Part-time	10.0%

Minimum degree required
CNA

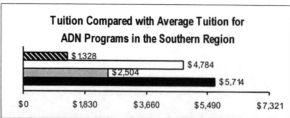

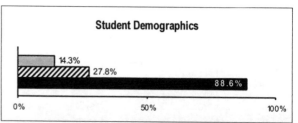

WESTERN OKLAHOMA STATE COLLEGE

Useful Facts

2801 N Main Street
Altus, OK 73521
(580) 477-7831
Carol Kendrix, RN, BSN, MSN

www.wosc.edu

Accreditation
Oklahoma Board of Nursing, National League for
Nursing Accrediting Commission (NLNAC)

Acceptance rate	58.5%		
Faculty-student ratio	1: 10		
Faculty	Full time	5	
	Part time	12	

Degrees conferred
Associate Degree

Tuition[1]		Student Demographics	
In state	$74	Female	90.8%
Out of state	$178	Under age 25	32.1%
Enrollments	109	Minority	22.4%
Graduations	44	Part-time	0.0%

Minimum degree required
High school diploma or GED

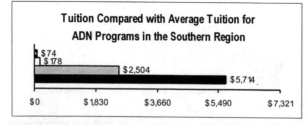

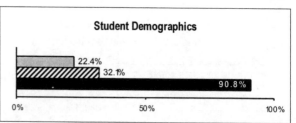

Oregon

BLUE MOUNTAIN COMMUNITY COLLEGE

Useful Facts*

PO Box 100
Pendleton, OR 97801
(541) 278-5879
Elizabeth Sullivan, RN, MS

www.bmcc.cc.or.us

Accreditation
Oregon State Board of Nursing

Acceptance rate	73.3%

Degrees conferred
Associate Degree

Tuition		Student Demographics	
In state	$1,332	Female	88.9%
Out of state	$3,996	Under age 25	42.0%
Enrollments	45	Minority	15.6%
Graduations	14	Part-time	0.0%

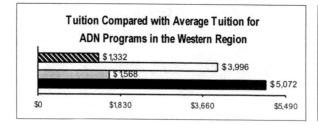

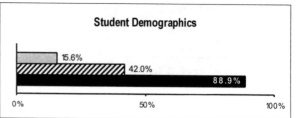

Key	Tuition Chart	⊠ Program - in state ☐ Program - out of state ☐ Average - in state ■ Average - out of state

Oregon

CENTRAL OREGON COMMUNITY COLLEGE — *Useful Facts**

2600 NW College Way
Bend, OR 97701
(541) 383-7546
Nancy Zavacki, RN, MSN

www.cocc.edu

Accreditation
Oregon State Board of Nursing

Degrees conferred
Associate Degree

Acceptance rate	36.4%

Tuition
In state	$5,885
Out of state	$16,585
Enrollments	74
Graduations	32

Student Demographics
Female	90.5%
Under age 25	19.0%
Minority	2.7%
Part-time	58.1%

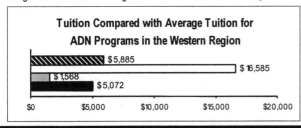

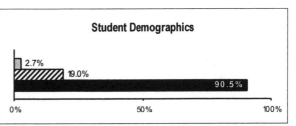

CHEMEKETA COMMUNITY COLLEGE — *Useful Facts*

4000 Lancaster Dr NE, PO Box 14007
Salem, OR 97305
(503) 399-5058
Kay Carnegie, RN, MS

www.chemeketa.edu

Accreditation
Oregon State Board of Nursing, National League
for Nursing Accrediting Commission (NLNAC)

Degrees conferred
Associate Degree

Acceptance rate	31.3%
Faculty-student ratio	1:7

Faculty
Full time	14
Part time	9

Tuition
In state	$2,550
Enrollments	125
Graduations	55

Student Demographics
Female	84.0%
Under age 25	22.4%
Minority	9.9%
Part-time	0.0%

Minimum degree required
High school diploma or GED

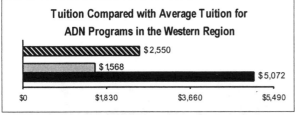

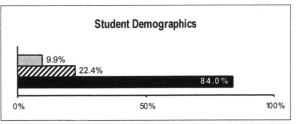

CLACKAMAS COMMUNITY COLLEGE — *Useful Facts**

19600 South Mollala Avenue
Oregon City, OR 97005
(503) 657-6958
Judith Anderson, RN, MS

www.clackamas.edu

Accreditation
Oregon State Board of Nursing

Degrees conferred
Associate Degree

Acceptance rate	41.7%

Tuition
In state	$1,665
Out of state	$5,895
Enrollments	72
Graduations	31

Student Demographics
Female	87.5%
Under age 25	38.0%
Minority	2.8%
Part-time	0.0%

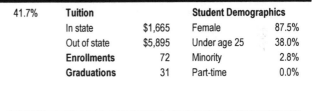

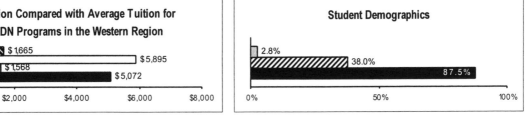

Demographics Chart: ■ Female ▨ Under age 25 ☐ Minority

Distance Learning

†The tuition reported for this program may be not be annualized.
*Data reported between 2001 and 2004.

Oregon

CLATSOP COMMUNITY COLLEGE
Useful Facts*

1653 Jerome Avenue
Astoria, OR 97103
(503) 338-2496
Karen Burke, RN, MS

www.ctrf.net/cccnurse

Acceptance rate	64.3%	**Tuition**	**Student Demographics**
		In state	$2,340	Female	86.0%
		Out of state	$6,000	Under age 25	52.6%
		Enrollments	57		
		Graduations	16	Part-time	21.1%

Accreditation
Oregon State Board of Nursing

Degrees conferred
Associate Degree

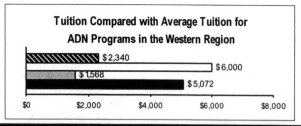

Tuition Compared with Average Tuition for ADN Programs in the Western Region
$2,340
$6,000
$1,568
$5,072

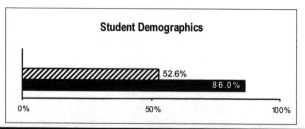

Student Demographics
52.6%
86.0%

COLUMBIA GORGE COMMUNITY COLLEGE

400 E Scenic Drive
The Dalles, OR 97058
(541) 506-6140
Marilyn McGuire Sessions, RN, MSN

www.cgcc.cc.or.us

Faculty	Full time	7
	Part time	6

Accreditation
Oregon State Board of Nursing

Degrees conferred
Associate Degree

LANE COMMUNITY COLLEGE
Useful Facts*

4000 East 30th Avenue
Eugene, OR 97405
(541) 463-5623
Anne O'Brien, RN, MSN

www.lanecc.edu/nursing

Acceptance rate	64.3%	**Tuition**	**Student Demographics**
		In state	$1,932	Female	82.6%
				Under age 25	0.0%
		Enrollments	138		
		Graduations	71	Part-time	0.0%

Accreditation
Oregon State Board of Nursing

Degrees conferred
Associate Degree

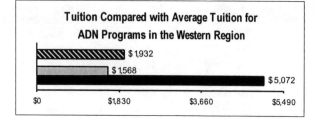

Tuition Compared with Average Tuition for ADN Programs in the Western Region
$1,932
$1,568
$5,072

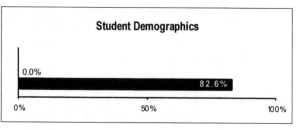

Student Demographics
0.0%
82.6%

Key | Tuition Chart | ⬚ Program - in state ☐ Program - out of state ▨ Average - in state ■ Average - out of state

Oregon

LINN-BENTON COMMUNITY COLLEGE — *Useful Facts*

6500 Pacific Blvd
Albany, OR 67306
(541) 917-4524
Faye Melius, MS

linnbenton.edu

Accreditation
Oregon State Board of Nursing

Acceptance rate		24.2%
Faculty-student ratio		1: 9
Faculty	Full time	8
	Part time	6

Tuition	
In state	$2,250
Out of state	$2,250
Enrollments	104
Graduations	44

Student Demographics	
Female	85.6%
Under age 25	20.2%
Minority	5.1%
Part-time	0.0%

Degrees conferred
Associate Degree

Minimum degree required
High school diploma or GED

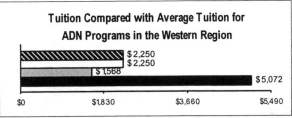

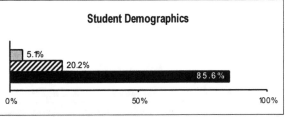

MT HOOD COMMUNITY COLLEGE — *Useful Facts*

26000 SE Stark
Gresham, OR 97030
(503) 491-6701
Janie Griffin, RN, MN, CPNP

www.mhcc.edu/nursing

Accreditation
Oregon State Board of Nursing

Acceptance rate		16.4%
Faculty-student ratio		1: 10
Faculty	Full time	8
	Part time	8

Tuition	
In state	$7,290
Out of state	$22,572
Enrollments	120
Graduations	51

Student Demographics	
Female	90.0%
Under age 25	8.3%
Minority	14.5%
Part-time	0.0%

Degrees conferred
Associate Degree

Minimum degree required
High school diploma or GED

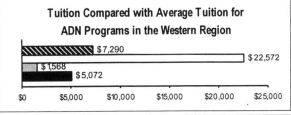

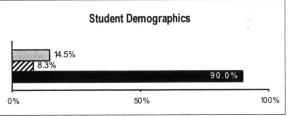

PORTLAND COMMUNITY COLLEGE — *Useful Facts*

12000 South West 49th Avenue
Portland, OR 97219
(503) 977-4205
Claudia Michel, RN, MN

www.pcc.edu/academ/nursing

Accreditation
Oregon State Board of Nursing, National League
for Nursing Accrediting Commission (NLNAC)

Acceptance rate		9.1%
Faculty-student ratio		1: 9
Faculty	Full time	18
	Part time	5

Tuition	
In state	$2,880
Out of state	$8,550
Enrollments	183
Graduations	93

Student Demographics	
Female	80.9%
Under age 25	18.6%
Minority	21.4%
Part-time	0.0%

Degrees conferred
Associate Degree

Minimum degree required
High school diploma or GED

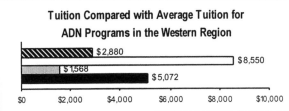

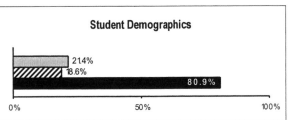

Demographics Chart	■ Female ▨ Under age 25 ☐ Minority	Distance Learning	†The tuition reported for this program may be not be annualized. *Data reported between 2001 and 2004.

Oregon

ROGUE COMMUNITY COLLEGE

3345 Redwood Highway
Grants Pass, OR 97527
(541) 956-7308
Linda Wagner, RN, MN

learn.roguecc.edu/alliedhealth/nursing/home.htm

Accreditation
Oregon State Board of Nursing, National League
for Nursing Accrediting Commission (NLNAC)

Acceptance rate		27.7%

Tuition			**Student Demographics**	
In state	$3,426		Female	85.0%
Out of state	$4,050		Under age 25	14.0%
Enrollments	60		Minority	6.7%
Graduations	26		Part-time	0.0%

Degrees conferred
Associate Degree

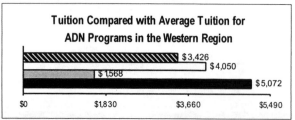

Tuition Compared with Average Tuition for ADN Programs in the Western Region

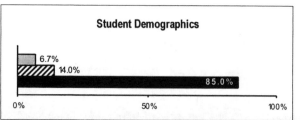

Student Demographics

SOUTHWESTERN OREGON COMMUNITY COLLEGE

1988 Newmark
Coos Bay, OR 97420
(541) 888-7340
Barbara Davey, RN, MS

southwestern.cc.or.us

Accreditation
Oregon State Board of Nursing

Degrees conferred
Associate Degree

TREASURE VALLEY COMMUNITY COLLEGE

650 College Boulevard
Ontario, OR 97914
(541) 881-8822
Maureen McDonough, RN, MS

tvcc.cc

Accreditation
Oregon State Board of Nursing

Acceptance rate		100.0%

Tuition			**Student Demographics**	
In state	$2,052		Female	100.0%
Out of state	$2,916		Under age 25	63.0%
Enrollments	19		Minority	5.3%
Graduations	17		Part-time	0.0%

Degrees conferred
Associate Degree

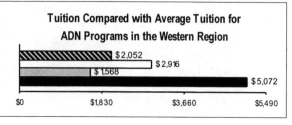

Tuition Compared with Average Tuition for ADN Programs in the Western Region

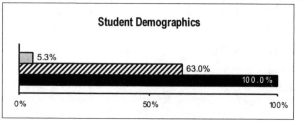

Student Demographics

Key | Tuition Chart | ▨ Program - in state ☐ Program - out of state ▤ Average - in state ■ Average - out of state

Oregon

UMPQUA COMMUNITY COLLEGE
Useful Facts

PO Box 967
Roseburg, OR 97470
(541) 440-4613
Sandra Hendy, RNC, MSN

www.umpqua.cc.or.us

Acceptance rate		58.3%
Faculty-student ratio		1: 11
Faculty	Full time	8
	Part time	6

Tuition	
In state	$3,120
Enrollments	124
Graduations	50

Student Demographics	
Female	79.8%
Under age 25	27.4%
Minority	4.8%
Part-time	21.0%

Accreditation
Oregon State Board of Nursing, National League for Nursing Accrediting Commission (NLNAC)

Degrees conferred
Associate Degree

Minimum degree required
High school diploma or GED

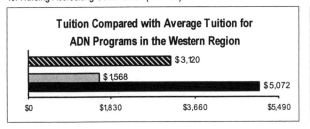

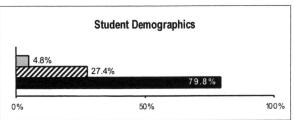

Pennsylvania

BUCKS COUNTY COMMUNITY COLLEGE
Useful Facts*

275 Swamp Road
Newtown, PA 18940
(215) 968-8326
Claire Keane, MSN, RN

www.bucks.edu

Acceptance rate	32.5%

Tuition	
In state	$2,550
Out of state	$7,650
Enrollments	215
Graduations	106

Student Demographics	
Female	83.7%
Under age 25	34.0%
Minority	7.5%
Part-time	89.3%

Accreditation
Pennsylvania State Board of Nursing, National League for Nursing Accrediting Commission (NLNAC)

Degrees conferred
Associate Degree

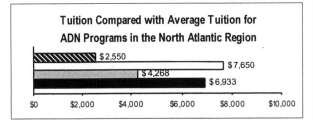

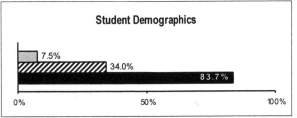

BUTLER COUNTY COMMUNITY COLLEGE
Useful Facts*

PO Box 1203, Oak Hills
Butler, PA 16003
(724) 287-8711
Elizabeth Gazza, RN, MSN, LCCE, FACCE

www.bc3.edu

Acceptance rate		40.4%
Faculty-student ratio		1: 12
Faculty	Full time	9
	Part time	7

Tuition	
In state	$1,608
Out of state	$4,824
Enrollments	156
Graduations	55

Student Demographics	
Female	89.7%
Under age 25	58.0%
Minority	3.2%
Part-time	62.2%

Accreditation
Pennsylvania State Board of Nursing, National League for Nursing Accrediting Commission (NLNAC)

Degrees conferred
Associate Degree

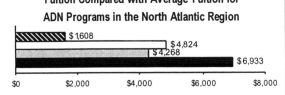

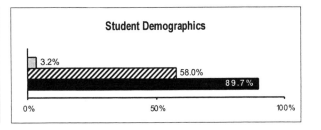

Demographics Chart	■Female ⧄Under age 25 ☐Minority	Distance Learning	†The tuition reported for this program may be not be annualized. *Data reported between 2001 and 2004.

Pennsylvania

CLARION UNIVERSITY
Useful Facts

1801 West First Street
Oil City, PA 16301
(814) 676-6591
Sally Bowser, MSN, RN

www.clarion.edu

Accreditation
Pennsylvania State Board of Nursing, National
League for Nursing Accrediting Commission
(NLNAC)

Acceptance rate		50.7%
Faculty-student ratio		1: 10
Faculty	Full time	11
	Part time	2

Degrees conferred
ASN

Tuition	
In state	$4,906
Out of state	$9,814
Enrollments	125
Graduations	74

Minimum degree required
High school diploma or GED

Student Demographics	
Female	87.2%
Under age 25	28.0%
Minority	1.6%
Part-time	0.0%

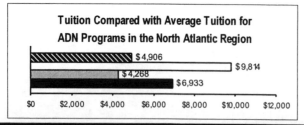

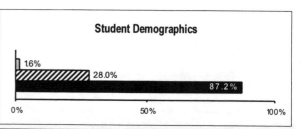

COMMUNITY COLLEGE OF ALLEGHENY COUNTY

595 Beatty Road
Monroeville, PA 15146
(724) 325-6875
Theresa Piekut, MSN, RNC

www.ccac.edu

Accreditation
Pennsylvania State Board of Nursing, National
League for Nursing Accrediting Commission
(NLNAC)

At the request of this nursing school, publication has been witheld.
Please contact the school directly for more information.

COMMUNITY COLLEGE OF BEAVER COUNTY
Useful Facts

1 Campus Drive
Monaca, PA 15061
(724) 775-8561
Linda Gallagher, MSN, RN

www.ccbc.edu

Accreditation
Pennsylvania State Board of Nursing, National
League for Nursing Accrediting Commission
(NLNAC)

Acceptance rate		44.2%
Faculty-student ratio		1: 14
Faculty	Full time	12
	Part time	2

Degrees conferred
Associate Degree

Tuition	
In state	$2,720
Out of state	$8,604
Enrollments	185
Graduations	61

Minimum degree required
High school diploma or GED

Student Demographics	
Female	88.1%
Under age 25	33.0%
Minority	6.7%
Part-time	89.2%

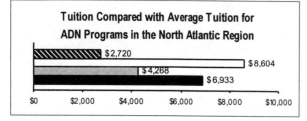

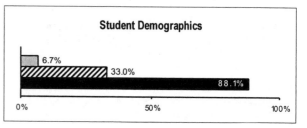

Key | Tuition Chart | ▨ Program - in state ☐ Program - out of state ▨ Average - in state ■ Average - out of state

Pennsylvania

COMMUNITY COLLEGE OF PHILADELPHIA — *Useful Facts**

1700 Spring Garden Street
Philadelphia, PA 19130
(215) 751-8853
Andrea Mengel, PhD, RN

www.ccp.edu

Acceptance rate	8.7%	**Tuition**		**Student Demographics**	
		In state	$3,104	Female	81.5%
		Enrollments	248	Minority	49.1%
		Graduations	114	Part-time	0.0%

Accreditation
Pennsylvania State Board of Nursing, National
League for Nursing Accrediting Commission
(NLNAC)

Degrees conferred
Associate Degree

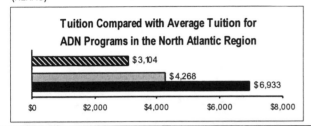

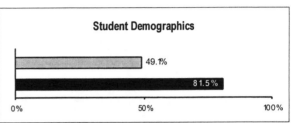

DELAWARE COUNTY COMMUNITY COLLEGE — *Useful Facts*

901 S Media Line Road
Media, PA 19063
(610) 359-5285
Lana deRuyter, MSN, RN

www.dccc.edu/faculty/ahn/index.htm

Acceptance rate	78.6%	**Tuition**		**Student Demographics**	
Faculty-student ratio	1:9	In state	$3,390	Female	91.8%
Faculty Full time	12	Out of state	$8,250	Under age 25	28.2%
Part time	47	**Enrollments**	305	Minority	11.9%
		Graduations	121	Part-time	91.8%

Accreditation
Pennsylvania State Board of Nursing, National
League for Nursing Accrediting Commission
(NLNAC)

Degrees conferred
Associate Degree

Minimum degree required
High school diploma or GED

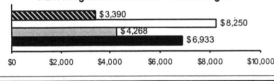

GWYNEDD-MERCY COLLEGE - *Minnesota Intercollegiate Nursing Consortium*

1325 Sumneytown Pike, PO Box 901
Gwynedd Valley, PA 19437
(215) 641-5539
Andrea Hollingsworth, PhD, RN

gmc.edu

Acceptance rate	25.2%	**Tuition**		**Student Demographics**	
		In state	$18,580	Female	93.1%
		Out of state	$18,580	Under age 25	73.4%
		Enrollments	349	Minority	9.3%
		Graduations	110	Part-time	18.9%

Accreditation
Pennsylvania State Board of Nursing, National
League for Nursing Accrediting Commission
(NLNAC)

Degrees conferred
Associate Degree

Minimum degree required
High school diploma or GED

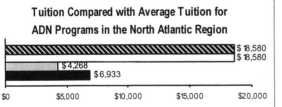

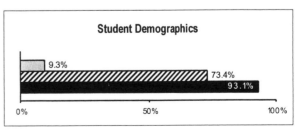

Demographics Chart	■ Female ▨ Under age 25 ▢ Minority	Distance Learning	¹The tuition reported for this program may be not be annualized.
			*Data reported between 2001 and 2004.

Pennsylvania

HARCUM COLLEGE

750 Montgomery Avenue
Bryn Mawr, PA 19010
(610) 526-6050
Marion Slater, PhD, RN

www.harcum.edu

Accreditation
Pennsylvania State Board of Nursing

Degrees conferred
Associate Degree

HARRISBURG AREA COMMUNITY COLLEGE - Harrisburg

1 HACC Drive	**Acceptance rate**	55.5%	**Tuition**	**Student Demographics**
Harrisburg, PA 17110	**Faculty-student ratio**	1: 8	In state	$2,700	Female	89.8%
(717) 780-2316	**Faculty** Full time	32	Out of state	$7,956	Under age 25	33.1%
Ronald Rebuck, MSN	Part time	47	**Enrollments**	432	Minority	11.0%
www.hacc.edu			**Graduations**	127	Part-time	68.1%

Accreditation
Pennsylvania State Board of Nursing, National
League for Nursing Accrediting Commission
(NLNAC)

Degrees conferred
Associate Degree

Minimum degree required
High school diploma or GED

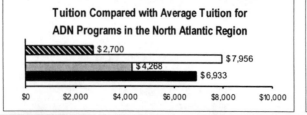

**Tuition Compared with Average Tuition for
ADN Programs in the North Atlantic Region**

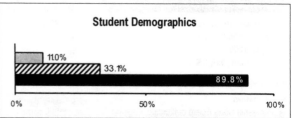

Student Demographics

LA ROCHE COLLEGE   *Useful Facts*

9000 Babcock Blvd	**Acceptance rate**	78.9%	**Tuition**	**Student Demographics**
Pittsburgh, PA 15237	**Faculty-student ratio**	1: 4	In state	$16,780	Female	81.6%
(412) 536-1173	**Faculty** Full time	4	Out of state	$16,780	Under age 25	63.2%
Rosemary McCarthy, PhD, RN	Part time	13	**Enrollments**	38	Minority	2.9%
www.laroche.edu			**Graduations**	6	Part-time	2.6%

Accreditation
Pennsylvania State Board of Nursing

Degrees conferred
Associate of Science in N

Minimum degree required
High school diploma or GED

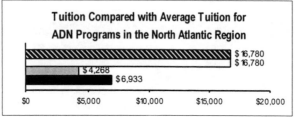

**Tuition Compared with Average Tuition for
ADN Programs in the North Atlantic Region**

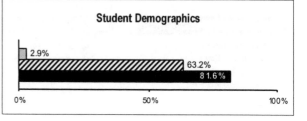

Student Demographics

Key | Tuition Chart | ▨ Program - in state ☐ Program - out of state ☐ Average - in state ■ Average - out of state

Pennsylvania

LEHIGH CARBON COMMUNITY COLLEGE - Morgan Center (Tomaqua)

4525 Education Park Dr
Schnecksville, PA 18078
(610) 799-1550
Nancy Becker, MS, RN

www.lccc.edu

Accreditation
Pennsylvania State Board of Nursing, National League for Nursing Accrediting Commission (NLNAC)

Acceptance rate	46.2%	
Faculty-student ratio	1: 8	
Faculty Full time	8	
Part time	13	

Degrees conferred
Associate Degree

Tuition	
In state	$1,140
Out of state	$3,420
Enrollments	42
Graduations	8

Minimum degree required
High school diploma or GED

Student Demographics	
Female	83.3%
Under age 25	38.1%
Minority	4.8%
Part-time	71.4%

Tuition Compared with Average Tuition for ADN Programs in the North Atlantic Region

$1,140
$3,420
$4,268
$6,933

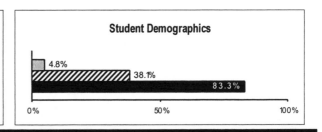
Student Demographics

4.8%
38.1%
83.3%

LEHIGH CARBON COMMUNITY COLLEGE - Schnecksville

4525 Education Park Dr
Schnecksville, PA 18078
(610) 799-1550
Nancy Becker, MS, RN

www.lccc.edu

Accreditation
Pennsylvania State Board of Nursing, National League for Nursing Accrediting Commission (NLNAC)

Acceptance rate	28.9%	
Faculty-student ratio	1: 8	
Faculty Full time	8	
Part time	13	

Degrees conferred
Associate Degree

Tuition	
In state	$1,140
Out of state	$3,420
Enrollments	78
Graduations	35

Minimum degree required
High school diploma or GED

Student Demographics	
Female	84.6%
Under age 25	17.9%
Minority	14.1%
Part-time	75.6%

Tuition Compared with Average Tuition for ADN Programs in the North Atlantic Region

$1,140
$3,420
$4,268
$6,933

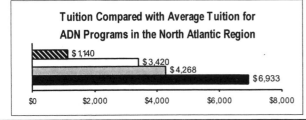

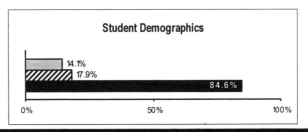
Student Demographics

14.1%
17.9%
84.6%

LOCK HAVEN UNIVERSITY OF PENNSYLVANIA - CLEARFIELD CAMPUS - Clearfield (3 locations)

201 University Drive
Clearfield, PA 16830
(814) 768-3451
Therese Sayers, MS, RN

www.lhup.edu

Accreditation
Pennsylvania State Board of Nursing, National League for Nursing Accrediting Commission (NLNAC)

Acceptance rate	20.7%	
Faculty-student ratio	1: 13	
Faculty Full time	6	
Part time	3	

Degrees conferred
Associate Degree

Tuition	
In state	$3,129
Out of state	$5,841
Enrollments	99
Graduations	91

Minimum degree required
High school diploma or GED

Student Demographics	
Female	85.9%
Under age 25	38.4%
Part-time	60.6%

Tuition Compared with Average Tuition for ADN Programs in the North Atlantic Region

$3,129
$5,841
$4,268
$6,933

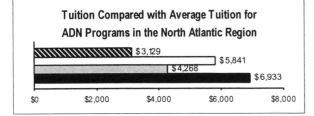

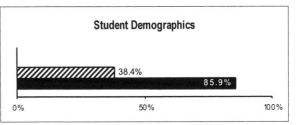
Student Demographics

38.4%
85.9%

Demographics Chart	■Female ☑Under age 25 ☐Minority	Distance Learning	†The tuition reported for this program may be not be annualized. *Data reported between 2001 and 2004.

Pennsylvania

LUZERNE COUNTY COMMUNITY COLLEGE - *Kulpmont*

1333 South Prospect St
Nanticoke, PA 18634
(570) 740-0463
Dana Clark, EdD, RN

www.luzerne.edu

Accreditation
Pennsylvania State Board of Nursing, National League for Nursing Accrediting Commission (NLNAC)

Acceptance rate	60.0%	
Faculty-student ratio	1: 13	
Faculty Full time	18	
Part time	15	

Tuition	
In state	$2,344
Out of state	$7,032
Enrollments	27
Graduations	22

Student Demographics	
Female	81.5%
Under age 25	25.9%
Part-time	0.0%

Degrees conferred
Associate Degree

Minimum degree required
High school diploma or GED

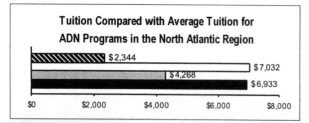

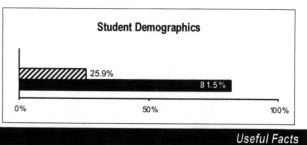

LUZERNE COUNTY COMMUNITY COLLEGE
Useful Facts

1333 South Prospect St
Nanticoke, PA 18634
(570) 740-0463
Dana Clark, EdD, RN

www.luzerne.edu

Accreditation
Pennsylvania State Board of Nursing, National League for Nursing Accrediting Commission (NLNAC)

Acceptance rate	16.2%	
Faculty-student ratio	1: 13	
Faculty Full time	18	
Part time	15	

Tuition	
In state	$2,344
Out of state	$7,032
Enrollments	295
Graduations	125

Student Demographics	
Female	86.4%
Under age 25	16.9%
Minority	2.0%
Part-time	0.0%

Degrees conferred
Associate Degree

Minimum degree required
High school diploma or GED

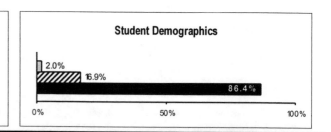

Student Demographics chart

MERCYHURST COLLEGE - NORTH EAST
Useful Facts

16 West Division Street
North East, PA 16428
(814) 725-6139
Susan Vitron, MSN, RN

www.mercyhurst.edu

Accreditation
Pennsylvania State Board of Nursing, National League for Nursing Accrediting Commission (NLNAC)

Acceptance rate	71.9%	
Faculty-student ratio	1: 22	
Faculty Full time	6	
Part time	3	

Tuition	
In state	$11,700
Out of state	$11,700
Enrollments	162
Graduations	47

Student Demographics	
Female	80.2%
Under age 25	41.4%
Minority	5.6%
Part-time	0.0%

Degrees conferred
Associate Degree

Minimum degree required
High school diploma or GED

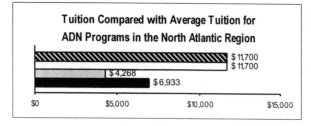

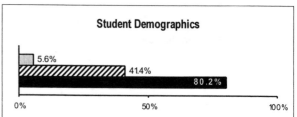

Key | Tuition Chart | ▨ Program - in state ☐ Program - out of state ☐ Average - in state ■ Average - out of state

Pennsylvania

MONTGOMERY COUNTY COMMUNITY COLLEGE — Useful Facts

340 DeKalb Pike
Blue Bell, PA 19422
(215) 641-6471
Beverly Welhan, DNSc, RN

www.mc3.edu

Accreditation
Pennsylvania State Board of Nursing, National
League for Nursing Accrediting Commission
(NLNAC)

Acceptance rate	75.0%
Faculty-student ratio	1: 8
Faculty Full time	17
Part time	24

Degrees conferred
Associate Degree

Tuition	
In state	$2,520
Out of state	$7,560
Enrollments	219
Graduations	115

Minimum degree required
High school diploma or GED

Student Demographics	
Female	87.2%
Under age 25	31.5%
Minority	14.9%
Part-time	90.9%

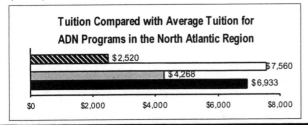

Tuition Compared with Average Tuition for ADN Programs in the North Atlantic Region

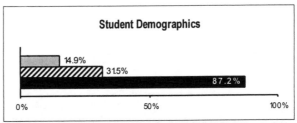

Student Demographics

MOUNT ALOYSIUS COLLEGE — Useful Facts*

7373 Admiral Peary Highway
Cresson, PA 16630
(814) 886-6393
Janet Grady, DrPH, RN

www.mtaloy.edu

Accreditation
Pennsylvania State Board of Nursing, National
League for Nursing Accrediting Commission
(NLNAC)

Acceptance rate	54.6%

Degrees conferred
Associate Degree

Tuition	
In state	$15,610
Out of state	$15,610
Enrollments	288
Graduations	109

Student Demographics	
Female	80.6%
Under age 25	46.0%
Minority	1.4%
Part-time	4.5%

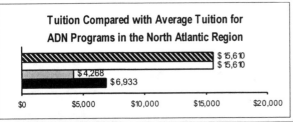

Tuition Compared with Average Tuition for ADN Programs in the North Atlantic Region

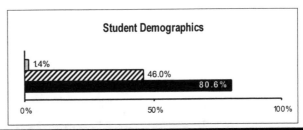

Student Demographics

NORTHAMPTON COMMUNITY COLLEGE - Bethlehem

3835 Green Pond Road
Bethlehem, PA 18020
(610) 861-5376
Kathleen Dolin, MSN, RN

www.northampton.edu

Accreditation
Pennsylvania State Board of Nursing, National
League for Nursing Accrediting Commission
(NLNAC)

Acceptance rate	8.2%
Faculty-student ratio	1: 10
Faculty Full time	6
Part time	20

Degrees conferred
Associate Degree

Tuition	
In state	$3,276
Out of state	$7,462
Enrollments	167
Graduations	63

Minimum degree required
High school diploma or GED

Student Demographics	
Female	92.8%
Under age 25	22.8%
Minority	16.4%
Part-time	89.8%

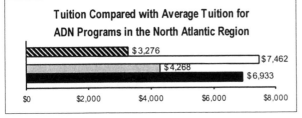

Tuition Compared with Average Tuition for ADN Programs in the North Atlantic Region

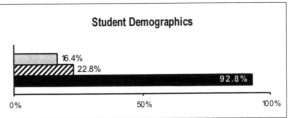

Student Demographics

Demographics Chart	■Female ▨Under age 25 ▢Minority	Distance Learning	†The tuition reported for this program may be not be annualized. *Data reported between 2001 and 2004.

Pennsylvania

PENNSYLVANIA COLLEGE OF TECHNOLOGY - *Williamsport*

One College Avenue
Williamsport, PA 17701
(570) 327-4525
Pamela Starcher, RN, MN, PhD(c)

www.pct.edu

Acceptance rate		19.5%
Faculty-student ratio		1: 5
Faculty	Full time	17
	Part time	32

Tuition	
In state	$10,080
Out of state	$12,660
Enrollments	151
Graduations	74

Student Demographics	
Female	89.4%
Under age 25	50.3%
Minority	4.6%
Part-time	54.3%

Accreditation
Pennsylvania State Board of Nursing, National League for Nursing Accrediting Commission (NLNAC)

Degrees conferred
Associate Degree

Minimum degree required
High school diploma or GED

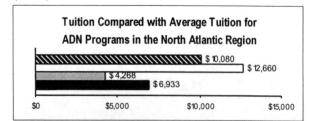

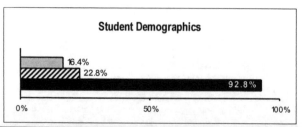

PENNSYLVANIA STATE UNIVERSITY - *University Park*

201 Health and Human Dev East
University Park, PA 16804
(814) 863-0247
Paula Milone-Nuzzo, RN, PhD, FAAN, FHHC

www.hhdev.psu.edu/nurs/nurs.htm

Acceptance rate		46.7%
Faculty-student ratio		1: 10
Faculty	Full time	64
	Part time	42

Tuition	
In state	$9,722
Out of state	$15,322
Enrollments	385
Graduations	173

Student Demographics	
Female	86.5%
Under age 25	47.5%
Minority	4.2%
Part-time	41.3%

Accreditation
Pennsylvania State Board of Nursing, National League for Nursing Accrediting Commission (NLNAC)

Degrees conferred
Associate Degree

Minimum degree required
High school diploma or GED

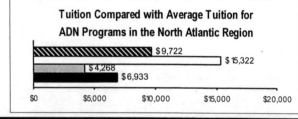

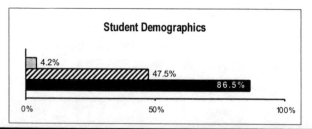

READING AREA COMMUNITY COLLEGE
Useful Facts

10 S 2nd Street
Reading, PA 19603
(610) 372-4721
Amelia Rodriquez, EdD, RN

www.racc.edu

Acceptance rate		8.5%
Faculty-student ratio		1: 6
Faculty	Full time	19
	Part time	9

Tuition	
In state	$2,010
Out of state	$4,020
Enrollments	135
Graduations	65

Student Demographics	
Female	84.4%
Under age 25	17.8%
Minority	12.9%
Part-time	14.8%

Accreditation
Pennsylvania State Board of Nursing, National League for Nursing Accrediting Commission (NLNAC)

Degrees conferred
Associate Degree

Minimum degree required
High school diploma or GED

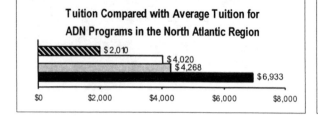

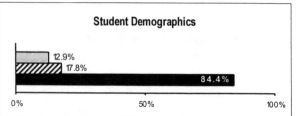

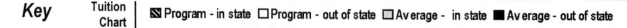

Key | Tuition Chart | ⊠ Program - in state ☐ Program - out of state ☐ Average - in state ■ Average - out of state

Pennsylvania

UNIVERSITY OF PITTSBURGH AT BRADFORD | Useful Facts

300 Campus Drive
Bradford, PA 16701
(814) 362-7640
Perla Ilagan, PhD, RN

www.upb.pitt.edu

Accreditation
Pennsylvania State Board of Nursing, National
League for Nursing Accrediting Commission
(NLNAC)

Acceptance rate	87.7%	
Faculty-student ratio	1: 10	
Faculty Full time	6	
Part time	7	

Degrees conferred
Associate Degree

Tuition	
In state	$12,664
Out of state	$25,208
Enrollments	99
Graduations	35

Minimum degree required
High school diploma or GED

Student Demographics	
Female	85.9%
Under age 25	64.6%
Minority	4.0%
Part-time	18.2%

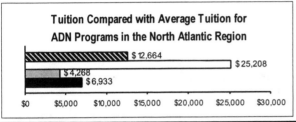

Tuition Compared with Average Tuition for ADN Programs in the North Atlantic Region

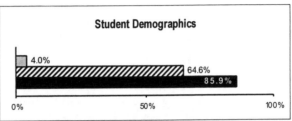

Student Demographics

WESTMORELAND CO COMMUNITY COLLEGE - Greene Co Education Center

400 Armbrust Road
Youngwood, PA 15697
(724) 925-4028
Patricia Mihalcin, RN, PhD

www.wccc-pa.edu

Accreditation
Pennsylvania State Board of Nursing, National
League for Nursing Accrediting Commission
(NLNAC)

Acceptance rate	66.7%	
Faculty-student ratio	1: 13	
Faculty Full time	13	
Part time	30	

Degrees conferred
Associate Degree

Tuition	
In state	$1,950
Out of state	$5,850
Enrollments	12
Graduations	6

Minimum degree required
High school diploma or GED

Student Demographics	
Female	91.7%
Under age 25	25.0%
Part-time	50.0%

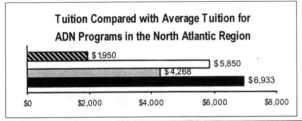

Tuition Compared with Average Tuition for ADN Programs in the North Atlantic Region

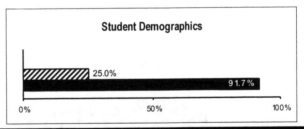

Student Demographics

WESTMORELAND CO COMMUNITY COLLEGE - Indiana

400 Armbrust Road
Youngwood, PA 15697
(724) 925-4028
Patricia Mihalcin, RN, PhD

www.wccc-pa.edu

Accreditation
Pennsylvania State Board of Nursing, National
League for Nursing Accrediting Commission
(NLNAC)

Acceptance rate	32.0%	
Faculty-student ratio	1: 13	
Faculty Full time	13	
Part time	30	

Degrees conferred
Associate Degree

Tuition	
In state	$1,950
Out of state	$5,850
Enrollments	43
Graduations	14

Minimum degree required
High school diploma or GED

Student Demographics	
Female	86.0%
Under age 25	34.9%
Part-time	60.5%

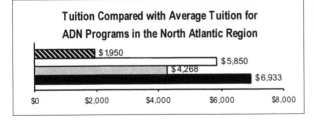

Tuition Compared with Average Tuition for ADN Programs in the North Atlantic Region

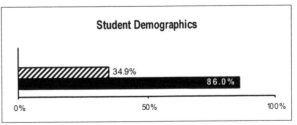

Student Demographics

Demographics Chart | ■Female ▨Under age 25 ☐Minority | **Distance Learning** | †The tuition reported for this program may be not be annualized.
*Data reported between 2001 and 2004.

Pennsylvania

WESTMORELAND CO COMMUNITY COLLEGE - *Youngwood*

400 Armbrust Road
Youngwood, PA 15697
(724) 925-4028
Patricia Mihalcin, RN, PhD

www.wccc-pa.edu

Acceptance rate		35.2%
Faculty-student ratio		1: 13
Faculty	Full time	13
	Part time	30

Tuition

In state	$1,950
Out of state	$5,850
Enrollments	305
Graduations	116

Student Demographics

Female	87.2%
Under age 25	37.4%
Minority	1.3%
Part-time	64.9%

Accreditation
Pennsylvania State Board of Nursing, National League for Nursing Accrediting Commission (NLNAC)

Degrees conferred
Associate Degree

Minimum degree required
High school diploma or GED

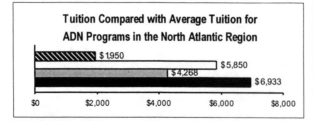

Tuition Compared with Average Tuition for ADN Programs in the North Atlantic Region

$1,950
$5,850
$4,268
$6,933

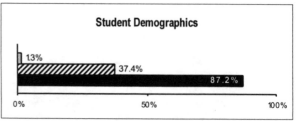

Student Demographics

1.3%
37.4%
87.2%

Rhode Island

COMMUNITY COLLEGE OF RHODE ISLAND   *Useful Facts**

1762 Louisquisset Pike
Lincoln, RI 02865
(401) 333-7102
Maureen McGarry, PhD

www.ccri.edu

Acceptance rate	5.4%

Tuition

In state	$2,000
Out of state	$5,874
Enrollments	508
Graduations	182

Student Demographics

Female	88.6%
Under age 25	17.4%
Minority	20.9%
Part-time	0.0%

Accreditation
Rhode Island Board of Nurse Registration & Nursing Education, National League for Nursing Accrediting Commission (NLNAC)

Degrees conferred
Associate Degree

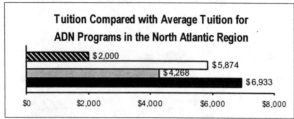

Tuition Compared with Average Tuition for ADN Programs in the North Atlantic Region

$2,000
$5,874
$4,268
$6,933

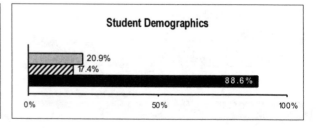

Student Demographics

20.9%
17.4%
88.6%

Key | Tuition Chart | ▨ Program - in state ☐ Program - out of state ▦ Average - in state ■ Average - out of state

South Carolina

CENTRAL CAROLINA TECHNICAL COLLEGE — *Useful Facts*

506 North Guignard Dr
Sumter, SC 29150
(803) 778-7822
Beverly Gulledge, RN, MN

www.cctech.edu

Acceptance rate		78.6%	**Tuition**		**Student Demographics**	
Faculty-student ratio		1: 7	In state	$2,700	Female	93.0%
Faculty	Full time	11	Out of state	$4,800	Under age 25	34.0%
	Part time	8	Enrollments	100	Minority	17.2%
			Graduations	51	Part-time	100.0%

Accreditation
South Carolina State Board of Nursing, National League for Nursing Accrediting Commission (NLNAC)

Degrees conferred
Associate Degree

Minimum degree required
High school diploma or GED

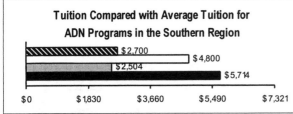

Tuition Compared with Average Tuition for ADN Programs in the Southern Region

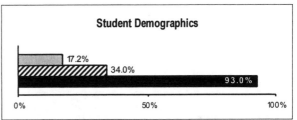

Student Demographics

FLORENCE DARLINGTON TECHNICAL COLLEGE — *Useful Facts**

PO Box 100548
Florence, SC 29501
(843) 661-8180
Latrell Fowler, RN, PhD

www.fdtc.edu

Acceptance rate	80.9%	**Tuition**		**Student Demographics**	
		In state	$1,100	Female	91.3%
		Out of state	$1,476		
		Enrollments	264	Minority	22.3%
		Graduations	103	Part-time	58.7%

Accreditation
South Carolina State Board of Nursing, National League for Nursing Accrediting Commission (NLNAC)

Degrees conferred
Associate Degree

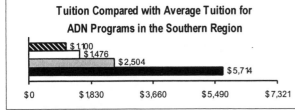

Tuition Compared with Average Tuition for ADN Programs in the Southern Region

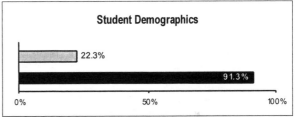

Student Demographics

GREENVILLE TECHNICAL COLLEGE — *Useful Facts*

PO Box 5616
Greenville, SC 29606
(864) 250-8382
Margaret Kroposki, PhD, RN

www.greenvilletech.com

Acceptance rate		81.1%	**Tuition**		**Student Demographics**	
Faculty-student ratio		1: 7	In state	$3,107	Female	89.9%
Faculty	Full time	37	Out of state	$6,707	Under age 25	31.8%
	Part time	33	Enrollments	365	Minority	18.4%
			Graduations	229	Part-time	63.8%

Accreditation
South Carolina State Board of Nursing, National League for Nursing Accrediting Commission (NLNAC)

Degrees conferred
Associate Degree

Minimum degree required
High school diploma or GED

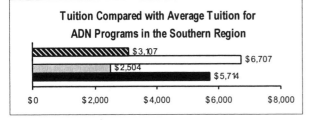

Tuition Compared with Average Tuition for ADN Programs in the Southern Region

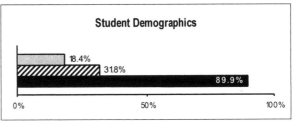

Student Demographics

Demographics Chart | ■Female ▨Under age 25 ☐Minority | **Distance Learning** 🖥 | †The tuition reported for this program may be not be annualized.
*Data reported between 2001 and 2004.

South Carolina

HORRY GEORGETOWN TECHNICAL COLLEGE

Useful Facts

2050 Highway 501 East
Conway, SC 29526
(843) 349-5383
Donna Richards, RN, PhD

hgtc.edu

Acceptance rate	30.0%	
Faculty-student ratio	1: 12	
Faculty	Full time	16
	Part time	8

Tuition
In state	$1,328
Out of state	$2,132
Enrollments	236
Graduations	93

Student Demographics
Female	91.5%
Under age 25	28.4%
Minority	25.0%
Part-time	95.8%

Accreditation
South Carolina State Board of Nursing, National League for Nursing Accrediting Commission (NLNAC)

Degrees conferred
Associate Degree

Minimum degree required
High school diploma or GED

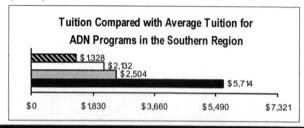

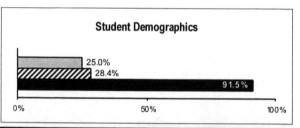

MIDLANDS TECHNICAL COLLEGE

Useful Facts

PO Box 2408
Columbia, SC 29202
(803) 822-3402
Janet Ancone, MSN, RN

www.midlandstech.edu/nursing

Acceptance rate	22.7%	
Faculty-student ratio	1: 11	
Faculty	Full time	31
	Part time	8

Tuition
In state	$3,624
Out of state	$8,712
Enrollments	370
Graduations	100

Student Demographics
Female	92.4%
Under age 25	32.7%
Minority	39.4%
Part-time	94.9%

Accreditation
South Carolina State Board of Nursing, National League for Nursing Accrediting Commission (NLNAC)

Degrees conferred
Associate Degree

Minimum degree required
High school diploma or GED

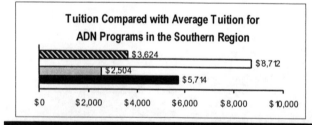

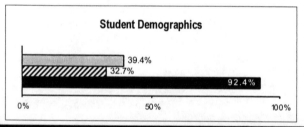

ORANGEBURG CALHOUN TECHNICAL COLLEGE

Useful Facts*

3250 St Mathews Rd
Orangeburg, SC 29118
(803) 535-1354
Delura Knight, MSN

www.octech.org

Acceptance rate	100.0%

Tuition
In state	$1,700
Out of state	$3,624
Enrollments	118
Graduations	43

Student Demographics
Female	94.9%
Under age 25	20.0%
Minority	15.4%
Part-time	62.7%

Accreditation
South Carolina State Board of Nursing, National League for Nursing Accrediting Commission (NLNAC)

Degrees conferred
Associate Degree

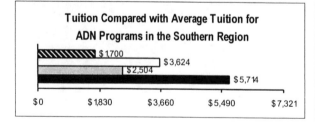

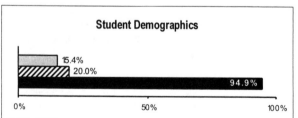

Key | Tuition Chart | ⧄ Program - in state ☐ Program - out of state ▨ Average - in state ■ Average - out of state

South Carolina

PIEDMONT TECHNICAL COLLEGE - *Greenwood*

Emerald Road Drawer 1467
Greenwood, SC 29648
(864) 941-8529
REBECCA KING, MSN, RN

piedmont technical college

Accreditation
South Carolina State Board of Nursing, National
League for Nursing Accrediting Commission
(NLNAC)

Acceptance rate		8.4%
Faculty-student ratio		1: 12
Faculty	Full time	14
	Part time	0

Degrees conferred
Associate Degree

Tuition	
In state	$4,200
Out of state	$4,500
Enrollments	174
Graduations	130

Minimum degree required
High school diploma or GED

Student Demographics	
Female	97.1%
Under age 25	25.9%
Minority	25.3%
Part-time	5.7%

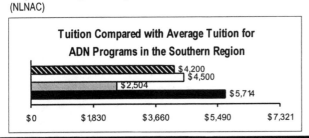

Tuition Compared with Average Tuition for ADN Programs in the Southern Region
$4,200 / $4,500 / $2,504 / $5,714

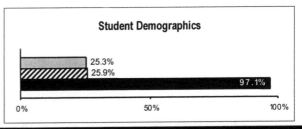

Student Demographics
25.3% / 25.9% / 97.1%

SPARTANBURG TECHNICAL COLLEGE

PO Box 4386
Spartanburg, SC 29305
(864) 592-4882
Susan Cherry-Casey, RN, MN

www.stcsc.edu

Accreditation
South Carolina State Board of Nursing

Faculty	Full time	10
	Part time	6

Degrees conferred
Associate Degree

TECHNICAL COLLEGE OF THE LOWCOUNTRY

PO Box 1288
Beaufort, SC 29901
(843) 525-8267
Sue Johnson, EdD, RN

www.tclnursing.org

Accreditation
South Carolina State Board of Nursing, National
League for Nursing Accrediting Commission
(NLNAC)

At the request of this nursing school, publication has been witheld.
Please contact the school directly for more information.

TRI -COUNTY TECHNICAL COLLEGE   *Useful Facts*

7900 Highway 76, PO Box 587
Pendleton, SC 29670
(864) 646-1343
Janet Fuller, RN, MSN

www.tctc.edu

Accreditation
South Carolina State Board of Nursing, National
League for Nursing Accrediting Commission
(NLNAC)

Acceptance rate		15.0%
Faculty-student ratio		1: 9
Faculty	Full time	11
	Part time	2

Degrees conferred
Associate Degree

Tuition	
In state	$2,450
Out of state	$5,820
Enrollments	104
Graduations	76

Minimum degree required
High school diploma or GED

Student Demographics	
Female	95.2%
Under age 25	19.2%
Minority	9.6%
Part-time	80.8%

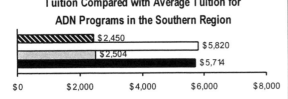

Tuition Compared with Average Tuition for ADN Programs in the Southern Region
$2,450 / $5,820 / $2,504 / $5,714

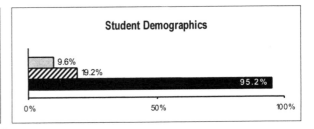

Student Demographics
9.6% / 19.2% / 95.2%

Demographics Chart	■Female ☑Under age 25 ☐Minority	Distance Learning 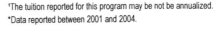	¹The tuition reported for this program may be not be annualized. *Data reported between 2001 and 2004.

South Carolina

TRIDENT TECHNICAL COLLEGE
Useful Facts

PO Box 118067
Charleston, SC 29423
(843) 574-6138
Muriel Horton, MSN, RN

www.tridenttech.edu/nursing

Accreditation
South Carolina State Board of Nursing, National
League for Nursing Accrediting Commission
(NLNAC)

Acceptance rate		100.0%
Faculty-student ratio		1: 11
Faculty	Full time	25
	Part time	19

Degrees conferred
Associate Degree

Tuition			Student Demographics	
In state	$2,850		Female	86.8%
Out of state	$5,486		Under age 25	31.3%
Enrollments	380		Minority	21.1%
Graduations	146		Part-time	86.3%

Minimum degree required
High school diploma or GED

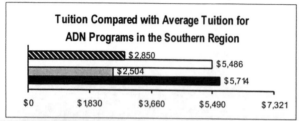

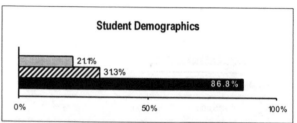

UNIVERSITY OF SOUTH CAROLINA - AIKEN
Useful Facts

471 University Parkway
Aiken, SC 29801
(803) 641-3263
L Julia Ball, RN, PhD

www.usca.edu

Accreditation
South Carolina State Board of Nursing, National
League for Nursing Accrediting Commission
(NLNAC)

Faculty-student ratio		1: 9
Faculty	Full time	15
	Part time	23

Degrees conferred
Associate Degree

Tuition			Student Demographics	
In state	$6,158		Female	85.4%
Out of state	$12,346		Under age 25	41.7%
Enrollments	48		Minority	16.7%
Graduations	19		Part-time	0.0%

Minimum degree required
High school diploma or GED

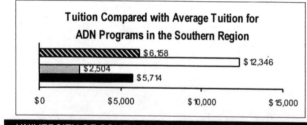

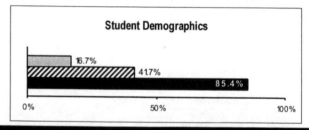

UNIVERSITY OF SOUTH CAROLINA - UPSTATE
Useful Facts

800 University Way
Spartanburg, SC 29303
(864) 503-5444
Marsha Dowell, PhD, RN

www.uscupstate.edu/academic/mbsn/index.shtml

Accreditation
South Carolina State Board of Nursing, National
League for Nursing Accrediting Commission
(NLNAC)

Faculty-student ratio		1: 10
Faculty	Full time	35
	Part time	15

Degrees conferred
Associate Degree

Tuition			Student Demographics	
In state	$6,416		Female	93.9%
Out of state	$13,254		Under age 25	24.2%
Enrollments	33		Minority	15.2%
Graduations	63		Part-time	100.0%

Minimum degree required
Other (please specify)

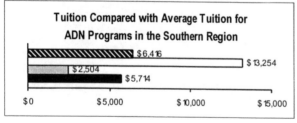

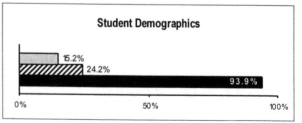

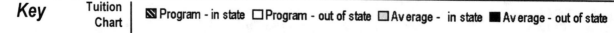

Key | Tuition Chart | ▨ Program - in state ▢ Program - out of state ▢ Average - in state ■ Average - out of state

South Carolina

YORK TECHNICAL COLLEGE — *Useful Facts*

452 South Anderson Road
Rock Hill, SC 29730
(803) 981-7067
Mary Laney, MSN, RNC

www.yorktech.com/department/nursing/department.htm

Acceptance rate		100.0%
Faculty-student ratio		1: 11
Faculty	Full time	10
	Part time	8

Tuition	
In state	$6,768
Out of state	$16,320
Enrollments	149
Graduations	33

Student Demographics	
Female	96.0%
Under age 25	30.9%
Minority	100.0%
Part-time	78.5%

Accreditation
South Carolina State Board of Nursing, National League for Nursing Accrediting Commission (NLNAC)

Degrees conferred
LPN or LVN, Associate Degree

Minimum degree required
High school diploma or GED

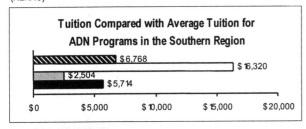

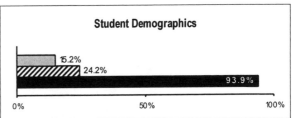

South Dakota

DAKOTA WESLEYAN UNIVERSITY — *Useful Facts*

1200 West University Avenue
Mitchell, SD 57301
(605) 995-2889
Gloria Thompson, RN, MS

www.dwu.edu/nursing

Acceptance rate		78.7%
Faculty-student ratio		1: 12
Faculty	Full time	11
	Part time	0

Tuition	
In state	$15,700
Out of state	$15,700
Enrollments	132
Graduations	29

Student Demographics	
Female	93.2%
Under age 25	54.5%
Minority	6.1%
Part-time	11.4%

Accreditation
South Dakota Board of Nursing, National League for Nursing Accrediting Commission (NLNAC)

Degrees conferred
Associate Degree

Minimum degree required
HS/GED for generic AA program; LPN for LPN-RN curriculum

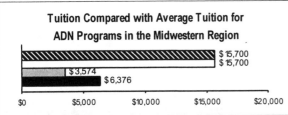

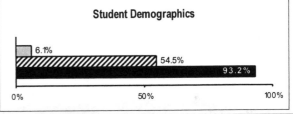

OGLALA LAKOTA COLLEGE — *Useful Facts**

1 Nursing Way, PO Box 861
Pine Ridge, SD 57747
(605) 867-5856
Sarah Coulter Dauuer, MSN, CNM, CPNP

www.olc.edu

Acceptance rate	64.3%

Tuition[1]	
In state	$65
Out of state	$65
Enrollments	26
Graduations	9

Student Demographics	
Female	96.2%
Under age 25	40.0%
Minority	76.9%
Part-time	0.0%

Accreditation
South Dakota Board of Nursing

Degrees conferred
Associate Degree

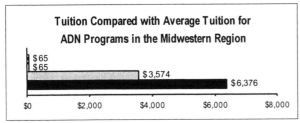

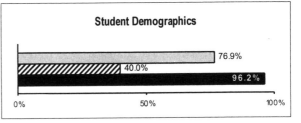

Demographics Chart	■ Female ▨ Under age 25 ☐ Minority	Distance Learning	[1]The tuition reported for this program may be not be annualized. *Data reported between 2001 and 2004.

South Dakota

PRESENTATION COLLEGE

1500 North Main Street
Aberdeen, SD 57401
(605) 229-8472
Linda Burdette, MS, RN, CNP

www.presentation.edu/nursing

Acceptance rate		87.5%
Faculty-student ratio		1: 10
Faculty	Full time	12
	Part time	20

Tuition		
In state	$11,400
Out of state	$11,400
Enrollments	12
Graduations	6

Student Demographics	
Female	75.0%
Under age 25	33.3%
Minority	66.7%
Part-time	25.0%

Accreditation
South Dakota Board of Nursing, National League for Nursing Accrediting Commission (NLNAC)

Degrees conferred
Associate Degree

Minimum degree required
High school diploma or GED

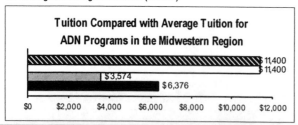

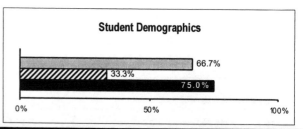

UNIVERSITY OF SOUTH DAKOTA

414 East Clark, Julian Hall 243
Vermillion, SD 57069
(605) 677-5006
June Larson, MS, RN

www.usd.edu/nursing

Acceptance rate		56.4%
Faculty-student ratio		1: 13
Faculty	Full time	41
	Part time	2

Tuition		
In state	$2,291
Out of state	$7,278
Enrollments	543
Graduations	213

Student Demographics	
Female	91.5%
Under age 25	44.8%
Minority	4.2%
Part-time	56.4%

Accreditation
South Dakota Board of Nursing, National League for Nursing Accrediting Commission (NLNAC)

Degrees conferred
Associate Degree

Minimum degree required
High school diploma or GED

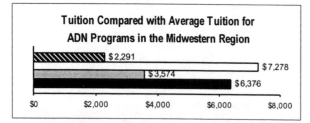

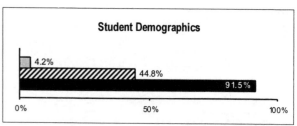

Tennessee

AQUINAS COLLEGE

4210 Harding Road
Nashville, TN 37205
(615) 222-4038
Linda Watlington, DSN, RN

www.aquinas-tn.edu

Acceptance rate		61.0%

Tuition		
In state	$4,620
Out of state	$4,620
Enrollments	128
Graduations	48

Student Demographics	
Female	85.2%
Under age 25	31.0%
Minority	8.6%
Part-time	73.4%

Accreditation
Tennessee State Board of Nursing, National League for Nursing Accrediting Commission (NLNAC)

Degrees conferred
Associate Degree

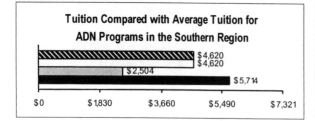

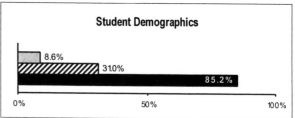

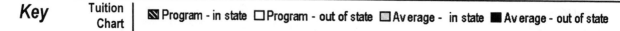

Key | Tuition Chart | ▨ Program - in state ☐ Program - out of state ▥ Average - in state ■ Average - out of state

Tennessee

CHATTANOOGA STATE TECHNICAL COMMUNITY COLLEGE — *Useful Facts*

4501 Amnicola Highway
Chattanooga, TN 37406
(423) 493-8721
Cynthia Swafford, EdD, RN

www.chattanoogastate.edu/nursing/nurmain.asp

Acceptance rate	23.7%	
Faculty-student ratio	1: 12	
Faculty	Full time	17
	Part time	6

Tuition	
In state	$2,342
Out of state	$8,556
Enrollments	248
Graduations	91

Student Demographics	
Female	86.3%
Under age 25	32.3%
Minority	10.6%
Part-time	0.0%

Accreditation
Tennessee State Board of Nursing, National League for Nursing Accrediting Commission (NLNAC)

Degrees conferred
Associate Degree

Minimum degree required
High school diploma or GED

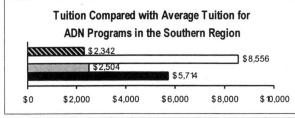

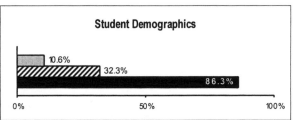

CLEVELAND STATE COMMUNITY COLLEGE — *Useful Facts*

PO Box 3570
Cleveland, TN 37320
(423) 478-6227
Patricia Purnell, EdD, MSN, RN

www.clevelandstatecc.edu

Acceptance rate	36.0%	
Faculty-student ratio	1: 12	
Faculty	Full time	10
	Part time	6

Tuition	
In state	$2,435
Out of state	$8,849
Enrollments	158
Graduations	48

Student Demographics	
Female	92.4%
Under age 25	44.3%
Minority	9.5%
Part-time	74.7%

Accreditation
Tennessee State Board of Nursing, National League for Nursing Accrediting Commission (NLNAC)

Degrees conferred
Associate Degree

Minimum degree required
High school diploma or GED

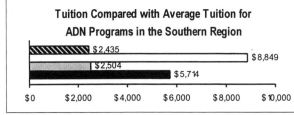

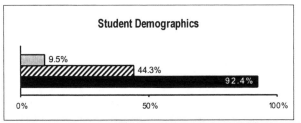

COLUMBIA STATE COMMUNITY COLLEGE — *Useful Facts*

1665 Hampshire Pike
Columbia, TN 38401
(931) 540-2600
Lois Ewen, PhD, MSN, BSN, RN

www.columbiastate.edu/nursing.htm

Faculty-student ratio	1: 14	
Faculty	Full time	15
	Part time	17

Tuition	
In state	$2,142
Out of state	$8,556
Enrollments	322
Graduations	126

Student Demographics	
Female	90.7%
Under age 25	39.4%
Minority	10.5%
Part-time	0.0%

Accreditation
Tennessee State Board of Nursing, National League for Nursing Accrediting Commission (NLNAC)

Degrees conferred
Associate of Applied Scie

Minimum degree required
High school diploma or GED

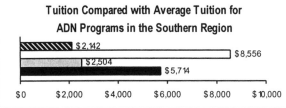

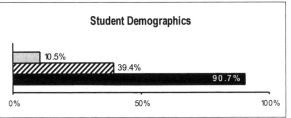

Demographics Chart | ■ Female ◪ Under age 25 ▢ Minority | **Distance Learning** 🖥️ | ¹The tuition reported for this program may be not be annualized.
*Data reported between 2001 and 2004.

Tennessee

DYERSBURG STATE COMMUNITY COLLEGE
Useful Facts

1510 Lake Road
Dyersburg, TN 38024
(731) 286-3398
Cindy Fisher, MSN, RN

www.dscc.edu/nursing

Acceptance rate		29.2%
Faculty-student ratio		1: 8
Faculty	Full time	9
	Part time	11

Tuition	
In state	$1,071
Out of state	$3,207
Enrollments	118
Graduations	58

Student Demographics	
Female	93.2%
Under age 25	35.6%
Minority	11.0%
Part-time	61.9%

Accreditation
Tennessee State Board of Nursing, National League for Nursing Accrediting Commission (NLNAC)

Degrees conferred
Associate Degree

Minimum degree required
High school diploma or GED

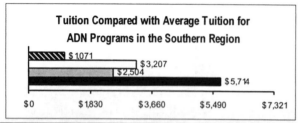

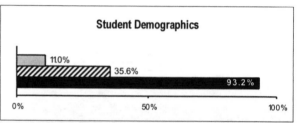

JACKSON STATE COMMUNITY COLLEGE
Useful Facts

2046 North Parkway
Jackson, TN 38301
(901) 425-2622
Leslie Sands, DSN, APRN, BC

jscc.edu

Acceptance rate		29.8%
Faculty-student ratio		1: 13
Faculty	Full time	21
	Part time	3

Tuition	
In state	$2,395
Out of state	$7,798
Enrollments	289
Graduations	84

Student Demographics	
Female	86.9%
Under age 25	46.4%
Minority	5.5%
Part-time	5.5%

Accreditation
Tennessee State Board of Nursing, National League for Nursing Accrediting Commission (NLNAC)

Degrees conferred
Associate Degree

Minimum degree required
High school diploma or GED

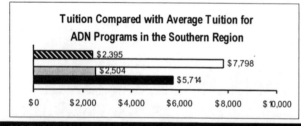

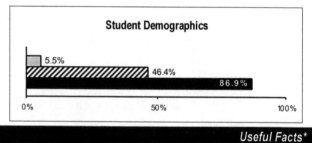

MOTLOW STATE COMMUNITY COLLEGE
Useful Facts*

PO Box 8500
Lynchburg, TN 37352
(931) 393-1631
Reba Walters, MSN, RN

www.mscc.edu

Acceptance rate	31.8%

Tuition	
In state	$1,600
Out of state	$6,392
Enrollments	105
Graduations	36

Student Demographics	
Female	88.6%
Under age 25	42.0%
Minority	3.8%
Part-time	0.0%

Accreditation
Tennessee State Board of Nursing, National League for Nursing Accrediting Commission (NLNAC)

Degrees conferred
Associate Degree

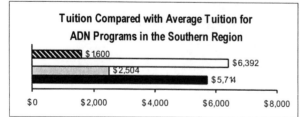

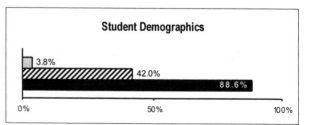

Key | Tuition Chart | ▨ Program - in state ☐ Program - out of state ☐ Average - in state ■ Average - out of state

Tennessee

ROANE STATE COMMUNITY COLLEGE — Useful Facts

276 Patton Lane
Harriman, TN 37748
(865) 882-4605
Priscilla Spitzer, MN, RN

www.roanestate.edu

Accreditation
Tennessee State Board of Nursing, National
League for Nursing Accrediting Commission
(NLNAC)

Acceptance rate	29.6%	
Faculty-student ratio	1: 12	
Faculty Full time	14	
Part time	11	

Tuition	
In state	$2,142
Out of state	$8,556
Enrollments	231
Graduations	109

Student Demographics	
Female	85.3%
Under age 25	35.5%
Minority	5.7%
Part-time	27.3%

Degrees conferred
Associate Degree

Minimum degree required
High school diploma or GED

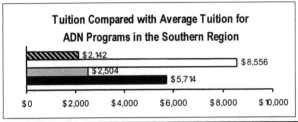

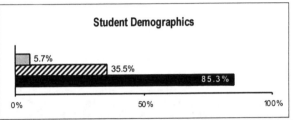

SOUTHERN ADVENTIST UNIVERSITY

PO Box 370
Collegedale, TN 37315
(423) 236-2942
L James, DSN, RN

nursing.southern.edu

Accreditation
Tennessee State Board of Nursing, National
League for Nursing Accrediting Commission
(NLNAC)

At the request of this nursing school, publication has been witheld.
Please contact the school directly for more information.

SOUTHWEST TENNESSEE COMMUNITY COLLEGE — Useful Facts

737 Union Ave
Memphis, TN 38103
(901) 333-5425
Mary Vines, MSN, APRN, BC

southwest.tn.edu/nursing

Accreditation
Tennessee State Board of Nursing, National
League for Nursing Accrediting Commission
(NLNAC)

Acceptance rate	10.0%	
Faculty-student ratio	1: 12	
Faculty Full time	13	
Part time	14	

Tuition	
In state	$2,142
Out of state	$8,556
Enrollments	235
Graduations	91

Student Demographics	
Female	86.0%
Under age 25	19.1%
Minority	51.9%
Part-time	42.6%

Degrees conferred
Associate Degree

Minimum degree required
High school diploma or GED

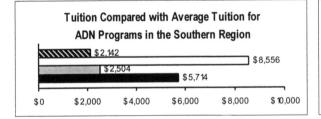

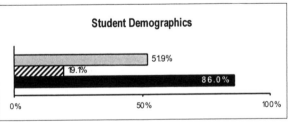

Demographics Chart	■Female ☒Under age 25 ☐Minority	**Distance Learning** 💻	¹The tuition reported for this program may be not be annualized. ²Data reported between 2001 and 2004.

Tennessee

TENNESSEE STATE UNIVERSITY
Useful Facts

3500 John A Merritt Boulevard, Box 9596
Nashville, TN 37209
(615) 963-5254
Mary Graham, EdD

www.tnstate.edu

Acceptance rate	67.8%
Faculty-student ratio	1: 7
Faculty Full time	26
Part time	14

Tuition
In state	$4,414
Out of state	$13,726
Enrollments	104
Graduations	68

Student Demographics
Female	90.4%
Under age 25	67.3%
Minority	67.3%
Part-time	0.0%

Accreditation
Tennessee State Board of Nursing, National League for Nursing Accrediting Commission (NLNAC)

Degrees conferred
Associate Degree

Minimum degree required
High school diploma or GED

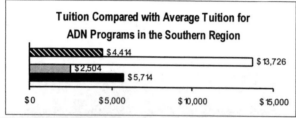

Tuition Compared with Average Tuition for ADN Programs in the Southern Region

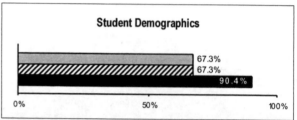

Student Demographics

WALTERS STATE COMMUNITY COLLEGE
Useful Facts

500 S Davy Crockett Parkway
Morristown, TN 37813
(423) 585-6983
Martel Rucker, MSN, RN

www.ws.edu

Acceptance rate	52.6%
Faculty-student ratio	1: 12
Faculty Full time	18
Part time	12

Tuition
In state	$2,142
Out of state	$6,414
Enrollments	280
Graduations	118

Student Demographics
Female	89.6%
Under age 25	32.5%
Minority	5.0%
Part-time	78.6%

Accreditation
Tennessee State Board of Nursing, National League for Nursing Accrediting Commission (NLNAC)

Degrees conferred
Associate Degree

Minimum degree required
High school diploma or GED

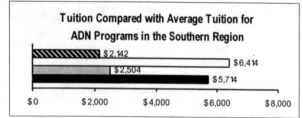

Tuition Compared with Average Tuition for ADN Programs in the Southern Region

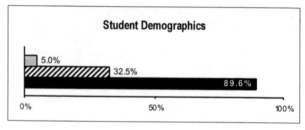

Student Demographics

Key | Tuition Chart | ▨ Program - in state ☐ Program - out of state ☐ Average - in state ■ Average - out of state

Texas

ALVIN COMMUNITY COLLEGE
Useful Facts

3110 Mustang Rd
Alvin, TX 77511
(281) 756-3634
Sally Durand, RN, MSN

www.alvincollege.edu

Accreditation
Texas Board of Nurse Examiners, National
League for Nursing Accrediting Commission
(NLNAC)

Acceptance rate		27.1%
Faculty-student ratio		1: 12
Faculty	Full time	8
	Part time	5

Tuition

In state	$840
Out of state	$3,300
Enrollments	127
Graduations	59

Student Demographics

Female	89.8%
Under age 25	36.2%
Minority	20.3%
Part-time	66.9%

Degrees conferred
Associate Degree

Minimum degree required
High school diploma or GED

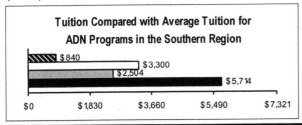
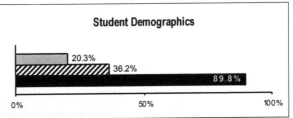

AMARILLO COLLEGE

PO Box 447
Amarillo, TX 79178
(806) 354-6010
Sheryl Mueller, MSEd, MSN, RN

www.actx.edu

Accreditation
Texas Board of Nurse Examiners, National
League for Nursing Accrediting Commission
(NLNAC)

At the request of this nursing school, publication has been witheld.
Please contact the school directly for more information.

ANGELINA COLLEGE - Lufkin

PO Box 1768
Lufkin, TX 75902
(936) 633-5445
Sharon Buffalo, RN, MSN

www.angelina.edu

Accreditation
Texas Board of Nurse Examiners

Acceptance rate		29.6%
Faculty-student ratio		1: 11
Faculty	Full time	13
	Part time	1

Tuition

In state	$1,232
Out of state	$2,562
Enrollments	149
Graduations	71

Student Demographics

Female	85.9%
Under age 25	28.2%
Minority	14.8%
Part-time	0.0%

Degrees conferred
Associate Degree

Minimum degree required
ADN or Diploma

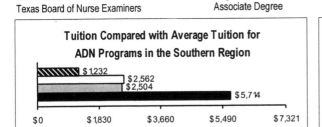
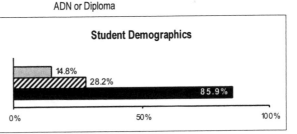

Demographics Chart	■Female ☒Under age 25 ▢Minority	Distance Learning	'The tuition reported for this program may be not be annualized. *Data reported between 2001 and 2004.

Texas

ANGELO STATE UNIVERSITY

ASU Station #10902
San Angelo, TX 76909
(325) 942-2224
Leslie Mayrand, PhD, RN, CNS

www.angelo.edu/dept/nursing

Accreditation
Texas Board of Nurse Examiners, National League for Nursing Accrediting Commission (NLNAC)

Acceptance rate	72.0%
Faculty-student ratio	1: 8
Faculty Full time	19
Part time	5

Degrees conferred
Associate Degree

Tuition	
In state	$4,285
Out of state	$12,565
Enrollments	180
Graduations	71

Minimum degree required
High school diploma or GED

Student Demographics	
Female	87.8%
Under age 25	65.0%
Minority	13.9%
Part-time	33.9%

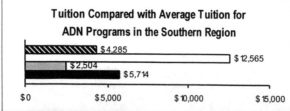

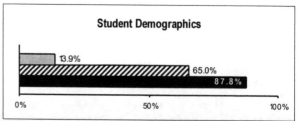

AUSTIN COMMUNITY COLLEGE - Austin

3401 Webberville Road
Austin, TX 78702
(512) 223-5787
Jean Ward, RN, MSN

www.austincc.edu

Accreditation
Texas Board of Nurse Examiners, National League for Nursing Accrediting Commission (NLNAC)

Acceptance rate	24.6%
Faculty-student ratio	1: 9
Faculty Full time	40
Part time	11

Degrees conferred
Associate Degree

Tuition	
In state	$1,170
Out of state	$5,520
Enrollments	420
Graduations	153

Minimum degree required
High school diploma or GED

Student Demographics	
Female	85.0%
Under age 25	13.8%
Minority	28.4%
Part-time	0.0%

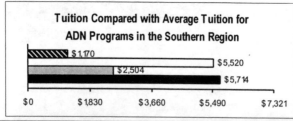

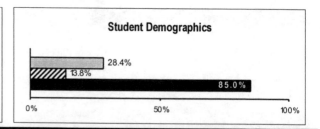

BLINN COLLEGE - Bryan

PO Box 6030, 2423 Blinn Blvd
Bryan, TX 77805
(979) 209-7204
Thena Parrott, PhD, RN

www.blinn.edu

Accreditation
Texas Board of Nurse Examiners, National League for Nursing Accrediting Commission (NLNAC)

Acceptance rate	45.6%
Faculty-student ratio	1: 9
Faculty Full time	13
Part time	4

Degrees conferred
Associate Degree

Tuition	
In state	$1,530
Out of state	$4,890
Enrollments	137
Graduations	36

Minimum degree required
High school/GED + prerequisite courses

Student Demographics	
Female	85.4%
Under age 25	45.3%
Minority	14.6%
Part-time	0.0%

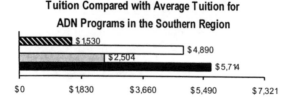

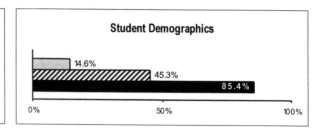

Key	Tuition Chart	▨ Program - in state ☐ Program - out of state ☐ Average - in state ■ Average - out of state

Texas

CENTRAL TEXAS COLLEGE - Killeen

PO Box 1800
Killeen, TX 76540
(254) 526-1300
Jeanette Jost, MSN, RN

www.ctcd.edu

Accreditation
Texas Board of Nurse Examiners, National League for Nursing Accrediting Commission (NLNAC)

Acceptance rate		40.7%
Faculty-student ratio		1: 7
Faculty	Full time	21
	Part time	17

Degrees conferred
Associate Degree, LPN or LVN

Tuition	
In state	$960
Out of state	$6,000
Enrollments	202
Graduations	70

Minimum degree required
High school diploma or GED

Student Demographics	
Female	90.6%
Under age 25	11.9%
Minority	25.0%
Part-time	14.4%

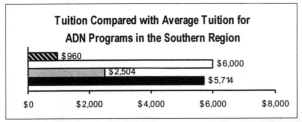

Tuition Compared with Average Tuition for ADN Programs in the Southern Region

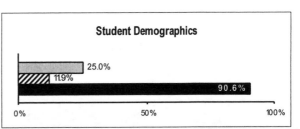

Student Demographics

CISCO JUNIOR COLLEGE

717 E Industrial Blvd
Abilene, TX 79602
(325) 794-4400
Jackolyn Morgan, MSN, RN

www.cisco.cc.tx.us

Accreditation
Texas Board of Nurse Examiners

Acceptance rate		81.6%
Faculty-student ratio		1: 3
Faculty	Full time	9
	Part time	2

Degrees conferred
Associate Degree

Tuition	
In state	$2,478
Out of state	$3,860
Enrollments	34
Graduations	32

Minimum degree required
LVN

Student Demographics	
Female	91.2%
Under age 25	17.6%
Minority	23.5%
Part-time	0.0%

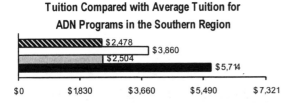

Tuition Compared with Average Tuition for ADN Programs in the Southern Region

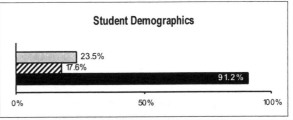

Student Demographics

COLLEGE OF THE MAINLAND

1200 Amburn Road
Texas City, TX 77591
(409) 938-1211
Gay Reeves, EdD, RN, MSN

www.com.edu

Accreditation
Texas Board of Nurse Examiners, National League for Nursing Accrediting Commission (NLNAC)

Acceptance rate		56.9%
Faculty-student ratio		1: 7
Faculty	Full time	9
	Part time	4

Degrees conferred
Associate Degree

Tuition	
In state	$780
Out of state	$2,670
Enrollments	73
Graduations	13

Minimum degree required
High school diploma or GED

Student Demographics	
Female	83.6%
Under age 25	39.7%
Minority	37.5%
Part-time	0.0%

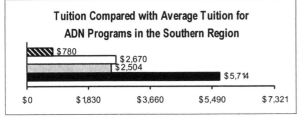

Tuition Compared with Average Tuition for ADN Programs in the Southern Region

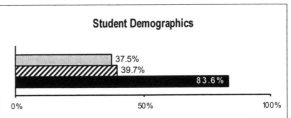

Student Demographics

Demographics Chart	■Female ☒Under age 25 ▢Minority	Distance Learning	¹The tuition reported for this program may be not be annualized. *Data reported between 2001 and 2004.

Texas

COLLIN COUNTY COMMUNITY COLLEGE

2200 W University Drive
Mc Kinney, TX 75071
(972) 548-6883
Linda Ard, PhD, RNc, CNS

www.ccccd.edu/nursing

Accreditation
Texas Board of Nurse Examiners, National
League for Nursing Accrediting Commission
(NLNAC)

Acceptance rate		15.2%
Faculty-student ratio		1: 6
Faculty	Full time	14
	Part time	8

Degrees conferred
Associate Degree

Tuition[1]		
In state	$37	
Out of state	$90	
Enrollments	113	
Graduations	48	

Minimum degree required
High school diploma or GED

Student Demographics	
Female	90.3%
Under age 25	18.6%
Minority	15.2%
Part-time	0.0%

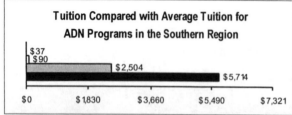

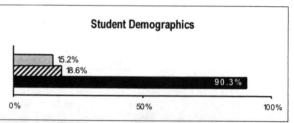

DEL MAR COLLEGE

101 Baldwin Blvd
Corpus Christi, TX 78404
(361) 698-1320
Donna Wofford, PhD, RN

www.delmar.edu/rn

Accreditation
Texas Board of Nurse Examiners, National
League for Nursing Accrediting Commission
(NLNAC)

Acceptance rate		44.2%
Faculty-student ratio		1: 13
Faculty	Full time	21
	Part time	17

Degrees conferred
Associate Degree

Tuition		
In state	$1,850	
Out of state	$5,960	
Enrollments	377	
Graduations	133	

Minimum degree required
High school diploma or GED

Student Demographics	
Female	84.1%
Under age 25	33.2%
Minority	47.6%
Part-time	98.1%

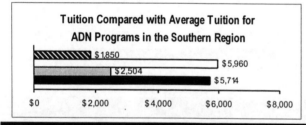

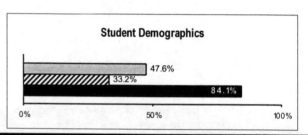

EL CENTRO COLLEGE

801 Main Street
Dallas, TX 75202
(214) 860-2414
Sondra Flemming, RN

www.elcentrocollege.edu

Accreditation
Texas Board of Nurse Examiners, National
League for Nursing Accrediting Commission
(NLNAC)

Acceptance rate	45.5%

Degrees conferred
Associate Degree

Tuition		
In state	$1,534	
Out of state	$4,484	
Enrollments	461	
Graduations	128	

Student Demographics	
Female	86.6%
Under age 25	28.0%
Minority	50.4%
Part-time	0.0%

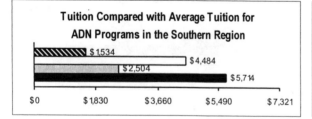

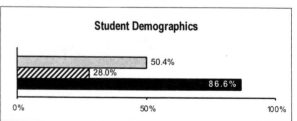

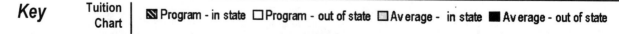

Key | Tuition Chart | ▧ Program - in state ☐ Program - out of state ▨ Average - in state ■ Average - out of state

Texas

EL PASO COMMUNITY COLLEGE - El Paso

PO Box 20500
El Paso, TX 79998
(915) 831-4530
Anita Rhodes, MSN, RN

www.epcc.edu

Accreditation
Texas Board of Nurse Examiners, National
League for Nursing Accrediting Commission
(NLNAC)

At the request of this nursing school, publication has been witheld.
Please contact the school directly for more information.

GALVESTON COLLEGE — *Useful Facts*

4015 Ave Q
Galveston, TX 77550
(409) 944-1387
Lillian Barron, RN, MSN, FNP

www.gc.edu

Accreditation
Texas Board of Nurse Examiners, National
League for Nursing Accrediting Commission
(NLNAC)

Acceptance rate	52.0%	**Tuition**		**Student Demographics**	
Faculty-student ratio	1: 7	In state	$900	Female	89.4%
Faculty Full time	17	Out of state	$1,800	Under age 25	29.8%
Part time	7	**Enrollments**	141	Minority	41.8%
		Graduations	57	Part-time	0.0%

Degrees conferred
Associate Degree

Minimum degree required
High school diploma or GED

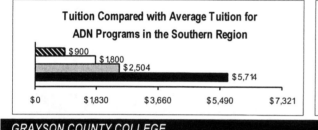

Tuition Compared with Average Tuition for ADN Programs in the Southern Region

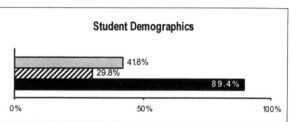

Student Demographics

GRAYSON COUNTY COLLEGE — *Useful Facts*

6101 Grayson Drive
Denison, TX 75020
(903) 786-9596
Dickie Gerig, RN, MS

www.grayson.edu

Accreditation
Texas Board of Nurse Examiners, National
League for Nursing Accrediting Commission
(NLNAC)

Acceptance rate	31.5%	**Tuition**[1]		**Student Demographics**	
Faculty-student ratio	1: 12	In state	$42	Female	90.8%
Faculty Full time	16	Out of state	$210	Under age 25	39.2%
Part time	3	**Enrollments**	217	Minority	21.2%
		Graduations	67	Part-time	82.0%

Degrees conferred
Associate Degree

Minimum degree required
High school diploma or GED

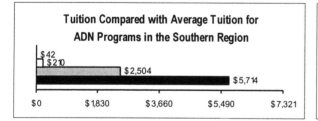

Tuition Compared with Average Tuition for ADN Programs in the Southern Region

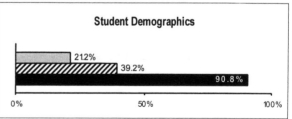

Student Demographics

Demographics Chart	■Female ▨Under age 25 ☐Minority	Distance Learning	[1]The tuition reported for this program may be not be annualized. *Data reported between 2001 and 2004.

Texas

HOUSTON BAPTIST UNIVERSITY
Useful Facts

7502 Fondren Road
Houston, TX 77074
(281) 649-3300
Nancy Yuill, PhD, RN

www.hbu.edu

Acceptance rate		6.8%
Faculty-student ratio		1: 9
Faculty	Full time	10
	Part time	5

Tuition	
In state	$12,000
Out of state	$12,000
Enrollments	18
Graduations	6

Student Demographics	
Female	88.9%
Under age 25	50.0%
Minority	50.0%
Part-time	0.0%

Accreditation
Texas Board of Nurse Examiners, National League for Nursing Accrediting Commission (NLNAC)

Degrees conferred
Associate Degree

Minimum degree required
High school diploma or GED

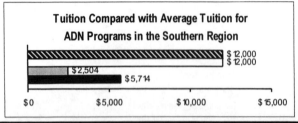

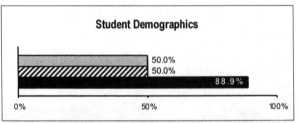

HOUSTON COMMUNITY COLLEGE SYSTEM

1900 Pressler Dr, Ste 344
Houston, TX 77030
(713) 718-7230
Roger Kline, MS, RN, MBA, BSN

www.hccs.edu

| Faculty | Full time | 21 |
| | Part time | 19 |

Accreditation
Texas Board of Nurse Examiners

Degrees conferred
Associate Degree

HOWARD COLLEGE - Big Spring

1001 N Birdwell
Big Spring, TX 79720
(432) 264-5107
Jessica Greni, RN, MSN

www.howardcollege.edu

Acceptance rate		14.5%
Faculty-student ratio		1: 7
Faculty	Full time	3
	Part time	1

Tuition	
In state	$1,020
Out of state	$1,840
Enrollments	25
Graduations	9

Student Demographics	
Female	76.0%
Under age 25	28.0%
Minority	36.0%
Part-time	0.0%

Accreditation
Texas Board of Nurse Examiners, National League for Nursing Accrediting Commission (NLNAC)

Degrees conferred
Associate Degree

Minimum degree required
High school diploma or GED

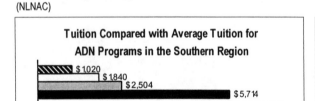

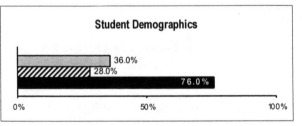

Key | Tuition Chart | ▨ Program - in state ☐ Program - out of state ▧ Average - in state ■ Average - out of state

Texas

KILGORE COLLEGE
Useful Facts

300 South High Street
Longview, TX 75601
(903) 753-2642
Barbara Brush, RN, BSN

www.kilgore.edu

Accreditation
Texas Board of Nurse Examiners, National
League for Nursing Accrediting Commission
(NLNAC)

Acceptance rate	28.0%

Degrees conferred
Associate Degree

Tuition
In state	$1,050
Out of state	$7,650
Enrollments	112
Graduations	46

Minimum degree required
High school diploma or GED

Student Demographics
Female	89.3%
Under age 25	26.8%
Minority	23.2%
Part-time	1.8%

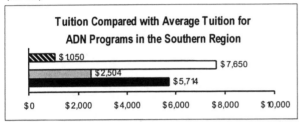

Tuition Compared with Average Tuition for ADN Programs in the Southern Region

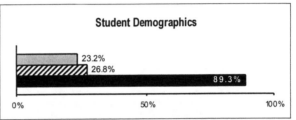

Student Demographics

LAMAR STATE COLLEGE - ORANGE
Useful Facts*

410 W Front Street
Orange, TX 77630
(409) 882-3307
Leah McGee, RN, MEd, MSN, C-FNP

www.orange.lamar.edu/nursing

Accreditation
Texas Board of Nurse Examiners

Acceptance rate	33.3%

Degrees conferred
Associate Degree

Tuition
In state	$2,760
Out of state	$10,536
Enrollments	40
Graduations	29

Student Demographics
Female	80.0%
Minority	30.0%
Part-time	0.0%

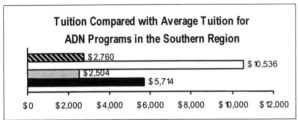

Tuition Compared with Average Tuition for ADN Programs in the Southern Region

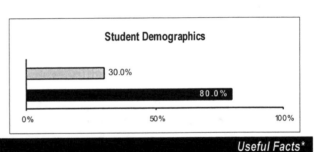

Student Demographics

LAMAR STATE COLLEGE - PORT ARTHUR
Useful Facts*

1500 Procter
Port Arthur, TX 77641
(409) 984-6354
Janet Hamilton, RN, MSN

www.pa.lamar.edu

Accreditation
Texas Board of Nurse Examiners

Acceptance rate		50.0%
Faculty-student ratio		1: 2
Faculty	Full time	14
	Part time	1

Degrees conferred
Associate Degree

Tuition
In state	$3,330
Out of state	$11,610
Enrollments	36
Graduations	27

Student Demographics
Female	75.0%
Under age 25	25.0%
Minority	30.3%
Part-time	100.0%

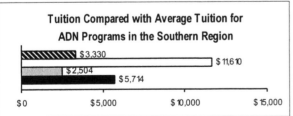

Tuition Compared with Average Tuition for ADN Programs in the Southern Region

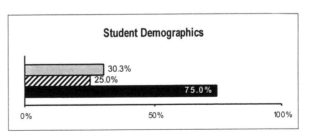

Student Demographics

Demographics Chart	■Female ▨Under age 25 ▢Minority	Distance Learning	†The tuition reported for this program may be not be annualized. *Data reported between 2001 and 2004.

Texas

LAMAR UNIVERSITY · Useful Facts

PO Box 10081
Beaumont, TX 77710
(409) 880-8817
Eileen Curl, PhD, RN

dept.lamar.edu/nursing

Accreditation
Texas Board of Nurse Examiners, National
League for Nursing Accrediting Commission
(NLNAC)

Acceptance rate	23.0%
Faculty-student ratio	1: 9
Faculty Full time	33
Part time	2

Degrees conferred
Associate Degree

Tuition	
In state	$3,834
Out of state	$10,458
Enrollments	87
Graduations	38

Minimum degree required
High school diploma or GED

Student Demographics	
Female	78.2%
Under age 25	27.6%
Minority	31.8%
Part-time	3.4%

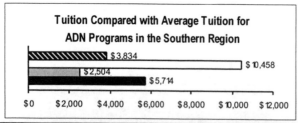

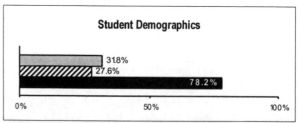

LAREDO COMMUNITY COLLEGE · Useful Facts

W End Washington Street, Box 256
Laredo, TX 78040
(956) 721-5262
Dianna Miller, MSN, RN

www.laredo.edu

Accreditation
Texas Board of Nurse Examiners, National
League for Nursing Accrediting Commission
(NLNAC)

Acceptance rate	72.0%
Faculty-student ratio	1: 7
Faculty Full time	12
Part time	1

Degrees conferred
Associate Degree

Tuition	
In state	$960
Out of state	$2,880
Enrollments	91
Graduations	22

Minimum degree required
High school diploma or GED

Student Demographics	
Female	69.2%
Under age 25	54.9%
Minority	95.6%
Part-time	0.0%

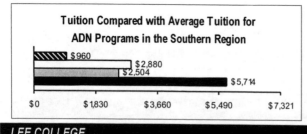

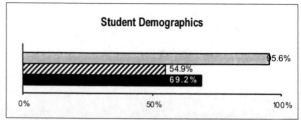

LEE COLLEGE · Useful Facts

511 S Whiting
Baytown, TX 77520
(281) 425-6449
Judy Etzel, MS, RN

www.lee.edu

Accreditation
Texas Board of Nurse Examiners, National
League for Nursing Accrediting Commission
(NLNAC)

Acceptance rate	25.0%
Faculty-student ratio	1: 14
Faculty Full time	10
Part time	4

Degrees conferred
Associate Degree

Tuition	
In state	$750
Out of state	$2,550
Enrollments	171
Graduations	44

Minimum degree required
High school diploma or GED

Student Demographics	
Female	80.7%
Under age 25	18.7%
Minority	57.6%
Part-time	0.0%

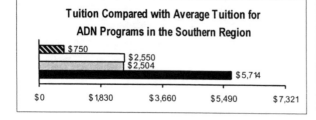

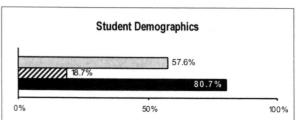

Key	Tuition Chart	▨ Program - in state ☐ Program - out of state ▨ Average - in state ■ Average - out of state

Texas

MCLENNAN COMMUNITY COLLEGE — *Useful Facts*

1400 College Dr
Waco, TX 76708
(254) 299-8349
Cherry Beckworth, RN, PhD

www.mclennan.edu/departments/hsp/adn

Accreditation
Texas Board of Nurse Examiners, National League for Nursing Accrediting Commission (NLNAC)

Acceptance rate	22.5%
Faculty-student ratio	1: 11
Faculty Full time	20
Part time	1

Degrees conferred
Associate Degree, LPN or LVN

Tuition	
In state	$1,590
Out of state	$3,390
Enrollments	231
Graduations	136

Minimum degree required
High school diploma or GED

Student Demographics	
Female	90.5%
Under age 25	37.2%
Minority	29.7%
Part-time	0.0%

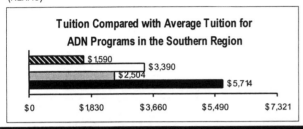

Tuition Compared with Average Tuition for ADN Programs in the Southern Region

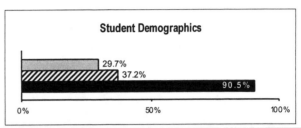

Student Demographics

MIDLAND COLLEGE - Midland

3600 North Garfield
Midland, TX 79705
(432) 685-4741
Kim Bezinque, RN-BC, MSN

midland.edu

Accreditation
Texas Board of Nurse Examiners, National League for Nursing Accrediting Commission (NLNAC)

Acceptance rate	14.1%
Faculty-student ratio	1: 11
Faculty Full time	10
Part time	5

Degrees conferred
Associate Degree

Tuition	
In state	$555
Out of state	$1,170
Enrollments	133
Graduations	66

Minimum degree required
High school diploma or GED

Student Demographics	
Female	82.0%
Under age 25	48.1%
Minority	26.2%
Part-time	40.6%

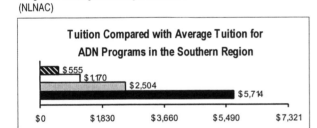

Tuition Compared with Average Tuition for ADN Programs in the Southern Region

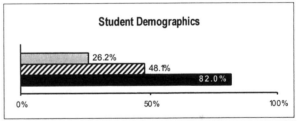

Student Demographics

NAVARRO COLLEGE - Corsicana

3200 West 7th Avenue
Corsicana, TX 75110
(903) 875-7584
Sara Washington, MS, RN

navarrocollege.edu

Accreditation
Texas Board of Nurse Examiners, National League for Nursing Accrediting Commission (NLNAC)

Acceptance rate	21.1%
Faculty-student ratio	1: 11
Faculty Full time	6
Part time	0

Degrees conferred
Associate Degree

Tuition	
In state	$605
Out of state	$1,225
Enrollments	64
Graduations	30

Minimum degree required
High school diploma or GED

Student Demographics	
Female	84.4%
Under age 25	31.3%
Minority	35.9%
Part-time	0.0%

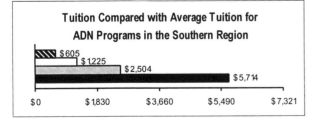

Tuition Compared with Average Tuition for ADN Programs in the Southern Region

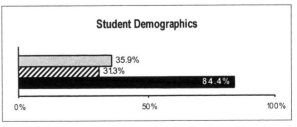

Student Demographics

Demographics Chart	■ Female ▨ Under age 25 ▢ Minority	**Distance Learning**	

¹The tuition reported for this program may be not be annualized.
*Data reported between 2001 and 2004.

Texas

NORTH CENTRAL TEXAS COLLEGE
Useful Facts

1525 W California
Gainesville, TX 76240
(940) 668-4264
Ann Blankenship, MS, RN

www.nctc.edu/what_we_teach/appsci/adn/adn.html

Acceptance rate	29.0%	
Faculty-student ratio	1: 15	
Faculty	Full time	8
	Part time	5

Tuition
In state	$1,770
Out of state	$2,730
Enrollments	157
Graduations	54

Student Demographics
Female	84.7%
Under age 25	31.2%
Minority	14.6%
Part-time	0.0%

Accreditation
Texas Board of Nurse Examiners, National League for Nursing Accrediting Commission (NLNAC)

Degrees conferred
Associate Degree

Minimum degree required
High school diploma or GED

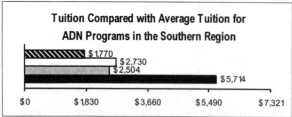

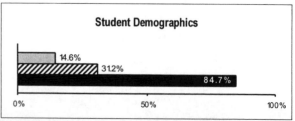

NORTH HARRIS COLLEGE - MEEP
Useful Facts

2700 WW Thorne Drive
Houston, TX 77073
(281) 618-5764
Berthine Mason, MN, RN

nursing.northharriscollege.com

Acceptance rate	23.8%	
Faculty-student ratio	1: 21	
Faculty	Full time	18
	Part time	6

Tuition
In state	$1,224
Out of state	$2,874
Enrollments	440
Graduations	156

Student Demographics
Female	93.2%
Under age 25	9.1%
Minority	34.9%
Part-time	0.0%

Accreditation
Texas Board of Nurse Examiners, National League for Nursing Accrediting Commission (NLNAC)

Degrees conferred
LPN or LVN, Associate Degree

Minimum degree required
High School diploma and 10 semester hours of Anatomy and physiology, psychology , college-level engl

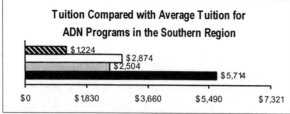

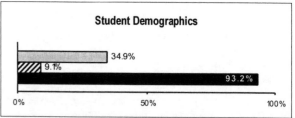

NORTHEAST TEXAS COMMUNITY COLLEGE
Useful Facts*

PO Box 1307
Mt Pleasant, TX 75455
(903) 572-1911
Cynthia Amerson, RN, MS, BSN

ntcc.edu

Acceptance rate	29.8%

Tuition
In state	$630
Out of state	$1,500
Enrollments	35
Graduations	20

Student Demographics
Female	85.7%
Under age 25	20.0%
Minority	2.9%
Part-time	0.0%

Accreditation
Texas Board of Nurse Examiners

Degrees conferred
Associate Degree

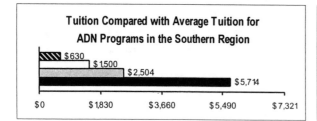

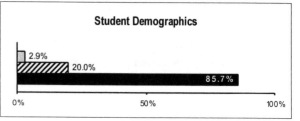

Key | Tuition Chart

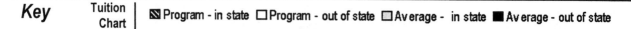

Program - in state □ Program - out of state □ Average - in state ■ Average - out of state

Texas

ODESSA COLLEGE

201 W University
Odessa, TX 79764
(432) 335-6463
Carmen Edwards, MSN, RN

www.odessa.edu/dept/nursing

Acceptance rate	81.8%	

Tuition		Student Demographics	
In state	$2,002	Female	71.5%
Out of state	$3,225	Under age 25	39.4%
Enrollments	137	Minority	45.9%
Graduations	64	Part-time	0.0%

Accreditation
Texas Board of Nurse Examiners, National League for Nursing Accrediting Commission (NLNAC)

Degrees conferred
Associate Degree

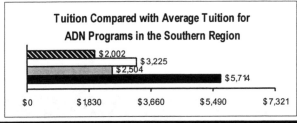

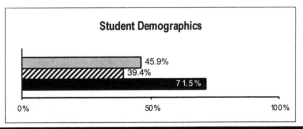

PANOLA COLLEGE - Carthage

820 W Panola
Carthage, TX 75633
(903) 694-4003
Barbara Cordell, PhD, RN

www.panola.edu

Acceptance rate	64.7%		
Faculty-student ratio	1: 7		
Faculty	Full time	15	
	Part time	2	

Tuition		Student Demographics	
In state	$630	Female	81.7%
Out of state	$630	Under age 25	38.5%
Enrollments	104	Minority	18.3%
Graduations	26	Part-time	17.3%

Accreditation
Texas Board of Nurse Examiners, National League for Nursing Accrediting Commission (NLNAC)

Degrees conferred
Associate Degree

Minimum degree required
High school diploma or GED

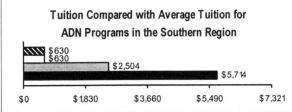

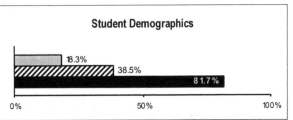

PARIS JUNIOR COLLEGE

2400 Clarksville St
Paris, TX 75460
(903) 782-0734
Marcia Putnam, RN, MSN

www.parisjc.edu

Acceptance rate	70.6%		
Faculty-student ratio	1: 10		
Faculty	Full time	6	
	Part time	0	

Tuition[1]		Student Demographics	
In state	$435	Female	89.5%
Out of state	$1,005	Under age 25	38.6%
Enrollments	57	Minority	15.8%
Graduations	43	Part-time	0.0%

Accreditation
Texas Board of Nurse Examiners, National League for Nursing Accrediting Commission (NLNAC)

Degrees conferred
Associate Degree

Minimum degree required
current LPN/LVN

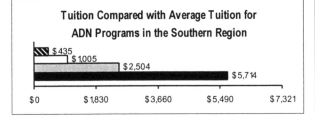

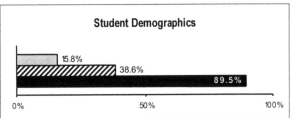

Demographics Chart	■ Female ▨ Under age 25 ▢ Minority	Distance Learning	[computer icon]	[1]The tuition reported for this program may be not be annualized. *Data reported between 2001 and 2004.

Texas

SAINT PHILIP'S COLLEGE

1801 Martin Luther King Drive
San Antonio, TX 78203
(210) 531-4730
Shirley Carson-Davis, RN, MSN, FNP, CNS

www.accd.edu/spc/spcmain/spc.htm

Accreditation
Texas Board of Nurse Examiners

Degrees conferred
Associate Degree

Tuition[1]		Student Demographics	
In state	$360	Female	85.0%
Out of state	$666	Under age 25	0.0%
Enrollments	20	Minority	65.0%
Graduations	16	Part-time	0.0%

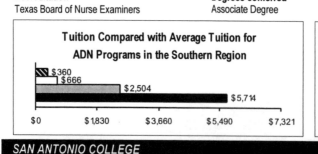

Tuition Compared with Average Tuition for ADN Programs in the Southern Region

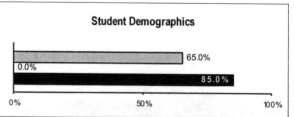

Student Demographics

SAN ANTONIO COLLEGE

1300 San Pedro Avenue
San Antonio, TX 78212
(210) 733-2375
Judy Staley, MSN, RNC, WHNP, FNP-BC

www.accd.edu/sac/nursing

Accreditation
Texas Board of Nurse Examiners, National
League for Nursing Accrediting Commission
(NLNAC)

Degrees conferred
Associate Degree

		Tuition		Student Demographics	
Acceptance rate	29.3%				
Faculty-student ratio	1: 11	In state	$1,472	Female	75.0%
Faculty Full time	44	Out of state	$5,072	Under age 25	11.7%
Part time	16	Enrollments	556	Minority	63.8%
		Graduations	293	Part-time	0.0%

Minimum degree required
High school diploma or GED

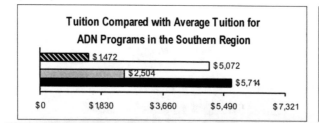

Tuition Compared with Average Tuition for ADN Programs in the Southern Region

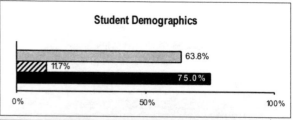

Student Demographics

SAN JACINTO COLLEGE CENTRAL

8060 Spencer Highway
Pasadena, TX 77501
(281) 476-1842
Edna Robinson, BSN, MS

www.sjcd.edu

Accreditation
Texas Board of Nurse Examiners, National
League for Nursing Accrediting Commission
(NLNAC)

Degrees conferred
Associate Degree

		Tuition		Student Demographics	
Acceptance rate	36.3%				
Faculty-student ratio	1: 15	In state	$1,110	Female	81.3%
Faculty Full time	20	Out of state	$2,775	Under age 25	41.8%
Part time	9	Enrollments	364	Minority	39.3%
		Graduations	179	Part-time	95.3%

Minimum degree required
High school diploma or GED

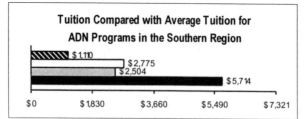

Tuition Compared with Average Tuition for ADN Programs in the Southern Region

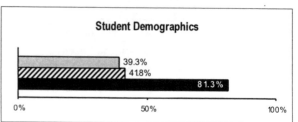

Student Demographics

Key | **Tuition Chart** | ▨ Program - in state ☐ Program - out of state ▨ Average - in state ■ Average - out of state

Texas

SOUTH PLAINS COLLEGE - Levelland

1401 College Ave
Levelland, TX 79336
(806) 894-9611
Sue Ann Lopez, RN, MSN

www.southplainscollege.edu

Accreditation
Texas Board of Nurse Examiners, National League for Nursing Accrediting Commission (NLNAC)

Acceptance rate	30.8%	
Faculty-student ratio	1 : 7	
Faculty Full time	24	
Part time	8	

Tuition	
In state	$1,712
Out of state	$2,852
Enrollments	196
Graduations	66

Student Demographics	
Female	83.7%
Under age 25	4.1%
Minority	35.2%
Part-time	0.0%

Degrees conferred
Associate Degree

Minimum degree required
High school diploma or GED

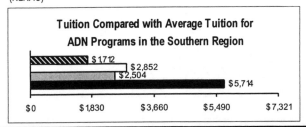
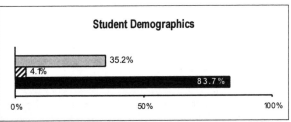

SOUTH TEXAS COLLEGE - McAllen

PO Box 9701
McAllen, TX 78501
(956) 683-3124
Paula Olesen, RN, MSN

stcc.cc.tx.us

Accreditation
Texas Board of Nurse Examiners

At the request of this nursing school, publication has been withheld.
Please contact the school directly for more information.

SOUTHWESTERN ADVENTIST UNIVERSITY   *Useful Facts*

100 W Magnolia
Keene, TX 76059
(817) 202-6235
Penny Moore, PhD, RN

www.swau.edu

Accreditation
Texas Board of Nurse Examiners, National League for Nursing Accrediting Commission (NLNAC)

Acceptance rate	49.5%	
Faculty-student ratio	1 : 8	
Faculty Full time	10	
Part time	7	

Tuition	
In state	$12,144
Out of state	$12,144
Enrollments	109
Graduations	28

Student Demographics	
Female	64.2%
Under age 25	51.4%
Minority	57.8%
Part-time	0.0%

Degrees conferred
Associate Degree

Minimum degree required
High school diploma or GED

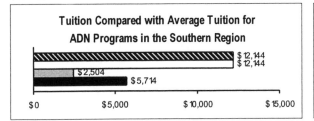
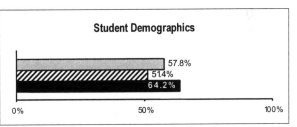

Demographics Chart	■ Female ▨ Under age 25 ☐ Minority	Distance Learning	🖥	¹The tuition reported for this program may be not be annualized. *Data reported between 2001 and 2004.

Texas

TARRANT COUNTY COLLEGE
Useful Facts

5301 Campus Drive
Fort Worth, TX 76119
(817) 515-4952
Irma Ray, RN, CS, PhD

www.tccd.edu/nursing

Accreditation
Texas Board of Nurse Examiners, National
League for Nursing Accrediting Commission
(NLNAC)

Acceptance rate		26.0%
Faculty-student ratio		1: 11
Faculty	Full time	30
	Part time	6

Degrees conferred
Associate Degree

Tuition	
In state	$1,104
Out of state	$3,600
Enrollments	368
Graduations	129

Minimum degree required
High school diploma or GED

Student Demographics	
Female	89.1%
Under age 25	26.4%
Minority	50.3%
Part-time	0.0%

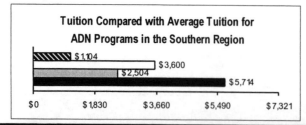

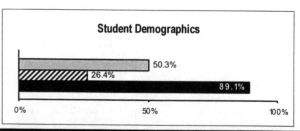

TEMPLE COLLEGE - Temple

2600 S First St
Temple, TX 76501
(254) 298-8667
Virginia Leak, MS, RN

www.templejc.edu

Accreditation
Texas Board of Nurse Examiners, National
League for Nursing Accrediting Commission
(NLNAC)

*At the request of this nursing school, publication has been withheld.
Please contact the school directly for more information.*

TEXARKANA COLLEGE
Useful Facts

2500 North Robison Rd
Texarkana, TX 75599
(903) 832-5565
Carol Hodgson, PhD, RN

www.texarkanacollege.edu

Accreditation
Texas Board of Nurse Examiners, National
League for Nursing Accrediting Commission
(NLNAC)

Acceptance rate		62.0%
Faculty-student ratio		1: 6
Faculty	Full time	22
	Part time	6

Degrees conferred
Associate Degree

Tuition	
In state	$1,400
Out of state	$2,500
Enrollments	156
Graduations	59

Minimum degree required
High school diploma or GED

Student Demographics	
Female	87.8%
Under age 25	47.4%
Minority	12.8%
Part-time	2.6%

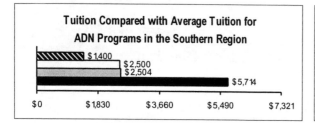

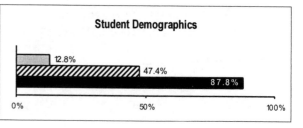

Key — Tuition Chart | ▨ Program - in state ☐ Program - out of state ▦ Average - in state ■ Average - out of state

Texas

THE UNIVERSITY OF TEXAS - BROWNSVILLE AND TEXAS SOUTHMOST COLLEGE — *Useful Facts**

80 Fort Brown
Brownsville, TX 78520
(956) 554-5071
Katherine Dougherty, EdD, RN

www.utb.edu

Acceptance rate	38.5%	

Tuition[1]
In state $26
Out of state $253
Enrollments 114
Graduations 68

Student Demographics
Female 75.4%
Under age 25 4.0%
Minority 82.5%

Accreditation
Texas Board of Nurse Examiners, National League for Nursing Accrediting Commission (NLNAC)

Degrees conferred
Associate Degree

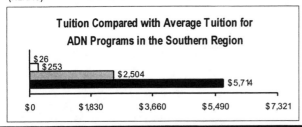

Tuition Compared with Average Tuition for ADN Programs in the Southern Region

$26
$253
$2,504
$5,714

$0 $1,830 $3,660 $5,490 $7,321

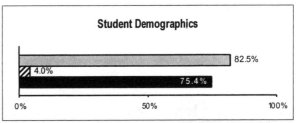

Student Demographics

82.5%
4.0%
75.4%

0%   50%   100%

TRINITY VALLEY COMMUNITY COLLEGE - *Kaufman*

800 Hwy 243 West
Kaufman, TX 75142
(972) 932-4309
Helen Reid, EdD, RN, MSN

www.tvcc.edu/healthscience

Acceptance rate 41.7%
Faculty-student ratio 1: 14
Faculty Full time 15
Part time 4

Tuition
In state $600
Out of state $1,950
Enrollments 238
Graduations 88

Student Demographics
Female 87.4%
Under age 25 27.7%
Minority 16.8%
Part-time 2.5%

Accreditation
Texas Board of Nurse Examiners, National League for Nursing Accrediting Commission (NLNAC)

Degrees conferred
Associate Degree

Minimum degree required
None

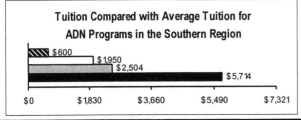

Tuition Compared with Average Tuition for ADN Programs in the Southern Region

$600
$1,950
$2,504
$5,714

$0 $1,830 $3,660 $5,490 $7,321

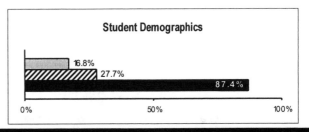

Student Demographics

16.8%
27.7%
87.4%

0%   50%   100%

TYLER JUNIOR COLLEGE - *Tyler*

1327 Baxter
Tyler, TX 75711
(903) 510-2869
Lylith Nicholson, PhD, RN

www.tjc.edu

Acceptance rate 31.5%

Tuition[1]
In state $360
Out of state $960
Enrollments 156
Graduations 56

Student Demographics
Female 76.3%
Minority 13.6%
Part-time 0.0%

Accreditation
Texas Board of Nurse Examiners

Degrees conferred
Associate Degree

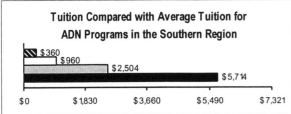

Tuition Compared with Average Tuition for ADN Programs in the Southern Region

$360
$960
$2,504
$5,714

$0 $1,830 $3,660 $5,490 $7,321

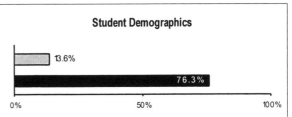

Student Demographics

13.6%
76.3%

0%   50%   100%

| Demographics Chart | ■Female ▨Under age 25 ▢Minority | Distance Learning | [1]The tuition reported for this program may be not be annualized. *Data reported between 2001 and 2004. |

Texas

VERNON COLLEGE - *Vernon*

4400 College Drive
Vernon, TX 76384
(940) 552-6291
Cathy Bolton, RN, BSN, MSN

www.vernoncollege.edu

Accreditation
Texas Board of Nurse Examiners

Degrees conferred
Associate Degree

VICTORIA COLLEGE - *Victoria*

2200 E Red River
Victoria, TX 77901
(361) 582-2551
LeAnn Wagner, RN, MSN

www.vc.cc.tx.us/dept/adn

Accreditation
Texas Board of Nurse Examiners, National
League for Nursing Accrediting Commission
(NLNAC)

*At the request of this nursing school, publication has been witheld.
Please contact the school directly for more information.*

WEATHERFORD COLLEGE   *Useful Facts*

225 College Park Drive
Weatherford, TX 76086
(817) 598-6309
Cheryl Livengood, RN, MSN

www.wc.edu

Accreditation
Texas Board of Nurse Examiners, National
League for Nursing Accrediting Commission
(NLNAC)

Degrees conferred
Associate Degree

Acceptance rate	20.3%	
Faculty-student ratio	1:7	
Faculty Full time	7	
Part time	4	

Tuition	
In state	$1,440
Out of state	$3,150
Enrollments	65
Graduations	65

Minimum degree required
High school diploma or GED

Student Demographics	
Female	89.2%
Under age 25	13.8%
Minority	9.4%
Part-time	53.8%

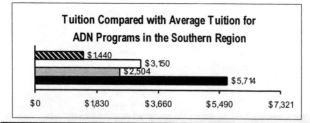

Tuition Compared with Average Tuition for ADN Programs in the Southern Region

$1,440 / $3,150 / $2,504 / $5,714

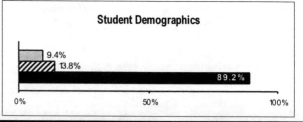

Student Demographics

9.4% / 13.8% / 89.2%

WHARTON COUNTY JUNIOR COLLEGE   *Useful Facts*

911 Boling Highway
Wharton, TX 77488
(979) 532-6404
Sarah Clark, RN, MS

wcjc.edu

Accreditation
Texas Board of Nurse Examiners

Degrees conferred
Associate Degree

Acceptance rate	17.6%	
Faculty-student ratio	1:12	
Faculty Full time	5	
Part time	0	

Tuition	
In state	$960
Out of state	$1,920
Enrollments	59
Graduations	24

Minimum degree required
High school diploma or GED

Student Demographics	
Female	89.8%
Under age 25	28.8%
Minority	25.9%
Part-time	0.0%

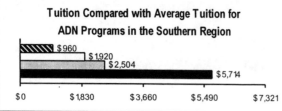

Tuition Compared with Average Tuition for ADN Programs in the Southern Region

$960 / $1,920 / $2,504 / $5,714

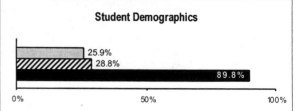

Student Demographics

25.9% / 28.8% / 89.8%

Key | Tuition Chart | ⧄ Program - in state ☐ Program - out of state ▨ Average - in state ■ Average - out of state

Utah

COLLEGE OF EASTERN UTAH   *Useful Facts*

451 East 400 North
Price, UT 84501
(435) 613-5347
Frances Swasey, RN, MN

www.ceu.edu/nursing

Acceptance rate	68.8%	
Faculty-student ratio	1: 3	
Faculty Full time	7	
Part time	0	

Tuition		**Student Demographics**	
In state	$1,611	Female	85.7%
Out of state	$6,752	Under age 25	38.1%
Enrollments	21	Minority	9.5%
Graduations	37	Part-time	0.0%

Accreditation
Utah State Board of Nursing, National League for
Nursing Accrediting Commission (NLNAC)

Degrees conferred
Associate Degree

Minimum degree required
LPN

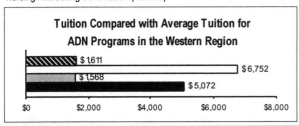
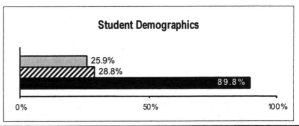

DIXIE STATE COLLEGE   *Useful Facts**

225 S 700 E
St George, UT 84770
(435) 652-7854
Jayne Moore, PhD, RN

www.dixie.edu/health

Acceptance rate	97.6%	
Faculty-student ratio	1: 3	
Faculty Full time	8	
Part time	15	

Tuition		**Student Demographics**	
In state	$1,524	Female	87.5%
Out of state	$6,672	Under age 25	42.5%
Enrollments	40		
Graduations	38	Part-time	0.0%

Accreditation
Utah State Board of Nursing, National League for
Nursing Accrediting Commission (NLNAC)

Degrees conferred
Associate Degree

Minimum degree required
LPN license

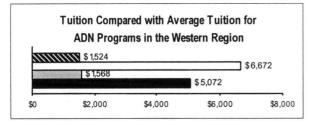
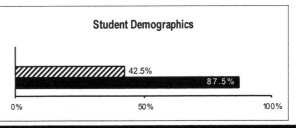

SALT LAKE COMMUNITY COLLEGE   *Useful Facts**

PO Box 30808
Salt Lake City, UT 84130
(801) 957-4043
Betty Damask-Bemenek, MN, RN

www.slcc.edu

Acceptance rate	62.9%

Tuition		**Student Demographics**	
In state	$2,175	Female	75.7%
Out of state	$6,674	Under age 25	11.0%
Enrollments	280	Minority	21.2%
Graduations	164	Part-time	0.0%

Accreditation
Utah State Board of Nursing, National League for
Nursing Accrediting Commission (NLNAC)

Degrees conferred
Associate Degree

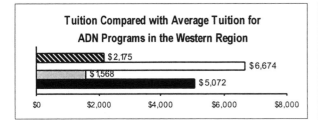
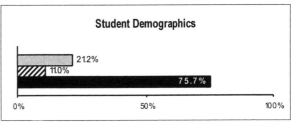

Demographics Chart	■Female ☒Under age 25 ☐Minority	Distance Learning	¹The tuition reported for this program may be not be annualized.
			*Data reported between 2001 and 2004.

Associate Degree Programs

Utah

800 West University Parkway
Orem, UT 84058
(801) 863-8192
Gary Measom, APRN, PhD
www.uvsc.edu/nurs

Acceptance rate		18.9%
Faculty-student ratio		1: 14
Faculty	Full time	18
	Part time	4

Tuition
In state	$2,580
Out of state	$9,030
Enrollments	230
Graduations	96

Student Demographics
Female	76.1%
Under age 25	52.6%
Minority	4.8%
Part-time	0.0%

Accreditation
Utah State Board of Nursing, National League for Nursing Accrediting Commission (NLNAC)

Degrees conferred
Associate Degree

Minimum degree required
Associate degree in a non-nursing field

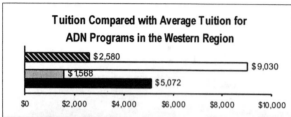

Tuition Compared with Average Tuition for ADN Programs in the Western Region

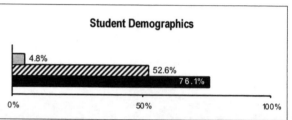

Student Demographics

3903 University Ave
Ogden, UT 84408
(801) 626-6833
Catherine Earl, postdoc, DPA, MSN, RN
www.weber.edu

Acceptance rate		32.7%
Faculty-student ratio		1: 9
Faculty	Full time	37
	Part time	4

Tuition
In state	$2,573
Out of state	$9,008
Enrollments	366
Graduations	331

Student Demographics
Female	87.2%
Under age 25	70.2%
Minority	7.1%
Part-time	0.0%

Accreditation
Utah State Board of Nursing, National League for Nursing Accrediting Commission (NLNAC)

Degrees conferred
Associate Degree

Minimum degree required
High school diploma or GED

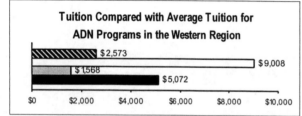

Tuition Compared with Average Tuition for ADN Programs in the Western Region

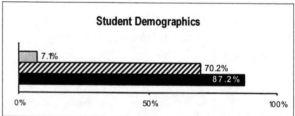

Student Demographics

Vermont

251 South Street
Castleton, VT 05735
(802) 468-1236
Susan Farrell, RN, MS, MAEd
www.castleton.edu/nursing

Acceptance rate	41.6%

Tuition
In state	$7,186
Out of state	$13,670
Enrollments	144
Graduations	36

Student Demographics
Female	91.7%
Under age 25	29.0%
Part-time	54.9%

Accreditation
Vermont State Board of Nursing, National League for Nursing Accrediting Commission (NLNAC)

Degrees conferred
Associate Degree

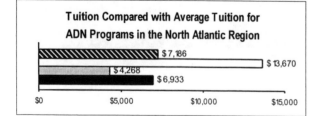

Tuition Compared with Average Tuition for ADN Programs in the North Atlantic Region

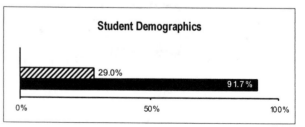

Student Demographics

Key | Tuition Chart | ▨ Program - in state ☐ Program - out of state ▨ Average - in state ■ Average - out of state

Vermont

SOUTHERN VERMONT COLLEGE

982 Mansion Dr
Bennington, VT 05201
(802) 447-4661
Holly Madison, MSN, BS

www.suc.edu/suc/index.htm

Enrollments	33
Graduations	24

Accreditation
Vermont State Board of Nursing, National
League for Nursing Accrediting Commission
(NLNAC)

Degrees conferred
Associate Degree

VERMONT TECHNICAL COLLEGE

PO Box 500
Randolph Center, VT 05061
(802) 447-5419
Patricia Menchini, RN, MS

www.vtc.edu

			Tuition		Student Demographics	
Acceptance rate		49.4%				
Faculty-student ratio		1: 3	In state	$7,680	Female	87.3%
Faculty	Full time	17	Out of state	$14,640	Under age 25	16.5%
	Part time	12	**Enrollments**	79	Minority	6.4%
			Graduations	65	Part-time	60.8%

Accreditation
Vermont State Board of Nursing, National
League for Nursing Accrediting Commission
(NLNAC)

Degrees conferred
Associate Degree

Minimum degree required
Practical Nursing Certificate

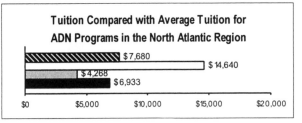

Tuition Compared with Average Tuition for ADN Programs in the North Atlantic Region
$7,680 / $14,640 / $4,268 / $6,933

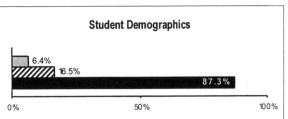

Student Demographics
6.4% / 16.5% / 87.3%

Virginia

BLUE RIDGE COMMUNITY COLLEGE - VIRGINIA

PO Box 80, 1 College Lane
Weyers Cave, VA 24486
(540) 234-9261
Loretta Wack, MSN, RN

www.br.cc.va.us/nursing

Accreditation
Virginia Board of Nursing, National League for
Nursing Accrediting Commission (NLNAC)

At the request of this nursing school, publication has been witheld.
Please contact the school directly for more information.

Demographics Chart	■ Female ☑ Under age 25 ☐ Minority	Distance Learning	💻	¹The tuition reported for this program may be not be annualized.
				*Data reported between 2001 and 2004.

Virginia

CHRV - JEFFERSON COLLEGE OF HEALTH SCIENCES
Useful Facts

PO Box 13186
Roanoke, VA 24179
(540) 224-6970
Lisa Allison-Jones, RN, MSN, PhD

www.jchs.edu

Accreditation
Virginia Board of Nursing, National League for
Nursing Accrediting Commission (NLNAC)

Acceptance rate		33.7%
Faculty-student ratio		1: 13
Faculty	Full time	14
	Part time	11

Tuition	
In state	$13,960
Out of state	$13,960
Enrollments	259
Graduations	87

Degrees conferred
Associate Degree

Minimum degree required
High school diploma or GED

Student Demographics	
Female	87.3%
Under age 25	46.7%
Minority	14.0%
Part-time	21.2%

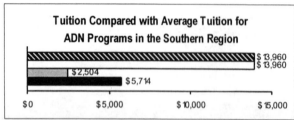

Tuition Compared with Average Tuition for ADN Programs in the Southern Region

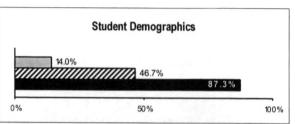

Student Demographics

DABNEY S LANCASTER COMMUNITY COLLEGE
Useful Facts

PO Box 1000
Clifton Forge, VA 24422
(540) 863-2843
Judy Coleman, MSN

www.dl.vccs.edu

Accreditation
Virginia Board of Nursing, National League for
Nursing Accrediting Commission (NLNAC)

Acceptance rate		77.8%
Faculty-student ratio		1: 7
Faculty	Full time	5
	Part time	1

Tuition	
In state	$2,040
Out of state	$6,450
Enrollments	41
Graduations	17

Degrees conferred
Associate Degree

Minimum degree required
PN preparation

Student Demographics	
Female	87.8%
Under age 25	12.2%
Part-time	65.9%

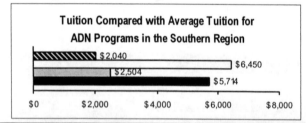

Tuition Compared with Average Tuition for ADN Programs in the Southern Region

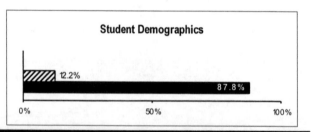

Student Demographics

GERMANNA COMMUNITY COLLEGE

2130 Germanna Highway
Locust Grove, VA 22508
(540) 423-9820
Jane Ingalls, PhD, RN

gcc.cc.va.us

Accreditation
Virginia Board of Nursing, National League for
Nursing Accrediting Commission (NLNAC)

*At the request of this nursing school, publication has been witheld.
Please contact the school directly for more information.*

| **Key** | Tuition Chart | ▨ Program - in state ☐ Program - out of state ▨ Average - in state ■ Average - out of state |

Virginia

J SARGEANT REYNOLDS COMMUNITY COLLEGE
Useful Facts

PO Box 85622
Richmond, VA 23285
(804) 523-5476
Frances Stanley, MSN

www.jsr.vccs.edu

Acceptance rate		35.0%
Faculty-student ratio		1: 13
Faculty	Full time	18
	Part time	18

Tuition	
In state	$2,123
Out of state	$6,546
Enrollments	340
Graduations	162

Student Demographics	
Female	88.2%
Under age 25	40.9%
Minority	38.0%
Part-time	52.9%

Accreditation
Virginia Board of Nursing, National League for
Nursing Accrediting Commission (NLNAC)

Degrees conferred
Associate Degree

Minimum degree required
High school diploma or GED

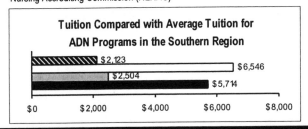

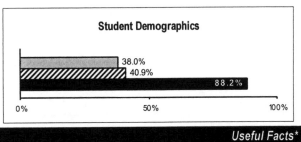

JOHN TYLER COMMUNITY COLLEGE
Useful Facts*

13101 Jefferson Davis Highway
Chester, VA 23831
(804) 706-5102
Barbara Laird, EdD, APRN, BC

www.jt.cc.va.us

Acceptance rate	84.4%

Tuition	
In state	$2,006
Out of state	$6,429
Enrollments	236
Graduations	84

Student Demographics	
Female	94.1%
Under age 25	15.0%
Minority	35.0%
Part-time	39.0%

Accreditation
Virginia Board of Nursing, National League for
Nursing Accrediting Commission (NLNAC)

Degrees conferred
Associate Degree

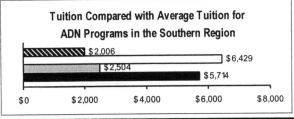

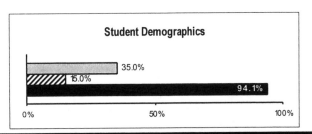

LORD FAIRFAX COMMUNITY COLLEGE - Middletown

173 Skirmisher Lane
Middleton, VA 22645
(540) 868-7281
Kathleen Wotring, RN, MSN

lf.vccs.edu

Acceptance rate	52.8%

Tuition	
In state	$3,637
Out of state	$13,706
Enrollments	208
Graduations	54

Student Demographics	
Female	94.7%
Under age 25	22.0%
Minority	15.9%
Part-time	16.3%

Accreditation
Virginia Board of Nursing

Degrees conferred
Associate Degree

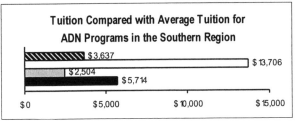

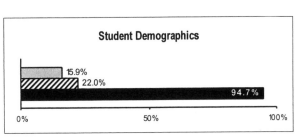

Demographics Chart	■Female ▨Under age 25 ☐Minority	Distance Learning		†The tuition reported for this program may be not be annualized. *Data reported between 2001 and 2004.

Virginia

MARYMOUNT UNIVERSITY

2807 N Glebe Road
Arlington, VA 22207
(703) 284-1580
Theresa Cappello, PhD, RN

www.marymount.edu

At the request of this nursing school, publication has been witheld.
Please contact the school directly for more information.

Accreditation
Virginia Board of Nursing, National League for
Nursing Accrediting Commission (NLNAC)

NEW RIVER COMMUNITY COLLEGE

PO Box 1127
Dublin, VA 24084
(540) 674-3600
LaRue Ridenhour, MS, RN

| **Faculty** | Full time | 2 |
| | Part time | 0 |

www.nr.cc.va.us/nursing

Accreditation
Virginia Board of Nursing

Degrees conferred
Associate Degree

NORFOLK STATE UNIVERSITY   *Useful Facts**

700 Park Avenue
Norfolk, VA 23504
(757) 823-9015
Bennie Marshall, EdD, CNA, BC

www.nsu.edu\nursing

Acceptance rate	43.5%
Faculty-student ratio	1: 21
Faculty Full time	12
Part time	12

Tuition	
In state	$4,300
Out of state	$14,255
Enrollments	381
Graduations	59

Student Demographics	
Female	94.2%
Under age 25	25.0%
Minority	93.4%
Part-time	8.1%

Accreditation
Virginia Board of Nursing, National League for
Nursing Accrediting Commission (NLNAC)

Degrees conferred
Associate Degree

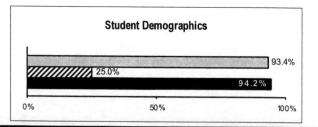

NORTHERN VIRGINIA COMMUNITY COLLEGE   *Useful Facts*

6699 Springfield Center Drive
Springfield, VA 22150
(703) 822-6580
Diane Wilson, MSN, RN

www.nvcc.edu/medical/health/nursing

Acceptance rate	83.0%
Faculty-student ratio	1: 11
Faculty Full time	20
Part time	10

Tuition¹	
In state	$68
Out of state	$220
Enrollments	281
Graduations	149

Student Demographics	
Female	87.2%
Under age 25	31.0%
Minority	37.0%
Part-time	0.0%

Accreditation
Virginia Board of Nursing, National League for
Nursing Accrediting Commission (NLNAC)

Degrees conferred
Associate Degree

Minimum degree required
High school diploma or GED

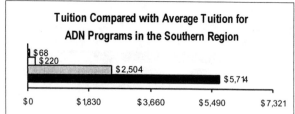

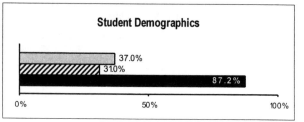

Key | Tuition Chart | ▨ Program - in state ☐ Program - out of state ☐ Average - in state ■ Average - out of state

Virginia

PATRICK HENRY COMMUNITY COLLEGE — *Useful Facts**

PO Box 5311
Martinsville, VA 24115
(276) 656-0248
Mildred Owings, MSN, RN, CS

www.ph.vccs.edu

Accreditation
Virginia Board of Nursing, National League for
Nursing Accrediting Commission (NLNAC)

Degrees conferred
Associate Degree

Acceptance rate	37.8%

Tuition		Student Demographics	
In state	$1,911	Female	88.4%
Out of state	$6,289	Under age 25	10.4%
Enrollments	95	Minority	15.8%
Graduations	35	Part-time	0.0%

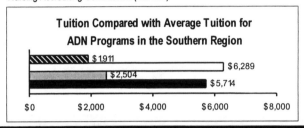

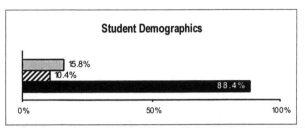

PAUL D CAMP COMMUNITY COLLEGE

PO Box 737
Franklin, VA 23851
(757) 569-6732
Candace Rogers, DSN, RN

www.pc.cc.va.us

Accreditation
Virginia Board of Nursing

Degrees conferred
Associate Degree

PIEDMONT VIRGINIA COMMUNITY COLLEGE — *Useful Facts*

501 College Drive
Charlottesville, VA 22902
(434) 961-5446
Kathleen Hudson, PhD, RN

www.pvcc.edu

Accreditation
Virginia Board of Nursing, National League for
Nursing Accrediting Commission (NLNAC)

Degrees conferred
Associate Degree

Acceptance rate		49.0%
Faculty-student ratio		1: 15
Faculty	Full time	9
	Part time	5

Tuition		Student Demographics	
In state	$2,040	Female	85.0%
Out of state	$6,420	Under age 25	34.1%
Enrollments	173	Minority	16.7%
Graduations	65	Part-time	90.2%

Minimum degree required
None

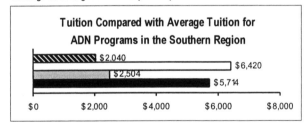

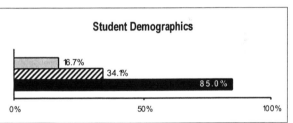

Demographics Chart	■ Female ▨ Under age 25 ☐ Minority	Distance Learning	¹The tuition reported for this program may be not be annualized. *Data reported between 2001 and 2004.

Virginia

SOUTHSIDE VIRGINIA COMMUNITY COLLEGE - *Keysville*

109 Campus Drive
Alberta, VA 23821
(434) 736-2060
Kristin Windon, RN, MSN, APRN, BC

www.southsidenurse.com

Acceptance rate		39.1%
Faculty-student ratio		1: 12
Faculty	Full time	5
	Part time	3

Tuition	
In state	$2,195
Out of state	$6,640
Enrollments	76
Graduations	21

Student Demographics	
Female	96.1%
Under age 25	31.6%
Minority	25.0%
Part-time	7.9%

Accreditation
Virginia Board of Nursing

Degrees conferred
Associate Degree

Minimum degree required
High school diploma or GED

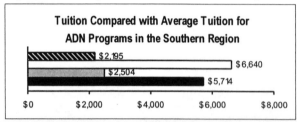

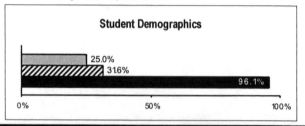

THOMAS NELSON COMMUNITY COLLEGE   *Useful Facts**

PO Box 9407
Hampton, VA 23670
(757) 825-2808
Sandra Marcuson, MS, RN

www.tncc.edu

Acceptance rate		57.5%

Tuition¹	
In state	$67
Out of state	$214
Enrollments	128
Graduations	36

Student Demographics	
Female	93.0%
Under age 25	33.0%
Minority	48.8%
Part-time	45.3%

Accreditation
Virginia Board of Nursing, National League for
Nursing Accrediting Commission (NLNAC)

Degrees conferred
Associate Degree

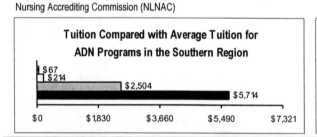

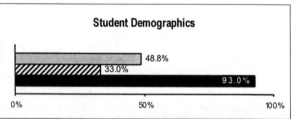

TIDEWATER COMMUNITY COLLEGE

7000 College Drive
Portsmouth, VA 23703
(757) 822-2308
Denise Bell, MSN

www.tcc.edu

Accreditation
Virginia Board of Nursing, National League for
Nursing Accrediting Commission (NLNAC)

At the request of this nursing school, publication has been withheld.
Please contact the school directly for more information.

Key	Tuition Chart	▨ Program - in state ☐ Program - out of state ▥ Average - in state ■ Average - out of state

Virginia

VIRGINIA APPALACHIAN TRICOLLEGE   *Useful Facts*

PO Box 828
Abingdon, VA 24212
(276) 739-2439
Kathy Mitchell, RN, MSN, BSN

www.me.vccs.edu/dept/ietech/nursing/index.html

Acceptance rate		45.0%
Faculty-student ratio		1: 17
Faculty	Full time	12
	Part time	18

Tuition[1]	
In state	$68
Out of state	$215
Enrollments	357
Graduations	117

Student Demographics	
Female	84.9%
Under age 25	31.9%
Minority	1.1%
Part-time	53.8%

Accreditation
Virginia Board of Nursing, National League for
Nursing Accrediting Commission (NLNAC)

Degrees conferred
Associate Degree

Minimum degree required
High school diploma or GED

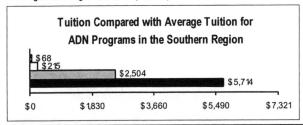

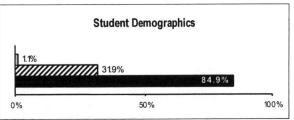

VIRGINIA WESTERN COMMUNITY COLLEGE

3097 Colonial Ave, PO Box 14007
Roanoke, VA 24038
(540) 857-6283
Martha Barnas, RN, MSN, MSEd

www.vw.vccs.edu

At the request of this nursing school, publication has been withheld.
Please contact the school directly for more information.

Accreditation
Virginia Board of Nursing, National League for
Nursing Accrediting Commission (NLNAC)

WYTHEVILLE COMMUNITY COLLEGE   *Useful Facts**

1000 East Main Street
Wytheville, VA 24382
(276) 223-4846
Rita Klimas, RN, BSN, MSN

www.wcc.vccs.edu

Acceptance rate		30.4%

Tuition[1]	
In state	$68
Out of state	$215
Enrollments	161
Graduations	96

Student Demographics	
Female	92.5%
Under age 25	38.5%
Minority	2.5%
Part-time	50.3%

Accreditation
Virginia Board of Nursing, National League for
Nursing Accrediting Commission (NLNAC)

Degrees conferred
Associate Degree

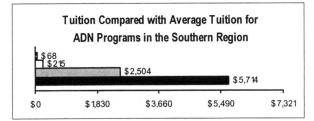

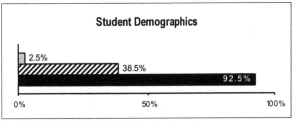

| Demographics Chart | ■Female ▨Under age 25 ▢Minority | Distance Learning | 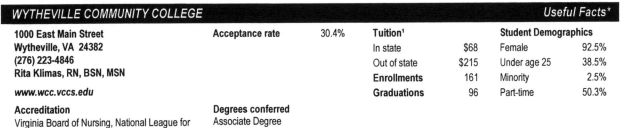 | [1]The tuition reported for this program may be not be annualized.
*Data reported between 2001 and 2004. |
|---|---|---|---|---|

Washington

BELLEVUE COMMUNITY COLLEGE
Useful Facts

3000 Landerholm Circle SE B134
Bellevue, WA 98033
(425) 564-2191
Maurice McKinnon, EdD, MA, RN

www.bcc.ctc.edu

Acceptance rate		16.3%
Faculty-student ratio		1: 13
Faculty	Full time	6
	Part time	4

Tuition	
In state	$2,523
Out of state	$7,731
Enrollments	107
Graduations	48

Student Demographics	
Female	86.0%
Under age 25	23.4%
Minority	17.8%
Part-time	0.0%

Accreditation
Washington State Nursing Care Quality
Assurance Comm., National League for Nursing
Accrediting Commission (NLNAC)

Degrees conferred
Associate Degree

Minimum degree required
High school diploma or GED

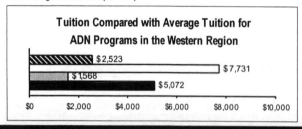

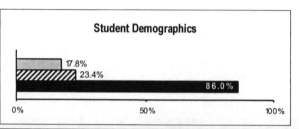

BELLINGHAM TECHNICAL COLLEGE

3028 Lindbergh Avenue
Bellingham, WA 98225
(360) 752-8433
Irene Farquhar, RN, MN

www.btc.ctc.edu

Accreditation
Washington State Nursing Care Quality
Assurance Comm.

Degrees conferred
Associate Degree

BIG BEND COMMUNITY COLLEGE
Useful Facts

7976 Bolling Street
Moses Lake, WA 98837
(509) 793-2130
Linda Wrynn, MSN, RN

www.bigbend.edu

Acceptance rate		43.8%
Faculty-student ratio		1: 7
Faculty	Full time	6
	Part time	2

Tuition	
In state	$2,592
Out of state	$3,024
Enrollments	48
Graduations	22

Student Demographics	
Female	85.4%
Under age 25	31.3%
Minority	11.4%
Part-time	0.0%

Accreditation
Washington State Nursing Care Quality
Assurance Comm., National League for Nursing
Accrediting Commission (NLNAC)

Degrees conferred
LPN or LVN, Associate Degree

Minimum degree required
High school diploma or GED

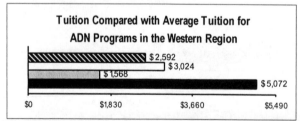

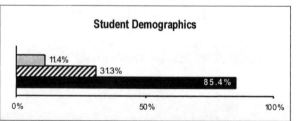

CENTRALIA COLLEGE

600 West Locust Street
Centralia, WA 98531
(360) 736-9391
Nola Ormrod, MSN, RN

www.centralia.ctc.edu

Accreditation
Washington State Nursing Care Quality
Assurance Comm.

Degrees conferred
Associate Degree

| **Key** | Tuition Chart | ▨ Program - in state   ☐ Program - out of state   ▦ Average - in state   ■ Average - out of state |

Washington

CLARK COLLEGE — *Useful Facts**

1800 East McLoughlin Boulevard
Vancouver, WA 98663
(360) 992-2192
Shelly Quint, RN, MS

www.clark.edu

Accreditation
Washington State Nursing Care Quality
Assurance Comm., National League for Nursing
Accrediting Commission (NLNAC)

Acceptance rate	6.2%

Degrees conferred
Associate Degree

Tuition
In state	$794
Out of state	$925
Enrollments	198
Graduations	78

Student Demographics
Female	89.4%
Under age 25	39.0%
Minority	7.6%
Part-time	0.0%

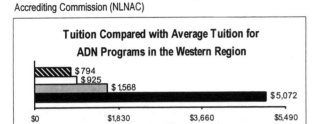

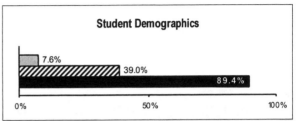

COLUMBIA BASIN COLLEGE — *Useful Facts*

2600 N 20th Avenue
Pasco, WA 99301
(509) 372-7681
Mary Hoerner, MN

www.columbiabasin.edu/nursing

Accreditation
Washington State Nursing Care Quality
Assurance Comm., National League for Nursing
Accrediting Commission (NLNAC)

Acceptance rate		47.7%
Faculty-student ratio		1: 10
Faculty	Full time	9
	Part time	1

Degrees conferred
Associate Degree

Tuition
In state	$2,502
Out of state	$3,402
Enrollments	98
Graduations	56

Minimum degree required
High school diploma or GED

Student Demographics
Female	84.7%
Under age 25	38.8%
Minority	17.3%
Part-time	0.0%

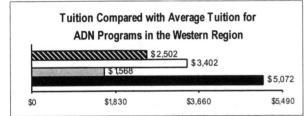

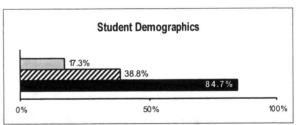

COMMUNITY COLLEGES OF SPOKANE — *Useful Facts**

N 2000 Greene St
Spokane, WA 99217
(509) 533-8622
Claudia Kroll, RN

www.pc.ctc.edu

Accreditation
Washington State Nursing Care Quality
Assurance Comm., National League for Nursing
Accrediting Commission (NLNAC)

Acceptance rate	27.5%

Degrees conferred
Associate Degree

Tuition
In state	$1,115
Out of state	$4,567
Enrollments	196
Graduations	68

Student Demographics
Female	86.2%
Under age 25	26.0%
Minority	3.1%
Part-time	32.7%

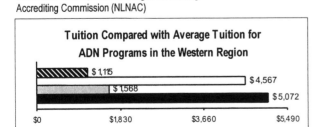

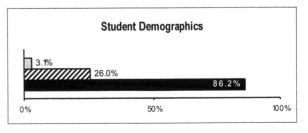

Demographics Chart	■ Female ▨ Under age 25 ☐ Minority	Distance Learning		†The tuition reported for this program may be not be annualized. *Data reported between 2001 and 2004.

Washington

EVERETT COMMUNITY COLLEGE

2000 Tower Street
Everett, WA 98201
(452) 388-9550
Patricia Black, EdD, RN

At the request of this nursing school, publication has been withheld.
Please contact the school directly for more information.

www.everettcc.edu

Accreditation
Washington State Nursing Care Quality
Assurance Comm., National League for Nursing
Accrediting Commission (NLNAC)

GRAYS HARBOR COLLEGE   *Useful Facts*

1620 Edward P Smith Drive
Aberdeen, WA 98520
(360) 538-4148
Penelope Woodruff, MS, RN

ghc.ctc.edu/nursing/index.htm

Accreditation
Washington State Nursing Care Quality
Assurance Comm., National League for Nursing
Accrediting Commission (NLNAC)

Acceptance rate	46.9%	
Faculty-student ratio	1: 5	
Faculty Full time	6	
Part time	0	

Tuition		
In state	$3,231
Out of state	$10,958
Enrollments	30
Graduations	30

Student Demographics	
Female	93.3%
Under age 25	20.0%
Minority	3.3%
Part-time	0.0%

Degrees conferred
Associate Degree

Minimum degree required
Certificate of Completion Practical Nursing

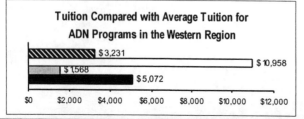

Tuition Compared with Average Tuition for ADN Programs in the Western Region

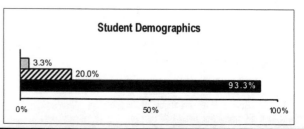

Student Demographics

HIGHLINE COMMUNITY COLLEGE   *Useful Facts**

2400 South 240th Street
Des Moines, WA 98198
(206) 878-3710
Barbara Smith, MN, RN

flightline.highline.edu/nursing

Accreditation
Washington State Nursing Care Quality
Assurance Comm., National League for Nursing
Accrediting Commission (NLNAC)

Acceptance rate	26.0%	
Faculty-student ratio	1: 8	
Faculty Full time	8	
Part time	9	

Tuition		
In state	$2,270
Out of state	$7,443
Enrollments	106
Graduations	65

Student Demographics	
Female	84.9%
Under age 25	26.4%
Minority	40.4%
Part-time	0.0%

Degrees conferred
Associate Degree

Minimum degree required
Completion of pre-requisite courses, those
earning high school and college credits
concurrently ok

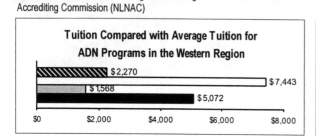

Tuition Compared with Average Tuition for ADN Programs in the Western Region

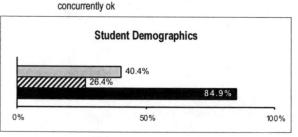

Student Demographics

Key | Tuition Chart | ▧ Program - in state ☐ Program - out of state ▨ Average - in state ■ Average - out of state

Washington

LOWER COLUMBIA COLLEGE — *Useful Facts*

1600 Maple Street
Longview, WA 98632
(360) 442-2861
Helen Kuebel, MSN, RN

lcc.ctc.edu/departments/nursing

Accreditation
Washington State Nursing Care Quality
Assurance Comm., National League for Nursing
Accrediting Commission (NLNAC)

Acceptance rate	32.5%
Faculty-student ratio	1: 13
Faculty Full time	11
Part time	5

Degrees conferred
Associate Degree

Tuition	
In state	$2,445
Out of state	$3,120
Enrollments	171
Graduations	69

Minimum degree required
High school diploma or GED

Student Demographics	
Female	81.3%
Under age 25	17.5%
Minority	9.0%
Part-time	0.0%

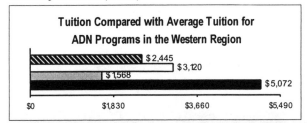

Tuition Compared with Average Tuition for ADN Programs in the Western Region
$2,445 / $3,120 / $1,568 / $5,072

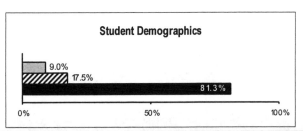

Student Demographics
9.0% / 17.5% / 81.3%

NORTH SEATTLE COMMUNITY COLLEGE — *Useful Facts**

9600 College Way North
Seattle, WA 98103
(206) 528-4562
Mary Sitterley, RN, MN, MEd

www.northseattle.edu/health/rnladder

Accreditation
Washington State Nursing Care Quality
Assurance Comm.

Faculty-student ratio	1: 2
Faculty Full time	3
Part time	13
Enrollments	23

Degrees conferred
Associate Degree

Student Demographics	
Female	87.0%
Under age 25	0.0%
Minority	34.8%
Part-time	0.0%

OLYMPIC COLLEGE — *Useful Facts*

1600 Chester Avenue
Bremerton, WA 98337
(360) 394-2757
Ellen Wirtz, MN, RN

www.oc.ctc.edu

Accreditation
Washington State Nursing Care Quality
Assurance Comm., National League for Nursing
Accrediting Commission (NLNAC)

Acceptance rate	27.2%
Faculty-student ratio	1: 9
Faculty Full time	9
Part time	6

Degrees conferred
ATA- Nursing

Tuition	
In state	$2,445
Out of state	$3,854
Enrollments	111
Graduations	51

Minimum degree required
None

Student Demographics	
Female	87.4%
Under age 25	34.2%
Minority	16.5%
Part-time	0.0%

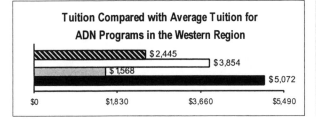

Tuition Compared with Average Tuition for ADN Programs in the Western Region
$2,445 / $3,854 / $1,568 / $5,072

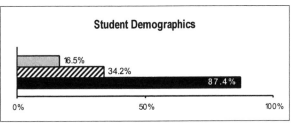

Student Demographics
16.5% / 34.2% / 87.4%

Demographics Chart	■ Female ▨ Under age 25 ▢ Minority	Distance Learning	†The tuition reported for this program may be not be annualized.
			*Data reported between 2001 and 2004.

Washington

PENINSULA COLLEGE

1502 E Lauridesen Blvd
Port Angeles, WA 98362
(360) 417-6455
Marca Davis, RN, MSN

www.pc.ctc.edu

Accreditation
Washington State Nursing Care Quality
Assurance Comm.

Degrees conferred
Associate Degree

Acceptance rate	56.8%

Tuition			Student Demographics	
In state	$2,070		Female	80.5%
Out of state	$2,467		Under age 25	20.0%
Enrollments	41		Minority	10.0%
Graduations	18		Part-time	0.0%

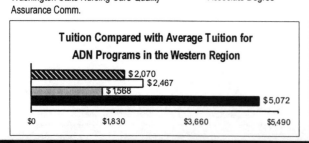

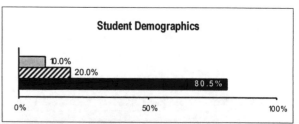

SEATTLE CENTRAL COMMUNITY COLLEGE

1701 Broadway
Seattle, WA 98122
(206) 344-4326
Maria Azpitarte, MS, RN

seattlecentral.org/profilies/pro_nursing.htm/

Accreditation
Washington State Nursing Care Quality
Assurance Comm., National League for Nursing
Accrediting Commission (NLNAC)

*At the request of this nursing school, publication has been withheld.
Please contact the school directly for more information.*

SHORELINE COMMUNITY COLLEGE

16101 Greenwood Avenue N
Greenwood, WA 98155
(206) 546-4720
Bette Perman, MN, RN

www.shoreline.edu/nurse.html

Accreditation
Washington State Nursing Care Quality
Assurance Comm., National League for Nursing
Accrediting Commission (NLNAC)

Degrees conferred
Associate Degree

Acceptance rate		18.0%
Faculty-student ratio		1: 11
Faculty	Full time	11
	Part time	12

Tuition		Student Demographics	
In state	$1,632	Female	84.5%
Out of state	$6,450	Under age 25	30.0%
Enrollments	194	Minority	17.5%
Graduations	84	Part-time	0.0%

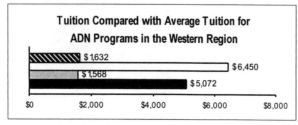

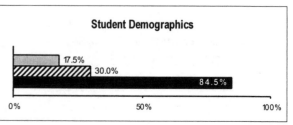

Key | Tuition Chart | ▨ Program - in state ☐ Program - out of state ▨ Average - in state ■ Average - out of state

Washington

SKAGIT VALLEY COLLEGE

2405 E College Way
Mount Vernon, WA 98273
(360) 416-7790
Cynthia Scaringe, MSN, RN

www.skagit.edu

Accreditation
Washington State Nursing Care Quality
Assurance Comm., National League for Nursing
Accrediting Commission (NLNAC)

At the request of this nursing school, publication has been witheld.
Please contact the school directly for more information.

SOUTH PUGET SOUND | Useful Facts

2011 Mottman Road South West
Olympia, WA 98512
(360) 754-7711
Marilyn Adair, MSN, RN

www.spscc.ctc.edu

Acceptance rate		31.4%
Faculty-student ratio		1: 9
Faculty	Full time	8
	Part time	6

Tuition		**Student Demographics**	
In state	$2,434	Female	80.8%
Out of state	$2,824	Under age 25	16.3%
Enrollments	104	Minority	15.0%
Graduations	35	Part-time	36.5%

Accreditation
Washington State Nursing Care Quality
Assurance Comm., National League for Nursing
Accrediting Commission (NLNAC)

Degrees conferred
LPN or LVN, Associate Degree

Minimum degree required
High school diploma or GED

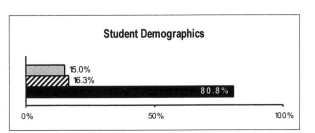

TACOMA COMMUNITY COLLEGE | Useful Facts

6501 South 19th Street
Tacoma, WA 98466
(253) 566-5225
Susan Ford, MN, RN

www.tacoma.ctc.edu/inst_dept/allied_health/nursweb/start.html

Acceptance rate		11.4%
Faculty-student ratio		1: 10
Faculty	Full time	9
	Part time	15

Tuition		**Student Demographics**	
In state	$2,543	Female	87.2%
Out of state	$7,751	Under age 25	34.8%
Enrollments	164	Minority	17.8%
Graduations	71	Part-time	17.1%

Accreditation
Washington State Nursing Care Quality
Assurance Comm., National League for Nursing
Accrediting Commission (NLNAC)

Degrees conferred
Associate Degree

Minimum degree required
30 credits of gen ed studies

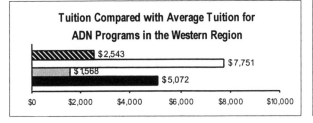
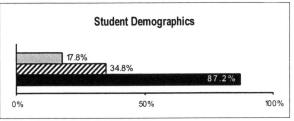

Demographics Chart	■Female ☒Under age 25 ▢Minority	Distance Learning	¹The tuition reported for this program may be not be annualized.
			*Data reported between 2001 and 2004.

Washington

WALLA WALLA COMMUNITY COLLEGE

500 Tausick Way
Walla Walla, WA 99362
(509) 527-4240
Marilyn Galusha, RN, MSN

wwcc.edu

Accreditation
Washington State Nursing Care Quality
Assurance Comm., National League for Nursing
Accrediting Commission (NLNAC)

Acceptance rate	52.5%	
Faculty-student ratio	1: 16	
Faculty Full time	12	
Part time	8	

Degrees conferred
Associate Degree

Tuition		
In state	$2,420	
Out of state	$3,520	
Enrollments	262	
Graduations	125	

Minimum degree required
High school diploma or GED

Student Demographics	
Female	83.2%
Under age 25	36.6%
Minority	7.6%
Part-time	0.0%

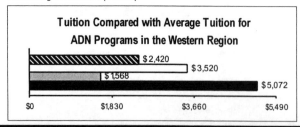

Tuition Compared with Average Tuition for ADN Programs in the Western Region
$2,420
$3,520
$1,568
$5,072
$0 $1,830 $3,660 $5,490

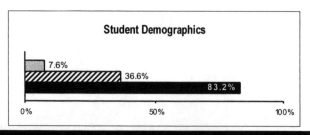

Student Demographics
7.6%
36.6%
83.2%
0%   50%   100%

WENATCHEE VALLEY COLLEGE

1300 Fifth Street
Wenatchee, WA 98801
(509) 682-6670
Linda Visser, MSN, RN

www.wvc.edu

Accreditation
Washington State Nursing Care Quality
Assurance Comm., National League for Nursing
Accrediting Commission (NLNAC)

Acceptance rate	49.1%	
Enrollments	153	
Graduations	67	

Degrees conferred
Associate Degree

Student Demographics	
Female	83.7%
Under age 25	30.0%
Minority	10.5%
Part-time	0.0%

YAKIMA VALLLEY COMMUNITY COLLEGE

S 16th Ave and Nob Hill Blvd
Yakima, WA 98907
(509) 574-4909
Rhonda Taylor, BSN, MSN

www.yvcc.edu/programs/nursing

Accreditation
Washington State Nursing Care Quality
Assurance Comm., National League for Nursing
Accrediting Commission (NLNAC)

At the request of this nursing school, publication has been witheld.
Please contact the school directly for more information.

Key | Tuition Chart | ▨ Program - in state ☐ Program - out of state ▨ Average - in state ■ Average - out of state

West Virginia

BLUEFIELD STATE COLLEGE
Useful Facts*

219 Rock Street
Bluefield, WV 24701
(304) 327-4144
Carol Cofer, MSN, MEd, RN, CS

www.bluefieldstate.edu

Accreditation
West Virginia Board of Examiners for Registered
Professional Nurses, National League for
Nursing Accrediting Commission (NLNAC)

Acceptance rate	21.1%

Degrees conferred
Associate Degree

Tuition		Student Demographics	
In state	$3,114	Female	81.4%
Out of state	$6,894	Under age 25	49.0%
Enrollments	145	Minority	6.2%
Graduations	67	Part-time	17.2%

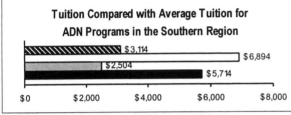

Tuition Compared with Average Tuition for ADN Programs in the Southern Region

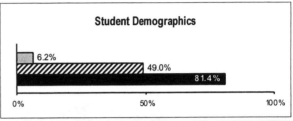

Student Demographics

DAVIS & ELKINS COLLEGE
Useful Facts

100 Campus Drive
Elkins, WV 26241
(304) 637-1314
R Cochran, DNSc, RN

www.davisandelkins.edu

Accreditation
West Virginia Board of Examiners for Registered
Professional Nurses, National League for
Nursing Accrediting Commission (NLNAC)

Acceptance rate		46.3%
Faculty-student ratio		1: 12
Faculty	Full time	6
	Part time	8

Degrees conferred
Associate Degree

Tuition		Student Demographics	
In state	$16,312	Female	86.9%
Out of state	$16,312	Under age 25	16.4%
Enrollments	122	Minority	4.1%
Graduations	47	Part-time	0.8%

Minimum degree required
High school diploma or GED

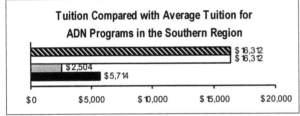

Tuition Compared with Average Tuition for ADN Programs in the Southern Region

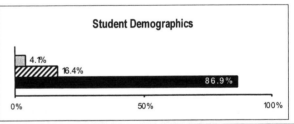

Student Demographics

FAIRMONT STATE COLLEGE
Useful Facts

1201 Locust Avenue
Fairmont, WV 26554
(304) 367-4767
Deborah Kisner, EdD, MSN, BSN,RN

www.fairmontstate.edu

Accreditation
West Virginia Board of Examiners for Registered
Professional Nurses, National League for
Nursing Accrediting Commission (NLNAC)

Acceptance rate		32.4%
Faculty-student ratio		1: 11
Faculty	Full time	14
	Part time	2

Degrees conferred
Associate Degree

Tuition		Student Demographics	
In state	$3,640	Female	87.0%
Out of state	$7,874	Under age 25	58.6%
Enrollments	169	Minority	2.4%
Graduations	75	Part-time	26.6%

Minimum degree required
High school diploma or GED

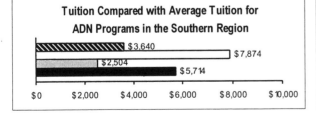

Tuition Compared with Average Tuition for ADN Programs in the Southern Region

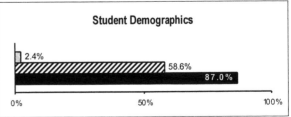

Student Demographics

Demographics Chart	■ Female ▨ Under age 25 ☐ Minority	Distance Learning		†The tuition reported for this program may be not be annualized. *Data reported between 2001 and 2004.

West Virginia

SHEPHERD COLLEGE

PO Box 3210
Shepherdstown, WV 25443
(304) 876-5341
Kathleen Gaberson, PhD, RN, CNOR, CNE

At the request of this nursing school, publication has been witheld.
Please contact the school directly for more information.

www.shepherd.edu

Accreditation
West Virginia Board of Examiners for Registered
Professional Nurses, National League for
Nursing Accrediting Commission (NLNAC)

SOUTHERN WEST VIRGINIA COMMUNITY AND TECHNICAL COLLEGE · *Useful Facts*

PO Box 2900
Mount Gay, WV 25637
(304) 792-7098
Pamela Alderman, MSN

www.southern.wvnet.edu

Acceptance rate	24.6%	
Faculty-student ratio	1: 11	
Faculty Full time	14	
Part time	2	

Tuition		**Student Demographics**	
In state	$1,634	Female	77.9%
Out of state	$6,486	Under age 25	37.8%
Enrollments	172	Minority	2.3%
Graduations	84	Part-time	0.0%

Accreditation
West Virginia Board of Examiners for Registered
Professional Nurses, National League for
Nursing Accrediting Commission (NLNAC)

Degrees conferred
Associate Degree

Minimum degree required
High school diploma or GED

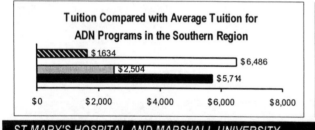

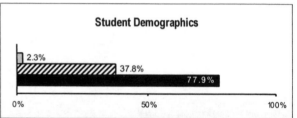

ST MARY'S HOSPITAL AND MARSHALL UNIVERSITY · *Useful Facts*

2900 First Avenue
Huntington, WV 25702
(304) 526-1415
Shelia Kyle, ASN, BSN, MS, MSN, EdD

www.stmarys.org/school_of_nursing.html

Acceptance rate	31.4%	
Faculty-student ratio	1: 10	
Faculty Full time	17	
Part time	1	

Tuition		**Student Demographics**	
In state	$4,000	Female	81.9%
Out of state	$6,300	Under age 25	44.0%
Enrollments	182	Minority	2.2%
Graduations	87	Part-time	3.8%

Accreditation
West Virginia Board of Examiners for Registered
Professional Nurses, National League for
Nursing Accrediting Commission (NLNAC)

Degrees conferred
Associate Degree

Minimum degree required
High school diploma or GED

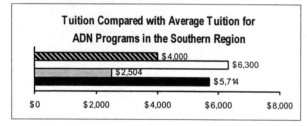

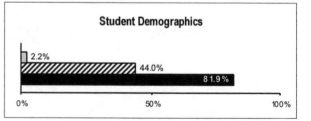

West Virginia

UNIVERSITY OF CHARLESTON — *Useful Facts**

2300 McCorkle Avenue, SE
Charleston, WV 25304
(304) 357-4835
Sandra Bowles, EdD, RN

www.ucwv.edu

Acceptance rate	44.8%	

Tuition		**Student Demographics**	
In state	$19,400	Female	75.9%
Out of state	$19,400	Under age 25	20.0%
Enrollments	54	Minority	10.0%
Graduations	54	Part-time	14.8%

Accreditation
West Virginia Board of Examiners for Registered
Professional Nurses, National League for
Nursing Accrediting Commission (NLNAC)

Degrees conferred
Associate Degree

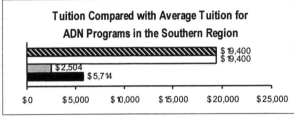
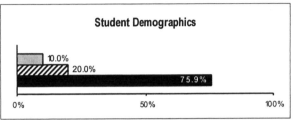

WEST VIRGINIA NORTHERN COMMUNITY COLLEGE — *Useful Facts**

1704 Market Street
Wheeling, WV 26003
(304) 233-5900
Linda Shelek, MSN, WHNP, CFNP

www.northern.edu/ai/schoolnursing

Acceptance rate	53.4%	

Tuition		**Student Demographics**	
In state	$1,680	Female	87.9%
Out of state	$5,592	Under age 25	10.0%
Enrollments	199		
Graduations	53	Part-time	0.0%

Accreditation
West Virginia Board of Examiners for Registered
Professional Nurses, National League for
Nursing Accrediting Commission (NLNAC)

Degrees conferred
Associate Degree

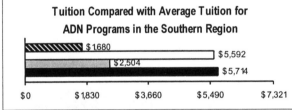
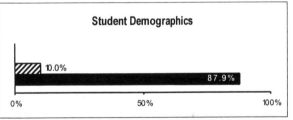

WEST VIRGINIA UNIVERSITY OF PARKERSBURG — *Useful Facts*

300 Campus Drive
Parkersburg, WV 26101
(304) 424-8300
Alita Sellers, PhD, RN

www.wvup.edu/nursing

Acceptance rate	35.9%	
Faculty-student ratio	1:9	
Faculty Full time	11	
Part time	7	

Tuition		**Student Demographics**	
In state	$834	Female	93.8%
Out of state	$2,946	Under age 25	61.5%
Enrollments	130	Minority	100.0%
Graduations	58	Part-time	0.0%

Accreditation
West Virginia Board of Examiners for Registered
Professional Nurses, National League for
Nursing Accrediting Commission (NLNAC)

Degrees conferred
Associate Degree

Minimum degree required
High school diploma or GED

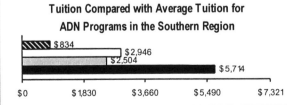
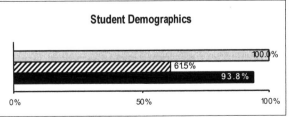

Demographics Chart	■ Female ⊠ Under age 25 ☐ Minority	**Distance Learning** 💻	¹The tuition reported for this program may be not be annualized. *Data reported between 2001 and 2004.

Wisconsin

BLACKHAWK TECHNICAL COLLEGE

6004 Prairie Road
Janesville, WI 53547
(608) 757-7678
Thomas Neumann, MS, RN

www.blackhawk.edu

Accreditation
Wisconsin Department of Regulation &
Licensing, National League for Nursing
Accrediting Commission (NLNAC)

Acceptance rate	49.6%
Faculty-student ratio	1: 10
Faculty Full time	9
Part time	3

Degrees conferred
Associate Degree

Tuition	
In state	$3,145
Out of state	$15,050
Enrollments	110
Graduations	37

Minimum degree required
High school diploma or GED

Student Demographics	
Female	96.4%
Under age 25	41.8%
Minority	6.4%
Part-time	96.4%

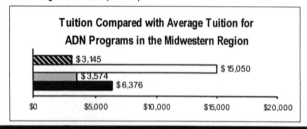

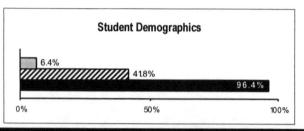

CARDINAL STRITCH UNIVERSITY

6801 North Yates Road
Milwaukee, WI 53217
(414) 410-4390
Nancy Cervenansky, PhD, RN, NCC

www.stritch.edu

Accreditation
Wisconsin Department of Regulation & Licensing

Acceptance rate	48.5%

Degrees conferred
Associate Degree

Tuition	
In state	$16,480
Out of state	$16,480
Enrollments	377
Graduations	60

Student Demographics	
Female	87.5%
Under age 25	38.7%
Minority	25.3%
Part-time	46.2%

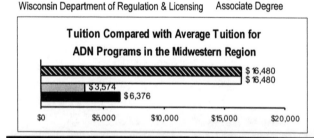

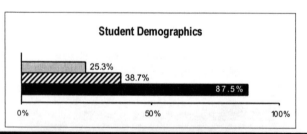

CHIPPEWA VALLEY TECHNICAL COLLEGE

620 West Clairemont Avenue
Eau Claire, WI 54701
(715) 833-6326
Ellen Kirking, RN, MSN

www.cvtc.edu

Accreditation
Wisconsin Department of Regulation &
Licensing, National League for Nursing
Accrediting Commission (NLNAC)

Acceptance rate	15.3%
Faculty-student ratio	1: 8
Faculty Full time	31
Part time	2

Degrees conferred
Associate Degree

Tuition	
In state	$3,120
Out of state	$17,860
Enrollments	269
Graduations	106

Minimum degree required
Nurse Aide Training

Student Demographics	
Female	91.1%
Under age 25	53.9%
Minority	3.4%
Part-time	75.5%

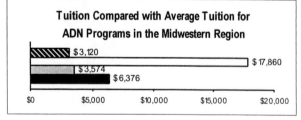

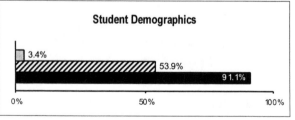

Key | Tuition Chart | ▨ Program - in state ☐ Program - out of state ▤ Average - in state ■ Average - out of state

Wisconsin

COLUMBIA COLLEGE OF NURSING

2121 East Newport Avenue
Milwaukee, WI 53211
(414) 961-4202
Katherine Dimmock, RN, MSN, EdD, JD

www.ccon.edu

Faculty-student ratio		1: 14
Faculty	Full time	14
	Part time	7

Accreditation
Wisconsin Department of Regulation & Licensing

Degrees conferred
Associate Degree

FOX VALLEY TECHNICAL COLLEGE   *Useful Facts**

1825 North Bluemound Drive
Appleton, WI 54912
(920) 831-4375
Carrie Thompson, MSN, RN

www.foxvalleytech.com/prog/nurassoc.htm

		Student Demographics	
		Female	94.3%
		Under age 25	38.0%
Enrollments	106	Minority	2.8%
Graduations	56	Part-time	67.0%

Accreditation
Wisconsin Department of Regulation & Licensing, National League for Nursing Accrediting Commission (NLNAC)

Degrees conferred
Associate Degree

GATEWAY TECHNICAL COLLEGE

3520 30th Ave
Kenosha, WI 53144
(262) 564-3074
Kathleen Russ, RN, BSN, MSN

www.gtc.edu

Accreditation
Wisconsin Department of Regulation & Licensing, National League for Nursing Accrediting Commission (NLNAC)

Degrees conferred
Associate Degree

LAKESHORE TECHNICAL COLLEGE   *Useful Facts*

1290 North Avenue
Cleveland, WI 53015
(920) 693-1661
Marilyn Kaufmann, PhD, RN

www.gotoltc.com

			Tuition		**Student Demographics**	
Acceptance rate		8.8%	In state	$2,415	Female	91.8%
Faculty-student ratio		1: 7	Out of state	$15,309	Under age 25	39.0%
Faculty	Full time	13	**Enrollments**	146	Minority	3.4%
	Part time	14	**Graduations**	50	Part-time	52.7%

Accreditation
Wisconsin Department of Regulation & Licensing, National League for Nursing Accrediting Commission (NLNAC)

Degrees conferred
Associate Degree

Minimum degree required
High school diploma or GED

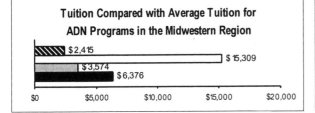

Tuition Compared with Average Tuition for ADN Programs in the Midwestern Region

$2,415
$15,309
$3,574
$6,376

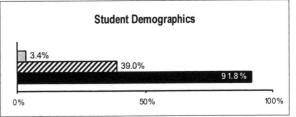

Student Demographics

3.4%
39.0%
91.8%

| **Demographics Chart** | ■ Female ▨ Under age 25 ▢ Minority | **Distance Learning** | | ⁺The tuition reported for this program may be not be annualized. *Data reported between 2001 and 2004. |

Wisconsin

MADISON AREA TECHNICAL COLLEGE
Useful Facts

3550 Anderson Street
Madison, WI 53704
(608) 246-6674
Marilyn Rinehart, MS, RN

www.matcmadison.edu

Accreditation
Wisconsin Department of Regulation &
Licensing, National League for Nursing
Accrediting Commission (NLNAC)

Acceptance rate		26.7%
Faculty-student ratio		1: 8
Faculty	Full time	31
	Part time	1

Degrees conferred
Associate Degree

Tuition	
In state	$4,838
Out of state	$13,057
Enrollments	264
Graduations	116

Minimum degree required
High school diploma or GED

Student Demographics	
Female	94.3%
Under age 25	12.1%
Minority	6.2%
Part-time	15.2%

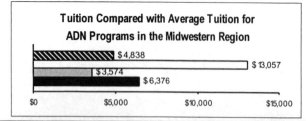

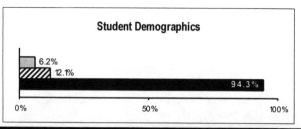

MID STATE TECHNICAL COLLEGE
Useful Facts

500 32nd Street North
Wisconsin Rapids, WI 54494
(715) 422-5510
Mary Moss, EdD, RN, MSN

www.mstc.edu

Accreditation
Wisconsin Department of Regulation &
Licensing, National League for Nursing
Accrediting Commission (NLNAC)

Acceptance rate		18.6%
Faculty-student ratio		1: 9
Faculty	Full time	16
	Part time	6

Degrees conferred
LPN or LVN, Associate Degree

Tuition	
In state	$2,300
Out of state	$4,600
Enrollments	176
Graduations	74

Minimum degree required
High school diploma or GED

Student Demographics	
Female	88.1%
Under age 25	22.2%
Minority	2.3%
Part-time	51.1%

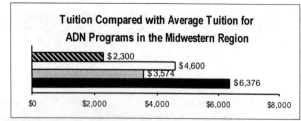

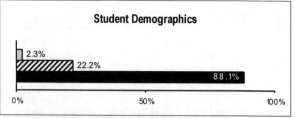

MILWAUKEE AREA TECHNICAL COLLEGE
Useful Facts

700 West State Street
Milwaukee, WI 53233
(414) 297-6241
Nancy Vrabec, PhD, RN, BC

www.matc.edu

Accreditation
Wisconsin Department of Regulation &
Licensing, National League for Nursing
Accrediting Commission (NLNAC)

Acceptance rate		77.3%
Faculty-student ratio		1: 8
Faculty	Full time	59
	Part time	25

Degrees conferred
Associate Degree

Tuition	
In state	$2,650
Out of state	$15,503
Enrollments	607
Graduations	155

Minimum degree required
High school diploma or GED

Student Demographics	
Female	89.0%
Under age 25	30.0%
Minority	37.6%
Part-time	94.1%

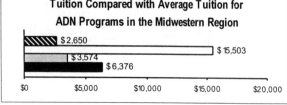

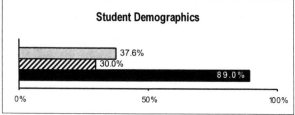

Key | Tuition Chart | ▨ Program - in state ☐ Program - out of state ☐ Average - in state ■ Average - out of state

Wisconsin

MORAINE PARK TECHNICAL COLLEGE
Useful Facts

2151 North Main Street
West Bend, WI 53090
(262) 335-5757
Anne Brett, PhD, RN

www.morainepark.edu

Accreditation
Wisconsin Department of Regulation &
Licensing, National League for Nursing
Accrediting Commission (NLNAC)

Acceptance rate		11.3%
Faculty-student ratio		1: 11
Faculty	Full time	18
	Part time	3

Degrees conferred
LPN or LVN, Associate Degree

Tuition	
In state	$2,280
Out of state	$12,363
Enrollments	208
Graduations	69

Minimum degree required
High school diploma or GED

Student Demographics	
Female	96.6%
Under age 25	14.9%
Part-time	8.7%

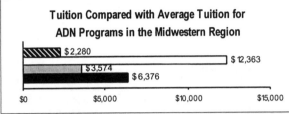

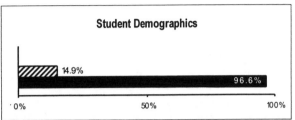

NICOLET AREA TECHNICAL COLLEGE
Useful Facts

PO Box 518
Rhinelander, WI 54501
(715) 365-4637
Lenore Mangles, MSN, RN

www.nicoletcollege.com/nursing/nursing.htm

Accreditation
Wisconsin Department of Regulation &
Licensing, National League for Nursing
Accrediting Commission (NLNAC)

Acceptance rate		28.3%
Faculty-student ratio		1: 9
Faculty	Full time	6
	Part time	0

Degrees conferred
Associate Degree

Tuition	
In state	$2,520
Out of state	$15,501
Enrollments	56
Graduations	28

Minimum degree required
High school diploma or GED

Student Demographics	
Female	92.9%
Under age 25	26.8%
Minority	1.8%
Part-time	10.7%

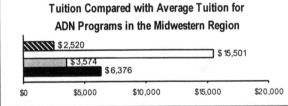

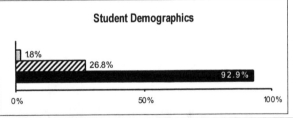

NORTH CENTRAL TECHNICAL COLLEGE
*Useful Facts**

1000 West Campus Drive
Wausau, WI 54401
(715) 675-3331
Jean Flood, MSN, RN

www.ntc.wi.us

Accreditation
Wisconsin Department of Regulation &
Licensing, National League for Nursing
Accrediting Commission (NLNAC)

Acceptance rate	9.6%

Degrees conferred
Associate Degree

Tuition[1]	
In state	$70
Out of state	$479
Enrollments	157
Graduations	57

Student Demographics	
Female	93.6%
Under age 25	46.0%
Minority	1.3%
Part-time	66.9%

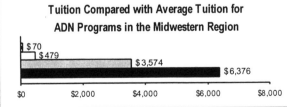

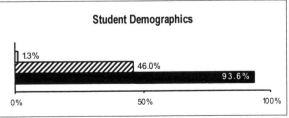

Demographics Chart	■Female ☒Under age 25 ☐Minority	Distance Learning	[1]The tuition reported for this program may be not be annualized. *Data reported between 2001 and 2004.

Wisconsin

NORTHEAST WISCONSIN TECHNICAL COLLEGE

2740 West Mason Street
Green Bay, WI 54307
(920) 498-5482
Kay Tupala, MS, RN

www.nwtc.edu

Faculty-student ratio		1: 9
Faculty	Full time	21
	Part time	19

Tuition	
In state	$2,576
Out of state	$2,718
Enrollments	286
Graduations	106

Student Demographics	
Female	94.4%
Under age 25	50.0%
Minority	3.1%
Part-time	16.8%

Accreditation
Wisconsin Department of Regulation &
Licensing, National League for Nursing
Accrediting Commission (NLNAC)

Degrees conferred
Associate Degree

Minimum degree required
High school diploma or GED

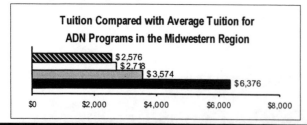
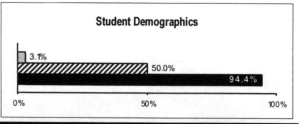

SOUTHWEST WISCONSIN TECHNICAL COLLEGE

1800 Bronson Boulevard
Fennimore, WI 53809
(608) 822-3262
Kathleen Gerrity, MSN, RN

www.swtc.edu

Acceptance rate	30.4%

Tuition	
In state	$2,528
Out of state	$14,640
Enrollments	108
Graduations	29

Student Demographics	
Female	92.6%
Under age 25	42.0%
Part-time	49.1%

Accreditation
Wisconsin Department of Regulation &
Licensing, National League for Nursing
Accrediting Commission (NLNAC)

Degrees conferred
Associate Degree

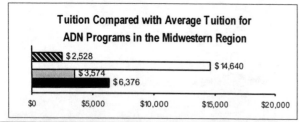
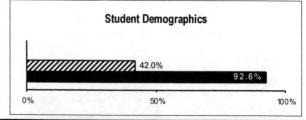

WAUKESHA COUNTY TECHNICAL COLLEGE

800 Main Street
Pewaukee, WI 53072
(262) 691-5368
Annette Severson, RN, MS

www.wctc.edu

Acceptance rate	66.7%

Tuition	
In state	$1,373
Out of state	$8,375
Enrollments	170
Graduations	44

Student Demographics	
Female	94.1%
Under age 25	30.0%
Minority	7.6%
Part-time	0.0%

Accreditation
Wisconsin Department of Regulation &
Licensing, National League for Nursing
Accrediting Commission (NLNAC)

Degrees conferred
Associate Degree

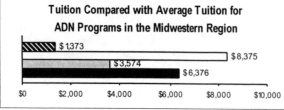
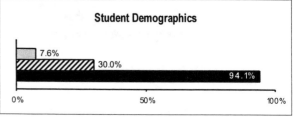

Key | Tuition Chart | ▨ Program - in state ☐ Program - out of state ☐ Average - in state ■ Average - out of state

Wisconsin

WESTERN WISCONSIN TECHNICAL COLLEGE

Useful Facts*

304 North 6th Street
La Crosse, WI 54602
(608) 785-9195
Mary Stolder, RN, MA, MS

www.wwtc.edu/adnursing

Acceptance rate	13.1%	

Tuition

In state	$2,310
Out of state	$14,640
Enrollments	120
Graduations	65

Student Demographics

Female	87.5%
Under age 25	12.0%
Minority	0.8%
Part-time	0.0%

Accreditation
Wisconsin Department of Regulation &
Licensing, National League for Nursing
Accrediting Commission (NLNAC)

Degrees conferred
Associate Degree

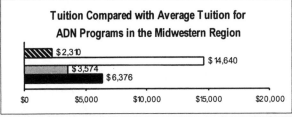

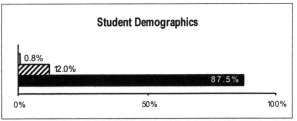

WISCONSIN INDIANHEAD TECHNICAL COLLEGE

Useful Facts*

505 Pine Ridge Drive
Shell Lake, WI 54871
(715) 468-2815
Piper Larson, MN, RN

www.witc.edu/pgmpages/nurseassoc/index.htm

Acceptance rate	64.4%	

Tuition

In state	$2,548
Enrollments	194
Graduations	50

Student Demographics

Female	94.3%
Under age 25	19.0%
Minority	2.6%
Part-time	45.9%

Accreditation
Wisconsin Department of Regulation &
Licensing, National League for Nursing
Accrediting Commission (NLNAC)

Degrees conferred
Associate Degree

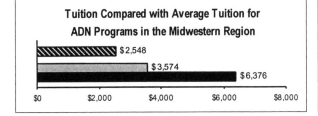

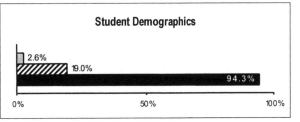

Demographics Chart	■ Female ▨ Under age 25 ☐ Minority	**Distance Learning**	¹The tuition reported for this program may be not be annualized. *Data reported between 2001 and 2004.

Wyoming

CASPER COLLEGE

125 College Drive
Casper, WY 82601
(307) 268-2717
Jolene Knaus, MS, RN

www.caspercollege.edu

| Acceptance rate | 52.8% |
| Faculty-student ratio | 1: 9 |

| Faculty | Full time | 12 |
| | Part time | 3 |

Tuition

In state	$1,536
Out of state	$4,296
Enrollments	121
Graduations	37

Student Demographics

Female	88.4%
Under age 25	26.4%
Minority	2.5%
Part-time	47.9%

Accreditation
Wyoming State Board of Nursing, National League for Nursing Accrediting Commission (NLNAC)

Degrees conferred
Associate Degree

Minimum degree required
High school diploma or GED

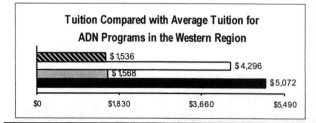

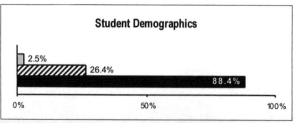

CENTRAL WYOMING COLLEGE

2660 Peck Avenue
Riverton, NA 82501
(307) 855-2226
Janet Harp, MSN, RN

cwc.edu

| Acceptance rate | 28.8% |

Tuition

In state	$1,800
Out of state	$4,440
Enrollments	61
Graduations	29

Student Demographics

Female	93.4%
Under age 25	8.0%
Minority	4.9%
Part-time	0.0%

Accreditation
Wyoming State Board of Nursing, National League for Nursing Accrediting Commission (NLNAC)

Degrees conferred
Associate Degree

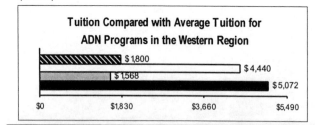

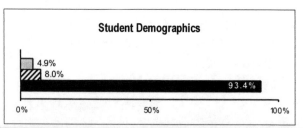

LARAMIE COUNTY COMMUNITY COLLEGE

1400 East College Drive
Cheyenne, WY 82007
(307) 778-1133
Carol Kabeiseman, MEd, MS, RN

www.lccc.wy.edu/nursing

| Acceptance rate | 48.2% |
| Faculty-student ratio | 1: 13 |

| Faculty | Full time | 10 |
| | Part time | 1 |

Tuition

In state	$1,956
Out of state	$4,716
Enrollments	137
Graduations	47

Student Demographics

Female	92.7%
Under age 25	35.8%
Minority	12.4%
Part-time	0.0%

Accreditation
Wyoming State Board of Nursing, National League for Nursing Accrediting Commission (NLNAC)

Degrees conferred
LPN or LVN, Associate Degree

Minimum degree required
High school diploma or GED

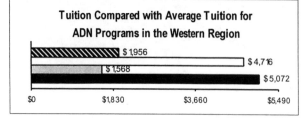

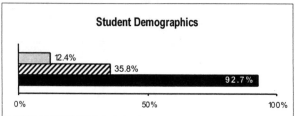

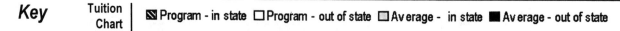

Key | Tuition Chart | ⧄ Program - in state ☐ Program - out of state ☐ Average - in state ■ Average - out of state

Wyoming

NORTHERN WYOMING COMMUNITY COLLEGE DISTRICT - Sheridan Campus

300 West Sinclair
Gillette, WY 82718
(307) 686-0254
Nancy Larmer, MSN, RN

At the request of this nursing school, publication has been witheld.
Please contact the school directly for more information.

www.sheridan.edu

Accreditation
Wyoming State Board of Nursing, National
League for Nursing Accrediting Commission
(NLNAC)

NORTHERN WYOMING COMMUNITY COLLEGE DISTRICT - Gillette Campus

300 West Sinclair
Gillette, WY 82718
(307) 686-0254
Nancy Larmer, MSN, RN

At the request of this nursing school, publication has been witheld.
Please contact the school directly for more information.

www.sheridan.edu

Accreditation
Wyoming State Board of Nursing, National
League for Nursing Accrediting Commission
(NLNAC)

NORTHWEST COLLEGE (WYOMING)   *Useful Facts*

231 West 6th Street
Powell, WY 82435
(307) 754-6479
Marlys Ohman, MN, RN

www.northwestcollege.edu

Accreditation
Wyoming State Board of Nursing, National
League for Nursing Accrediting Commission
(NLNAC)

Acceptance rate	29.9%	
Faculty-student ratio	1: 10	
Faculty Full time	5	
Part time	2	

Tuition	
In state	$1,368
Out of state	$2,064
Enrollments	62
Graduations	24

Student Demographics	
Female	83.9%
Under age 25	33.9%
Minority	3.2%
Part-time	6.5%

Degrees conferred
Associate Degree

Minimum degree required
Diploma

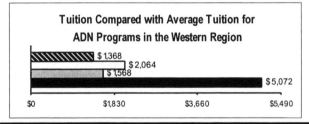

Tuition Compared with Average Tuition for ADN Programs in the Western Region
$1,368
$2,064
$1,568
$5,072
$0 $1,830 $3,660 $5,490

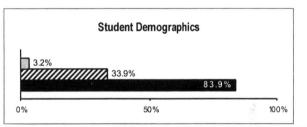

Student Demographics
3.2%
33.9%
83.9%
0%   50%   100%

WESTERN WYOMING COMMUNITY COLLEGE

2500 College Drive
Rock Springs, WY 82901
(307) 382-1801
Marlene Ethier, MS,RN

At the request of this nursing school, publication has been witheld.
Please contact the school directly for more information.

www.wwcc.cc.wy.us

Accreditation
Wyoming State Board of Nursing, National
League for Nursing Accrediting Commission
(NLNAC)

Demographics Chart	■Female ☑Under age 25 ▢Minority	Distance Learning	¹The tuition reported for this program may be not be annualized.
			*Data reported between 2001 and 2004.

Contact Information for Boards of Nursing

Alabama Board of Nursing
770 Washington Avenue   Phone: (334) 242-4060
RSA Plaza, Ste 250   FAX: (334) 242-4360
Montgomery, AL 36130-3900
N Genell Lee, MSN, JD, RN, Executive Officer
www.abn.state.al.us

Alaska Board of Nursing
550 West Seventh Avenue Suite 1500   Phone: (907) 269-8161
Anchorage, Alaska 99501-3567   FAX: (907) 269-8196
Dorothy Fulton, MA, RN, Executive Administrator

www.dced.state.ak.us/occ/pnur.htm

American Samoa Health Services
Regulatory Board   Phone: (684) 633-1222
LBJ Tropical Medical Center   FAX: (684) 633-1869
Pago Pago, AS 96799
Toaga Atuatasi Seumalo, MS, RN, Executive Secretary

Arizona State Board of Nursing
1651 E Morten Avenue, Suite 210   Phone: (602) 889-5150
Phoenix, AZ 85020   FAX: (602) 889-5155
Joey Ridenour, MN, RN, Executive Director
www.azboardofnursing.org

Arkansas State Board of Nursing
University Tower Building   Phone: (501) 686-2700
1123 S University, Suite 800   FAX: (501) 686-2714
Little Rock, AR 72204-1619
Faith Fields, MSN, RN, Executive Director
www.state.ar.us/nurse

California Board of Registered Nursing
1625 North Market Boulevard, Suite N-217   Phone: (916) 322-3350
Sacramento, CA 95834-1924   FAX: (916) 574-8637
Ruth Ann Terry, MPH, RN, Executive Officer
www.rn.ca.gov

California Board of Vocational Nurse and Psychiatric Technicians
2535 Capitol Oaks Drive, Suite 205   Phone: (916) 263-7800
Sacramento, CA 95833   FAX: (916) 263-7859
Teresa Bello-Jones, JD, MSN, RN, Executive Officer
www.bvnpt.ca.gov

Colorado Board of Nursing
1560 Broadway, Suite 880   Phone: (303) 894-2430
Denver, CO 80202   FAX: (303) 894-2821
Linda Volz, Program Director
www.dora.state.co.us/nursing

Connecticut Board of Examiners for Nursing
Dept of Public Health   Phone: (860) 509-7624
410 Capitol Avenue, MS# 13PHO FAX: (860) 509-7553
PO Box 340308
Hartford, CT 06134-0328
Jan Wojick, Board Liaison
Nancy L Bafundo, BSN, MS, RN, Board President
www.state.ct.us/dph

Delaware Board of Nursing
861 Silver Lake Blvd   Phone: (302) 739-4522
Cannon Building, Suite 203   FAX: (302) 739-2711
Dover, DE 19904
Iva Boardman, MSN, RN, Executive Director
www.professionallicensing.state.de.us/boards/nursing

District of Columbia Board of Nursing
Department of Health   Phone: (202) 724-4900
717 14th Street, NW, Suite 600 FAX: (202) 727-8241
Washington, DC 20005
Karen Scipio-Skinner, MSN, RN, Executive Director
www.dchealth.dc.gov

Florida Board of Nursing
Mailing Address: Phone: (850) 245-4125
4052 Bald Cypress Way, BIN C02 FAX: (850) 245-4172
Tallahassee, FL 32399-3252

Physical Address:
4042 Bald Cypress Way, Room 120
Tallahassee, FL 32399
Vacant, Executive Director
www.doh.state.fl.us/mqa

Georgia State Board of Licensed Practical Nurses
237 Coliseum Drive   Phone: (478) 207-1640
Macon, GA 31217-3858   FAX: (478) 207-1633
Brig Zimmerman, Executive Director
www.sos.state.ga.us/plb/lpn

Georgia Board of Nursing
237 Coliseum Drive   Phone: (478) 207-1640
Macon, GA 31217-3858   FAX: (478) 207-1660
Sylvia Bond, RN MSN, MBA, Executive Director
www.sos.state.ga.us/plb/rn

Guam Board of Nurse Examiners
Regular mailing address
PO Box 2816
Hagatna, Guam 96932

Phone: (671) 735-7406
(671) 725-7411
FAX: (671) 735-7413

Street address (for Fed Ex & UPS)
651 Legacy Square Commercial Complex,
South Route 10, Suite 9
Mangilao, Guam 96913
Lillian Perez-Posadas, Interim Executive Officer

Hawaii Board of Nursing
King Kalakaua Building
335 Merchant Street, 3rd Floor
Honolulu, HI 96813

Phone: (808) 586-3000
FAX: (808) 586-2689

Kathleen Yokouchi, MBA, BBA, BA, Executive Officer
www.hawaii.gov/dcca/areas/pvl/boards/nursing

Idaho Board of Nursing
280 N 8th Street, Suite 210
PO Box 83720
Boise, ID 83720

Phone: (208) 334-3110
FAX: (208) 334-3262

Sandra Evans, MA, Ed, RN, Executive Director
www2.state.id.us/ibn

Illinois Department of Professional Regulation
James R Thompson Center
100 West Randolph, Suite 9-300
Chicago, IL 60601

Phone: (312) 814-2715
FAX: (312) 814-3145

Vacant, Nursing Act Coordinator
www.dpr.state.il.us

Illinois Department of Professional Regulation
320 W Washington St, 3rd Floor
Springfield, IL 62786

Phone: (217) 782-8556
FAX: (217) 782-7645

Indiana State Board of Nursing
Professional Licensing Agency
402 W Washington Street, Room W072
Indianapolis, IN 46204

Phone: (317) 234-2043
FAX: (317) 233-4236

Tonja Thompson, Director of Nursing
www.state.in.us/hpb/boards/isbn

Iowa Board of Nursing
RiverPoint Business Park
400 SW 8th Street
Suite B
Des Moines, IA 50309-4685

Phone: (515) 281-3255
FAX: (515) 281-4825

Lorinda Inman, MSN, RN, Executive Director
www.state.ia.us/government/nursing

Kansas State Board of Nursing
Landon State Office Building
900 SW Jackson, Suite 1051
Topeka, KS 66612

Phone: (785) 296-4929
FAX: (785) 296-3929

Mary Blubaugh, MSN, RN, Executive Administrator
www.ksbn.org

Kentucky Board of Nursing
312 Whittington Parkway, Suite 300
Louisville, KY 40222

Phone: (502) 429-3300
FAX: (502) 429-3311

Charlotte F Beason, EdD, RN, CNAA, Executive Director
www.kbn.ky.gov

Louisiana State Board of Practical Nurse Examiners
3421 N Causeway Boulevard, Suite 505
Metairie, LA 70002

Phone: (504) 838-5791
FAX: (504) 838-5279

Claire Glaviano, BSN, MN, RN, Executive Director
www.lsbpne.com

Louisiana State Board of Nursing
3510 N Causeway Boulevard, Suite 601
Metairie, LA 70002

Phone: (504) 838-5332
FAX: (504) 838-5349

Temporary Address:
5207 Essen Lane, Suite 6
Baton Rouge, LA 70809

Phone: (225) 763-3570
(225) 763-3577
FAX: (225) 763-3580

Barbara Morvant, MN, RN, Executive Director
www.lsbn.state.la.us

Maine State Board of Nursing
Regular Mailing Address:
158 State House Station
Street Address:161 Capitol Street
Augusta, ME 04333

Phone: (207) 287-1133
FAX: (207) 287-1149

Myra Broadway, JD, MS, RN, Executive Director
www.maine.gov/boardofnursing

Maryland Board of Nursing
4140 Patterson Avenue   Phone: (410) 585-1900
Baltimore, MD 21215   FAX: (410) 358-3530
Donna Dorsey, MS, RN, Executive Director
www.mbon.org

Massachusetts Board of Registration in Nursing
Commonwealth of Massachusetts   Phone: (617) 973-0800
239 Causeway Street, Second Floor   (800) 414-0168
Boston, MA 02114   FAX: (617) 973-0984
Rula Faris Harb, MS, RN, Executive Director
www.mass.gov/dpl/boards/rn

Michigan/DCH/Bureau of Health Professions
Ottawa Towers North   Phone: (517) 335-0918
611 W Ottawa, 1st Floor   FAX: (517) 373-2179
Lansing, MI 48933
Diane Lewis, MBA, BA, Policy Manager for Licensing Division
www.michigan.gov/healthlicense

Minnesota Board of Nursing
2829 University Avenue SE   Phone: (612) 617-2270
Minneapolis, MN 55414   FAX: (612) 617-2190
Shirley Brekken, MS, RN, Executive Director
www.nursingboard.state.mn.us

Mississippi Board of Nursing
1935 Lakeland Drive, Suite B   Phone: (601) 987-4188
Jackson, MS 39216-5014   FAX: (601) 364-2352
Delia Owens, RN, JD, Executive Director
www.msbn.state.ms.us

Missouri State Board of Nursing
3605 Missouri Blvd   Phone: (573) 751-0681
PO Box 656   FAX: (573) 751-0075
Jefferson City, MO 65102-0656
Lori Scheidt, BS, Executive Director
pr.mo.gov/nursing.asp

Montana State Board of Nursing
301 South Park   Phone: (406) 841-2340
PO Box 200513   FAX: (406) 841-2305
Helena, MT 59620-0513
Sandra Dickenson, Executive Director
mt.gov/dli/bsd/license/bsd_boards/nur_board

Nebraska Dept of Health and Human Services Reg & Licensure
Nursing and Nursing Support   Phone: (402) 471-4376
301 Centennial Mall South   FAX: (402) 471-1066
Lincoln, NE 68509-4986
Charlene Kelly, PhD, RN, Executive Director
Nursing and Nursing Support Web Site:
www.hhs.state.ne.us/crl/nursing/nursingindex.htm

Nevada State Board of Nursing
5011 Meadowood Mall #201   Phone: (775) 688-2620
Reno, NV 89502-6547   FAX: (775) 688-2628
Debra Scott, MS, RN, Executive Director
www.nursingboard.state.nv.us

New Hampshire Board of Nursing
21 South Fruit Street, Suite 16   Phone: (603) 271-2323
Concord, NH 03301-2341   FAX: (603) 271-6605
Margaret Walker, MBA, BSN, RN, Executive Director
www.state.nh.us/nursing

New Jersey Board of Nursing
PO Box 45010   Phone: (973) 504-6586
124 Halsey Street, 6th Floor   FAX: (973) 648-3481
Newark, NJ 07101
George Hebert, Executive Director
www.state.nj.us/lps/ca/medical.htm

New Mexico Board of Nursing
6301 Indian School Road, NE, Suite 710   Phone: (505) 841-8340
Albuquerque, NM 87110   FAX: (505) 841-8347
Allison Kozeliski, RN, Executive Director
www.state.nm.us/clients/nursing

New York State Board of Nursing
Education Bldg
89 Washington Ave, 2nd floor – West wing
Albany, NY 12234   Phone: (518) 474-3817
Barbara Zittel, PhD, RN, Executive Secretary FAX: (518) 474-3706
www.nysed.gov/prof/nurse.htm

North Carolina Board of Nursing
3724 National Drive, Suite 201   Phone: (919) 782-3211
Raleigh, NC 27602   FAX: (919) 781-9461
Polly Johnson, MSN, RN, Executive Director
www.ncbon.com

North Dakota Board of Nursing
919 South 7th Street, Suite 504   Phone: (701) 328-9777
Bismarck, ND 58504   FAX: (701) 328-9785
Constance Kalanek, PhD, RN, Executive Director
www.ndbon.org

Northern Mariana Islands
Commonwealth Board of Nurse Examiners   Phone: (670) 664-4812
PO BOX 501458   FAX: (670) 664-4813
Saipan, MP 96950
Rosa M Tuleda, Associate Director of Public Health & Nursing

Ohio Board of Nursing
17 South High Street, Suite 400   Phone: (614) 466-3947
Columbus, OH 43215-3413   FAX: (614) 466-0388
Betsy J Houchen, RN, MS, JD, Exec Dir
www.nursing.ohio.gov

Oklahoma Board of Nursing
2915 N Classen Boulevard, Suite 524   Phone: (405) 962-1800
Oklahoma City, OK 73106   FAX: (405) 962-1821
Kimberly Glazier, MEd, RN, Executive Director
www.youroklahoma.com/nursing

Oregon State Board of Nursing
800 NE Oregon Street, Box 25m Suite 465 Phone: (971) 673-0685
Portland, OR 97232   FAX: (971) 673-0684
Joan Bouchard, MN, RN, Executive Director
www.osbn.state.or.us

Pennsylvania State Board of Nursing
PO 2649   Phone: (717) 783-7142
Harrisburg, PA 17105-2649   FAX: (717) 783-0822
Laurette D Keiser, RN, MSN, Executive Secretary/Section Chief
www.dos.state.pa.us/bpoa/cwp

Puerto Rico
Commonwealth of Puerto Rico   Phone: (787) 725-7506
Board of Nurse Examiners   FAX: (787) 725-7903
Mailing Address:
Office of Regulations and Certifications of Health Professionals
PO Box 10200
Santurce, PR 00908-0200

Physical Address:
800 Roberto H Todd Ave, Room 202, Stop 18
Santurce, PR 00908

Roberto Figueroa, RN, MSN, Executive Director of the Office of
Regulations and Certifications of Health Care Professions

Rhode Island Board of Nurse Registration and Nursing Education
105 Cannon Building   Phone: (401) 222-5700
Three Capitol Hill   FAX: (401) 222-3352
Providence, RI 02908
Vacant, Executive Officer
www.health.ri.gov

South Carolina State Board of Nursing
110 Centerview Drive   Phone: (803) 896-4550
Suite 202   FAX: (803) 896-4525
Columbia, SC 29210
Dottie Buchanan
www.llr.state.sc.us/pol/nursing

South Dakota Board of Nursing
4305 South Louise Ave, Suite 201   Phone: (605) 362-2760
Sioux Falls, SD 57106-3115   FAX: (605) 362-2768
Gloria Damgaard, RN, MS, Executive Secretary
www.state.sd.us/doh/nursing

Tennessee State Board of Nursing
425 Fifth Avenue North   Phone: (615) 532-5166
1st Floor - Cordell Hull Building   FAX: (615) 741-7899
Nashville, TN 37247
Elizabeth Lund, MSN, RN, Executive Director
www.tennessee.gov/health

Texas Board of Nurse Examiners
333 Guadalupe, Suite 3-460   Phone: (512) 305-7400
Austin, TX 78701   FAX: (512) 305-7401
Katherine Thomas, MN, RN, Executive Director
www.bne.state.tx.us

Utah State Board of Nursing
Heber M Wells Bldg, 4th Floor   Phone: (801) 530-6628
160 East 300 South   FAX: (801) 530-6511
Salt Lake City, UT 84111
Laura Poe, MS, RN, Executive Administrator
www.commerce.state.ut.us

Vermont State Board of Nursing
81 River Street   Phone: (802) 828-2396
Heritage Building   FAX: (802) 828-2484
Montpelier, VT 05609-1106
Anita Ristau, MS, RN, Executive Director
www.vtprofessionals.org/opr1/nurses

Virgin Islands Board of Nurse Licensure

PO Box 4247, Veterans Drive Station   Phone: (340) 776-7397
St Thomas, VI 00803   FAX: (340) 777-4003
Diane Viville, Executive Secretary

Virginia Board of Nursing

6603 West Broad Street   Phone: (804) 662-9909
5th Floor   FAX: (804) 662-9512
Richmond, VA 23230-1712
Jay Douglas, RN, MSM, CSAC, Executive Director
www.dhp.virginia.gov

Washington State Nursing Care Quality

Assurance Commission   Phone: (360) 236-4700
Department of Health   FAX: (360) 236-4738
HPQA #6
310 Israel Rd SE
Tumwater, WA 98501-7864
Paula Meyer, MSN, RN, Executive Director
wws2.wa.gov/doh/hpqa-licensing/HPS6/Nursing

West Virginia State Board of Examiners for Licensed Practical Nurses

101 Dee Drive   Phone: (304) 558-3572
Charleston, WV 25311   FAX: (304) 558-4367
Lanette Anderson, RN, BSN, JD, Executive Director
www.lpnboard.state.wv.us

West Virginia Board of Examiners for Registered Professional Nurses

101 Dee Drive   Phone: (304) 558-3596
Charleston, WV 25311   FAX: (304) 558-3666
Laura Rhodes, MSN, RN, Executive Director
www.wvrnboard.com

Wisconsin Department of Regulation and Licensing

1400 E Washington Avenue, RM 173   Phone: (608) 266-0145
Madison, WI 53708   FAX: (608) 261-7083
Kimberly Nania, PhD, MA, BS, Director, Bureau of Health Service Professions
www.drl.state.wi.us

Wyoming State Board of Nursing

2020 Carey Avenue, Suite 110   Phone: (307) 777-7601
Cheyenne, WY 82002   FAX: (307) 777-3519
Cheryl Lynn Koski, MN, RN, CS, Executive Director
nursing.state.wy.us